Terrorism,
2008–2012

W9-AMC-941

MONTGOMERY COLLEGE
ROCKVILLE CAMPUS LIBRARY
ROCKVILLE, MARYLAND

Terrorism, 2008–2012

A Worldwide Chronology

Edward Mickolus

McFarland & Company, Inc., Publishers
Jefferson, North Carolina

2082423

JAN 1 4 2015

MONTGOMERY COLLEGE
ROCKVILLE CAMPUS LIBRARY
ROCKVILLE MARYLAND

ISBN 978-0-7864-7763-0 (softcover : acid free paper) ∞
978-1-4766-1467-0 (ebook)

LIBRARY OF CONGRESS CATALOGUING DATA ARE AVAILABLE

BRITISH LIBRARY CATALOGUING DATA ARE AVAILABLE

© 2013 Edward Mickolus. All rights reserved

*No part of this book may be reproduced or transmitted in any form
or by any means, electronic or mechanical, including photocopying
or recording, or by any information storage and retrieval system,
without permission in writing from the publisher.*

Cover images © 2014 Thinkstock

Manufactured in the United States of America

*McFarland & Company, Inc., Publishers
Box 611, Jefferson, North Carolina 28640
www.mcfarlandpub.com*

To the people
who devote their lives to
keeping everyone else safe

TABLE OF CONTENTS

INTRODUCTION

With the publication of this volume, I, singly or in tandem, have written some twenty chronologies of terrorism and biographies of terrorists in the past three-plus decades. While I have hoped that each volume would be the last in the series, individuals willing to follow their fellow thugs into these pages continue to come forward.

Using a comprehensive definition, this chronology considers terrorism to be the use or threat of use of violence by any individual or group for political purposes. The perpetrators may be functioning for or in opposition to established governmental authority. A key component of international terrorism is that its ramifications transcend national boundaries, and, in so doing, create an extended atmosphere of fear and anxiety. The effects of terrorism reach national and worldwide cultures as well as the lives of the people directly hurt by the terrorist acts. Violence becomes terrorism when the intention is to influence the attitudes and behavior of a target group beyond the immediate victims. Violence becomes terrorism when its location, the victims, or the mechanics of its resolution result in consequences and implications beyond the act or threat itself.

The period 2008 to 2012 saw the continuation of trends identified in previous years, although it also saw the failure of some long-held analytic predictions. Some predictions were made by pundits who are paid for spouting opinions and issuing slogans masquerading as insights and not for developing understanding. But others were made by respected academics who look at patterns from history and might miss the "black swan" problem noted by Nassim Nicholas Taleb, such as the 9/11 attacks.

Most attacks continue to be low-level, unsophisticated bombings and shootings with terrorists going after targets of opportunity rather than mounting complex operations that are the stuff of Hollywood movies and novels. Some operations, most notably the three-day siege of Mumbai by jihadis in November 2008 and the takeover of an Algerian gas production facility in January 2013, underscore that not all terrorists opt for the easy hit.

Al Qaeda affiliates made kidnapping into a mobile murder rather than the barricade-and-hostage method it had been in the 1970s and 1980s.

We can put to bed the myth that has become "common knowledge" among the commentariat about terrorist behavior and anniversary dates. Despite media certainty, there is no evidence that terrorists conduct follow-up attacks on religious holidays, holidays for the target's nationalities, feast days of major terrorists, arrest dates of terrorists, or anniversaries of terrorist events. Al Qaeda has conducted no further attacks on, say, September 11 (anniversary of 9/11), July 7 (anniversary of the London subway attacks), or March 11 (anniversary of the Madrid train attacks). Pundits celebrate anniversary dates; terrorists do not. Terrorists know that the media will herald an upcoming date, and security services, heeding the counsel of their public affairs offices, will put on a display of preventive zeal. All for naught. Terrorists attack on the date that they believe will work now, not one that worked in the past.

Much was made of the coincidental date of the attack on the U.S. diplomatic facility in Benghazi, Libya, on September 11, 2012, in which four U.S. diplomats, including the U.S. ambassador, were murdered. With tens of thousands of terrorist attacks having been logged during the period covered by this chronology series, date overlap is unavoidable. It is noteworthy that although Islamists were credited with the attack, none of the groups claiming credit cited any link to the September 11, 2001, attacks. Moreover, there was no evidence of involvement by al Qaeda, per se.

Al Qaeda continued its transformation from a tightly controlled organization bowing to the whims of one individual to a loose confederation of like-minded jihadi zealots. On occasion, al Qaeda "central"—the group immediately surrounding Osama bin Laden and Ayman al-Zawahiri, plus the al Qaeda operations chief of the day (they keep getting killed)—bequeaths associate status on a franchise and permits it to use the al Qaeda brand. Hence, the growth of al Qaeda in the Islamic Maghreb, al Qaeda in the Arabian Peninsula (AQAP), and al Qaeda in Iraq (AQI). Although al-Shabaab in Somalia has not adopted the al Qaeda name, it, too, seems to have acquired second circle status. Other groups with close ties to al Qaeda, including Jemaah Islamiyah in Indonesia and Abu Sayyaf in the Philippines, have yet (at least, as of this writing) to obtain formal franchise status. Similarly, despite the similarity of their stated goals and interconnections of its membership, al Qaeda has not included the Chechens, Islamic Movement of Uzbekistan, or Uighurs as formal franchise spinoffs. Still other wannabes travel to the caves and training centers of al Qaeda to seek weapons, training, and the blessing of the core group.

Among theses wannabes has been a disturbing number of American citizens, many of them Western-looking and American-accented radicals steeped in U.S. culture and able to move more easily in the American environment. While excellent law enforcement work has led to the arrests and imprisonment of dozens of these individuals, it is clear that al Qaeda continues to believe that the Westernization of its operational cadre offers opportunities for attacks on the "far enemy"—the U.S. homeland.

The question of what to do with terrorists plagued the Bush and Obama administrations during this period. Media upset over interrogation methods and incarceration procedures led to calls for a catch-and-release policy, changes to questioning methods (on the dubious proposition that terrorists would commit themselves to similar limitations on their handling of hostages), and a shift to kinetic responses. Air strikes took out many leaders of al Qaeda central and its affiliates in Yemen, while scores were released from Guantanamo Bay military prison. Still others awaited trial as judicial scholars and other observers pondered whether a military or civilian court was the more appropriate forum. Several released from Guantanamo Bay to their home governments, who ultimately declared them no longer a threat, soon became leaders of terrorist organizations, with membership in the Gitmo alumni association giving instant street credibility among their brethren.

Aspects of the detainees' defenses continued to divert media attention. Many of the Guantanamo detainees claimed, in essence, that their training in al Qaeda camps in then Taliban-governed Afghanistan was a mere *praycation*, not terrorist-related. Others, most notably the "high value" detainees such as Khalid Sheikh Muhammad, Mustafa Ahmad al-Hawsawi, and Ramzi Binalshibh, attempted to make their hearings an opportunity to spout their propaganda rather than offer a true defense of their actions.

Governments wrestled with the juridical treatment of the prosecutable and perhaps non-prosecutable detainees as well as alumni of prisons. Countries tried various solutions with differing amounts of legislative oversight and domestic, public, international, and legal support.

The United States explored sending many Guantanamo Bay detainees to willing countries and substantially reduced its prison population. The merits of military commissions and civilian criminal trials were weighed, and sometimes tried in test cases. Ahmed Khalfan Ghailani, accused in the August 7, 1998, bombing of U.S. embassies in Kenya and Tanzania, narrowly missed a not guilty verdict on all 285 charges, being convicted of only a single charge of conspiracy in a civilian criminal court. "Not in my backyard" was the frequent lament of officials of cities on the short list of possible court fora for other trials of high value detainees.

Various civil rights and human rights groups spent more time worrying about the treatment of those charged—and sometimes not yet charged—with terrorism than with the effects on the victims and diverted resources of governments battling terrorist predators. The American Civil Liberties Union challenged the U.S. administration's dead-or-alive order for Anwar al-Aulaqi (variant al-Awlaki) who was connected to the perpetrators of several foiled and successful attacks and believed by many to be al Qaeda in the Arabian Peninsula's inspirational successor to Osama bin Laden. Rather than spend up to $80 million in litigation expenses and tying up the time of investigators defending against charges of undue interrogation meth-

ods, the British government agreed to an out-of-court financial settlement with fifteen Guantanamo Bay former detainees and one who was still incarcerated. A Polish government agency declared "victim" status for Abd-al-Rahim al-Nashiri, a high-value al Qaeda detainee.

Law enforcement and intelligence officers continued their stunning record of successes against terrorist threats. While there were several near misses, and, unfortunately, some successes by terrorists, on the whole, the period was one of few actual attacks on the U.S. homeland. It was not for lack of trying by the terrorists.

This record of success was easy for the media to ignore, as a streak of luck, particularly when the failed December 25, 2009, underwear bombing and the May 1, 2010, Times Square fizzle underscored that terrorists only need one win and have a different view of what constitutes success. Self-appointed terrorism experts within the media's *punditocracy* bloviated about "connecting the dots," as if the exceptionally intricate work of terrorism analysis merits reduction to such simplistic sloganeering. Piecing together tidbits post facto to fit a predetermined argument is easy. Figuring out what's happening when you're trying to monitor more than half a million names (which appear in several federal databases) in a tsunami of data and vet often conflicting threat information is another matter. The commentariat never provides any ideas on precisely what should be changed. Non-accountable amateur blognoscenti saying ex cathedra "connect the dots," "be creative," "get more and better intelligence," "all we need is better HUMINT," "just penetrate them," or "collaborate" without offering specifics is hardly illuminating uncharted, heretofore unconsidered territory. But the search for blame is easier than the discovery of effective antiterrorist methods.

The drawdown of U.S. and coalition forces in Iraq and (as of this writing) planned drawdown in Afghanistan has come at a time when terrorist attacks are on an oscillating pattern in Iraq, but an upward path in Afghanistan. Many observers wonder whether the troubling trends in Iraq will continue when the local security services are on their own against the terrorists. Very preliminary evidence suggests that the terrorists won't go away quietly. Al Qaeda in particular continued its expansion to new regions, with the successor to an Algerian Islamist group taking the name of al Qaeda in the Islamic Maghreb (AQIM) and a slice of Mali the size of Texas. Al Qaeda in Iraq sponsored the growth of the al Nusrah Front, an Islamist rebel group that expanded operations during the seemingly unending Syrian civil war. Meanwhile, an al Qaeda-like group, Boko Haram, was responsible for hundreds of murders in northern Nigeria, specializing in multiple casualty bombings of churches and attacks on government facilities. The Taliban in Afghanistan and Pakistan continued their depredations, while al Qaeda in Iraq exploited security gaps. Despite air strike attacks that decimated al Qaeda central leadership and drew down the leadership of al Qaeda in the Arabian Peninsula, plus the reversal of fortunes of al-Shabaab in Somalia, the overall movement continued to pose major threats in their regions. Al-Shabaab sympathizers attacked targets in Kenya while backing away from its earlier redoubts in Mogadishu. Most observers cited AQAP as the most likely to attempt to conduct attacks on the U.S. homeland, while individual homegrown radicalized Islamists continued to be stymied by the excellent work of the FBI. Increases in the treasury of AQIM—thanks to the millions acquired from ransom payments for Western hostages and smuggling operations—increased the operational potential of al Qaeda.

The major event in the ongoing al Qaeda narrative was the death of Osama bin Laden in a daring SEAL Team 6 raid on his compound in Abbotabad, Pakistan, on May 2, 2011. An exultant U.S. administration also celebrated the killing in August 2011 of al Qaeda in the Arabian Peninsula operations chief Anwar al-Aulaqi. These deaths and several more attributed to drone strikes siphoned the strength of al Qaeda's central leadership and that of its most operationally active affiliate, but were accompanied by much second-guessing from the sidelines. An embarrassed Pakistani government complained about a violation of sovereignty, while civil libertarians questioned whether there are detailed rules for determining when an American citizen can be targeted overseas.

Bin Laden's successor, Ayman al-Zawahiri, peppered the Internet with commentary on a host of issues, some related to al Qaeda's raison d'être, some a mere attempt to appear relevant or at least offer a proof of life, as jihadis operated with increasing independence of the original al Qaeda. Al-Zawahiri's ascension posed new issues for the organization as his management style was viewed by some as abrupt, and the propaganda shop lamented a charisma gap between al-Zawahiri and his predecessor. Al Qaeda affiliates were slow to pledge *bayat*—personal loyalty—to al-Zawahiri. Air strikes severely limited the group's succession planning; a litany of al-Zawahiri deputies was killed off.

One al Qaeda franchise that was especially active was the Arabian Peninsula group, operating out of the lawless areas of Yemen with some spillover amongst radical Saudis. Al-Aulaqi, with excellent knowledge of American culture, conducted propaganda operations aimed at recruiting Americans to some success. Some observers worried that he would elbow even bin Laden out as the major Islamist terrorist leader in the coming years. His simple message—try anything, you don't need our approval—portended a terrorist movement far more difficult to penetrate, with no central command calling the shots. Although al-Aulaqi's death took out a major spokesman for the al Qaeda cause, many lone wolves, including Americans, continue to pop up, cherishing al-Aulaqi's message of going it alone.

Tectonic change in the Middle East during the Arab Spring of 2011 sidelined al Qaeda to mere jeerleaders calling for continued efforts against corrupt leaders. The overthrow of several regimes, including the violent overthrow of Mu'ammar al-Qadhafi in Libya, left al Qaeda without a say in the direction of the new Middle East. Al-Qadhafi's death also removed a leading figure in the history of state sponsorship of terrorism. As time went on, however, jihadis with and without direct al Qaeda ties found ways to exploit the continuing instability in the region, seen in particular as a diminution of security service capabilities. Some services were more sympathetic to the jihadis' goals, if not their methods, than their authoritarian predecessors. Some felt constrained to rein in their public cooperation with the United States and other Western services out of concern for anti–Western "street" opinion. Still others have yet to achieve the levels of professionalism of their predecessors.

Al Qaeda in the Islamic Maghreb's inroads in Mali and fears of likely AQIM expansion of its territory leading to a takeover of the rest of Mali led Paris to give up its wait for a promised West African military response to the crisis and in January 2013 initiate a military intervention to roll back AQIM. The millions of dollars in hostage ransoms and the huge territorial expanse available led many to worry that AQIM could give like-minded jihadis a safe haven and training opportunities rivaling those of the Taliban-era Afghanistan. AQIM's imposition of an especially harsh interpretation of sharia, featuring destruction of holy sites and amputations, made the French action popular among the local population.

Terrorists continue to use the Internet in ways not initially conceived of by security services. Trends identified earlier in this series—particularly with regards to its use in propaganda and clandestine messaging—have expanded. Increased use of blogs in Internet culture has been mimicked by terrorists, who now sport online magazines. The al Qaeda in the Arabian Peninsula's *Inspire*, written in part by American al Qaeda members, has been a vanguard in the attempt to get Western kids hooked on the jihad by using cultural references.

While the al Qaeda diaspora gets the bulk of media attention, non-jihadi terrorists have not given up. The Revolutionary Armed Forces of Colombia (FARC), thanks to assistance from the neighboring government of Venezuela, leads the Latin American leftist cadres for longevity and audacity, while the Basque Nation and Liberty (ETA), despite arrests of its leaders on both sides of the French-Spanish border, garners headlines as one of Europe's long-term terrorist groups. Even splinters of the Irish Republican Army and like-minded affiliates have continued conducting occasional operations. FARC was not without its difficulties, however, losing several senior leaders plus sustaining an embarrassing rescue operation via government trickery of longtime hostage former presidential candidate Ingrid Betancourt. ETA unilaterally called another ceasefire in 2011. Hamas and Hizballah, while maintaining terrorist operational capabilities, have learned that the responsibilities of governance put them in a different phase of organizational development from that of simple revolutionary rhetoric and bomb-throwing. Lone wolves on the right also appear, most notably in Norway, where Anders Breivik's bombing and shooting spree in July 2011 killed sixty-eight people, mostly teens. The Breivik case also raises the issue as to whether lone wolves should be classified and treated as insane or as political terrorist groups with a membership of one.

The current volume follows the same format and method as the previous ones. As in earlier volumes, the international terrorist incidents and airline hijackings are identified by an eight-digit code. The first six digits identify the date on which the incident became known as a terrorist attack to someone other than the terrorists themselves (e.g., the date the letter bomb finally arrived at the recipient's office, even though terrorists had mailed it weeks earlier, or the date on which investigators determined that an anomalous situation was terrorist in nature). The first two numbers indicate the year, the next two the month and the following two the day. For example, 110701 would indicate an event that occurred on July 1, 2011. The final two digits ratchet the number of attacks that took place on that date. On dates on which multiple attacks occurred in the same location, a dash is followed by the number of the last events in the series. For example, three attacks in the same location on the same date would be noted as XXXXXX01-03. In instances in which either the day of the month or the month itself is unknown, "99" is used in that field.

The book is divided into three sections: Incidents, Updates, and Bibliography. The Incidents section provides a chronology and description of international terrorist activity for a given time period, based solely on publicly available sources. This series of chronologies is not intended to be analytical, but rather comprehensive in scope. As such, the Incidents section also includes descriptions of noninternational attacks that provide the security and political context in which international attacks take place. In some cases, the international terrorists mimic the tactics of their stay-at-home cohorts. Often, these are the same terrorists working on their home soil against domestic targets, rather than foreign targets. Domestic attacks often serve as proving grounds for techniques later adopted for international use. I have therefore included material on major technological, philosophical, or security advances, such as

the use of letter bombs; food tampering; major assassinations; attempts to develop, acquire, smuggle, or use precursors for an actual chemical, biological, radiological, or nuclear weapon; key domestic and international legislation and new security procedures; key arrests and trials of major figures; and incidents involving mass casualties. Noninternational entries do not receive an eight-digit code.

The Updates section provides follow-up material to incidents first reported prior to January 1, 2008. For example, updates include information about the outcome of trials for terrorist acts occurring prior to 2008 and "where are they now" information about terrorists and their victims. The update is identified by the original incident date, and I have included enough prefatory material to give some context and to identify the original incident in the earlier volumes.

The information cutoff date for this volume is December 31, 2012.

The Bibliography section includes references drawn from the same public sources that provide the incidents, literature searches, and contributions sent by readers of previous volumes. It does not purport to be comprehensive. The citations are grouped into topic areas chosen to make the Bibliography more accessible and include print and web-based material. The Bibliography gives citations on key events and may be referenced for more detail on specific attacks described in the Incidents section.

For those who prefer to run textual searches for specific groups, individuals, or incidents, a digital version of the 1960–2007 chronology is available from Vinyard Software, Inc., 502 Wandering Woods Way, Ponte Vedra, Florida 32081-0621, or e-mail via vinyardsoftware@hotmail.com. The data set comes in a WordPerfect and Word textual version and looks remarkably like the volumes in this series of hardcopy chronologies. A numeric version offers circa 150 numeric variables describing the international attacks from 1968 to 2012. The data sets can be purchased by specific year of interest. See www.vinyardsoftware.com for further details.

Vinyard also offers the Data on Terrorist Suspects (DOTS) project with a detailed biographical index of every terrorist suspect named in the previous volumes of this chronology.

Comments about this volume's utility and suggestions for improvements for its likely successors are welcome and can be sent to me via vinyardsoftware@hotmail.com. Please send your terrorism publication citations to me at Vinyard to ensure inclusion in the next edition of the bibliography.

Once again, there are many individuals who have contributed to this research effort. Of particular note are Susan Simmons, who edited this volume, and my family, who once again wondered if there was still a dining room table buried underneath the files used to produce this work.

2008–2012 INCIDENTS

2008

2008—Azerbaijan—Authorities halted a plot to bomb the Israeli Embassy in Baku, arresting several terrorists, including two Lebanese citizens who were operating under orders from Hizballah and the Iranian Revolutionary Guard Corps.

January 2008—Lebanon—A suspected al Qaeda member was arrested.

January 2008—Yemen—On July 11, 2010, a Yemeni appeals court confirmed the death sentences against four al Qaeda terrorists who attacked the U.S. Embassy in March 2008 and killed two Belgian female tourists in January 2008. They were convicted in 2009. The court upheld fifteen-year sentences for ten other terrorists, including four Syrians and a Saudi, for orchestrating the attacks. 08019901

January 1, 2008—Sudan—John Granville, 33, a USAID employee, and his driver, Abdelrahman Abbas Rahama, 40, were shot to death in Khartoum at 4:00 a.m., the day after the African Union–UN force assumed peacekeeping responsibilities in Darfur. Granville was from Buffalo, New York. He was shot five times in the hand, shoulder, and belly, and died on the operating table. He was returning from a New Year's party hosted by the British Embassy. Sudanese authorities denied it was terrorist-related. On January 4, the previously-unknown Ansar al-Tawhid (Companions of Monotheism) claimed credit. On February 9, Sudanese security forces arrested two suspects. Sudan announced on August 8 that five suspects would stand trial, beginning on August 17. One of the accused was a former Sudanese army officer who had been sacked. On June 24, 2009, a Sudanese court sentenced four Sudanese men to hang for the murders; a fifth was sentenced to two years in prison. Four of the men sentenced to death for Granville's murder escaped from the national prison through a sewage pipe on June 11,

2010, killing a Sudanese police officer and wounding another. One of the escapees was recaptured and another was killed in Somalia.

On January 8, 2013, the U.S. Department of State added to its terrorist watch list two of the killers, Abdelbasit Alhaj Alhassan Haj Hamad and Mohamed Makawi Ibrahim Mohamed. State blocked any of their U.S.-based property and froze their assets. Americans were prohibited from engaging in transactions with them. 08010101

January 1, 2008—Burundi—Gunmen killed one French aid worker and wounded another in Ruyigi. The two women in their 30s were volunteers with Action Against Hunger, a French charity. 08010102

January 2, 2008—Algeria—A car bomb exploded as it sped toward the police station in Naciria, killing four people and injuring twenty, including eight police officers.

January 2, 2008—Kosovo—A bomb exploded at the offices of the Serbian Komercijalna Bank in Dragas in southern Kosovo, causing considerable damage but no injuries.

January 4, 2008—Morocco—Fifty Islamists were sentenced to up to twenty-five years for plotting bombings and robberies.

January 4, 2008—Portugal—The thirtieth annual Dakar Rally, a race across the Sahara Desert that was scheduled to start in Lisbon on January 5, was canceled because of terrorist threats by al Qaeda in the Islamic Maghreb, previously known as the Salafist Group for Preaching and Combat, an Algerian group. Organizers also cited the recent murder of a French family in Mauritania by al Qaeda-linked terrorists. The race, organized by the France-based Amaury Sport Organization, would have held eight stages in Mauritania, finishing on January 20 in Dakar, Senegal. Circa 550 cars, trucks, and motorcycles were scheduled to compete in the 5,760 mile race, which had previously been called the Paris-Dakar.

January 5, 2008—Somalia—Ten Somali gunmen armed with pistols kidnapped acting Libyan Ambassador Naji Ahmed Subeyr and chief of staff Fatahi Mohammed Mustafa as they shopped in Mogadishu's Bakara market. They were freed hours later. 08010501

January 6, 2008—Qatar—U.S. al Qaeda member Adam Gadahn said in an Internet video that President Bush should be greeted with bombs and booby-trapped vehicles, not flowers, during his upcoming visit to the Middle East.

January 9, 2008—United States—The Treasury Department, citing Executive Order 13438, announced financial sanctions against a senior Iranian general and three Iraqi exiles based in Iran and Syria for fomenting violence in Iraq.

Iranian Brig. Gen. Ahmed Foruzandeh, leader of the Quds Force (variant Qods Force) operations in Iraq, had allegedly directed assassinations of Iraqis and ordered Iranian intelligence to provoke sectarian violence. Quds is the foreign operations branch of the Revolutionary Guards. He also financed operations by Shi'ite and Sunni extremists against U.S. forces and drove explosives and other war materiel into Iraq for use in suicide bombings. Treasury said he organized training courses for Iraqi militants in Iranian campus.

Abu Mustafa al-Sheibani is a leader of Shi'ite extremists based in Iran. His network includes hundreds of members in several pro–Iranian insurgent groups in the south that specialize in roadside bombs against Americans and sabotage of U.K. forces in the area.

Ismail Hafez al-Lami, alias Abu Dura, a leader of Shi'ite extremists based in Iran, leads a pro–Iranian group that targets Iraqi officials, Sunni leaders, and others. His group was responsible for the kidnap, torture, and murder of Sunnis in Iraq's Ministry of Higher Education in 2006.

Mish'an al-Jaburi, a former member of the Iraqi Parliament, fled to Syria after he embezzled government funds. He supports Iraqi insurgents and owns al-Zawra, a TV station critical of the coalition that has aired al Qaeda recruitment videos. Al-Zawra's assets were also included in the Treasury announcement.

January 10, 2008—Pakistan—A suicide bomber killed twenty-three and wounded forty-seven others near the Lahore High Court. Most of the casualties were attorneys mustering for a pro-democracy march.

January 11, 2008—United States—Three former leaders of the defunct Care International, a Muslim charity, were convicted in Boston on federal tax and fraud charges for using tax exemptions to hide support for religious militants and overseas terrorists since its creation in 1993. The trio were charged with making false statements, tax code violations, and conspiracy to defraud the government. Convicted on all counts were Emadeddin Muntasser, 43, Care International's founder, and Muhammed Mubayyid, 42, a former treasurer. Former Care International president Samir al-Monla was convicted on all counts except making a false statement. The group faced ten to nineteen years in prison. The prosecution noted Monla's meetings with Afghan warlord Gulbadeen Hekmatyar, who had been designated a global terrorist by the State Department. The group had been deemed the successor to the al-Kifah Refugee Center, which allegedly was tied to the bombers of the World Trade Center in February 1993. David Duncan, one of Muntasser's attorneys, planned to appeal.

January 11, 2008—Nigeria—Militants bombed an oil tanker near Port Harcourt. The Movement for the Emancipation of the Niger Delta was suspected.

January 12, 2008—Gaza Strip—Following the visit by President Bush to the West Bank earlier in the week, gunmen from the previously unknown Army of Believers, the al Qaeda branch on the land of Palestine, left leaflets at a private American school in Beit Lahiya. The group did not specifically claim credit for smashing windows, burning buses, and looting computers. 08011201

January 14, 2008—Thailand—Muslim rebels were suspected in the ambush of a Thai army patrol that killed all eight soldiers, one of whom was later beheaded. A bomb hidden on the road flipped over their Humvee. The attackers then fired on the trapped soldiers, killing them all in Chanae District of southern Narathiwat Province.

January 14, 2008—Afghanistan—At 6:00 p.m., gunmen attacked the luxury 177-room Serena Hotel in Kabul, throwing grenades and firing assault rifles, killing six people as they chased after Western guests who hid in the gym. Another six people were injured. One terrorist blew himself up; another was shot to death. It was not clear what happened to the other two Taliban terrorists mentioned by Taliban spokesman Zabiullah Mujahid. Among the dead were an American and a Norwegian journalist. The Norwegian Embassy was hosting a meeting at the hotel for Norwegian Foreign Minister Jonas Gahr Stoere, who was unhurt. The UN secretary general said Stoere was the target of the attack. Afghan officials blamed a

Pakistani insurgent and arrested four suspects, including an attacker who wore a police uniform during the assault. 08011401

January 15, 2008—Thailand—A bomb hidden on a motorcycle exploded at a market in Yala Province, killing twenty-seven people. Muslim rebels were suspected.

January 15, 2008—Lebanon—A bomb exploded next to an unmarked U.S. Embassy vehicle, killing two Lebanese and a Syrian citizen and wounding at least twenty passersby, shopkeepers, and office workers, and destroying six cars. The driver of the embassy's armored SUV was injured as the bomb exploded as the vehicle passed by the blue Honda car bomb on a coastal road north of Beirut in the Bourj Hammoud industrial district. Mathew Clason, a Minnesotan who arrived a fortnight earlier to work at the National Evangelical Church, was among the injured. 08011501

January 15, 2008—Afghanistan—The Taliban said that suicide bombers would attack Kabul restaurants frequented by Westerners.

January 16, 2008—United States—Former member of the U.S. House of Representatives Mark Deli Siljander (R–Michigan), 56, who had also served on the U.S. Mission to the UN in 1987, was named in a forty-two-count indictment issued by a federal grand jury in Kansas City for money laundering, conspiracy, and obstructing justice for lying to the FBI about lobbying senators on the Senate Finance Committee on behalf of the Islamic American Relief Agency (IARA) that sent more than $130,000 to Gulbuddin Hekmatyar, an al Qaeda and Taliban supporter who had been designated by the U.S. as a global terrorist. The indictment, unsealed in the U.S. District Court in Kansas City, Missouri, said the IARA paid him $50,000 in money that had been stolen from the U.S. Agency for International Development. He had not been registered as a lobbyist for a decade. The IARA, which had been based in Columbia, Missouri, was named by the U.S. Department of the Treasury in 2004 as a terrorist financier. Siljander is the founder and chairman of Global Strategies in Great Falls, Virginia, a PR and marketing firm. His book *A Deadly Misunderstanding: A Congressman's Quest to Bridge the Muslim-Christian Divide* was due to be published by HarperOne in June 2008. Each of the six counts he faced carried twenty-year sentences.

January 18, 2008—Sri Lanka—The Liberation Tigers of Tamil Eelam (LTTE) were suspected of having shot to death ten Sinhalese civilians in the south.

January 18, 2008—Yemen—Al Qaeda was suspected of firing on a four-vehicle convoy of tourists in Wadi Daw'an, a desert mountain valley in Hadramawt region, killing two Belgian women and their Yemeni driver and injuring four people. Among the dead was Claudine Van Caille, 65. Survivor Karina Lambert said four gunmen hiding behind a parked pickup truck fired on the group. 08011801

January 18, 2008—United States—The World Bank closed five of its offices throughout Washington, DC, after receipt of three telephoned bomb threats.

January 18, 2008—Pakistan—A suicide bombing at a Shi'ite prayer hall in Peshawar killed nine.

January 19, 2008—Pakistan—Karachi authorities arrested five militants and confiscated explosives that were to be used in suicide bombings against religious commemorations. Police found in the rented house more than 13 pounds of explosives used in suicide vests, 4 pounds of steel ball bearings, 2 pounds of nails, several hand grenades, handguns, a detonator, and cyanide that was to be used to poison drinks at refreshment sites along the Shi'ite mourners' procession route. Mohammad Aijaz, the group's leader, had been conducting training courses and taught at a camp in South Waziristan. His four accomplices trained at a camp in the tribal area in 2007.

January 19, 2008—Spain—As part of Operation Cantata, police arrested twelve Pakistanis, an Indian, and a Bangladeshi suspected of plotting an Islamic radical attack in Barcelona. Police raided the Torek Ben Ziad mosque, a nearby Muslim prayer house, a bakery in Raval, and several Barcelona apartments. Interior Minister Alfred Perez Rubalcaba said that they "belonged to a well-organized group that had gone a step beyond radicalization," as evidenced by police discovery of material for making bombs, four timing devices, a small bag of ball bearings, batteries, and cables. Some authorities said some detainees belonged to the Pakistan-based Tabligh Jamaat. Among the detainees were a Torek Ben Ziad imam and a 70-year-old man. One Pakistani legal resident of Spain, Maroof Ahmed Mirza, is an imam. TVE reported that the group was to attack four Barcelona targets, including a prayer house frequented by supporters of the late former Pakistani Prime Minister Benazir Bhutto and the Barcelona subway system. ABC News reported on January 25 that authorities in France and other European Union countries were searching for other members of the cell who had traveled from Spain to

Waziristan, Pakistan. Spain later said that it had seized only an ounce of explosives, which was probably for training purposes, rather than an imminent attack. Rafqat Ali, 27, a construction worker, and Sheikh Saeed Akhtar, 52, a shop worker, were later released. Police also detained Mohammad Ayud, 63, and Maroof Ahmed Mirza, 38, believed to be ideological leaders of the group. Three would-be Tablighi Jamaat suicide bombers were Mohamed Shoaib, Mehmooh Khalib, and Imran Cheema, who came to Barcelona from Pakistan between October 2007 and mid–January 2008. Other detainees included Mohamed Tarik, Qadeer Malik, Hafeez Ahmed, Roshan Jamal Khan and Shaib Iqbal. The press reported that a French agent, F-1, had infiltrated the group and found that it took orders from Baitullah Mehsud, head of the Taliban Movement of Pakistan that assassinated former Pakistani Prime Minister Benazir Bhutto on December 27, 2007. The group was planning attacks in Spain, Germany, France, and Portugal, according to the Associated Press.

On November 12, 2009, Madrid began the trial of eleven Islamic militants regarding a plot to conduct a suicide attack on the Barcelona metro. Prosecutors sought eighteen-year jail terms for the ringleaders, Mahroof Ahmed Mirza, who was to choose the place and time for the Barcelona attacks, and Mohammad Ayud Elahi Bibi. They were connected with the now-late Pakistani Taliban leader Baitullah Mehsud of the radical Tehrik-e-Tabligh movement. If Mehsud's demands following the metro attack were refused, further attacks would have been conducted in Europe. Four defendants showed up in Barcelona shortly before the attacks were to take place; two of them were from Pakistan. The Tehrik-e-Tabligh movement claimed responsibility for the Barcelona plot on its Web site and in a video. Six others faced sixteen years in prison if convicted of membership in a terrorist group and possession of explosives. The rest faced lesser terms for other supporting roles.

On December 15, 2009, the three-judge National Court convicted eleven Islamist militants of membership in a terrorist group, but acquitted them of conspiracy to attack the Barcelona metro system in January 2008. Two were found guilty of possession of explosives; the other nine were acquitted of that charge. The judges ruled that the plot had not advanced far enough to constitute a "specific" conspiracy by the al Qaeda-linked group of ten Pakistanis and an Indian (other reports said nine Pakistanis and two Indians), since the group had not picked a date and place and didn't possess a sufficient amount of explosives. Authorities said the plotters were going to conduct suicide bombings against the metro, with followup attacks in Spain, Germany, France, Portugal, and the United Kingdom if demands from the Pakistani Taliban and al Qaeda were unheeded. The group faced eight to fourteen-year prison terms. The defense team included attorney Jacobo Teijelo, who planned to appeal to the Supreme Court. The ringleader was identified as Imam Maroof Ahmed Mirza, 40.

January 20, 2008—Germany—Berlin police arrested four Arab men acting suspiciously near Jewish institutions. Three were soon released. The fourth was held on unrelated charges.

January 26, 2008—Afghanistan—Cyd Mizell, 49, a burqa-clad American female foreign aid worker who was working for the Asian Rural Life Development Foundation, was kidnapped with her driver in Kandahar at 8:00 a.m. while she was being driven to work. She taught English at Kandahar University and embroidery at a local girls' school. On February 27, her employer said it feared she was dead, although it had no evidence. No group claimed credit, and the Taliban denied involvement. Mizell was from Eureka, California. 08012601

January 26, 2008—Jordan—George Habash, 81, founder of the Popular Front for the Liberation of Palestine, died of a heart attack.

January 27, 2008—China—Police foiled terrorist plans by the East Turkestan Islamic Movement separatists when they raided an apartment building in Urumqi city's Tianshan District in Xinjiang. Two suspects were killed and fifteen others arrested. Police found homemade arms and explosives, terrorism training equipment, and religious materials. The separatist Uighurs planned attacks for February 5, the anniversary of the 1997 Uighur riots against Chinese rule. Chinese authorities added on March 8, 2008, that the terrorists had planned to disrupt the Beijing Olympics.

January 28, 2008—Pakistan—A missile fired by what the news media said was a U.S. Predator drone killed senior al Qaeda field commander Abu Laith al-Libi, 41, who was also a leader in the Libyan Islamic Fighting Group, and other Islamists, including seven Arabs and six Central Asians including Turkmen, at a house in North Waziristan. He had appeared in a video with Ayman al-Zawahiri in November 2007.

January 29, 2008—France—Authorities in Hendaye arrested Ainhoa Adin Jauregui, a Basque Nation and Liberty (ETA) member believed behind attacks in the 1990s that killed three people.

January 29, 2008—United States—At least nineteen addresses of the Church of Scientology in Los Angeles and Orange counties received envelopes containing white powder over several days. Streets were closed and evacuated.

January 31, 2008—United States—A New Haven, Connecticut judge ruled that prosecutors can claim that Hassan Abu-Jihaad, 31, made coded references to terrorist plots. Abu-Jihaad was accused of leaking a document on the location and vulnerabilities of a navy battle group to suspected terrorist supporters in London. The trial was scheduled to begin on February 25, 2008. On February 28, 2008, retired Rear Adm. David Hart, Jr., testified that the navy would have changed plans if it had known that the classified details of the battle group's movements had been leaked.

February 2008—Pakistan—Terrorists attacked the offices of British aid agency Plan International in Mansehra, killing three Pakistani workers. 08029901

February 1, 2008—Mauritania—Three to six gunmen fired from their car on the Israeli Embassy at 2:20 a.m., injuring four people, including a Mauritanian who lives nearby and three French citizens, outside VIP, a neighboring nightclub. A French woman who works for a non-governmental organization was airlifted for medical treatment in France. The terrorists dropped two firearms and two grenades before fleeing in a gun battle with guards. 08020101

February 1, 2008—Iraq—The U.S. military doubted reports that two female suicide bombers had Down syndrome. However, they had undergone psychiatric treatment before setting off bombs in a pet market on the northeast outskirts of Baghdad that killed nearly one hundred people.

February 3, 2008—Germany—Police found neo–Nazi graffiti ("Hass"—German for "Hate"—and "SS" runes) at the scene of a fire at the Turkish Cultural Center in Ludwigshafen where nine people, including five children, died. The building was home to two Turkish families.

February 4, 2008—Sri Lanka—Tamil Tiger rebels were suspected in the bombing of a bus that killed twelve people 150 miles northeast of Colombo.

February 4, 2008—Worldwide—Millions of people demonstrated against the Revolutionary Armed Forces of Colombia's atrocities. The demonstrations occurred in Caracas, Washington, Paris, Sydney, New York, and dozens of other cities.

February 4, 2008—Israel—At 10:30 a.m., a Palestinian suicide bomber wearing an explosive belt killed an Israeli woman and injured more than twenty others, including his accomplice, in Dimona, 40 miles from the Gaza Strip. An Israeli officer shot the wounded terrorist five times before he could set off the belt. Abu Walid, spokesman for the al-Aqsa Martyrs Brigades, claimed credit, saying the terrorists lived outside Gaza City and the central Gaza city of Khan Younis. Abu Obeida, spokesman for the Izz al-Din al-Qassam Brigades, a Hamas group, also claimed credit. One of the terrorists was Loay al-Lahwani. The dead Israeli was later identified as Lyubov Razdolskaya, 73, who worked in the physics department of Ben Gurion University. A retaliatory Israeli air raid killed nine Hamas fighters in Gaza.

February 5, 2008—Somalia—A grenade was thrown into a crowded residential neighborhood in Bossaso, killing twenty-one and wounding one hundred. Most of the casualties in Puntland were believed to be Ethiopians on their way to find work in the Arabian Peninsula, which lies across the Gulf of Aden. 08020501

February 6, 2008—Iraq—The media ran footage from five captured al Qaeda in Iraq videos that showed children, some as young as six years old, learning how to shoot, kidnap, use mortars, attack homes and cars, and murder. The videos were seized in a raid on December 4 in Khan Bani Saad in Diyala Province. A December 8 raid netted a movie script that included children interrogating and executing hostages.

February 7, 2008—Algeria—Al Qaeda in the Islamic Maghreb claimed credit for killing eight paramilitary gendarmes in Draa Aragayen in the desert province of El Oued, 300 miles southeast of Algiers. The group claimed it captured the gendarmes' weapons, bulletproof vests, and night vision binoculars. The group said, "The operation came as revenge for the killing of our brothers in the recent clashes in the southern region, so the apostates know that they will pay a dear price for every martyr of ours that falls."

February 8, 2008—Germany—Bernhard Falk, Vice President of the Federal Crime Office, said al Qaeda members based on the Pakistan-Afghanistan border were planning attacks in Germany.

February 10, 2008—Afghanistan—Norway closed its embassy because of terrorist threats from al Qaeda.

February 10, 2008—Iraq—Two CBS News journalists—a Briton and an Iraqi—were kidnapped from their hotel in Basra by twenty armed men wearing security service uniforms. The Iraqi was freed on February 14; the status of the Briton remained unknown. On April 14, 2008, British journalist Richard Butler was freed in an Iraqi Army raid on a house in Basra. He had been on an assignment for *60 Minutes*. Butler reported, "The Iraqi army stormed the house and overcame my guards, and they burst through the door. I had my hood on, which I had to have on all the time, and they shouted something at me and I took my hood off. I'm looking forward to a decent meal and getting back to my family and my friends at CBS." 08021101

February 11, 2008—East Timor—In a drive-by, rebel soldiers shot at the official residence of the president in a 4:30 a.m. attack, hitting 1996 Nobel Peace Prize winner Jose Ramos-Horta, 58, in the stomach. Coup attempt leader Maj. Alfred Reinaldo and another rebel were killed by guards who returned fire. A guard also died. Reinaldo had been wanted on murder charges in a 2006 case. He was charged with murder in 2006 but escaped from jail with fifty other inmates. Ramos-Horta was flown to Darwin, Australia, for treatment of his gunshot wounds to the chest, back, and stomach.

Simultaneously, rebels in a car fired at the home of Prime Minister Xanana Gusmao, who was unhurt. Eleven people were questioned in the attacks. Interim President Vicente Guterres declared a state of emergency.

February 11, 2008—Pakistan—Tariq Azizuddin, the Pakistani ambassador to Afghanistan, was reported missing in a northwest frontier province of Pakistan and was believed kidnapped as he was driving back to Kabul from Peshawar. Hours earlier, two Pakistani Atomic Energy Commission maintenance workers and their driver were kidnapped near Mir Ali, less than 100 miles from the Afghanistan-Pakistan border. The Pakistani media said that he had been captured by the Pakistani Taliban, which was demanding the release of Mansour Dadullah. Azizuddin, his driver, and his bodyguard appeared on a video on *al-Arabiya* television on April 19, 2008, saying that they had been kidnapped. They were shown accompanied by three masked gunmen. He said, "For twenty-seven days, we have lived comfortably.... They take care of us, and they respect us." Azizuddin, his driver, and his bodyguard were released on May 16 by Tehrik-e-Taliban in North Waziristan. He told the newspaper *Dawn* that he had been captured by sixteen gunmen who were armed with several weapons, including a suicide bomber's

jacket. He was held in three locations inside the tribal area of Pakistan. Government officials denied Pakistani Taliban leader Mehsud's claim that they had agreed to free several dozen of his followers.

February 11, 2008—Pakistan—Authorities captured Mansour Dadullah, the Taliban's leader in southern Afghanistan, who was an associate of Osama bin Laden, in a firefight in Baluchistan.

February 12, 2008—Denmark—Authorities in Arhus arrested a Dane of Moroccan origin and two Tunisians believed planning to assassinate Kurt Westergaard, a Danish *Morgenavisen Jyllands-Posten* newspaper cartoonist who was one of twelve cartoonists who had enraged Muslims in September 2005 with caricatures of Mohammed. The Dane was suspected of violating Danish antiterrorist laws. The Tunisians were to be expelled. The next day, in an Internet reposting of a video originally dated February 2006, Mohamed Hassan, alias Abu Yehia Libi, an al Qaeda fugitive, called on Muslims to attack Denmark, Norway, and France for running the cartoons. Hassan had escaped with three other terrorists from a U.S. military prison at Bagram Air Base, Afghanistan, in 2007. Meanwhile, Denmark closed several of its embassies in predominantly Muslim countries, including Indonesia and Pakistan. Protestors attacked other diplomatic missions in Iran and Syria.

February 12, 2008—Syria—Hizballah terrorist leader Imad Mughniyeh was killed in an explosion when a bomb went off in a Mitsubishi Pajero in Damascus. Two other people were injured. Israel denied involvement. He was suspected in the 1983 bombing of the U.S. Embassy in Beirut, the 1983 truck bombing of the U.S. Marine barracks in Beirut that killed 241 people, and the June 14, 1985, hijacking of TWA flight 847 in which U.S. Navy diver Robert Dean Stethem was shot to death. He was on the FBI's Most Wanted Terrorists list. Various groups threatened to retaliate.

February 12, 2008—Somalia—A German employee of the German relief organization Agro Action was kidnapped from his car in Sanag in northern Somalia following a gun battle between his bodyguards and local gunmen. A foreign woman traveling with the German was not kidnapped. Sanag is claimed by Puntland and the breakaway Republic of Somaliland. Somaliland troops freed him a few hours later. Two of the kidnappers were wounded, as was his driver. 08021201

February 13, 2008—United States/Syria—The United States extended financial sanctions against

Syria, broadening the number of Syrian officials whose assets can be blocked.

February 13, 2008—Iraq—A woman posing as a journalist with an English-speaking accomplice claimed that they had an interview with a prominent Iraqi tribal leader who works with U.S. forces. She set off a suicide bomb, killing four bodyguards protecting Sheikh Ifan al-Issawi. Her brother had been a suicide bomber in 2004.

February 14, 2008—Philippines—Authorities foiled a plot by al Qaeda-linked Abu Sayyaf and Jemaah Islamiyah militants to assassinate President Gloria Macapagal Arroyo during a visit to the country's premier military academy.

February 15, 2008—Mexico—Organized crime was suspected of setting off a bomb in Mexico City that killed one person and wounded two. The dead man had a hand blown off, suggesting that he was carrying the bomb.

February 15, 2008—Gaza Strip—An explosion in the Bureij refugee camp home of Ayman Atallah al-Fayed killed the senior Islamic Jihad (IJ) activist, along with eight other people, and wounded forty. IJ blamed Israel, although some Palestinians suggested that his arms cache exploded.

February 15, 2008—Gaza Strip—A dozen masked gunmen overpowered two security guards and blew up the eight thousand-volume library of the Young Men's Christian Association (YMCA). A second bomb was defused. The guards were later released. 08021501

February 15, 2008 India—Hundreds of Maoist rebels attacked six police compounds—including four police stations, a training academy, and an armory—in Nayagarh District, killing thirteen police officers and one civilian.

February 16, 2008—Somalia—Islamic insurgents fired mortars at the official residence of Somali President Abdullahi Yusuf, 73, who was unharmed.

February 17, 2008—Afghanistan—A bomb exploded in a crowd at a dogfight in Kandahar, killing more than one hundred people.

February 18, 2008—Afghanistan—The Taliban claimed credit for a Toyota Corolla car bomb that exploded in a crowded market in Spin Boldak, Kandahar, 100 yards from the Pakistan border, killing thirty-eight and wounding thirty-one, including three Canadian soldiers.

February 20, 2008—Morocco—Authorities announced the arrest of thirty-two people during the week in a crackdown on a terrorist network linked to al Qaeda that planned to assassinate

Cabinet members, army officers, and members of the local Jewish community. Some of the group belonged to al-Badil al-Hadari, an Islamist party whose banning was announced the same day. The group had conducted holdups and sold stolen goods. One member worked with European criminals to steal $25.65 million from an armored truck in Luxembourg in 2000. The group also stole gold jewelry in Belgium, melting it down and selling it via a goldsmith who belonged to the group. The group was led by Abdelkader Belliraj, who was arrested, as was political leader Mostafa Lmounatassime; Abdelhafid Sriti, a correspondent for Hizballah's *al-Manar* television; a university professor; and a police superintendent. Belliraj lived in Belgium.

February 22, 2008—United States—At 1:55 p.m., Antoine Lowery, 30, of the District of Columbia, drove a white Chevrolet pickup truck with a snowplow at a high rate of speed off the George Washington Memorial Parkway into a security gate at the headquarters of the Central Intelligence Agency. He was taken into custody after jumping out of the truck and saying, "The truck is going to blow up ... I have a bomb." He also counted down from five to zero several times. No bomb was found. He was released before being charged on February 26. He was rearrested, and on March 6, he appeared at the U.S. District Court in Alexandria on a felony charge of making a bomb threat. U.S. Magistrate Judge Barry Poretz ordered him detained pending a hearing. A federal grand jury indicted him on charges of threatening to assault a federal law enforcement officer, making a bomb threat, and engaging in unauthorized use of a vehicle. He faced a ten-year sentence, three years of supervised release, and a $250,000 fine if convicted. On May 16, he pleaded guilty to making a bomb threat. Sentencing was scheduled for August 8.

February 22, 2008—Tunisia—Al Qaeda in Islamic North Africa claimed credit for kidnapping two Austrian tourists, Wolfgang Ebner, 51, a tax consultant from Hallein, and Andrea Kloiber, 43, his girlfriend. They remained in captivity as of March 11, the date the group released an audiotape to al-Jazeera. Salah Abu Mohammed said the group was avenging Western cooperation with Israel. "We tell Western tourists that at the same time they are flowing into Tunisian lands seeking joy, our brothers are being slain in Gaza by the Jews with the collaboration of the Western states.... The mujahideen have previously warned and alerted them that the apostate Tunisian state cannot and will not be able to protect you, and the hands of the mujahideen can reach you wherever you are on the Tunisian soil." The tourists began their tour in La Goulette on February 10 and were scheduled to go to the Sahara area. They might have left Tunisia during their trip. As of June 11, they were believed to be in Mali. 08022201

February 27, 2008—Qatar—Ayman al-Zawahiri delivered a ten-minute Internet video eulogy for Abu Laith al-Libi, calling him the "knight who only dismounted from his steed's back in order to join the blessed caravan of the martyrs." In the tape, entitled *An Elegy to the Martyred Commander Abu Laith al-Libi*, he observed that "no chief of ours had died of a natural death, nor has our blood been spilled without a response. Al Qaeda field commander al-Libi died in Pakistan on January 28, 2008, in a missile attack. The Sahab Web posting also promised an interview of al-Zawahiri.

February 27, 2008—United States—Las Vegas police found ricin, an anarchist cookbook opened to a page on ricin, castor beans, a respirator, filters, a painter's mask, laboratory glassware, syringes, a notebook on ricin production, and firearms—including two semiautomatic pistols, a rifle, and a pistol with a suppressor—in a storage unit and in the Extended Stay America hotel room that had been used two weeks earlier by a man who was hospitalized for more than two weeks in critical condition. FBI agents searched the Riverton, Utah, suburban home where the hospitalized Roger Von Bergendorff, 57, once lived. On March 21, one of the police officers who inspected the hotel room tested positive for ricin. Von Bergendorff's coma had worn off on March 14. On April 16, he was arrested in Las Vegas and charged with possession of a biological toxin, possession of unregistered firearms, and possession of firearms not identified by serial number. His cousin, Thomas Tholen of Riverton, Utah, had been indicted earlier in April by a federal grand jury in Salt Lake City, Utah, for failing to report production and possession of ricin. Von Bergendorff, an artist, had lived in his cousin's basement. Prosecutors said that during his FBI interrogation, he admitted that "there have been people who have made him mad over the years and he had thoughts about causing them harm to the point of making some plans. However, he maintained that he never acted on those thoughts or plans." He told a federal judge that it was "not in my blood" to use the ricin. He faced thirty years in prison and a $750,000 fine. He was ordered to remain in custody until a preliminary hearing on May 2, when he pleaded not guilty to possession of a biological toxin and weapons

charges. He was represented by attorney Paul Riddle. His trial was scheduled for June 17. On August 4, the wheelchair-bound defendant pleaded guilty to federal charges of possessing a biological toxin. He faced thirty-seven months in federal prison.

February 28, 2008—Pakistan—A 2:00 a.m. missile strike near Kaloosha village in South Waziristan killed ten suspected al Qaeda and Taliban members and wounded seven others. The destroyed house belonged to Pashtun tribesman Sher Mohammad Malikkheil, alias Sheroo, who had known links with the Islamists. He was a member of the Yargulkhel subtribe of the Wazir tribe.

February 29, 2008—Iraq—Chaldean Catholic Archbishop Paulos Faraj Rahho was abducted in Mosul by gunmen who attacked his car, killing his driver and two guards. His body turned up in a shallow grave a fortnight later. On May 18, the Iraqi Central Criminal Court sentenced to death Ahmed Ali Ahmed, alias Abu Omar, a leader of al Qaeda in Iraq, for the murder.

March 2008—Colombia—Authorities announced on March 7 that earlier in the month, members of the Revolutionary Armed Forces of Colombia killed one of their commanders, Manuel Jesus Munoz, alias Ivan Rios, in a mountainous, coffee-growing region in north central Colombia. His bodyguard, Pedro Pablo Montoya, shot him, then severed Munoz's right hand and presented it, his ID card, and a computer to an army column. The United States had offered $5 million for his arrest on drug trafficking charges. The killing took place a week after the killing of Luis Edgar Devia (see March 1, 2008 incident).

March 1, 2008—Ecuador—Colombian troops killed Luis Edgar Devia, 59, alias Raul Reyes, one of the seven members of the Secretariat of the Revolutionary Armed Forces of Colombia (FARC), in a firefight and air strike near the border with Ecuador. Also killed were sixteen other members of FARC, including Guillermo Torres, a commander and a singer-songwriter, and Franklin Aisalla, an Ecuadoran FARC operative. Ecuadoran troops detained Diana Gonzalez of FARC, who was wounded in the clash.

The next day, Venezuelan President Hugo Chavez closed his embassy in Bogota and sent tanks, planes, and ten battalions to the border. Ecuador expelled the Colombian ambassador and also mobilized troops.

Colombia claimed that captured FARC documents and computer files showed that Chavez had paid $300 million to FARC, detailed drug deals, and listed FARC's efforts to acquire 50 kilograms of uranium. Interpol reported that the government had not tampered with the computer disks. Colombian officials said that they had confiscated more than 210,000 rounds of Venezuelan-made ammunition in FARC camps since 2003. Authorities had seized three laptop computers, two external hard drives, and three USB memory sticks. The hardware contained 610 gigabytes, including 210,888 images, 22,481 Web sites, hundreds of spreadsheets, thousands of video files, 37,872 written documents, and 7,989 e-mail addresses.

March 1, 2008—Algeria—Security forces killed twenty-five members of the Algerian al Qaeda affiliate after they had chased thirty of them who were planting roadside bombs in the Tizi-Ouzou and Bejaie regions.

March 3, 2008—Somalia—At 3:30 a.m., the U.S. Navy fired two missiles at al Qaeda member Saleh Ali Saleh Nabhan's hideout in Dhobley. Reports differed on casualties; the *Los Angeles Times* said at least six were killed and ten wounded; CNN said three women and three children were killed and twenty people were wounded. The *Times* also said the target was Hassan Turki, a leader of a Somali Islamist militia who was listed by the U.S. Department of State in 2004 as having links to al Qaeda and running military training camps in Somalia.

March 3, 2008—United States—The ecoterrorist Earth Liberation Front (ELF) was suspected of torching five $2 million luxury homes in the Street of Dreams development in Woodinville, a Seattle suburb. A sign with the letters ELF and "Built green? Nope black!" was found at the scene. There were no injuries but $7 million in damage was reported.

March 4, 2008—United States—*MSNBC* reported that the Transportation Security Administration's *Mass Transit System Threat Assessment* warned local law enforcement officials that terrorists were considering attacking mass transit systems, including passenger rail systems, "because they are accessible to large numbers of the public and are notoriously difficult to secure."

March 4, 2008—Nigeria—Gunmen attacked a highway construction crew, kidnapping a foreign worker in the south. The gunmen shot a soldier protecting the workers outside Port Harcourt. The Movement for the Emancipation of the Niger Delta was suspected. 08030401

March 5, 2008—China—At 10:00 a.m., Xia Tao, a man carrying explosives, hijacked a bus with ten Australian tourists in Xi'an, in the northwest Shaanxi Province. He released nine hostages but kept a 48-year-old woman from New South Wales and the group's Chinese translator. He had demanded free passage on another bus to the airport. He negotiated for three hours before police shot him to death at a toll plaza at the airport. No hostages were harmed. 08030501

March 6, 2008—United States—A bomb exploded at 3:43 a.m. in front of an armed forces recruiting station in Times Square, New York City, breaking windows but causing no injuries. Witnesses saw a man wearing a backpack dismount a bicycle, leave something at the entrance, and pedal away. The low order explosive was contained in a military-style ammunition box. Surveillance video showed the bicyclist showing up at 3:37 a.m. and leaving two minutes later. Police later received a blue 10-speed bike they believed was involved. Before the bombing, anarchist writings and photos of spots around the city, including the recruitment station and the Times Square police station, were found in several bags.

Several Congressional offices, mostly of Democratic members of the House of Representatives, received a letter that contained a photograph of a man standing in front of the pre-bombed recruiting station and a note saying, "We did it. Happy New York." The letters were more than thirty pages long and had serial numbers suggesting that several hundred had been printed. One letter had a California return address. The FBI said on March 7 that the letters and bomb were not linked. The FBI had interviewed the Los Angeles man who sent the two hundred-plus letters. He was not charged.

Authorities later said the bombing might have been the work of two of four men in a car who fled from a car at a Canada border crossing. Authorities found bags that contained passports of four people, along with the anarchist writings and photographs.

March 6, 2008—Thailand—Police arrested Tajikistan-born Russian arms dealer Victor Bout, 41, the model for Nicholas Cage's character in *Lord of War*. The U.S. Drug Enforcement Administration (DEA) had issued a warrant for his arrest. The United States charged him with conspiracy to smuggle missiles and rocket launchers to Revolutionary Armed Forces of Colombia rebels. The former Soviet Air Force officer was alleged by British intelligence to have provided arms to the Taliban and al Qaeda. The U.S. government added that he made a $50 million profit from his sales to the Taliban. On April 26, 2010, a Thai criminal court dismissed the former KGB major's claim that his arrest was illegal because of DEA involvement in the bust.

March 6, 2008—Philippines—The government announced the arrest of three suspected Middle Eastern militants who were plotting to bomb the embassies of the United States, United Kingdom, Australia, and Israel. One plotter was arrested in Manila; two others were separately captured in the south. They were believed linked to Jemaah Islamiyah and Abu Sayyaf. One suspect was Jordanian. One suspect was arrested at the Manila airport on February 15. Police said the plot was not linked to another plot to assassinate President Gloria Macapagal Arroyo. 08030601

March 6, 2008—Israel—At 8:30 p.m. Ala Abu Dehein, 25, a Palestinian bus driver from East Jerusalem's Jabel Mukaber neighborhood, walked into west Jerusalem's Merkaz HaRav yeshiva, a three-story Jewish seminary school, and fired an AK-47 and a pistol, killing eight rabbinical students and wounding another nine. Yitzhak Dadon, a part-time student, claimed he shot him to death, although the police credited an army officer and two undercover policemen. The students were ages 15 to 26. Dehein held an Israeli ID card. He was engaged to be married in the summer of 2008. Police took nine of his relatives into custody for questioning. The 84-year-old institute is an ideological base for the settler movement. Hamas praised the attack, but waffled on whether it was involved. Hizballah said a previously-unknown group named for Imad Mughniyeh claimed credit. Thousands of Palestinians in Gaza celebrated in the streets. 08030602

March 6, 2008—South Africa—Five members of the staff of Mokothedi Mpshe, acting chief of a prosecutor's office, became ill after handling a poisoned letter sent to the office. He had been heading corruption cases against politicians and government leaders, including African National Congress President Jakob Zuma and national police commissioner Jackie Selebi. Mpshe had not touched the letter. Staffers developed rashes and headaches but returned to work after the weekend.

March 7, 2008—Spain—The Basque Nation and Liberty was suspected in the shooting death of Isafas Carrasco, 42, in the Basque town of Arrasate as he left his home with his wife and daughter. No one claimed credit. The former city councilman was killed two days before the national elections.

March 7, 2008—China—Xinjiang's governor announced on March 8 that a flight crew prevented an attempt by more than one person to crash China Southern flight CZ6901 from Urumqi, capital of Xinjiang Province. The plane left Urumqi at 10:35 a.m. on Friday. The plane made an emergency landing in Lanzhou at 12:40 p.m. No passengers were reported injured. Two passengers were taken into custody. "Inflammable material" was found in the plane's restroom. Authorities later said that a 19-year-old Uighur woman was detained after trying to set a fire in the airplane's restroom and crash the flight. 08030701

March 11, 2008—Pakistan—A suicide bomber damaged the Lahore headquarters of the Federal Investigation Agency, which handles illegal immigration and smuggling, killing 28 people and injuring more than 170. A second suicide bomber struck a residential section of Lahore, killing another 3.

March 15, 2008—Pakistan—At 8:45 p.m., a bomb exploded at the Luna Caprese, an Italian restaurant in Islamabad that is frequented by foreigners, including Americans and Chinese. Two people were killed, including a Turkish woman, and eleven were wounded, including five Americans who work at the U.S. Embassy, a staff member of the British High Commission (embassy), a Canadian, a Japanese citizen, and three Pakistanis, including a couple dining and a waiter. Two Pakistanis were in critical condition and four Americans were in stable condition. A local al Qaeda affiliate was suspected. The press reported the next day that four of the injured Americans were FBI agents, including the legal attaché, assistant legal attaché, and a supervisor. 08031501

March 18, 2008—Yemen—The United States closed its embassy in Sana'a after three mortar rounds exploded at a nearby girls' high school at 12:40 p.m. Local authorities said it was a private affair not connected with terrorism, although the State Department said it was "directed against our embassy." The press said a Yemeni security guard was killed and more than a dozen girls were injured; the Interior Ministry said five soldiers and thirteen school girls were injured, three seriously. An al Qaeda cell led by Hamza al-Dayan was believed responsible. He fled the scene with three accomplices. On March 20, authorities arrested five suspects. Al-Dayan remained at large.

On April 20, 2008, Sana'a authorities arrested Muhammad Yaqout, a member of the Egyptian Jihad group suspected of being connected with terrorists who attack U.S. targets in Sana'a. Authorities said he was behind the two mortar attacks against the U.S. Embassy on March 18 and a residential compound housing U.S. and other

Western citizens on April 6. He had been arrested in August 2007 after a suicide car bombing killed eight Spanish tourists in Marib on July 2, 2007. He was released after two months.

In March 2009, Yemen began the trial in a Sana'a courthouse of sixteen suspected al Qaeda members, including fourteen Yemenis and two Syrians, on twenty-three terrorism charges, including the March 2008 mortar attack on the U.S. Embassy that instead hit the neighboring girls' school, and killings of foreigners, including the January 2008 murder of two female Belgian tourists, attacks on a foreigners' residential compound in Hadramout Province, and a gun battle with police in which an al Qaeda leader was killed.

On July 11, 2010, a Yemeni appeals court confirmed the death sentences against four al Qaeda terrorists who attacked the U.S. Embassy in March 2008 and killed two Belgian female tourists in January 2008. They were convicted in 2009. They had killed a school guard in a nearby building during the embassy attack. The court upheld fifteen-year sentences for ten other terrorists, including four Syrians and a Saudi, for orchestrating the attacks. 08031801

March 18, 2008—Somalia/United States—The United States designated the al-Shabaab militant wing of the Islamic Courts movement as a foreign terrorist group, calling it al Qaeda's main link to Somalia.

March 19, 2008—Israel—On April 10, Shin Bet announced that Aham Rial, 21, and Ana Salum, 21, two Palestinians from Nablus, had confessed to plotting to poison food they would serve at the Grill Express restaurant near the Diamond Exchange in Ramat Gan. They were members of the al-Aqsa Martyrs Brigade in Nablus, which also asked them to smuggle a suicide bomber into Israel. The duo were arrested on March 19. They were in the country illegally and lacked work permits.

March 19, 2008—Qatar—In a five-minute audiotape, entitled *The Response Is What You See, Not What You Hear*, posted on the Internet, Osama bin Laden condemned "those who are wise at the European Union" for supporting the United States in Afghanistan and for permitting publications of cartoons of the prophet Muhammad. "You were overboard in your unbelief and freed yourselves of the etiquettes of dispute and morals of fighting and went to the extent of publishing these insulting drawings. This is the greater and more serious tragedy, and the reckoning for it will be more severe." Muslims did not mock Jesus, according to bin Laden. "The laws of men which

clash with the legislation of Allah the Most High are null and void, aren't sacred and don't matter to us." He said the "crownless king in Riyadh" could have stopped the cartoons' publication "if it matter to him.... If there is no check on the freedom of your words, then let your hearts be open to the freedom of our actions." He also noted that "your publications of these drawings came in the framework of a new crusade in which the Pope of the Vatican has played a large, lengthy role and is a confirmation from you that the war continues." He said that European leaders were "testing Muslims." "These savage acts haven't ended the war, but rather, increase our determination to cling to our right, avenge our people and expel invaders from our country." "How it saddens us that you target our villages with your bombing: those modest mud villages which have collapsed onto our women and children. You do that intentionally, and I am witness to that. All of this ... without right and in conformity with your oppressive ally who, along with his aggressive policies, is about to depart the White House." "Animosity among people is very old but wise people ... have always been keen on maintaining the manners of disagreement and the ethics of fighting ... but you have abandoned many of these ethics although you use them as slogans." But "brutality" further made Muslims determined to "avenge our folk and eject the invaders from our countries." "The responses will be what you see and not what you hear and let our mothers bereave us if we do not make victorious our messenger of God." The audio coincided with Muhammad's birthday, and with the fifth anniversary of the coalition invasion of Iraq.

March 20, 2008—Qatar—In his second audiotape within twenty-four hours, Osama bin Laden observed that "Iraq is the perfect base to set up the jihad to liberate Palestine," and that its neighbors should "do their best in supporting their mujahideen brothers in Iraq." "My speech to you is about the siege of Gaza and the way to liberate it.... The Gaza siege is a direct result of Annapolis," site of the November 2007 summit of Israeli and Palestinian leaders. He called on Palestinians to ignore its political parties that are "mired in trickery of the blasphemous democracy ... Palestine cannot be retaken by negotiations and dialogue, but with fire and iron." And if a Muslim cannot fight in "the land of al-Quds" (Palestine), then "the nearest field of jihad today to support our people in Palestine is the Iraqi field." Those living in Syria, Lebanon, Jordan, and Saudi Arabia should "help in support of their mujahideen brothers in Iraq, which is the greatest opportunity and the biggest task."

March 23, 2008—Qatar—Ayman al-Zawahiri released a four-minute, forty-four-second audiotape on Islamist Web sites, calling on Muslims to attack Americans and Israelis to "liberate" Gaza in defense of Palestine.

> Muslims, today is your day. Strike the interests of the Jews, the Americans, and all those who participated in the attack on Muslims. Monitor the targets, collect money, prepare the equipment, plan with precision and then—while relying on God—assault, seeking martyrdom and paradise... Let us strike their interests everywhere, just as they gathered against us from everywhere, and let them know that every dollar they spend on the killing of Muslims, and for every bullet they fire at us, a volcano will turn back on them... There will be shed blood instead in return... They cannot expect to support Israel, then live in peace while the Jews are killing our fugitive and besieged people... Today there is no room for he who says that we should only fight the Jews in Palestine... If you let the people of Gaza be killed today, while you shout and demonstrate, tomorrow the event will turn around and the Crusaders and the Jews will kill you instead, and others will do nothing but shout back and demonstrate.

He said Egypt was cooperating with Israel in sanctioning Hamas.

> The plot was well-planned against Gaza. The bombs of the Jews are over the heads of its people, the Israeli tanks are aiming at their chests and the Egyptian border guards and security officers are aiming at their backs, preventing any kind of supplies to them, narrowing the routes to their food supplies and medication, preventing help to reach them and prohibiting them from evacuating their injured and protecting their families, locking them down from the south and the west so that the Jews take their full opportunity to kill and imprison whoever they wish and to destroy whatever they want.

He said the Egyptian leader "repeats the same dirty role" as the Lebanese Phalangists. "The roles are the same, even if the faces change—the same betrayal even if the names have changed." He also complained about the publication of a cartoon insulting the Prophet Muhammad, saying, "They will never be able to insult and make a mockery out of our Prophet, peace and prayers of Allah be upon him."

March 24, 2008—Egypt—The *Global Patriot*, a U.S. cargo ship under short term charter for the U.S. Navy's Military Sealift Command, fired on a small Egyptian boat while in the Suez Canal,

killing Mohammed Fouad, 27, a father of three. The vessel had been approached by several small boats, who were warned off via a flare. The small boat continued to approach, and two warning shots were fired.

April 2008—Malaysia/Indonesia—In mid–April, Malaysian authorities arrested Jemaah Islamiyah (JI) leaders Dr. Agus Purwanto and Abdur Rohim and sent them to Indonesia for their possible roles in fomenting violence in Poso. Abdur Rohim was believed to have replaced Zarkasih as the leader of JI.

April 2008—Nigeria—In mid–April, the Movement for the Emancipation of the Niger Delta claimed credit for attacking a pipeline operated by a Royal Dutch Shell joint venture that shut down a small amount of oil production. 08049901

April 1, 2008—United States—Officials at Orlando International Airport found pipe bomb making materials in the luggage of Kevin Brown, 32, a Jamaican who had been acting suspiciously near the Virgin Atlantic and Jamaica Airlines ticket counters in Terminal A. He had been scheduled to fly on Air Jamaica flight 80 to Montego Bay. He was held on one count of carrying an incendiary device or explosive onto a plane. His baggage held two galvanized pipes, end caps, two containers of BBs, batteries, two containers of nitromethane, a laptop, and bomb-making literature. He was in the United States legally. At his appearance in federal court in Orlando the next day, his was silent. His attorney said he wanted to show friends how to build explosives the way he learned in Iraq.

April 1, 2008—Turkey—Authorities conducted raids in eight Istanbul districts, arresting forty-five people suspected of al Qaeda involvement and plotting attacks.

April 1, 2008—Somalia—Gunmen kidnapped a Briton and a Kenyan who were working for the India-based Genesys International Corporation, which conducted aerial surveys for the United Nations to prepare maps of the area. The contract workers were kidnapped on the main road between Saakow and Bualle, 200 miles southwest of Mogadishu. 08040101

April 2, 2008—Qatar—In the first of two chat sessions, al Qaeda deputy Ayman al-Zawahiri addressed some of the nine hundred questions that had been posted to him earlier on Islamist Web sites. His responses were posted as a ninety-minute *al-Sahab* audio on a Web site. These are excerpts:

> Talib Jami'i Tib al-Jazaa'ir, an Algerian medical

student, noted that the December 11, 2007, suicide attacks on the UN offices in Algiers killed forty-one people, including eighteen employees, including three foreigners, and asked, "I want al-Zawahiri to answer me about those who kill the people in Algeria. What is the legal evidence for killing the innocents?" Another individual asked, "Excuse me, Mr. Zawahiri, but who is it who is killing with Your Excellency's blessing the innocents in Baghdad, Morocco, and Algeria?" Al-Zawahiri denied their innocence.

> Rather, according to the communiqué from the brothers in al Qaeda in the Islamic Maghreb, they are from the Crusader unbelievers and the government troops who defend them.... We haven't killed the innocents, not in Baghdad, nor in Morocco, nor in Algeria, nor anywhere else.... And if there is any innocent who was killed in the mujahideen's operations, then it was either unintentional error or out of necessity as in cases of al-Tatarrus [taking human shields by the enemy].... Rather, the enemies of al Qaeda kill innocents, because the enemy intentionally takes up positions in the midst of the Muslims for them to be human shields for him.... We don't kill innocents. In fact, we fight those who kill innocent—the Americans, the Jews, the Russians, the French and their agents.... Were we insane killers of innocents as the questioner claims, it would be possible for us to kill thousands of them in the crowded markets.

Al-Zawahiri continued, "The United Nations is an enemy of Islam and Muslims. It is the one which codified and legitimized the setting up of the state of Israel and its taking over of the Muslims' lands." The UN had permitted "crusaders" to enter Afghanistan and Iraq, permitted the separation of East Timor from Indonesia, but "it doesn't recognize that [right] for Chechnya, nor for all the Muslim Caucasus, nor for Kashmir, nor for Ceuta and Melilla, nor for Bosnia."

"Sheikh Osama bin Laden is healthy and well, by the grace of Allah. The prejudiced ones always try to spread false information about him being ill, but even if Osama bin Laden doesn't become ill, he must die one day, whereas Allah's religion will remain until Allah inherits the Earth and everything on it."

Mudarris Jughrafiya asked, "Why have you, to this day, not carried out any strike in Israel? Or is it easier to kill Muslims in the markets? Maybe it is necessary to take some geography lessons, because your maps only show the Muslim's states." Al-Zawahiri responded that al Qaeda had attacked Israeli interests in Tunisia and Kenya, "I expect the jihadi influence to spread after the Americans' exit from Iraq, and to move towards Jerusalem." He called for attacks against Israel. "We promise Muslim brothers that we will strive as much as we can to deal blows to the Jews inside Israel and outside it."

He noted that the Saudi government would soon crumble, because it is "swimming against the tide of history," as is the government of Egypt, a "corrupt, rotten regime [that] cannot possibly continue." Riyadh's "link to the international crusade is doomed.... The jihadist movement in the Peninsula will return, God willing." "We call the nation in Egypt and other parts to hit crusader and Jewish interests wherever they are to force the invaders to leave Muslim land, and to stop supporting corrupt regimes." He counseled patience to those who awaited the end of the Egyptian regime, citing the Arabic proverb, "The days will reveal to you what you didn't know, and news will come to you from those who didn't have it." "Severity of repression might delay change but it cannot stop it.... What matters is to prepare for change, being patient, willingness to make sacrifice and seizing opportunities."

He condemned a prominent Muslim scholar, Yusuf al-Qaradawi.

He also criticized Hamas, saying it should not participate in Gaza's secular government. "I took a gradual approach with them, but they didn't heed the opinion of their brothers." He noted that the killing of Israeli children "is not permitted" in rocket attacks.

Muslims should join "open jihad fields such as Somalia, Iraq, Algeria, and Afghanistan.... Be careful about ... the major sin of not rising for jihad."

"The myth of unipolar world is over. The strikes on New York and Washington are identifying marks of this collapse, but empires do not collapse in a minute and could take decades. The collapse of the Soviet Union is the closest example."

The audio posting was accompanied by a forty-six-page English-language transcript of the session.

April 6, 2008—Yemen—Four explosive projectiles were fired at a housing complex for foreign oil workers in Sana'a's Haddah neighborhood. No injuries were reported when three rounds went off inside the compound and another exploded outside the building. The U.S. Embassy ordered non-emergency employees to leave the country. Authorities arrested seven people in the case, suggesting they had al Qaeda connections. The little-known Jund al-Yemen Brigades said the attack was to avenge the death of Taliban military commander Mullah Dadullah in 2007 in Afghanistan.

On April 20, 2008, Sana'a authorities arrested Muhammad Yaqout, a member of the Egyptian Jihad group suspected of being connected with terrorists who attack U.S. targets in Sana'a. Authorities said he was behind two mortar attacks against the U.S. Embassy on March 18 and a residential compound housing U.S. and other Western citizens on April 6. He had been arrested in August 2007 after a suicide car bombing killed eight Spanish tourists in Marib on July 2, 2007. He was released after two months. 08040601

April 6, 2008—Sri Lanka—Fourteen people, including former Olympic marathoner K. A. Karunaratne, national athletics coach Lakshman de Alwis, and a government minister were killed and ninety others were wounded when a suicide bomber attacked the opening of a marathon outside Colombo. The Liberation Tigers of Tamil Eelam were suspected.

April 7, 2008—Malaysia—A knife-wielding Bangladeshi man injured several passengers on a GMG Airlines flight from Kuala Lumpur, Malaysia, to Dhaka, Bangladesh. The pilot landed at Don Muang International Airport in Bangkok at 10:00 a.m. The attacker and victims were treated for minor injuries.

April 9, 2008—Israel—After setting off a mortar barrage, four gunmen breached the Israel border with Gaza and attacked the Nahal Oz oil distribution center that supplies the fuel for Gaza, killing two civilian workers, including Oleg Lipson. Two of the militants were killed; the other two escaped. Israel blamed Hamas, although the attack was claimed by the Popular Resistance Committee, Islamic Jihad, and Fatah's al-Muhjahedeen Brigades. The Popular Resistance Committee said the joint operation had been designed to kidnap an Israeli soldier. The next day, Israel suspended fuel shipments.

April 10, 2008—China—The government announced the arrests in March and April of thirty-five people in the Xinjiang Uighur Autonomous region who were planning to set off terrorist bombs in Beijing and Shanghai in May during the Beijing Summer Olympics. Chinese authorities said they had found jihadist propaganda and bomb-making equipment in Xinjiang in January.

April 12, 2008—Iran—An explosion at the Shohada religious center of Rahpouyan Vesal (Followers of the Road to Join Up with God) at 9:00 p.m. during the weekly address by cleric Mohammad Enjavinejad killed nine and injured sixty-six people in the men's section of the mosque in Shiraz. Individuals posting to the group's Web site blamed Wahhabis, although investigators were not certain that a bomb was involved.

April 13, 2008—Somalia—Gunmen killed a Briton, two Kenyans, and a Somali in an 11:00 p.m. attack on school grounds in Beledweyne during an attack on the town by Islamic militants. 08041301

April 16, 2008—Spain—Judge Ismael Moreno of the National Court indicted Syrian-born Imad Eddin Barakat Yarkas, 44; Syria-born Muhamed Galeb Kalaje Zouaydi, 47; and Bassam Dalati Satut, 48, on suspicion of financing terrorist cells.

April 17, 2008—Spain—Basque Nation and Liberty set off a bomb in Balbao, injuring seven police officers outside a ruling Socialist Party locale. A warning phone call came a few minutes before the 6:00 a.m. explosion.

April 17, 2008—United Kingdom—Bristol authorities conducted two controlled detonations after arresting a 19-year-old on terrorism charges.

April 17, 2008—Qatar—Ayman al-Zawahiri released a sixteen-minute audiotape on the Internet, in which he said that the U.S. occupation of Iraq was a failure that the Bush administration would have to pass on to its successor. "Where the American invasion stands now, after five years, is failure and defeat." "If the American forces leave, they will lose everything. And if they stay, they will bleed to death." He said that halting troop withdrawals for forty-five days "is all a silly episode to disguise failure in Iraq and so Bush would avoid making a decision on withdrawing troops—which is considered to be a declaration of crusaders' defeat in Iraq—and move forward the problem to be the next president's issue." He also chastised Sunnis who joined the Americans against the terrorists in Iraq, saying, "Weren't these Awakening [Councils] supposed to hasten the departure of the American forces, or are these Awakenings in need of someone to defend them and protect them?" He noted, "Iraq nowadays is the most important battlefield on which our mujahideen are waging a war against the forces of the Zionist-Christian Crusade. Therefore, supporting the mujahideen in Iraq and especially the Islamic State of Iraq is a most important duty." He criticized Shi'ite cleric Muqtada al-Sadr, saying he "has become the laughing stock of the world" and an Iranian "toy." He complained about Egypt's "exploitation of Muslims." "Corruption and stealing have gotten to the point of making people hungry and preventing them from basic food. Making people hungry in Egypt ... is a part of the U.S.-Zionist plan ... to make Muslims subservient." He said the Democratic presidential candidates were "trying to deceive their people by saying that they will withdraw their troops from Iraq by talking to Iran."

April 19, 2008—Israel—Three Hamas suicide bombers set off two car bombs, wounding thirteen Israeli soldiers at the Kerem Shalom border crossing between Israel and the Gaza Strip at 6:00 a.m. during Passover.

April 19, 2008—Iraq—An individual claiming to be Abu Hamza al-Muhajir, alias Abu Ayyub al-Masri, head of al Qaeda in Iraq, said on an Internet audiotape that the group would launch a month-long offensive against U.S. troops. "We call on our beloved ones ... that each unit should present the head of an American as a gift to the charlatan Bush ... in addition to one of the apostate servants and slaves of the Awakening (Councils) during a one-month period.... As long as our hearts are together, obeying a leader that we trust ... then I swear to God, if America brought all its armies and its men and women to fight us, we will win."

April 21, 2008—Indonesia—A court sentenced Abu Dujana, military leader of Jemaah Islamiyah, to fifteen years in prison for illegal possession of firearms and explosives and of harboring suspected terrorists. The Arabic speaker was believed involved in the 2002 Bali nightclub bombings and other terrorist attacks, including those on the Australian Embassy and J. W. Marriott hotel. He trained in Afghanistan where he met Osama bin Laden. He had been captured in June 2007.

April 21, 2008—Spain—Basque Nation and Liberty phoned in a warning before a bomb damaged the recreation center of the ruling Socialist Party in the Basque town of Elgoibar. No injuries were reported in the 3:25 a.m. explosion.

April 21, 2008—Nigeria—The Movement for the Emancipation of the Niger Delta (MEND) said that it had blown up two pipelines it claimed were operated by the Chevron Corporation and a Royal Dutch Shell PLC joint venture in southern Rivers state. MEND asked actor George Clooney and former U.S. President Jimmy Carter to mediate. 08042101-02

April 21, 2008—Pakistan—Two UN Food Program workers were kidnapped in the Kyber Agency region. They were rescued by Pakistani authorities in a gun battle in which one paramilitary soldier was killed and seven others were wounded. 08042103

April 22, 2008—Qatar—Ayman al-Zawahiri released a two-hour audiotape on the Internet as the second installment of his answers to some nine hundred questions that had been posted on jihadi Web sites. He called on Muslims to join al Qaeda in Iraq. He claimed al Qaeda was planning attacks on Western targets plus Japan, which helps the "crusader campaign." Japan helped "under the banner of the crusader coalition ... therefore it participated in the crusader campaign against the lands of Islam. Our Islamic faith urged us to resist the injustice and aggression even if they were the most powerful on Earth. Should Japan take a lesson from this? ... We think that any country that joined aggression on Muslims must be deterred."

He alleged that Iran was behind the conspiracy myth that Israel was behind 9/11 saying Tehran and Hizballah were trying to discredit Sunni al Qaeda. He claimed Hizballah's *al-Manar TV* started the rumor, observing, "The purpose of this lie is clear ... that there are no heroes among the Sunnis who can hurt America as no else did in history. Iranian media snapped up this lie and repeated it. Iran's aim here is also clear: to cover up its involvement with America in invading the homes of Muslims in Afghanistan and Iraq."

He deemed al Qaeda in Iraq, also known as the Islamic Nation of Iraq, "the primary force opposing the crusaders and challenging Iranian ambitions." He mentioned global warming as reflecting "how criminal, brutal and greedy the Western crusader world is, with America at the top." Global warming "would make the world more sympathetic to and understanding of the Muslims' jihad against the aggressor America."

He said that "there are no women in al Qaeda jihadi group, but the women of the mujahideen are playing a heroic role in taking care of their houses and sons."

Regarding Afghanistan, he noted, "residents of the provinces and various regions welcome the Taliban and urge them to come to purify their regions of corruption; this is the secret of Taliban quick deployment and gripping control of 95 percent of Afghanistan. The crusaders and their agents in Pakistan and Afghanistan are starting to fall."

Muslims may not live permanently in the West because they would "have permanent stay there under the laws of the infidels."

The terrorism research center at West Point reported that 1,868 questions had been submitted.

April 23, 2008—Denmark—The Foreign Ministry closed its embassies in Algeria and Afghanistan after receiving further threats because of newspapers reprinting on February 13 a cartoon viewed by Muslims as demeaning Muhammad.

April 23, 2008—Germany—Some 130 police officers arrested nine citizens, ages 27 to 47, in Berlin, Bonn, and other locations, who were suspected of trying to convert others to radical Islam. The suspects were affiliated with the Multi-Kultur-Haus, an Islamic center in Neu-Ulm in the south that had been shut down in 2005 after authorities found material calling for jihadi suicide attacks in Iraq.

April 24, 2008—Nigeria—The Movement for the Emancipation of the Nigerian Delta said it had sabotaged a pipeline of Royal Dutch Shell in southern Rivers State. 08042501

April 25, 2008—Israel—A Palestinian gunman shot to death two Israeli guards at a factory on the border of Israel and the West Bank at 7:00 a.m. Hamas was among the groups that claimed credit for the attack at the entrance to the industrial zone of Nitzanei Shalom. The gunmen escaped.

April 26, 2008—Iraq—Abdullah Saleh al-Ajmi, 29, born in Almadi, Kuwait, set off a suicide bomb in Mosul near a police patrol. His was one of three suicide bombings that day that killed a total of seven people, including two police officers, and wounded twenty-eight others. He had been released from Guantanamo in 2005. He had been flown to Guantanamo from Bagram Air Base in Afghanistan on January 17, 2002. Numerous pundits noted that the Guantanamo detainees still posed a threat of terrorist recidivism if released.

April 27, 2008—Lebanon—Hizballah detained Karim Pakzad, a French delegate to the Socialist International meeting in Beirut. He was held for a few hours and released. 08042701

April 27, 2008—Afghanistan—Taliban gunmen killed three people, including a member of Parliament, Fazel Rahman Samkanai, and a 10-year-old boy, and wounded eleven when they fired mortars at a reviewing stand at an Afghan National Day celebration in an attempt to assassinate President Hamid Karzai. A second group of Taliban gunmen fired guns into the VIP stands from the third-floor room of a three-story hotel 500 yards from the parade ground. Karzai was unhurt. Among the injured were army officers, police officers, civilians, and parliamentarian Muhammad Daud Zazai. Several suspects were arrested in the attack in front of the Eid Gah Mosque; another two were killed. Among the dead was Nasir Ahmad Latifi, leader of the Qizilbash ethnic minority. Within a day, authorities had detained one hundred people for questioning. At least sixteen Afghans, including eight government employees, admitted involvement, and twenty government employees were suspended.

On April 30, hundreds of Afghan intelligence agents raided a Taliban redoubt in western Kabul. Seven people were killed, including three of the intelligence agents. One of those killed had supplied weapons in the assassination attempt. Among those killed was Homayoun, suspected of directing an attack on the Serena Hotel in Kabul in January 2008. He was linked to Jalaladdin Haqqani, who has al Qaeda ties. Six other suspects were detained in separate raids. On May 4, authorities arrested two Afghan government employees for alleged involvement.

On June 26, the Afghan government publicly accused the Pakistani Inter-Services Intelligence (ISI) agency of organizing the attack, a charge quickly denied by the Pakistani government. The Afghan government cited confessions of sixteen detainees and cell phone contacts.

May 1, 2008—Somalia—A U.S. air strike at 2:00 a.m. on Dusa Mareb killed Aden Hashi Ayro, an Islamist commander who led al-Shabaab militants and was believed to be the senior al Qaeda leader in Somalia, and another individual. His group had conducted daily attacks on government troops and their Ethiopian allies. In late February, the United States had designated the group a terrorist organization.

May 2, 2008—Yemen—A bomb on a motorcycle exploded in a crowd of worshipers leaving Friday prayers at a mosque, killing eighteen and wounding forty-eight in Saada in a mountainous Shi'ite populated northern border with Saudi Arabia. The area is host to a rebellion by the al-Zaydi sect that began in 2004.

May 5, 2008—Turkey—Peritan Derseem, a spokesman for PEJAK, the Iranian wing of the Kurdistan Workers' Party (PKK) threatened to launch suicide attacks against U.S. interests to punish the United States for sharing intelligence with Turkey after Turkey bombed rebel bases on Mount Qandil on the Iran-Iraq border, killing 150 Kurdish rebels. Derseem said only six were killed. She said that although some rebels wanted to conduct suicide attacks, the group's leadership had yet to approve them. "We have changed our stand toward the United States government and we are standing against them now. Maybe someday ... individual combatants might launch suicide attacks inside Iraq and Turkey, and even against American interests." She said PEJAK was operationally independent of the mainstream PKK.

May 7, 2008—Colombia—Carlos Mario Jimenez, 42, one of the three members of the directorate of the right-wing United Self-Defense Forces of Colombia (AUC), who commanded the

Central Bolivar Bloc of six thousand rebels who ran a cocaine trafficking operation, was extradited to the United States. A judge had blocked the extradition in April 2008, but the judiciary's senior administrative panel overruled him on May 6. He was to be charged with cocaine trafficking and financing a terrorist group. He was the first AUC leader to be extradited.

May 13, 2008—Colombia—Bogota announced the extradition of thirteen senior paramilitary leaders of the right-wing United Self-Defense Forces of Colombia to the United States. They had been accused of ordering the murders of thousands of people, including peasants, leftist politicians, journalists, and union activists. While in Colombian jails, they ran a cocaine trafficking organization. They included Salvatore Mancuso; Rodrigo Tovar, alias Jorge 40; Diego Fernando Murillo, alias Don Berna; Hernan Giraldo; and Ramiro Vanoy.

May 13, 2008—India—Seven bicycle bombs went off within twelve minutes and within 500 yards of each other in Jaipur, killing at least sixty and injuring scores of others. Other bombs were defused. Disgruntled Muslim youths were suspected. The first bomb went off at 7:35 p.m. outside a police station and near a market. A second bomb went off near a sweet shop. One bomb went off outside the Hanuman temple, a Hindu place of worship. Others exploded at a jewelry market and close to the Hawa Mahal (Palace of Winds).

May 14, 2008—Pakistan—U.S. Predator drones fired Hellfire missiles at two male guesthouses in Damodola, Banjaur, killing al Qaeda operative Abu Suleiman al-Jaziery—an Algerian "high value target"—among several local fighters and foreigners. Authorities believed he was planning attacks outside Pakistan. The death toll ranged from eleven to thirty. Faqir Mohammed, deputy leader of Pakistan's Taliban movement, vowed revenge.

May 14, 2008—France—A judge convicted five Frenchmen, a Moroccan, and an Algerian on terrorism charges of "criminal association with a terrorist enterprise" for sending a dozen French fighters to training camps for al Qaeda in Iraq. Sentences ranged from eighteen months to seven years. Three defendants were released for time served. Each confessed to traveling to Iraq. They had faced ten-year sentences. Farid Benyettou, 27, the group's leader, was sentenced to six years for providing weapons, training, and travel through Syria to Iraq for young men he had recruited via religious teaching. He was a former janitor turned street preacher. Boubakeur el-Hakim, whose brother was killed in Iraq, received seven years.

May 14, 2008—Iraq—At 6:00 p.m. a 12-year-old suicide bomber killed twenty-three people and injured twenty-five in an attack against relatives of Col. Faisal Ismail al-Zobaie, Fallujah's police chief and repentant insurgent, during the funeral for al-Zobaie's uncle, a school principal. The uncle was murdered when insurgents demanded to know whether he was al-Zobaie's uncle. Abu al-Laith al-Jubori, spokesman for al Qaeda in Iraq, claimed credit for the funeral attack in the Zobaa area west of Baghdad.

May 15, 2008—Iraq—At 5:00 p.m., gunmen fired on a car carrying three Iranian Embassy staffers on their way to visit the Kadhimiya Shi'ite shrine in northwestern Baghdad, wounding them and their local driver. Two of the victims were seriously wounded. 08051501

May 16, 2008—Qatar—In the span of three days, Osama bin Laden released onto a jihadi Web site a ten-minute audiotape and a twenty-two-minute audiotape, accompanied by a stock photo of him in a white robe and turban next to a photo of the al-Aqsa mosque. One tape, entitled *The Causes of Conflict on the Sixtieth Anniversary of the State of Israeli Occupation*, coincided with the sixtieth anniversary of the founding of the state of Israel. "The participation of Western leaders with the Jews in this celebration confirms that the West backs this Jewish occupation of our land, and that they stand in the Israeli corner against us." He observed that "we will continue, God permitting, our struggle against the Israelis and their allies. We are not going to give up an inch of the land of Palestine as long as there is one true Muslim on Earth." "This is evidence that Palestine is our land, and the Israelis are invaders and occupiers who should be fought." "To Western nations ... this speech is to understand the core reason of the war between our civilization and your civilizations. I mean the Palestinian cause." "The Palestinian cause is the major issue for my (Islamic) nation. It was an important element in fueling me from the beginning and the nineteen others [presumably the 9/11 hijackers] with a great motive to fight for those subjected to injustice and the oppressed." He said the Western media was "portraying the Jewish invaders, the occupiers of our land, as the victims, while it portrayed us as the terrorists. Sixty years ago, the Israeli state didn't exist. Instead, it was established on the land of Palestine raped by force. Israelis are occupying invaders whom we should fight." "Peace talks that started sixty years ago are just meant to deceive the idiots. After all the destruction and the killings ... your leaders talk about principles. This is unbearable."

Mentioning former Israeli Prime Minister Menachem Begin, he suggested that "instead of punishing him over his crimes ... he was awarded a Nobel Prize." He criticized leaders who achieved power "either by a military coup or with backing from foreign forces. Those kings and leaders sacrificed Palestine and al-Aqsa to keep their crowns." He said these leaders were "wolves" and "agents of the crusaders." "Every day, the herd wishes the wolves would stop preying on it." "They have decided that peace with the Zionists is their strategic option so damn their decision." "Even if all the leaders have sacrificed the Palestinian issue in its entirety, we are not relieved of the responsibility.... Each one of us is responsible for the death of our vulnerable people in Gaza where scores have died because of the blockade." Egyptian militants should end the blockade of Gaza: "They are the only ones close to its borders, and they must work on breaking this siege." Arab leaders have not fought "even a single serious war to get Palestine back." He said Hassan Nasrallah, Hizballah's leader, had not tried hard enough. "The truth is the opposite. If he was honest and has enough (resources), why then he did not support the fight to liberate Palestine." He also complained about Nasrallah acquiescing to UN deployment of peacekeepers in Lebanon "to protect the Jews." "In our time now, the real terrorism and armed robbery is done by the leader of the strongest military power humanity has ever known."

May 18, 2008—Pakistan—A Taliban suicide bomber killed eleven and wounded twenty-two outside a bakery near the gate of the Punjab Regimental Center, a Northwest Frontier Province army base in Mardan city. Four soldiers guarding the base were among the dead. The attack took place during peace negotiations between the new government and the Taliban. Authorities believed the attack was conducted by a local Taliban splinter faction.

May 18, 2008—Colombia—Nelly Avila Moreno, alias Karina, 45, Revolutionary Armed Forces of Colombia's most prominent female military commander, ended twenty-four years with the rebels by surrendering with her lover to the authorities. She had lost an eye in combat.

May 20, 2008—France—Police in Bordeaux detained Basque Nation and Liberty (ETA) political and military leader Javier Lopez Pena, 49, and three other ETA members: Ainhoa Ozaeta Mendiondo (she allegedly read the group's March 2006 cease-fire declaration); Jon Salaberria, a former regional legislator for ETA's Batasuna political wing; and Igor Suberbiola, a member of ETA's

youth wing. Lopez had been the object of a twenty-five-year manhunt. He was believed behind the decision to end the ETA cease-fire by bombing an airport parking garage in Madrid in December 2006 that killed two people. Police had followed an ETA lawyer to the hideout, where they confiscated four handguns, a computer, and bomb-making materials.

May 21, 2008—Spain/France—Authorities arrested two more Basque Nation and Liberty (ETA) members: Jose Antonio Barandiaran, former mayor of Andoain in the Spanish Basque region, and a French national who had rented the Bordeaux apartment to the ETA members.

May 21, 2008—Morocco—Police in Fez and Nador arrested eleven members of an al Qaeda network sending fighters to Iraq. They were also sending them to terrorist training camps run by al Qaeda in the Islamic Maghreb. Authorities said they were connected to a group involved with a network in Belgium that had been broken up in February. Authorities were unaware of plans for a terrorist attack in Belgium.

May 22, 2008—United Kingdom—Police arrested Nicky Reilly, 22, a "radicalized" Muslim convert from Plymouth, England, for trying to set off a bomb in the Giraffe restaurant in Exeter just before noon. He was believed to be a mentally ill, "introverted loner" who had been manipulated by radicals. He had changed his name to Mohammed Rasheed in 2007. He sustained cuts to his eye and face after his bomb exploded. Two other unexploded devices were found near the restaurant. No one else was injured. He had spent time in a mental hospital and had the mental age of a 10-year-old. He was believed to suffer from schizophrenia and Asperger's syndrome. He made three bombs from caustic soda, paraffin, and nails in a tin box. Before the attempted bombing, he received a text message of encouragement. Police arrested two men at gunpoint outside an open-air café in Plymouth on May 23. On October 15, 2008, Reilly, listed as Mohammed Saeed-Alim, pleaded guilty via video link from prison to London's Central Criminal Court. Sentencing was scheduled for later.

May 26, 2008—Sri Lanka—A parcel bomb hidden in the luggage rack of a crowded commuter train in Panadura, 17 miles from Colombo, killed seven and wounded eighty-four others when it went off at 5:30 p.m. Many were office workers in evening rush hour. The Liberation Tigers of Tamil Eelam was suspected.

May 26, 2008—Nigeria—The Movement for the Emancipation of the Niger Delta claimed that it had "successfully sabotaged another major trunk pipeline" of the Shell Petroleum Development Company in Rivers State. "Minutes after the sabotage, our fighters encountered a military gunboat which opened fire blindly on the advance guard. We flanked them in a counter-attack and killed in close combat all the drunken soldiers numbering eleven, collecting their weapons, ammunitions, and bulletproof vests before using dynamite to sink the gunboat with its dead occupants." The government denied that its soldiers had been killed. 08052601

May 27, 2008—United States—The United States imposed financial sanctions against the Pakistan-based Lashkar-e-Tayyiba (LeT), blocked its assets, and prohibited Americans from doing business with four leaders of the group: Muhammad Saeed, the group's leader; Zaku-ur-Rehman Lakhi, chief of operations; Haji Muhammad Ashraf, chief of finance; and Mahmoud Mohammad Ahmed Bahaziq, a main financier.

May 28, 2008—Nepal—The royalist Ranab Sena set off a bomb in Katmandu that injured six.

May 29, 2008—Nepal—Suspeced royalists set off three bombs in Katmandu, causing no injuries.

May 30, 2008—Philippines—A cell phone–detonated bomb exploded outside Edwin Andrews Air Base in Zamboanga, killing a man and a woman and wounding nineteen. The bomb damaged three cars and a lawmaker's office; two of his employees were wounded, including Voltaire Mahatol. Four Filipino employees of AMORE, a private group implementing USAID-funded community power projects, were wounded. The al Qaeda-linked Abu Sayyaf Group was suspected in attacking commuters waiting to hitch a ride on a C-130 cargo plane.

June 1, 2008—Somalia—Al-Shaabab militiamen were suspected of firing mortars at the plane carrying Somali transitional President Abdullahi Yusuf Ahmed as it was taking off from Mogadishu Airport at 11:00 a.m. No one was injured. The group is a splinter of the Islamic Courts Union.

June 1, 2008—Iraq—A suicide bomber set off an explosion at a police checkpoint in Hit that killed nine people. Authorities on June 8 dismantled the group behind the attack, seizing fifty explosive belts. The first to confess was a Palestinian; other foreigners were also involved. The U.S. Army said it made forty-nine arrests following the attack.

June 2, 2008—Pakistan—A white Toyota Corolla with fake diplomatic license plates exploded in front of the Danish Embassy in Islamabad, killing four to eight people, including two police-

men and a Pakistani cleaner at the Embassy and wounding twenty-four to thirty-five, all Pakistanis, including a handyman and two office workers. Other reports said that one foreign national and a child died and that among the wounded was a Brazilian citizen of Pakistani descent. Western diplomats said one of the dead had dual Pakistani-Danish citizenship. Among the dead was a security guard working at the neighboring UN Development Program building. The 1:00 p.m. blast damaged the residences of the Dutch ambassador and the Australian defense attaché, located near the Danish Embassy, as well as the UN-funded Devolution Trust for Community Empowerment, a local development organization. Anjum Masood, field operations manager for the Trust, was wounded, as was Anwar Butt, a manager with the UN Development Program. Twenty cars were destroyed. Norway and Sweden closed their embassies. It was not clear initially whether it was a suicide bomb, timebomb, or a remotely-detonated device, although authorities later settled on it being a suicide bomb.

Mustafa Abu al-Yazid, an Afghanistan-based operative for al Qaeda, later claimed credit on the Internet for the 44-pound bomb; the Danish Security and Intelligence Service (PET) confirmed that al Qaeda or an affiliate were the main suspects. The claimant warned that more attacks would come if Denmark did not apologize for publishing what were deemed anti–Muhammad cartoons. He said this attack would "only be the first drop of rain." Al-Yazid said the attack was "revenge against the infidel government" for "degrading drawings of the prophet." He cited a recent bin Laden audio recording in which he said that "if there is no check on your freedom of words, then let your hearts be open to the freedom of our actions."

On September 25, 2010, a Pakistani court acquitted three men of involvement in the bombing, saying there was insufficient evidence against them. 08060201

June 4, 2008—Qatar—Ayman al-Zawahiri released an eleven-minute video on the Internet, marking the anniversary of the June 1967 Six Day War, usually referred to in Arabic as *naksa* (the setback). In a tape entitled *In Memory of the Naksa: Break the Siege of Gaza*, he called on Muslims to conduct holy war to break the Israeli economic blockade of the Gaza Strip, saying, "Salvation of the Muslim nation is through the march of its sons on the path of jihad.... The sons of the nation should break the shackles of the treacherous regimes and move to wage jihad, which has become a duty.... Step up your martyrdom-seeking operations and increase your missiles and ambushes, as there is no solution but this." He accused Arab regimes of responsibility for the 1967 defeat, saying they were "impotent and unable to protect the Muslim nation, its sanctuaries and its wealth." The war "unveiled that [Arab] regimes had no principles ... except holding to their seats (of power)." He said Egyptian leaders were "criminal traitors" and said, "The brother from Gaza is refused entry [by Egypt], while an Israeli tourist is allowed to enter without a visa.... You have the right to enter Egypt whenever you like and destroy the treacherous siege. Those who confront you should not blame anyone but themselves." The video showed al-Zawahiri's picture next to that of a man holding an injured infant.

June 4, 2008—Sri Lanka—An explosive went off on a train track, injuring twenty-three commuters on a train going from Panadura to Colombo.

June 4, 2008—Algeria—Bombs went off at a military barracks and at a café in a beach neighborhood of Algiers, wounding six people.

June 5, 2008—Pakistan—Police raided an Islamist militant safe house in Nowshera. In the subsequent gunfight, a police driver and a militant were injured. Several militants fled.

June 5, 2008—Pakistan—Police in Rawalpindi arrested six Islamists, including three would-be suicide bombers, and confiscated 2,200 pounds of explosives from three vehicles—two Toyota Land Cruisers and a Toyota Corolla. The group planned on attacking "sensitive installations," including the Rawalpindi office of President Pervez Musharraf. The Land Cruisers were each carrying 1,100 pounds of explosives.

June 5, 2008—Algeria—A roadside bomb killed six soldiers in Boumerdes.

June 6, 2008—Sri Lanka—A remotely-detonated bomb exploded on a bus in Moratuwa, a southern suburb of Colombo, killing twenty-one commuters and injuring fifty-three. The Liberation Tigers of Tamil Eelam (LTTE) was suspected. The LTTE was also suspected in the bombing of a bus in the Kandy suburb of Polgolla that killed one person. Police later defused a Claymore mine at the same location.

June 7, 2008—Afghanistan—*BBC* journalist Abdul Samad Rohani was kidnapped in the Lashkar Gar region of Helmand Province. His body was found the next day. He had been kidnapped with an Italian journalist, who was freed after the government agreed to release five jailed Taliban members. 08060701

June 8, 2008—Algeria—Two bombs exploded at a train station in Beni Amrane, 60 miles east of Algiers, killing thirteen people, including a French engineer, and eight soldiers and three Algerian firefighters hit by the second blast five minutes later. An unknown number of others were injured. The French engineer, 57, and his Algerian driver were killed in the first explosion. He was working on a renovation project to expand the number of lines at the station. Both bombs appeared to be remotely detonated. Al Qaeda in Islamic North Africa was suspected. The Algerian Defense Ministry later said only the French citizen and his local driver were killed. 08060801

June 10, 2008—Spain—Police in Barcelona, Pamplona, and the northeastern province of Castellon arrested eight Algerian-born men ranging in age from 27 to 39 who were suspected of funding and providing logistical support to the Algerian-based al Qaeda in the Islamic Maghreb. Police also detained ten others suspected of assisting the main cell. Authorities seized 7,000 Euros (worth circa $10,800) and found evidence of monetary transfers to Algeria, bank books, telephone cards, CDs, videos, and other documents. The Interior Ministry's spokesman said the group was "devoted to financing, recruitment, and sending warriors to conflict zones." In addition to money, the group was believed to have provided night-vision goggles, cell phones, satellite navigation devices, and other electronic equipment to individuals in Algeria.

June 12, 2008—United States—The U.S. Supreme Court ruled 5–4 that suspected terrorists and foreign fighters incarcerated at Guantanamo Bay by the U.S. military have the right to challenge their detention in federal court. The majority included Justices Kennedy, Stevens, Souter, Ginsburg, and Breyer. Strong dissents were cast by Chief Justice Roberts and Justices Scalia, Thomas, and Alito. The appeals had been filed by noncitizens, including lead plaintiffs Lakhdar Boumediene, a Bosnian, and Fawzi al-Odah, a Kuwaiti, who questioned the constitutionality of the October 2006 Military Commissions Act. Salim Ahmed Hamdan's attorney said he would file an appeal asking that charges be dropped.

June 13, 2008—Spain/United States—Spain extradited to the U.S. arms dealer Monzer al-Kassar, who was accompanied on the Madrid-New York City flight by U.S. Drug Enforcement Administration officers. He was held on charges of supplying millions of dollars of weapons to Revolutionary Armed Forces of Colombia rebels to attack U.S. forces in Colombia. He had been arrested in

Madrid in June 2007. The Spanish National Court approved his extradition in October 2007. The Court said that since the 1970s he had provided weapons to armed groups in Nicaragua, Brazil, Bosnia, Iran, and Iraq, inter alia. The Spanish government gave its final approval in early June 2008. The indictment charged him with conspiracy to support terrorists, conspiracy to kill U.S. soldiers, conspiracy to acquire and use antiaircraft missiles, and money laundering. The United States agreed not to seek the death penalty or life without parole, punishments that are not available in Spanish law. He had been acquitted in Spain in 1995 of supplying assault rifles used by the Palestinians who shipjacked the Italian cruise ship *Achille Lauro* in 1985, killing an American.

June 13, 2008—Afghanistan—Circa 870 prisoners escaped at 9:30 p.m. from Sarposa Prison, the Kandahar city jail, after a Taliban suicide fighter set off explosives in a vehicle at the gates. Another pedestrian suicide bomber set off his explosives at the rear of the prison. Thirty gunmen on motorbikes fired rockets and guns while all of the jail's prisoners breached the walls. Several police officers were killed. At least 350 of the prisoners were believed to belong to the Taliban.

June 13, 2008—United States—Ahmed Abdellatif Sherif Mohammed, 26, an Egyptian college student who made an instructional video on making remote-controlled devices into bombs agreed to plead guilty to a federal charge of providing material support to terrorists. Prosecutors agreed to drop the other charges. He and fellow former University of South Florida student Youssef Samir Megahed were arrested after a traffic stop in South Carolina in August 2007 during which police found explosives in the trunk of the car Mohammed was driving. Megahed still faced charges of illegally transporting explosives and possession of a destructive device.

June 13, 2008—United States—A federal jury in Ohio, after three days of deliberations, convicted Mohammad Amawi, 28, Marwan el-Hindi, 45, and Wassim Mazloum, 27, of plotting to kill U.S. soldiers in Iraq. A former Army Special Forces soldier posing as a radical recorded the men talking about training in explosives, guns, and sniper tactics for about two years beginning in 2004. U.S. District Judge James G. Carr did not set a sentencing date. The trio faced life in prison. They had been raising money for their jihad against U.S. troops.

June 16, 2008—United Kingdom/United Arab Emirates—The British government warned its nationals in the United Arab Emirates that terrorists might be planning attacks against their interests, including places frequented by expatriates and foreign travelers, residential compounds, and "military, oil, transport, and aviation interests."

June 17, 2008—Iraq—At 6:00 p.m., a bomb hidden in a minibus exploded at a bus terminal at a crowded market area in the heavily Shi'ite Huriya District of northwest Baghdad, killing fifty-one and wounding seventy-five.

June 18, 2008—United States—The U.S. Department of the Treasury designated two Venezuelans as supporters of Hizballah, freezing their assets and prohibiting Americans from conducting business transactions with the duo. They included Ghazi Nasr al-Din, a Venezuelan diplomat posted in the Venezuelan Embassy in Beirut, Lebanon; he had earlier worked in the Venezuelan Embassy in Damascus, Syria. The United States said he had arranged for Hizballah members to travel to a training course in Iran. The other designee was Fawzi Kan'an, a Caracas-based owner of two travel agencies who was a "supporter and a significant provider of financial support to Hizballah." He had "met with senior Hizballah officials in Lebanon to discuss operational issues including possible kidnapping and terrorist attacks." He reportedly also traveled with Hizballah operatives for training in Iran.

June 19, 2008—Nigeria—The Movement for the Emancipation of the Niger Delta (MEND) attacked the Bonga oil field, some 65 miles from land, but were prevented from entering a computer control room which they had hoped to destroy. Royal Dutch Shell shut down production of the field, which produces 200,000 barrels per day. MEND said it had captured an American worker on a supply vessel nearby. Two sailors were injured in the attack.

Meanwhile, militants not affiliated with MEND sabotaged a Chevron Corporation pipeline in the Niger Delta, causing the company to shut down its onshore oil production, leading to production losses of 120,000 barrels per day. 08061901-02

June 21, 2008—Somalia—Hassan Mohamed Ali, a Somali who headed the UN High Commissioner for Refugees facility in Somalia, was abducted during the night by six men who broke into his Mogadishu home. He was freed on August 27. 08062101

June 22, 2008—Iraq—At 12:30 p.m. a female Iraqi suicide bomber killed fifteen, including seven police officers—among them a captain—and wounded more than forty-five, including ten Iraqi police officers, near a courthouse and government outpost in central Baquba in Diyala Province. She was wearing an explosive vest packed with ball bearings. Authorities blamed al Qaeda in Mesopotamia, a group of takfiri Sunni extremists who attack Shi'ites, believing them to be heretics. She was the sixteenth female suicide bomber in Diyala Province and the twenty-first female suicide bomber in Iraq in 2008. One of the wounded police officers was Jassim Mohammed al-Saedi, who said the police were moving prisoners to court.

June 23, 2008—United Kingdom—Parliament approved the Court of Appeals's ruling in May that the People's Mujahideen of Iran should be taken off the list of terrorist groups. The group was still considered to be a terrorist group by the United States and the European Union. The group now has greater freedom to organize and raise money in the United Kingdom.

June 24, 2008—Somalia—Pirates boarded a yacht that had run out of gas in the Red Sea's Gulf of Aden and took four European hostages: a man, a woman, their child, and their yacht's pilot. Ahmed Yusuf Yasin, vice president of the breakaway Republic of Somaliland, said the hostages were taken into hills around Las Qoray, a fishing town claimed by Puntland, a self-declared autonomous state, and Somalia. The hostages were believed to be either French or German. 08062401

June 24, 2008—Iraq—At 9:20 a.m., a bomb went off at a meeting of the Sadr City District Council, killing four Americans, an Italian interpreter, and six Iraqis, who were outside the room. The four Iraqi council members inside the room survived. Steven L. Farley, 57, a State Department contract employee from Guthrie, Oklahoma, had served for several years in the Naval Reserve and volunteered to join the State Department in April 2007. Another dead American was a civilian contract worker for the Department of Defense. Two U.S. soldiers were also killed. Ten Iraqis and another U.S. soldier were injured. The bomb broke the legs of Qasim Abdul Zahra, a council member. The U.S. military suspected "special groups"—Iranian-backed militias—and caught three men with explosive residue on their hands. Authorities believed the target was Hassan Hussein Shammah, deputy council chief, who was also wounded. 08062402

June 25, 2008—Saudi Arabia—The Riyadh government announced that it had arrested 701 suspected al Qaeda-linked terrorists since the beginning of the year. Some had planned a car bombing of an oil installation. At least 181 were later released for lack of proof of links to terrorist networks. The other 520 remained in custody. Authorities had confiscated money, weapons, and ammunition. One man was arrested while trying to raise money in Yanbu.

June 26, 2008—Pakistan—Islamist radicals torched a hotel at Pakistan's lone ski resort in the Swat Valley, near the Afghanistan border. They broke into the state-run hotel at the Malam Jabba resort, sacked it, and set it alight.

June 27, 2008—North Korea/United States—The United States removed the Democratic People's Republic of Korea from its list of states that support terrorists after North Korea blew up the cooling tower of its Yongbyon nuclear plant in front of CNN cameras.

June 28, 2008—Somalia—A Swede and a Dane who worked for the Swedish Rescue Services Agency (SRSA) were taken hostage by Islamist Courts Union militants in Hudor, a town near the Ethiopia border. They were released within hours. The duo educate people about the dangers of unexploded landmines. SRSA is a Swedish government foreign aid organization working at the request of the UN in Somalia. Seven people, including the district commissioner, were injured in the battle for Hudor. 08062801

July 1, 2008—Algeria—Abdelmalek Droukdel, alias Abou Mossab Abdelouadoud, leader of the al Qaeda affiliate in Algeria, told the *New York Times* that "We found America building military bases in the south of our country and conducting military exercises, and plundering our oil and planning to get our gas. Therefore, it became our right and our duty to ... declare clearly the American interests are legitimate targets.... Everyone must know that we will not hesitate in targeting it whenever we can and wherever it is on this planet." French, Spanish, and "Jewish" interests were also on his target list. "The large proportion of our mujahideen comes from Algeria. And there is a considerable number of Mauritanians, Libyans, Moroccans, Tunisians, Malians, and Nigerians."

July 2, 2008—Israel—Hussam Edwyat, 34, a Palestinian constructor worker, killed three Israelis and injured forty others at lunchtime when he rammed his yellow Caterpillar earthmover into cars and buses on Jaffa Road in Jerusalem, where he had lived and worked side-by-side with Jews. Police officer Eli Mizrahi jumped into the vehicle's cab and shot him twice at close range, killing him. Among those killed were Elizabeth Goren Friedman, 54; a 30-year-old woman; and Jean Relevy, 68, a handyman. Neighbors said Edwyat had dated a Jewish woman for several years and had fathered her child; his relatives claimed his only two children were by his Palestinian wife. Police revealed he had a criminal record of drug charges and domestic abuse, for which he served two years in prison. Several terrorist groups claimed credit, although police suggested he was politically motivated but acted alone. He had lived in the Arabic Sur Baher neighborhood in Jerusalem.

July 3, 2008—Indonesia—Authorities arrested twelve militants, including three foreigners, in Palembang, while they were planning to attack a café in Bukittinggi, a tourist city in West Sumatra. They found a cache of explosives, including bomb-making materiel and guns. One of those detained was an English teacher and bomb maker linked to Mas Selemat Kastari, a Jemaah Islamiyah leader who escaped from a Singapore jail in March. Others were associated with a group led by Noordin Mohammad Top.

July 4, 2008—Belarus—A homemade bomb injured fifty people when it sprayed nuts and bolts into an open-air concert attended by President Alexander Lukashenko, who was unhurt. Another unexploded bomb was found nearby. On July 16, Minsk police conducted a house-by-house search. Liberal and nationalist opposition leaders said a dozen people had been detained. As of April 2011, no motive had been determined.

July 6, 2008—Somalia—Gunmen fired on people exiting a mosque in Mogadishu, killing Osman Ali Ahmed, head of the UN Development Program for Somalia, and wounding his son and another man. 08070601

July 6, 2008—Pakistan—A suicide bomber killed ten to fifteen people and injured twenty-two in a crowd of ten thousand conservative Islamist protestors and mourners commemorating a raid on the radical Red Mosque in Islamabad in 2007. On July 4, al Qaeda's al-Sahab media wing had released a video tribute to the Mosque's leaders, including previously-related messages from Osama bin Laden and Ayman al-Zawahiri.

July 7, 2008—Afghanistan—A car bomb killed 41 people and injured 150 others when it exploded at the entrance to the Indian Embassy in Kabul. Investigators said evidence at the scene suggested the involvement of a foreign intelligence agency. Some observers blamed the Pakistani Inter-Services Intelligence (ISI) service. Pakistan denied involvement; Prime Minister Yousaf Raza Giliani promised to investigate the accusations. The *Washington Post* reported on August 1, 2008, that U.S. intelligence officials believed ISI had pro-

vided logistical assistance to the bombers, who were linked to Jalaluddin Haqqani, a Pashtun and pro-Taliban insurgent leader. Among the dead were an Indian defense attaché, a political information officer, two Indian security officials, and nine police officers. Among the injured was the 13-year-old daughter of Mohammed Sabeer, who could not find his three other children following the explosion. 08070701

July 7, 2008—Georgia—Four people died and five were injured when a bomb exploded in secessionist Abkhazia, the fifth bombing of the week. Georgian spokesmen denied charges of involvement.

July 8, 2008—Sudan—Hundreds of horseback-riding gunmen ambushed a convoy of sixty United Nations–African Union (UN-AU) peacekeepers, killing seven and wounding seven in Darfur in a two-hour firefight. The riders were joined by forty trucks carrying mounted machine guns and antitank and antiaircraft weapons. Several of the UN-AU trucks exploded. At least two soldiers and police officers were wounded. Most of the injured UNAMID peacekeepers were Rwandans. 08070801

July 9, 2008—Turkey—At 11:00 a.m., at least one gunman fired at the U.S. Consulate in Istanbul. In the ensuring five-minute gun battle, three guards and three gunmen were killed, and a police officer and a tow truck driver were injured. No Americans were harmed. The gunmen had driven up in a white vehicle. One walked up to a guard and shot him in the head. They then fired a pump-action shotgun and pistols. A fourth gunman escaped in the getaway car; police believed he might have been wounded. Al Qaeda was suspected, although Interior Minister Besir Atalay said all of the attackers were Turks. By the next day, authorities had detained four suspects, including the suspected gunman. One of the dead terrorists, Erkan Kargin, had been in Afghanistan. On July 13, authorities arrested and charged Dursun P. with membership in a terrorist organization and involvement in the attack. 08070901

July 9, 2008—Turkey—Kurdish separatists kidnapped three German mountain climbers on Mount Agri in the east. The Kurdistan Workers' Party (PKK) was blamed. The kidnappers said, "We are not the enemies of the German people, and we have not mistreated any of the hostages. Unless the German government announces it has stopped its enemy-like politics towards PKK and the Kurds, we will not release the German citizens." The PKK released them on July 20. The hostages were identified as Helmut Johann.

Martin Georpe, and Lars Helmer Reime. 0807 0902

July 11, 2008—Israel—Just before midnight, a gunman wounded two Israeli policemen on patrol at the Lion's Gate in Jerusalem's Old City. The attack was believed to be a Palestinian nationalist operation. A video camera captured the attack, but did not show the attacker's face.

July 11, 2008—Nigeria—Two German employees of the construction firm Julius Berger were kidnapped in the Niger Delta. On August 14, 2008, MEND claimed that "an elite commando unit from the Movement for the Emancipation of the Niger Delta [MEND] concluded a successful rescue of two German hostages and staff of Julius Berger." 08071101

July 13, 2008—Somalia—Gunmen in a local militia shot to death a World Food Program staffer in Buale in the south. The gunmen had demanded payment for truckers ferrying aid to impoverished inhabitants.

July 15, 2008—Sudan—The UN Security Council announced that two hundred gunmen on horses and in forty vehicles "using sophisticated weaponry and tactics" attacked a UN peacekeeping patrol, killing one peacekeeper. 08071501

July 18, 2008—Afghanistan/United States—Aafia Siddiqui, 36, a Pakistani mother of three with a bachelor of science degree in biology from Massachusetts Institute of Technology (MIT) and a doctorate in neuroscience from Brandeis, grabbed a U.S. soldier's M-4 rifle from the floor and fired two shots at a group of Americans after being detained outside the Ghazni governor's compound for questioning at a Ghazni police station. She was shot and wounded. Her purse contained "numerous documents describing the creation of explosives, chemical weapons, and other weapons involving biological material and radiological agents." There were also "descriptions of various landmarks in the United States, including in New York City," such as the Statue of Liberty, Brooklyn Bridge, and Empire State Building, U.S. "military assets," and excerpts from *The Anarchist Arsenal*. She was charged in U.S. District Court in Manhattan on August 5, 2008, with one count of attempting to kill U.S. military officers and FBI agents in Afghanistan and one count of assault. She faced twenty years per charge if convicted. She was represented by attorney Elaine Whitfield Sharp.

She had left the United States for Afghanistan with her three children in March 2003, when the FBI said she was wanted for questioning for al

Qaeda connections, particularly regarding Adnan G. el-Shukrijumah. Her name also was raised during interrogations of Khalid Sheikh Mohammed. In 2004, FBI Director Robert Mueller identified her as "an al Qaeda operative and facilitator" who was one of seven people sought for potential terrorist attacks in the United States. She was believed to have worked with and married al Qaeda terrorist Ammar al-Baluchi before his April 2003 arrest in Pakistan. While still living in Boston with her then-husband, a Pakistani doctor, the duo founded the Institute of Islamic Research and Teaching, which the United States said funded terrorist front charities.

On January 19, 2010, the trial on seven counts of attempted murder and other charges began in the U.S. District Court for the Southern District of New York. She was represented by attorney Charles Swift. On February 3, 2010, after three days of deliberations, she was convicted on all seven counts. Sentencing was scheduled for May. She faced life in prison.

On September 23, 2010, a U.S. court sentenced Aafia Siddiqui to eighty-six years in prison. Hundreds of demonstrators in Pakistan protested the ruling.

July 18, 2008—Afghanistan—In a nighttime raid, gunmen kidnapped two French aid workers from their house in Daikundi Province. 08071801

July 20, 2008—Spain—Basque Nation and Liberty (ETA) set off five bombs in northern Spain, causing no injuries. An ETA member had phoned in warnings on four of the bombs.

July 20, 2008—Colombia—Millions of Colombians in hundreds of anti–Revolutionary Armed Forces of Colombia protests throughout the country demanded the release of hundreds of hostages held by the rebels. Protests were also held in dozens of locations outside the country, including New York, Washington, DC, and Paris. Hundreds of thousands of protestors jammed into Bogota; many wore symbolic chains.

July 21, 2008—China—A bomb exploded at 7:10 a.m. in a bus pulling into the Panjiawan bus stop on Kunming's main street. Wang Dezhi, a woman, was killed, and her fiancé's left arm was injured. A 74-year-old paying to get on the bus was lacerated by flying glass. A young man had gotten off the bus seconds earlier, leaving behind a black bag that held the bomb. At 8:05 a.m., a second bomb exploded on another bus on West Renmin Road. Two people were killed and fourteen were injured in the two attacks.

Commander Seyfullah ("Sword of God") claimed credit for the Turkestan Islamic Party in a video released on July 26 and entitled *Our Blessed Jihad in Yunnan*. Seyfullah said the group planned "to target the most critical points related to the Olympics. We will try to attack Chinese central cities severely, using the tactics that have never been employed." Observers believed the group is a cover name for the East Turkestan Islamic Movement. The Uighur speaker also claimed credit for a Shanghai bus explosion, a July 17 attack with an explosives-carrying tractor in Wenzhou, and a July 17 bombing of a plastics factory in Guangzhou. Observers noted inaccuracies in his statements, including that the Guanghou explosion was on March 13 in a vehicle repair plant and residential building, killing seven and wounding thirty; and that the Wenzhou explosion on May 17 involved a man who rammed his tractor into a gambling establishment and killed nineteen.

July 22, 2008—Israel—At 2:00 p.m., Ghasan Abu Teir, 23, yet another Palestinian construction worker, took his earthmover down Jerusalem's King David Street, injuring sixteen people, one seriously, before being shot to death by military reservist Yaakov Asael, 53. The attack occurred a block from the King David Hotel, where presidential candidate Barack Obama was to stay the next evening. Teir crashed the earthmover into a bus and tried to tip it over with the shovel. He then crashed into passenger cars, damaging four within 150 yards. Teir's family said he had no political affiliation and was a religious man who dropped out after eighth grade.

July 25, 2008—India—Nine bombs exploded in Bangalore within fifteen minutes, killing two and wounding at least twenty. The next day, police defused another bomb near a popular shopping mall. The bombs were unsophisticated and contained nuts and bolts. A woman and a day laborer were killed at a bus stop in Maiwala.

July 26, 2008—India—At least sixteen bombs exploded during the night in Ahmadabad, killing 56 and wounding 161. Among those killed was the father of Yash Vyas, 6, himself hospitalized by the blast. Yash's brother was also hurt. The bombs went off in two waves: one near a market, a second near a hospital. One was hidden on a bus. Several were hidden in metal lunch boxes. The first bomb went off on a bicycle at 6:40 p.m. in Maninagar. Islamic militants were suspected. By the next day, police had rounded up thirty suspects.

A little-known group sent an e-mail to Indian television stations, saying, "Await five minutes for the revenge of Gujarat." In 2002, riots in that state killed one thousand people, most of them Muslims. Ahmadabad is Gujarat's capital. The note said, "In the name of Allah, the Indian Mujahideen strike again! Do whatever you can, within five minutes from now, feel the terror of death!" Some observers questioned the authenticity of the note, observing that it came from a French Yahoo account and was written in English by Guru al-Hindi ("Teacher of Indians"). Such a mélange of Arabic and Hindi is an odd construction.

By August 16, Indian police had arrested ten suspects affiliated with the banned Students Islamic Movement of India (SIMI) on charges of waging war against the state and murder. Police said the SIMI is another name for the Indian Mujahideen. Among those arrested were Mufti Abu Bashir and an employee of a software firm who had masterminded the attacks.

July 27, 2008—Turkey—Two bombs went off 15 meters from each other in the Gungoren suburb of Istanbul at 10:00 p.m., killing 17, including 5 children, and injuring 150 others. A stun grenade went off in a telephone booth and lured onlookers and rescuers to the area, where a second bomb exploded 40 meters away ten minutes later. The government blamed Kurdish rebels, but Zubeyir Aydar, a Kurdistan Workers Party leader, said Turkish nationalists were behind the attacks. One of the dead was Seyma Ozkan, 12, who ran to her balcony to see what the first explosion was about; a piece of shrapnel from the second bomb pierced her heart. Kazim Buyuk, 65, was hit in the leg by the first bomb.

July 28, 2008—Iraq—Four women set off explosives hidden under their abbayas, killing 51 and injuring more than 250. In Kirkuk, 15 died in a bombing at a Kurdish political demonstration. Subsequent fighting between Kurds, Arabs, and Turkmens killed 12 more and injured 187. At 8:00 a.m., three other suicide bombers attacked Shi'ites in Baghdad's Karrada neighborhood within five minutes, hitting a tent where pilgrims were being fed, at a checkpoint for women, and at a Shi'ite march. The Baghdad bombings killed 24 and injured 79. Authorities blamed al Qaeda in Iraq.

July 28, 2008—Pakistan—The news media reported that a pre-dawn U.S. missile strike on a compound at a former religious school near Azam Warsak, a village in South Waziristan in northwestern Pakistan, killed six people, including possibly Midhat Mursi, alias Abu Khabab al-Masri, a senior al Qaeda figure. Local officials said four Egyptians and two Pakistanis were killed. Television news media later reported that possibly among the dead was Ayman al-Zawahiri.

July 29, 2008—United States—Aware that police were about to search his bedroom, Collin McKenzie-Gude, 19, went to White Flint Mall in southern Maryland, attacked a 78-year-old man, and tried to steal his car. A defense attorney said McKenzie-Gude later turned himself in to police. Patrick Yevsukov, a close friend who pleaded guilty to making and possessing pipe bombs and cooperated with police, said that the former Bethesda honor student was plotting to assassinate Barack Obama during the 2008 presidential campaign. He planned to plant bombs in the road to halt the convoy, then shoot him with an AR-15 rifle that police found in his bedroom. McKenzie-Gude pleaded guilty in Montgomery Circuit Court to attempted carjacking.

On September 3, 2009, McKenzie-Gude pleaded guilty to possessing bomb-making chemicals found in his bedroom along with three high-powered rifles, two shotguns, hundreds of rounds of ammunition, a manual showing how to kill someone from 200 meters away, 50-plus pounds of chemicals, and a map with markings around Camp David.

In a December 7, 2009, filing, prosecutors said documents found on his thumb drive indicated that he also planned to kill Meghan Haney—Yevsukov's mother—and another student if a gun deal failed. Sentencing was scheduled for January 7, 2010; he faced eight years in prison. On January 7, 2010, U.S. District Judge Peter J. Messitte postponed sentencing of McKenzie-Gude on charges of storing bomb-making materials in his bedroom closets. His attorney, Steven Kupferberg, wanted to call to the stand Patrick Yevsukov regarding a plot to kill President Obama. Prosecutors wanted McKenzie-Gude to serve another six and a half years. A hearing was set for January 14, 2010. McKenzie-Gude had pleaded guilty in a separate state court to a charge of attempted carjacking and was to be sentenced separately for that conviction. Yevsukov had pleaded guilty to two counts of the manufacture or possession of a destructive device and was to be sentenced soon. On January 19, McKenzie-Gude was sentenced to sixty-one months; the judge said he deserved seventy-eight months, but credited him for the seventeen months served since his arrest.

On May 12, 2010, Circuit Court Judge Michael D. Mason sentenced McKenzie-Gude to an additional year in prison for assaulting Dermot Owens in the attempted carjacking. On May 26, 2010, Montgomery County Circuit Judge Louise G. Scrivener placed Patrick Yevsukov on three years' supervised probation. The 4.0 student at the University of Baltimore wanted to attend law school. He was represented by attorney Rene Sandler.

August 2008—Afghanistan—In mid-month, an American working for the Army Corps of Engineers was kidnapped and held in an insurgent stronghold 30 miles west of Kabul. In mid–October 2008, U.S. Special Forces soldiers conducted a nighttime rescue operation that freed him and killed several insurgents. It was the first time U.S. troops had rescued a hostage in Afghanistan. 08089901

August 2008—Pakistan—Chinese engineer Long Xiaowei was kidnapped. He was freed on February 14, 2009, days before President Asif Ali Zardari's planned visit to China. 08089902

August 1, 2008—Syria—Brig. Gen. Mohammed Suleiman, 49, was shot to death near the port city of Tartous. He orchestrated Syrian weapons shipments to Hizballah. Exiled former Vice President Abdul Halim Khaddam's Free Syria Web site said a sniper on a yacht fired the four shots. An Israeli newspaper said Suleiman was also in charge of Syria's nuclear program.

August 3, 2008—United States—Two bombs exploded at the University of California at Santa Cruz. A firebomb was set at a house porch, forcing an animal experimenter and his family to escape via a second-story window. Another bomb destroyed a researcher's car. Police deemed the attacks "domestic terrorism."

August 3, 2008—Algeria—A suicide car bomber wounded twenty-five people in Tizi Ouzou. Al Qaeda in the Islamic Maghreb claimed credit, saying, "We tell the sons of France and the slaves of America, and their masters, too, that our finger is on the trigger and the convoys of martyrs are longing to rampage your bastions in defense of our Islamic nation."

August 4, 2008—China—Two individuals drove a dump truck into a group of seventy police officers jogging near the Yiquan Hotel in Kashgar, then threw explosives at the wounded, killing sixteen and injuring sixteen. One bomb detonated early, blowing off the terrorist's arm. The second terrorist threw a bomb near the gate of the police station. The Turkestan Islamic Party had threatened to disrupt the Olympics. China said the 8:00 a.m. attack was conducted by terrorists and arrested the two Uighur attackers, ages 28 and 33, at the scene. One attacker tried to slash the arresting officers. Police found another ten bombs, a homemade handgun, and four knives in the vehicle. Authorities said the duo left wills saying that they were willing to give up their lives in jihad against the government. One more police officer later died. On August 9, 2009, China executed the two members of the East Turkestan Islamic Movement in front of four thousand observers in Kashgar Stadium.

August 4, 2008—Jordan—A military court sentenced ten men to up to five years in jail for planning to attack U.S. and Iraqi forces in Iraq. Two men were tried in absentia. The others were arrested inside Jordan or at the Syria border. The group met in a shop in Zarqa to watch videos of suicide attacks in Iraq and listen to speeches by al Qaeda leaders.

August 6, 2008—Guantanamo Bay—A military jury found Salim Ahmed Hamdan, bin Laden's former driver, guilty of supporting terrorism but acquitted him of conspiracy to commit terrorist acts. The next day, he was sentenced to sixty-six months in prison.

August 8, 2008—China—On the date of the opening of the Beijing Olympics, the Turkestan Islamic Party released a third video threatening attacks and calling on Muslims to avoid travel in the area. Spokesman Abdullah Mansour said, "We oppose implementing the Chinese Communist system in our homeland of East Turkestan because this system is based on atheism."

August 10, 2008—China—Bomb-throwing Muslim terrorists left at least eleven people dead in Xinjiang region in western China. Ten terrorists and one security guard died in the dozen pre-dawn bombings of a police station, government buildings, the China Construction Bank, and the Three Eagle Shoe City shopping center in Kuqa County. Police killed seven of the attackers; three others blew themselves up. Police arrested another two and were searching for three more. The bombs were fashioned with bent pipes, gas canisters, and liquid gas tanks. In one attack, the terrorists drove a three-wheeled vehicle into a public security bureau compound, setting off explosives at 2:30 a.m., killing a security guard and injuring two police officers and two civilians. At 8:30 a.m., police found five individuals hiding under a counter in a nearby market. When confronted, the men threw bombs at the police. Police shot two to death; the other three killed themselves.

August 12, 2008—China—At 9:00 a.m., a terrorist jumped from a passing vehicle at a security checkpoint and stabbed to death three security officials in Yamanya town in Xinjiang region. He wounded a fourth before escaping.

August 12, 2008—Afghanistan—Unconfirmed Pakistani press reports indicated that Mustafa Abu al-Yazid, alias Sheik Saeed, al Qaeda's senor commander in Afghanistan, was killed in a gun battle with Pakistani soldiers.

August 12, 2008—Pakistan—A roadside bomb aimed at Air Force personnel killed fourteen people, including seven Air Force officers, injured several other people, and damaged a bridge in Peshawar. Islamist Tehrik-e-Taliban Pakistan terrorists were suspected. The government had been engaging in operations against the group and al Qaeda. A security official claimed that al Qaeda commander Abu Saeed al-Masri was killed in Bajaur.

August 12, 2008—Qatar—Ayman al-Zawahiri issued a rare English-language audio in which he accused Pakistani leaders of kowtowing to the United States, observing, "Let there be no doubt in your minds that dominant political forces at work in Pakistan today are competing to appease ... the modern-day crusaders in the White House and are working to destabilize this nuclear-capable nation under the aegis of America."

August 13, 2008—Afghanistan—At 10:30 a.m., five Taliban gunmen fired assault rifles in ambushing a two-car convoy of female foreign aid workers with the New York–based International Rescue Committee in Pul-i-Alam city in Logar Province, killing Nicole Dial, 30, a dual American-Trinidad citizen; Jacqueline Kirk, 40, a dual Canadian-British citizen; a Canadian woman initially identified as an Irish aid worker; and their Afghan driver, Mohammad Aimal, 25 of Kabul. The Taliban said the aid workers were spies trying to undermine the country. The trio were returning from meetings with officials in Sayed Habibullah in Logar Province, where they were exploring setting up an education program for mentally and physically disabled children. 08081301

August 13, 2008—Lebanon—Fatah al-Islam set off a bomb packed in a briefcase next to a bus on Masarif Street in Tripoli at 8:00 a.m., killing fourteen, including nine Lebanese soldiers and two civilians, and injuring more than fifty others. The remotely-detonated bomb was filled with nuts and bolts. Police blamed Hizballah.

August 14, 2008—Iraq—A female suicide bomber set off explosives in Iskandariyah among Shi'ite pilgrims on their way to the Shabaniyah religious festival in Karbala, killing eighteen and wounding sixty-eight. Kamil Kadhim, 29, was struck by a ball bearing. Police were suspicious of the woman who was wearing thick clothes on a very hot evening, but when they approached her, she set off the bomb, killing three police officers and others.

August 15, 2008—Colombia—Leftist rebels set off a bomb at a small town festival, killing seven and wounding fifty.

August 18, 2008—United Kingdom—Aabid Hussain Khan, 23, and Sultan Muhammad, 23, were found guilty of possessing a large number of articles and information, including al Qaeda propaganda and guides on how to make poisons and suicide vests. The next day, Khan, the ringleader of the cell, was sentenced to twelve years; Muhammad was sentenced to ten years.

August 19, 2008—Algeria—An al Qaeda in the Islamic Maghreb suicide bomber drove a car bomb into an Algerian police academy in Issers, 35 miles east of Algiers, killing forty-eight people—all but one were civilians—and wounding another forty-five.

August 19, 2008—Northern Ireland—A bomber used a rocket-propelled grenade loaded with Semtex against police officers on patrol 80 miles southwest of Belfast. The Semtex may have been part of a Provisional Irish Republican Army cache that was decommissioned as part of the 1998 Good Friday peace accord.

August 19, 2008—Afghanistan—Some one hundred Taliban attackers killed ten French paratroopers on patrol in a mountain ambush near Sarobi, 40 miles east of Kabul. The gunmen injured another twenty-one French soldiers. The Taliban lost thirteen fighters; fourteen were injured. Another group of six suicide bombers tried to attack Camp Salerno, a NATO base in Khost Province, killing ten Afghans and wounding thirteen. A second bomb was defused.

August 20, 2008—Algeria—Al Qaeda in the Islamic Maghreb synchronized suicide bombers killed twelve people. A pre-dawn car bomb went off outside a military command post in Bouira, 60 miles southeast of Algiers, wounding seven soldiers and one police officer. Fifteen minutes later, a car bomb went off next to a passenger bus outside a central Bouira hotel, killing twelve Algerians and injuring thirty-four. The attack targeted contractors working on a dam project. Bus passengers worked for SNC-Lavalin, a Canadian engineering and construction firm based in Montreal. 08082001

August 20, 2008—Pakistan—Several suicide bombers set off explosives at entry points to the nuclear weapons complex at the Wah Cantonment, reportedly a nuclear weapons assembly plant, according to a research paper published by Bradford University's Shaun Gregory.

August 21, 2008—Philippines—Leaders of a Muslim rebel group rejected the government's call, as part of a peace agreement, for the surrender of Abdullah Macapaar and Ameril Umbra Kato, who led attacks that killed dozens of people.

August 21, 2008—Pakistan—Pakistani Taliban suicide bombers killed sixty and injured one hundred in an attack at the country's largest army munitions factory in Wah. One bomb went off at 2:30 p.m. when two suicide bombers walked up to the main gate of the Pakistan Ordinance Factory and detonated their suicide vest. A third bomber set off explosives at another gate. Most of the dead were civilian workers killed during a shift change.

August 22, 2008—United Kingdom—Authorities arrested three men in the north during an investigation into death threats posted on a Web site in January by al Qaeda in Britain against Prime Minister Gordon Brown and former Prime Minister Tony Blair.

August 23, 2008—Somalia—Gunmen kidnapped Canadian journalist Amanda Lindhout, Australian journalist Nigel Brennan, their Somali driver, and two Somali guards while they were traveling southwest of Mogadishu. The two journalists were freed on November 25, 2009. It was not disclosed whether a ransom had been paid. 08082301

August 24, 2008—United States—Authorities arrested three men in suburban Denver who reportedly had discussed several assassination plots against Democratic presidential nominee Barack Obama and possessed high-powered rifles, camouflage, and other gear. On August 26, the trio was charged with gun and drug violations. Authorities said the threat was more "aspirational than operational." The prosecutor said the threats, "hateful and bigoted though they were, involved a group of meth heads, methamphetamine abusers, all of whom were impaired at the time." The Democratic National Convention began on August 25 in Denver.

Shawn Robert Adolf, 33, faced thirty-three years in prison for illegal possession of a firearm, body armor, and possession of meth with intention to distribute. He was arrested at the Cherry Creek Hotel in Glendale, where he was staying with a woman who joined him to take meth.

Tharin Robert Gartrell, 28, faced two years on gun and drug charges. He was arrested at 1:30 a.m. on August 24 when police saw him driving erratically. They found two rifles, eighty-five rounds of ammunition, a bulletproof vest, and meth lab items. He said the guns belonged to the two others, who had been parrying at a local Hyatt.

Nathan Dwaine Johnson faced eleven years for illegal possession of firearms and meth. Police arrested him at the Hyatt. He told Secret Service agents that Adolf said he could kill Obama with a sniper rifle on Inauguration Day. On December 17, 2008, Johnson pleaded guilty in Denver federal court to a charge of possession of a firearm by a prohibited person. He faced up to thirty-seven months in prison. Sentencing was set for March 20, 2009.

August 26, 2008—Pakistan—A bomb went off on a bridge in Bannu, throwing a bus carrying Pakistani police and government workers over the railing and into a riverbed 30 feet below. Eight people were killed. Insurgents were blamed.

August 26, 2008—Pakistan—Gunmen fired on the armored vehicle of Lynne Tracy, principal officer at the U.S. Consulate in Peshawar, as she was leaving her home in the University Town district at 8:00 a.m. to go to work. She was unharmed. The car returned to the house. Three employees were in the car. 08082601

August 26, 2008—Afghanistan—Japanese aid worker Kazuya Ito, 31, who worked for the Japan-based Peshawar-kai aid agency, was kidnapped in Nangarhar. His bullet-riddled body was found the next day in Shewa. The Afghan Interior Ministry claimed its police forces had staged a rescue attempt. 08082602

August 27, 2008—Sudan—A man carrying a knife hijacked a B-37 carrying one hundred people, including Darfur Transitional Authority officials, after takeoff from Nyala, South Darfur, en route to Khartoum. He and a colleague diverted it to Kufra, Libya, where he released the passengers but kept six crew as hostages. They later surrendered after negotiations with Libyan authorities. The Sudanese Liberation Army denied involvement. 08082701

August 27, 2008—China—Two policemen and six assailants died when police searching for a separatist woman in a cornfield were attacked by knife-wielding rebels, who also wounded two police officers.

August 28, 2008—United States—The U.S. Treasury Department added Joseph Kony, leader of the Ugandan Lord's Resistance Army, to its list of specially designated global terrorists, which imposes financial sanctions.

September 2008—Nigeria—The Movement for the Emancipation of the Niger Delta (MEND) released ill British oil worker Robin Barry Hughes

on April 19, 2009. MEND said he was "handed over to contacts who in turn handed him over to his employers," Hydrodrive. No ransom was requested. The group said it was releasing him because of "health and age considerations," but that Mathew John Maguire, who was kidnapped with Hughes, "will remain in our custody until further notice." The group had initially demanded the release by Nigeria of MEND member Henry Okah, who was detained in 2008 and charged with treason.

MEND reneged on a pledge to release Maguire, of Wirral, Birkenhead, Merseyside, United Kingdom, on his birthday, June 1, 2009. The 35-year-old was captured from a boat carrying him to an oil rig. His father had used a Nigerian Web site to contact them. Rebel spokesman Jomo Gbomo posted a note to the Web site saying that the hostage would be released after 258 days in captivity provided the kidnappers' safety was guaranteed. On June 12, 2009, MEND said it had released Maguire to Port Harcourt authorities. A private security official confirmed the release. 08099901

September 2008—Pakistan—Ambassador-designate Abdul Khaliq Farahi was freed in Khost, Afghanistan, on November 13, 2010, and returned to his government. He had been kidnapped in September 2008 while on his way home in a Karachi suburb after having been named Afghanistan's ambassador to Pakistan. His driver was killed in the attack. 08099902

September 2, 2008—Sri Lanka—Some forty-eight people were killed and fifty-seven wounded in battles between Liberation Tigers of Tamil Eelam (LTTE) rebels and the Army's 57th Division, who wrested control of LTTE's nerve center in Mallavi.

September 3, 2008—Pakistan—Gunmen fired at the motorcade of Pakistani Prime Minister Yousuf Raza Gilani as his Mercedes limousine was en route to picking him up at the airport. Two bullets hit the driver's window as it was driving on the main highway between Islamabad and Rawalpindi.

September 12, 2008—United States/Venezuela— The United States announced that former Interior Minister Ramon Rodriguez Chacin, military intelligence director Hugo Carvajal, and Henry de Jesus Silva, director of intelligence and prevention services, had assisted the Revolutionary Armed Forces of Colombia (FARC) to obtain weapons to attempt to overthrow Colombian President Alvaro Uribe. Rodriguez reportedly was in contact with FARC leaders Luciano Marin, alias Ivan Marquez, and Rodrigo Londono, alias Timochenko.

The U.S. Treasury Department placed financial sanctions on the trio.

September 13, 2008—India—Five bombs placed in trash cans and on bicycles and an auto-rickshaw exploded in crowded markets in New Delhi within twenty-five minutes, killing at least twenty-three and injuring more than one hundred. Among the dead was the 10-year-old daughter of Fareeda Sheik Liaqat, 35. The first ammonium nitrate bomb went off at 6:15 p.m. near a car in an electronics market. One of the sites was the upscale Greater Kailash market. The Indian Mujahideen claimed credit by sending from a Mumbai suburb an e-mail that said, "Within five minutes from now ... this time with the Message of Death, dreadfully terrorizing you for your sins. And thus our promise will be fulfilled, Insh'allah. Do whatever you want and stop us if you can." The e-mail said that there would be nine explosions; police defused four other bombs. The bombs were packed with ball bearings and used timers. Shop owner Ejaz Ahmad, 32, was injured.

Within a day, police had arrested ten suspects. Police said Abdul Suban Tauqir, a software engineer, was suspected of sending the e-mail.

Two of the suspects were killed in an 11:00 a.m. raid on their New Delhi safe house on September 19. Police officer Mohan Chand Sharma, 44, died and several were seriously injured. A third suspect was detained; two others escaped. Police said one of the dead terrorists was Mohammad Atif, who was a leader in the New Delhi bombings and several others in three other towns in 2008. He was believed associated with Abdul Sbhan Qureshi, alias Tauqeer, a computer expert and member of a radical Indian student group. Police seized bomb-making equipment, an AK-47 assault rifle and two pistols. Indian authorities detained Zeesham Ahmed, a graduate student of business management who scored high in commercial law and organizational behavior.

On September 24, Indian police arrested Mohammed Arif Shaikh, founder of the Indian Mujahideen, along with four others who were in possession of explosives, ammunition, and detonators, while they were planning an attack on Mumbai.

On October 24, police arrested four Hindus on charges of involvement in the motorcycle bombing in Malegaon, near Mumbai, that killed five people. One of the suspects was Pragya Singh, 36, who said she was a sadhvi (saint). She was in her late 20s and had been associated with the student wing of the Hindu nationalist Bharatiya Janata Party and the women's wing of Vishwa Hindu Parishad (World Hindu Council). She

owned the motorcycle used in one of the bombings. Ganesh Sovani was her attorney.

By November 23, ten Hindus, including Army Lt. Col. Srikant Prasad Purohit, were in custody. Authorities said Purohit trained Hindu activists in combat techniques and explosives. Avinash Bhide served as his attorney.

Police said most of the detainees were associated with the Abhinav Bharat (New India), which advocated the creation of a Hindu nation and said the government was soft on Muslim terrorism. The group's president is Himani Savarkar, 62.

September 15, 2008—Australia—A Melbourne jury convicted a Muslim cleric and five followers of forming a terrorist group that considered conducting "violent jihad" by assassinating former Prime Minister John Howard and attacking sports events, including a football game that attracts one hundred thousand people and the Formula One Grand Prix. Four others were found innocent of membership in the group. The jury was still deliberating on the fate of two others. Those convicted faced life terms. Among them was Abdul Nacer Benbrika, 48, an Algerian-born cleric who led the cell. He was represented by Remy Van de Wiel.

September 15, 2008—Philippines—Gunmen kidnapped six people from their two vehicles on a road near Kabangalan village on Basilan Island. Two of the people escaped. A few hours later, the kidnappers released two people, including Ludy Borja Dekit, 37, an employee of a Richmond, Virginia–based aid agency. Two remained as hostages. 08091501

September 15, 2008—Mexico—Terrorists threw two grenades into a crowd celebrating Mexico's Independence Day in Morelia, Michoacan, killing seven and injuring more than one hundred. Mexican drug gangs were believed responsible. On September 26, Mexican federal prosecutors arrested three Zeta Gulf drug cartel gang members who confessed to throwing the grenades.

September 17, 2008—Yemen—At 9:15 a.m., six gunmen wearing military uniforms attacked the U.S. Embassy in Sana'a, killing thirteen when they fired rocket-propelled grenades and automatic weapons and set off two vehicle bombs at the main gate. Among the dead were six guards and four civilians, plus Susan Elbaneh, 18, a Yemeni American from New York who had married a Yemeni in a traditional arranged marriage less than a month earlier. She was a cousin of Jaber Elbaneh, who is on the FBI's Most Wanted Terrorists list. The six gunmen also died. Al Qaeda was suspected. Police detained twenty-five people for questioning, but authorities later said it would not institute more stringent security measures. Authorities said on November 1 that the six gunmen had trained in al Qaeda camps in Hadramut and Marib Provinces. Three of them had been in Iraq. 08091701

September 19, 2008—Germany—Authorities arrested two men near Frankfurt for plotting to blow up U.S. targets in 2007 and charged them with membership in a terrorist group. Omid Shirkhani, 27, a German citizen of Afghan descent, had trained at Islamic Jihad Union camps on the Afghanistan-Pakistan border in the spring and summer of 2007. Hueseyin Ozgun, 27, a Turk, had traveled to the same area in 2007 but was detained by Pakistani security forces before he could reach the camp. He was returned to Germany. The duo had shared bank account information and a debit card with the trio (Fritz Martin Gelowicz, Adem Yilmaz, and Daniel Martin Schneider) arrested on September 4, 2007, for planning bombings against U.S. targets.

September 19, 2008—Egypt—Gunmen kidnapped five Germans, five Italians, and a Romanian tourist and eight Egyptian guides and drivers during a safari while they were camping and took them into Sudan. Two of the Italians were in their 70s. The kidnappers demanded $6 million ransom for the group, which was taken from the Gilf al-Kebir plateau near the Great Sand Sea noted for its cave paintings. The hostages were rescued on September 29 in a joint Egyptian-Sudanese operation near the Sudan-Chad border; no ransom was paid. The Egyptian Defense Minister said half of the kidnappers are dead. 08091901

September 20, 2008—Mauritania—The army found the bodies of a dozen soldiers who had been ambushed in the desert the week before by the local al Qaeda branch. The victims had been shot and their throats slit.

September 20, 2008—Pakistan—A suicide dump truck bomb carrying a ton of explosives went off at Islamabad's Marriott Hotel, killing at least 60 and injuring 266. Some observers said that the death toll would reach at least 100. At least 21 foreigners, including the Czech Republic's ambassador, were among the casualties. Several guards who had examined the truck were killed. Two Department of Defense employees were dead, a contractor was missing, and three State Department officers were hurt. Pakistani authorities said the attackers had targeted the official residence of Prime Minister Yousaf Raza Gilani, a block away from the hotel. Authorities blamed terrorists from South Waziristan, saying Baitullah Mehsud, leader

of the Tehrik-e-Taliban, was the chief suspect. By October 24, police had arrested four men in Punjab who were suspected of "indirect involvement" in the bombing. The government blamed Lashkar-i-Jhangvi for assisting the attackers. 08092001

September 20, 2008—Ethiopia—Gunmen kidnapped two foreign Doctors for the World in Ethiopia's Ogaden Province, smuggled them across the border into Somalia, and held them for 108 days before releasing them on January 6, 2009, in Mogadishu, Somalia. Keiko Akahane, 32, a Japanese doctor, and Willem Sools, 27, a Dutch nurse, appeared unharmed. Akahane told reporters, "Every day I was afraid we might get killed. In the first week, the month, we didn't know when we'd get killed—was it tonight or tomorrow night? Every time we heard the guns, we thought 'This is the end.'" 08092002

September 21, 2008—Nigeria—The Movement for the Emancipation of the Niger Delta declared a unilateral cease-fire following appeals from elders and politicians in the southern region. The group said it would resume attacks if its base camps were raided by the military.

September 21, 2008—Spain—A car bomb exploded at the Ondarroa police station, injuring ten people. Another bomb went off in Vitoria, the Basque region's capital. Police blamed the Basque Nation and Liberty (ETA). Three days earlier, a court had banned a pro-independence Basque political party for its ETA links.

September 22, 2008—Israel—A Palestinian resident of East Jerusalem crashed his car into a group of soldiers near the Old City of Jerusalem, injuring thirteen before he was shot to death.

September 24, 2008—Somalia—Islamist insurgents fired mortar rounds into a base of African Union peacekeepers and surrounding neighborhoods in Mogadishu, killing eleven civilians and injuring forty. No soldiers were harmed.

September 24, 2008—Russia—Ruslan Yamadayev, 46, a former Chechen rebel commander in the mid–1990s who defected to the Russians in 1999 and served in the Russian parliament, was shot to death during the night when a gunman walked up to his black Mercedes while waiting in traffic near the British Embassy in Moscow. Passenger Lt. Col. Sergei Kizyun, a retired Chechen military officer, was critically wounded. The assailant fled in a getaway car.

September 25, 2008—Germany—Federal prosecutors issued arrest warrants for Eric Breininger, 21, a German citizen and Muslim convert, and Houssain al-Malla, 23, a Lebanese, who had reentered Germany after attending camps in Pakistan and Afghanistan. They were suspected of involvement with the Islamic Jihad Union.

September 25, 2008—Israel—At 1:00 a.m., a pipe bomb planted outside his Jerusalem home lightly wounded Zeev Sternhel, 70s, in his leg. The Holocaust survivor is a leading Israeli political scientist and critic of Jewish settlement of the West Bank. Police found fliers in his neighborhood offering $320,000 for the death of any member of Peace Now, which he had supported in opposing Jewish settlements. Police blamed the extreme right and members of the settlers' movement. Itamar Ben-Gvir, spokesman for the National Jewish Front, said, "I don't denounce this incident, but say categorically that we are not involved."

September 26, 2008—Germany—At 6:55 a.m., German troops boarded Royal KLM flight 1804 at Cologne-Bonn airport as it was prepared to leave the gate for Amsterdam and arrested Abdirazak B., a Somali, 23, and Omar D., a Somali-born German, 24, who were planning terrorist attacks. The duo had left notes in their apartments saying that they were willing to die for jihad. The two were scheduled to fly to Uganda via Amsterdam, then on to Pakistan, where many Germany-based radicals had attended terrorist training camps.

September 26, 2008—Pakistan—Police attacked a Karachi insurgent safe house. In the ensuing gun battle, three suicide bombers blew themselves up, also killing a handcuffed prisoner.

September 26, 2008—Pakistan—A bomb derailed a train in Punjab, killing four and wounding fifteen.

September 27, 2008—United Kingdom—London police arrested three men on suspicion of the commission, preparation, or instigation of acts of terrorism.

September 27, 2008—India—At 2:15 p.m., a small bomb exploded in a New Delhi hardware and electronics market, killing one and wounding eighteen. Two men on a motorcycle dropped a plastic bag containing a lunchbox and sped away. Police said it contained a crude, low-intensity bomb. A small boy was killed when he picked up the bomb, causing it to detonate. He had called out, "Uncle, you have left your bag behind."

September 27, 2008—Syria—At 8:45 a.m., a suicide bomber detonated a GMC Suburban carrying 440 pounds of explosives in the Sayeda Zaineb neighborhood of Damascus, killing seventeen. The vehicle had crossed into the country a day earlier from an unnamed Arab country. The southern neighborhood was near a Shi'ite shrine which draws pilgrims from Iran and other countries. The area was home to hundreds of thousands of Iraqi war refugees. Takfir was suspected.

September 27, 2008—Algeria—A car bomb killed three and injured seven.

September 28, 2008—Pakistan—Polish engineer Piotr Stanczak was kidnapped. On October 14, 2008, the kidnappers released a video of him. They claimed to have killed him on February 7, 2009, after a deadline had passed; the group had demanded the release of sixty prisoners and the withdrawal of Pakistani forces from the area. Poland's foreign minister said internal Pakistani government bickering hampered efforts to stop Stanczak's eventual beheading. Stanczak, a geologist, left behind a child. 08092801

September 29, 2008—Lebanon—Fatah al-Islam was suspected in the remote detonation of a Renault car bomb near a bus full of Lebanese soldiers that killed five and wounded more than thirty during the morning rush hour on a road leading to several schools. No one claimed credit. The bomb contained ball bearings.

October 1, 2008—Lebanon—By October 8, two American journalists who had not been seen since October 1 were believed to be missing. Holli Chmela, 27, and Taylor Luck, 23, had been vacationing in the area. Both worked for the *Jordan Times* and had been expected to have returned from Beirut and Tripoli to Amman by October 4. They had arrived in Lebanon on September 29. They had also planned a side trip by taxi to Syria. On October 9, they were discovered in custody in Damascus, Syria, having tried to sneak into the country with smugglers. They were released in good condition.

October 3, 2008—Pakistan—The government said a 10:00 p.m. U.S. missile strike had killed twenty-four people, including twenty-one insurgents, among them sixteen Arabs, five Pakistani Taliban fighters, two women, and a child in North Waziristan. The *Washington Post* reported that the attack was aimed at Taliban leaders and Afghan brothers Daud Jan and Abdur Rehman in Muhammad Khel village, 20 miles west of Miranshah.

October 3, 2008—Iraq—Mahir Ahmad Mahmud Judu al-Zubaydi, alias Abu Assad, alias Abu Rami, an emir of al Qaeda in Iraq, was killed in a gun battle with U.S. troops in the northern Baghdad neighborhood of Adhamiyah. He was believed to be behind a series of bombings in Baghdad, including a car bombing and suicide bombing on October 2 that targeted people outside Shi'ite mosques. He was the al Qaeda in Iraq (AQI) leader in Rusafa, an eastern Baghdad district. A woman with him was also killed. He had left Ansar al-Islam to join AQI in 2004. He was behind several car bombings and mortar attacks in Sadr City in 2006 and 2007, including the fall 2006 bombing that killed more than two hundred. He was also believed behind a May 1, 2008, bombing in Baghdad that killed a U.S. soldier and wounded three others.

October 4, 2008—Pakistan—Adam Gadahn, alias Azzam al-Amriki, released a thirty-two-minute As-Sahab video on the Internet mentioning Pakistan, U.S. economic problems, and fighting in Kashmir. He said, "It's time for you to put aside tribal, ethnic and territorial differences and petty worldly disputes not just for now but forever and unite to restore the glories of your forefathers and hasten, Allah willing, the defeat of the Zionist-crusader enemy and the establishment of the Islamic state, the Ummah, so eagerly anticipated." Turning to a "victory in Kashmir" that will occur some day, he observed,

> It is the liberation of the jihad there from this interference which, Allah willing, will be the first step towards victory over the Hindu occupiers of that Islam land.... The enemies of Islam are facing a crushing defeat, which is beginning to manifest itself in the extended crisis their economy is experiencing. The crisis, whose primary cause, in addition to the abortive and unsustainable crusades they are waging in Afghanistan, Pakistan and Iraq, is they are turning their backs on Allah's revealed laws, which forbid interest-bearing transactions, exploitation, greed, and injustice in all its forms and demand the worship of Allah alone to the exclusion of all false gods, including money and power.

October 5, 2008—Iraq—Abu Qaswarah, alias Abu Sara, the Swedish-Moroccan deputy chief of al Qaeda in Iraq (AQI) since June 2007 and its leader in the north, was killed in Mosul in a clash with coalition forces. Four other AQI members died in the battle which began during a raid on a safe house in which the terrorists initiated fire on the soldiers. An explosive belt detonated inside the house, killing five AQI insurgents, three women, and three children. He was believed to have planned attacks against U.S. and Iraqi forces in Mosul, including a foiled attack on the Mosul Civic Center in September 2008. Authorities later announced that his name was Muhammad Moumou, 43, a Moroccan who obtained Swedish citizenship in 1994 and who was listed as a terrorist by the United States, UN, and European Union.

The U.S. Department of the Treasury named him a terrorist facilitator on December 7, 2006. He was born in Fez, Morocco, and became a close associate of Abu Musab al-Zarqawi, serving as his chemical and biological weapons liaison in Europe. He trained at al Qaeda's Khalden camp in Afghanistan in the mid–1990s. He was arrested in Denmark in March 2004 for suspected involvement in the 2003 suicide bombings in Casablanca that killed thirty-three people. He had ties to the radical Brandbergen Mosque in Stockholm. He had also lived in London, Stockholm, and Haninge, Sweden. His Swedish passport was due to expire in December 2009.

October 6, 2008—Sri Lanka—A Liberation Tigers of Tamil Eelam suicide bomber killed retired Maj. Gen. Janaka Perera and twenty-six others at an opposition United National Party office in Anuradhapura. Another eighty were injured.

October 6, 2008—Pakistan—A suicide bomber set off an explosives vest at the Bhakkar home of opposition parliamentary leader Rashid Akbar Nawani, killing twenty and injuring thirty-five. The guests were celebrating Eid al-Fitr, the end of Ramadan. Nawani was slightly injured. Some television stations said thirty-five were killed and fifty-three injured.

October 6, 2008—Somalia—Two Kenyan Agriculture Ministry employees and their local driver were kidnapped near the southwestern border. The driver was soon released. 08100601

October 7, 2008—Guantanamo Bay—U.S. District Judge Ricardo M. Urbina ruled that seventeen Uighurs held at the Guantanamo facility who had been deemed no threat to the United States could not be held indefinitely. They were ordered to be released by October 10 to seventeen Uighur families in the Washington, DC, area who had agreed to house them temporarily. The Justice Department filed an emergency appeal saying that the order violated separation-of-powers and presented national security concerns. The Justice Department said that the seventeen had trained at East Turkistan Islamic Movement (ETIM) camps. The ETIM had been designated a terrorist organization after the seventeen had been detained in Pakistan nearly seven years ago. The next day, a three-judge panel of the U.S. Court of Appeals for the District of Columbia Circuit granted the Justice Department request for an emergency administrative stay of the release.

October 8, 2008—Somalia—Gunmen kidnapped a British oil worker affiliated with the Canadian-based Africa Oil Corporation. He was detained near Bossaso, a center of kidnappings and piracy. Security forces surrounded the kidnappers and freed the Briton in a gun battle in which one bandit was killed and another wounded. The Briton was unharmed. 08100801

October 9, 2008—United States—A federal judge in Miami sentenced two United Self Defense Forces of Colombia paramilitary leaders to long prison terms after they pleaded guilty to cocaine conspiracy charges. Ramiro Vanoy Murillo, 60, received more than twenty-four years in prison. Francisco Javier Zuluaga Lindo, 28, received nearly twenty-two years.

October 11, 2008—United States—The Bush Administration took North Korea off its list of countries that support terrorism, following years of negotiation regarding Pyongyang's nuclear weapons program. North Korea had agreed to not restart its reactor. North Korea had been on the list since 1987. Still on the list were Iran, Syria, Sudan, and Cuba.

October 12, 2008—Afghanistan—Canadian Broadcasting Corporation journalist Mellissa Fung, 35, was kidnapped while reporting as a freelancer. She was traveling with her translator and driver after interviewing refugees in a camp near Kabul. Local media covered the kidnapping, but the international media did not, following a request from the CBC and the Canadian Embassy suggesting that coverage would complicate the case. She was freed in good health in Kabul on November 8 at 7:30 p.m. She said that she was held in a small cave in which she could hardly stand. For the first weeks, she was held under guard. During the last week, her ankles and wrists were shackled. Tribal elders and provincial council members interceded for her release. No ransom was paid. 08101201

October 13, 2008—Mexico—In the early morning, two gunmen threw a grenade and fired at the U.S. Consulate General in Monterrey. The grenade did not explode. Several bullets hit the front gate and windows of the building. Police later found six bullet casings from a pistol. Authorities speculated that it could have been a drug cartel, foiled border crossers, or other amateurs. 08101301

October 15, 2008—Turkey—A drunken Uzbek passenger tried to hijack a Turkish Airlines A-320 carrying 164 Russians and 3 others from Antalya, Turkey, to St. Petersburg, Russia. He had claimed to have a bomb, but was overpowered by the passengers. No bomb was found. The plane landed on time at 3:20 p.m. at St. Petersburg's Pulkovo Airport. 08101501

October 16, 2008—Israel—Israeli troops shot and killed a suspected Palestinian male bomber in a West Bank village.

October 16, 2008—Pakistan—Khalid Habib, an operations coordinator for al Qaeda in the tribal region along the Pakistan-Afghanistan border, was believed killed in a missile strike in Saam, Wana, South Waziristan, that killed four civilians and wounded seven others. He was believed to be a deputy to Mustafa Abu al-Yazid, alias Sheikh Said, commander of al Qaeda in Afghanistan.

October 19, 2008—Sudan—Nine Chinese oil workers were kidnapped in the southwestern Kordofan Province, next to Darfur. No group claimed credit, although the Sudanese Foreign Ministry blamed the Justice and Equality Movement, a Darfur rebel group which denied involvement. On October 27, the kidnappers killed five of the hostages. Two others escaped; the other two were being held. Chinese officials announced the next day that four of the hostages died in a failed rescue attempt. 08101901

October 19, 2008—Somalia—Gunmen shot to death a Somali engineer employed by the UN as he walked home from a mosque with friends in Hudur. 08101902

October 20, 2008—Afghanistan—Two gunmen on a motorcycle killed Gayle Williams, 34, who had worked for Serving Emergency Relief and Vocational Enterprises, a U.K.-based Christian charity, in an 8:00 a.m. drive-by shooting in Kabul. She was walking to work in the Kart-e-Char neighborhood when they fired automatic weapons at her. A Taliban spokesman Zabiullah Muhahi said, "This woman came to Afghanistan to teach Christianity to the people of Afghanistan. Our leaders issued a decree to kill this woman." She had British and South African nationalities. 08102001

October 21, 2008—China—Police requested the extradition of eight members of the East Turkestan Islamic Movement thought to be hiding in Pakistan and Afghanistan. The Chinese men were believed to have plotted attacks during the August 8–24 Olympic Games, including bombings in China, the Middle East, and South Asia.

October 21, 2008—Saudi Arabia—The government indicted 991 suspected members of al Qaeda in the Arabian Peninsula who had conducted thirty attacks since 2003 in an effort to destabilize the regime.

October 22, 2008—United States—Members of the Sheriff's Office in Crockett County, Tennessee, arrested two neo–Nazi skinheads who planned to assassinate Democratic presidential candidate Barack Obama, kill eighty-eight black people, and decapitate fourteen other victims. Police had foiled an attempt to rob a gun store and attack a predominantly African American high school. The duo were identified as Daniel Cowart, 20, of Bells, Tennessee, and Paul Schlesselman, 18, of Helena–West Helena, Arkansas. They were held without bond. Authorities confiscated a high-powered rifle, a sawed-off shotgun, a handgun, and several swords and knives from the rural Tennessee home of Cowart's grandparents, where the duo were staying. They were charged with possession of an unregistered firearm, conspiracy to steal firearms from a federally licensed gun dealer, and threatening a presidential candidate.

Cowart and Schlesselman met online a month earlier via a mutual friend. The duo planned to use nylon rope and ski masks in robberies and home invasions across several states in a killing spree. At the end, they planned to dress in white tuxedos and white top hats and drive their car at speed, firing a .308-caliber rifle at Obama from the windows. However, the day after they met, they failed in an attempted robbery of a home in Bells, Tennessee, when they noticed a dog and two vehicles on the premises. For practice, they fired at a window of the Church of Christ of Beech Grove in Brownsville, Tennessee. They then chalked swastikas and other racially motivated words and symbols on the hood of their car.

The numbers eighty-eight and fourteen are symbolic to white supremacists. Fourteen is the number of words in a phrase attributed to a white supremacist who said, "We must secure the existence of our people and a future for white children." The eight refers to the eighth letter of the English alphabet. Double Hs are the initials for Heil Hitler.

The two pleaded not guilty on November 6 in front of a federal magistrate in Memphis to charges of conspiracy and firearms offenses. They were held without bail in a Tennessee prison. They faced more than a decade in prison. On November 20 they were charged in a superseding indictment with civil rights conspiracy. Cowart was also charged with damage to religious property and use of a firearm during a violent crime. On November 26, Daniel Cowart and Paul Schlesselman pleaded not guilty to the new federal charges.

On January 14, 2010, Paul Schlesselman pleaded guilty in a Jackson, Tennessee, courtroom to one count of conspiracy, one count of threatening to kill and harm a presidential candidate, and one count of possession of a firearm in furtherance of a crime of violence. Sentencing was scheduled for April 2010, when he faced ten years. Co-defendant Daniel Cowart remained in custody.

On March 29, 2010, in a plea agreement, Daniel Cowart pleaded guilty to eight to ten counts of conspiracy, threatening a presidential candidate, and federal firearms violations. Cowart faced twelve to eighteen years in prison. Co-defendant Paul Schlesselman was to be sentenced on April 15.

October 24, 2008—United States—Afghan citizen Haji Juma Khan, 54, pleaded not guilty in the U.S. District Court in Manhattan to charges of leading an international narcotrafficking group that funded the Taliban. He was detained in Indonesia the previous day on an Interpol notice, having arrived in Jakarta from Dubai. His group had produced enough morphine base to supply American heroin demand for more than two years.

October 25, 2008—Afghanistan—A local security guard working at the DHL shipping firm office in Kabul shot to death the firm's country director and his deputy before committing suicide. A Briton and a South African were killed. The shooter was hired a month earlier from a Pashtun area north of Kabul. Many Taliban members are Pashtuns, but the Taliban denied involvement.

October 28, 2008—Sri Lanka—Liberation Tigers of Tamil Eelam rebels conducted an air strike against a power station near Colombo, darkening the city.

October 28, 2008—Spain—Police detained four Basque Nation and Liberty members suspected of planning an attack in Navarra region. Police confiscated weapons and explosives.

October 29, 2008—Canada—A court in Ottawa found Canadian software engineer Momin Khawaja guilty of involvement in a plot to bomb nightclubs, trains, and a shopping center in the United Kingdom. Sentencing was scheduled for November 18; he faced life in prison.

October 29, 2008—Somalia—Shirwa Ahmed, 27, a Minneapolis-based Somali and naturalized U.S. citizen was believed to have gone to Somalia to conduct one of the October 29 suicide bombings in breakaway Somaliland and the Puntland region that killed more than twenty people. He blew himself up in a suicide bombing in northern Somalia. His attack was one of five simultaneous bombings that day attributed to al-Shabaab, which has al Qaeda links. The FBI returned his remains to his family in Minneapolis in late fall 2008. More than a dozen young Somalis had disappeared from the Minneapolis area around that time.

At least seven Somalis from Minneapolis were reported missing on November 4. One of them, a 17-year-old, reportedly took his passport with him and arrived in Nairobi, Kenya, the next day. He called his parents on November 6 to say that he was in Mogadishu, Somalia. He had not been heard from since November 27, 2008.

October 30, 2008—India—Eleven bombs exploded between 11:10 a.m. and noon in Assam, killing 61 and wounded 350. The first explosions went off in a fruit and vegetable market, in a parking lot, a bazaar, and near a rail station. Others went off in Guwahati, the state capital. Observers suspected the banned independence group United Front of Assam (ULFA), which denied involvement. Others suggested it was armed Islamists based in Bangladesh.

October 30, 2008—Afghanistan—Three individuals attacked the Ministry of Information and Culture in Kabul, killing five and seriously injuring twenty-one at 11:00 a.m. One individual shot two guards near the entrance before setting an explosives vest in a hall on the ground floor. The others, one dressed in an Afghan police uniform, went to separate parts of the building. One worker heard the sound of a Kalashnikov being fired. Authorities stopped a bomber from setting off his explosives vest. The third gunman remained at large two hours later. The Taliban said it was targeting foreign advisors working in the building. 08103001

October 31, 2008—Cameroon—A local militia group kidnapped ten mostly foreign oil workers and threatened to kill them if progress wasn't made on setting up autonomy talks with the government. Ebi Dari, the militia's commander, said that the group had grabbed six Frenchmen, two Cameroonians, one Senegalese, and one Tunisian from a boat off the coast. 08103101

October 31, 2008—Pakistan—Gunmen kidnapped Afghan businessman Zia ul–Haq Ahadi and brother of Afghan Finance Minister Anwar-ul-Haq Ahadi near his home in Hayatabad. 0810 3102

November 2008—Afghanistan—A Dutch journalist was kidnapped. He was freed on November 7 after about a week in captivity. 08119901

November 1, 2008—Afghanistan—Gunmen kidnapped Joanie de Rijke, who was working on a story for Belgium's *P* magazine, outside Kabul. She was freed unharmed a week later. 08110101

November 3, 2008—Afghanistan—Gunmen kidnapped French aid worker Dany Egreteau, 32, in Kabul. They released a video of him pleading for his life. He was freed on December 3, 2008. French President Nicolas Sarkozy said he was "doing well." 08110301

November 5, 2008—Somalia—Gunmen ambushed a convoy in Dusa Marreb, 360 miles north of Mogadishu, as it was traveling to Kenya and took four European aid workers—two French citizens, a Belgian, and a Bulgarian working for the French group Action Against Hunger—and two Kenyans hostage. The hostages had been on their way to the airport. On August 11, 2009, the kidnappers released the four aid workers and two pilots. 08110501

November 6, 2008—Pakistan—A Taliban suicide bomber killed seventeen people and wounded forty others at a meeting of tribesmen hosted by an anti-insurgent militia. Another two people were killed in a separate suicide bombing.

November 6, 2008—Russia—A bomb exploded when a minibus taxi pulled up outside a market in Vladikavkaz, North Ossetia, killing eleven people.

November 10, 2008—Kenya—Somali gunmen kidnapped two Italian nuns in El Wak just before dawn on the Somalia-Kenya border. Caterina Giruado, 67, and Maria Teresa Olivero, 60, were freed unharmed on February 19, 2009. No ransom was paid. 08111001

November 10, 2008—Afghanistan—The Taliban kidnapped David Rohde, 41, a *New York Times* reporter, outside of Kabul, as he was en route to interview a Taliban commander in eastern Logar Province. He had arrived in Afghanistan earlier that month to work on a history of U.S. involvement in Afghanistan. He won a Pulitzer Prize in 1996 for his reporting on the Srebrenica massacre in Bosnia, and was part of a *NYT* team that won a Pulitzer Prize in May 2009 for coverage of Afghanistan and Pakistan in 2008. The *NYT* hired Boston-based American International Security Corporation (AISC), led by former CIA senior operations chief Duane Clarridge, to secure Rohde's release.

A Taliban spokesman told CNN in May 2009 that it had provided two "proof of life" videos and had demanded negotiations for the release of its leaders in U.S. custody and a multi-million dollar ransom.

On June 19, 2009, Rohde and local reporter Tahir Ludin, 35, climbed over the wall of the compound where they were held in North Waziristan, Pakistan. A Pakistani military spokesman said that the Pakistan military was involved in freeing them, but did not provide details. The duo found a Pakistani army scout near Miran Shah, North Waziristan, who brought them to a local army base. Their driver, Asadullah Mangal, 24, did not escape. No ransom was paid and no prisoners were released.

Some forty news organizations, including al-Jazeera, had agreed to keep the story quiet until his release. 08111002

November 11, 2008—Iraq—U.S. forces killed Hammadi Awdah Abd Farhan, alias Hajji Hammadi, an al Qaeda in Iraq (AQI) leader in a gun battle that began when they raided his safe house in western Baghdad's Mansour neighborhood. He was behind several attacks, including the suicide bombing on June 26, 2008, that killed three U.S. Marines, two interpreters, and more than twenty Iraqis in Karmah. Among the dead was Lt. Col. Max A. Galeai of Pago Pago, American Samoa, commander of the U.S. Marines in the area. Farhan had videotaped the explosion. He was also behind the death of Army Reserve then–Pfc. Keith Matthew Maupin, 20, who was kidnapped on April 9, 2004, during an attack on his fuel convoy. Maupin's remains were found in March 2008 in an agricultural area northwest of Baghdad. Farhan was the emir of AQI in the Karmah and Abu Ghraib areas west of Baghdad. He was also involved in several assassinations of Sons of Iraq (SOI) members in Baghdad; SOI is an organization of repentant AQI insurgents who now fight AQI. Five suspects were captured following the gun battle.

November 12, 2008—Pakistan—The Taliban was suspected when an Iranian diplomat was kidnapped on his way to work in Peshawar. His driver was shot. 08111201

November 12, 2008—Pakistan—American aid worker Stephen Vance, 52, and his driver were shot to death in Peshawar. He was working on an Agency for International Development project to bring economic development to the tribal region. Vance was leaving for work from his home in the University Town area. The California native had worked for the previous six months for the Silver Spring, Maryland-based Cooperative Housing Foundation International. Survivors included a wife and five children, who had lived with him in Mongolia, East Timor, and the former Soviet Union. The Pakistani Taliban took credit. 08111202

November 14, 2008—Pakistan—Gunmen fired on a car in Peshawar carrying Japanese journalist Motoki Yotsukura of the daily *Asahi Shimbun*, wounding him in the leg. His Pakistani assistant was also injured. 08111401

November 14, 2008—Kosovo—A bomb was thrown at the building housing the office of the European Union's special representative in Pristina, breaking windows and damaging cars. 0811 1402

November 17, 2008—France—Police arrested Garikoitz Aspiazu Rubina, alias Txeroki (Cherokee), a senior leader of the most violent faction of the Spanish Basque Nation and Liberty, and a girlfriend while they were sleeping in Cauterets, a Pyrenees ski resort. Rubina was believed behind a plot to kill Spanish King Juan Carlos and ordering the bombing of a parking lot in Spain.

November 19, 2008—Qatar—In an eleven-minute As-Sahab video posted on the Internet, al Qaeda deputy Ayman al-Zawahiri said to President-elect Barack Obama, "You have reached the position of president, and a heavy legacy of failure and crimes awaits you. You were born to a Muslim father, but you chose to stand in the ranks of the enemies of the Muslims and pray the prayer of the Jews, although you claim to be a Christian, in order to climb the rungs of leadership in America." He said Obama compared unfavorably with Malcolm X, saying, "As for Malik al-Shabazz (Malcolm X) ... he condemned the crimes of the Crusader West against the weak and oppressed.... That's why ... Malik al-Shabazz ... was killed." He called Secretary of State Condoleezza Rice, former Secretary of State Colin Powell, and Obama "house Negros," which refers to African Americans who kowtow to white interests. Al-Zawahiri called Obama's election "an admission of defeat in Iraq.... If you still want to be stubborn about America's failure in Afghanistan, then remember the fate of Bush and Pervez Musharraf, and the fate of the Soviets and the British before them. And be aware that the dogs of Afghanistan have found the flesh of your soldiers to be delicious, so send thousands after thousands to them."

November 20, 2008—United States—U.S. District Judge Richard J. Leon ruled that five of the six Algerians held at Guantanamo Bay Naval Base must be released. He said the government had not proved that they were "enemy combatants." The Algerians were arrested in Bosnia and held at the Naval Base since January 2002 on suspicion of planning to bomb the U.S. Embassy in Sarajevo. They were also accused of planning to go to Afghanistan to fight against the coalition. Judge Leon said that the evidence against them was flimsy and based on an unnamed source of indeterminate reliability who appeared in a classified document. However, he ordered that the government could continue to detain al Qaeda facilitator

Belkacem Bensayah, as the evidence against him was based on corroborated intelligence. Bosnia had indicated that the men would be permitted to return. They were identified as Lakhdar Boumediene, Mohamed Nechle, Mustafa Ait Idir, Hadj Boudella, and Saber Lahmar.

November 20, 2008—Thailand—A bomb exploded at 3:30 a.m. at Government House, the prime minister's office complex in Bangkok, which antigovernment People's Alliance for Democracy demonstrators had occupied since late August. A 48-year-old man was killed and twenty-three others injured when the explosive went off on the canvas of a large marquee and sprayed shrapnel on those sleeping below. Police believed a grenade was involved. The protestors rejected negotiations saying they would continue their action until the government collapsed.

November 22, 2008—Pakistan—Rashid Rauf, a British Pakistani citizen who was involved in an al Qaeda plot to blow up ten British planes in 2006, was killed in a missile strike in Ali Khel in North Waziristan. Four other suspected terrorists, including three foreigners, were also killed.

November 24, 2008—United States—A federal jury in Dallas convicted five former leaders of the Texas-based Holy Land Foundation for Relief and Development (HLF), which had been the largest Muslim charity in the United States, of 108 criminal charges. The case began with a raid in December 2001 on the HLF headquarters in Richardson, Texas, when federal authorities seized HLF assets. The group had been accused of sending more than $12 million to Hamas. The case had originally listed more than one hundred unindicted co-conspirators.

November 26, 2008—United States—The FBI and Department of Homeland Security (DHS) warned state and local officials that "uncorroborated but plausible information" received in late September indicated that al Qaeda might have discussed attacking New York City transit systems. DHS spokeswoman Amy Kudwa said, "Neither DHS nor FBI has any specific information to confirm that this plot has developed beyond aspiration planning." Authorities in New York, Washington, and five other major cities with subway systems were considering increasing police presence.

November 26, 2008—Afghanistan—A suicide car bomb exploded 200 yards away from the main entrance to the U.S. Embassy. One person was killed and six wounded in the attack against a U.S. convoy. The embassy was hosting a Thanksgiving Day footrace.

November 26–28, 2008—India—At 9:00 p.m., at least ten college-aged male terrorists in two rubber dinghies traveled from a hijacked ship off shore and landed in Mumbai, where they went to ten public facilities and set off explosives and fired automatic weapons. In the attacks and ensuing battles with Indian commandoes attempting to rescue several dozen Indian and Western hostages, at least 200 people were killed—including 22 foreigners, among them 6 Americans, a Briton, an Australian, a German, an Italian, and a Japanese—and 9 of the terrorists, and another 350 people were wounded, including 2 Canadians. Indian authorities expected these figures to increase as more bodies were discovered.

Reports differed as to the number of terrorists in the attack party, the number who survived, and their affiliations. The previously unknown Deccan Mujahideen claimed credit via an e-mail to India's news media. Indian authorities said that the two surviving terrorists were British citizens of Pakistani descent. They were being interrogated regarding the identities of the other terrorists, what groups were involved, and whether Pakistan was involved. Other reports said only one terrorist—a Lashkar-i-Taiba "foot soldier" from Pakistan's Punjab area—survived. Yet another report said three terrorists were detained. Conducting simultaneous attacks is an al Qaeda hallmark, but al Qaeda does not take hostages. Some observers suggested the involvement of Lashkar-i-Taiba ("Army of the Pious") and Jaish-i-Muhammad ("Soldiers of Muhammad"), two Muslim extremist groups in Pakistan. Others saw a Kashmiri separatist connection.

Sources varied regarding the number of terrorists involved. Initial reports suggested fifteen; later reports said only ten.

Police later determined that the terrorists had hijacked a ship named the *Kuber*, shot the man in charge, and steamed to Mumbai. The terrorists were carrying photographs of the sites to be attacked. Some had lived in Mumbai a few months earlier, pretending to be students while surveilling the sites.

The gunmen set off explosives at the sites to give the impression that there were far more attackers involved. The sites included facilities in an affluent southern section of Mumbai, the heart of its financial district:

- Leopold Café, which the terrorists shot up first, at 9:30 p.m., before moving on to the Taj. The restaurant is frequented by tourists. Seven people, including three foreigners, died.
- Chhatrapathi Shivaji Terminus railway station, which two gunmen attacked at 10:00 p.m.,

killing forty-eight people and wounding many more in a twenty-minute attack. Shashank Shinde, 46, was killed while he was patrolling the station and attempted to tackle the assault rifle-wielding terrorists. Upon leaving, the terrorists fired at the *Times of India* and the Municipal Corporation of Greater Mumbai buildings. The two terrorists took over a police vehicle by killing three officers and wounding a fourth. The police officers had been responding to a call from the Cama Hospital. The lone survivor was police constable Arun Jadhav, who played dead.

- Metro movie theater, which was attacked at 10:30 p.m. by the two railway gunmen, who arrived by the hijacked police vehicle. They threw grenades and fired at passengers and pedestrians, killing ten and injuring thirty. The terrorists returned to their car and drove along Mahatma Gandhi Road, past the Bombay Stock Exchange, on their way to the Taj Hotel. But police intercepted them at Chowpatty, a beach on the city's far west side. Police killed one gunman and arrested Azam Amir Kasab, 21, a Pakistani.

- Thirty-six-floor Oberoi Trident Hotel, where at least twenty-four people were killed in an initial attack at 10:15 p.m. Indian authorities said they had killed two gunmen at the site. Among the dead were former University of Maryland art professor Alan Scherr, 58, and his daughter, Naomi, 13, of central Virginia's Nelson County, who were shot execution-style. They were visiting India with the Synchronicity Foundation, a Virginia-based meditation group. At 10:40 a.m. on November 28, India's National Security Guard killed two gunmen. By midnight of November 28, police had found forty-one dead bodies. At least ninety-eight hostages had been rescued. Among the injured hostages was Linda Ragsdale, a children's book illustrator from Nashville, who was with Synchronicity. A bullet had grazed her spine. Two other Synchronicity members were wounded. American Andreina Varagona was shot in the shoulder. Subash Waghela was hit in the abdomen and left hand; he died later that day.

- Waterfront landmark Taj Mahal Palace and Tower Hotel, which at least three terrorists attacked at 10:15 p.m. The terrorists fired on diners at the Sea Lounge restaurant, aiming at tourists. Its 105-year-old Moorish-style rooftop dome was engulfed in flames and smoke. The terrorists knocked on doors of the 565-room hotel, calling for American and British

citizens to come out. Some 250 guests, including Americans, Europeans, and South Koreans, took cover on the rooftop, where they were trapped for four hours. Commandoes began a rescue operation at 4:30 a.m. Seven hours after the attack began firefighters rescued more than fifty hotel guests. Authorities secured the fire exit, and the rest of the hostages fled down the stairs and through windows. A running gun battle ensued. At 2:30 a.m. on November 28, Indian Marine commandoes entered the building, where they saw more than thirty bodies and several wounded people. At least ten members of the kitchen staff were killed, including Vijay Rao Banja, father of two and a senior chef. Among the dead was Sabina Sehgal Saikia, an editor with the *Times of India* newspaper, who died in her room on the fifth floor of the Taj Mahal Palace and Tower Hotel.

After a sixty-hour siege, one wing of the hotel was gutted. At least eleven commandoes died in the gunfire. Among them was Hemant Karkare, chief of Mumbai's counterterrorism squad. The commandoes killed four terrorists, but one remained hiding. Four hundred hostages were freed. Police later captured the last terrorist. Authorities found backpacks filled with ammunition and grenades, credit cards from several banks, and an identity card from Mauritius. Among the injured was Commando Rajveer Singh, 33, who sustained a gunshot wound to his left hand and severe burns on his face when a gunman in room 471 resisted arrest. Also injured was Rangoli Garg, 18, who sustained a leg wound.

- Cama and Albless Hospital, which the terrorists attacked between 10:45 and 11:15 p.m. Two terrorists were captured after they hijacked a police van to escape from the hospital. Three hospital workers and two police officers died.

- Gokuldas Tejpal Hospital, which the terrorists attacked between 10:45 and 11:15 p.m.

- Mazegaon Dockyard was the scene of a midnight bombing.

- Nariman House, a business and residential complex, where at 4:30 a.m. on November 27, the terrorists took hostages at the Chabad-Lubavitch Jewish Center, including eight Israelis and an American rabbi and his wife. Later that day, commandoes surrounded the facility. The terrorists killed U.S. citizen Rabbi Gavriel N. Holtzberg, 29, and his wife, Rivka, 28, both of whom were born in Israel and were raised in the Crown Heights neighborhood of Brooklyn, New York. Three other hostages—

U.S. citizen Leibish Teitlebaumat; dual national American-Israeli Bentzion Chroman; and an unidentified Israeli woman—also died at the center. At 11:30 a.m. on November 28, commandoes airlifted to the building's roof and dropped smoke bombs. By 7:00 p.m. fighting was over and one commando had died. Haresh Gohil, a civilian, was killed near the center. Sandra Samuel, a cook, rescued Moshe Holtzberg, almost 2, from the center.

- Northern district's Ramada Hotel and the Vile Parle.

Police later seized the explosives-laden mothership. At least fifteen police officers died in the attacks, as well as Balasaheb Bhosale, a police official who tried to stop a gunman at a rail station.

Surviving terrorist Azam Amir Kasab said that the terrorist group members had trained for a year before the attack at a Lashkar camp in Pakistan. He admitted membership in Lashkar, renamed Jamaat-ud-Dawa in 2005. He claimed the group staged from Karachi, Pakistan. The terrorists killed the crew of a fishing trawler, slitting the throat of the captain, killing the four other crew members, and dumping their bodies over the side. They then took a speedboat and a rubber dinghy to the shoreline. They split up into four teams, some hailing two taxis to get to their first targets.

On November 30, government officials said the official casualty numbers were 174 people dead and 239 wounded. Home Minister Shivraj Patil resigned.

The gunmen had used several electronic devices to keep in touch with each other and monitor media coverage and police plans. They used Global Positioning System equipment, carried CDs with high-resolution satellite images, and switched SIM cards (subscriber identity cards) in multiple cell phones.

Authorities said a third of the victims were Muslims. Indian Muslim leaders refused to permit the nine dead terrorists to be buried in Muslim cemeteries.

Indian police charged Tauseef Rehman, 28, of Calcutta, and Mukhtar Ahmed Sheik, 35, from Jammu and Kashmir, with fraud and conspiracy for using a false ID card to buy twenty-two SIMs that were used by the terrorists during the attacks. Ahmed allegedly was a member of an irregular Jammu and Kashmir police force who was working undercover to penetrate Lashkar-e-Taiba. Police also hoped to question Faheem Ahmed Ansari, a Mumbai native, who had been arrested in February for an attack on a police training camp in Rampur, Uttar Pradesh. He had claimed to have surveilled targets for another Lashkar-e-Taiba plan.

Police said Lashkar-e-Taiba leaders Zaki ur–Rehman Lakhvi, variant Lakhwi, and Yusuf Muzammil, directed the Mumbai attacks. India requested their extradition, as well as that of Hafiz Sayeed, Lashkar's alleged leader.

Kasab claimed he had trained at four Lashkar camps near Muzzafrabad, Mansera, Muritke, and Karachi during the previous nine to twelve months. Police said he would be charged on twelve counts of murder, criminal conspiracy, and waging war against the state. As of Christmas, although he was held on twelve charges, he was not yet formally charged and was ordered by a judge to remain in police custody for two more weeks.

Police identified one of the dead terrorists as Abu Ismail and the commando who was killed defending Indian civilians as Sandeep Unnikrishnan. Nashville residents Rudrani Devi and Linda Ragsdale were hospitalized for more than a week. Canadians Helen Connolly and Michael Rudder were expected to recover from their injuries.

On December 8, Pakistani authorities raided a Lashkar camp in Muzzafrabad, arresting twenty-two individuals, including Lakhvi, believed to be behind the Mumbai attacks.

Police said that nine of the gunmen came from central Punjab Province of Pakistan. Three came from Okara, three from Multan, two from Faisalabad, one from Sialkot, and Ismail Khan, 26, the group's leader, from northwest Pakistan's Dera Ismail Khan city. They identified the attackers as Ajmal Amir from Faridkot, Abu Ismail from Dera Ismail Khan, Hafiz Arshad and Babr Imran from Multan, Javed from Okara, Shoaib from Narowal, Nazih and Nasr from Faisalabad, Abdul Rahman from Arifwalla, and Fahad Ullah (or Fahadullah) from Dipalpur Taluka. All were between the ages of 20 and 28.

On December 9, Pakistani police placed Jaish-i-Muhammad leader Masood Azhar under house arrest. He had been under house arrest in connection with the December 2001 attack on the Indian parliament but was never charged and was freed eleven months later.

On December 12, Pakistan banned the Jamaat-ud-Dawa, which the United States had earlier designated as a Lashkar front group, and put Jamaat-ud-Dawa's founder Hafiz Sayeed under house arrest.

Indian police were investigating the possible roles of Indian nationals in the attack. Sabauddin Ahmed, 29, might have provided safe houses and brought the terrorists across the border. He had been arrested earlier in 2008 in connection with a grenade attack on a police camp.

Terrorist Shadullah phoned Indian television from room 1856 of the Oberoi Trident Hotel to say, "We demand the release of all mujahideen put in jails. Then will we release these people. Otherwise, we will destroy this place.... You must have seen what's happening here.... Release them, and we, the Muslims who live in India, should not be harassed.... Things like demolition of Babri Masjid and killings should stop."

Terrorist Imran Babar phoned an Indian television station during the attack on the Jewish facility, citing the 2002 riots in Gujarat that killed more than one thousand people, the 1992 destruction of the centuries-old Babri mosque by Hindu mobs, and India's control over part of Kashmir. "Are you aware of how many people have been killed in Kashmir? Are you aware of how your army has killed Muslims? We die every day. It's better to win one day as a lion than die this way.... You call their [Israeli] army staff to visit Kashmir. Who are they to come to J and K? [Jammu and Kashmir] This is a matter between us and the Hindus, the Hindu government. Why does Israel come here?"

Pakistani authorities said on December 31, 2008, that Lashkar-e-Taiba detainee Zarar Shah had confessed to involvement. India said he was involved in the planning of the attacks.

On February 12, 2009, Pakistani Interior Minister Rehman Malik told a news conference in Islamabad that "some part of the conspiracy has taken place in Pakistan." Six of the Mumbai conspirators, including Lashkar-i-Taiba senior member Zaki-ur-Rehman Lakhvi, had been arrested and were held in local custody. Two other suspects were at large. The surviving gunman, a Pakistani, was in Indian custody. He said that all of the accused would be tried in Pakistan. He noted that "the Internet phone calls between the terrorists were set up by a militant operating from Barcelona, who was later lured to Pakistan on a pretext and arrested." An individual sent $238 from a Spanish account to register a domain name registered in Houston; another domain name was registered in Russia. A satellite phone the terrorists had used was registered "in a Middle Eastern country." The conspirators used Austrian SIM cards to transfer data between the phones. Pakistani Federal Investigation Agency officials traced the registration of one of the three phones to a shop, whose owner identified the bank account of Hamad Ameen Sadiq, the "main operator" of the conspiracy.

On February 25, 2009, India charged surviving terrorist Ajmal Amir Kasab with thirteen crimes, including murder, "waging war against India," and entering a train station without a ticket. He faced the death penalty. Two unnamed Pakistani Army officials accused of training the gunmen were also charged. Indian citizens Fahim Ansari and Sabauddin were accused of providing maps for the attacks. The charge sheet ran to 11,280 pages, citing more than two thousand witnesses, and named thirty-seven others alleged to have planned the attacks.

On April 15, 2009, trial judge M.L. Tahiliyani barred Ajmal Amir Kasab's attorney from representing him because of a conflict of interest, moments before the trial was to open in a special court set up inside a Mumbai prison. New defense attorney Abbas Kazmi Kasab in his opening statement withdrew Kasab's February confession, which he claimed was signed under duress. He also claimed Kasab was under 17 and should be tried in a juvenile court. Prosecutor Ujjwal Nikam said Kasab had said three times that he was 21. The judge rejected the defense's motion. On April 24, Judge M. L. Tahiliyani ruled that a radiologist and a forensic dentist would examine Kasab to determine whether he was a minor to be tried in a juvenile court.

Indian authorities announced on April 28, 2009, that medical tests, including a dental exam and bone-density scans, conducted on Ajmal Amir Kasab indicated that he was more than 20 years old. He had claimed that he was younger than 17 at the time of the attacks. On May 6, 2009, he pleaded not guilty to eighty-six charges, including murder and waging war against India. He faced the death penalty.

On June 2, 2009, the Lahore High Court in Pakistan ruled that there was insufficient evidence to hold Hafiz Sayeed, 59, leader of Jamaat-ud-Dawa and founder of the Lashkar-i-Taiba group, under house arrest. The latter group was believed to be behind the Mumbai attacks. Jamaat was banned but reemerged under the name Falah-i-Insaniat. India had charged him in absentia; there were no charges against him in Pakistan.

During his trial, Mohammed Ajmal Kasab testified on July 20, 2009, that Zaki-ur-Rehman Lakhvi, Pakistani head of the Lashkar-e-Tayyiba, had plotted the attacks. He pleaded guilty to all eighty-six charges and said that he was "ready to die." Kasab had withdrawn an earlier confession. He was represented by defense attorney Abbas Kazmi, who was surprised by the plea. Kasab said he trained in Lashkar camps in Muzaffarabad, Kashmir, and in Manshera in the northwest.

Pakistani authorities arrested two more suspected planners of the attack on August 29, 2009, bringing the total in custody to seven.

Pakistan, on September 21, 2009, placed cleric Hafiz Muhammad Saeed, head of Jamaat-ud Dawa, which is believed to be the front group for Lashkar-e-Taiba, under house arrest in connection with the case. He had been charged with making hate speeches against the state and holding illegal gatherings. The government had said that it would charge seven suspects. On October 12, 2009, a court in Lahore dropped criminal charges against Hafiz Muhammad Saeed, whom Indian said had masterminded the Mumbai siege. The court dismissed the charges for lack of evidence. Saeed was the founder of Lashkar-e-Taiba. He was represented by attorney A. K. Dogar.

On November 25, 2009, a court in Rawalpindi, Pakistan charged seven individuals with acts of terrorism, money laundering, supplying funds for terrorism, and providing tools for terrorism. All pleaded not guilty. They all faced the death penalty. They were identified as mastermind Zaki-ur-Rehman Lakhvi, Umar Abjul Wajid, Shahid Jameel Riaz, Jameel Ahmed, Mohammad Younas Anjum, Mazhar Iqbal, and Hammad Amin Sadiq. Jameel Ahmed was represented by attorney Alyas Saddiqi. An HBO documentary in November 2009 reported that the terrorists had called themselves the Army of the Righteous.

On December 9, 2009, U.S. citizen David Coleman Headley was charged in Chicago with helping the Mumbai attackers, videotaping targets—including the Taj Mahal and Oberoi hotels, the Leopold Café, the Jewish outreach center, and the train station—and briefing the attackers. He even took boat trips to scout out the town's main harbor; a trip the terrorists later followed in the operation. He surveilled the National Defense College in Delhi in March 2009. He pleaded not guilty to nine felony counts in the Mumbai attack and three other counts for plotting an attack on the Danish newspaper that in 2005 ran the Muhammad cartoons. The charges included providing material support for terrorism, conspiracy to bomb public places, and aiding and abetting the murder of six U.S. nationals. He faced the death penalty. He waived his right to a grand jury indictment. He was represented by defense attorney John Theis. India was expected to request extradition. Prosecutors said Tahawwur Hussain Rana had asked Headley to congratulate the killers.

In 1998, Headley was convicted of and sentenced to fifteen months for conspiring to smuggle Pakistani heroin into the United States.

On December 18, 2009, lone surviving terrorist Ajmal recanted his confession, saying he was a mere tourist who was arrested three weeks before the attack and was tortured into the confession.

The next day, the HBO documentary *Terror in Mumbai* reported that Ajmal had been sold to the terrorists three months before the attack by his father so that his brothers and sisters could marry.

On January 14, 2010, Tahawwur Rana and David Coleman Headley were charged in a twelve-count indictment on charges of planning a violent attack on Danish newspaper *Jyllands Posten* and helping in the Mumbai attack. They remained in federal custody in Chicago. The indictment also charged retired Pakistani military officer Abdur Rehman Hashin Syed and terrorist leader Ilyas Kashmiri. Headley was represented by attorney John Theis. Rana was represented by Patrick Blegen. Headley faced twelve counts, including six of conspiracy to murder and maim people in India and provide material support to a foreign terrorist organization. He faced the death penalty. Rana was charged with three counts of providing material support to a foreign terrorist organization and faced life in prison. Kashmiri and Abdur Rehman were charged with conspiracy to murder and maim people in Denmark and faced the death penalty.

During his trial on January 18, 2010, lone surviving gunman Mohammed Ajmal Kasab told the court that four of the gunmen were Indian, despite government claims that all of the terrorists were Pakistanis. One was from Indian-administered Kashmir, one from Gujarat, and two others from Mumbai. He had withdrawn his confession in December 2009.

On February 11, 2010, Shahid Azmi, attorney of Fahim Ansari, an Indian who had been accused of aiding the Mumbai terrorists, was shot to death near his home in the Mumbai suburbs.

On March 18, 2010, David Coleman Headley pleaded guilty in U.S. District Court in Chicago to charges that he had scouted the targets for the Mumbai attack and a planned attack against a Danish newspaper in which suicide bombers would attempt to kill everyone in the building. He also scouted targets in Pune and Goa. He specifically pleaded guilty to twelve counts of conspiring to bomb public places in India, to murder and maim people in India and Denmark, to provide material support to foreign terrorist plots and to provide material support to Lashkar-e-Taiba, and to aiding and abetting the murder of U.S. citizens in India. At-large Ilyas Kashmiri told him that the Danish attackers should behead captives and throw the heads out of the office. Headley agreed to testify against co-defendant Tahawwur Hussain Rana. The Department of Justice agreed not to seek the death penalty against Headley. The United States said Indian investigators would be given access to Headley, but he would not be extradited to India, Pakistan, or Denmark. India demanded unfettered access. The plea agreement indicated that he had been put in contact with an al Qaeda cell in Europe.

On May 3, 2010, a Mumbai court issued a 1,522-page verdict that convicted Ajmal Amir Kasab of "waging war on India." He had been convicted of most of the eighty-six counts against him, including murder, arms smuggling, and conspiracy. He and an accomplice gunned down 58 people and wounded 104 others at the train station. The next day, he was sentenced to death. His attorney, K. P. Pawar, had requested life in prison. At least 610 witnesses had testified during his trial. Judge M. L. Tahiliyani acquitted two Indians of helping plot the attacks; the prosecutor said he would appeal the acquittals. India had charged 38 people in the case.

On May 25, 2010, Pakistan's Supreme Court ruled that Hafiz Sayeed, a founder of Lashkar-i-Taiba, should remain free because the government did not have enough evidence to imprison him. The government had requested reversal of lower court decisions to release him from house arrest.

On February 21, 2011, the Mumbai High Court upheld Kasab's death sentence and the acquittals on charges of conspiracy of Fahim Ansari and Sabauddin Ahmed for a lack of "corroborative" evidence.

On April 25, 2011, prosecutors in the U.S. District Court in Chicago charged four Pakistanis— Sajid Mir, Abu Qahafa, Mazhar Iqbal, and Maj. Iqbal—in a superseding indictment with aiding and abetting the murder of U.S. citizens in India, conspiracy to murder and maim, and providing material support to Lashkar-e-Taiba in connection with the Mumbai attack. Mir, Qahafa, and Mazhar Iqbal were also charged with conspiracy to bomb public places. None of them were in U.S. custody. David Coleman Headley claimed that Maj. Iqbal was a member of Pakistan's Directorate for Inter-Services Intelligence (ISI). Prosecutors said Mir was Headley's handler; Qahafa trained others in combat techniques, and Mazhar Iqbal was a Lashkar commander who passed messages to Headley via defendant Tahawwur Rana.

On May 23, 2011, David Coleman Headley told the Chicago court in the terrorism trial of Tahawwur Rana that the ISI recruited him and played a key role in the Mumbai attacks. He told the court that "ISI provided assistance to Lashkar: financial, military and moral support." He said that ISI Maj. Iqbal chose the targets—including the Chabad House—the route, and a safe house, and that Iqbal

was also involved in the plot to attack *Jyllands-Posten* in Denmark.

On June 21, 2012, police arrested Sayed Zabiuddin Ansari at New Delhi airport as he arrived from Saudi Arabia. He was suspected of facilitating the attack. An international arrest warrant was issued for him in 2009. Police believed his voice was heard in the Pakistan control room guiding the Mumbai killers. He was heard saying in Hindi on a tape "This is just a trailer, the entire movie is yet to come." Police said he had lived in Saudi Arabia for the past two years and was "talent-spotting" for another "massive attack" in India. He had been deported from Saudi Arabia. On June 27, Indian Home Minister Palaniappan Chidambaram said that Ansari confirmed Pakistani state support for the attacks, saying two ISI agents were among the five people in the terrorist control room with Ansari during the attack.

The High Court of Mumbai upheld Mohammed Ajmal Kasab's conviction and sentence in February 2011. On August 29, 2012, the Indian Supreme Court upheld his death sentence. On November 21, 2012, India hanged Kasab at Yerwada Jail in Pune. On November 29, 2012, the Pakistani Taliban threatened to attack India in retaliation for the execution.

On January 24, 2013, U.S. District Judge Harry Leinenweber in a federal court in Chicago sentenced David Headley to thirty-five years in prison. 08112601-10

November 26, 2008—Qatar—Al Qaeda's propaganda arm released on the Internet another video interview of Ayman al-Zawahiri, who did not mention the Mumbai attacks.

November 26, 2008—Somalia—Pirates kidnapped British journalist Colin Freeman and Spanish photojournalist Jose Cendon, both working for London's *Daily Telegraph* newspaper, in Bosasso. They were freed on January 4, 2009. The two Somali journalists who were kidnapped with them were unaccounted for. 08112611

November 26, 2008—Afghanistan—Dawa Khan Menapal of Radio Free Europe/Radio Liberty and local television reporter Aziz Popal, both Afghan journalists, were kidnapped in Ghazni Province but released three days later. 08112612

November 30, 2008—Iraq—A bomb destroyed the National Public Radio armored car in Iraq. The bomb, which was attached to the car, caused no injuries to Ivan Watson, 33, the U.S. reporter working for NPR and three Iraqi colleagues— producer and translator Ali Hamdani and two drivers. Iraqi soldiers arrested an egg vendor thought to have family links to an al Qaeda in Iraq member. 08113001

December 2008—Nigeria—Two Russian expatriates were kidnapped by gunmen in the Niger Delta. The duo escaped from their captors in mid–February 2009. After wandering for several days, they were rescued by Nigerian soldiers. 08129901

December 3, 2008—India—Authorities found a bag containing 20 pounds of explosives at the Mumbai train station that had been attacked on November 26. Police did not know if it was left during the attack.

December 8, 2008—Spain—French police arrested three Basque Nation and Liberty members, including Aitzol Iriondo Yarza, 30, believed to be the new military leader of the group following the November arrest in France of Garikoitz Aspiazu Rubina, alias Txeroki.

December 8, 2008—United States—At a pretrial hearing for the 9/11 defendants at Guantanamo Bay, five of the defendants offered to plead guilty to murder and war crimes, but withdrew the offer when the judge said it might undercut their preference for a death penalty. Khalid Sheik Mohammed, Tawfiq bin Attash, Ramzi Binalshibh, Mustafa Ahmed al-Hawsawi, and Ammar al-Baluchi, alias Ali Abdul Aziz Ali, wanted to be viewed as martyrs by being executed. The Pentagon charge sheet, released in May, accused them of "conspiracy, murder in violation of the law of war, attacking civilians, attacking civilian objects, intentionally causing serious bodily injury, destruction of property in violation of the law of war, terrorism, and providing material support for terrorism."

December 10, 2008—Mexico—Gunmen kidnapped Miami-based Felix Batista, 55, an American anti-kidnapping negotiator. He apparently knew the kidnappers, embracing one (according to video surveillance) before getting into their white sport utility vehicle, which drove away. He was a consultant for the Houston-based consulting firm ASI Global and had resolved nearly one hundred kidnapping cases in Latin America. He had stepped out to take a cell phone call at the El Principal restaurant in Saltillo. He had met with Mexican business executives regarding anti-kidnap measures. He had been in the K&R (kidnap and ransom) industry for more than twenty years. Mexican research firms said there are five hundred kidnappings per month in the country. Some officials at the state attorney general's office said that Batista had met with Jose Pilar Valdez,

owner of a local security firm, who had been kidnapped hours earlier. 08121001

December 11, 2008—Belgium—Belgian police detained fourteen people of Moroccan descent with links to a Belgian al Qaeda cell that might have been planning an attack at a European summit meeting in Brussels. Police conducted overnight raids at sixteen locations in Brussels and Liege, seizing computer equipment. A federal prosecutor said one of the detainees "was possibly planning a suicide attack," but the location was unknown. A detainee had made a farewell video. Three of the detainees had been to Afghanistan and Pakistan. The next day, a Belgian magistrate ordered the continuation of the custody of six Belgian citizens who were among the fourteen detainees, including Malika el-Aroud, widow of Abdessater Dahmane, one of the two men who killed Ahmed Shah Massoud, head of the anti–Taliban Northern Alliance in Afghanistan on September 9, 2001. She had posted Islamist propaganda on the Internet. Belgian police called her "an al Qaeda living legend." Her current husband was also arrested.

On December 15, a French citizen of Tunisian origin was charged with illegal association "related to a terrorist enterprise. He had been arrested in Grenoble, France. He was believed to have assisted in running the Minbar Web site, which Belgian authorities said was an Islamic propaganda outlet.

December 14, 2008—Niger—Robert Fowler, a former Canadian diplomat now serving as the UN's special envoy to Niger, was reported missing. The vehicle in which he, an aide, and their driver were traveling was found abandoned 30 miles northeast of Niamey. On February 18, 2009, al Qaeda in the Islamic Maghreb (AQIM) claimed it was holding Fowler and his aide, Louis Guay, both Canadians, as well as four Western European tourists who were kidnapped on January 22, 2009. Abu Mohammed, the group's spokesman, told al-Jazeera, "We announce to the general public that the mujahideen reserve the right to deal with the six kidnapped according to Islamic sharia law." They were freed on April 22, 2009. Canada denied paying a ransom. AQIM's Omar Ould Hamaha was involved in the kidnapping. Fowler wrote a memoir, *A Season in Hell: My 130 Days in the Sahara with al Qaeda.* He said the kidnappers took possession of his car in "a slick, violent, well-coordinated and impeccably executed grab." He was fed bowls of rice, slept on the sand, and was frequently moved. Fowler said of his kidnappers, "There's no doubt of their faith: They would sit chanting in the full Sahara sun for hour after hour.... They are realists in the sense that they understand realpolitik. They understand pressure on governments." Moustapha Chafi, an adviser to several governments in the region, was involved in negotiations for Fowler's release. 08121401

December 16, 2008—France—Paris police found five sticks of old dynamite in the Printemps department store near the Gare St. Lazare train station. No detonator was attached to the dynamite. An unknown group had warned that the bombs had been placed and said it would conduct other attacks if France did not withdraw its soldiers from Afghanistan. In a French-language note sent to Agence France Press, the Afghan Revolutionary Front said, "Get this message to your president of the republic so he withdraws these troops from Afghanistan before the end of February 2009. Otherwise, we will be in action again in your capitalist department stores, and this time without warning." The note specified where the dynamite could be found. On December 10, a caller to *Le Monde* had made similar threats. 08121601

December 19, 2008—Greece—Masked youths threw firebombs at the French Institute in Athens. 08121901

December 20–21, 2008—India—Police in Kashmir arrested three Pakistani men who were planning to drive a bomb-laden vehicle into a building in India.

December 28, 2008—Pakistan—A suicide bomber killed thirty-four people at a polling station near the Swat Valley. He had pretended he was having car trouble and asked the victims to push it before he set off the explosives.

December 29, 2008—United States—A letter addressed to President-elect Barack Obama arrived at the State Revenue Department building in Springfield, Illinois. It contained the HIV-infected blood of Ethiopian refugee Saad Hussein, 27, who had included his Chicago return address. He said this "was his way of seeking help from the government."

December 31, 2008—Denmark—Two Israeli citizens were injured in a shopping mall shooting in Odense, on the island of Fyn. One was hit in the hand; the other in the leg. Their injuries were not life-threatening. The motive was a mystery. On January 1, 2009, Danish police arrested a Lebanese-born Danish citizen of Palestinian descent on suspicion of shooting the two Israelis. He pleaded not guilty to a charge of attempted murder. 08123101

December 31, 2008—Spain—An hour after the Basque Nation and Liberty phoned a warning, a car bomb exploded outside the Basque-run EiTB regional television station in Bilbao at 11:00 a.m. Five hundred people had evacuated the building. One person suffered an ear injury. The TV station remained on the air. Police found the vehicle's owner tied to a tree in the woods outside Bilbao.

2009

2009—Somalia—On October 6, 2012, three years after his kidnapping by local jihadis, bearded Denis Allex, reportedly a French intelligence officer, released a four-minute video titled *Message to François Hollande* in which he read a script in French. "I record this message, which I direct to you personally in the month of July 2012, three years after my abduction, three years away from my family, my wife, and my children; three years of solitude," reads the English transcript of his statement.

January 2009—Colombia—The Revolutionary Armed Forces of Colombia bombed a Blockbuster video store in Bogota, killing two. 0901 9901

January 1, 2009—Pakistan—The U.S. media reported that a CIA Predator strike killed Kenyan citizen Fahid Mohammed Ally Msalam, alias Usama al-Kini, al Qaeda's chief of operations in Pakistan, and his deputy, Sheikh Ahmed Salim Swedan, in a Hellfire missile strike on a building being used for explosives training. The air strike occurred near Karikot, South Waziristan Province. The duo was suspected of involvement in several recent suicide bombings in Pakistan, as well as the August 1998 bombings of U.S. embassies in Kenya and Tanzania.

January 2, 2009—Sri Lanka—Government troops captured Kilinochchi, the de facto capital of the terrorist Liberation Tigers of Tamil Eelam (LTTE). Authorities met minimal resistance, suggesting that the LTTE guerrillas had retreated to jungle bases. The next day, troops bombed the port of Mullaitivu, the rebel's last stronghold. The LTTE had begun its separatist insurgency in 1983. Since then, nearly seventy thousand people had been killed. LTTE political leader Balasingham Nadesan said that the group would keep fighting.

Meanwhile, an LTTE suicide bomber set off a motorcycle near the Sri Lanka Air Force headquarters in Colombo, killing two airmen and wounding thirty other people, including nine airmen.

January 5, 2009—Greece—Just before dawn, two gunmen fired automatic weapons at riot police outside the Ministry of Culture in Athens, severely wounding one police officer. The Revolutionary Struggle claimed credit.

January 6, 2009—Qatar—In an audiotape posted on the Internet, al Qaeda deputy Ayman al-Zawahiri said that the Israeli incursion into Gaza was the fault of U.S. President-elect Barack Obama. "These raids are Obama's gift to you before he takes office." "This is Obama, whom the American machine of lies tried to portray as the rescuer who will change the policy of America.... He kills your brothers and sisters in Gaza mercilessly and without affection." He said the Israeli assault was a "link in the chain of the crusade against Islam and Muslims," led by President Obama.

January 13, 2009—Austria—A spokesman for Chechen President Ramzan Kadyrov, 33, on April 29, 2010, denied Austrian police speculation of involvement in the January 2009 murder of Chechen dissident Umar Israilov in Vienna. Austria arrested three Chechens who were likely to be indicted. The Vienna Public Prosecutor's office said, "In this final report there is circumstantial evidence that connects the killing to Mr. Kadyrov and other people in his surroundings. The police say that leads to the assumption that Mr. Kadyrov ordered at least the kidnapping and maybe the killing of Mr. Israilov." Minutes after the shooting, a suspect made an eleven-second phone call to Shaa Turlayev, a senior aide to the Chechen president. The Austrian police said Turlayev met in Austria with some of the murder suspects three months before the attack. One of the suspect's cell phones contained a photo of a suspect next to Kadyrov. Israilov had served as a chief witness in a case against Kadyrov at the European Court of Human Rights. The Chechen government noted that Israilov had been a rebel leader.

January 14, 2009—Greece—Revolutionary Struggle said it would continue conducting terrorist attacks. It claimed credit for the December 23, 2008, attack on a riot police bus and the January 5, 2009, wounding of a police officer in front of the Ministry of Culture.

January 14, 2009—Qatar—Osama bin Laden, in an audiotape entitled *A Call for Jihad to Stop the Aggression on Gaza* that was posted on the Internet, called on Muslims to attack Israel and said he would open "new fronts" against the United States. He complained that Arab leaders had not aided beleaguered Gazans, and the Arab leaders had been "avoiding their responsibility" to liberate Palestine. "If you are not persuaded to fight, then open the way to those who are persuaded." He said President Obama would receive a "heavy inheritance" from President Bush. "If he withdraws

from the war, it is military defeat. And if he continues it, he drowns in economic crisis. How can it be that [President Bush] passed over to him two wars, not one war, and he is unable to continue them? We are on our path to open other fronts, with permission from Allah."

January 15, 2009—Philippines—Abu Sayyaf kidnapped three International Committee of the Red Cross aid workers and threatened to behead them if the government did not pull its troops out of most of southern Jolo Island. The group ultimately freed the Swiss, Italian, and Filipino hostages. The last hostage, Italian engineer Eugenio Vagni, was freed on July 12, 2009. 09011501

January 20, 2009—Indonesia—Three firebombs were thrown at the Egyptian Embassy, causing a small fire but no injuries. Egypt had kept its border with Gaza closed during the recent Israeli incursion.

January 20, 2009—United States—*Politics Daily* reported on January 5, 2010, that Bush administration officials learned of a plot by Somali terrorists to detonate explosives during the inauguration of incoming President Barack Obama. It was later determined that a rival Somali group had faked the information to provoke the United States to attack its foe.

January 22, 2009—Mali—Members of al Qaeda in the Islamic Maghreb (AQIM) kidnapped four Europeans (two Swiss, a German, and a British tourist) in an attack on their convoy near the border with Niger. The tourists had attended a Tuareg festival. The AQIM gunmen fired at the tires of the tourists' car, forcing it to stop. On February 18, 2009, Abu Mohammed, AQIM spokesman, told al-Jazeera, "We announce to the general public that the mujahideen reserve the right to deal with the six kidnapped according to Islamic sharia law." On April 22, 2009, AQIM posted its demands on an Islamist Web site and called for the United Kingdom to "release Sheikh Abu Qatada, who is unjustly held, for the release of its British citizen. We give it twenty days as of the issuance of this statement. When this period expires, the mujahideen will kill the British hostage." The previous week, AQIM has released German citizen Marianne Petzold and Swiss citizen Gabriella Greitner. The group said it would hold Grietner's husband "until we have achieved our legitimate demands." AQIM had earlier demanded the release of twenty AQIM prisoners in Mali and elsewhere. The demand was later extended another fifteen days to May 30.

On June 3, 2009, the group said it had killed British hostage Edwin Dyer on May 31, one day after expiration of its second deadline. The al-Falojah Web site carried a two-page message in Arabic in which the group observed that "the British captive was killed so that he, and with him the British state, may taste a tiny portion of what innocent Muslims taste every day at the hands of the Crusader and Jewish coalition to the east and the west of the world." The group had demanded a $14 million ransom for Dyer and a Swiss hostage. Dyer had worked in Austria and spoke fluent German. He was on a German travel operator's tour in West Africa and was kidnapped after attending a cultural festival in Anderamboukane, Mali.

On June 16, 2009, Mali's army killed several al Qaeda members in an attack on a terrorist camp near the Algeria border. 09012201

January 26, 2009—Europe—The European Union (EU) took the People's Mujahideen Organization of Iran off its list of terrorist groups and lifted its economic and financial sanctions. The government of Iran said the decision promoted terrorism. France appealed the decision. This was the first delisting by the EU.

January 26, 2009—United States—Two Sri Lankan immigrants—Nadarasa Yogarasa and Sathajhan Sarachandran—pleaded guilty in a New York court to providing material support to terrorists when they tried to supply hundreds of thousands of dollars worth of surface-to-air missiles and assault weapons to the Liberation Tigers of Tamil Eelam. Charges against two other Sri Lankan immigrants—Sahilal Sabaratnam and Thiruthanikan Thanigasalam—were expected to go forward.

February 2009—Mexico—Al-Jazeera ran a video showing Kuwaiti dissident Abdullah al-Nafisi telling a room of colleagues in Bahrain that al Qaeda was surveilling the U.S. border with Mexico, observing,

> Four pounds of anthrax—in a suitcase this big—carried by a fighter through tunnels from Mexico into the United States are guaranteed to kill 330,000 Americans within a single hour if it is properly spread in population centers there. What a horrifying idea. 9/11 will be small change in comparison. Am I right? There is no need for airplanes, conspiracies, timings, and so on. One person, with the courage to carry 4 pounds of anthrax, will go to the White House lawn, and will spread this "confetti" all over them, and then we'll do these cries of joy. It will turn into a real celebration.

The *Washington Times* reported on June 3, 2009, that the individual was an al Qaeda recruiter and that the group was also considering working with right-wing white militia groups.

February 2009—United States—The Treasury Department froze the assets of the Maryland-based Tamil Foundation charity, saying that its officials funneled money to the Liberation Tigers of Tamil Eelam.

February 1, 2009—Italy—Police arrested three men for beating and torching a 35-year-old Indian immigrant man who was sleeping on a bench in a seaside town near Rome. He was hospitalized with severe burns.

February 2, 2009—Pakistan—Gunmen kidnapped American UN official John Solecki, chief of the UN refugee office in Quetta. They shot to death Syed Hashim Raza, his driver, in an 8:30 a.m. ambush of Solecki's car in Baluchistan Province as Solecki was on his way to work. Solecki had worked for the UN High Commissioner for Refugees (UNHCR) in Baluchistan for two years. The Pakistani militant separatist kidnappers released a twenty-second video of a blindfolded Solecki on February 13, threatening to kill him within seventy-two hours unless Pakistani authorities released 141 women from prison. He was heard saying, "This is a message to the United Nations. I am not feeling well. I'm in trouble. Please help me resolve this problem soon so that I can gain my release." The Baluchistan Liberation United Front kidnappers also sent a letter to a local news agency, echoing the death threat. The UNHCR said that he had a serious medical condition that could threaten his life. Solecki, whose hands and feet were bound, was found otherwise unharmed on April 4, 2009, near the Afghanistan border in western Pakistan. The body of separatist politician Ghulam Mohammed Baloch, who had assisted in Solecki's release, was found in the southwest on April 9, six days after he was abducted. The remains of two of his kidnapped colleagues were discovered with him. 09020201

February 3, 2009—Qatar—Al Qaeda deputy chief Ayman al-Zawahiri released an audiotape on the Internet in which he said that President Obama "said he was concerned about the killings of civilians in Gaza. We thank Mr. Obama for his concern, which we received with thousands of shells and ... white phosphorus."

February 9, 2009—Sri Lanka—A Liberation Tigers of Tamil Eelam woman set off a bomb while being frisked by a female soldier processing refugees at a camp in Vishvamadu, killing twenty-eight and wounding sixty. Among the dead were twenty soldiers and eight women and children.

February 13, 2009—Iraq—A woman wearing an explosives-laden vest killed thirty-five Shi'ite pilgrims and injured another sixty-seven at a checkpoint in Mussayib, 35 miles south of Baghdad, en route to Karbala in southern Iraq. Local authorities suspected Sunni insurgents.

February 17, 2009—Equatorial Guinea—Sixteen Nigerians used two speedboats in an attack on the presidential compound, triggering a gun battle in which several attackers drowned and another was killed.

February 18, 2009—Greece—A powerful fertilizer car bomb exploded at Citibank's Athens offices. On March 11, 2009, the leftist Revolutionary Struggle claimed credit. Police said the bomb had enough explosives to destroy the four-story building. 09021801

February 19, 2009—United Kingdom—The European Court of Human Rights ruled that the United Kingdom was guilty of unlawfully detaining six Algerians, a Jordanian, a Tunisian, and a stateless individual without trial under post–9/11 antiterrorism laws and ordered the government to pay them awards ranging from $2,155 to $4,944 plus legal costs. Among them were Abu Qatada and Mahmoud Abu Rideh.

February 20, 2009—Sri Lanka—The Liberation Tigers of Tamil Eelam were suspected when two planes attacked Colombo, killing three people and injuring at least forty-eight. The injured included M. F. Raheem, who had a bullet removed from his left arm. One bullet-riddled plane crashed into a building housing the Inland Revenue Department, killing the pilot and a bystander, the 14-year-old daughter of Chandregra Kamgomene. The building is near the headquarters of the Air Force. Another plane was shot down near the international airport, 22 miles north of Colombo, at 10:30 p.m., killing the pilot.

February 20, 2009—Thailand—More than twenty Muslim insurgents armed with automatic rifles beheaded two soldiers after ambushing ten soldiers who were escorting teachers to school in southern Yala Province.

February 20, 2009—Pakistan—A suicide bomber killed at least thirty people and injured scores of others in an attack in Dera Ismail Khan in the northwest against a funeral procession for a slain Shi'ite cleric.

February 22, 2009—Somalia—Islamist insurgents killed eleven Burundian soldiers and injured fifteen others in an attack on an African Union peacekeeping force compound in Mogadishu. The insurgents fired mortars before two suicide bombers, one in a car bomb, set off their explosives. The al-Shabaab group claimed credit. 09022201

February 22, 2009—Egypt—A bomb exploded at 6:00 p.m. in the Khan el-Khalili market, a central Cairo bazaar frequented by tourists, killing a French woman and wounding at least twenty people, including thirteen French citizens, three Saudis, three Egyptians, and a German. Reports differed as to whether it was a grenade thrown by terrorists from a nearby hotel or a bomb hidden under a bench. Authorities defused a second nearby bomb. The market had been attacked by a suicide bomber in April 2005, killing twenty-one people, including an American and two French citizens. 09022202

March 2009—West Bank—Israeli soldiers shot to death a Palestinian youth who had thrown a firebomb at their vehicle.

March 1, 2009—Guinea-Bissau—A bomb exploded in the office of Armed Forces Chief of Staff Gen. Batiste Tagme na Waie, a rival to the president, killing him and wounding five other senior military officers, two of them critically. After the attack, all local radio stations were ordered to immediately suspend their programs. His predecessor, Gen. Verissimo Correia Seabra, had been shot and killed by soldiers in October 2004.

March 2, 2009—Guinea-Bissau—President Joao Bernardo Vieira, 69, was assassinated by gunfire. Looting broke out at the presidential palace. He had become president in 1980 following a military coup. He was elected president in the country's first free elections in 1994, but was ousted five years later in a coup. He was re-elected in 2005. The army said that this was not a coup, but rather an attack by a group of "isolated" soldiers who were to be arrested.

March 3, 2009—Pakistan—At least a dozen gunmen armed with rifles, grenades, and rocket launchers ambushed the visiting Sri Lankan cricket team's bus, killing six police officers, the civilian driver of a Pakistan Cricket Board vehicle, and another civilian, and wounding seven players, a coach, and an umpire in a fifteen-minute gun battle 300 yards from Lahore's Gaddafi Stadium. Sri Lankan players Thilan Samaraweera and Tharanga Paranavitana were treated for bullet wounds at the local hospital. Umpire Ahsan Raza was wounded in the abdomen. Five players, including team captain Mahela Jayawardene and British assistant coach Paul Farbrace, sustained minor injuries. Bus driver Mohammed Khalil accelerated through the gunfire and drove to the safety of the stadium. All of the gunmen escaped, apparently unharmed. They left behind machine guns, RPGs, plastic explosives, and backpacks filled with dried fruit, mineral water, and walkie-talkies, suggesting that they might have intended to make a stand and take hostages. No group claimed credit. Suspects included Lashkar-i-Taiba and the Liberation Tigers of Tamil Eelam. Lahore's police chief said the attackers resembled Pashtuns. Lashkar-i-Taiba spokesman Abdullah Ghaznavi denied responsibility. On June 17, 2009, Pakistani police arrested Mohammad Zubair, a member of the Punjabi Taliban, a splinter of Lashkar-e-Jhangvi. 09030301

March 5, 2009—Israel—Mar'i al-Rdaidah, 26, a Palestinian man from east Jerusalem, carjacked a construction vehicle on a major road and swung a police car into the air, then crashed it into a bus. He was shot to death by bystanders and police. Two officers inside the car were slightly injured. It was not known whether al-Rdaidah was a member of any terrorist group.

March 6, 2009—France/Spain—French authorities handed to Spanish authorities Ignacio Pedro Santesteban Goikoetxea, alias Einstein, who had been arrested in 2000 in southwestern France. Spain wanted the Basque Nation and Liberty electronics expert on terrorism charges.

March 7, 2009—Northern Ireland—At 9:20 p.m. two gunmen dressed as pizza deliverymen attacked a British Army base in Massereene, County Antrim, killing two soldiers and seriously wounding two other soldiers and two real pizza deliverymen. One of the injured pizza deliverymen was a 32-year-old from Poland who was in critical condition. Authorities said that the two soldiers, who were within hours of deploying to Afghanistan, were shot execution-style while they were on the ground. The dead soldiers were identified as Mark Quinsey, 23, and Cengiz "Patrick" Azimkar, 21. The two gunmen escaped in a car driven by a third individual. They were believed to be in their early 20s. The British Army's Special Reconnaissance Regiment had arrived earlier in the week to monitor Irish Republican Army (IRA) splinter groups that were believed to be planning an attack before St. Patrick's Day. The Real IRA claimed credit on March 8 in a phone call to the Irish *Sunday Tribune*, using the group's code word, saying that the British soldiers "occupied the north of Ireland." That day, police in Randalstown, 5 miles from the army base, were investigating a car that might have been used by the gunmen.

By March 13, police had arrested three suspects, one 17 and another 37 (on March 15, the *Washington Post* reported their ages as 41, 32, and 21). Colin Duffy, 41, an IRA dissident who lived in Lurgan, was arrested on March 14. His arrest sparked rioting involving youths who threw Molotov cocktails at police; no one was injured. Duffy

was convicted in 1993 of murdering a British soldier; the case was later dismissed when a key witness was identified as a loyalist paramilitary soldier. In 1997, Duffy was charged with killing two police officers; those charges were also dropped. His previous defense attorney, Rosemary Nelson, died in a 1999 car bombing.

On March 25, Lord Chief Justice Brian Kerr ordered the immediate release of six suspected IRA dissidents, ruling that their eleven-day detention was illegal because the lower court judge who extended their detention to a fortnight had failed to consider whether the arrests were lawful. Police released but rearrested Duffy, who was charged on March 25 with killing the two soldiers. Specific charges were two kinds of murder, five kinds of attempted murder, and one count of possession of a firearm and ammunition with intent to endanger life. 09030701

March 10, 2009—Greece—A bomb exploded at Citibank's northwest Athens offices, causing damage but no injuries. On March 11, 2009, the leftist Revolutionary Struggle claimed credit. 09031001

March 10, 2009—United States—A military judge in Guantanamo Bay released the pleadings of several 9/11 defendants. Khalid Sheikh Mohammed and his fellow defendants said the charges were "badges of honor, which we carry with pride.... Your intelligence apparatus, with all its abilities, human and logistical, had failed to discover our military attack plans before the blessed 11 September operation. We are terrorists to the bone."

March 10, 2009—Northern Ireland—Continuity IRA, an Irish Republican Army splinter faction, claimed credit for the fatal shooting of Constable Stephen Paul Carroll, 48, in Craigavon. Police arrested a man in his 20s; two more had been arrested by March 15. Hundreds of mourners attended Carroll's funeral.

On March 23, police arrested a 17-year-old in the case. He appeared in court that morning charged with belonging to the banned Continuity IRA. On March 24, police charged a 37-year-old suspect with murder and possession of a firearm.

March 11, 2009—Sri Lanka—An apparent Liberation Tigers of Tamil Eelam suicide bomber attacked a Muslim procession during a religious holiday, killing fourteen people and critically wounding a government minister.

March 11, 2009—Ecuador—Police captured Sixto Antonio Cabana, a Revolutionary Armed Forces of Colombia (FARC) commander who was wanted by the United States on charges of running cocaine smuggling operations. It was Ecuador's first arrest of a FARC member since it broke diplomatic relations with Colombia a year earlier over a raid by Colombian authorities into Ecuador.

March 12, 2009—Sudan—Gunmen kidnapped three Medecins San Frontieres (Doctors Without Borders) staffers—a Canadian nurse, an Italian doctor, and French coordinator Raphael Meunier—along with two Sudanese workers during the night in Serif Umra Province in northern Darfur. The two Sudanese were soon freed. The trio was working for the group's Belgian section. The previous week, the Sudanese government had ordered thirteen aid groups to leave the country after the International Criminal Court had issued an arrest warrant for war crimes and crimes against humanity against Sudanese President Omar Hassan al-Bashir. The kidnappers demanded a ransom. The foreigners were freed on March 15 (some reports said March 13). No ransom was paid to the Eagles of al-Bashir. 09031201

March 12, 2009—Netherlands—Dutch police received an anonymous warning of a plot by Moroccan immigrants to bomb an Amsterdam shopping district. Police arrested six men and one woman. One man had connections to the March 11, 2004, Madrid train bombers. Police released all seven the next day.

March 12, 2009—France—A Paris appeals court overruled the 2007 convictions on charges of "criminal association with a terrorist enterprise of former Guantanamo Bay detainees Ridouane Khalid, Brahim Yadel, Khaled ben Mustafa, Nizar Sassi, and Mourad Benchellali." The court held that French DST agents overstepped their authority in questioning the five at the U.S. military prison facility in 2002 and 2004. Prosecutors planned an appeal to the Court of Cassation. The five were arrested in Afghanistan in 2001 and were repatriated to France in 2004 and 2005. In their 2007 trial, they had admitted receiving military training in Afghan camps.

March 13, 2009—Afghanistan—Taliban spokesman Mohammed Ibrahim Hanafi, self-proclaimed commander in Helmand Province, told CNN that the group would execute foreign aid workers as spies or hold them hostage for the release of Taliban fighters. "If we get someone, that it how we will deal with it under our new constitution." He also called on "Afghan brothers not to work with NGOs."

March 14, 2009—Qatar—Al Jazeera Television broadcast an audiotape from Osama bin Laden in which he called Israeli actions against Hamas in Gaza a "holocaust." "The Gaza holocaust is an historic event and a tragic turning point. The road of returning al-Aqsa needs righteous leadership." He claimed that "it was clear that some of the Arab leaders have collaborated with the Crusader-Zionist alliance against our people, those whom America calls the moderate leaders. We must disown ourselves from all those" governments. He called for Muslims to aid Iraqi insurgents in efforts to "liberate" Iraq "so they can defeat the greatest ally to the Zionists." After that, they could move on to Jordan to "liberate all of Palestine from the sea to the river" from Israel.

March 15, 2009—West Bank—Gunmen shot to death two Israeli policemen during the night near the Massua settlement, a Jewish enclave in the Jordan Valley. Palestinian nationalists were suspected. The police vehicle was found upside down.

March 15, 2009—Yemen—Terrorists threw a bomb at tourists posing for photograph near the ancient fortress city of Shibamd, killing four South Korean tourists and their guide. 09031501

March 16, 2009—Somalia—Kidnappers released a Somali and three foreign staff members who were working in Wajid for a UN humanitarian organization. The four had been en route from semiautonomous Puntland to Kenya when they were kidnapped. 09031601

March 17, 2009—Sudan—Gunmen attacked a vehicle and shot to death a UN–African Union peacekeeper in the Darfur region. 09031701

March 19, 2009—Qatar—Osama bin Laden issued an audiotape in which he called Somali President Sheik Sharik Sheik Ahmed a tool of the United States and called for his overthrow. A group of Somali Islamic clerics rejected the suggestion.

March 22, 2009—United Kingdom—Passengers from Emirates flight EK011 flying from Dubai to London's Gatwick Airport were evacuated after landing at 6:45 a.m. Ten minutes earlier, a passenger found a threatening note. Bomb techs inspected the plane. The airport was temporarily closed.

March 22, 2009—Israel—Authorities found a 200-pound car bomb that malfunctioned near a Haif's Lev Hamifrtz shopping center. Police heard a small explosion, which could have been the detonator, inside a Subaru in the mall's parking lot. The bomb was packed with ball bearings. The car had been stolen from East Jerusalem. A little-known group from Galilee claimed credit.

March 24, 2009—Qatar—In a video, al Qaeda deputy chief Ayman al-Zawahiri called for Sudanese to begin a "long guerrilla war" against President Umar al-Bashir, whom the International Criminal Court (ICC) had charged with war crimes. "The Sudanese regime is too weak to defend the Sudan, so you must do what was done by your brothers in Iraq and Somalia. So make preparations, by training, equipping, storing, and organizing for a long guerrilla war, for the contemporary Crusade has bared its fangs at you." He complained about Sudan's 1996 decision to expel Osama bin Laden. "The Bashir regime is reaping what it sowed." He said that al-Bashir's "former trail-mates" have "revolted against him." He said the ICC decision was a pretext for a Western invasion. "You are being targeted so Islam can be eliminated from the Sudan."

March 26, 2009—Somalia—A bomb exploded around noon at the Bakaraha market in Mogadishu, injuring Interior Minister Abdukadir Ali Omar in the leg and killing one of his secretaries. Al-Shabaab was suspected.

March 27, 2009—Pakistan—A suicide bomber attacked a crowded mosque in Jamrud in the Khyber tribal agency in the northwest, killing fifty-one and injuring several more. Authorities said the death toll could hit seventy.

March 30, 2009—Pakistan—Baitullah Mehsud, an Islamist leader from the South Waziristan tribal area, claimed credit for the Taliban Movement of Pakistan attack on a policy academy in Lahore. Eleven people died in the attack on the police academy. He said that his group was going to conduct an "astonishing" attack in Washington in revenge for more than thirty strikes by U.S. UAVs against terrorist sanctuaries.

April 2009—Iraq—A suicide bombing at the Imam Wais area of a restaurant where Iranian pilgrims were gathered for lunch killed more than fifty Iranians and injured dozens of others. 0904 9901

April 2009—Pakistan—As of April 13, James McLintock, 44, a British convert to Islam, had been held for two weeks in Peshawar on suspicion of involvement in assisting British Muslim militants to make contacts in Pakistan.

April 2009—United States—Pakistani Taliban leader Baitullah Mehsud falsely claimed credit for a mass shooting at the American Civic Association in Binghamton, New York.

April 5, 2009—Pakistan—A suicide bomber at the entrance to a crowded mosque in Chakwal city in Punjab Province, 50 miles south of Islamabad, killed twenty-two people, wounded dozens, including at least one police officer, and damaged a car and four motorcycles. A little known group believed tied to the Pakistani Taliban claimed credit.

April 7, 2009—Saudi Arabia—In raids in several areas, including near the Yemen border, the government arrested eleven al Qaeda–linked insurgents and confiscated arms. Authorities said the cell planned attacks and kidnappings.

April 8, 2009—United Kingdom—Police arrested a dozen men, including ten Pakistanis who entered the United Kingdom on student visas, another Pakistani, and a Briton, in raids on eight locations in Manchester, Liverpool, and other locales. Operation Pathway arrests took place at an internet café and a residence in Manchester, a guest house and home improvement store in Chlitheroe, and a library at John Moores University in Liverpool. They were from the North West Frontier Province of Pakistan and were members of a suspected al Qaeda cell planning an attack in Manchester. They were in their late teens to 41 years old. Police continued a search for their bomb factory.

The country's most senior counterterrorism official, Assistant Commissioner Bob Quick, head of Special Operations at Scotland Yard, resigned after being photographed carrying secret antiterrorist documents, which could be read clearly by passersby. The raids had to be conducted quickly after the inadvertent leak of the materials. Quick had used the documents to brief the prime minister regarding the suspects, who had been under surveillance for a month. The documents included such details as "AQ driven attack planning within the UK" and "Merseyside—Dynamic entry, firearms."

On April 11, police released without charge an 18-year-old suspect, who was then questioned by immigration authorities from the Border Agency. On April 21, 2009, police released nine of the eleven Pakistani suspects into the custody of the British Border Agency, who wanted the group deported on grounds of national security. On April 22, the final two suspects were freed. None of them were charged. Authorities wanted to deport eleven of the twelve.

April 12, 2009—Egypt—Egyptian and Israeli authorities claimed that Hizballah was planning to attack Israeli tourists at Sinai Peninsula resorts. Egypt said it had arrested forty-nine Hizballah members between November and January. They were led by Lebanese citizen Sami Shihab and smuggled weapons and ammunition, plotted attacks, and spied. Egypt's *Al Ahram* said the network included twelve Egyptians plus individual citizens from Palestine, Lebanon, Syria, and Sudan. The authorities discovered $2 million and stockpiles of weapons and ammunition. They had rented a building in Cairo and properties in southern Egypt, along the Israel border and in Red Sea tourist resorts. They were also in a villa on the Suez Canal, from where they could "monitor and target ships."

April 13, 2009—Gaza Strip—An unmanned Palestinian fishing boat crammed with hundreds of pounds of explosives detonated off the coast of Gaza but caused no casualties. Israeli authorities said terrorists were planning to attack a naval patrol in the area. Al-Jazeera reported that the previously unknown Secret Special Units, a Palestinian group, used a remote-control device to set off the bomb.

April 14, 2009—Turkey—Security forces arrested two Kurdish rebels for plotting bombings in the west.

April 16, 2009—India—Maoist rebels attacked fourteen polling stations and vehicles carrying election officials, killing seventeen people in the east and central regions of the country.

April 18, 2009—France—Police from Spain and France arrested Jurdan Martitegi Lizaso, 28, the suspected leader of the Basque Nation and Liberty (ETA), and two accomplices in Montauriol village near Perpignan in southeastern France. He was linked to three car bombings, including one in September 2008 in Santona that killed an army officer and injured six other people. Police had followed a local ETA leader from Spain to France, where he met with Martitegi for two hours to learn about handling explosives and weapons. He was among those arrested. Police seized three pistols, two vehicles, and explosives from the detained trio. Nine members of ETA had been arrested in recent days; five leaders had been arrested in France in the previous fortnight.

April 18, 2009—Spain—Hours after the arrest in France of Martitegi, police arrested six other Basque Nation and Liberty suspects whose ages ranged from 25 to 31.

April 19, 2009—Somalia—Gunmen in the Bakool region kidnapped two staff members—a Dutch and a Belgian—of the Belgian chapter of Doctors Without Borders. 09041901

April 19, 2009—India—Soldiers killed five militants in a shootout in Assam. Three were believed to be from a splinter of the National Democratic Front of Bodoland, while the other two were from the Muslim United Liberation Tigers of Assam. Police seized weapons and ammunition in the raid.

April 20, 2009—Jamaica—A mentally disturbed gunman in his 20s got past a security guard and walked onto CanJet (a Canadian carrier) flight 918, a B737 that had arrived from Halifax, Canada, with 174 Canadian passengers and 8 crew members and was scheduled to fly to Santa Clara, Cuba, from Montego Bay's Sangster International Airport. As he was taking the passengers hostage, he fired a bullet that grazed the co-pilot's face. After robbing passengers, he allowed them to depart, but kept 6 crew hostage and demanded to be flown off the island. Two of those crew members locked themselves in the cockpit. The hijacker's father and Prime Minister Golding were among those who negotiated with him. Eight hours later, troops stormed the plane and arrested the hijacker at 7:00 a.m. No one else was injured. Among the passengers was Christian Gosselin, one of a twenty-five-person wedding party. He and his girlfriend were among those released. Also on the plane was passenger Brenda Grenier. Gosselin said the hijacker demanded money from all of the passengers. 09042901

April 20, 2009—Spain—A bomb exploded at 9:00 a.m. in a stolen van outside construction company Ferrovial Agroman's building in northeast Madrid, following a 7:37 a.m. warning phone call by Basque Nation and Liberty (ETA) to the Red Cross. No injuries were reported but thirty vehicles were damaged. The firm is involved in building a high speed train line in the Basque region, which ETA has opposed. On February 9, 2005, the ETA bombed a glass-façade office building in the same neighborhood, causing dozens of injuries.

April 20, 2009—Qatar—Ayman al-Zawahiri posted to an Islamist Web site a screed against U.S. President Barack Obama, saying he was the same as his predecessor. "America came to us with a new face, with which it is trying to fool us. He is calling for change, but (he aims) to change us so that we abandon our religion and rights…. Obama did not change the image of America among Muslims…. America is still killing Muslims." He complained that the United States was sending more troops to Afghanistan, even though it was losing in Iraq and Afghanistan. He told Hamas not to bow to Egyptian pressure and that Palestinians should attack Israelis around the world. "If circumstances were difficult in one place they are easier in other places. Our enemies, crusaders and Jews, are scattered everywhere."

April 21, 2009—United States—The FBI announced it had added to its Ten Most Wanted Terrorists Daniel Andreas San Diego, 31, an animal rights activist who had attempted to close a U.K. animal testing company. He was wanted for bombing two biotech firms in San Francisco that are linked to Huntingdon Life Sciences, in Cambridgeshire, United Kingdom. He was believed to be carrying a handgun. The FBI offered a reward of $250,000 for information leading to his arrest. His chest tattoo features burning hillsides with the words, "It only takes a spark." A tattoo of burning and collapsed buildings graces his back. The FBI called him "a well-known San Francisco Bay area animal rights extremist involved with the Stop Huntington Animal Cruelty campaign, commonly referred to as SHAC." SHAC was founded in the United Kingdom in 1999 and moved to the United States the next year.

He was accused of placing an explosive booby trap at the entrance of the Chiron Life Science Centre building in California in 2003. Other explosives went off before they could be defused. He was also believed involved with the nail bombing of the Shaklee Corporation, also in California, a few weeks later.

April 22, 2009—Germany—A Berlin court began a trial of three Germans and a Turk who had by September 2007 accumulated enough chemicals to make a half ton of explosives, which were to be used in bombings of U.S. military bases, dance clubs, bars, and other American hangouts in Germany. Those accused were Fritz Gelowicz, 29; Adem Yilmaz, 30, a Turk who grew up in Germany; and Daniel Schneider, 22, a Muslim convert. While overseas, the group met a recruiter for the Pakistan-based Islamic Jihad Union, which had been accused of bombing the U.S. and Israeli embassies in Tashkent, Uzbekistan, in 2004. The four were charged with membership in a foreign terrorist organization.

April 26, 2009—Brazil—Sao Paolo police detained an unnamed Arab resident of Brazil who ran a Web site that could be linked to terrorists. The site included anti–U.S. screeds in Arabic. He was suspected of being an al Qaeda member and being a facilitator of its international communications. Police seized his computers. A court ordered his release after he was jailed for three weeks.

April 30, 2009—Netherlands—On Queen's Day, a 38-year-old man tried to crash his car into a bus carrying Queen Beatrix at a parade in Apeldoorn, killing six people, including a military policeman, and injuring twelve others, including two teens

and a 9-year-old girl. Princess Maxima and Prince Willem Alexander were among those who watched him drive past police barriers into Dutch festival attendees. The driver, who acknowledged that he was trying to attack the Queen and her family, died the next day. He had no history of mental illness. Neighbors said he had recently been fired and was facing eviction. He was not believed to be linked to a terrorist group. No explosives were found.

May 2009—Kenya—The Somalia-based Islamist group al-Shabaab kidnapped an outspoken cleric from a refugee camp 50 miles inside Kenya. 0905 9901

May 2009—United Arab Emirates—The *Washington Times* reported on September 17, 2009, that Emirates authorities had broken up an al Qaeda terrorist ring that planned attacks in Dubai. The plot originated in Ras al-Khaimah, the comparatively poor member of the seven-nation United Arab Emirates. The terrorists had video surveillance of the Dubai Towers and had designated suicide bombers, who had yet to make martyrdom videos. The Israeli press claimed the Iranian government was behind the plot. The *Times* reported that Muhammad Ali al-Mansuri, former Minister of Public Lands for Ras al-Khaimah and now a human rights lawyer, was arrested on June 7 but was bailed out.

May 12, 2009—United States—A Miami federal jury convicted five of the remaining Liberty City Six in their third trial of charges of planning to blow up the Sears Tower in Chicago. Sentencing was scheduled for July 27, 2009. The group had been arrested in June 2006.

May 12, 2009—Italy—Italian authorities delivered arrest warrants for Marcel Gendron, 34, alias the Engineer, a French engineer and computer specialist and Islamic convert, and cellmate Bassam Ayachi, 63, a Syrian-born French citizen, on suspicion of being al Qaeda representatives in Europe who were planning attacks in the United Kingdom and France. The duo were already in a prison in Bari, Italy, held on charges of organizing illegal immigration. Their bugged cell conversations indicated that they were planning a plane attack on Charles de Gaulle Airport and had a "ton of grenades." They had been stopped in November 2008 in Bari after disembarking from a ferry from Greece. Hiding in their vehicle were five illegal immigrants—two Palestinians and two Syrians—who were sent back to Greece. The two had links to a dozen other people who were arrested in December in France and Belgium and who were being investigated for international terrorism and training and recruiting for terrorist purposes. French and Belgian police suspected the duo of recruiting and sending volunteers to fight in the jihad in Afghanistan. The duo were represented by attorney Ornella Romito. Both had resided in Belgium for several years.

May 17, 2009—Greece—Incendiary bombs exploded outside a private security firm, a car dealership, and a company selling surplus military equipment.

May 18, 2009—Sri Lanka—Government troops ended the decades of Liberation Tigers of Tamil Eelam (LTTE) terrorism with the death of the group's leader, Velupillai Prabhakaran, 54. Troops also killed his son, Charles Anthony, who was head of the LTTE's tiny air force; Pottu Amman, the group's intelligence chief; and Soosai, the head of the "Sea Tiger" naval wing. The survivors, on a patch of jungle the size of a football field, surrendered.

May 20, 2009—Argentina—The government issued an international arrest warrant for Samuel Salman El Reda, a Colombian of Lebanese descent, in connection with the July 1994 bombing of a Jewish charities building in Buenos Aires that killed eighty-five and injured three hundred.

May 20, 2009—United States—The FBI arrested James Cromitie, 53, David Williams, Onta Williams, and Haitian citizen Laguerre Payen, all of Newburgh, New York, in connection with a plot to set off a car bomb at a Jewish temple in the Bronx and fire guided missiles at military planes at the New York Air National Guard base in Newburgh. The undercover operation had lasted a year. The four Muslim extremists were charged with conspiracy to use weapons of mass destruction against the United States and conspiracy to acquire and use antiaircraft missiles. Police Commissioner Raymond W. Kelly told reporters that Cromitie, the ringleader, had more than two dozen arrests on minor charges in New York. They were arrested at 9:00 p.m. while planting inert bombs in cars outside the Riverdale Jewish Center and the Reform Riverdale Temple. They had intended to then drive 60 miles to the Newburgh Air National Guard base, where they would fire a missile which also had been made inert. An informant had told Cromitie that he was a representative of Jaish-e-Muhammad. On June 14, 2010, Judge Colleen McMahon of the U.S. District Court for the Southern District indefinitely delayed the trial, saying that prosecutors had not provided relevant information to the defense during discovery. She also scheduled a bail hearing and was willing to hear a petition to dismiss the

eight counts, for which they faced life in prison. Samuel Braverman was among the defense lawyers. On October 18, 2010, the four defendants were convicted of plotting to blow up New York City synagogues and shoot down military planes. A jury deliberated eight days. The four faced life in prison. On September 7, 2011, Laguerre Payen, 29, was sentenced to twenty-five years in prison.

May 22, 2009—Iraq—The body of Jim Kitterman, American citizen and president of Janus Construction, a small company he formed in 2008, was found in a car in Baghdad's Green Zone. He had worked in Iraq for the Houston-based KBR construction company and the Kuwait-based Peregrine Development companies in Iraq for several years. The former U.S. Navy chief petty officer had been stabbed several times as well as bound at the hands and blindfolded. 09052201

May 23, 2009—Pakistan—Armed men kidnapped a French tourist in Baluchistan. They handed him over to authorities on August 21, 2009. 09052301

May 25, 2009—Iraq—Terrence Barnich, 56, deputy director of the U.S. Department of State's Iraq Transition Assistance Office in Baghdad, a U.S. soldier, and a civilian Defense Department contractor were killed when a roadside mine exploded as their convoy was leaving the construction site of a U.S.-funded water treatment plant in Fallujah. Two other people were wounded. Barnich had arrived in Iraq in January 2007. 0905 2501

May 27, 2009—Pakistan—A car bomb exploded in the morning outside two police buildings and a Lahore office of the Pakistani Inter-Services Intelligence (ISI) agency on Mall Road, killing 30 people, including 9 police officers, and injured 250. Gunmen crashed their car through a security barrier, jumped out, and fired on the ISI office. After a gun battle, the car blew up. The gunmen continued firing and threw grenades fifteen minutes after the detonation of 200 pounds of explosives, which damaged an emergency response center (Rescue 15), the ISI office, and operating rooms of a neighboring hospital. The Taliban and Islamists were suspected; no immediate claims were made. Two people were arrested.

May 27, 2009—United States—Shukri Abu Baker, 50, and Ghassan Elashi, 55, two founding members of the Holy Land Foundation for Relief and Development, were sentenced to sixty-five years in prison for funneling millions of dollars to Hamas. They had been convicted in November

2008 on 108 counts, including funding schools and social welfare programs controlled by Hamas. Three other members of the group were also sentenced.

May 28, 2009—Iran—A bomb exploded in the second-largest Shi'ite mosque in Zahedan, killing 25 and wounding 125. Jundallah claimed credit. Less than thirty-six hours later, three suspects were hanged in front of the mosque.

May 30, 2009—Iran—A homemade bomb was found and defused on a domestic flight from Ahvaz to Tehran. Rumors suggested former president Mohammad Khatami, who was campaigning for president, was on board.

May 31, 2009—United States—At 10 a.m., a gunman shot to death George R. Tiller, 67, a late-term abortion doctor who was serving as an usher at Reformation Lutheran Church in Wichita. The gunman fled in a car. Hours later, police arrested a suspect.

Tiller had been shot in both arms by a protestor in 1993, and his clinic was bombed in 1985. The shooter, abortion protester Rachelle "Shelly" Shannon, remains in prison. Tiller had begun conducting abortions in 1973. He ran Women's Health Care Services, one of only three clinics that perform late-term abortions. In March 2009, he was acquitted on charges of performing late-term abortions without getting a second medical opinion.

Hours after the deadly attack, police stopped and detained Scott Roeder, 51, of Merriam, Kansas, as he was driving the getaway car on Interstate 35. He had posted a note in May 2007 on Operation Rescue's Web site, calling on people to question the church's hierarchy. He was held in Sedgwick County Jail. He had been arrested in April 1996 in Shawnee County, Kansas, with bomb components in his car. He was convicted in June 1996 of criminal use of explosives and sentenced to sixteen months; he was discharged in March 1998 and the conviction was overturned that year when a court ruled that the car's search was improper. His father said his son was a member of the Montana Freemen, an anti-government group. Roeder pleaded not guilty on July 27, 2009, to murdering Tiller. Roeder was ordered held on a $20 million bond. Trial was scheduled for September 21, 2009. Scott Roeder phoned the Associated Press from his jail cell to take credit for George Tiller's murder, saying, "Because of the fact pre-born children's lives were in imminent danger, this was the action I chose.... I have been told so far at least four women have changed their minds, that I know of, and have chosen to have

the baby. So even if one changed her mind it would be worth it. No, I don't have any regrets." Roeder was charged with first degree murder and aggravated assault.

Tiller's family announced on June 9 that it would not reopen his Kansas Women's Health Care Services abortion clinic.

On January 29, 2010, jurors deliberated for thirty-seven minutes before convicting Scott Roeder of premeditated, first-degree murder and aggravated assault for pointing a gun at two ushers at Tiller's church after the shooting. He was represented by attorney Mark Rudy. Roeder faced a mandatory sentence of life in prison, with the possibility of parole after twenty-five years. Sentencing was scheduled for March 9, 2010. The prosecution said it would pursue a "hard fifty" sentence, requiring him to serve at least fifty years before parole eligibility. On April 1, 2010, the court sentenced Scott Roeder to life in prison, eligible for parole only after fifty years. He showed no remorse at the sentencing hearing, saying that God "will avenge every drop of innocent blood."

May 31, 2009—Iran—Authorities defused a bomb on a Kish Air flight from Ahvaz to Tehran with 131 people on board.

May 31, 2009—Nigeria—The Movement for the Emancipation of the Niger Delta claimed that it had destroyed several Chevron oil pipelines and thus put a storage facility out of commission. 09053101

June 2009—Kenya—Western officials warned expatriates to stay away from Nairobi malls because of possible suicide attacks. A few weeks later, the Somalia-based Islamist group al-Shabaab threatened to destroy Nairobi's "tall glass buildings." 09069901-02

June 2009—Italy—Authorities issued arrest warrants for two Tunisians, two Moroccans, and an Algerian plotting attacks on a church and a subway line.

June 2009—Afghanistan—On August 7, 2012, Reuters and other U.S. news media reported that the U.S. administration was considering transferring five senior Taliban figures from Guantanamo Bay prison to Qatar in exchange for Sgt. Bowe Bergdahl. Among the detainees was Mullah Mohammed Fazl, a former Taliban deputy minister of defense, believed behind the killing of thousands of Shi'ites; Noorullah Noori, a former top military commander; Abdul Haq Wasiq, a former deputy intelligence minister; and Khairullah Khairkhwa, a former interior minister.

June 2009—Mauritania—In late June, al Qaeda in the Islamic Maghreb claimed credit for shooting Christopher Leggett, an American, on a Nouakchott street. Three Mauritanians were charged with murder in early August 2009; one was wearing a suicide belt that did not explode when he was arrested in July. 09069903

June 1, 2009—Iran—Arsonists torched the Zahedan branch of the Mehr Finance and Credit Institution, killing five people.

June 1, 2009—United States—Abdulhakim Mujahid Muhammad, born Carlos Bledsoe, 24, was arrested moments after shooting at recruiters outside a military recruiting office in Little Rock, Arkansas. He killed William Long, 24, of Conway, Arkansas, and wounded Quinton Ezeagwula, 18, of Jacksonville, Arkansas. Police said Muhammad had probably acted on "political and religious motives." The two soldiers had recently completed basic training and were serving in the office as part of the Hometown Recruiting Assistance Program. The FBI was investigating reports of his 2006–2007 links to a small mosque in Columbus, Ohio, that had been visited by convicted terrorists Iyman Faris (convicted in 2003 of planning to bomb the Brooklyn Bridge), Nuradin Abdi (convicted in 2007 of planning to blow up an Ohio shopping mall), and Christopher Paul (convicted in 2008 of conspiracy to bomb targets in the United States and Europe). He had been arrested in Yemen in 2008 and was imprisoned there for several months for overstaying his visa and holding a fraudulent Somali passport. While in Yemen, he might have attended the Damaj Institute, which was frequented by radicalized U.S. converts, including John Walker Lindh, the "American Taliban" captured in Afghanistan in 2001. Muhammad was represented by attorney Jim Hensley, who said Muhammad was teaching English to Afghan war refugees in Yemen. Muhammad had used Google Maps to find recruiting centers in New York, Atlanta, Louisville, and Philadelphia, plus Jewish institutions, a day care center, a post office, and a Baptist church. He pleaded not guilty to the shooting, despite earlier reports that he had confessed upon arrest.

Abdulhakim Mujahid Muhammad, on July 31, 2009, again pleaded not guilty to charges that he fatally shot Pvt. William Andrew Long. Prosecutors said they would seek the death penalty. A Pulaski County, Arkansas, judge set a February 15, 2010, trial date. The defendant twice phoned the Associated Press about the shooting, saying that he had killed Long, but it was not a murder because U.S. military actions in the Middle East justified it.

On January 21, 2010, he asked a Memphis judge

to change his plea to guilty and said that he was a soldier in al Qaeda in the Arabian Peninsula who conducted "a jihadi attack" in retribution for the killing of Muslims by U.S. troops. "I wasn't insane or post-traumatic nor was a I forced to do this act," he wrote in pencil, saying he was a member of "Abu Basir's Army," believed to refer to Naser Abdel-Karim al-Wahishi, alias Abu Basir, head of the Yemeni branch of al Qaeda. Muhammad had spent sixteen months in Yemen beginning in fall 2007, allegedly to teach English and learn Arabic. While there, he married a Yemeni woman. Yemen deported him to the United States in January 2009. He was represented by attorney Claiborne Ferguson. Muhammad was charged with capital murder, attempted capital murder, and ten counts of unlawful discharge of a firearm. Prosecutors said they would seek the death penalty.

June 2, 2009—Iran—Rebels killed a passenger when they fired on a bus in the southeast.

June 2, 2009—Qatar—Ayman al-Zawahiri, al Qaeda's second in command, released on Islamist Web sites a twelve-minute audiotape entitled *Tyrants of Egypt and America's Agents Welcome Obama* in which he said that U.S. President Barack Obama is not welcome in Egypt because of its alliance with Israel. He called the president an enemy of Muslims for his support for "Zionist aggression," sending more soldiers to Afghanistan, ordering bombings in the tribal areas of Pakistan, and administering a "bloody campaign against Muslims" in Pakistan's Swat Valley. He said Obama was invited to Cairo by the "torturers of Egypt" and "slaves of America." "His bloody messages were received and are still being received by Muslims, and they will not be concealed by public relations campaigns or by farcical visits or elegant words." He labeled Obama,

> that criminal who came seeking, with deception, to obtain what he failed to achieve on the ground after the mujahideen ruined the project of the Crusader America in Iraq, Afghanistan, and Somalia.... The White House declared that Obama will send a message from Egypt to the Islamic world but they forget that his messages were already received when he visited the Western Wall and wore the Jewish yarmulke and when he prayed their prayers.... His administration continued to reject the appliance of the Geneva Conventions regarding Muslim prisoners in the crusade war against Islam that they call the war on terror.... His bloody messages were received and they are still coming and they will not be obstructed either by the public relations campaign, the shenanigan visits, or the articulate words.

June 3, 2009—Qatar—While U.S. President Barack Obama was visiting Saudi Arabia and later addressing an audience at Cairo's al-Azhar University, al-Jazeera aired a four-minute audiotape from Osama bin Laden in which the al Qaeda leader attacked U.S. policy on Pakistan. Bin Laden said Obama is "walking the same road of his predecessors to build enmity against Muslims and increasing the number of fighters, and establishing more lasting wars." He claimed Obama had ordered Pakistani President Asif Ali Zardari,

to prevent the people of Swat from implementing sharia law through killing and bombing and destruction.... All this led to the displacement of about a million Muslims—elderly, women and children—from their villages and homes to become refugees in tents. They became refugees in tents after they were honored in their own home.... This basically means that Obama and his administration put new seeds of hatred and revenge against America. The number of these seeds is the same as the number of those victims and refugees in Swat and the tribal area in northern and southern Waziristan. Obama has followed the steps of (Bush) who established wars with other nations. American people should prepare themselves for coming wars.... The American people need to prepare to only gain what those seeds bring up.... Let the American people prepare to continue to reap what has been planted by the heads of the White House in the coming years and decades."

He said the war is "fulfilling an American, Jewish and Indian plot.... Zardari and Ishfaq Kiyan are working on diverting the Pakistani Army from its missions which are protecting Islam and its people and instead they fight Islam and Muslims specially the Pashtun and Bloush tribes in Swat valley, though most of the Pakistani people reject this unjust war. Zardari did this in response to the ones paying him in the White House—not 10 percent but multiple folds of that."

Moving on to India, he observed that it is "easy for India to subject the disassembled territories of Pakistan, one after another, for its own benefit, like the case of eastern Pakistan [Bangladesh] before, or even worse. This way, America eases its worry towards Pakistan's nuclear weapons."

I have also a few words to America and may the wise hear, I will disclose the reasons why people are eager to fight America and why the hatred always increases. I say that the freemen who conducted the 9/11 attacks weren't displaced by the U.S. Army and haven't tasted the unjust of America, but they heard what had happened to people in Palestine. That's why they left their universities and homes and went toward America to fight and punish it. You can imagine what

would the freemen (al Qaeda members) do if they were touched by the unjust of America.

June 9, 2009—Pakistan—Three to five terrorists in a Toyota Corolla and a pickup truck fired weapons to get onto the grounds of the 5-star Pearl Continental Hotel in Peshawar, then set off a 500 kilogram car bomb, killing themselves and eleven people, including a Nigerian who worked for the United Nations and Aleksandar Vorkapic, an official with the Office of the UN High Commissioner for Refugees, who was from Belgrade, Serbia, and wounding fifty others. The terrorists destroyed thirty cars and caused extensive damage to the hotel, destroying ten rooms and damaging fifty others. The hotel frequently hosts foreigners and diplomats. Police detained two hotel security guards for questioning. 09060901

June 10, 2009—United States—A federal judge in Atlanta, Georgia, convicted Syed Haris Ahmed, 24, of conspiracy to support terrorists. He had gone to Washington, DC, in April 2005, where he made short digital videos of the U.S. Capitol, Pentagon, George Washington National Masonic Memorial, the World Bank, and fuel tanks near I-95 in northern Virginia.

June 10, 2009—United States—At 12:44 p.m., white supremacist James Wenneker von Brunn, 88 (thereby setting a new record), from Annapolis, Maryland, doubleparked his red Hyundai on 14th Street and walked into the Holocaust Museum with a 70-year-old Winchester .22-caliber rifle and fired three shots, killing African American security guard Stephen Tyrone Johns, 39, of Temple Hills, Maryland, and wounding another guard. Two officers from Wackenhut Services, Jason McCuiston and Harry Weeks, fired back eight .38-caliber rounds, hitting von Brunn, who was expected to survive. Von Brunn was taken into custody and charged with murder. The Mensa member had written several anti–Semitic screeds, in print and on the Internet.

The Holocaust denier had on December 7, 1981, tried to kidnap members of the Federal Reserve Board of Governors but was captured carrying weapons outside a board meeting at Fed headquarters at 20th Street and Constitution Avenue, NW, in Washington, DC. He told the court that he was trying to place the board under "legal, nonviolent citizen's arrest," although he was carrying a revolver, sawed-off shotgun, and knife. He was sentenced in 1983 to more than four years in prison for attempted armed kidnapping. He was released in 1989.

Von Brunn had captained a PT boat in the Pacific in World War II.

During his September 2, 2009, court hearing, von Brunn opposed a psychiatric evaluation. U.S. District Judge Reginald Walton denied him bail and ordered a psych evaluation within thirty days at a facility in Butner, North Carolina. Von Brunn was represented by public defender A. J. Kramer. Prosecutors said he had planned the attack for months and intended for it to be a suicide mission that would "send a message to the Jewish community" that the Holocaust was a hoax. On January 6, 2010, von Brunn died at a North Carolina hospital.

June 11, 2009—Yemen—Houthi Shi'ite rebels stopped a bus and seized twenty-four medical workers, who were from India, Egypt, the Sudan, and the Philippines, in Amran Province. The gunmen demanded the release of tribesmen arrested in a war between the government and the rebels in 2008. The hostages were released unharmed. 09061101

June 11, 2009—Italy—Police arrested six suspected leftists who were planning a terrorist attack in La Maddalena, an island off Sardinia, which had been scheduled to host the G-8 Summit in July. Among the detainees was a man who earlier was investigated on suspicion of providing support to the Italian Red Brigades.

June 11, 2009—Colombia—Authorities captured Martin Cuero, the fourth-ranking leader of the leftist Revolutionary Armed Forces of Colombia (FARC), in the northwestern city of Calarca. He was a senior aide to FARC leader Mono Jojoy. Cuero had belonged to FARC for twenty years and liaised with Colombian drug traffickers to funnel money to weapons purchases. He was wanted on charges of murder, terrorism, and rebellion.

June 12, 2009—Yemen—Authorities arrested Hassan Hussein bin Alwan, a Saudi, whom the government described as "the biggest and the most influential" financier for al Qaeda in Yemen and Saudi Arabia. The date of the arrest was not disclosed. He was believed to have financed attacks in two neighboring countries. Yemen charged him with forming a terrorist group in Yemen and financing its activities. 09061201

June 12, 2009—Yemen—Houthi Shi'ite rebels in northern Saada Province kidnapped seven Germans, a Briton, and a South Korean—among them three children under the age of 6—from a hospital where the six adults worked for the World Wide Services Foundation, a Dutch international medical relief group. On June 15, Yemeni officials in the Noshour Valley in Safrah district in Saada Province found the bodies of three kidnapped women—South Korean teacher Eom Young-sun and German nurse trainees Rita Stumpp and Anita Gruenwald—all in their 20s. The Germans had attended a Bible school and Eom had attended a Christian missionary school in South Korea. The *Yemen Post* had claimed that seven hostages were killed, but SABA reported the next day the belief that six were still alive. Houthi rebels accused drug traffickers and regional tribesmen of the murders. Fox News blamed al Qaeda and Said Ali al-Shihri, an Islamist extremist who was the group's number 2 leader in the Arabian Peninsula. The Saudi had been released from Guantanamo Bay military prison in November 2007 and sent to a Saudi rehabilitation program for repentant Islamist terrorists. He was also believed to have been involved in the September 2008 attacks that left sixteen dead near the U.S. Embassy in Sana'a, Yemen. 09061202

June 12, 2009—Italy/United States—American and Italian authorities arrested a group of hackers who allegedly stole from phone companies around the world. The illegal profits apparently funded terrorist activities. A federal grand jury in New Jersey indicted three people who live in the Philippines, including one man who has been linked to al Qaeda. The trio was accused of providing Pakistani nationals in Italy with access to stolen phone lines. The company that paid the hackers also financed the communications of terrorists in the November 2008 Mumbai attacks. Italian officials arrested five Pakistanis in raids on ten call centers suspected of involvement. Among those arrested were a husband-and-wife team who managed call centers in Brescia, Italy—Mohammad Zamir, 40, and Shabina Kanwal, 38.

June 12, 2009—United Kingdom—A London court sentenced Arunchalam Chrishanthakumar to two years in prison after the British Liberation Tigers of Tamil Eelam (LTTE) leader was convicted of supplying bomb-making equipment to the LTTE.

June 12, 2009—United States—The Department of Justice announced that it had sent three Saudi detainees who had been held at Guantanamo Bay to their home country. The trio—Khalid Saad Mohammed, Abdalaziz Kareem Salim al-Noofayaee, and Ahmed Zaid Salim Zuhair—would be subject to Saudi judicial review before entering a rehabilitation program.

June 13, 2009—Qatar—Adam Yahiye Gadahn, alias Azzam, the American al Qaeda spokesman, released another video admitting that he had Jewish roots. "Let me here tell you something about myself and my biography, in which there is a benefit and a lesson.... Your speaker has Jews in his ancestry, the last of whom was his grandfather." He noted that his grandfather was a "Zionist" and "a zealous supporter of the usurper entity, and a prominent member of a number of Zionist hate organizations. He used to repeat to me what he claimed are the virtues of this entity and encouraged me to visit it, specifically the city of Tel Aviv, where relatives of ours live." His grandfather gave him Prime Minister Benjamin Netanyahu's book *A Place Among the Nations*, about which Gadahn said the "rabid Zionist" posits "feeble arguments and unmasked lies to justify the Jews' rape of Muslim Palestine." Referring to the Zionists, Gadahn asks, "How can a person with an ounce of self-respect possibly stand in the ranks of criminals and killers who have no morals, no mercy, no humanity and indeed, no honor.... Isn't it shameful enough for a person to carry the citizenship of America, the symbol of oppression and tyranny and advocate of terror in the world?" [Gadahn did not notice the unintended irony, given his position in the al Qaeda organization.] Gadahn called on his fellow Muslims for "our weapons, funds, and jihad against the Jews and their allies everywhere." He criticized U.S. President Barack Obama, observing that the "Zio-Crusader alliance" was fighting his "brothers" in "open faced aggression" attributable to Obama, who offers "other deceptive, false, and sugarcoated words of endearment and respect." Gadahn spoke Arabic with English subtitles; As-Sahab Media released an English transcript.

June 15, 2009—Nigeria—The Movement for the Emancipation of the Niger Delta (MEND) warned the International Football Association (FIFA) to "rethink" allowing Nigeria to host the upcoming under–17 World Cup series from October 24 to November 15. "The safety of international players and visitors cannot be guaranteed due to the current unrest," MEND said in an e-mail. 09061501

June 15, 2009—Nigeria—The Movement for the Emancipation of the Niger Delta (MEND) said it had attacked Chevron's Abiteve oil flow station in the Niger Delta at 2:00 a.m. as part of its "Hurricane Piper Alpha" campaign against the government. MEND claimed it had sparked a fire that was consuming the entire facility. 09061502

June 17, 2009—Nigeria— The Movement for the Emancipation of the Niger Delta (MEND) claimed it blew up Shell's major crude oil trunk in Bayelsa State as part of its campaign "to cripple the entire oil and gas export of the Federal Republic of Nigeria." MEND said the company should "vacate the Niger Delta region to avoid collateral damage to their investment and death to staff." Shell halted production "to avoid potential environmental impact."

June 18, 2009—Algeria—Gunmen believed affiliated with the local al Qaeda organization shot to death eighteen paramilitary policemen and a civilian.

June 18, 2009—Somalia—Islamists killed National Security Minister Omar Hashi Aden, four other government officials, and eighteen other people in a suicide car bomb attack at a hotel frequently by government officials. He was meeting with other government officials and clan leaders in Beledweyne, 200 miles north of Mogadishu, near the Ethiopia border. The government blamed al Qaeda, saying that at least two hundred foreign fighters, mostly from Yemen and Pakistan, were aiding al-Shabaab, the al Qaeda affiliate, which claimed credit for the attack.

June 19, 2009—Nigeria—The Movement for the Emancipation of the Niger Delta (MEND) attacked a Nigerian military gunboat and bombed a major oil pipeline owned by the Italian gas company Agip in Bayelsa State. MEND said, "All the soldiers numbering seven (7) were dispossessed of their weapons. The gunboat was also stripped of its weapons before it was disabled by explosives. The soldiers pleaded for their lives to be spared and we did."

June 19, 2009—Spain—The Basque Nation and Liberty (ETA) set off a car bomb in a parking lot in Arrigorriaga, about 30 miles south of Bilbao, killing Spanish police officer Eduardo Puelles, a senior figure in the fight against ETA. The group called him a "torturer," saying, "he was also the one responsible for pressuring young independence activist militants on the street for their collaboration by means of threats."

June 21, 2009—Nigeria—Royal Dutch Shell reported that three of its oil pipelines in the eastern part of the Niger Delta in Nigeria had been attacked. One offshore facility was "engulfed in fire," according to the Movement for the Emancipation of the Niger Delta.

June 22, 2009—Russia—A car bomb injured Yunus-Bek Yevkurov, 45, president of Ingushetia, west of Chechnya, as his motorcade was on a road outside Nazran. One person was killed and several others, including his brother, were injured. Reports differed as to whether a suicide bomber drove into the convoy or a parked car was remotely detonated. The former military intelligence officer had offered amnesty to the insurgents.

June 25, 2009—Colombia—Police and an air force task force attacked a rebel camp in the Amazon jungle, killing twenty-five Revolutionary Armed Forces of Colombia members, including Juan Carlos Usuga, alias El Enano (The Dwarf).

June 25, 2009—Nigeria—The Movement for the Emancipation of the Niger Delta (MEND) took credit for attacking a Royal Dutch Shell pipeline and warned Russia not to invest in Nigeria. Hours later, Nigerian President Umaru Yar'Adua offered amnesty to MEND if they would hand over their weapons and renounce armed struggle. 09062501

June 29, 2009—Nigeria—The Movement for the Emancipation of the Niger Delta took credit for a "massive explosion" at the Forcados terminal, one of Royal Dutch Shell's two main export terminals. MEND said it had sunk a Nigerian military patrol boat with more than twenty soldiers on board. 09062901

June 29–30, 2009—Afghanistan—The Taliban was believed to have kidnapped U.S. Army Pfc. Bowe Robert Bergdahl, 23, an airborne infantryman, after his shift in Paktika Province during the night. He was believed to be the only American soldier in Taliban captivity. The group released a video of him on July 19. Another one surfaced on December 25, 2009. A seated Bergdahl was wearing a U.S. military helmet, uniform, and sunglasses. Text read, "An American soldier imprisoned by the Mujahideen of the Islamic Emirate of Afghanistan." During the video, he said he was born in Sun Valley, Idaho, and provided his rank, birth date, blood type, his unit, and mother's maiden name before reading a verbal attack on the U.S. conduct of the war in Afghanistan and its relations with Muslims. He was forced to say,

> I'm afraid to tell you that this war has slipped from our fingers and it's just going to be our next Vietnam unless the American people stand up and stop all this nonsense…. To all you soldiers out there who are getting ready to come over here for the first time because of the stupidity of our country and leaders … you are fighting very smart people who know exactly how to kill us and are extremely patient…. I bear witness I was continuously treated as a human being, with dignity, and I had nobody deprive me of my clothes and take pictures of me naked. I had no dogs barking at me or biting me, as my country has done to their Muslim prisoners in the jail that I have mentioned.

The video also showed prisoners in U.S. custody being abused. At the end of the video, Taliban spokesman Zabihullah Mujahid added demands for a "limited number of prisoners" to be exchanged for Bergdahl. On April 7, 2010, the Taliban released a seven-minute video of Pfc. Bowe Bergdahl saying that he wanted to return to his family in Idaho and that the war was not worth the cost of lives. On December 8, 2010, the Taliban released the fourth video of Bergdahl, with bags under his eyes and an abrasion on his left cheek.

June 30, 2009—France—Al Qaeda posted on Islamist Web sites a threat to attack France "by every means and wherever we can reach them" in reaction to official French statements against the wearing of burqas in public. Abu Musab Abdul Wadud, self-identified commander of al Qaeda in the Islamic Maghreb, said, "We will not tolerate such provocations and injustices, and we will take our revenge from France." The statement, dated June 28, came five days after President Nicolas Sarkozy told parliamentarians that "the problem of the burqa is not a religious problem. This is an issue of a woman's freedom and dignity. This is not a religious symbol. It is a sign of subservience; it is a sign of lowering. I want to say solemnly, the burqa is not welcome in France." Parliament began an investigation into whether the burqa threatened the secular nature of the French constitution. Al Qaeda said France was

> committing all of these grievances in a time when we see their women flooding our nations, filling our shores, poorly dressed and nude in a deliberate defiance to the feelings of Muslims and in clear contempt to the teachings of the Islamic faith, traditions, and norms. Our Muslim brothers in France in particular and in Europe in general are increasingly troubled by the practices of the French politicians and their leaders, and their constant harassments of our people regarding the burqa issue. Yesterday they targeted the veil, today the burqa and maybe tomorrow their evil hands could be extended to defame our pillars of faith, like praying, fasting, or the pilgrimage.

July 2009—Yemen—A court on July 7, 2010, found Mansour Daleel, 18, and Mubarak al-Shabwani, 23, guilty of ambushing and looting a military truck and carrying weapons and killing a civilian, a policeman, and three soldiers in a gun battle after the initial attack. Prosecutors said they also attacked a convoy and killed two senior police officials, including the director of political security, in November 2009. The duo were arrested in December 2009 in Maarib Province. The duo admitted membership in al Qaeda. Daleel said he would appeal.

July 2009—Kenya—Gunmen kidnapped three aid workers affiliated with Action Against Hunger in the northeast and took them across the border into Somalia. Their whereabouts were unknown as of mid–August 2009. 09079901

July 2, 2009—Afghanistan—The *Washington Times* reported that Pakistani Taliban leader Baitullah Mehsud was buying children, including 7-year-olds, from their parents for between $7,000 to $14,000 to serve as suicide bombers.

July 3, 2009—Sudan—Aid workers Hilda Kawuki, 42, and Sharon Commins, 33, were kidnapped in Kutum. On October 18, 2009, they were freed in good health. They were initially interviewed in Kutum. No ransom was paid for the employees of the Irish aid agency GOAL. 0907 0301

July 6, 2009—Philippines—A bomb in Mindanao killed six people. Abu Sayyaf was suspected.

July 7, 2009—Philippines—Two bombs exploded in Mindanao, killing a total of six people and injuring fifty-three. Abu Sayyaf was suspected.

July 8, 2009—Nigeria—The Movement for the Emancipation of the Niger Delta sabotaged oil pipelines run by Royal Dutch Shell and Agip, an Italian firm. 09070801-02

July 9, 2009—Qatar—Abu Mansour al-Amriki, an American al Qaeda member who has often served as one of its spokesmen, issued a twenty-minute English-language audiotape entitled *The Beginning of the End*. Al-Amriki said that al-Shabaab, the Somali al Qaeda affiliate, was stronger than ever. Condemning President Barack Obama's efforts to create a "new beginning" with the Muslim world, the speaker said, "Despite the fact that you have been ... forced [by Muslim fighters] to at least pretend to extend your hand in peace to the Muslims, we cannot and shall not extend our hands. Rather, we shall extend to you our swords, until you leave our lands." "Let this not come as a surprise to those who are mesmerized by Obama's speech in Cairo, our positions ... have not changed in the least. If we study his words carefully, we can note very clearly that this new beginning is still heavily based upon American interests.... Not because he loves the Muslims he lived with in Indonesia, as a boy, but rather, it is because the only way to defeat the Muslims is by distracting them with his temporary life." He said Obama's speechwriters were responsible for "one major miscalculation.... A Muslim doesn't look to peace, security, education, work, or the love of any other number of things as his ultimate goals. Instead, a Muslim is always working and striving to please the one true Creator." "As you have presented to us a new beginning, we reply by saying that by the permission of Allah, this beginning is ... the beginning

of the end—the end of the tyranny and oppression so common to America. This is the cause of the entire Muslim [world], and it is being carried even by those who are considered legal citizens of your own country, according to your own laws." "As far as your claims with regard to improving some of the policies of Bush, you are claiming that Guantanamo Bay will be closed down early next year. We won't be satisfied until all the Guantanamos ... around the world have been closed, and all of the Muslim prisoners—male and female—have been released. You claim that you will fully pull out all of your troops from Iraq by 2012. We won't be satisfied until you pull out all of your troops from all of the Muslim lands." He mentioned an al-Shabaab member who was killed in Somalia, observing, "We want to inform his family that he was one of the best brothers here. We need more like him, so if you can encourage more of your children and more of your neighbors, anyone around, to send people like him to this jihad it would be a great asset for us."

July 10, 2009—Mexico/Colombia—Interpol issued a worldwide extradition "red notice" in which Colombia asked for the arrest of Mexican student Lucia Morett, 28, who survived the March 2008 Colombian bombing of an Ecuadoran camp of the Revolutionary Armed Forces of Colombia. Bogota wanted her for organized crime, transnational crime, and terrorism. She ran for congress in Mexico's elections on July 5, but did not win, thereby not gaining parliamentary immunity.

July 11–12, 2009—Indonesia—Attacks on the U.S.-owned PT-Freeport mining company killed an Australian mine technician and two Indonesians. 09071101, 09071202

July 12, 2009—Nigeria—The Movement for the Emancipation of the Niger Delta (MEND) set alight an oil depot and loading tankers in Lagos, killing five people in its first attack outside the Delta region. Jomo Gbomo, spokesman for the MEND, claimed that "led by a pillar of fire, heavily armed MEND fighters today ... carried out an unprecedented attack on the Atlas Cove Jetty in Lagos State. The depot and loading tankers moored at the facility are currently on fire."

July 12, 2009—United States—A federal grand jury unsealed the indictments of Salah Osman Ahmed, 26, and Abdifatah Yusuf Isse, 25, both of Minnesota, charged on one count each of providing material support to terrorists and conspiracy to kill, kidnap, maim, or injure people overseas between September 2007 and December 2008 in the recruiting of Somali al-Shabaab militants in the United States. The jury also charged Ahmed with two counts of making false statements to investigators when he told FBI agents that he had traveled alone on a flight to Somalia when, in fact, he and another person went together "so that they could fight jihad in Somalia." Authorities arrested Ahmed, who lived in New Brighton and worked as a security guard. Isse had been arrested in the spring in Seattle. At least a dozen young Somali men had disappeared from Minneapolis; three had been killed in Somalia. Among them was Shirwa Ahmed, 27, who blew himself up in October 2008, killing twenty-nine others. Burhan Hassan, 17, went missing in October 2008 and was killed in Somalia in June 2009. Zakaria Maruf, 30, and Jama Sheikh Bana, 20, died in a gun battle in Mogadishu on July 10, 2009.

Isse had pleaded guilty in April to one count of providing material support to terrorists.

On July 28, 2009, Ahmed pleaded guilty to providing material support to terrorists. Other charges—one count of conspiracy to kill, kidnap, maim, and injure and two counts of lying to the FBI—were to be dropped at sentencing as part of the plea deal. He faced fifteen years in prison. He was represented by attorney Jim Ostgard, who said his client intended to battle Ethiopian soldiers, not fight alongside terrorists.

July 13, 2009—Nigeria—Government officials freed the Movement for the Emancipation of the Niger Delta leader Henry Okah to meet an insurgent demand. The group's main arms smuggler was arrested in September 2007 in Luanda, Angola, and was later extradited to Nigeria.

July 14, 2009—Somalia—Ten gunmen stormed the Sahafi Hotel International in Mogadishu and seized two French security advisors—Marc Aubriere and Denis Allex—who were working with the Somali government. Some reports said they were training Somali intelligence and defense officers. The gunmen disarmed the hotel's security guards, then went on a room-to-room search for the Frenchmen, who had registered as journalists. The blindfolded and bound hostages were taken on foot to the Bakara market. Al-Shabaab, an al Qaeda–linked group, was suspected of kidnapping the French citizens who had arrived in the country nine days earlier. There was no immediate claim of responsibility; no ransom was demanded. An al-Shabaab spokesman said the duo would be tried under sharia law. The government said the pair was taken out of Mogadishu.

On September 17, 2009, al-Shabaab issued demands for the release of Allex—Aubriere, held by the militia Hezb-ul-Islam, had escaped three weeks earlier—calling for Paris to stop supporting the transitional government, release al-Shabaab prisoners, and withdraw African Union peacekeepers, French antipiracy warships patrolling the Somali coast, and French security companies operating in the country.

On January 12, 2013, French commandoes failed in a nighttime rescue raid in Bulomarer, Somalia. Hostage Denis Allex, a member of the French General Directorate for External Security (DGSE), reportedly died in the raid, as did a French soldier. The French government said the kidnappers killed Allex during the raid. Other reports said Allex and another French soldier were missing and might have been killed. At least seventeen al-Shabaab members were killed. Al-Shabaab claimed that Allex was alive, would be "judged within two days" for the attack, and would probably be executed. The group also claimed a wounded French soldier was in its hands. "In the end, it will be the French citizens who will taste the inevitable bitter consequences of the irresponsible attitude of their government with regard to the hostages." On January 16, the terrorists said they had sentenced Allex to death. On January 17, 2013, they claimed they had executed him at 11:30 a.m. on January 16. Sheikh Abdiasis Abu Musab, the group's military operations spokesman, said, "Let Muslims enjoy his execution and the French cry."

President Obama sent a letter to Congress noting that United States fighter jets flying from Camp Lemonnier in Djibouti "provided limited technical support" to the French rescue team. 09071401

July 15, 2009—Nigeria—The Movement for the Emancipation of the Niger Delta (MEND) called a sixty-day cease-fire to its attacks on oil installations and kidnapping of foreigners. But the group threatened to go back to fighting after charging that seven military joint task force (JTF) gun boats with heavily armed troops were headed toward a camp near the border of the coastal states of Delta and Ondo. MEND spokesman Jomo Gbomo said,

> If this information from a very reliable source within the JTF happens to be true, the cease-fire will be called off with immediate effect.... We are monitoring the armada and sincerely hope that the planned attack will be converted to a war exercise.... A compulsory prelude to talks is the withdrawal of the military joint task forces from the Gbaramatu communities and the return of all the displaced persons back to their various homes. Hopefully, the cease-fire period will create an enabling environment for progressive dialogue.

July 15, 2009—Qatar—Ayman al-Zawahiri, al Qaeda's deputy leader, released a nine-minute English-language audio message entitled *My Muslim Brothers and Sisters in Pakistan* on Islamist Web sites. He called upon Pakistanis to support Islamists in countering U.S. influence in Pakistan.

> I believe that every honest and sincere Muslim in Pakistan should seriously contemplate ... Pakistan's present state and expected future, because the blatant American crusader interference in Pakistan's affairs ... has reached such an extent that it now poses a grave danger to Pakistan's future and very existence.... If we stand by passively without offering due support to the mujahideen, we shall not only contribute to the destruction of Pakistan and Afghanistan, but we shall also deserve the painful punishment of almighty Allah.... It is the individual duty of every Muslim in Pakistan to join the mujahideen, or at the very least, to support the Jihad in Pakistan and Afghanistan with money.

He said Islamists plan "to establish Pakistan as a political entity standing as a citadel of Islam in the subcontinent.... The scholars of Islam have unanimously agreed that if the infidel enemy enters a Muslim country, it is the duty of all of its inhabitants, and when needed their neighbors, to mobilize for Jihad. The Americans are today occupying Afghanistan and Pakistan, so it is the duty of every Muslim in Pakistan to rise up to fight them." He called the Pakistani government:

> A clique of corrupt politicians and a junta of military officers who are fighting to remain on the American pay list by employing Pakistan's entire military and all its resources in the American crusade against Islam.... The current ruling class in Pakistan is lining up under the cross of the modern Crusade and competing for American bribes. Hence, the actual ruler of Pakistan is the American ambassador, who pays the bribes and issues the orders.... The only hope to save Pakistan from this disastrous fate of Jihad [because other institutions are] either sunk in the swamp of corruption or are too helplessly crippled and paralyzed to bring about any change.

He said the Americans feared the use of nuclear weapons by Islamists. "This is why the Western Crusade, headed by America and served by the puppet rulers of our countries with their armies, security organizations, media, judiciary and jails, aims at halting the escalating jihadi tide in the Muslim World. The crusade aims at eradicating the growing jihad nucleus in order to break up this nuclear capable country, and transform it into tiny fragments, loyal to and dependent on the neocrusaders."

July 15, 2009—Kenya—The Somalia-based Islamist group al-Shabaab broke into a Kenyan school and told the children to quit their classes and join jihad.

July 16, 2009—Pakistan—Gunmen shot to death Zil-e-Usman, 59, a Pakistani field officer for the UN High Commissioner for Refugees, as he was coming out of an office in the Kacha Garhi camp near Peshawar. He was hit in the chest in a gun battle in which a security guard was killed and another employee was wounded in what appeared to be a botched kidnapping attempt. He had worked for UNHCR for twenty-five years. 09071601

July 16, 2009—Egypt—In the corridors of the meeting of the Non-Aligned Movement's summit, Pakistani Prime Minister Yousaf Raza Gillani and Indian Prime Minister Moanmohan Singh announced an agreement to "share real-time, credible and actionable" counterterrorist intelligence.

July 17, 2009—Colombia—Police found a video in a Revolutionary Armed Forces of Colombia (FARC) computer that showed the FARC deputy chief reading the deathbed manifesto of FARC founder Manuel Marulanda, in which he said that the group provided funding to the 2006 election campaign of Ecuadoran President Rafael Correa.

July 17, 2009—Indonesia—The Jemaah Islamiyah (JI) was suspected of the 7:48 a.m. bombing of the luxury Ritz-Carlton and JW Marriott hotels in Jakarta, killing nine and wounding fifty, including at least thirteen foreigners from Italy, South Korea, Canada, Hong Kong, India, Japan, Norway, the Netherlands, India, Australia, New Zealand, Singapore, and the United Kingdom. Eight were from the United States. Among the dead were:

- Australian Trade Commission officer Craig Senger
- Perth businessman Nathan Verity
- Timothy David Mackay, 62, a New Zealander who headed Indonesian operations for cement products manufacturer PT Holcim

The wounded included:

- Kevin Moore, American general manager of Husky Oil North Sumbawa
- Jim Castle, an American business consultant and head of CastleAsia who had lived in Indonesia since 1977 and was an advisor to the U.S.-Indonesia Society. He was a major promoter of investment in Indonesia. He suffered some hearing damage.
- a Chevron employee
- two directors of the Phoenix-based PT-Freeport McMoRan Copper & Gold Inc., who were injured at the Ritz-Carlton

Police defused another bomb found in a laptop in room 1808 of the Marriott hotel. It was set to go off. Analysis of the bombers' DNA matched that of the homemade bomb found on floor 18.

The second floor windows of the Ritz were blown out, suggesting the bomb was planted inside the hotel's Airlangga restaurant. The Marriott bomb went off in the basement. The two hotels are 50 meters apart—an underground passageway connects them.

Suicide bombers were later suspected, and authorities believe the attacks were the work of Malaysian fugitive Noordin M. Top, who leads a breakaway faction of JI. A man who checked into room 1808 two days earlier gave his name as Nurdin. He offered a $1,000 cash deposit, claiming he had no credit card.

In a security video, a man in a cap could be seen pulling a wheeled suitcase across the Ritz's lobby and entering a restaurant. Seconds later, the bomb went off.

The Marriott was hosting a meeting of foreign executives of major companies in Indonesia organized by the consultancy firm CastleAsia, which is headed by an American. The Manchester United football team, which had been scheduled to stay at the Ritz-Carlton, canceled its visit to Indonesia.

Authorities said that the homemade high-explosive bombs were filled with nails.

On July 29, Noordin Top posted responsibility claims on Web sites on behalf of al Qaeda in Indonesia. One statement on an Islamist Web site said the Ritz attack was by "one of our mujahideen warriors against the American lackeys and stooges visiting the hotel.... God has given us a blessing for us to find a way to attack the biggest hotel that America owns in the Indonesian capital of Jakarta—the Ritz-Carlton, where security was very tight making it very difficult to initiate the attack that we did." He noted that the Manchester United soccer team "players are Christians and therefore do not deserve Muslims' money and respect." He said the Marriott target was Americans with ties to the Kadin, the Indonesian Chamber of Commerce and Industries.

On August 7, Detachment 88 troops tracking down Noordin Mohammad Top raided an apparent terrorist safe house in the Central Java town of Temanggung, conducting a gun battle with at least four individuals. The raid began after two people believed to be nephews of its owner were arrested earlier that day. Top was initially reported to have died in the eighteen-hour exchange of fire. Authorities later identified the decedent as Ibrohim, a florist at the Ritz-Carlton, who was suspected to have been the inside man. 09071701-02

July 17, 2009—Indonesia—Two hours after the hotel bombings, a car bomb exploded near a shopping complex in northern Jakarta.

July 18, 2009—Kenya—Three foreign aid workers were kidnapped near the Somalia border. 0907 1801

July 19, 2009—Indonesia—On September 17, 2009, Indonesian commandos raided a Jemaah Islamiyah (JI) hideout in Solo, Central Java, killing JI leader Noordin Muhammad Top and Bagus Budi Pranoto, who were wanted for the hotel bombings.

July 21, 2009—Lebanon—The Lebanese Army arrested ten members of a terrorist group suspected of planning attacks abroad. Most of the detainees were non–Lebanese Arabs. Some had used business cover for their operations, which were designed to aid "radical elements" from Fatah al-Islam and give them fake documents to get into the Ein el-Hilweh Palestinian refugee camp, target the United Nations Interim Force in Lebanon (UNIFIL) troops, smuggle wanted terrorists from the Ein el-Hilweh camp to other countries, provide them with fake documents and money, and surveil money exchange centers and jewelry stores as robbery targets. 09072101

July 22, 2009—United States—The FBI announced that Long Island, New York, native Bryant Neal Vinas, alias Ibrahim, Bashir al-Ameriki, and Ben Yameen al-Kandee, 26, had pleaded guilty as "John Doe" in a sealed courtroom in Brooklyn on January 28, 2009, to conspiracy to murder Americans, to providing material support to a foreign terrorist organization, and to receiving military-type training from a foreign terrorist organization in connection with a September 2008 rocket attack on a U.S. military base in Afghanistan. Vinas along with others fired rockets at the military base during a 2008 attack. He was also accused of giving information about the New York transit system and the Long Island Railroad to al Qaeda. He was arrested in Peshawar, Pakistan, in November 2008. He apparently received five months of military training from al Qaeda in the mountains of Waziristan in 2008. His mother said she had not seen him since he moved out at age 18 after his parents divorced. His father is Peruvian-born.

European investigators linked him to Moez Garsallaoui, a Tunisian Islamist militant and husband of Malika el-Aroud, at training camps in Pakistan; and with a Belgian cell that included Hicham Beyayo, who was arrested in December 2008 in Belgium. In July 2008, Garsallaoui talked of cross-border attacks on U.S. bases. Beyayo provided authorities with information on the training he received, according to Len Kamdang, his attorney.

Vinas joined the U.S. Army in 2002 but washed out after three weeks at Fort Jackson, South Carolina. He converted from Catholicism—he might have earlier served as an altar boy—to Salafi Islam in 2004. He attended the Islamic Association of Long Island in Selden, New York, where others remembered him as polite and soft-spoken. He left New York on September 11, 2007, and arrived in Lahore the next day. He soon met al Qaeda militants in Pakistan and decided that month to wage jihad in Afghanistan. After a few weeks, he and twenty insurgents surveilled an American combat outpost in Afghanistan's Kunar Province, but decided not to fire their mortars because of American air patrols circling overhead. He went on to Mohmand, Pakistan, where he was asked to become a suicide bomber. Agreeing, he went to Pakistan for further instruction, but was told that he needed more religious training.

Upon graduating, Vinas moved to Waziristan, meeting al Qaeda members from Saudi Arabia and Yemen. From March to July 2008, he attended three al Qaeda courses on how to fire an AK-47, an RPG, and handguns. He learned how to use C4 and TNT explosives and make suicide bombing vests. He apparently did not take the electives in forgery, poison, and advanced bombing. In September 2008, he joined a group near the Afghanistan border to fire rockets at the U.S. base. In one attack, radio problems aborted the mission; in the other, the rockets fell short. He spent several weeks in the Waziristan mountains meeting with al Qaeda leaders to discuss attacks in the West. He left the Pakistani tribal areas in October 2008 to find a wife in Peshawar, where he was arrested a few weeks later. He said he had met a few Belgian and French citizens in early 2008, who trained with him in al Qaeda camps. Belgian prosecutors interviewed him in March 2009 in support of their case against six militants who were arrested in December 2008. He was in the custody of the U.S. Marshals Service.

Belgian prosecutors told CNN that one of Vinas's contacts, Walid Othmani, 25, a Frenchman, spent time with him. Othmani was arrested in Europe. He was charged in France with participation in a criminal conspiracy with the aim of preparing a terrorist act.

July 22, 2009—Indonesia—PT Freeport, an American copper and gold mining firm, denied press reports that two people were killed in an attack on a twelve-bus convoy in easternmost Papua Province. The firm said a vehicle was wrecked, and one person and several were wounded, but no shots were fired. However, when police and mechanics arrived to assist, shots were fired at them, and three people were wounded in the gunbattle. The Antara News Agency claimed two people were killed in an attack on the convoy. 09072201

July 22, 2009—Iraq—Gunmen ambushed a three-bus convoy of Iranian pilgrims in the Imam Wais area about 43 miles northeast of Diyala's provincial capital of Baquba, killing five and wounding thirty-five. Sunni extremists were believed responsible for the attacks on the Shi'ites. 09072202

July 23, 2009—Afghanistan—U.S. officials said that Saad bin Laden, 27, third-oldest son of al-Qaida leader Osama bin Laden, may have been killed in a U.S. air strike in Pakistan in late spring. No body or DNA evidence was recovered to prove it. He went to Iran after 9/11 and was held under a form of house arrest from 2003 to 2008, before turning up in Pakistan. On January 16, 2009, the U.S. Treasury imposed financial sanctions on the Saudi, saying Americans would be barred from engaging in financial transactions with him. Officials claimed he worked with Khalid Sheikh Muhammad and participated in the planning of the March 2002 bombing of the Djerba synagogue in Tunisia in which seventeen were killed. He was also believed to have facilitated communications between Ayman al-Zawahiri and the Iranian Quds Force after al Qaeda's attack on the U.S. Embassy in Yemen in 2008.

July 24, 2009—Belgium—Gunmen hijacked a helicopter, forcing the pilot to land in the courtyard of a prison near Bruges. Inmates Mohammed Johry, Abdel Had Kahjary Mulloul, and Ashraf Sekkaki escaped. Sekkaki had more than sixteen convictions for violence, including bank robbery and kidnapping. A 22-year-old Moroccan accomplice had to stay behind because the helicopter was full. Helicopter pilot Ludwig Louwagie was unhurt. He said a couple had booked the helicopter for a sightseeing tour, but once off the ground, the man pulled a gun and took away his headset. On August 1, the trio robbed a bank, a gas station, and two storage facilities in only two hours. 09072401

July 26, 2009—Nigeria—The Movement for the Emancipation of the Niger Delta released its remaining six hostages, but rejected the government's offer of amnesty.

July 26, 2009—Egypt—Egypt's prosecutor general charged twenty-six, including two Lebanese, a Sudanese, and five Palestinians, for spying for the Lebanese group Hizballah, as well as plotting terrorist attacks and aiding militants in the Gaza Strip. The group members were arrested in April. The case was to be tried in the State Security Emergency Court. The prosecutor called for Lebanon to arrest senior Hizballah official Mohammed Qabalan and three Egyptians. The defendants were represented by attorney Montasser al-Zayat. Some eighteen suspects were charged with providing Hizballah since 2005 with information about Suez Canal schedules, tourist destinations in the Sinai, and tourist travel routes. Two suspects had worked in the Suez Canal shipping industry. Others were Egyptians living on the Gaza border. The Lebanese funded the cell and gave it technical expertise to collect information and acquire explosives "for activities to destabilize security and public order." Egypt's official state news agency said Qabalan disbursed $38,000 to Egyptian operatives to buy explosives and hide them in Sinai. Three suspects were charged with digging tunnels under the Egypt-Gaza border with the intention of smuggling people and goods. Others were charged with providing safe houses for militants smuggled across the border. The prosecutor accused five members of Egypt's banned Muslim Brotherhood of belonging to the Hizballah cell.

July 26, 2009—Russia—A suicide bomber killed six people and ten civilians while trying to enter a concert hall in Grozny minutes before the start of a play. Four police officers stopped him 130 feet from the hall; all were killed. Some eight hundred spectators were evacuated. A Turkish construction manager and a Georgian died in the hospital. 09072601

July 27, 2009—United States—U.S. District Judge Gerald Bruce Lee sentenced an unrepentant Ahmed Omar Abu Ali, 28, to life in prison. The al Qaeda member had joined the group in Saudi Arabia in 2002 and plotted to assassinate then–President George W. Bush. In 2008, the 4th U.S. Circuit Court of Appeals in Richmond ordered a new sentencing hearing, saying his thirty-year sentence was too lenient. His attorney, Joshua Dratel, planned an appeal.

July 27, 2009—United States—Authorities in North Carolina arrested seven men who were then charged in court in Raleigh with providing material support to terrorism and conspiracy to murder, kidnap, maim, and injure people abroad. Daniel Patrick Boyd, alias Saifullah ("Sword of God"), 39, a North Carolina drywall contractor, had trained in Pakistan and Afghanistan and

fought Soviets there between 1989 and 1992, according to the unsealed indictment. He reportedly encouraged others to engage in jihad. Two suspects were his sons: Zakariya Boyd, 20, and Dylan Boyd, alias Mohammed, 22. The other defendants were Anes Subasic, 33; Mohammad Omar Aly Hassan, 22; and Ziyad Yaghi, 21. The six were U.S. citizens who lived in North Carolina. Yaghi and Subasic are naturalized U.S. citizens. Hysen Sherifi, 24, a native of Kosovo and a U.S. legal permanent resident of North Carolina, was also charged. The indictment said Boyd and several of the defendants traveled to Israel in 2007 to engage in "violent jihad." Boyd was also accused of trying to raise money in 2008 to fund others' travel overseas for jihad. Sharifi allegedly went to Kosovo to engage in violent jihad, according to the indictment. Several of the defendants, including Daniel Patrick Boyd, were also charged with practicing military tactics on a private property in Caswell County in June to July 2009. A Justice Department official said Daniel Boyd had "conspired with others to recruit and help young men travel overseas in order to kill." Authorities mentioned a cache of several semiautomatic weapons, including an AK-47 assault rifle and carbines modeled after military-issue M14s and M16s. The defendants faced life in prison.

Authorities were searching for another U.S. citizen, whose name has been redacted from court documents but was identified by the news media as Jude Kenan Mohammad, 20, from Raleigh, who was believed to be hiding in Pakistan. The North Carolina resident traveled to Pakistan on October 3, 2008, to "engage in violent jihad," according to the indictment.

The indictment also said Boyd lied to the FBI and Customs and Border Protection agents at the Atlanta, Georgia, and Raleigh airports in 2007 regarding his trip to Israel and that he had traveled to Gaza in March 2006 "to introduce his son to individuals who also believed that violent jihad was a personal obligation on the part of every good Muslim." The indictment said Sherifi went to Kosovo in July 2008, Yaghi to Jordan in October 2006, and the eighth defendant to Pakistan in October 2008. All the trips were taken to "engage in violent jihad."

Daniel Boyd and his brother, Charles, were convicted in 1991 of bank robbery in Peshawar, Pakistan. The duo was also accused of carrying ID cards for the Afghan guerrilla group, Hezb-e-Islami (Party of Islam). They were sentenced to have their right hands and left feet cut off for the robbery, but the country's Supreme Court overturned their convictions on the urging of the U.S.

Department of State. Daniel Boyd and his wife, Sabrina, were profiled in the *Washington Post* in 1991.

The *New York Times* reported that Boyd, the son of a Marine, sent an e-mail to Sherifi about dying as a martyr in a suicide attack. The *Washington Post* reported that the arrests occurred after learning that Daniel and Sabrina Boyd and their two sons might be moving to Jordan.

FBI agents seized from Daniel Boyd's house and truck an antiterrorism handbook used by emergency response units, four gas masks, $13,000 in cash, an anti–U.S. fatwa, and more than twenty-seven thousand rounds of ammunition, including armor-piercing bullets. Authorities also found a trench under a deck of the house which a witness claimed was a bunker to store weapons. On August 5, Federal Magistrate Judge William Webb denied bail to six defendants. The seventh suspect's hearing was postponed because he was appointed a new attorney. Daniel Boyd was heard on a May 2009 tape talking about hitting Wells Fargo trucks and banks to finance jihad.

On September 23, 2009, MSNBC reported that Daniel Patrick Boyd and Hysen Sherifi were indicted for plotting to kill U.S. soldiers at the U.S. Marine Corps base at Quantico, Virginia. They had obtained maps of the base, according to a superseding indictment. The original indictment said only that they had plotted international terrorism and conspired to support terrorism. The new indictment added weapons charges against Daniel Boyd, Hysen Sherifi, and Zakariya Boyd.

On February 9, 2011, Daniel Boyd pleaded guilty in federal court in New Bern, North Carolina, to conspiracy to assist violent jihadists and to participate in attacks in foreign countries. Sentencing was scheduled for May 2011. He faced fifteen years in prison on the single count of conspiracy to provide material support to terrorists and a life sentence for conspiracy to "murder, kidnap, maim, and injure persons in a foreign country." On August 15, 2011, Dylan Boyd, Mohammad Omar Aly Hassan, Ziyad Yaghi, Hysen Sherifi, and Anes Subasic, all from North Carolina, pleaded not guilty to multiple felony counts that they had planned terrorist attacks against a Marine base in Virginia and overseas.

On December 20, 2011, the court sentenced Zakariya Boyd, 22, to nine years in federal prison and Dylan Boyd, 25, to eight years. Each had pleaded guilty to conspiracy to provide support to terrorists, which carried a maximum of fifteen years in prison and $250,000 fine.

July 27, 2009—India—A landmine went off under a police van in the Dantewada district of Chhattisgarh State, killing six police officers and injuring three others who were returning from duty. Maoist Naxalite rebels were blamed.

July 28, 2009—Colombia/Venezuela—Venezuela denied allegations that a cache of Revolutionary Armed Forces of Colombia (FARC) arms seized in 2008 from a guerrilla base had come from Venezuela. The rockets had been made in Sweden by Saab Bofors Dynamics. Colombian Vice President Francisco Santos argued that AT4 shoulder-launched anti-tank weapons purchased by Venezuela had ended up in FARC hands. Venezuela announced that it would withdraw its ambassador from Bogota and freeze diplomatic relations.

July 30, 2009—Nigeria—Following a week of violence in which more than four hundred people were killed, Nigerian troops raided the northern Nigerian compound of the Boko Haram Islamist sect that wants to impose sharia. The violence began after troops had arrested some sect members. The group attacked police, military, and government facilities in Bauchi State; violence spread to three other states. During a gun battle, troops killed one hundred militants, including Ustaz Mohammed Yusuf, the sect's leader (authorities later said he was shot and killed in custody), who was hiding in a goat's pen at the home of his in-laws. On July 29, troops took over the group's compound in Maiduguri, Borno, and killed the group's deputy chief.

July 30, 2009—Ecuador/Colombia—Ecuadoran officials released excerpts from the twenty-page diary of deceased Revolutionary Armed Forces of Colombia (FARC) deputy leader Raul Reyes in which he said that FARC had donated to Ecuadoran President Rafael Correa's 2006 campaign. Reyes observed in 2008 that "trusting Correa was suicide." The diary claimed that Ecuadoran officials, including former head of security Gustavo Larrea, former under-secretary for governing Ignacio Chauvin, retired Col. Jorge Brito, and dentist Luis Ayala, accepted FARC money and had connections with Mexican drug gangs. The Ecuadoran government denied the allegations and asked the Organization of American States to investigate. The diary covered July 2007 to February 23, 2008. Reyes died in a bombing attack in early March 2008.

July 30, 2009—Spain—A remotely-detonated Basque Nation and Liberty bomb hidden under a parked car killed two Civil Guards driving by outside barracks on the Mediterranean island of Mallorca.

August 1, 2009—United States—Authorities evacuated thousands of travelers from New York's La Guardia Airport Central Terminal from 5:20 a.m. until 9:00 a.m. after Scott McGann, 32 (who lived on New York streets for a year), apparently intoxicated, was spotted at a security checkpoint carrying a backpack stuffed with wires and two six-volt batteries. Port Authority police told him not to move, but he instead tried to push a switch which activated nothing. He was placed in custody. He had tickets on a United Airlines flight to Chicago and a connector to Oakland, where he has family. The backpack also had other electronic devices and personal items. His rap sheet included three prior arrest in the New York area, including two in 2008 and one in June 2009 involving tampering with evidence and resisting arrest. The bomb squad determined that it was a hoax device and blew it apart with a water cannon. Likely charges included placing a false bomb in a transportation facility and making terroristic threats.

August 1, 2009—United Kingdom—London's *Daily Telegraph* reported that MI5 had fired six Muslim recruits. Two attended training camps in Pakistan where they might have met al Qaeda recruiters; they had trained at MI5 for several weeks. The other four had unexplained gaps of up to three months in their resumes. MI5 spokesmen said none of them had actually started work.

August 2, 2009—Pakistan—Authorities charged Sufi Mohammad, father-in-law of Swat Valley Taliban leader Maulana Fazlullah, with criminal charges of aiding terrorism, sedition, and conspiracy against the government. The charges carry a minimum life sentence and a maximum of death. Mohammad had given a speech in April 2009 in which he condemned democracy and elections and deemed the constitution un–Islamic. The cleric had helped negotiate a failed peace deal with the Swat Taliban.

August 3, 2009—Qatar—In a ninety-minute videotape entitled *The Realities of Jihad and the Fallacies of Hypocrisy* that was released to Islamist Web sites, al Qaeda deputy chief Ayman al-Zawahiri said "Obama wants a Palestinian state that works as a branch for the Israeli government." He observed,

> Israel is a crime that needs to be wiped out.... The promises of the two states and ending the settlements were made by Bush, so what's new? This is the continuation of the same Zionist crusader crime against Muslims since the end of World War II.... Obama can come with all the eloquent words he has, but it is nothing but illu-

sions.... The mujahideen opened the doors to start a new relationship, but [the Americans] insist that their relationships with the Muslim world must be based on hurting us and oppressing us.... What new did Obama bring us? He brought us the bombing of Gaza where one thousand martyrs died. He brought us the destruction in Afghanistan, Iraq, and Pakistan. What else? He expanded the American prisons so they can absorb more innocent Muslims.... We are not idiots to accept meaningless flexible words. Obama is the new face with the same old crimes.

He said the truce offered to President Bush still was available, but U.S. forces must leave Afghanistan and all Muslim countries in the Middle East. "These offers were dealt with impolitely but are still valid, and the offer is fair. But they want a relationship with us based on suppression. Obama is like a wolf whose fangs tear your flesh and whose paws slit your face and then he calls on you to talk about peace." He noted that post 9/11 antiterrorism efforts had failed. "After seven and a half years, their campaign failed in Iraq and in Afghanistan just like it failed in Somalia and will fail in Pakistan.... The only reason the American administration changed its policy from Bush's motto that you are either with them or against them to Obama's saying that he wants to deal with the Islamic world based on a new policy [is] because of the heavy losses that they suffered from by the hands of the mujahideen." He predicted that the mujahideen will go on fighting. "They will face that campaign no matter how long it will last, even till Judgment Day. No surrender, no defeat, no submission, no retreat when it comes to the right of the Muslims and their pride." He praised Afghan insurgents for challenging the United States, calling the action "an achievement by itself because it stood for its pride, dignity and lands.... What's happening in Afghanistan is a lesson, which the Muslim world should learn. American forces have been defeated by the Taliban." He also said that Tehran "never supported the Palestinians in Gaza, they didn't launch any rocket to aid them as they promised to do if Israel attacks Lebanon—or is it that the Palestinians are second-class citizens? ... Iran is ready to sell out the Muslims anytime and aid the crusaders in their campaign against them."

August 4, 2009—Australia—Some four hundred police officers executed nineteen search warrants in nine Melbourne neighborhoods and arrested four Australian suspects, some of Lebanese and Somali descent, believed planning an attack on a military base with automatic weapons, deemed by police "the most serious terrorist attack on Australian soil." The group was believed linked to al-Shabaab of Somalia. Several other people were detained for questioning regarding the planned suicide attack on the Holsworthy Barracks in western Sydney. The terrorists would have shot as many people as they could until they were themselves killed. They had sought support from Islamic leaders to issue a fatwa in support of the attack. One of the men had participated in the Somali insurgency. The men, aged 22 to 26, had been spotted surveilling the barracks. Police charged Nayed El Sayed, 25, from Glenroy, with conspiring to plan or prepare for a terrorist act. He did not enter a plea nor request bail when he appeared in Melbourne Magistrates' Court on August 4. Police were also questioning Saney Aweys and a fifth man, 33, already in custody. Aweys and the three other suspects were not immediately charged.

August 4, 2009—Argentina—A bomb exploded at 2:30 a.m. at a Chilean LAN Airlines ticket office in Buenos Aires, causing moderate damage to a door, window, and furniture, but no injuries. The owner of a pickup truck was arrested. A hooded person leaving a package in front of the office was seen on a security video. 09080401

August 6, 2009—Nigeria—The government announced an amnesty for rebels, guaranteeing them a pardon and a job. By August 25, the Movement for the Emancipation of the Niger Delta (MEND) claimed the amnesty deal was a charade, but one thousand rebels turned in buckets of bullets and boxes and boxes of machine guns and rocket launchers. MEND commander Ebikabowei "Boyloaf" Ben said his group was committed to dialogue. The amnesty was scheduled to last until October 4. MEND threatened further attacks on the oil industry at the end of its sixty-day ceasefire on September 15.

August 7, 2009—Sri Lanka—Authorities arrested Selvarajah Pathmanathan, the new head of the Liberation Tigers of Tamil Eelam (LTTE), who succeeded Velupillai Prabhakaran, founder of LTTE, who was killed on May 18 in a gun battle with the government. Pathmanathan had run the LTTE's arms and smuggling operations for decades.

August 8, 2009—Indonesia—A raid in the Jakarta suburbs thwarted a planned assassination attempt on Indonesian President Susilo Bambang Yudhoyono. Authorities found a cache of 100 kilograms of explosives, bomb-making materials, and a truck. Detachment 88 troops killed two militants linked to the 2004 Australian Embassy bombing.

August 8, 2009—Indonesia—Authorities in north Jakarta arrested Suryana, alias Yayan, alias Gepeng, on suspicion of terrorism.

August 8, 2009—Mauritania—A suicide bomber killed himself and wounded two embassy security guards who were jogging near the walls of the French Embassy during the night. Al Qaeda in the Islamic Maghreb was suspected of having brought in militants from Mali. A government-linked Web site said the Mauritanian bomber yelled, "Allahu akbar" before blowing himself up. 09080801

August 9, 2009—Spain—Two bombs exploded at the La Rigoletta restaurant on the Paseo del Portitxol street in front of the Can Pere Antoni beach in Palma de Mallorca, the capital of Mallorca Island, at 3:00 p.m., causing no injuries. The Basque Nation and Liberty warned police. The first bomb was in a bag in the women's rest room. The second exploded soon after.

August 9, 2009—India—The Badminton England team withdrew from the World Badminton Championships in Hyderabad after threats by the Laskhar-e-Taiba (Urdu for "Soldiers of the Pure"). Badminton Scotland vowed to stay, as did three Welsh Badminton players. 09080901

August 11, 2009—Kuwait—Authorities arrested six Kuwaiti members of an al Qaeda–linked group planning to attack Camp Arifjan, a U.S. military logistics and supply base in the desert 38 miles south of Kuwait City, as well as Kuwait security agencies and other targets. The six confessed to purchasing a truck and filling it with chemicals and gas cylinders, which they would then crash into the camp. The camp is used as a staging area for operations into Iraq. The six had made martyrdom videos claiming credit for the attack. One of the detainees was believed involved in the 2002 armed attack on Marines training in Failaka Island that killed one and injured another. 09081101

August 12, 2009—Somalia—Gunmen in central Somalia shot to death eight Muslim missionaries near a large mosque in Galkayo, Puntland. Seven were from Tabliq in Pakistan; the fifth was from Somalia. 09081201

August 17, 2009—Russia—A suicide truck bomber drove through the gates of a police building in Ingushetia and set off his explosives, killing 20 and injuring 130, including 10 children. The 440 pounds of TNT destroyed the Nazran police headquarters when police were arriving for morning roll call. Terrorists fired at police fleeing the fire, killing another three police officers. Local police had been tipped off but were unable to find the truck. Ingushetia President Yunus-Bek Yevkurov blamed Islamist militants.

August 19, 2009—Saudi Arabia—The government announced that it had arrested forty-four al Qaeda–linked suspects during the past year.

August 19, 2009—Iraq—In the bloodiest day in Baghdad since U.S. troops withdrew, suicide truck bombs exploded at the Finance Ministry, the Foreign Ministry, and three other locations, killing one hundred people and wounding hundreds of others. Authorities detained eleven senior security officials for questioning. Members of an insurgent cell were also arrested. On August 23, Iraqi officials released a confession by Wissam Ali Kadhim Ibrahim, 57, a former Ba'athist police official, who said he was acting on orders of Sattam Farhan, a Ba'athist exile living in Syria. Ibrahim said the truck bomb was built in Khalis, northeast of Baghdad. He claimed $10,000 was given to a man who let the truck pass through Diyala Province checkpoints. Ibrahim had served as a town police chief in Diyala. On August 26, Iraq and Syria recalled their ambassadors. Iraq demanded that Syria extradite two of the Iraqi suspects, Sattam Farhan and Mohammed Younis al-Ahmed, a former senior member of Saddam Hussein's regime, living in Syria.

August 22, 2009—Pakistan—A car bombing in Peshawar killed two people, including the spokesman for Ansar ul-Islam. Two suspects were arrested.

August 22, 2009—Nigeria—A fortnight after the start of a sixty-day amnesty, hundreds of Movement for the Emancipation of the Niger Delta insurgents turned in their weapons, mortar shells, and gunboats.

August 23, 2009—Pakistan—The government announced that it had arrested thirteen people, including three Pakistani Taliban members wearing suicide vests inside a bus station in Sargodha. They were planning on attacking two Shi'ite mosques, police stations, and a Norwegian telecommunications company in Punjab. Other terrorists were planning to attack the parliament building, the intelligence service, and other federal institutions. Those detained included the leader of the Pakistani Taliban in Punjab. Police also announced the arrest of seven Lashkar-e-Jhangvi members carrying suicide vests and ammunition in Karachi. Authorities seized explosives, assault weapons, and heroin at their Karachi hideout.

Meanwhile, a suicide bomber in Peshawar killed three and injured fifteen, including two women and seven children. Police stopped him when they saw him acting suspiciously. In the ensuing gunfight, he ran out of bullets and blew himself up, destroying five houses.

August 26, 2009—United States—The press reported on October 26 that six Harvard University Medical School Pathology Department researchers were poisoned by coffee tainted with sodium azide, a chemical preservative. Symptoms included dizziness, tinnitus, and passing out; they can also include rapid breathing and nausea. It was unclear whether the poisoning was intentional. The lab had not received threats by animal rights protestors.

August 27, 2009—Saudi Arabia—Abdullah Hassan Tali al-Assiri, 23, a suicide bomber carrying a cell phone bomb (other reports said it was hidden in his colon) slightly injured Prince Muhammad bin Nayef, assistant interior minister for security affairs, at his palace in Jeddah. Authorities said the "wanted militant" had earlier said he wanted to turn himself in. The bomb went off while he was passing security guards at 11:30 p.m. Nayef had said he could go past the guards as a sign of good faith in turning himself in. Nayef runs the country's antiterrorism program. Al Qaeda in the Arabian Peninsula claimed credit. The Saudi government announced that al-Assiri hid his 100 grams of PETN plastic explosives in his underwear—not his rectum, as had been earlier reported—hoping that cultural taboos against intrusive searches would protect him.

August 28, 2009—Germany—German federal prosecutors arrested Kadir T., a German of Turkish origin who was a suspect in a plot by the Uzbek militant group Islamic Jihad Union (IJU) to attack U.S. troops in Germany, including those at Ramstein Air Base. He had tried to acquire a video camera and night-vision equipment for the group, shipping them to Waziristan in Pakistan. Four IJU members, known as the Sauerland Group, three of whom were arrested in September 2007, were on trial for plotting attacks against the United States.

August 28, 2009—Qatar—Ayman al-Zawahiri released a twenty-two-minute video, entitled *Path of Doom*, on radical Islamist Web sites in which he called on Pakistanis to back Islamic militants in tribal areas against American "crusaders" and the Pakistani Army. He observed,

> The war in the tribal areas and Swat [Valley] is an inseparable part of the crusaders' assault on the Muslims the length and breadth of the Islamic world.... This is the battle, briefly and plainly; and this is why anyone who supports the Americans and Pakistan Army—under any pretext, ploy or lie—is in fact standing with, backing and supporting the crusaders against Islam and Muslims. [The United States] wants

to eliminate the Mujahideen (Islamic militants) in the tribal areas so they can seek to smother the Jihad in Afghanistan. [However] no people abandon Jihad without Allah giving them a general punishment.... There is no honor for us except through Jihad.... People of Pakistan ... back the jihad and mujahideen with your persons, wealth, opinion, expertise, information, and prayers and by exhorting others to help them and preach their message.

August 28, 2009—Pakistan—Authorities arrested four Swedes and seven Turks planning to travel to North Waziristan to join al Qaeda operatives hiding there. One of the Swedes was identified as Mehdi-Muhammed Ghezali, who had earlier been held at Guantanamo Bay. He had been arrested in Pakistan in 2001 and was released in 2004 by the United States.

August 29, 2009—Sudan—Gunmen kidnapped a Nigerian man and a Tanzanian woman who were working for the joint UN–African Union force in Darfur. It was the first time UNAMID staff had been abducted. The two were freed on December 13, 2009. The kidnappers were not publicly identified. 09082901

August 17–September 14, 2009—China—As of September 14, authorities had recorded 530 stabbings with hypodermic needles by Uighurs in Urumqi of Han Chinese. China's Academy of Military Medical Sciences said that the syringes contained nothing lethal—no viruses, radioactive substances or harmful chemicals—and no illnesses nor infections were reported. On September 12, three people were sentenced to up to fifteen years for the stabbings.

September 2009—Sweden—Abdirh Abdi Hussein, 25, a Somali hip-hop artist in Rinkeby who campaigns against al-Shabaab, was attacked on the street by a masked man who slashed him on the forehead. The attacker said in Somali, "Leave us alone or we'll kill you." No suspect had been found as of January 2010. 09099901

September 2, 2009—Greece—The Revolutionary Struggle was suspected when a car bomb injured one person in front of the Athens Stock Exchange. Police, acting on a tip, had evacuated the building.

September 2, 2009—Peru—Shining Path rebels shot down an air force helicopter trying to evacuate soldiers wounded in a rebel ambush in the Andes mountains, killing the pilot and co-pilot, both of whom held the rank of major, and wounding a third. A second helicopter rescue mission was scheduled. Machine-gun fire hit the helicopter's rotor, causing it to crash upside down.

September 4, 2009—United States—The Earth Liberation Front (ELF) used a stolen excavating machine to pull down two KRKO radio station towers in Snohomish County, Washington. The station remained on air via a backup transmitter site. ELF said, "AM radio waves cause adverse health effects including a higher rate of cancer, harm to wildlife, and the signals have been interfering with home phone and intercom lines." It called itself "an international underground organization that uses direct action in the form of economic sabotage to stop the systematic exploitation and destruction of the planet. Since its inception in North America in 1996, ELF has inflicted well over $150 million in damages to corporations and governmental agencies that are profiting from the destruction of the Earth." The group's public spokesman, Jason Crawford, told the press, "When all legal channels of opposition have been exhausted, concerned citizens have to take action into their own hands to protect life and the planet."

September 4, 2009—Germany—The United Press International reported that former Red Army Faction (RAF) member Verena Becker had been arrested in her Berlin apartment in connection with the April 1977 murder of Siegfried Buback. She reportedly had been paid $70,000 by the German intelligence service for tips that led to the arrests of several terrorists. Although RAF terrorists Christian Klar, Knut Folkerts, Guenter Sonnenberg, and Brigitte Mohnhaupt were convicted of planning and carrying out the killing, several observers had questioned the verdict. Becker had been sentenced to life in prison in 1977 for seriously injuring a police officer, but was pardoned in 1989. When she and Sonnenberg were arrested, they had the Buback murder weapon, but she was never tried in the case. She then alerted police to the hiding places of Klar and Mohnhaupt.

September 5, 2009—Afghanistan—Gunmen kidnapped *New York Times* reporter Stephen Farrell, 46, a dual Irish-U.K. national who was covering a NATO air strike on a Taliban-held area south of Kunduz. While interviewing villagers, one of them yelled, "Taliban," and Abdul Hamshid, Farrell's driver, panicked and ran off with the car keys. Gunmen hit Afghan journalist and translator Sultan Munadi with a Kalashnikov rifle, but the hostages were otherwise well-treated. The International Committee of the Red Cross, Muslim cleric Mullah Saleem, tribal elders, and relatives of kidnapped Afghan journalist Sultan Munadi, 34, negotiated with the kidnappers. After his release, Farrell wrote on his blog, "It became a tour of a Taliban-controlled district of Afghanistan, and that control appeared total.... At no point did we see a single NATO soldier, Afghan policeman, soldier, or any check to the Taliban's ability to move at will.... We were paraded to the children in the street: the infidel and his translator, to be laughed at and mocked." However, the kidnappers' "operational security was hopelessly inept." In cell phone calls, the Taliban referred to Farrell, "heedless of who was, almost certainly, monitoring the calls.... They drove with headlights full on at night as they moved us from house to house, at least three different buildings a day." During their third night of captivity, there apparently was a rescue attempt, but the kidnappers moved them to another location within minutes.

Local Afghans helped British troops in NATO's International Security Assistance Force locate the hostages, whom they freed in a commando raid on September 9, during which Munadi; Corporal John Harrison, 29, a member of the British Parachute Regiment; a woman; and a child died. The Media Club of Afghanistan complained about Munadi's death, saying the rescue was "reckless and double-standard behavior" because it was designed to save the Westerner's life and Munadi's body was left behind.

Farrell had been kidnapped in April 2004 in Falluja, Iraq, while on assignment for the *Times of London*.

On October 5, 2010, authorities detained a Taliban commander believed to be a district leader in Chahar Darah in Kunduz Province. He was believed to be implicated in the kidnapping. The detained Taliban leader was connected to senior leaders of the Islamic Movement of Uzbekistan. 09090501

September 8, 2009—Yemen—Four Yemenis, aged 20 to 33, were arrested near the U.S. Embassy in Sana'a when police found them carrying grenades, automatic weapons, and ammunition in two vehicles. They were residents of Damag and members of a large radical Sunni madrassa.

September 9, 2009—Mexico—At 1:40 p.m., Jose Flores Pereira, 44, a Bolivian drug addict and alcoholic who claimed to be a church minister, hijacked Aeromexico flight 576, a B-737-800 flying from Cancun with 7 crew and 104 American, Mexican, and British passengers. He demanded to speak to Mexican President Felipe Calderon. The hijacker said the date of 9/9/09 was significant, saying that 9/9/9 is 666 upside down. He said the divine reference made him want to alert Mexico City to an earthquake. The plane landed in Mexico City five minutes ahead of schedule. He had claimed to be one of three hijackers and that his cardboard box contained a bomb. After an hour standoff, authorities stormed the plane and escorted him and several other men off in handcuffs; the latter were soon released. The bomb was colored lights attached to a can. Police later said Flores had been convicted of armed robbery in Mexico, had lived in Mexico for seventeen years, and had attended a religious meeting in Cancun a week earlier. His wife of eighteen years, Elisa Melger, 38, mother of their three sons, said he had not used drugs or alcohol during the previous seventeen years. 09090901

September 9, 2009—Jamaica—Honorary British Consul to Montego Bay John Terry, 64, was found dead in his home in Mount Carey, St. James. Police said he had a wound to his head. Terry had been an honorary consul for thirteen years.

September 12, 2009—United States—The body of part-time census worker and teacher Bill Sparman, 51, was founded hanging from a tree near a cemetery in a remote patch of the Daniel Boone National Forest in Clay County in rural southeastern Kentucky. The word "Fed" was scrawled on his chest. The FBI was investigating whether he was a victim of anti-government violence.

September 13, 2009—Qatar—As-Sahab Media posted an eleven-minute videotape on Islamist Web sites in which Osama bin Laden asked the American people to "lend me your ears" and said,

Reasonable people knew that Obama is a powerless man who will not be able to stop the war as he promised, but instead he will drag it to the maximum possible extent.... To the American people, this is my message to you: a reminder of the reasons behind 9/11 and the wars and the repercussions that followed and the way to resolve it.... From the beginning, we have stated many times ... that the cause of our disagreement with you is your support of your allies, the Israelis, who are occupying our land in Palestine. Your stance, along with some other grievances, are what led us to carry out the events of 9/11.... Prolong the wars as much as you like. By God, we will never compromise on it [Palestine], ever.... If you think about your situation well, you will know that the White House is occupied by pressure groups... Rather than fighting to liberate Iraq, as Bush claimed, it [the White House] should have been liberated.... The time has come for you to liberate yourselves from fear and the ideological terrorism of neo-conservatives and the Israeli lobby.

Noting that Defense Secretary Robert Gates and Gen. David Petraeus were holdovers from the

Bush Administration who "promote the previous policies of fear to market the interest of big companies," he claimed,

> The bitter truth is that the neo-conservatives continue to cast their heavy shadows upon you.... If you stop the war, then fine. Otherwise we will have no choice but to continue the war of attrition against you on all possible axes [variant "on every front"), like we exhausted the Soviet Union for ten years until it collapsed with grace from Allah the Almighty and became a memory of the past.... Ask yourselves to determine your position: is your security, your blood, your children, your money, your jobs, your homes, your economy, and your reputation dearer to you than the security of the Israelis, their children, and their economy? If you choose safety and stopping wars, as opinion polls show you do, then this requires you to work to punish those on your side who play with our security. We are ready to respond to this choice on aforementioned sound and just bases. [Obama] has followed the steps of his predecessor in antagonizing Muslims ... and laying the foundation for long wars ... Obama and his administration have sowed new seeds of hatred against America. Let the American people prepare to harvest the crops of what the leaders of the White House plant in the next years and decades.

He also said an unnamed retired CIA officer had written *Confessions of a Killer for Hire* and could explain the reasons for 9/11. He said not understanding the Israeli issue "cost you a lot without any result whatsoever.... This position of yours, combined with some other injustices, pushed us to undertake the events of September 11." If Americans realized the "suffering from the injustice of the Jews ... you will realize that both our nations are victims of the policies of the White House," and a "hostage" to interest groups and companies. He noted, "You are waging a hopeless and losing war, a war in which the end is not visible on the horizon.... We will continue our war of extermination against you on all possible fronts."

September 14, 2009—United States—The Joint Terrorism Task Force in New York raided two Queens apartments after visits the previous week by airport shuttle bus driver Najibullah Zazi, 24, a suspected associate of al Qaeda. No arrests were made and no explosives were found. Zazi had moved to Colorado eight months earlier. Police confiscated a computer and several cell phones. On September 19, after Zazi had consulted an attorney and refused to continue the three-day interrogation, the FBI arrested him on charges of making false statements to federal agents. The

legal permanent resident admitted receiving weapons and explosives training from al Qaeda in Federally Administered Tribal Areas (FATA), Pakistan in 2008. Authorities also arrested Zazi's father, Mohammed Wali Zazi, 53, a naturalized U.S. citizen, in Denver; and Imam Ahmad Wais Afzali, 37, of Queens, New York City, also a permanent resident from Afghanistan, on charges of making false statements to federal agents, which carries a penalty of eight years in prison. The media suggested he was involved in a plot to set off hydrogen peroxide-based explosives somewhere in the United States, perhaps against transportation centers such as a large railroad or bus station. Authorities seized a video of New York's Grand Central Terminal. Prosecution documents filed with the court indicated that Zazi's laptop computer contained e-mailed instructions about how to build explosives and detonators. Zazi, born in Afghanistan in 1985, moved to Pakistan at age 7 and emigrated to the United States in 1999. He returned to Pakistan in 2007 and 2008 to visit his wife, according to his attorney, Arthur Folsom. The defense team included spokeswoman Wendy Aiello. A federal magistrate set bail at $50,000 for the elder Zazi when the trio first appeared in court. Afzali was represented by attorney Ronald L. Kuby. Affidavits said Afzali warned Najibullah Zazi that his phone was being monitored. Afzali's bond was set at $1.5 million. The media said the New York Police Department (NYPD) had used Afzali as an informant, but ultimately charged him, saying he had tipped off Zazi and coached him on what to say under interrogation. The press said the NYPD and FBI clashed over his use and when to arrest Zazi.

Authorities said they were seeking another dozen suspects.

On September 24, a federal grand jury in the Eastern District of New York indicted the younger Zazi for conspiracy to use weapons of mass destruction (explosive bombs) against persons or property in the United States and deemed him a flight risk. Zazi faced a life sentence for having, between August 1 and September 21, 2008, "knowingly and intentionally conspired with others to use one or more of the explosives." The affidavit said Zazi and others "traveled in interstate and foreign commerce, used e-mail and the Internet, and that this offense and the results of the offense would have affected interstate and foreign commerce." The government claimed, "Zazi received detailed bomb-making instructions in Pakistan, purchased components of improvised explosive devices, and traveled to New York City on September 10, 2009, in furtherance of his criminal plans." He went overseas to receive bomb-making instructions, conducted Internet research on explosives' components and purchased components "necessary to produce TATP (Triacetone Triperoxide) and other explosive devices." Nine pages of handwritten notes stored on Zazi's computer "contain formulations and instructions regarding the manufacture and handling of initiating explosives, main explosives charges, explosives detonators, and components of a fusing system." A Denver court dismissed the false statement charges so that he could face the more serious terrorism charge. Najibullah Zazi pleaded not guilty via attorney J. Michael Dowling in Brooklyn's U.S. District Court to the bomb-conspiracy charges on September 29. Judge Raymond J. Dearie issued a permanent order of detention. Authorities were also investigating the relation to the case of a dozen backpacks found in one of the raided apartments and an attempt to rent a U-Haul truck.

On October 4, prosecutors said Najibullah Zazi and others had flown to Peshawar, Pakistan, on August 28, 2008. His colleagues, including Naiz Khan of Queens, New York, were subsequently put under surveillance when they returned to the United States. Meanwhile, a grand jury in New York was exploring expanding the charges against Zazi, who had pleaded not guilty in U.S. District Court in Brooklyn to charges of conspiring with others to detonate explosives in the United States. Prosecutors said Zazi had purchased large quantities of beauty supplies with bomb-making ingredients. The Associated Press reported on October 15, 2009, that he was suspected of having contacts with Mustafa Abu al-Yazid, 53, alias Abu Saeed al-Masri, alias Sheikh Said, an Egyptian founder of al Qaeda who headed the group's finance committee before 9/11.

On November 2, 2009, Imam Ahmad Wais Afzali, 37, pleaded not guilty to lying to the FBI.

On January 8, 2010, taxi driver Zarein Ahmedzay was indicted by a grand jury and pleaded not guilty to lying to the FBI about his visits to Pakistan and Afghanistan. He was represented by attorney Michael Marinaccio. On January 9, 2010, Bosnian immigrant Adis Medunjanin, 25, pleaded not guilty to charges of conspiracy to commit murder in a foreign country and receiving military training from al Qaeda. He was ordered held without bond until his detention hearing, scheduled for January 14, 2010. The duo, who lived in Queens, New York, were arrested earlier in the week by FBI's Joint Terrorism Task Force and were tied to Najibullah Zazi.

Medunjanin was arrested and his passport confiscated on January 7 after he rear-ended another car while driving 90 miles per hour on an approach to the Whitestone Bridge linking Queens and the Bronx. He sustained minor injuries. He had called 911 before the accident, saying in Arabic, "We love death more than you love life ... Allah Akbar." He was represented by attorney Robert Gottlieb. Medunjanin came to the United States in 1994 and became a citizen in 2002. He and Zazi attended the same high school and frequented the same mosque.

On January 14, 2010, Zazi's uncle, Naqib Jaji, 38, was quietly arrested. He had lived in Queens before moving to Denver. He was arraigned before Judge Raymond J. Dearie of the U.S. District Court. He was released from custody on January 22. He was indicted on a sealed felony charge. He was represented by attorney Donald D. DuBoulay. The *New York Times* suggested that Jaji was cooperating with authorities.

On February 1, 2010, Denver police arrested Zazi's father, Mohammed Wali Zazi, at his suburban home after a previous charge of lying to the government was dropped while he was out on bail. Mohammed Zazi was charged with trying to dispose of chemicals and other evidence. A new indictment unsealed in a Brooklyn federal court accused him of conspiring with others to destroy or hide "glasses, masks, liquid chemicals, and containers" that were evidence in the foiled plot.

Najibullah Zazi pleaded guilty on February 22, 2010, in the U.S. District Court in Brooklyn to conspiracy to use weapons of mass destruction, to commit murder in a foreign country, and to provide material support for a terrorist organization. He faced a life term at sentencing on June 25, 2010. Zazi was represented by attorney Michael Dowling. Justice Department officials said Zazi and his confederates had planned for their subway attack to occur on September 14, 15, or 16. He told the court, "In spring 2008, I conspired with others to join the Taliban, to fight along with the Taliban against the United States. We were recruited to al Qaeda instead." He said he "had discussions with al Qaeda about targets including the New York City subway system.... In early September 2009, I drove to New York with materials to build bombs.... The plan was to use materials in the subway once the bomb was ready."

On February 25, 2010, Adis Medunjanin, 25, and Zarein Ahmedzay, 25, already in custody, were charged in the U.S. District Court in Brooklyn with plotting with Flushing High School classmate Zazi to conduct three coordinated bombings on Manhattan subways during rush hour. The duo pleaded not guilty to new charges of conspiracy to use weapons of mass destruction, conspiracy to commit murder in a foreign country, and providing material support for a terrorist organization. The duo faced life in prison if convicted. Admedzay was represented by attorney Michael A. Marinaccio. Medunjanin was earlier charged with conspiracy to commit murder in a foreign country and receiving military training from a terrorist organization. Ahmedzay had been charged with lying about his August 2008 to Pakistan with Zazi.

On March 4, 2010, Imam Ahmad Wais Afzali pleaded guilty to lying to the FBI regarding his alerting Najibullah Zazi to the investigation. Under the terms of his plea agreement, the charge was reduced from lying to federal agents "during the course of a terror investigation"—which carries a maximum sentence of eight years in prison—to simply lying to federal agents, which carries a lesser maximum sentence of five years. The plea agreement recommended a sentence of zero to six months in prison. Sentencing was scheduled for April 8. He would then leave the United States within ninety days of completion of any sentence.

On April 12, 2010, the media reported Pakistani authorities arrested an unnamed Pakistani as a fourth suspect weeks earlier.

On April 23, 2010, Zarein Ahmedzay pleaded guilty in a Brooklyn courtroom to federal charges of conspiracy to use weapons of mass destruction and providing material support to al Qaeda. He faced life in prison. He said that the suicide attacks were to occur during Ramadan. He said he, Zazi, and Adis Medunjanin met on the Pakistan-Afghanistan border in August 2008 with Saleh al-Somali, al Qaeda's chief of international operations, and Rashid Rauf, a senior al Qaeda operative. Rauf had planned a 2006 plot to destroy ten airliners flying from the United Kingdom to the United States. Rauf was killed in a missile strike in November 2008. Al-Somali was killed in a missile strike in December 2009.

On July 5, 2010, Imam Ahmad Afzali and his wife left on a 2:00 p.m. flight to live in Saudi Arabia as part of his plea deal. He had earlier pleaded guilty to one charge of lying to federal agents about tipping off Zazi. He was represented by attorney Ron Kuby.

On July 7, 2010, the United States charged Pakistani citizen Tariq ur-Rehman with aiding Najibullah Zazi's plot to bomb the New York subway system and conduct attacks in shopping centers in Manchester, United Kingdom. He said on July 8, 2010, that he would fight extradition from Pakistan.

On July 8, 2010, U.S. federal prosecutors charged Adnan el-Shukrijumah, 34, a senior al Qaeda leader, with masterminding the above plots.

On July 8, 2010, Norwegian police announced the arrests of three suspected al Qaeda members—two in Oslo and one visiting a Duisburg kindergarten near Frankfurt, Germany. They were suspected of planning terrorist attacks. Norwegian police said the trio included a 39-year-old Chinese Uighur who was a naturalized Norwegian; a 37-year-old Iraqi Kurd; and a 31-year-old Uzbek asylum-seeker who had come to Norway. Germany planned to extradite the Iraqi to Norway. The two foreign nationals had legal resident permits for Norway. The Uzbek, who had been in Norway since 2002, was represented by attorney Kjell Dahl. The Uighur and the Iraqi had been in Norway since 1999. The three had been under surveillance for more than a year and were believed members of the Turkistan Islamic Party, a Uighur separatist group operating in Waziristan, Pakistan. The Uighur was believed to have visited Waziristan within the previous two years and contacted al Qaeda. They were working on a peroxide-based explosive. A U.S. official suggested that Saleh al-Somali was involved in "conjuring it up." The Norwegian authorities made the arrests after learning that the Associated Press was going to expose the case, although the news service said it was going to wait to publish until the arrests were made.

September 14, 2009—Somalia—In a 1:00 p.m. raid on Baraawe, southern Somalia, U.S. Special Operations commandos killed Saleh Ali Saleh Nabhan, believed to have been behind the November 28, 2002, bombing of a Mombasa hotel, the August 7, 1998 bombings of the U.S. embassies in Kenya and Tanzania, and to have personally fired a missile at an Israeli jet at the Mombasa airport on November 28, 2002. The 30-something Mombasa-born Yemeni went on to become a senior instructor for Somali Islamist recruits belonging to al-Shabaab, including some Americans, and was liaison to senior al Qaeda leaders in Pakistan. Four military helicopters carried commandos firing .50 caliber machine guns and other automatic weapons at two trucks in the desert, killing six foreign fighters, including Nabhan, and three Somali al-Shabaab members. Nabhan was linked to Fazul Abdullah Mohamed, al Qaeda's East Africa operations chief.

September 15, 2009—Iran—Reuters reported that senior al Qaeda advisor Mustafa Hamid, alias Abu Walid al-Masri, called on the Taliban to kidnap foreign civilians in Afghanistan to obtain the release of prisoners held by the coalition. The Internet document apparently was written in late July and was entitled *U.S. Soldier in Afghanistan: The First Step for the Release of All Prisoners of the War on Terror.*" Hamid had been detained in Iran since 2003 but maintained contacts with jihadi Web sites.

September 16, 2009—China—The Public Security Ministry raided a bomb-making factory in Aksu, Xinjiang, some 430 miles southwest of the regional capital of Urumqi, arresting six suspects and confiscating twenty bombs.

September 17, 2009—Indonesia—Relying on a tip, Indonesian commandos raided a terrorist hideout in Solo, Central Java, killing Tanzim Qaedat al-Jihad (Organization for the Base of Jihad) leader Noordin Muhammad Top, 41, and three other terrorists during a six-hour shootout. A large bomb exploded in the house four hours into the siege. Police found 440 pounds of explosives, an M-16 rifle, a laptop computer, and documents linking Jemaah Islaymiah and al Qaeda.

Also killed was Bagus Budi Pranoto, wanted for the July 2009 suicide bombings of the JW Marriott and Ritz-Carlton hotels in Jakarta that killed nine people and wounded more than fifty others; Adib Susilo, who had rented the safe house; and Aryo Sudarsono, a protégé of Top.

September 17, 2009—Somalia—Al-Shabaab terrorists drove two stolen UN-marked trucks laden with explosives into a meeting between senior Somali and African Union officials at a fortified base in Mogadishu, killing at least twenty-one people, including fifteen peacekeepers, among them Maj. Gen. Juvenal Niyoyunguruza of Burundi, the deputy commander of the African Union peacekeeping force, and seriously injuring several other commanders and the Somali police chief. The bombs went off at a fuel depot and the office of a U.S. logistics company. The group said the attack was in retaliation for the September 14, 2009, attack that killed Saleh Ali Saleh Nabhan. The trucks were stolen in either Baidoa or Jowhar. The next day, the Islamists threatened further attacks. A Somali official said six other UN vehicles were missing.

On September 25, a Somali Mursade subclan Web site, dayniile.com, said one of the suicide attackers was an American who had lived in Washington State until 2007, when he left the United States to join the group. 09091701

September 17, 2009—Afghanistan—A Taliban car bomb killed six Italian troops, including Capt. Antonio Fortunato, and ten Afghan civilians and injured more than fifty when the driver crashed his Toyota sedan into an Italian military convoy at a traffic circle near Kabul's international airport. On September 21, a service was held for the Italian troops in St. Paul's Basilica in the Vatican.

September 18, 2009—Germany—Al Qaeda posted a twenty-six-minute video threatening that if voters did not push political parties to withdraw Germany's 4,200 troops from Afghanistan, "there will be a rude awakening" after the September 27 elections. Addressing himself to Chancellor Angela Merkel, the German-speaking terrorist said,

In a democracy, only the people can order its soldiers home. But if the German people decides for the continuation of the war, it has passed judgment upon itself and showed the whole world that in a democracy civilians are not innocent after all. If the German people wants to live in security again, it has the opportunity now.... The parliamentary election is the people's only opportunity to shape the policy of the country.... With the withdrawal of the last German soldiers, the last mujaheed also will be withdrawn from Germany.

Muslims should "stay away from anything not vital for the two weeks after the elections.... Keep your children close to you." Authorities later said the clean shaven suit-and-tie wearing terrorist was Bekkay Harrach, 32, a German-Moroccan born in Morocco and raised in Bonn, who had traveled to the West Bank in 2003.

September 18, 2009—Pakistan—A suicide bomber drove his vehicle into a hotel in Kohat in the North West Frontier Province, killing more than thirty and wounding dozens.

September 19, 2009—Qatar—Fugitive Taliban leader Mullah Omar posted a video on the Internet in which he complained that his regime's treatment of women had been misinterpreted by the West.

September 19, 2009—Colombia/United States—Colombia extradited to Florida Nancy Conde Rubio, 37, who led a finance and supply operation for the Revolutionary Armed Forces of Colombia (FARC). She faced charges of terrorism in a U.S. federal court. She was the former girlfriend of a FARC member who helped guard fifteen hostages, including Ingrid Betancourt and three U.S. military contractors, who were rescued by the Colombian military in July 2008. Conde's intercepted phone calls helped locate the rebel hideout.

September 20, 2009—Somalia—Al-Shabaab posted on extremist Web sites a forty-eight-minute video entitled *Labaik ya Osama* (*At your service, Osama*), in which the group formally pledged allegiance to Osama bin Laden and al Qaeda. Members of the group were shown training, engaging in gun battles, and chanting bin Laden's name. The video showed Omar Hammami, alias Abu Mansoor al-Amriki, who was born in Mobile, Alabama.

September 20, 2009—Germany—Al Qaeda released the week's second anti–Germany video, criticizing its military presence in Afghanistan. Authorities said the speaker was a masked Bekkay Harrach, 32, a German Moroccan who was clean shaven and wearing a suit and tie in an earlier clip in which he said Germany faced a "rude awakening" if it did not end its "war" in Afghanistan. Four days later, the United States urged Americans in Germany to exercise caution by keeping a low profile. The travel alert remained in effect until November 11, two weeks after Germany's federal elections. The United Kingdom also issued a travel alert regarding Germany.

On September 25, Stuttgart police and the Division for State Security Protection arrested a 25-year-old unemployed Turkish man whom they accused of uploading the video, which had been accessed nearly four thousand times. The suspect, who lives alone, was not believed to have been involved in producing the video, was actively involved in Web sites, and was a supporter of Islamic activities who had been under surveillance for some time.

September 21, 2009—Pakistan—The government claimed police had stopped a plan to assassinate provincial Education Minister Sarfar Hussain Babak and attack government facilities and security forces. Police engaged four militants in a gun battle that ended when a teen suicide bomber blew himself up. An informant had said that insurgents were holed up in a government high school in the North West Frontier Province. Three men escaped, including one who was wounded.

September 22, 2009—Russia—A court sentenced to terms of up to ten years ten mostly teenaged skinheads who had been convicted in Moscow earlier in September for the hate crime murder of a Kyrgyz national and the attempted murders of Chinese, Kyrgyz, and Uzbek citizens.

September 22, 2009—Qatar—Al Qaeda released a 106-minute video entitled *The West and the Dark Tunnel,* in which Ayman al-Zawahiri said that the Muslim world would overthrow U.S. President Barack Obama. He observed, "America has come in a new, hypocritical face. Smiling at us, but stabbing us with the same dagger that Bush used. God willing, your end will be at the hands

of the Muslim nation, so that the world and history will be free of your crimes and lies." The video included several appearances by Adam Gadahn, alias Azzam al-Amriki, who said "The important question is will Obama and his Democrats learn from his predecessor's mistakes or will they go on repeating them until they too leave office in humiliation and disgrace. Unfortunately, for the Democrats, and judging by their first seven and a half months at the helm of the sinking American ship, the prognosis doesn't look good."

September 22, 2009—South Africa—The U.S. Embassy, consulates in Johannesburg, Cape Town and Durban, and other U.S. aid and development offices throughout the country were ordered closed for two days after receipt of unspecified information provided by U.S. security officials.

September 23, 2009—United States—Undercover FBI agents arrested prison parolee Michael Finton, 29, alias Talib Islam, of Decatur, Illinois, for plotting to set off a truck bomb at the federal building in Springfield, Illinois, and kill its occupants. The detainee had no ties to known terrorist groups and his case was apparently unrelated to the ongoing cases in Dallas, New York, and Denver. Finton drove what he thought was a ton of explosives to the Paul Findley Federal Building and Courthouse in Springfield. Exiting the truck, he got into a waiting car with an undercover agent. A few blocks away, he tried to remotely detonate the bomb. No explosion occurred, and he was handcuffed. Finton took as his role model convicted American Taliban John Walker Lindh and said he wanted to train overseas as a jihadi fighter. An individual in Saudi Arabia funded Finton's trip to Saudi Arabia in April and May 2008. The sting operation started in 2009. Two weeks before the attempted bombing, Finton met with an undercover agent who told him the truck would contain a ton of explosives. Finton said civilian casualties would be justified. On October 7, a federal grand jury indicted him on charges of attempted murder of a federal officer or employee and attempted use of a weapon of mass destruction against property owned by the United States. 09092301

September 24, 2009—United States—Hosam Maher Husein Smadi, 19, a Jordanian, was arrested following a sting operation for plotting to bomb the sixty-story Fountain Place office tower in Dallas, Texas. Authorities said he had hoped to stage his attack on September 11. He made violent postings on an extremist chat site. He told undercover FBI agents about his plans. At his hearing on September 25, Judge Irma Ramirez set a probable cause hearing for October 5. He entered the

United States illegally and lived in Texas. He tried to set off an explosive attached to a vehicle at the base of the skyscraper. FBI officers posing as members of an al Qaeda sleeper cell were in touch with him for several months. Smadi wanted to attack the Dallas-Fort Worth airport but changed to the skyscraper that houses Wells Fargo Bank. The affidavit indicated that in a chat, Smadi told the FBI, "I have decided to change the target. God willing, the strike will be certain and strong. It will shake the currently weak economy in the state and the American nation, because this bank is one of the largest banks in the city." He claimed to be a soldier of Osama bin Laden and wanted to commit violent jihad. The FBI undercover agents tried to talk him into nonviolent methods, but, "Smadi again communicated his continuing commitment for violent jihad," according to the affidavit. He surveilled the bank in July, then told an undercover agent he would attack it on September 11. However, he waited until the end of Ramadan on September 20. He received an inert explosive from an undercover agent, drove a car into the parking garage of the tower, then tried to detonate the fake bomb via his cell phone. Instead, the number rang a phone in the FBI's possession. He faced a charge of attempting to use a weapon of mass destruction, which carries a sentence of life in prison and a $250,000 fine. On October 26, 2009, Smadi pleaded not guilty to two counts of attempting to use a weapon of mass destruction by plotting to bomb a skyscraper in Dallas, Texas. On May 25, 2010, Hosam Maher Husein Smadi agreed to a thirty-year prison sentence in exchange for pleading guilty to attempted use of a weapon of mass destruction in his foiled truck bombing. 0909 2401

September 25, 2009—Germany—Al Qaeda's As-Sahab media branch released another five-minute bin Laden video, in which he told Europeans,

> Justice demands that you lift your oppression and withdraw your troops [from Afghanistan] and reason demands that you don't hurt your neighbors. If today Europe is suffering the travails of the economic crisis, then how do you think you will fare after America pulls out, Allah permitting, for us to retaliate from the oppressor on behavior of the oppressed? ... An intelligent man doesn't waste his money and sons for a gang of criminals in Washington and it is a shameful thing for a person to be in a coalition whose supreme commander has no regard for human life and who intentionally bombs villagers from the air.... Then the Humvees come along, and when it becomes

clear to them that those killed were children, American generosity gushes forth in all its abundance and they give the victims' relatives $100 for every child killed. [Europeans would] understand the causes of the bloody events in Madrid and London [if they saw what the United States was doing in Afghanistan.] You are aware that oppression topples those who commit it and injustice has unhealthy consequences for the unjust. So on what basis are you violating what you talk about holding in high esteem, like justice and human rights?

The video included German subtitles.

September 28, 2009—Qatar—Al Qaeda deputy chief Ayman al-Zawahiri released a twenty-eight-minute video on Islamist Web sites in which he eulogized Baitullah Mehsud, the former leader of the Pakistani Taliban, who was killed in an air strike on August 5 in South Waziristan, Pakistan. He observed,

> Baitullah managed to create a massive Jihadi movement that launched wars, ambushes and battles against the crusaders and their agents in Afghanistan. He also managed to clearly show that the Pakistani government is not Islamic but instead an infidel treacherous government working as a servant to the crusaders.... To the Americans I say, you killed Mehsud, but you will not kill Islam or the Jihad. Islam doesn't end by the death of one man.... Jihad will go on until the liberation of Afghanistan and until you run away defeated from our land. The global peace and security will not be achieved unless you withdraw from the lands of the Muslims.

Al-Zawahiri also took the opportunity to insult U.S. President Barack Obama, who is popular in the Muslim world. "Here is Obama, the fraud, who pretended to be affected by the suffering of the Palestinians and then allows the settlements to flourish in the West Bank and in Jerusalem ... while pressing the weak (Arab) leaders to offer more concessions.... Is the reality of the criminal Obama now clear to us? Or do we need more crimes in Kabul, Baghdad, Mogadishu, and Gaza to be sure of his criminal nature?" He also took a swipe at German Chancellor Angela Merkel, who had told the German parliament that German troops in Afghanistan were supporting international peace and security, and all of NATO. "International peace and security will not be realized until you get out from the lands of Muslims and stop interfering in their affairs." He said that Turkey, command of the month in Afghanistan for NATO, was "participating in shedding Muslim blood."

October 2009—Israel—American-born ultra–Orthodox settler Yaakov "Jack" Teitel, 37, was arrested on terrorist charges for a series of attacks that began in 1997 against Arabs, police officers, leftists, messianic Jews, and homosexuals. Police called him a "Jewish terrorist"; his lawyer, Adi Keidar, said the West Bank settler needed psychiatric help. Keidar said Teitel admitted shooting a Palestinian man in 1997 and laying explosive devices. He also falsely admitted involvement in other crimes, such as the August 2009 shooting at a Tel Aviv gay youth club that killed two people. Teitel claimed to be doing God's work, trying to eradicate profanities against God. Teitel was arrested in Jerusalem after hanging posters in support of the Tel Aviv attack. Police spokesman Micky Rosenfeld likened him to "a serial killer. This guy was a Jewish terrorist who targeted different types of people. He was deeply involved in terrorism on all different levels." Teitel entered Israel as a tourist in 1997, smuggling a handgun on board a British Airways flight to Tel Aviv.

The first attack was the 1997 fatal shooting of Samir Balbisi, an east Jerusalem cab driver. Two months later, the same gun was used to shoot and kill a Palestinian shepherd in the South Hebron Hills. In 2008, he planted a bomb inside a package delivered to a house of a messianic Jewish family. Ami Ortiz, a 15-year-old boy, suffered serious injuries when the bomb went off. In September 2008, Teitel left explosives at the doorstep of Israel Prize winner Zeev Sternhell. The prominent left-wing activist was slightly wounded.

On November 12, 2009, Teitel was indicted on two charges of murder, four counts of attempted murder, and other charges, including carrying and manufacturing weapons. His lawyer, Adi Keidar, said Teitel had confessed to crimes he was not involved in.

October 1, 2009—Germany—Authorities arrested Adnan V., 24, a man with dual Turkish-German citizenship. He was suspected of recruiting supporters for al Qaeda and of procuring bomb-making materials. Police searched an Offenbach apartment and a Frankfurt business.

October 3, 2009—United States—Authorities arrested David Coleman Headley, 49, a U.S.-born resident of Chicago, at O'Hare Airport as he was ready to board a plane to Pakistan. He had lived in Pakistan as a youth. He changed his name from Daood Gilani in 2006 to avoid suspicion when he traveled. He told the FBI that he had planned to attack a building occupied by *Morgenavisen Jyllands-Posten*, a Danish newspaper in Copenhagen that in 2005 had published cartoons of the prophet Muhammad. He reportedly had conspired to do so during a meeting in January 2009

in the Federally Administered Tribal Area region of northwestern Pakistan with Ilyas Kashmiri, operational chief of the 313 Brigade commando group—an al Qaeda affiliate in Pakistan—and former Pakistani military officer Tahawwur Hussain Rana, 48. The affidavit said Headley traveled to Denmark to surveil the newspaper for attacks, which the trio called "the Mickey Mouse Project." Authorities found in his checked bags a memory stick with ten videos of the entrance to the Copenhagen newspaper, military sites, and Copenhagen's central train station. The group talked about assassinating the paper's cartoonist and cultural editor, who they incorrectly believed was Jewish. After a predatory strike that was reported—incorrectly—to have killed Kashmiri, Headley turned to another group, Lashkar-e-Taiba. Headley was represented by John Theis. Headley was charged with conspiracy to murder and maim in a foreign country.

Rana was arrested on October 18 and charged with conspiring to support terrorists. Rana, owner of First World Immigration Services, which authorities said was a front to explain purchases made by the unemployed Headley, was represented by attorney Patrick W. Blegan. Pakistan-born Rana became a Canadian citizen who lived in Chicago. He and Headley attended a military school in Hasan Abdal, Pakistan.

October 4, 2009—Qatar—Al Qaeda deputy Ayman al-Zawahiri posted a ten-minute eulogy to Libyan terrorist Ali Mohammed Abdel-Aziz al-Fakheri, alias Ibn al-Sheikh al-Libi, who he called "a veteran fighter in repelling the attacks of the hypocrite agents who were working for the crusaders against the mujahideens." Al-Libi had falsely claimed a link between al Qaeda and Saddam Hussein's regime. Human rights activists claimed al-Libi died in May, killed,

> on behalf of the American criminal monster, who fools us as the smiling Obama who seeks peace and the defender of human rights.... Obama claims to respect human rights and condemn torture, and here I will not ask him about the expansion of the Bagram prison, and will not ask how he forgave the crimes of the CIA executioners. I will not ask him about his decision not to release the detainee abuse photos and will not ask him about the program to hand over detainees to other countries to be tortured, and will not ask him about the assassination teams that are deployed to assassinate anyone who is suspected to be an extremist.

Al-Zawahiri threatened a continuation of attacks, calling U.S. officials, "murderers, criminals, vampires.... We will bleed your blood and drain your economy until you stop your crimes, you arrogant tyrants, and we will, God willing, avenge the killing of each mujahideen, widow and orphan Muslim." He called on the United States to "apologize and pay financial and moral compensation" for those detained. "This is the least to be accepted from you and from your government."

October 5, 2009—Pakistan—At noon, a suicide bomber in his 20s and wearing a paramilitary Frontier Corps uniform set off a vest containing 15 pounds of explosives in a reception area at the World Food Program (WFP) offices in Islamabad, killing five—four Pakistani women and an Iraqi man—and wounding eight. The UN temporarily closed its WFP office. Officials said the dead were finance assistant Mohammed Wahab, senior finance assistant Abid Rehman, receptionist Gulrukh Tahir, office assistant Farzana Barkat, and Iraqi national Botan Ahmed Ali al-Hayawi, an information and communications technology officer. Azam Tariq, Pakistani Taliban spokesman, claimed credit. 09100501

October 6, 2009—India—Maoist Naxalite rebels beheaded police officer Francis Induwar after the government refused to release London-educated Maoist leader Kobad Ghandy.

October 6, 2009—Uganda—Somali Defense Minister Yusuf Mohamed Siad was kidnapped as he walked out of a Kampala mosque. 09100601

October 7, 2009—Germany—At 6:00 a.m., more than 150 German investigators raided twenty-seven apartments in Berlin, searching for "potentially violent Islamic extremists." The raids concentrated on fifteen suspects believed plotting bombings in Russia to be directed by a Berlin-based Islamic organization. Some may have been involved in "jihadi training" in camps along the Pakistan-Afghanistan border. Over the past week, three suspects were banned from leaving through Berlin's Tegel Airport. Most of the suspects were Germans, but the group included Turkish, Algerian, Lebanese, Dutch, and Romanian nationals. Police seized computers, memory devices, and clothes.

October 7, 2009—China—Al Qaeda strategist Abu Yahia al-Libi posted an Arabic-language video on Islamist Web sites in which he called on China's Uighurs to engage in jihad against the Chinese government. He said "There is no way for salvation and to lift this oppression and tyranny unless you ... seriously prepare for jihad in the name of God and carry your weapons against the ruthless brutal invader thugs," referring to Hans in western China's Xinjiang Province. Re-

ferring to recent violence in the area, he observed, "What we saw and heard in the recent events in Turkistan was not accidental and didn't happen overnight. This is an intifada [an uprising] and a usual response to the decades of oppression, the organized cleansing and the systematic repression until the people had enough.... This was not the first uprising that the oppressed Muslim people carried out, because they keep grieving and struggling to preserve their identity against the aggressors." He called upon the world's Muslims to support the Uighurs. He predicted that China would fail the same way the Soviets failed in their invasion of Afghanistan, saying, "To you, the state of atheism and obstinacy: You are coming to an end and you will face the same fate of the Russian bear of disintegration and division. You will encounter the same defeat when your nation will fight in its own backyard the humble minority of Muslims who are stronger in faith."

October 8, 2009—Afghanistan—At 8:30 a.m., the Taliban set off a suicide car bomb on the corner of Passport Lane and the Indian Embassy near the Interior Ministry, killing seventeen—including two Afghan police officers and fifteen civilians—and wounding sixty-three. Three guards posted around the embassy's fortified wall were slightly injured by shrapnel. The Ali Abad Hospital cared for eighteen of the injured, including Golam Sakhih, 46, a gardener at a nearby hotel, who had shards of glass in his leg. None of the embassy employees were hurt. Hours later, the UN Security Council unanimously condemned the attack and extended the mandate of NATO-led military forces for a year. The Taliban said an Afghan drove the SUV and intended to attack the embassy. The Taliban claimed the bomb killed thirty-five, including senior Indian Embassy officials and international and Afghan police officers. Indian pundits blamed Pakistan's Inter-Services Intelligence. 09100801

October 8, 2009—France—Police in Vienne (near Lyon), France arrested Adlene Hicheur, 32, a French particle physicist born in Setif, Algeria, and Halim, his 25-year-old brother, on suspicion of passing information on possible terrorist targets in France to members of al Qaeda in the Islamic Maghreb. He was working on an antimatter project at the Large Hadron Collider, the world's most powerful particle accelerator, in the 17-mile-long tunnel under the France-Switzerland border. The Collider is at CERN, Europe's particle physics lab near Geneva. He was a postdoc at the Swiss Federal Institute of Technology in Lausanne since 2003. The scientist had written of his desire to carry out attacks. As of October 14, Halim had been released and Adlene had not been charged. Adlene received his doctorate in 2003 from the University of Savoid in Annecy, France. He was an author on more than one hundred physics papers. He had worked at the Rutherford Appleton Laboratory at Chilton, Oxfordshire, United Kingdom.

October 8, 2009—India—More than two hundred Maoist Naxalite rebels ambushed forty-five police commandos in Laheri village in Maharashtra State, killing seventeen of them in a three-hour gun battle and taking their weapons.

October 9, 2009—Pakistan—In a morning attack, a suicide car bomber in Peshawar killed 52 people and injured 106 when his 50 kilograms of explosives went off near a bus stop in the Khyber Bazaar.

October 10, 2009—Pakistan—Nine Amjad Farooqi gunmen took thirty-nine civilian and military hostages at the army headquarters in Rawalpindi. The initial gun battle killed four gunmen and six guards. The gunmen wore camouflage and used a minivan to attack the headquarters checkpoint. The gunmen demanded the release of several militants in Pakistani custody. The hostages were freed after a twenty-two-hour siege in which three soldiers and three hostages were killed and five injured. One terrorist wearing a suicide vest was shot to death. Two others blew themselves up in another part of the building. The press reported that twenty people, including nine terrorists and eight soldiers, died in the incident. Aqil, aka Dr. Usman, who led the attack, was injured when he set off explosives and was captured. He was believed to have masterminded the March 2009 attack on the Sri Lankan cricket team in Lahore, Pakistan. He was also believed to have been involved in the July 2007 attempt to attack the airplane of former Pakistani President Pervez Musharraf. He was from Pakistani's Punjab Province, as were four other militants. Five were from South Waziristan.

October 10, 2009—Pakistan—An Amjad Farooqi bomb targeted against a military vehicle at a security checkpoint in the Shangla district in the Swat Valley killed forty-one and injured forty-five.

October 11, 2009—Northern Ireland—The Irish National Liberation Army, a Provisional Irish Army splinter group, renounced violence and said it would soon hand over weapons and use "exclusively peaceful means." It vowed to cooperate with Canadian Gen. John D. Chastelain, leader of the international disarmament commission overseeing the disarming of the loyalist and republican terrorists.

October 11, 2009—Somalia—Sheik Da'ud Mohamed Garane, al-Shabaab's appointed governor of Gedo region in Somalia, threatened to attack targets in Kenya. He told two hundred people in southwestern Somalia, "Our intelligence sources have already confirmed that Kenya is giving training and military equipment to Somali men in three different areas along its border with Somalia. These men are being prepared to attack the peaceful positions we control. But let me tell Kenya that we will do all we can to prevent that to happen."

October 11, 2009—Philippines—Irish priest Michael Sinnott was kidnapped during an evening stroll in his garden at his missionary home on Mindanao Island by four or five members of the Moro Islamic Liberation Front. They threw him into a pickup which they drove to a beach, got out, burned the vehicle, and escaped with him in a speedboat. He was freed on November 12. Manila said no ransom was paid. 09101101

October 12, 2009—India—Maoist Naxalite terrorists blew up a railway track and a bridge, fired at a bus, blocked a highway, and burned down a truck before fleeing in mineral-rich Jharkhand State. They also called for a two-day strike over a planned government offensive in two of the eleven rebel strongholds chosen for the operation.

October 15, 2009—Pakistan—Five Amjad Farooqi attacks in Lahore, Kohat, and Peshawar killed thirty-nine people. At 9:00 a.m. at the Federal Investigation Agency in Lahore, a terrorist used grenades and a rifle to enter a broken main gate and kill six people. The Taliban bombed a police station in Khoat and a government residence in Peshawar. Half of the dead were security police; ten militants died and two were captured.

October 16, 2009—Australia—Five men—Mohamed Ali Elomar, Abdul Rakib Hasan, Khaled Cheikho, Moustafa Cheikho, and Mohammed Omar Jamal, aged 25 to 44, who were arrested in a November 2005 raid on a home, were convicted in the Supreme Court of New South Wales in Sydney of "conspiracy to do acts in preparation for a terrorist act or acts." Some three hundred witnesses testified during the record ten-month, $27.5 million trial. They had pleaded guilty at the start of their trial. The jury deliberated for twenty-three days. Sentencing was scheduled for December 14, 2009. They faced life in prison. Prosecutors used eighteen hours of taped phone conversations that showed the group was planning a terrorist attack in Australia. They were linked to four others who had earlier pleaded guilty to acquiring weapons, hydrochloric acid, and bombs for an attack. Three of them had trained at paramilitary camps in western New South Wales to prepare for the attacks. The prosecution said that the attack would be revenge for Australia's sending troops to Iraq and Afghanistan. They had stockpiled thirty thousand rounds of ammunition, bomb-making equipment, and explosive chemicals, along with extremist literature, instructional DVDs for building homemade bombs, and suicide bomb-belts. One of the men had links to Lashkar-e-Taiba in Pakistan.

October 18, 2009—Iran—Jundallah (Soldiers of God) was suspected when a suicide bomber killed forty-two people, including five senior commanders of the Revolutionary Guard and more than twenty tribal leaders, in the Pishin district of Sistan-Baluchistan Province, near the Pakistan border. Among the dead were Gen. Noor Ali Shoushtari, deputy commander of the Guard's ground force, and Rajab Ali Mohammad-Zadeh, a chief provincial Guard commander for the area. Some local Web sites suggested more than sixty were killed. More than two dozen others were wounded. The commanders were in a car en route to a meeting with local tribal leaders. Press TV claimed there was an explosion at the meeting at the inauguration of the Local Achievements Exhibition in Pishin and another one at another convoy of Guards.

October 19, 2009—Spain—Spain arrested two armed Basque Nation and Liberty (ETA) suspects, including Aitor Elizaran Aguilar, 30, who ran ETA's political policy-making branch, and a woman, Oihana San Vicente, 32, who worked in ETA's political apparatus. Spain credited a joint French-Spanish operation for the takedown. The duo carried fake IDs and were driving a car stolen the previous week.

October 20, 2009—Pakistan—Six people were killed and twenty-nine wounded when suicide bombers detonated explosives in the men's and women's sections of International Islamic University.

October 20, 2009—United States—The Supreme Court announced it would determine whether judges have the power to release Guantanamo Bay prisoners into the United States if deemed not be enemy combatants. The case, *Kiyemba v. Obama*, involved the Uighurs still held at the prison facility.

October 21, 2009—United States—Tarek Mehanna, 27, a dual Egypt-U.S. citizen pharmacist

who lived with his parents in Sudbury, Massachusetts, was charged with one count of conspiracy to provide material support for terrorists. He distributed a video that he said showed the "mutilation and abuse" of the bodies of U.S. personnel in Iraq and the setting off of a roadside bomb in Iraq that killed U.S. soldiers. An FBI agent said that Mehanna "reveled in the death of United States servicemen overseas." The acting U.S. Attorney for Massachusetts said that Mehanna and other conspirators wanted to kill one or two members of the U.S. administration, fire automatic weapons at mall entrances and then kill first responders. The mall plot fell through when the conspirators could not get automatic weapons via Islamic convert Daniel Maldonado, who was said to have contacts with gang members. Mehanna faced fifteen years in prison and a $250,000 fine. His two co-conspirators included Ahmad Abousamra and another man whose identity was not released. The prosecution team said the trio traveled to Pakistan, Iraq, Syria, and Yemen and sought training from the Taliban. The prosecution said that the "conspiracy to kill, kidnap, maim, or injure persons or damage property in a foreign country, and extraterritorial homicide of a U.S. national" started in 2001 and lasted until May 2008. Mehanna was represented by attorney J. W. Carney, Jr. The affidavit said the conspirators planned "violent jihad against American interests and ... would talk about fighting jihad and their desire to die on the battlefield ... the co-conspirators attempted to radicalize others and inspire each other by, among other things, watching and distributing jihadi videos." Mehanna had been arrested in November 2008 as he was about to board a flight at Logan International Airport in Boston and indicted in January 2009 on charges of lying to a joint terrorism task force regarding Maldonado, who was captured by Kenyan troops while fighting with al Qaeda in Somalia. Maldonado was sentenced to ten years after pleading guilty to receiving military-type training from al Qaeda.

Mehanna was held without bail on October 21, 2009, by Magistrate Judge Leo T. Sorokin of the federal court in Boston. A detention and probable cause hearing was scheduled for October 30.

October 22, 2009—Sudan—Several armed men kidnapped Gauthier Lefevre, a French staffer for the International Committee of the Red Cross (ICRC), near Al-Geneina in West Darfur. His ICRC vehicle was clearly marked with Red Cross logos. 09102201

October 22, 2009—Northern Ireland—A bomb exploded at a British Territorial Army base in

North Belfast at 1:00 a.m., causing no injuries. Irish Republican Army splinter groups were suspected.

October 22, 2009—Algeria—Terrorists ambushed a convoy of private security contractors with the Canadian engineering and construction firm SNC-Lavalin in a remote mountainous area near Tizi Ouzou. Seven Algerian police officers died and two others were wounded in the attack east of Algiers. No foreigners were harmed. The local al Qaeda affiliate was suspected. 09102202

October 22, 2009—Nigeria—Royal Dutch Shell offered to provide training and financial assistance to repentant rebels who accepted the government's amnesty for the Movement for the Emancipation of the Niger Delta militants.

October 22, 2009—Pakistan—At 9:30 a.m., two Taliban gunmen on a motorcycle fired at an unarmored Pakistani army jeep stuck in traffic in residential Islamabad, killing Brig. Moeenuddin Ahmed Haider, who was on bereavement leave (his father-in-law had died) from a posting with the UN peacekeeping force in the Sudan, and another military officer in the vehicle. The driver was critically wounded; some reports said he was killed. Haider was on his way to army headquarters in Rawalpindi. The gunmen escaped.

October 23, 2009—Italy—Libyan citizen Mohamed Game was seriously wounded when he set off a homemade bomb at an Italian military barracks in Milan. An Italian soldier was slightly injured. Game and his two accomplices did not fit the normal profile of a homegrown terrorist, being moderately involved in local religious activities. 09102301

October 23, 2009—Pakistan—Five civilians and two security personnel were killed and thirteen injured when a suicide bomber riding a bicycle set off his explosives at the Kamra checkpoint near the Pakistan Aeronautical Complex, a military facility 40 miles northwest of Islamabad. Some observers believed the site is associated with the country's nuclear weapons program.

At least fifteen people were wounded, nine seriously, in a car bomb explosion near the upscale Swan restaurant in Peshawar's residential Hayatabad neighborhood. Police arrested two suspects at the scene.

Sixteen people died when a bus which they were taking to a wedding hit a roadside bomb in the Mohmand tribal region.

October 25, 2009—Nigeria—The Movement for the Emancipation of the Niger Delta announced an indefinite cease-fire.

October 25, 2009—Iraq—Bombs exploded outside government buildings in Baghdad, killing 160 people, including 30 Iraqi children riding on a bus, and injuring 540 people, including 3 American security contractors. One bomb went off at 10:15 a.m. outside Baghdad's Provincial Council governorate building, another at the Justice Ministry, at 10:30 a.m. Among the dead were 30 children in a minibus outside the Justice Ministry building. That bomb was hidden in a white Department of Water pickup that was stolen in Falluja. The Islamic State of Iraq claimed credit.

On October 31, a man being questioned for the bombings grabbed a guard's gun while being escorted to get a drink of water, wounded the guard, broke into an investigator's office, and fatally shot investigator Maj. Arkan Hachim, who returned fire after he was wounded and shot the suspect to death. 09102501

October 27, 2009—United Kingdom—Seven former Guantanamo Bay detainees asked the High Court in London to reject the government's request for secret sessions on their allegations that they were tortured at Gitmo, Pakistan, Afghanistan, and Morocco. The ex-detainees were Binyam Mohamed, Bisher al-Rawi, Jamil el-Banna, Richard Belmar, Omar Deghayes, Moazzam Begg, and Martin Mubanga.

October 28, 2009—United States—The FBI fatally shot Luqman Ameen Abdullah, 53, alias Christopher Thomas, leader of a radical fundamentalist Sunni Islam separatist group and the radical mosque Masjid al-Haqq, in a gun battle at a warehouse in Dearborn, Michigan, after he and ten followers failed to surrender on several criminal charges, including conspiracy to sell stolen goods and illegal possession and sale of firearms. In three raids, police arrested six of his followers on charges of illegal possession and sale of firearms and conspiracy to sell stolen goods. Abdullah was an imam of a faction of Ummah ("Brotherhood"), a radical group whose primary mission is to establish an Islamic state within the United States. Some of his followers converted to Islam while in prison. He told them stealing was acceptable so long as they prayed. He skimmed 20 percent of the profits from furs, electronics, and other items his followers fenced. A search of his duplex yielded weapons, including an M-16.

October 28, 2009—Pakistan—A car bomb packed with 250 pounds of explosives went off in the Mina Bazaar in old town Peshawar, killing one hundred people, including sixty women and children, and injuring more than two hundred during a visit to Pakistan by U.S. Secretary of State

Hillary Clinton. Many buildings, including a mosque, collapsed, and scores of stores were set on fire. No group claimed credit, although the Taliban was suspected.

October 28, 2009—Afghanistan—At 5:45 a.m., three Taliban gunmen wearing suicide vests and police uniforms were shot to death by UN guards after killing eight people, including six UN workers—among them five foreigners—including an American security guard and two members of the Afghan security forces at Kabul's Bakhtar guesthouse hosting UN staffers. Nine UN staffers were injured. The gunmen used grenades and rockets in the attack. Taliban spokesman Zabiullah Mujahid said the raid aimed at warning people to avoid participating in the November 7 runoff presidential election. Twenty poll-watchers were staying at the facility. Oamrullah Saleh, chief of Afghan intelligence, said that the attack was the work of Afghan warlord Jalaluddin Haqqani's group and al Qaeda member Ajmal, who was hiding in Waziristan. Saleh said that eight Afghans were arrested, including an imam who provided safe haven. The three suicide attackers were from Pakistan's Swat Valley. 09102801

October 28, 2009—Somalia—Islamic gunmen attempted to assassinate Somali President Sheikh Sharif Sheikh Ahmed in a gun battle with African Union peacekeepers that left five people dead and sixteen injured on Maka Al-Mukarama, which links the airport and the presidential palace in Mogadishu. He was returning from Yemen when the convoy took mortar fire.

October 29, 2009—Pakistan—The Pakistani military found a passport of Said Bahaji, a 9/11 suspect, in Sherwangai, a South Waziristan town captured from Taliban terrorists. The passport of the German citizen of Moroccan descent included an August 2001 Pakistani visa. Bahaji entered Karachi, Pakistan, on September 4, 2001. He had lived with 9/11 hijack leader Muhammad Atta in Germany. Bahaji was a member of a cell in Hamburg that funded the 9/11 hijackers. He is wanted in Germany and Spain on terrorism charges.

Soldiers also found a Spanish passport for Raquel Burgos Garcia, who is married to Amer Azizi, a Moroccan member of al Qaeda suspect in the 9/11 attacks in 2001 and the 3/11 Madrid train bombings in 2004. Her family had not heard from her since 2001. Her passport had visas to India and Iran. Authorities also found a Moroccan document with her photo.

November 2009—Mali—Al Qaeda in the Islamic Maghreb (AQIM) kidnapped a French man in Menaka. In early March 2010, AQIM released Pierre Camatte following a Mali court decision to release four jailed AQIM members. 09119901

November 1, 2009—Saudi Arabia—Authorities in Riyadh searching a vacant house found an al Qaeda weapons cache that included 281 assault rifles and 51 ammunition boxes.

November 2, 2009—Pakistan—A suicide bomber rode up in a motorcycle and set off explosives outside a National Bank branch where people had queued up for their monthly checks, killing thirty-five, including two women and four soldiers, and injuring sixty-five, including nine soldiers, in the Cannt area of Rawalpindi. The bank is near the army's headquarters.

A separate suicide bomber injured seventeen people at the Babu Sabu police checkpoint in Lahore.

November 3, 2009—Israel—Israeli Navy commandos stopped the Antigua-flagged cargo ship *Francop*, which was loaded with hundreds of tons of arms heading from Iran to Syria. The arms, which Israel said were destined for Hizballah, included more than forty containers of missiles, rockets, light arms, and mortars.

November 5, 2009—United States—At 1:00 p.m. yelling "God is Great" in Arabic, Muslim psychiatrist and Army Maj. Nidal Malik Hasan, 39, shot to death thirteen people and wounded forty-three at the Soldier Readiness Center of Fort Hood, Texas, before being wounded by four bullets in a gun battle with civilian police Sgt. Kimberly Munley, 34, who was injured in the thighs and a wrist, and army civilian police Sgt. Mark Todd, who arrived minutes after she did. Many of the wounded had multiple gunshot wounds. The 36th Engineer Brigade suffered the majority of casualties. Hasan carried two pistols and more than a half-dozen magazines of ammunition, firing at least one hundred rounds at unarmed soldiers. Initial reports of more than one gunman proved false; two individuals detained for questioning were soon released.

Hasan was born at Arlington Hospital, Virginia, to parents who emigrated from Jordan. He graduated from William Fleming High School in Roanoke, Virginia, then enlisted in the U.S. Army. He graduated from Virginia Tech in 1997 with a biochem major, then picked up a doctorate in psychiatry from the Uniformed Services University of the Health Sciences in Bethesda. Hasan had served at Walter Reed Army Medical Center for eight years, working with veterans suffering post-traumatic stress. Hasan had counseled soldiers at the psychiatric facility on campus. He had poor fitness reports as a psychiatrist. He had attended the Muslim Community Center in Silver Spring, Maryland, for daily prayers, often in his army fatigues. He had often railed against the U.S. war on terror, saying it was actually a war against Muslims, and had complained about being scheduled to go to Afghanistan the next month. An individual with the screen name Nidal Hasan had posted praises of suicide bombers on the Internet six months earlier. He had wanted a discharge from the army, having endured anti–Muslim harassment since 9/11. He was single with no children and described by many as a loner.

One of Hasan's pistols, a $1,100 FN Herstal Five-Seven that can handle thirty-round magazines, came from Guns Galore in Killeen, Texas.

Among the dead were:

- Spec. Jason Dean Hunt, 22, who had served for three and a half years, including a tour in Iraq. He was married in August in Oklahoma City.
- Pfc. Michael Pearson, 21, scheduled to deploy to Afghanistan as a bomb disposal specialist
- Pvt. Francheska Velez, 21, en route from Iraq to Chicago after learning she was pregnant with her first child. She had disarmed bombs in Iraq. Her father was Colombian and her mother Puerto Rican. She had been in the army for three years.
- Nurse practitioner Russell Seager, 51, from Mount Pleasant, Wisconsin, was preparing to deploy to Iraq. In August, he was profiled by WUWM–Milwaukee Public Radio.
- Physician's assistant Michael G. Cahill, 62, a retired chief warrant officer in the National Guard and a physician's assistant for twenty-two years. He had worked as a contract civilian employee for six years at Fort Hood. He was four years from retiring.
- Sgt. Amy Krueger, 29, from rural Wisconsin, who dropped her studies in social work a week after 9/11 to enlist in the army. She had earlier deployed to Afghanistan, where she was slated to return in December. She was with the Madison, Wisconsin-based 467th Medical Detachment.
- Pfc. Aaron Nemelka, 19, had been in the army for over a year and had signed up to defuse bombs. He was a 2008 graduate of West Jordan (Utah) High School.
- Pfc. Kham Xiong, 23, from St. Paul, Minnesota, whose father fought the Communists during the Vietnam War. He was the first casualty, waiting to get a flu shot and a vision test.
- Staff Sgt. Justin M. DeCrow, 32, a thirteen-year veteran who had decided to become a civilian. He had been deployed in South Korea. He had known his wife, Marikay, since first grade.

- Retired Maj. John P. Gaffaney, 56, a psychiatric nurse for the San Diego government for twenty years who had spent three years before successfully persuading a review board for the National Guard to return him to active duty despite his hearing loss. He had reported to Fort Hood on November 1.
- Spec. Frederick Greene, 29, from Mountain City, Tennessee, nicknamed "Silent Soldier," was to deploy to Afghanistan. He had been married less than two years and enlisted six months after the wedding. He served in the 16th Signal Company at Fort Hood.
- Army Reserve Lt. Col. Juanita Warman, 55, a single mother with two daughters and six grandchildren, who worked her way through the University of Pittsburgh. She had orchestrated the creation of the post-traumatic stress disorder program of the Yellow Ribbon Reintegration Program. The physician's assistant and nurse was to deploy to Iraq. She hailed from Havre de Grace, Maryland. She was buried in Section 59 of Arlington National Cemetery.
- Maj. Libardo Eduardo Caraveo, 52, an army psychologist from Ciudad Juarez, Mexico, and Woodbridge, Virginia, who had arrived at Fort Hood the day before he was murdered. He was slated to deploy to Afghanistan. He was a graduate of the University of Texas at El Paso, first in his family to attend college. He earned his doctorate in psychology from the University of Arizona.

The wounded included:

- Pfc. Najee Hull
- Pvt. Joseph Foster

Investigators determined that Hasan had held his mother's funeral at the Dar al-Jihrah Islamic Center in Falls Church, Virginia, on May 31, 2001, the same mosque that 9/11 hijackers Nawaf al-Hazmi and Hani Hanjour had attended the previous month. Since-radicalized Imam Anwar al-Aulaqi had served at the mosque at that time. Al-Aulaqi moved on to London, where he preached Islamist extremism. Having moved on to Yemen, he exchanged e-mails with Hasan, and praised Hasan's attack. Hasan also visited radical Islamist Web sites.

On November 13, Hasan's lawyer, retired Army Col. John Galligan, said his client was paralyzed from the waist down, had severe pain in his hands, and likely would never walk again.

The same day, Hasan was charged with thirteen counts of premeditated murder, which carries the death penalty. On December 2, 2009, Hasan was charged with an additional thirty-two counts of attempted premeditated murder of the thirty soldiers and two civilians who were injured.

On April 9, 2010, Nidal Hasan was airlifted from a San Antonio military hospital to Bell County Jail in Belton, where he would be kept in isolation under twenty-four-hour watch in a 12×15 foot cell in the jail infirmary.

Hasan made his first Article 32 courtroom appearance on June 1, 2010, but the trial was delayed for four months.

On October 5, 2010, Hasan was ordered to undergo a mental evaluation to determine his fitness to stand trial. John Galligan served as Hasan's lead attorney.

On November 6, 2012, 148 victims and family members sued the federal government for compensation and sued al-Aulaqi's estate for compensation and punitive damages.

November 5, 2009—Afghanistan—A Norwegian journalist and his Afghani translator were kidnapped in the east near the Pakistan border while filming a documentary. He phoned the Norwegian Embassy the next day to report his kidnapping. The duo were freed on November 12. 09110501

November 8, 2009—Pakistan—A Taliban suicide car bomber killed twelve people, including Matni-area Mayor Abdul Malik, a little girl, and five young men, and injured thirty-six, including the mayor's son, when the terrorist set off 10 kilograms of explosives in Adazai, 10 miles south of Peshawar. Malik had earlier been a Taliban supporter, but switched sides. Taliban spokesman Omar claimed credit, saying, "Our local fighters carried out this attack. He had set up a militia. He was supporting killings of our men. He was interfering in our matters."

Meanwhile, Islamabad police shot to death a would-be suicide bomber at a checkpoint.

November 9, 2009—Pakistan—A suicide bomber set off his rickshaw near a group of Peshawar policemen, killing three people and wounding five.

November 10, 2009—Pakistan—A suicide bomber drove his red car, loaded with 110 pounds of explosives, into a donkey cart at a congested traffic circle in Charsadda, 18 miles north of Peshawar, killing twenty-six, including six children and three women, and injuring sixty. Police Chief Mohammed Riaz Khan, whose two-car convoy was leaving the area, said he was the target.

November 11, 2009—Somalia—Abdi Hassan Abdi, a Somali, tried to board a Daallo Airlines flight scheduled to fly from Mogadishu airport to Hargeisa, then Djibouti, and then Dubai, with a plastic bag containing 600 grams of ammonium nitrate and a half liter of concentrated sulfuric acid in a plastic bottle, along with a syringe containing 5 milliliters of an unidentified liquid. He was the last person to board the flight. African Union peacekeeping forces arrested Abdi after they searched him and discovered the chemicals. They handed him over to the Somali National Security Agency. The case was similar to a Nigerian's attempt to bomb a Northwest Airlines flight from Amsterdam to Detroit on Christmas Day. 0911 1101

November 12, 2009—Pakistan—Two motorcycle riders shot to death Abul Hassan Jaffri, Pakistani director of public relations for the Iranian Consulate in Peshawar, near his home as he was on his way to work. No group claimed credit for killing the Shi'ite Muslim, although Iran blamed Jundallah. 09111201

November 13, 2009—United States—Attorney General Eric Holder announced that 9/11 suspects Khalid Sheik Mohammed, Ramzi Bin al-Shibh, Walid bin Attash, Ali Abdul Aziz Ali, and Mustafa Ahmed al-Hawsawi would be tried in New York City. Five other Guantanamo Bay detainees—Omar Khadr, Mohammed Kamin, Ibrahim al-Qosi, Noor Uthman Muhammed, and Abd al-Rahim al-Nashiri—would be tried at military commissions.

November 13, 2009—Italy—Authorities announced the arrests of seventeen people involved in a terrorist financing ring. Italian police arrested six people on charges of criminal association and falsifying documents. Austrian arrested two others; the investigation involved police in the United Kingdom, France, Spain, Switzerland, Austria, and Algeria. The group raised 1 million Euros during three years via muggings, burglaries, and other thefts, sending the money to Algeria. The group created fake IDs to travel between North Africa and Europe.

November 13, 2009—Pakistan—A suicide car bomber killed sixteen and wounded more than thirty in an attack at the gate of the Inter-Services Intelligence directorate headquarters in Peshawar.

November 15, 2009—Germany—The Federal Criminal Police Office announced that they believed that Jan Schneider, alias Hamza, a Kazakhstan-born ethnic German convert to Islam, may be traveling to Afghanistan and planning to attack German military or civilian targets in Afghanistan.

November 18, 2009—Pakistan—A suicide bomber killed nineteen outside a Peshawar court house. He had arrived by taxi at a lower courthouse and was being searched by police at the gate when he set off his explosives.

November 19, 2009—Pakistan—Two police officers were killed after a remotely-detonated bomb went off shortly after midnight, destroying a police vehicle and wounding four others in Peshawar.

November 22, 2009—Northern Ireland—A 400-pound car bomb left by Provisional Irish Republican Army (IRA) dissidents outside a police reform headquarters in Belfast failed to go off.

Meanwhile, police arrested four other IRA dissidents after a gun battle.

November 23, 2009—United States—The federal government charged eight suspects with recruiting at least twenty young Somali Americans from Minnesota to join the al-Shabaab Islamist insurgency in Somalia. Mahamud Said Omar, a U.S. permanent resident, had been arrested two weeks earlier in the Netherlands. He had funded airfare and AK-47s for several of the youths to join the al Qaeda affiliate. The United States requested his extradition. The seven others were outside the United States and not in custody. Among them were Cabdulaahi Ahmed Faarax and Abdiweli Yassin Isse, who were charged on October 9, a day after they told a U.S. border agent that they were going from San Diego to Tijuana, Mexico. The FBI said they had conspired to recruit and pay for six Somali Americans to go abroad in December 2007. One of their recruits was Shirwa Ahmed, 27, a Minneapolis college student who blew himself up in one of five coordinated attacks that killed twenty-two UN aid workers in Somalia in October 2008. Charged with conspiracy to support terrorism and kill outside the United States, firearms offenses, and solicitation to commit violent crime were Ahmed Ali Omar, Khalid Mohamud Abshir, Zakaria Maruf, Mohamed Abdullahi Hassan, and Mustafa Ali Salat. They were all U.S. permanent residents who left for Somalia between December 2007 and August 2008. A key trainer for the recruits was Saleh Ali Nabhan, 30, a liaison to al Qaeda in Pakistan.

November 24, 2009—Spain—Hundreds of police officers in four northern provinces arrested thirty-four people believed to be members of the outlawed Segi (literally meaning "to continue"), the youth wing of the Basque Nation and Liberty (ETA). None were yet considered full-fledged members of ETA but could become so. Many of the suspects were picked up in Bilbao and San Sebastian. Police searched forty-six homes and twenty-one youth centers, seizing pro–ETA publications, material, instruction manuals to make firebombs, and computers.

November 24, 2009—United States—A federal grand jury in Philadelphia indicted four men in a plot to support Hizballah through illegal schemes, including buying twelve hundred Colt M-4 machine guns. Hassan Hodroj—a member of Hizballah's political council—and his son-in-law Dib Hani Harb, both of Beirut, sought to send the weapons from Philadelphia to Syria but were thwarted by an undercover operation. Hodroj was a Hizballah spokesman and head of its Palestinian issues portfolio. Harb, Moussa Ali Hamdan of Brooklyn, and Hasan Antar Karaki of Beirut were also charged with seeking to send counterfeit money and cash generated by the sale of phony passports to Hizballah. The four were believed to be overseas. Another six were indicted for a separate scam that entailed trafficking in stolen cell phones, laptops, automobiles, fake Nike tennis shoes, and Sony PlayStation 2 video game systems that would finance the shipment of antiaircraft missiles to Syria. The chief suspect in the case, who was arrested on November 21, paid $20,000 to an undercover officer in July as a deposit on machine guns and Stinger shoulder-fired missiles. Eight others were charged with lesser offenses, including trafficking in stolen or counterfeit goods. Authorities had thirteen suspects in custody and were looking for eleven others.

November 27, 2009—Russia—A 15-pound bomb planted on a rail line derailed the Nevsky Express train between Moscow and St. Petersburg, killing at least 26 people and injuring 130 others some 200 miles northwest of Moscow in a wooded area near Uglovka. Three carriages were thrown from the tracks in the 9:30 p.m. explosion. Among the dead was Boris Yevstratikov, chief of the Russian federal reserve; a former senator; and Sergei Tarasov, chairman of the state road agency. Among the injured were passengers Igor Pushkaryov, 32; and Yekaterina Ivanova, who waited four hours to be removed from the train that was carrying 650 passengers and 20 staff. At least 92 people were hospitalized; 21 were listed in serious condition.

The next day, a smaller bomb partly exploded, briefly disrupting rescue operations but causing no injuries.

An attack on the train in 2007 caused 27 injuries but no deaths.

Muslim extremists, North Caucasus militants, and Russian ultranationalists were all suspected in the attack. Police released a sketch of a suspect and a description of an accomplice; the duo was spotted near the area in the days before the attack occurred. The sketch showed a man in his early 50s with light skin and wearing a red wig. The male accomplice was in his early 30s. Police found a possible hideout where four people had stayed and recovered DNA samples.

Chechen Islamists led by Doku Umarov posted a claim of responsibility on the Web site kavkaz-center.com, which often runs messages of support for the rebels. Russian news services said the suspects included Pavel Kosolapov, an ethnic Russian who converted to Islam, who was accused in the 2007 bombing of the same train. He remained at large. He was also believed to have been involved in some of the attacks since 2004 on subway trains, bus stops, and rock festivals.

On March 6, 2010, Russian authorities said that the eight Islamists who were killed and ten captured on March 2 and 3, 2010, were behind the Nevsky train bombing, as well as fifteen other attacks. Police found explosive components in a raid in Ingushetia Province. DNA taken from the rebels matched that found at the scene of the train bombing. Among those killed was Alexander Tikhomirov, a young radical preacher.

November 29, 2009—Mauritania—Al Qaeda in the Islamic Maghreb (AQIM) kidnapped three Spanish aid workers—two men and a woman from the Barcelona Solidarity Action humanitarian organization—from their thirteen-vehicle aid convoy. The group announced via an audiotape on December 7 that it had kidnapped them and released an audio on December 14 saying that they were in "good health." However, the Spanish government announced in late December that aid worker Albert Vilalta, 45, was injured. The press said he was shot three times in his left leg while trying to flee during the abduction, and that the government sent medicine for him with the help of area tribal leaders. AQIM later said the trio was being treated in accordance with sharia law and planned to free "our detainees from your jails." The AQIM claimed that two cells abducted the three Spaniards about 105 miles north of Nouakchott, near Nouadhibou, and in a separate incident, a Frenchman in neighboring Mali, to the east. The Spanish Foreign Ministry said it had not received any demands. 09112901

December 2009—Niger—Late in the month, al Qaeda–linked bandits murdered four Saudi tourists hunting birds in the desert of Tillaberi in the west. One Saudi shot at the gunmen, part of a thirty-member gang led by a local arms smuggler. Two other Saudis were wounded. *Al-Sharq al-Awsat* reported that the gunmen planned to sell them to al Qaeda in the Islamic Maghreb leader

Mokhtar Belmokhtar, alias The Uncatchable. 09129901

December 3, 2009—Guinea—Junta leader Capt. Moussa "Dadis" Camara was slightly wounded when a renegade faction of his presidential guard opened fire on him. Vice President and Defense Minister Gen. Sekouba Konate returned from Lebanon to serve as acting president.

December 3, 2009—Somalia—A male suicide bomber dressed as a woman in a black burqa set off his bomb at a graduation ceremony of doctors at Banadir University in Mogadishu, killing twenty-four people, including nine students, parents, two journalists, a professor, two doctors, and three government officials, and wounding fifty-five. The terrorist walked up to a speakers' panel, said, "Peace," and set off the bomb. Among the dead was Minister of Higher Education Ibrahim Hassan Addou, a Somali American who once taught at American University; Education Minister Abdullahi Wayel; and Health Minister Qamar Aden. Sports Minister Suleman Olad Robie was hospitalized in critical condition. The government blamed al-Shabaab and said the killer was a Danish citizen of Somali descent. The bomber's father identified a photo of the dead terrorist. 09120301

December 3, 2009—Syria—A bomb went off in the morning on a bus in the Zinab neighborhood of Damascus near a Shi'a shrine, killing and wounding dozens. A bombing in the same area killed seventeen people in September 2008.

December 4, 2009—Pakistan—The Tehrik-i-Taliban Pakistan claimed credit when four gunmen attacked a mosque in Rawalpindi frequented by military personnel, killing forty and wounding eighty in the gun and grenade assault. Most of the victims were children. Two suicide bombers blew themselves up during a prayer service. The first stood up in the front row and set off his explosives. Several other attackers threw grenades and shot from the back of the mosque. The second attacker then blew himself up. Two gunmen were killed by authorities. Among the dead was Bilal Riaz, son of retired general Nasim Riaz, who was praying with him.

December 4–5, 2009—Sudan—Gunmen shot to death five Rwandan soldiers in a series of attacks on the UN–African Union peacekeeping forces in Darfur. 09120401, 09120501

December 7, 2009—Turkey—A radical wing of the separatist Kurdish Workers Party (PKK) claimed credit when gunmen fired automatic weapons at a military vehicle, killing seven Turkish soldiers and injuring three others near Resadiye in Tokat Province, Antolia. The ambush followed weeks of street protests across the country.

December 7, 2009—Pakistan—Bombs in Lahore and Peshawar killed forty-six and wounded one hundred. A suicide bomber killed ten outside a Peshawar courthouse. Two remotely-detonated bombs went off in Lahore's Moon Market at 9:00 p.m., killing thirty-six people, including a 2-year-old, and injuring one hundred, including Mohammad Nauman. Authorities later said one of the bombs was set off by a suicide bomber.

December 7, 2009—United States/Pakistan—Pakistani authorities raided a home in Sargodha, about 120 miles south of Islamabad, and arrested five Muslim U.S. citizen students from Alexandria, Virginia, who were suspected of planning terrorist attacks, obtaining terrorist training, and seeking to join the Jaish-e-Mohammed, Lashkar-e-Jangvi, and Jamaat ud-Dawa militant organizations. The arrests occurred at the home of Khalid Farooq Chaudry (father of Umar Farooq Chaudry), an activist with ties to the banned Jaish-e-Mohammed. The detainees told arresting officers, "We are here for jihad." The groups did not trust the five's bona fides when initially contacted in August and sent them away. The individuals included two Pakistani Americans, two Ethiopian Americans (also reported as Yemeni Americans), and an Egyptian American. Some had been born in the United States. They had told their parents that they were attending a local conference, but the parents became suspicious when they called their cell phones and got an overseas ring tone. They immediately contacted the FBI, local imams, and the Council on American-Islamic Relations (CAIR). The five arrived in Karachi on November 30, then went to Lahore and later Sargodha. The five were identified as:

- Umar Farouq Chaudhry, 24, Pakistani American originally from Sargodha, who had maintained links with an Islamic extremist organization. His mother claimed that he was in Pakistan to marry and said he was a student at George Mason University. The detained father owns a small computer sales and repair business called Geeks and Wireless.
- Waqar Hussain Khan, variant Hassan Khan, 22, Pakistani American who was convicted in Fairfax, Virginia, in 2008 of embezzlement for stealing packages from the UPS store where he worked. He received a one-year suspended sentence.
- Ahmad Abdullah Minni, 20, Ethiopian American who had been contacted by Pakistani Taliban recruiter Saifullah after he praised jihadi videos on YouTube. The family runs a day care center out of their home.
- Aman Hasan Yamer, 18, Ethiopian American
- Ramy Zamzam, 22, Howard University dental student of Egyptian background. Friends said he was involved with local charities. Zamzam received a bachelor of science degree from Howard in chemistry and biology in 2009.

Pakistani police said Zamzam was the ringleader. He refused to answer questions for hours. He had tried to raise money to build mosques in the United States. He left behind an eleven-minute video which some believed was a suicide bomber testament. In the video, the narrator referred to "the ongoing conflict in the world, and that young Muslims have to do something."

Other names given for them included Yasir Zamzam, Aman Yasir, Ahmed Abdullah Waqar, and Eman Hassan.

The five had exchanged coded e-mails for months with Saifullah and got in touch with him when they arrived in Pakistan on November 30. Police found that they were carrying a map of Miranshah, a town in Waziristan, where al Qaeda is based. Authorities confiscated their laptops, external hard drives, cell phones, and an iPod.

The five had met as members of a youth group at the Islamic Circle of North America Mosque in Alexandria, Virginia.

On December 14, 2009, Pakistan's High Court in Lahore blocked them from being deported or handed over to the FBI until it had time to review the case. A court in Sargodha ordered the group held for ten days for interrogation. On December 25, a Pakistani court extended their detention for another ten days. Authorities said the group had mentioned a Pakistani nuclear power plant in Punjab Province in their e-mail account. They also found maps of a Pakistani air force base in Sargodha and sensitive installations at Chashma Barrage nearby. The area includes a major water reservoir and Chinese-installed power plants. On December 31, 2009, Pakistani police said they would ask a court to charge the five and would seek life sentences. They were scheduled for a January 4, 2010, court appearance in Sargodha.

At the January 4, 2010, hearing of the five Americans, a Pakistani court gave the prosecution two weeks to prepare charges. The five northern Virginians said that they would fight terrorism charges. While they claimed to be jihadists, they said they were not planning terrorist attacks. The next hearing was set for January 18.

On March 17, 2010, Pakistani authorities

charged the five with five counts, three of which carry a life term. Prosecutors said they were planning to attack a Pakistani nuclear plant and an air base, targets in Afghanistan, and "territories of the United States." The specific charges included planning to wage war against powers in alliance with Pakistan, planning to commit terrorist acts in the territories of Afghanistan and the United States, and contributing money to banned organizations. Evidentiary hearings were scheduled for March 31, 2010.

The trial opened on March 31, 2010, with the defense saying the government had fabricated the evidence. The prosecution said that the five communicated via shared e-mail account ramadanhaji 99@yahoo.com. Defense attorney Hassan Katchela said he would present exculpatory evidence on June 9; the prosecution had rested on May 14.

On June 24, 2010, a Pakistani court convicted the five on charges of criminal conspiracy and funding a banned terrorist organization and sentenced them to ten years in prison. They were each fined $820. Defense attorney Hassan Katchela said he would appeal. The government also planned to appeal the sentences, hoping for twenty years.

December 8, 2009—Pakistan—Two U.S. Predator missiles hit a white car being driven to the Afghanistan border, killing Saleh al-Somali, a senior al Qaeda operations planner who ran the group's attacks outside the Afghanistan-Pakistan region, and another Arab man near Miran Shah in North Waziristan Province. The *Washington Post* reported that he was believed to have plotted attacks against the United States and Europe.

December 8, 2009—Iraq—The Islamic State of Iraq, also known as al Qaeda in Iraq (AQI), claimed credit for setting off four bombs around 10:00 a.m. near education facilities, judicial complexes, and other targets in Baghdad that killed 127 and wounded more than 500. The group said it had hit "bastions of evil and dens of apostates." The group claimed it was "determined to uproot the pillars of this government" and "the list of targets has no end." The government blamed remnants of Saddam Hussein's Baath Party and AQI. One of the bombs was set against the Rafaidyan Bank that was used as the temporary headquarters of the Finance Ministry, which was destroyed in August 2009. A small blue pickup truck was driven into an alley near the building, after which it was detonated. Another bomb hit the Judicial Institute, which trains judges. Another went off in the Karkh district courthouse's parking lot, after an attacker drove through a checkpoint. The courthouse abuts a fine arts academy near a children's cultural center. Another bomb went off in the Dora neighborhood near a technical institute.

December 9, 2009—Thailand—Five bombs went off before the landing of a helicopter carrying Malaysian Prime Minister Najib Razak and Thai Prime Minister Abhisit Vejjajiva during a joint visit to the border town of Bukit Ta to open the Thai-Malay Friendship Bridge over the Sunai Lukok River. Among the wounded were four soldiers, two Marines, five police officers, and three local defense officers, who were trying to remove booby-trapped banners with separatist slogans. Four bombs went off in Yala; another went off in nearby Narathiwat Province. 09120901

December 11, 2009—Qatar—Adam Gadahn, the U.S.-born al Qaeda spokesman, released an English-language video on Islamist Web sites in which he said that the United States and Pakistan were responsible for a recent wave of bombings that had been attributed to al Qaeda–linked groups. He claimed al Qaeda "condemned and continue to condemn" all attacks by Western powers or "secular political forces." He added, "We express our condolences to the families of the Muslim men, women, and children killed in these criminal acts and we ask Allah to have mercy on those killed and accept them as shohadaa (martyrs).… We also express the same in regard to the unintended Muslim victims of the mujahideen's operations against the crusaders and their allies and puppets, and to the countless faceless and nameless Muslim victims of the murderous crusades" in Afghanistan, Pakistan's Waziristan regions, and Swat Valley, and elsewhere. He warned against assisting the United States in the newly-announced troop surge, saying,

> Those who have made the foolish decision to stand with America and its allies in their losing war against Islam … you have not only betrayed Islam and Muslims and left the fold of faith, but you have also caused the destabilization of nations and the displacement … of thousands of weak and oppressed people.… The blood of countless Muslims is on your hands, and the security and very future of the countries you claim to defend and serve has been placed in jeopardy because your external enemies are taking advantage of your heedlessness as you fight and kill your fellow countrymen for American dollars.

December 15, 2009—Pakistan—A car bomb killed twenty-two people (seventeen men, three women, and two children) and injured sixty, three critically, at a market in Dera Ghazi Khan. The terrorist set off the explosives in front of the home of former provincial governor Sardar Zulfiqar Muhammad Khosa, who is now the senior advisor to the chief minister of Punjab. Twenty shops were destroyed.

December 15, 2009—Afghanistan—In mid-morning, a car bomb killed eight people in Kabul's upscale Wazir Akbar Khan neighborhood. It was apparently targeted against former vice president Ahmed Zia Massoud, brother of the late commander of the Northern Alliance, Ahmed Shah Massoud, who was assassinated by al Qaeda two days before 9/11. The bomb went off outside the former VP's residence, killing two guards and four female civilians, and injuring dozens. The Heetal Hotel, popular among Westerners, was also damaged.

December 15, 2009—Afghanistan—A bomb killed five Afghans and a Nepalese man at the Paktia office of a contractor working on U.S. development projects. 09121501

December 15, 2009—Afghanistan—A facility of the United States firm DAI was bombed in Gardez, killing five Afghan security guards. 09121502

December 15, 2009—Ecuador—The government released its 131-page Angostura report, which indicated that Gustavo Larrea, who served as Interior and Security Minister under President Rafael Correa, had direct links with the Revolutionary Armed Forces of Colombia (FARC). The report said former Deputy Interior Minister Jose Ignacio Chauvin and television journalist and Alianza Pais legislator Maria Augusta Calle also were tied to FARC. The report said that retired general and former ambassador to Venezuela Rene Vargas Pazzos rented a farm west of Quito to the FARC, which used it to refine cocaine.

December 16, 2009—Ghana/United States—U.S. Drug Enforcement agents and Ghanaian authorities arrested three French-speaking Malian men in their 30s believed to be running cocaine to finance al Qaeda. They were sent to New York on December 16, charged with smuggling drugs through the Sahara to Spain to raise money for al Qaeda, al Qaeda in the Islamic Mahgreb (AQIM), and the Revolutionary Armed Forces of Colombia (FARC). U.S. Magistrate Jude James C. Francis, IV, in New York ordered them held without bail after they did not enter pleas to charges of narcoterrorism conspiracy and conspiracy to provide material support to terrorists by moving hundreds of kilograms of cocaine. Oumar Issa, Harouna Toure, and Idriss Abelrahman were believed to be members of AQIM. The U.S. Drug Enforcement Administration (DEA) used informants posing as supporters of FARC. In August 2009, DEA started the sting operation. In September, a French-speaking DEA informant

posed as "a Lebanese radical committed to opposing the interests of the United States, Israel, and, more broadly, the West and its ideals," according to court papers. He met Issa in Ghana, saying that FARC wanted to securely smuggle drugs through western and northern Africa to Europe. The suspects said their transportation protection fee was 3,000 Euros (circa $4,200) per kilogram. The charge sheet noted that "Issa confirmed that the protection would come from al-Qaeda and the people that would protect the load would be very well armed." Issa was represented by attorney Julia Gatto. They faced life in prison.

The court filing said Toure served as the business leader of an organization that worked closely with AQIM. Per the government affidavit, "Toure stated that he has worked with al Qaeda to transport and deliver between one and two tons of hashish to Tunisia and that his organization and al Qaeda have collaborated in the human smuggling of Bangladeshi, Pakistani, and Indian subjects into Spain." In taped conversations, Toure mentioned kidnap attempts against Europeans and obtaining foreign visas. Abelrahman allegedly led a militia of eleven armed men who provided security for the drug shipments. He confided anti–U.S. sentiments to the DEA's informants. Issa was alleged to be a fixer for a criminal ring operating in Togo, Ghana, Burkina Faso, and Mali. Toure and Abelrahman met the DEA informants in November in Ghana, claiming to be "kings" of the desert and "warriors of God." DEA said Toure told an undercover informant one route would be through Algeria and Morocco; another would be through Algeria to Libya.

December 17, 2009—Yemen—Security forces raided three terrorist safe houses in Sana'a and Abyan Province, killing thirty-four terrorists and arresting seventeen others with ties to al Qaeda. ABC News claimed two U.S. Predator cruise missiles had been used in the raids. Among the dead was Mohammed Saleh al-Kazemi, a senior al Qaeda figure in Yemen, and Hani Abdo Shaalan, a Yemeni who was released from Guantanamo Bay in June 2007. The 30-year-old was among four al Qaeda members killed in a December 17, 2009, raid by Yemeni authorities north of Sana'a. He was planning to bomb the U.K. Embassy and other Western sites. He had traveled to Afghanistan via Pakistan in July 2001. He became a chef's assistant at a Taliban camp and was at Tora Bora during the U.S. air campaign. He was captured by Pakistani forces near the Afghanistan border.

December 17, 2009—Qatar—One of the four wives of al Qaeda deputy chief Ayman al-Zawahiri,

Omaima Hassan, published a statement on Islamist Web sites, her first. Her seven-page screed called on "Muslim sisters" to assist with supporting jihad, which she believes is "an obligation for all Muslims, men and women, but the way of fighting is not easy for women. Our main role—that I ask God to accept from us—is to preserve the mujahideen in their sons, and homes, and boost their confidence, and to help them raise their children in the best way." But women can also become suicide bombers who conduct "martyrdom missions." Women should continue to wear Muslim head coverings (hijabs) and ignore the Western media.

Meanwhile, As-Sahab released Ayman al-Zawahiri's sixty-five-page *The Morning and the Lantern*, a critique of the Pakistani government.

December 18, 2009—Pakistan—A suicide attacker set off explosives outside a mosque frequented by police in the Lower Dir region after Friday prayers, killing ten people and wounding twenty-five. No group claimed credit, although the Pakistani Taliban was suspected.

December 18, 2009—Poland—Far-right terrorists were linked with the theft of the "Arbeit Macht Frei" ("Work Sets You Free") sign at the entrance to the Auschwitz death camp, now a museum. A week later, Polish police found the sign, which had been cut into three pieces, and arrested five men, initially described as "ordinary criminals." They had dropped the "I" in "Frei," leading to their capture. *Aftonbladet* reported that the group had been commissioned by Swedish neo–Nazis who would sell the sign to a Nazi memorabilia collector, then use the money to finance terrorist attacks in Sweden, including bombings of the Riksdagen (Stockholm's parliament building), as well as the foreign ministry and the home of Prime Minister Fredrik Reinfeldt. The neo–Nazis reportedly had Russian weapons, explosives, and machine guns and a five-man assault team. On January 8, 2010, Anders Högström, founder of Sweden's anti-immigrant National Socialist Front in 1994, claimed that he organized the theft for an unnamed collector who was willing to pay hundreds of thousands of dollars. On January 3, the British *Daily Mirror* said it was a rich Briton. But after finding out about the plot, Högström claimed he instead informed police. Högström left the far-right movement in 1999. Krakow police said they were already arresting the thieves when the anonymous phone call was received. Polish prosecutors said they wanted to question three Swedish residents. Authorities said the leader of the gang, Marcin A, had worked at

Högström's family estate in southern Sweden. On March 18, 2010, a Warsaw court convicted three men—two of them brothers—of the theft and sentenced them to eighteen to thirty months. 09121801

December 19, 2009—Nigeria—The Movement for the Emancipation of the Niger Delta said one of its boats had attacked a major pipeline west of Port Harcourt belonging to either Chevron or Royal Dutch Shell. Shell said it had no reports of such an attack. The group said the October 25 cease-fire was void for the next thirty days. 0912 1901

December 21, 2009—Colombia—The Teofilo Forero unit of the Revolutionary Armed Forces of Colombia (FARC) was believed responsible for the kidnap and murder of Luis Francisco Cuellar Carvajal, governor of the department of Caqueta, Colombia, who was kidnapped from his home at 10:00 p.m. Colombian troops found his bloody body, his throat slit, the next day, on his sixty-ninth birthday. One of his bodyguards was killed during the kidnapping, the fifth time Cuellar had been kidnapped. Cuellar was kidnapped by eight to ten men in military uniforms who drove a pickup to his home as Cuellar was settling into bed around 10:15 p.m. After killing the guard, they opened the front door using explosives. They then drove the hostage to the mountains bordering Florencia, the local capital. After President Uribe ordered the military to find the kidnappers, the terrorists killed Cuellar. In the previous kidnappings, Cuellar had been released after payment of a ransom.

December 24, 2009—Yemen—Yemeni and U.S. forces attacked a meeting of senior al Qaeda operatives, who might have included Anwar al-Aulaqi, who was in touch with the gunman responsible for the Fort Hood shootings on November 5, 2009, and apparently was in touch with would-be Christmas 2009 airline bomber Umar Farouk Abdulmutallab. Authorities suggested that thirty militants were killed, including al-Aulaqi. Also killed were two al Qaeda leaders—Nasser al-Wuhayshi, who had been Osama bin Laden's personal secretary and ran al Qaeda's operations on the Arabic Peninsula; and his deputy, Said Ali al-Shihri, a Saudi who had been released from Guantanamo Bay military prison. Authorities said it would take days to identify the dead and wounded. Al-Aulaqi's house in Shabwa Province was demolished in the attack. A Yemeni journalist, Abdul Elah Hider al-Shaya, said he had talked on the phone with al-Aulaqi after the attack.

December 24, 2009—West Bank—Gunmen shot to death Rabbi Meir Hai, 45, a teacher and father of seven, as he drove near his home in the Shavei Shomron settlement. On December 26, the Israeli Defense Forces killed six Palestinians, including three in Nablus believed to have been involved in the attack. Police said the trio was involved with the al-Aksa Martyrs Brigade. One of them, Annan Sleiman Moustafa Tsubakh, 36, was hiding in a crawlspace in his house with two assault rifles, two handguns, and ammunition. The other three were crawling along the border wall planning an attack.

December 25, 2009—Netherlands/United States—Umar Farouk Abdulmutallab, a Nigerian, 23, tried to light a powdery substance in seat 19A on Northwest Airlines flight 253, an Airbus 330 that originated in Amsterdam that was about to land in Detroit. Two people spotted him and a third—Jasper Schuringa, a filmmaker from Amsterdam—and the flight attendants jumped him after the device ignited. A faulty detonator stymied the explosion. He was treated for second and third degree burns on his thighs at the burn unit of the University of Michigan Medical Center. Schuringa also was hospitalized after the attack.

The Nigerian told authorities he wanted to set off a bomb over the United States. He tried to set off the explosives with a syringe sewn into his underwear; the media immediately labeled him the Underwear Bomber. The explosives were taped to his leg. He said he had been equipped and trained by an al Qaeda bomb maker in Yemen and that there were "others like him" in Yemen.

He had left Lagos, Nigeria, the previous day on a KLM flight to Amsterdam's Schipol Airport and boarded the flight in Amsterdam, having not undergone secondary screening. A Delta Airlines (Northwest and Delta have merged) official initially said a passenger had set off firecrackers on the plane at Detroit Metropolitan Airport, causing minor injuries among the 278 passengers. Initial reports differed as to whether the device was an incendiary or an explosive.

The next day, Scotland Yard searched an apartment block at University College, London, where a person named Umar Farouk Abdulmutallab was a mechanical engineering student from September 2005 to June 2008.

While not on the U.S. Transportation Security Administration (TSA) no-fly list or FBI's Terrorist Screening Database (TSDB), Abdulmutallab is in the National Counterterrorism Center's TIDE (Terrorist Identities Datamart Environ-

ment) records of terrorist suspects. His father, Alhaji Umaru Mutallab, a prominent retired Nigerian bank executive, had warned the U.S. Embassy in Nigeria on November 19 about his son's "radicalization," prompting his addition in the terrorism database; CNN claimed that the father had talked to someone at CIA. The U.S. Embassy in London had issued the son a visa in 2008.

Al Qaeda in the Arabian Peninsula (AQIM) said it was retaliating for U.S. support to Yemeni antiterrorist efforts. It said Abdulmutallab had "penetrated all modern and sophisticated technology and devices and security barriers in airports of the world, with courage and bravery, without fearing death and with seeking the help of Allah."

Abdulmutallab told investigators that he had the personal blessing for the operation of Anwar al-Aulaqi, a Yemen-based cleric with al Qaeda ties who had been in contact with Nidal Hasan, who on November 5, 2009, shot to death thirteen people at Fort Hood. Some reports said that Abdulmutallab and al-Aulaqi had been in the same Yemeni prayer room.

He was the youngest of sixteen children of his father and the son of the second of his father's two wives. He grew up in Kaduna, Nigeria. He obtained an engineering degree from City University in London. He later studied for an advanced business degree in Dubai. He father agreed to let him go to Yemen in July to study Arabic. In August he told his family that he had dropped out but would stay in Yemen for unknown reasons. Days later he texted to say that he was cutting all ties with his family. The Yemeni government verified that he was in the country from early August to early December and had a visa to study at the Sana'a Institute for the Arabic Language. He paid cash for the ticket on the December 24 KLM flight to Amsterdam at the KLM office in Accra, Ghana, on December 16, 2009. Nigerian authorities said he snuck into the country on December 24.

Investigators said he brought 80 grams of pentaerythritol tetranitrate (PETN), a powerful plastic explosive, on board the flight. The material was enough to punch a hole in the side of the plane if it had exploded.

He was charged in the U.S. District Court for Eastern Michigan with attempting to destroy an aircraft and with placing a destructive device on board a plane. Each count carries a twenty-year sentence. He was jailed in Milan, Michigan, 45 miles south of Detroit, until a bond hearing. He was assigned public defender Miriam Siefer. He was scheduled to appear in a federal court in Michigan on January 8, 2010.

Authorities determined that an individual named Farouk1986 (perhaps Abdulmutallab) had posted to an Internet forum, www.gawaher.com, three hundred messages from 2005 to 2007 (when he was in a British boarding school in Togo), including one in January 2005 that lamented that he "never found a true Muslim friend.... I have no one to speak too [sic].... No one to consult, no one to support me, and I feel depressed and lonely. I do not know what to do. And then I think this loneliness leads me to other problems." He indicated that he had been in the United States (he might have traveled to Washington in July 2004 and Houston in August 2008.). He had considered studying at Stanford, UC–Berkeley, or Cal-Tech, but he scored only 1200 on the SAT. He logged 287 Facebook friends. He frequently sought the counsel of others on how to live an upstanding Muslim lifestyle.

U.K. Home Secretary Alan Johnson said Abdulmutallab had been watchlisted in May 2009 and banned from entering the United Kingdom.

On January 6, 2010, Umar Farouk Abdulmutallab was charged with six federal counts, including attempted use of a weapon of mass destruction, which carries a life sentence; attempted murder within the special aircraft jurisdiction of the United States; willful attempt to destroy and wreck an aircraft within the special aircraft jurisdiction of the United States; willfully placing a destructive device in, upon, and in proximity to an aircraft, within the special aircraft jurisdiction of the United States; and two counts of possession of a firearm or destructive device in furtherance of a crime of violence. Authorities said he had sewn into his underwear the high explosives Pentaerythritol (PETN), Triacetone Triperoxide (TATP), and other ingredients. Judge Nancy Edmunds was assigned to the case in the Eastern District of Michigan.

On January 6, 2010, a federal grand jury indicted Abdulmutallab on six counts, including attempted use of a weapon of mass destruction, attempted murder, willful attempt to destroy or wreck an aircraft, and use of a firearm in a crime of violence. He faced life in prison.

Pundits noted that evidence that should have been considered included that he had purchased a one-way ticket with cash and had no luggage, that he was in touch with radical Imam al-Aulaqi, and that National Security Agency had a report indicating that AQIM was planning a holiday attack using a Nigerian named Umar Farouk. Other reports disputed the no-luggage, no-cash story.

In a one-minute audiotape released on January 24, 2010, Osama bin Laden said he endorsed the Christmas 2009 attempt to blow up a Northwest flight.

National Public Radio reported on January 25, 2010, that Abdulmutallab had contacts with two of the men involved in terrorist plots in the United Kingdom. Waheed Zaman was involved in the 2006 plot to set off liquid bombs on seven passenger planes en route to the United States and Canada. They might have met via programs sponsored by the Islamic Student Society at the London Metropolitan University; Zaman was president of the society. Abdulmutallab was president of University College London's Islamic Society in 2007. Abdulmutallab was also linked to a man arrested in 2007 in a plot to kidnap and behead a British Muslim soldier.

On January 21, 2010, Malaysia arrested four Syrians, two Nigerians, two Malaysians, a Yemeni, and a Jordanian tied to an international terrorist network with ties to Abdulmutallab. They were among the fifty people arrested while attending a weekly Islamic class with Aiman al-Dakkak, a Syrian university lecturer in his 50s, at a home near Kuala Lumpur. Al-Dakkak and his family had lived in Malaysia since 2003, when he came to Malaysia to pursue a second doctorate in Islamic studies. His son, Mohamed Hozifa, in his 20s, was among the ten detainees. Some were students at a Malaysian university in Gombak. The others were freed. Among them was Muhamad Yunus Zainal Abidin.

On April 26, 2010, ABC *World News* reported that a newly-discovered video produced by AQIM showed Umar Farouk Abdulmutallab training with al Qaeda in Yemen, firing weapons at such targets as a Jewish star, a U.K. flag, and the letters UN, and speaking in Arabic about the upcoming attack. He said in the video, "The enemy is in your lands with their armies, the Jews and the Christians and their agents.... God said if you do not fight back, He will punish you and replace you."

National Counterterrorism Center director Michael E. Leiter told the Aspen Institute's Homeland Security Forum on June 30, 2010, that Anwar al-Aulaqi "had a direct operational role" in the bombing attempt. Another U.S. official said al-Aulaqi was the link between the bomber and his trainers.

On September 13, 2010, Abdulmutallab fired his lawyers and suggested he wanted to plead guilty to some of the charges.

On December 15, 2010, federal prosecutors in Detroit added the charges of conspiracy to commit an act of terrorism transcending national boundaries and possession of an explosive device in furtherance of crime of violence. Abdulmutallab faced a life sentence. A new arraignment was scheduled for December 16 in federal court in Detroit. Initial charges included attempted use of a weapon of mass destruction and willful attempt to destroy and wreck an aircraft within the jurisdiction of the United States, but did not specifically say "terrorism." On January 25, 2011, U.S. District Judge Nancy G. Edmunds set a trial date of October 4, 2011. He was represented by attorney Anthony Chambers.

On February 10, 2012, the U.S. Department of Justice released a memo indicating that Anwar al-Aulaqi personally directed the underwear bomber plot of December 25, 2009.

On February 16, 2012, Abdulmutallab was sentenced in U.S. District Court in Detroit to life in prison without possibility of parole. 09122501

December 27, 2009—Pakistan—Two suicide bombers killed ten people and wounded scores of others. One bomb went off at the home of Sarfaraz Khan, a local official in the Kurram area of a semiautonomous tribal region, killing him, his 13-year-old son, three young nephews, and possibly his wife. A second bomb went off when a suicide bomber set off his explosives outside a prayer hall in Muzzaffarabad, Kashmir, during Ashura, killing eleven and injuring more than eighty.

December 28, 2009—Pakistan—A Pakistani Taliban suicide bomber killed forty-four people and injured another sixty among the thousands of Shi'ites who were commemorating Ashura via a procession along M. A. Jinnah Road in Karachi. An earlier blast in the northeast killed seven others.

December 28, 2009—Spain—Interior Minister Alfredo Perez Rubalcaba warned that Basque Nation and Liberty could be planning a major attack or a high-profile kidnapping. Madrid raised the nationwide terrorism alert to level two. The highest level is four, when the military would be deployed against an imminent threat.

December 29, 2009—Yemen—An al Qaeda in the Arabic Peninsula Web site called on all Muslims to join the "mast [intentional pun] media campaign" by providing information helpful in attacking U.S. naval interests, including vessels at sea, how crews are serviced by other nations, naval nuclear weapons, and navy personnel and their families. "The lions of al Qaeda flirted with the American Navy several years ago when they targeted the destroyed Cole! Now, with the help of God, every American naval vessel in the seas and oceans: aircraft carriers, submarines, and all of its war machines within range of al Qaeda—will be destroyed, God willing."

December 30, 2009—Afghanistan—A Taliban terrorist wearing an explosives belt under his clothes killed seven American civilians and a Jordanian (a separate report said he was an Afghan civilian) and wounded eight people, including six Americans, at the heavily fortified military Forward Operating Base Chapman in Khost Province. Reports differed as to whether the terrorist walked into the base dining room or gym.

Taliban spokesman Zabiullah Mujahid the bomber was an Afghan National Army soldier wearing a military uniform. ABCNews.com reported on January 2, 2010, that the bomber was a Pakistani member of the Wazir tribe who had visited the facility several times. Initial reports said he would be driven by Arghawan, the base Afghan security director, two hours from the Ghulam Khan border crossing to the base. Because he was with Arghawan, he was not searched. Arghawan also died in the explosion. ABC News claimed that the Taliban in Pakistan had told the Associated Press that the informant had offered to become a double agent for them and that the bombing was in revenge for drone attacks against senior Taliban leaders. The news service speculated that the perpetrators belonged to the Taliban faction led by Sirajuddin Haqqani, son of Jalaluddin Haqqani, whose group also kidnapped Pfc. Bowe Bergdahl in late June 2009.

The White House announced on December 31, 2009, that President Barack Obama sent a message to the Agency workforce, in which he said,

I write to mark a sad occasion in the history of the CIA and our country. Yesterday, seven Americans in Afghanistan gave their lives in service to their country. Michelle and I have their families, friends, and colleagues in our thoughts and prayers. These brave Americans were part of a long line of patriots who have made great sacrifices for their fellow citizens, and for our way of life. The United States would not be able to maintain the freedom and security that we cherish without decades of service from the dedicated men and women of the CIA. You have helped us understand the world as it is, and taken great risks to protect our country. You have served in the shadows, and your sacrifices have sometimes been unknown to your fellow citizens, your friends, and even your families. In recent years, the CIA has been tested as never before. Since our country was attacked on September 11, 2001, you have served on the front lines in directly confronting the dangers of the 21st century. Because of your service, plots have been disrupted, American lives have been saved, and our Allies and partners have been more secure. Your triumphs and even your names may be unknown to your fellow Americans, but your service is deeply appreciated. Indeed, I know firsthand the excellent quality of your work because I rely on it every day. The men and women who gave their lives in Afghanistan did their duty with courage, honor and excellence, and we must draw strength from the example of their sacrifice. They will take their place on the Memorial Wall at Langley alongside so many other heroes who gave their lives on behalf of their country. And they will live on in the hearts of those who loved them, and in the freedom that they gave their lives to defend. May God bless the memory of those we lost, and may God bless the United States of America.

CIA.gov reported the same day that CIA Director Leon Panetta said,

Those who fell yesterday were far from home and close to the enemy, doing the hard work that must be done to protect our country from terrorism. We owe them our deepest gratitude, and we pledge to them and their families that we will never cease fighting for the cause to which they dedicated their lives—a safer America. Families have been our Agency's first priority. Before sharing this information with anyone else, we wanted to be in contact with each of them. This is the most difficult news to bear under any circumstances, but that it comes during the holidays makes it even harder. In coming days and weeks, we will comfort their loved ones as a family. They are in our thoughts and prayers—now and always.... Yesterday's tragedy reminds us that the men and women of the CIA put their lives at risk every day to protect this nation. Throughout our history, the reality is that those who make a real difference often face real danger.

The Web site also said that "Director Panetta credited U.S. military doctors and nurses with saving the lives of those wounded in the attack. In honor and memory of the dead, he requested that the flags at CIA Headquarters be flown at half-staff."

On January 7, 2010, Mustafa Abu Yazid, al Qaeda's commander of operations in Afghanistan and its number 3 leader, claimed credit via Islamist Web sites, saying it was avenging the deaths of Baitullah Mehsud, leader of the Taliban in Pakistan who was killed in a missile strike last August, and al Qaeda operatives Saleh al-Somali and Abdullah al-Libi.

Al-Jazeera reported that the bomber was Jordanian Humam Khalil Abu-Mulal al-Balawi, a Jordanian doctor who became a double agent. Al-Balawi came from the same hometown as the deceased leader of al Qaeda in Iraq, Abu Musab al-Zarqawi. The Jordanians had believed that he had been rehabilitated and were using him to find Ayman al-Zawahiri, according to CNN. Al Qaeda named him as Hamam Khalil Mohammed Abu Malal, alias Abu Dujana Khorasani. It said he was a well-known Islamist author and a preacher on jihadi Web sites. "May God accept him as a martyr who was able to infiltrate the Americans' forts.... We ask God to bless the people who follow your path, Abu Dujana. Let them know that your brothers are following your path and they will not have peace of mind until they slaughter the Americans and let the Islamic nation be proud for having men like you among its sons."

Several groups have claimed responsibility for the attack, including the Taliban in Afghanistan. Hakimullah Mehsud, Pakistani Taliban chief, also said in an e-mail that his group was avenging Baitullah Mehsud's killing. He was believed to have died from his wounds in a U.S. missile strike on January 17, 2010.

On January 2, 2010, AOL.com ran video showing the bomber's video will. The suicide bomber was wearing a military uniform and holding a gun.

The Jordanian and the American intelligence services offered me millions of dollars to work with them and to spy on mujahideen ["holy warriors"] here, but hamd'allah ["thanks be to God"] I came to the mujahideen and I told them everything. We arranged together this attack. What we strive for cannot be exchanged for all the wealth in the world. This attack will be the first of the revenge operations against the Americans.... We say that we will never forget the blood of our Emir Beitullah Mehsud, God's mercy on him. To retaliate for his death in the United States and outside the United States will remain an obligation on all emigrants who were harbored by Beitullah Mehsud.... God's combatant never exposes his religion to blackmail and never renounces it, even if he is offered the sun in one hand and the moon in the other.

He had posted on September 2009 on an al Qaeda Web site, "If [a Muslim] dies in the cause of Allah, he will grant his words glory that will be permanent marks on the path to guide to jihad, with permission from Allah. If love of jihad enters a man's heart, it will not leave him even if he wants to do so. What he sees of luxurious palaces will remind him of positions of the martyrs in the higher heaven."

Mustafa Abul-Yazid, leader of al Qaeda in Afghanistan and the group's overall number 3, posted to a Web site on January 7, 2010, that bomber Humma Khalil Mohammed Abu-Mulal al-Balawi, 36, a doctor, "detonated his explosive belt, concealed from the eyes of those who do not believe in the Hereafter, in a gathering of American and Jordanian intelligence men.... He avenged our martyrs, and as he wrote in his final testament, may God have mercy on him: Taking revenge for the leader the Amir Beitullah Mehsud and the leaders Abu Saleh al-Somali and Abdallah Said al-Libi and their brothers, may God have mercy on them." Al-Yazid said that the bomber wrote in his will that he was avenging "our righteous martyrs." He said this was a "successful epic" and that the group would fight the United States "until they inflict upon them the greatest and most astonishing deaths and wounds.... May God accept him as a martyr who was able to infiltrate the Americans' forts. We ask God to bless the people who follow your path, Abu Dujana. Let them know that your brothers are following your path and they will not have peace of mind until they slaughter the Americans and let the Islamic nation be proud for having men like you among its sons."

The *New York Times* reported on January 2 that the Afghan Taliban claimed that the bomber was a disillusioned Afghan National Army soldier, which the Afghan Defense Ministry denied. WSJ.com reported on January 3 that a senior Afghan Taliban leader said, "We attacked this base because the team there was organizing drone strikes in Loya Paktia and surrounding area. We attacked on that particular day because we knew the woman who was leading the team [was there]." The *Los Angeles Times* on January 9 said Balawi was born in Kuwait and arrested in Jordan in 2009 attempting to enter the Gaza Strip as part of a medical relief team.

The Pakistani Taliban also claimed credit. The press suggested involvement of the Haqqani network, a Taliban splinter.

Forward Operating Base Chapman was named for 1st Special Forces Group Sgt. 1st Class Nathan Chapman of Puyallup, who died on January 4, 2002, the first American soldier killed in the war.

Humma Khalil Abu-Mulal al-Balawi, from Zarqa, Jordan, had frequently posted on jihadi Web sites, including the password-protected al-Hisba site, where he used the name Abu Dujana al-Khurasani, according to the *Wall Street Journal* on January 5. He was recruited into al Qaeda. Sometime in 2008 or 2009, he approached Jordanian intelligence (or was arrested and interrogated regarding his support for extremists) and was recruited as a double agent to report on the whereabouts of Ayman al-Zawahiri, according to the *Washington Times*. Other press reports said that he approached the Jordanian service and offered his services.

CIA Director Leon Panetta wrote in the *Washington Post* on January 10, 2010, that the bomber

was about to be searched by security officers when he set off his bomb outside a gym on the compound. The *Los Angeles Times* reported on January 9 that most of the CIA officers were 50 feet away but that the blast was particularly powerful and the device included shrapnel.

On January 6, the Associated Press and *Newsweek Turkiye* reported that Defne Bayrak, 31, Turkish journalist wife of the bomber, phoned Turkish media to say that her husband saw the United States as an adversary, as did she. (Reuters on January 7 reported that she was the author of *Osama bin Laden: Che Guevara of the East*.) The Istanbul-based Bayrak said her husband planned to become a surgeon in Turkey. She said he was a Kuwaiti-born Palestinian. They met in an Internet chat room and married during his last year of medical school in 2001. They had two little girls while he worked in Jordanian hospitals. He was one of a group of Jordanian doctors who offered to aid Hamas in Gaza and besieged Palestinians during the Israeli assault on Hamas. He also had contacts with the Jordanian Muslim Brotherhood. Newsweek.com reported on January 4 that he had been an administrator for the al-Hesbah Forum, a major al Qaeda Web site. He had said he wanted to die in a jihad against Israel and the United States, according to Mohammed Yousef, a high school classmate in Jordan. The Jordanian GID arrested him in March (or January) 2009 following his Internet postings as Abu Dujana al-Khurasani. He was jailed for three days, then left Jordan, claiming he was going to study surgery in Pakistan. Bayrak said that did not work out, and he got another job. He apparently then traveled to Afghanistan. Bayrak took their two daughters from Jordan to Istanbul in October 2009. On January 1, 2010, she received an anonymous call from a person she believed was in Pakistan who told her, "Your husband did this for Allah. We will broadcast a video of his celebrated martyrdom on the Web and you will watch him."

The video appeared soon afterward in which al-Balawi said, "We will never forget the blood of our emir Baitullah Mehsud. We will always demand revenge for him inside America and outside."

MSNBC.com reported on January 4 that al-Balawi told the Vanguards of Khurasan, an al Qaeda Web site,

When you ponder the verses and hadiths that speak about jihad and its graciousness, and then you let your imagination run wild to fly with what Allah has prepared for martyrs, your life becomes cheap for its purpose, and the extravagant houses and expensive cars and all the decoration of life becomes very distasteful in your eyes.... They say "there's love that kills." And I only see that as truthful in the love for jihad, as this love is either going to kill you in repentance should you choose to sit away from jihad, or will kill you as a martyr for the cause of Allah if you choose to go to jihad, and the human must choose between these two deaths.

The Washington Post on January 5 expanded on the story, saying he had told the Vanguards that,

I have had a predisposition for love of jihad and martyrdom since I was little. If love of jihad enters a man's heart, it will not leave him even if he wants to do so.... If the name of a martyr they knew is mentioned in front of them, you find that blood has frozen in their veins as though it were a dew drop in the mouth of a beautiful flower. You find that the weeping in their straying looks is more eloquent than screams.

The Associated Press reported on January 4 that he had posted on a jihadi Web site, "No words are more eloquent than those proven by acts, so that if a Muslim survives, he will be one who proves his words with acts. If he dies in the cause of Allah, he will grant his words glory that will be permanent marks on the path to guide to jihad, with permission from Allah."

On January 7, the Associated Press noted that an Islamic Web site ran an article Abu Dujana wrote on December 29, 2008, in which he commented on seeing a photo of two Islamic women lying dead in a pool of blood. "Anyone who sees such painful picture and does not rush to fight should consider his manhood and masculinity dead. I have never wished to be in Gaza, but now I wish to be a bomb fired by the monotheists or a car bomb that takes the lives of the biggest number of Jews to hell."

On January 8, the *New York Times* reported that muslm.net ran a blog by Abu Dujana al-Khorasani with the headline, "When Will My Words Drink My Blood?" He wrote, "My words will die if I do not save them with my blood. My articles will be against me if I don't prove to them that I am not a hypocrite. One has to die to make the other live. I wish I could be the one to die."

A Pakistani television network on January 9 also ran a video clip of him meeting with Pakistani Taliban leader Hakimullah Mehsud, saying, "The emigrant for the sake of God will not put his religion on the bargaining table and will not sell his religion even if they put the sun in his right hand and the moon on his left." Mehsud had claimed credit for the attack on behalf of Tehrak-e-Taliban Pakistani, according to CNN on January 4.

PBS.com and ABCNews.com reported on January 5, 2010, that the dead included:

- Harold Brown, Jr., 37, a former Navy SEAL originally from Massachusetts, who left behind a wife and three children, aged 12, 10, and 2. He had served in the army and his family said he had worked for the State Department. He had also worked for Science Applications International Corporation (SAIC). His obituary in the *Worcester Telegram and Gazette* on January 9 noted that he was born in Boston, Massachusetts, and graduated from Nashoba Regional High School in 1990. He earned an associate of arts degree in Liberal Arts from Mt. Wachusett Community College, a bachelor of arts degree in political science from George Washington University, and a master of business administration from the University of Phoenix. He served with the U.S. Army in Bosnia, the Gulf War, and Operation Iraqi Freedom. He was a runner and fitness enthusiast who was a member of the Knights of Columbus.
- Scott Roberson, 39, a security officer from Ohio who left behind an 8-months-pregnant wife, Molly. Their daughter will be named Piper. The former Navy SEAL had been an undercover narcotics officer for the Atlanta police department. Cleveland.com reported on January 2 that he earned a degree in criminology from Florida State University and had been a contractor with the UN security forces in Kosovo. He later protected high-risk officials in Iraq. His sister told 11Alive.com on January 2 that he was a member of the Iron Pigs—a national motorcycle club for law enforcement and firefighters—and a founding member of the Metro Atlanta Police Emerald Society.

Newsweek.com and the Associated Press reported on January 6 that two of the dead were employees of Xe, formerly Blackwater:

- Jeremy Wise, 35, a former Navy SEAL from Virginia Beach, Virginia.
- Dane Clark Paresi, 46, a Portland, Washington, native and retired U.S. Army master sergeant who lived in DuPont, near Fort Lewis. KATU.com reported that Paresi grew up on Mount Scott, graduated from Portland's Marshall High School in 1982, and began army basic training the next day. He served twenty-seven years in the army, deploying with Special Forces to war zones including Afghanistan, Iraq, and Somalia. He earned the Bronze Star, the National Defense Service Medal with Bronze Star, and the Meritorious Service Medal, along with Bronze Service Stars for tours in Mauritania, the Philippines, Iraq,

Bosnia, Rwanda, Southeast Asia, Kenya, and Afghanistan. He retired from 1st Special Forces Group at Fort Lewis in 2008. He left behind a wife—MindyLou—and two daughters—Alexandra, 24, and Santina, 9—along with his parents and five siblings. He was buried with full military honors at Willamette National Cemetery, a quarter mile from his boyhood home.

Associated Press and FederalNewsRadio.com on January 7 reported that one of the dead was:

- Elizabeth Hanson, 30, who hailed from Rockford in northern Illinois. She was not married or engaged. She graduated from Keith Country Day School in Rockford in 1997. Her class photo included a quotation from novelist Ursula K. LeGuin, "It is good to have an end to journey toward; but it is the journey that matters, in the end." She attended Colby College in Maine, majoring in Economics and writing a senior thesis entitled *Faithless Heathens: Scriptural Economics of Judaism, Christianity and Islam*. She minored in Russian language and literature, according to the *New York Times* of January 7.

Daren James LaBonte's family later decided to report on his death and tell a little about his life but not about the work he was doing:

- LaBonte grew up in Connecticut, playing baseball and football at Brookfield High School. He turned down an offer from the Cleveland Indians to join the army upon his graduation from high school in 1992. He joined the First Battalion, 75th Ranger Regiment. He later graduated from Columbia College of Missouri and earned a master of arts degree in Criminal Justice from Boston University in May 2006. He had worked as a police officer in Libertyville, Illinois, and with the U.S. Marshals before joining the FBI. He worked briefly in the FBI's New York field office, before leaving in 2006. His daughter, Raina, would turn age 3 in November 2010. He was buried at Arlington National Cemetery.

The Associated Press and FederalNewsRadio.com on January 7, 2010, reported that one of the wounded was the deputy station chief of Kabul and that the dead Khost base chief was a 45-year-old member of the Alec Station created before 9/11 to track down bin Laden. She left behind three small children.

The *Washington Post* reported on January 10 that Paresi and Wise were approaching al-Balawi as he exited his car for a security check. Al-Balawi kept his hand in his pocket, and pushed a plunger, detonating the bomb that fired thousands of steel pellets, killing several Americans outside and injuring six CIA officers inside a nearby building.

In a memorial ceremony held on February 5, 2010, in a huge tent at the Quadrangle of CIA Headquarters, President Obama called the dead "American patriots who loved their country and gave their lives to defend it.... There are no words that can ease the ache in your hearts. But to their colleagues and all who served with them—those here today, those still recovering, those watching around the world, I say: Let their sacrifice be a summons. To carry on their work. To complete this mission. To win this war and to keep our country safe." The Director of the CIA, Leon Panetta, added, "They are the heart and soul of this great country. Their devotion to duty is the foundation of our country.... We will carry this fight to the enemy.... Our resolve is unbroken, our energy undiminished and our dedication to each other and to our nation unshakable." The White House issued the following press release on February 5, 2010:

President Obama and CIA Director Panetta Speak at CIA Memorial Service

The Central Intelligence Agency today held a memorial service at its headquarters for the seven Americans killed in eastern Afghanistan on December 30th. Family members and more than a thousand Agency officers gathered in attendance, along with guests including President Obama and senior officials from the Intelligence Community, the White House, and the Pentagon, as well as members of Congress.

President Obama spoke of the country's gratitude to the families. "Everything you instilled in them—the virtues of service and decency and duty—were on display that December day. That is what you gave them. That is what you gave to America. And our nation will be forever in your debt." He told CIA officers that their "seven heroes" were at the vanguard of a mission vital to national security. "Let their sacrifice be a summons. To carry on their work. To complete this mission. To win this war, and to keep our country safe."

CIA Director Leon E. Panetta paid tribute to the talent and accomplishments of the fallen, telling their loved ones that Agency officers "simply cannot do these jobs-we can't do these jobs-without the love and support of our families." He called the seven "genuine patriots" who "lived up to our highest principles," and pledged that CIA would strive to be worthy of them. Panetta added: "As they worked to protect lives, they sacrificed their own. For this, we honor them-now and always.... We will carry this fight to the enemy. Our resolve is unbroken, our energy undiminished, and our dedication to each other and to our nation, unshakable."

President Obama gave the following remarks at the memorial for the CIA officers at CIA Headquarters in Langley, Virginia:

America's intelligence agencies are a community, and the CIA is a family. That is how we gather here today. I speak as a grateful Commander-in-Chief who relies on you. There are members of Congress here who support you. Leaders—Leon Panetta, Steve Kappes—who guide you. And most of all, family, friends and colleagues who love you and grieve with you.

For more than sixty years, the security of our nation has demanded that the work of this agency remain largely unknown. But today, our gratitude as citizens demands that we speak of seven American patriots who loved their country and gave their lives to defend it: [Names redacted.]

They came from different corners of our country—men and women—and each walked their own path to that rugged base in the mountains. Some had come to this work after a lifetime of protecting others—in law enforcement, in the military; one was just a few years out of college.

Some had devoted years, decades, even, to unraveling the dark web of terrorists that threatened us; others, like so many of you, joined these ranks when 9/11 called a new generation to service. Some had spent years on dangerous tours around the globe; others had just arrived in harm's way.

But there, at the remote outpost, they were bound by a common spirit. They heard their country's call and answered it. They served in the shadows and took pride in it. They were doing their job and they loved it. They saw the danger and accepted it. They knew that the price of freedom is high and, in an awful instant, they paid that price.

There are no words that can ease the ache in your hearts. But to their colleagues and all who served with them—those here today, those still recovering, those watching around the world—I say: Let their sacrifice be a summons. To carry on their work. To complete this mission. To win this war, and to keep our country safe.

To their parents—it is against the natural order of life for parents to lay their children to rest. Yet these weeks of solemn tribute have revealed for all to see—that you raised remarkable sons and daughters. Everything you instilled in them—the virtues of service and decency and duty—were on display that December day. That is what you gave them. That is what you gave to America. And our nation will be forever in your debt.

To the spouses—your husbands and wives raised their hand and took an oath to protect and defend the country that they loved. They fulfilled that oath with their life. But they also took your hand and made a vow to you. And that bond of love endures, from this world to the next. Amidst grief that is sometimes unbearable, may you find some comfort in our vow to you—that this agency, and this country, will stand with you and support you always.

And to the beautiful children—I know that this must be so hard and confusing, but please always remember this. It wasn't always easy for your mom or dad to leave home. But they went to another country to defend our country. And they gave their lives to protect yours. And as you grow, the best way to keep their memory alive and the highest tribute you can pay to them is to live as they lived, with honor and dignity and integrity.

They served in secrecy, but today every American can see their legacy. For the record of their service—and of this generation of intelligence professionals—is written all around us. It's written in the extremists who no longer threaten our country—because you eliminated them. It's written in the attacks that never occurred—because you thwarted them. And it's written in the Americans, across this country and around the world, who are alive today—because you saved them.

And should anyone here ever wonder whether your fellow citizens truly appreciate that service, you need only remember the extraordinary tributes of recent weeks: the thousands of Americans who have sat down at their computers and posted messages to seven heroes they never knew; in the outpouring of generosity to the memorial foundation that will help support these proud families.

And along a funeral procession in Massachusetts, in the freezing cold, mile after mile, friends and total strangers paying their respects, small children holding signs saying, "Thank You." And a woman holding up a large American flag because, she said simply, "He died for me and my family."

As a nation, we pledge to be there for you and your families. We need you more than ever. In an ever-changing world where new dangers emerge suddenly, we need you to be one step ahead of nimble adversaries. In this information age, we need you to sift through vast universes of data to find intelligence that can be acted upon swiftly. And in an era of technology and unmanned systems, we still need men and women like these seven—professionals of skill and talent and courage who are willing to make the ultimate sacrifice to protect our nation.

Because of them, because of you, a child born in America today is welcomed into a country that is proud and confident, strong and hopeful—just as Molly Roberson welcomed her daughter Piper this week, both of whom join us today. Piper will never know her dad, Scott. But thanks to Molly, she will know what her father stood for—a man who served his country, who did his duty, and who gave his life to keep her safe.

And on some distant day, years from now, when she is grown, if Piper—or any of these children—seeks to understand for themselves, they'll need only come here—to Langley, through these doors, and stand before that proud Memorial Wall that honors the fallen.

And perhaps they'll run their fingers over the stars that recall their parent's service. Perhaps they'll walk over to that Book of Honor, turn the pages, and see their parent's names. And at that moment of quiet reflection, they will see what we all know today—that our nation is blessed to have men and women such as these. That we are humbled by their service, that we give thanks for every day that you keep us safe.

May God bless these seven patriots, may he watch over their families. And may God bless the United States of America.

On February 27, 2010, radical Islamist Web sites featured a longer forty-three-minute cut of al-Balawi's confessor video in Arabic and English versions. It was dated Safar 1431, which includes any date between January 16, 2010, and February 13, 2010. An introduction by As-Sahab said President Obama's 2009 address in Cairo had deceived "sim pletons," adding "it wasn't long before these fools woke up to Obama's crimes, which are no less ugly than the crimes of his predecessor." Al-Balawi said that he had been targeting Jordanian intelligence. "We planned for something but got a bigger gift—a gift from God—who brought us ... a valuable prey: Americans, and from the CIA. That's when I became certain that the best way to teach Jordanian intelligence and the CIA a lesson is with the martyrdom belt.... So it wasn't planned this way. The target was Abu Zaid, but the stupidity of Jordanian intelligence and the stupidity of American intelligence is what has turned it into a valuable prey. It's a blessing from Allah." He said, "Look, this is for you. It's not a watch. It's a detonator to kill as many as I can, God willing." He told As-Sahab Media that he tried to join the jihad in Iraq, but then was recruited by the Jordanians. "Actually, Jordanian intelligence—may God send consecutive curses on it—is the one who gave me a large amount of money, it is the one who paid for my ticket, and it is the one who helped me to forge some documents I needed to get a Pakistani visa.... They tried to entice me with money and offered me amounts reaching into the millions of dollars." He instead used the money to fund the mujahideen terrorists. "So this is a new era for the Mujahideen, God willing, in which the Mujahideen will use intelligence-based tactics and methods which rival or even exceed those of the security apparatuses of the strongest of states, like Jordan and American, with the permission of Allah, Lord of the worlds.... You can only get a maximum number of kills for a minimum number of martyrs and losses in the ranks of the Mujahideen with a martyrdom operation." He said Jordanian intelligence had helped target al Qaeda and Hizballah leaders. "The Jordanian intelligence apparatus has a record which emboldens them to such behavior, but with Allah's permission, after this operation, they will never stand on their feet again.... There is no solution to the situation in Jordan other than mobilizing to the land of jihad to learn the arts of war and train in them, then return to Jordan and begin operations." He said he had tricked the Jordanians, observing, "I cut ties for four months, then came back to them with some videos taken with leaders of the Mujahideen, so that they would think that I was leaking videos and betraying the Mujahideen.... The bait fell in the right spot, and they went head over heels with excitement ...[I would] throw in some accurate information which we thought the enemy probably already had knowledge of."

On March 8, 2010, Hussein al-Yemeni, a senior al Qaeda bomb expert and trainer believed to have been behind the Khost attack, was among more than a dozen people killed in an air strike in Miram Shah, North Waziristan, Pakistan. He was believed to have been an intermediary between al Qaeda in the Arabian Peninsula, the Taliban, and the Haqqani network in Afghanistan and Pakistan, serving as a conduit for funds, messages, and recruits. He was in his late 20s or early 30s. He had been imprisoned in Yemen between 2005 and 2007 and went to Pakistan after his release.

On April 30, 2010, extremist Web sites posted a twenty-nine-minute audio, entitled *O Hesitant One, It Is an Obligation*, by al-Balawi, in which he said that Islamic countries were "plagued with despotic leaders" who were anti-jihad. "How long will love for jihad to be just a dream, little more than a hobby which you do on your off-time?" He said he had recorded the message on December 29, 2009.

On Memorial Day, May 31, 2010, the American Airpower Museum in Farmingdale, New York, sent a B-17 bomber to drop flowers into the waters off Manhattan near Ground Zero in memory of the Khost victims. Michael J. Sulick, Director of the CIA's National Clandestine Serice, threw two dozen red roses into the water.

During the CIA's memorial ceremony, the names of those killed in Khost were publicly identified as chief of base Jennifer Lynne Matthews, 45, of Fredericksburg, buried at Arlington National Cemetery; Daren James LaBonte, 35, of Alexandria; Scott Michael Roberson, 39; Harold E. Brown, Jr., 37; Elizabeth Hanson, 30; and security contractors Jeremy Jason Wise, 35; and Dane Clark Paresi, 46. Twelve new stars were added to the Memorial Wall, bringing the constellation of heroes to 102 stars, 40 of whom remained unidentified to the public.

On August 20, 2010, federal authorities filed sealed criminal charges in U.S. District Court in the District of Columbia against Pakistani Taliban leader Hakimullah Mehsud for the Khost attack. The charges were unsealed on September 1, 2010. He was charged with conspiracy to murder a U.S. national while outside the United States and conspiracy to use a weapon of mass destruction against a U.S. national while outside the United States.

On October 19, 2010, CIA's Office of Public Affairs released Director Leon E. Panetta's statement on the Khowst attack, entitled *Lessons from Khowst*, to the public:

Last December, our Agency family lost seven courageous and talented colleagues in a terrorist attack at Forward Operating Base Chapman in Khowst, Afghanistan. These dedicated men and women were assigned to CIA's top priority—disrupting and dismantling al-Qa'ida and its militant allies. That work carries, by its very nature, significant risk. CIA is conducting the most aggressive counterterrorism operations in our history, a mission we are pursuing with a level of determination worthy of our fallen heroes. We will sustain that momentum and, whenever possible, intensify our pursuit. We will continue to fight for a safer America.

Earlier this year, I directed that a task force of seasoned Agency professionals conduct a review of the Khowst attack. The purpose was to examine what happened, what lessons were learned, and what steps should be taken to prevent such incidents in the future. In addition, I asked Ambassador Thomas Pickering and Charlie Allen, a highly accomplished former Agency officer, to conduct an independent study of the Khowst attack and to review the work of the task force. They concurred with its findings. One of CIA's greatest strengths is our ability to learn from experience, refine our methods, and adapt to the shifting tactics of America's enemies.

The review is now complete, and I would like to thank those who participated. They did our Agency a great service. It was, to be sure, a difficult task—especially since key insights perished with those we lost. Perfect visibility into all that contributed to the attack is therefore impossible. But based on an exhaustive examination of the available information, we have a firm understanding of what our Agency could have done better. In keeping with past practice, we will provide the Khowst report to the Office of Inspector General.

In highly sensitive, complex counterterrorism operations, our officers must often deal with dangerous people in situations involving a high degree of ambiguity and risk. The task force noted that the Khowst assailant fit the description of someone who could offer us access to some of our most vicious enemies. He had already provided information that was independently verified. The decision to meet him at the Khowst base—with the objective of gaining additional intelligence on high priority terrorist targets—was the product of consultations between Headquarters and the field. He had confirmed access within extremist circles, making a covert relationship with him—if he was acting in good faith—potentially very productive. But he had not rejected his terrorist roots. He was, in fact, a brutal murderer.

Mitigating the risk inherent in intelligence operations, especially the most sensitive ones, is essential to success. In this case, the task force determined that the Khowst assailant was not fully vetted and that sufficient security precautions were not taken. These missteps occurred because of shortcomings across several Agency components in areas including communications, documentation, and management oversight. Coupled with a powerful drive to disrupt al-Qa'ida, these factors contributed to the tragedy at Khowst. Each played an important role; none was more important than the others. Based on the findings of the task force and the independent review, responsibility cannot be assigned to any particular individual or group. Rather, it was the intense determination to accomplish the mission that influenced the judgments that were made.

There are no guarantees in the dangerous work of counterterrorism, but the task force identified six key areas that deserve greater focus as we carry out that vital mission. We will:

- Enforce greater discipline in communications, ensuring that key guidance, operational facts, and judgments are conveyed and clearly flagged in formal channels.
- Strengthen our attention to counterintelligence concerns while maintaining a wartime footing.

- Apply the skills and experience of senior officers more effectively in sensitive cases.
- Require greater standardization of security procedures.
- More carefully manage information sharing with other intelligence services.
- Maintain our high operational tempo against terrorist targets, even as we make adjustments to how we conduct our essential mission.

I have approved 23 specific actions recommended by the task force, some of which I ordered implemented months ago. They provide for organizational and resource changes, communications improvements, tightened security procedures, more focused training, and reinforced counterintelligence practices. These include:

- Establishing a War Zone Board made up of senior officers from several components and chaired by the Director of the National Clandestine Service. It will conduct a baseline review of our staffing, training, security, and resources in the most dangerous areas where we operate.
- Assembling a select surge cadre of veteran officers who will lend their expertise to our most critical counterterrorism operations.
- Creating an NCS Deputy within the Counterterrorism Center, who will report to the Director of the Counterterrorism Center and ensure a more integrated effort across Agency offices.
- Conducting a thorough review of our security measures and applying even more rigorous standards at all our facilities.
- Expanding our training effort for both managers and officers on hostile environments and counterintelligence challenges.
- Creating an integrated counterintelligence vetting cell within our Counterterrorism Center that focuses on high-risk/high-gain assets, evaluates potential threats, assesses "lessons learned," and applies the latest technology and best practices to counterterrorism operations.
- Designating a senior officer to ensure that all the recommendations are indeed implemented.

We've now taken a hard look at what happened and what needed to be done after the tragedy at Khowst. While we cannot eliminate all of the risks involved in fighting a war, we can and will do a better job of protecting our officers. Drawing on the work of the task force and its insights, it's time to move forward. Nothing in the report can relieve the pain of losing our seven fallen colleagues. By putting their lives on the line to pursue our nation's terrorist enemies, they taught us what brav-

ery is all about. It is that legacy that we will always remember in our hearts. 09123001

December 30, 2009—Afghanistan—Four Canadian troops, including Sgt. George Miok, Sgt. Kirk Taylor, and Cpl. Zachery McCormack, and Michelle Lang, 34, a Canadian health reporter with the *Calgary Herald*, on assignment for Canwest News Service, were killed when their armored vehicle was hit by a bomb. The group was visiting community reconstruction projects 4 miles outside Kandahar during the afternoon. Lang had been in the country for only nineteen days, on her first assignment in Afghanistan. 09123002

December 31, 2009—Afghanistan—The French Foreign Ministry said two French journalists and their local guides were missing. On February 14, 2010, the Taliban posted on a jihad Web site a video of the two kidnapped journalists pleading for Paris to negotiate for their release. On April 12, 2010, the Taliban threatened to kill kidnapped French journalists Herve Ghesquiere and Stephane Taponier and their driver, who had been held for more than one hundred days, if a Taliban video was not broadcast on French television and France did not release detainees. Ghesquiere, reading from a script in English, said, "The French President, Mr. Nicolas Sarkozy, must understand that we are now in danger of death. I repeat: the French president much negotiate very quickly. Otherwise, we will be executed soon." Taponnier read from a French script. The Taliban said it had submitted a list of their "most ordinary detainees to the government of France for release as an exchange for the two Frenchmen and their Algerian colleague." It added, "There is no other option for the release of the said detainees except the option of a detainees exchange." The group said that the detainees were "miserable" and "living a life under torture and brutalities." On June 29, 2011, after 547 days of captivity, France 3 Television French journalists Herve Ghesquiere and Stephane Taponier and their interpreter Reza Din were released. 09123101

December 31, 2009—Yemen—After a gun battle, authorities arrested Mohammed Abdu Saleh al-Haudali, 35, an al Qaeda member, in the village of Deer Jaber in the Bajel district northeast of Sana'a.

Elsewhere, Mohammed Ali Al-Henk, an al Qaeda operative, was captured in the Arhab district north of Sana'a.

2010

January 2010—Turkey—Authorities arrested more than 120 suspected al Qaeda members in raids in east and central Anatolia.

January 1, 2010—Denmark—Armed with an ax and a knife, a 28-year-old Somali man with ties to the al Qaeda-related al-Shabaab broke into the Aarhus home of cartoonist Kurt Westergaard, 75, during the night. The Danish artist's 2005 cartoon of the Prophet Muhammad wearing a bomb-shaped turban generated several death threats over the years. Westergaard pressed an alarm and hid with his 5-year-old granddaughter in a safe room while the attacker yelled "Revenge!" and "Blood!" Police arrived two minutes later and shot the Somali in the hand and knee when he brandished the ax. The man's wounds were serious but not life-threatening. The Somali was charged with two counts of attempted murder against Westergaard and a police officer. He denied the charges. The court banned publication of the defendant's name. He was represented by attorney Niels Christian Strauss. The Somali man had earlier been granted asylum and received a residency permit to stay in Denmark. The Danish Security and Intelligence Service (DSIS or PET) local intelligence service said he was suspected of terrorist activities in east Africa and had been under surveillance.

Westergaard had been the subject of several other threats. In October 2009, charges were brought against two Chicago-based men for planning to kill Westergaard and *Jyllands Posten*'s former cultural editor. In 2008, local police arrested two Tunisians plotting to kill him, but neither was prosecuted. One was deported and the other was released in late December 2009 after an immigration board rejected the DSIS's efforts to expel him from Denmark.

On February 3, 2011, a Danish court sentenced Mohamed Geele, a Somali man, to nine years in prison after convicting him two days earlier of attempted terrorism, attempted manslaughter, and attacking a police officer with a knife and an ax, in his attack on Westergaard. Geele was to be permanently expelled from Denmark when his prison term is complete. Prosecutors had sought a twelve-year sentence. Danish authorities said Geele had links to an East African Islamist militia allied with al Qaeda. 10010101

January 1, 2010—Pakistan—A suicide bomber drove an SUV packed with 550 pounds of explosives into the middle of a village volleyball game in the village of Shah Hassan Khel in the Lakki Marwat district of North Waziristan, killing ninety-six people and injuring more than one hundred. Village leaders had formed private militias to battle the Pakistani Taliban and had recently turned in twenty-four extremists to authorities. The villagers vowed to continue to fight the Taliban.

January 3, 2010—Yemen—The United Kingdom and United States announced closures of their embassies in the wake of al Qaida terrorist threats. The United States had information that eight terrorists had been planning an attack. Three were killed by Yemeni forces; another was captured wearing a suicide vest. The next day, Japan, France, Spain, and Germany limited services at their embassies. France closed its embassy to the public. Japan halted consular services.

January 3, 2010—Kenya—Authorities arrested Jamaican-born Muslim cleric Abdullah el-Faisal, whose online sermons were listened to by would-be underwear bomber Umar Farouk Abdulmutallab, during a preaching tour. Kenyan authorities said he was a threat to national security. El-Faisal was the imam on the London mosque attended by would-be shoe bomber Richard Reid and would-be twentieth 9/11 hijacker Zacarias Moussaoui. In 2003, the United Kingdom convicted him of inciting racial hatred in speeches that called for killing Hindus, Christians, Jews, and Americans and sentenced him to seven years. He was also accused of influencing one of the July 2005 London transit system bombers. The United Kingdom deported him to Jamaica in May 2007. Kenya deported him on January 7 to Nigeria. He was scheduled to fly on to Gambia and then on to Jamaica, but airlines in Nigeria refused to take him. He was returned to Kenya. Kenyan authorities drove him to Tanzania—from where he had arrived in Kenya—but authorities there refused entry. Several countries, including the United States, refused overflight privileges. On January 21, Kenya finally flew el-Faisal to Jamaica.

January 4, 2010—Yemen—Following a gun battle at the Raydah hospital in the Arhab region, authorities captured three wounded al Qaeda members suspected of threatening Western targets. Authorities arrested four people suspected of taking the wounded terrorists to the hospital and hiding them there. The trio included Muhammad al-Hanq, emir of the Arhab cell of al Qaeda in the Arabian Peninsula. Yemeni authorities were also looking for his close relative, Nazih al-Hanq.

January 5, 2010—United States—A Transportation Security Administration (TSA) worker on January 24 admitted planting a plastic bag of white powder in the carry-on luggage of Rebecca Solomon, 22, a University of Michigan student who was flying from Philadelphia to Detroit. The TSA employee said it was a prank. TSA fired him.

January 6, 2010—Egypt—In a drive-by shooting, gunmen opened fire outside an Egyptian Coptic Christian church in Naga Hammadi City at 11:30

p.m., killing a Muslim police officer and six Copt civilians and injuring seven others during the denomination's celebration of Christmas Eve. On January 15, 2011, Mohamed El-Kamouny, one of three defendants, was sentenced for his part in the attack. Sentencing for the other two was set for February 2011.

January 6, 2010—Russia—At 7:55 a.m., a suicide bomber drove into a traffic police station during roll call in Makhachkala, capital of Dagestan, killing six police officers and injuring sixteen others. Other officers used a police vehicle to block him from driving into the compound's interior, so he set off the explosives. Some 150 officers were lined up for roll call. Alexander Bastrykin, the head of Russia's Investigative Committee in the Russian Prosecutor General's Office, said that 513 terrorist acts were conducted in the first ten months of 2009 in the Northern Caucasus.

January 6, 2010—Afghanistan—Shortly after 6:00 a.m., Taliban gunmen wearing green police uniforms and suicide vests and armed with guns and grenades attacked the Bekhtar guest house, a three-story hotel in Kabul where UN elections advisors were staying. John Christopher "Chris" Turner of Kansas City, Missouri, who works for a trucking company on contract to the U.S. military, grabbed an AK-47, herded twenty-five guests to the laundry room, and, along with a Nepalese man and UN guards, fired at the terrorists. During the two-hour gun battle, five UN staffers, two security guards, the brother-in-law of Afghan governor Gul Agha Sherzai, and the three terrorists died. Among the dead was an American. Another nine UN employees were injured; Turner was burned slightly. Taliban spokesman Zabiullah Mujahid phoned the Associated Press to claim credit. 1001 0601

January 6, 2010—Afghanistan—A mile from the UN guest house, a rocket struck the "outer limit" of the presidential palace but caused no casualties. Two more rockets landed in the grounds of the upscale Serena Hotel, used by many foreigners. One unexploded rocket filled the hotel lobby with smoke.

January 8, 2010—United Kingdom—British police arrested three people who had made an oral threat at 9:15 p.m. to the crew on an Emirates Airlines plane as it was taxiing for takeoff for Dubai. Police boarded the plane with sniffer dogs. The trio, aged 36, 48, and 58, were held on suspicion of making a bomb threat.

January 8, 2010—Angola—Forces for Liberation of the State of Cabinda (FLEC) rebels fired Kalashnikov machineguns on the bus taking Togo's national soccer team to the Africa Cup of Nations tournament shortly after crossing the border with the Congo. The Angolan bus driver, an assistant coach, and the squad's spokesperson died. Two players and seven other people were injured. The players were goalkeeper Kodjovi Obilale, who was shot in the chest and stomach, and a defense player, who took two shots in the back. Obilale was flown to a South African hospital. Ten security guards in two chase cars returned fire for thirty minutes. Despite entreaties by captain and star striker Emmanuel Adebayor and the rest of the team to play on, the government pulled its team. Togo had been scheduled to play against Ghana in Cabinda. The Togolese government demanded an apology for the tournament directors and the government of Angola. On January 11, Angola arrested two suspects. 10010801

January 8, 2010—Afghanistan—Three rockets were fired at the U.S. Consulate in Herat, causing no casualties. One rocket hit the building housing the consulate. 10010802

January 8, 2010—Nigeria—Gunmen attacked a Chevron pipeline that carries crude oil out of Chevron's seven swamp fields in the Delta region.

January 8, 2010—Pakistan—Eight terrorists were killed when their suicide vest exploded in their house in Baldia, an ethnic Pashtun neighborhood in Karachi. Police seized guns, more suicide vests, and grenades.

January 9, 2010—Malaysia—Arsonists brought to six the number of churches that were firebombed during Muslim protests of a court ruling that permitted a Catholic newspaper to use the word Allah as a term for God. Firebombs damaged the Good Shepherd Lutheran Church in southwestern Kuala Lumpur. In an earlier attack, the Metro Tabernacle was badly damaged. The government appealed the court's decision and contributed $148,000 to relocate the Tabernacle. The next day, two more churches were firebombed. No one was hurt. By January 11, at least ten acts of violence had been logged.

January 9, 2010—China—MSNBC reported that an individual dropped two bottles of corrosive acid into a crowd near Temple Street in the Kowloon area of Hong Kong at 9:30 p.m., injuring thirty people, including children and tourists. Similar acid attacks since December 2008 had injured more than one hundred people. The next day authorities arrested a Chinese man in his 30s, who was on the roof of a nearby building along with caps to the bottles believed to have been used in the attack. Authorities were offering a $39,000 reward for information.

January 9, 2010—Greece—A bomb exploded in a trash bin outside the parliament building in Athens during the evening, causing no casualties. A caller told *Eleftherotypia* newspaper that a bomb was placed outside the building and another inside the neighboring Hotel Grande Bretagne.

January 9, 2010—Pakistan—A U.S. missile strike in North Waziristan killed Jamal Saeed Abdul Rahim, a Palestinian with possible Lebanese citizenship who was a member of Abu Nidal and possibly of al Qaeda. He was wanted by the United States for his role in the September 5, 1986, hijacking of Pan Am 73 during a stop in Karachi in which twenty people, including two Americans, were killed when the terrorists threw grenades and fired automatic weapons at the passengers. He was tried and convicted in Pakistan, but he and three accomplices were released in January 2008. The four were placed on the FBI's Most Wanted Terrorist List in 2009.

January 10, 2010—Afghanistan—A roadside bomb exploded outside the vehicle of *Sunday Mirror* defense correspondent Rupert Hamer, 39, killing him, a U.S. Marine, and an Afghan National Army soldier and wounding photographer Philip Coburn, 43, and five Marines. The duo was embedded with the U.S. Marine Corps and was with a patrol near Nawa in the south. The two had flown to Afghanistan on December 31 for what was scheduled to be a month-long stay. Hamer left behind a wife and three children, aged 6, 5, and 19 months. He had been with the *Mirror* for a dozen years, covering the U.K. armed forces in the Middle East, central Asia, Oman, Bahrain, Iraq, and Afghanistan. Coburn, an eight-year veteran with the paper, had covered Afghanistan, Iraq, Rwanda, and Hurricane Katrina in the United States. 10011001

January 10, 2010—Portugal/France/Spain—Police in France and Portugal arrested four members of the Basque Nation and Liberty (ETA). In the first operation, Spanish Civil Guards in Bermillo de Sayago near the Portugal border, stopped a man driving a van that contained explosives, weapons, and documentation. During the search, the driver stole a police car and fled to Portugal, where he was arrested by local authorities. Police also arrested a woman driving a sedan who was the van's lookout. French police detained a man and a woman, both armed, who removed 2,000 Euros from an ETA hideout in a forest near Chadrat in central France.

January 10, 2010—Afghanistan—A roadside bomb killed three Afghan aid workers employed by a German relief agency in Uruzgan Province. 10011002

January 12, 2010—Iran—A remotely-detonated bomb attached to a motorcycle killed Massoud Ali Mohammadi, 50, outside his northern Tehran home. Two other people were wounded. Neighbors thought there had been an earthquake. No one claimed credit. The government blamed the Mujahideen-e-Khalq (alias People's Mujahideen Organization of Iran, National Liberation Army of Iran, National Council of Resistance, Organization of the People's Holy Warriors), Israel, and the United States. Mohammadi, a specialist in particle and theoretical physics, taught neutron physics at Tehran University, but had no ties to the government nuclear enrichment program. He was one of 240 university professors (and a total of 419 scientists) who signed a letter supporting the opposition candidate, Mir Hussein Moussavi, before the June 2009 election. He had been involved in the Jordan-based UN Synchrotron-light for Experimental Science and Applications in the Middle East (SESAME) project, which involves scientists from Iran, Israel, and other Middle Eastern countries. Fashi was convicted in August 2011 and ordered to be executed. Iran's Supreme Court upheld the execution order. On May 15, 2012, Iran hanged Majid Jamali Fashi, 24, who had been accused of being a Mossad agent, for the murder. On June 17, 2012, Tehran announced the arrests of twenty suspects linked to the assassinations of five Iranian nuclear experts killed since early 2010.

Tehran state television on August 5, 2012, ran a broadcast of confessions of fourteen suspects, including eight men and six women, in the killing of five Iranian nuclear scientists. Suspect Behzad Abdoli said he had been trained in Israel, observing, "I entered Turkey and then was taken to Cyprus by ship. From there, I entered Israel." Suspect Arash Kheradkish said he was trained in attaching magnetic bombs to moving cars. Other suspects were Jamali Fashi and Maziar Ebrahimi.

January 12, 2010—Yemen—Security forces killed Abdullah al-Mehdarhad, leader of a Yemeni al Qaeda cell, in a gun battle after his group was surrounded at his house in the Habban region of Shabwa Province.

January 12, 2010—Nigeria—Gunmen ambushed a bus traveling from Port Harcourt to Afam, killed a police constable, wounded a driver, and kidnapped three Britons and a Colombian, all of whom worked for Royal Dutch Shell Oil. They were freed on January 19. The Movement for the

Emancipation of the Niger Delta denied involvement. 10011201

January 14, 2010—Jordan—A roadside bomb exploded near a convoy of Israeli diplomats on their way home for the weekend, causing no injuries. 10011401

January 14, 2010—Pakistan—The press suggested that a U.S. missile strike on a former madrassa in Pasalkot, South Waziristan, might have killed Pakistani Taliban leader Hakimullah Mehsud, although the group denied it. At least ten Taliban were killed. On January 16, Taliban spokesman Azim Tariq played a tape for Reuters in which an individual who sounded like Mehsud said, "I am neither wounded nor dead. I am fine."

January 14, 2010—Pakistan—The *New York Times* reported that a drone-fired missile hit a compound in the Shaktu area of South Waziristan, killing Philippine Abu Sayyaf terrorist Abdul Basit Usman. The Filipino bomb-making expert was linked to Jemaah Islamiyah. The U.S. Department of State said he was responsible for bombings in 2006 and 2007 in the Philippines that killed fifteen people. A $1 million reward had been offered for his capture.

January 15, 2010—Yemen—Six al Qaeda operatives were killed in a 2:30 p.m. air raid on two vehicles near Alajasher on the border between Saada and al-Jawf provinces in the country's far north. Among the dead was Qassim al-Raimi, variant Qasim al-Raymi, the group's military commander and third-ranking member of al Qaeda in the Arabian Peninsula (AQAP) in Yemen. He allegedly planned to kill the U.S. ambassador to Yemen and was involved in the 2007 suicide bombing that killed eight Spanish tourists. Also believed dead were Abu Ayman al-Masri, Ammar Ubadah al-Waeli, Ayeth Jaber al-Shebwani, and Saleh al-Tayes. Al-Shebwani was in charge of recruitment and provided logistical support to all foreign nationals recruited in AQAP in Yemen.

January 17, 2010—Pakistan—A follow-up air strike against Hakimullah Mehsud on two vehicles was believed to have injured him. Some tribesmen in the Orakzai area said he died of his wounds and was buried there.

January 18, 2010—Afghanistan—Seven Taliban terrorists attacked the presidential palace, the ministries of finance, mines, and justice, and the Serena Hotel in Kabul. In the attack five were killed and seventy-one injured, including thirty-five civilians. All seven terrorists died. The Taliban said it was thirty-one dead officials, five dead Taliban, and thirty-one injured. Two of the terrorists

were killed at the Feroshgah-e-Afghan Shopping Center. Two bombs went off at 9:50 a.m., while fourteen members of President Hamid Karzai's Cabinet were being sworn in. A terrorist set off a suicide bomb at a traffic circle nearby. Five minutes later, three attackers hiding weapons and suicide vests ran into a shopping complex across from the Justice Ministry. One terrorist got into an ambulance and drove to the traffic circle outside the Education Ministry, where he blew himself up. Three terrorists in a building next to a movie theater conducted a gun battle with police. Local authorities on January 24 arrested the ringleader of the group and suggested that al Qaeda had coordinated the attack. Authorities said the ringleader and several others confessed to the attack by the Haqqani network. They also said ammonium nitrate was used in the attack.

January 20, 2010—Dubai—The body of Mahmoud al-Mabhouh, one of the founders of Hamas's military wing, the Izzedine al-Assam Brigades, was found in a hotel. Local officials said a "professional criminal gang" was responsible. Mabhouh's corpse was sent to Damascus, Syria, where he had lived since fleeing the Gaza Strip in 1989. Hamas blamed Israel. Mabhouh had entered Dubai on January 19. His brother claimed that Mabhouh had suffered electric shocks, poisoning, and strangulation. He had been involved in the kidnap and murder of two Israeli soldiers in 1989. Israel also said he was involved in smuggling rockets from Iran to terrorists in Gaza.

On February 15, 2010, Dubai Police Chief Lt. Gen. Dhahi Khalfan Tamim identified six individuals carrying fake British passports bearing the names of Israeli citizens, three Irish citizens, a German, and a French citizen as being suspects in the assassination. The suspects included one woman. He said the emirate would seek international arrest warrants; the eleven names were later placed on the Interpol Red List. Gen. Tamim also said two Palestinians were held for having provided logistical assistance, but as of February 18, they had not been charged. Dubai said that the eleven left the country within twenty-four hours, fleeing to Europe, Asia, and South Africa. The next day, governments of those countries were questioning the Dubai investigation. At least four people living in Israel, including Paul Keeley, shared names with suspects identified by Dubai police, but three of the four said they were not the people in the photos released by Dubai, and the daughter of the fourth said it was a mistake. On February 18, 2010, Dubai's police chief said there was a 99 percent chance that Mossad was responsible. On February 24, Dubai said it was seeking another fifteen suspects, making the total twenty men and six women. Some fourteen suspects used MetaBank credit cards issued in the United States. The New York–based Payoneer firm issued some of the credit cards used by the suspects; the firm has offices in Tel Aviv. Dubai police officials said on February 28 that the Hamas member had been injected in the thigh with succinylcholine, a fast-acting muscle relaxant, before being suffocated. Dubai also said it had arrested a third Palestinian suspect.

On March 3, 2010, Dubai's police chief said he would seek Interpol arrest warrants for Israel's prime minister and intelligence director. By March 9, Interpol had issued twenty-seven Red Notices, which help national police authorities to circulate arrest warrants in other countries.

On March 23, 2010, the British government expelled an unnamed senior Israeli diplomat over the alleged use of twelve false U.K. passports in the assassination.

On June 12, Polish authorities arrested Uri Brodsky, suspected of working for Mossad in Germany. They believed he helped issue a fake German passport in Cologne to a member of the hit team who had identified himself as Michael Bodenheimer and falsely claimed that his Jewish family had fled Nazi Germany.

On August 5, 2010, the Polish court of appeals announced that it would extradite to Germany an alleged Israeli agent "accused of helping to get false documents for the man who is thought to have killed the Hamas leader in Dubai." He had been arrested two months earlier on a European warrant for procurement of a false German passport. As of early August, Dubai police had identified thirty-three suspects, who used British, Irish, French, Australian, and German passports.

January 21, 2010—India—Airports were placed on high alert amid reports that al Qaeda-linked Lashkar-e-Taiba terrorists were plotting to hijack a plane belong to Air India or Indian Airlines flying to a neighboring South Asian country. Indian media said detainee Amjad Khawaja, a leader of Harkat-ul-Jihad-al-Islami, had tipped his police interrogators. He had been arrested in Chennai, India, the previous week. The threat report later morphed into a plot to crash a plane from Mumbai or Delhi into London and to arrange attacks by suicide bombers on paragliders. Indian Home Ministry official U. K. Bansal told reporters, "We have intelligence reports that Lashkar-e-Taiba has purchased fifty paragliding kits from Europe with an intention to launch attacks on India." The

United Kingdom raised its threat level from "Substantial" to "Severe," its second-highest level.

January 22, 2010—Turkey—In several pre-dawn raids, authorities arrested 120 people suspected of links with al Qaeda, including some senior members of the group's Turkish branch, including Serdal Erbasi, alias Abu Zehr, head of the Ankara cell. Police seized weapons, explosives, medical equipment, and fake ID cards and passports in sixteen cities. The *Zaman* newspaper said they were planning to attack Turkish targets and the Kabul regional command center of the NATO-led security mission in Afghanistan. Turkish forces took over the rotating command of the center in November 2009. The previous week, police in Ankara and Adana arrested forty suspects.

January 22, 2010—United Kingdom—The government raised its terrorism threat level to "Severe," its second-highest level.

January 22, 2010—Iraq—A U.S.-Iraq raid in Mosul led to the death of al Qaeda in Iraq leader Saad Uwayid Obeid Mijbil al-Shammari, alias Abu Khalaf, who had broken free from his restraints and attacked his guard. He had been involved in smugglings hundreds of suicide bombers via Syria since 2006. Military authorities said he was also a financier and arms supplier for the group.

January 23, 2010—United Kingdom—Part of Manchester Airport was evacuated after the discovery of unidentified white powder in carry-on luggage destined for London.

January 23, 2010—Iraq—Gunmen kidnapped American citizen Issa T. Salomi. He had grown up in Iraq before fleeing in 1991. He worked as a U.S. Army linguist since 2007. The group released a video with its demands for the release of four terrorists and the prosecution of "Blackwater mercenaries." The Shi'ite group League of the Righteous (Asaib al-Haq) released him on March 25, saying the Iraqi government had agreed to release four detainees. 10012301

January 24, 2010—Qatar—In a one-minute audiotape broadcast on al-Jazeera, Osama bin Laden claimed credit for the December 25, 2009, bombing attempt against the Northwest flight and threatened further attacks against the United States. Analysts doubted that the central leadership of al Qaeda was aware of the attack in advance. Bin Laden addressed U.S. President Barack Obama, saying, "The message delivered to you through the plane of the heroic warrior Umar Farouk Abdulmutallab was a confirmation of the previous messages sent by the heroes of the September 11. If our messages had been able to reach you through words, we wouldn't have been delivering them through planes." He said, "From Osama to Obama: America will never dream of security unless we will have it in reality in Palestine. God willing, our raids on you will continue as long as your support for the Israelis continues. Peace be upon those who follow guidance."

January 25, 2010—Iraq—Shortly before 4:00 p.m., suicide bombers attacked the Hamra, Babylon, and Sheraton hotels, killing thirty-six people and wounding dozens. The *Washington Post*'s bureau is in the Hamra Hotel; three of its Iraqi employees were wounded. Several other Western news organizations are headquartered in the Hamra and the Sheraton. In the final attack, on the Hamra, two men walked up to a checkpoint and fired pistols at the four guards. One gunman lifted the security barrier, allowing a white Kia minivan with explosives to enter. A guard shot the driver, killing him and stopping the vehicle 50 yards from the hotel building. An accomplice remotely detonated the explosives. Among the injured were Wissam Mahmoud, who works at the Hamra, *Washington Post* staffer Naseer Fadhil, and *Washington Post* office manager Abu Mohammed. Observers blamed members of the former Ba'ath Party. 10012501-03

January 26, 2010—Iraq—A suicide bomber drove his truck into the Iraqi Interior Ministry's forensics division, killing 38 people. At least 150 people were injured in this and the previous day's hotel bombings. The Baghdad Operations Command said 9 people were killed and 67 wounded. Al Qaeda in Iraq was blamed.

January 27, 2010—Iraq—Gunmen fired on buses transporting Iranian pilgrims in the south, killing two. 10012701

January 29, 2010—Qatar—In a new tape aired by al-Jazeera, Osama bin Laden blamed the United States and other industrialized nations for global warming. He said the world should boycott U.S. products and stop using the dollar to break the U.S. economy. He observed, "The effects of global warming have touched every continent. Drought and deserts are spreading, while from the other floods and hurricanes unseen before the previous decades have now become frequent." He said corporations,

> Are the true criminals against the global climate" putting "tens of millions into poverty and unemployment.... People of the world, it's not right for the burden to be left on the mujahideen (holy warriors) in an issue that causes harm to everyone.... Boycott them to save your-

selves and your possessions and your children from climate change and to live proud and free.... The world is held hostage by major corporations, which are pushing it to the brink. World politics are not governed by reason but by the force and greed of oil thieves and warmongers and the cruel beasts of capitalism.

To end this crisis, the "wheels of the American economy" should be stopped. "This is ... if the peoples of the world stop consuming American goods.... We must also stop dealings in the dollar and get rid of it as soon as possible. I know that this has great consequences and grave ramifications, but it is the only means to liberate humanity from slavery and dependence on America." He also demanded "punishing and holding to account" corporation chiefs, saying, "this should be easy for the American people to do, particularly those who were affected by Hurricane Katrina or those who lost their jobs, since these criminals live among them, particularly in Washington, New York, and Texas." He mentioned the December 18 climate conference in Copenhagen, Denmark. He also mentioned Iraq, Afghanistan, and Palestine.

February 2010—United Kingdom—Authorities arrested Rajib Karim. His trial began on February 1, 2011, in London. The Bangladesh-born 31-year-old U.K. citizen, a British Airways worker, had exchanged messages with radical Muslim cleric Anwar al-Aulaqi in 2009 and 2010 regarding a plot to blow up planes, preferably in the United States. Prosecutors said al-Aulaqi quizzed him on "limitations and cracks in present airport security systems.... Our highest priority is the United States. Anything there, even on a smaller scale compared to what we may do in the United Kingdom, would be our choice." Karim was arrested in February 2010. He admitted offering to participate in terrorist operations, making a jihadi recruitment video, and fund-raising for terrorism. He denied he knew that the information he provided would be used for terrorism. Karim, his wife, and baby son came to Britain in 2006, settling in Newcastle in the northeast of England. He was soon accepted into a graduate entrant program at British Airways, eventually ending up as a software engineer. His brother, Tehzeeb Karim, travelled to Yemen and met with al-Aulaqi.

February 1, 2010—Iraq—A female suicide bomber killed at least forty-one people and injured more than one hundred in an attack on Shi'ite Muslim pilgrims in northern Baghdad. Women were being searched in a crowded tented area along the main road in Bab al-Sham. Among the dead were the three women who were conducting the searches.

The injured included Mohammed Haider, age 2. Al Qaeda in Iraq (AQI) was suspected.

On February 18, 2010, Iraqi security forces arrested AQI member Mohammed Shaker Mahmoud, 30, at his home in Al-Mukhaissah village in Diyala Province for recruiting female suicide bombers.

February 2, 2010—United States—In the annual worldwide threat briefing to the Senate Select Committee on Intelligence, senior intelligence officials testified that it was virtually certain that al Qaeda or its allies would attempt to attack the United States in the next six months.

February 3, 2010—Russia—Moscow announced that it had killed Makhmoud Mokhammed Shaaban, 49, an Egyptian militant in Dagestan who had set up the al Qaeda chapter in the North Caucasus. The federal security service said it had also killed one of his fellow gunmen. The state-run RIA news agency said Georgia had assisted him, but the Tbilisi government denied the charges.

February 5, 2010—Pakistan—A motorcycle bomb exploded in Karachi on a bus filled with Shi'ite Muslims, killing twenty and injuring sixty-nine. Another motorcycle bomb went off in front of the emergency room at Karachi's Jinnah Hospital where the first attack's victims were being treated, killing thirteen and wounding ninety-two. At least thirty-three were killed in the two blasts.

February 8, 2010—Qatar—Said al-Shihri, deputy chief of al Qaeda in the Arabian Peninsula, posted on an extremist Web site that "American and Crusader interests are everywhere and their agents are moving everywhere.... Attack them and eliminate as many enemies as you can."

February 10, 2010—Nigeria—The previously-unknown Joint Revolutionary Council of the Niger Delta claimed credit for attacking the Tura manifold owned by Royal Dutch Shell in Abonnema. The manifold connects several pipelines to the Bonny Export Terminal. Authorities said the attack failed and that explosives were confiscated. 10021001

February 10, 2010—United Kingdom—The Appeals Court rejected the Foreign and Commonwealth Office's attempt to keep secret a seven paragraph summary of forty-two classified documents provided to MI5 by the CIA in 2009 regarding the treatment of Ethiopian national Binyam Mohamed during interrogation in Pakistan in May 2002.

February 11, 2010—Pakistan—Two suicide bombings in the Bannu district of the North West Frontier Province killed fifteen people, including nine police officers and six civilians, and wounded at least twenty-five, including eleven police officers, among them Bannu Police Chief Iqbal Marwat, and fourteen civilians. The second blast, eight minutes after the first, claimed the most casualties, coming when police arrived at the scene of the first bombing.

February 12, 2010—West Bank—Israeli soldiers shot to death Fayez Faraj, 41, a Palestinian who tried to stab them in Hebron.

February 13, 2010—India—At 7:30 p.m., a waiter attempted to open an unattended package which exploded, killing ninety-eight, including four foreigners, and wounding sixty in the German Bakery in Pune's Koregaon Park. The dead included an Iranian and an Italian. The dozen wounded foreigners included citizens of Yemen, Sudan, Taiwan, and Germany. The bakery is a tourist hangout near the Osho Ashram, which was surveiled by David Coleman Headley as a potential terrorist target. 10021301

February 16, 2010—Pakistan—The Western news media reported that Pakistani and U.S. intelligence services in Karachi on February 10 had captured Mullah Abdul Ghani Baradar, the Taliban's top military commander, the Taliban's number 2 and the most important Taliban leader to be captured since 9/11. Authorities believed he ran the Quetta Shura (leadership council) and oversaw Taliban operations across southern and western Afghanistan. He had been the deputy defense minister during the Taliban regime. He was believed to have issued the code of conduct that was given to Taliban field commanders. On February 24, 2010, Pakistan refused to hand him over to the FBI, but said that he could be extradited to Afghanistan.

February 17, 2010—Spain—Police arrested suspected Basque Nation and liberty (ETA) member Faustino Marcos Alvarez, 38, on a southbound train from France soon after it crossed into Spain at the town of Port-Bou in northern Spain. He was carrying a .38 revolver with thirteen bullets, three forged Spanish identity cards, two forged French identity cards, a laptop computer, and about $8,000 in cash. He had been a fugitive since 2002 when he fled after police dismantled an ETA unit in Spain's northern Basque region.

February 21, 2010—Philippines—In a morning raid, Philippine Marines killed six Abu Sayyaf militants, including rebel commander Albader Parad, in Sulu Province. He had been involved in the 2009 kidnapping of Red Cross workers; all three were later released. The Marines recovered four firearms.

February 22, 2010—Qatar—In an Internet video, Ayman al-Zawahiri said in an audio recording,

> Let every free Turkish Muslim who is keen on protecting his fellow Muslims know that the Turkish forces will serve the Crusader campaign in Afghanistan, which is burning the villages, destroying the houses, and killing the women and the children, occupying the lands of the Muslims, fighting the Sharia and spreading lewdness, debauchery, and corruption. The Turkish troops will carry out the same operations in Afghanistan that the Jews are carrying out in Palestine, so how would the pious, free Turkish Muslim people accept such a crime against Islam and the Muslims?

The video included a martyrdom video will by Muaath al-Turki, who praised the 9/11 attacks, asked his family for forgiveness, and said that he "can die only once for the sake of jihad." The video said he had attacked the U.S. base in Khost, Afghanistan, killing eight U.S. soldiers and a dozen Afghans, a claim the U.S. military denied.

February 24, 2010—Pakistan—A missile strike in Dargah Mandi in North Waziristan, Pakistan, killed thirteen terrorists, including Qari Mohammad Zafar, who was wanted for questioning in the March 2, 2006, bombing near the U.S. Consulate in Karachi that killed three Pakistanis and U.S. diplomat David Foy. The United States had put a $5 million reward out for the pro–Taliban Zafar, who was a member of Lashkar-e Jangvi.

February 26, 2010—Italy—Police arrested an Italian with a criminal record and ten Kurds, most of them from Turkey, in the central and northern sections of Italy on suspicion of recruiting for the Kurdistan Workers' Party (PKK). Police conducted searches of sixteen other sites

February 26, 2010—Afghanistan—The Taliban attacked a Kabul luxury nine-story Safi Landmark Hotel and two guest houses—including the Park Residence Guesthouse and an Indian-owned guest house—frequented by foreigners, killing at least seventeen, including some foreigners and three police officers, and injuring thirty-eight. The first bomb went off in a van outside the Aria guesthouse. A second bomber detonated his explosives inside the building. The other bombers entered the Park Residence; one set off his explosives and the other hid before firing on Afghan security forces arriving at the scene. A gun battle raged for four hours after the 6:30 a.m. bombings. Taliban spokesman Zabihullah Mujahid said five Taliban

suicide bombers were involved. On March 2, 2010, Afghan intelligence spokesman Sayed Ansari claimed that Laskhar-i-Taiba, the group believed responsible for the Mumbai attacks of November 26–28, 2008, was behind the guest houses attacks. He said the suicide bombers spoke Urdu and were searching for Indian victims. Other observers said the Haqqani network was responsible for the attacks. Indian officials suggested the two groups worked together. The attacks killed six Indians, including two army doctors and an engineer, along with eight Afghans, an Italian diplomat, and a French filmmaker. 10022601

February 27, 2010—Philippines—Abu Sayyaf and Muslim separatist rebels attacked Tubigan village on Basilan Island with grenade launchers and automatic rifles, killing one militiaman and ten civilians while the residents slept.

February 27, 2010—Thailand—Small explosive devices went off during the evening at four banks in Bangkok, a day after the high court ordered the seizure of $1.4 billion of exiled former leader Thaksin Shinawatra's assets in a corruption case.

February 28, 2010—France—French and Spanish police arrested Basque Nation and Liberty (ETA) leader Ibon Gogeascoechea Arronategui, 54, and two ETA colleagues—Gregorio Jimenez Morales, 55, and Beinat Aguinagalde Ugartemendia, 26—in Cahan, Normandy, in northern France. The police had established surveillance on a cottage that had been rented using faked IDs. Police said the terrorists were planning an attack Inside Spain. Authorities seized three firearms, false documents, explosives, money, a stolen car, and computer equipment. Gogeascoechea was wanted for placing explosives around the Guggenheim Museum in Bilbao in 1997. Jimenez was wanted in connection with a failed rocket attack on a former Spanish prime minister in 2001. Aguinagalde was wanted for the murders of a Basque politician in March 2008 and of a businessman in December 2008.

March 2010—Afghanistan—Two gunmen wearing suicide vests and carrying assault rifles climbed over a wall around a USAID contractor's office in Lashkar Gah, Helmand Province, then fired into the office where an American and four Afghans ran an agricultural project. The only person in the office, an Afghan secretary, survived two shots to the stomach. Security guards killed the terrorists before they could set off their devices. 10039901

March 2010—Afghanistan—Late in the month, a convoy of employees of the U.S.-based Chemonics firm was ambushed south of Lashkar Gah; three Afghans were killed. 10039902

March 2010—Pakistan—The previously-unknown Asian Tigers claimed credit for kidnapping a British journalist and two former Pakistani intelligence officers who had traveled to Pakistani's mountainous northwest. Also kidnapped was Sultan Amir Tarar, alias Colonel Imam, who was suspected of assisting the Taliban and al Qaeda. Also held was a Pakistani documentary filmmaker. On April 30, 2010, Pakistani authorities said the kidnappers had shot to death former intelligence officer Khalid Khawaja, 58. He had been a bin Laden supporter. He had served as a squadron commander in Pakistan's air force and was an intermediary between the government and al Qaeda. He had been a legal advisor to the five northern Virginia students who had been accused of terrorism in Pakistan. He was also involved in the 2007 storming of the Red Mosque. The Taliban released the Briton in April 2010. Tarar died in Taliban captivity in mid–January 2011. The Taliban said it was a heart attack; others said he was murdered by his kidnappers. The Taliban demanded a ransom for his body. 10039903

March 2010—Portugal—Basque Nation and Liberty member Andoni Zengotitabengoa was arrested at Lisbon's airport before he could fly to Venezuela with a faked Mexican passport.

March 2, 2010—Philippines—Police in Manila captured three Abu Sayyaf terrorists wanted for arson and robbery during bombing attacks in Mindanao. They were detained in their Manila safe house, which contained grenades, detonating cords, and blasting caps.

March 3, 2010—Iraq—Three bombs went off in Diyala Province at government and medical buildings during the morning, killing at least thirty-three people and injuring fifty-five. The first car bomb went off at an Iraqi police station at 9:45 a.m. in Baqubah. A suicide bomber a few minutes later set off his car bomb near the main provincial building, destroying the offices of former Prime Minister Ibrahim al-Jafari's political party. As the wounded were being transported to the emergency room, a suicide bomber on foot set off his explosives at the main gate to the hospital. Ali al-Tameemi, head of the Diyala health center, was injured in his left hand. Al Qaeda in Iraq was suspected.

March 4, 2010—Strait of Malacca—Singapore's Navy Information Fusion Center warned that terrorists might conduct an attack in the Strait against oil tankers. Malaysian authorities conducted an anti-piracy drill in the area.

March 4, 2010—Yemen—The government arrested eleven al Qaeda in the Arabian Peninsula members in Sana'a following a gun battle in which one man was killed.

March 6, 2010—Pakistan—Authoritites announced the arrest in Karachi of al Qaeda operative Adam Gadahn of Riverside, California, but later withdrew the claim, saying the detainee was the previously unknown Abu Yahya Mujahideen al-Adam, an al Qaeda member from Pennsylvania.

March 7, 2010—Pakistan—American al Qaeda spokesman Adam Gadahn posted on jihadi Web sites a video in which he called on Muslims in the U.S. military to emulate Maj. Nidal Malik Hasan, who shot to death thirteen people at Fort Hood on November 5, 2009. He viewed Hasan as "the ideal role model for every repentant Muslim in the armies of the unbelievers and apostate regimes."

March 8, 2010—Pakistan—A suicide car bomber crashed through a perimeter wall and detonated 1,100 pounds of explosives, killing thirteen and wounding eighty at the Lahore building that houses a special investigative unit that interrogates key terrorism suspects. Some forty counterterrorist officials were inside the building, which collapsed. The Pakistani Taliban was suspected.

March 9, 2010—United States—The Justice Department claimed that Colleen Renee LaRose, alias Jihad Jane, alias Fatima LaRose, 46, of Pennsylvania and five other individuals had allegedly planned a martyrdom operation to kill Swedish cartoonist Lars Vilks. She faced a life sentence and $1 million fine after her indictment for conspiracy to provide material support to terrorists and kill a person in a foreign country, making false statements to a government official and attempted identity theft. She had been arrested in Philadelphia on October 15, 2009, and was held at the Federal Detention Center there on charges of attempting to transfer a passport stolen from her boyfriend, Kurt Gorman.

The Justice Department said she and five unindicted co-conspirators recruited men on the Internet "to wage violent jihad in South Asia and Europe, and recruited women on the Internet who had passports and the ability to travel to and around Europe in support of violent jihad." In June 2008, she had posted a comment on YouTube as Jihad-Jane saying she was "desperate to do something somehow to help" Muslims. From December 2008 to October 2009, she was in e-communication with the five men, developing plans "which included martyring themselves, soliciting funds for terrorists, soliciting passports, and avoiding travel restrictions (through the collection of passports and through marriage) in order to wage violent jihad." She allegedly had contacted violent jihadis in South Asia and throughout Europe. The indictment said she had stolen a U.S. passport to "facilitate an act of international terrorism" and had been ordered "to kill a citizen and resident of Sweden, and to do so in a way that would frighten 'the whole Kufar [nonbeliever world].'" She was represented by federal public defender Mark Wilson. On March 18, 2010, she pleaded not guilty; the trial was set for May. If convicted, she faced life in prison and a $1 million fine. The same day, the *Philadelphia Inquirer* claimed that she had confessed and was working on a plea deal.

LaRose was born in 1963 and lived in Montgomery County, Pennsylvania. The 4 foot, 11 inch, 100-pound middle school dropout was charged in 2002 in Pennsylvania with public drunkenness and disorderly contact. She was also charged with writing bad checks and driving while intoxicated (DWI) in South Texas, where she lived with Sheldon "Buddy" Barnum, who she had married in 1980 when he was 32 and she was 16. She had been married at least twice. She had cared for her boyfriend Gorman's ailing father in a suburb where she had few friends. She left her live-in boyfriend in Pennsburg, outside Philadelphia, in August 2009, shortly after the father's death, and traveled to Ireland and Sweden, possibly to launch the attack. She told e-friends she could "blend in" because of her blond hair, blue eyes, and small frame. On September 30, 2009, she told her Sweden-based jihadi fiancé, who was in an artists' enclave, that it would be "an honour and great pleasure to die or kill for [him] ... only death will stop me here that I am so close to the target!"

On March 3, Irish police in Waterford and Cork had arrested four men and three women—one an American female Muslim convert identified as Jamie Paulin-Ramirez, 31—ranging in age from their mid–20s to late 40s, plotting to kill Lars Vilks. The other suspects were living legally as refugees in Ireland. The detainees included Danijel Orsov, 26, a Croat and a Muslim convert; Nadah Sameh, a Libyan woman in her 30s; and Ghamraffan Slimane and his wife, Ilef, an Algerian couple in their late 40s who were the only people arrested who were not living in Waterford. The couple operated a bakery in Cork. On March 12, Ireland extended the detention of three suspects for three more days. On March 15, Ireland charged Ali Charaf Damache, a ten-year resident of Ireland originally from Algeria, and Abdul Salam Monsour Khalil al-Jahani, from Libya, with minor offenses. Damache made a menacing telephone call; Jahani was charged with

failing to produce a valid ID document. They were scheduled to appear in court on March 19, possibly to face new charges, including conspiracy to murder. Observers suggested LaRose was in contact with the suspects.

Authorities suggested that suburban Denver mother Paulin-Ramirez was motivated by love for an Algerian Muslim rather than terrorism when she went to Ireland on September 11, 2009, and married a Muslim she had met online. She and La Rose had connected in online chat rooms. She was a nursing student and medical aide before converting to Islam. Ireland released the Leadville, Colorado, resident on March 18. She had been living in Waterford with Libyan citizen Abdul Salam al-Jahani since the fall of 2009 and was several months pregnant. She moved into a Dublin hotel with her 6-year-old son, Christian, from a previous marriage. She had previously been married to three Mexican men (she divorced one who beat her; the other two were deported for being illegal immigrants). She was born in a Kansas City suburb, where her parents divorced when she was young. She had a hearing disorder and was often targeted by bullies. The son told his grandparents that he'd been taught to shoot and had his own sword and knife. Paulin-Ramirez had changed Christian's name to Wahid.

On April 2, Paulin-Ramirez was arrested in Philadelphia and charged along with LaRose with conspiracy to provide material support to terrorists. The indictment is a superseding document to a previous indictment that had charged only LaRose, who pleaded not guilty to the original four charges. LaRose was also charged with making false statements to a government official and attempted identity theft. Paulin-Ramirez was represented by attorney Jeremy H. Gonzalez Ibrahim. The indictment said the two e-mailed each other the previous summer. LaRose asked her friend to join her in Europe at a "training camp." Paulin-Ramirez arrived on September 12, 2009, with "the intent to live and train with jihadists." She married an unidentified co-conspirator whom she had never met. La Rose faced life in prison and a $1 million fine; Paulin-Ramirez faced fifteen years and a $250,000 fine.

On April 7, 2010, Jamie Paulin-Ramirez shook her head to plead not guilty to one count of conspiracy to provide material support to terrorists. She was silent so that her voice in court could not be compared to any potential teltaps. She faced a maximum of fifteen years in jail. Ramirez's trial was set for May 2. She was represented by defense lawyer Jeremy Ibrahim.

On February 1, 2011, Colleen LaRose pleaded

guilty to all counts at a federal change-of-plea hearing in Philadelphia. LaRose was indicted in 2009 on conspiring to support terrorists, commit murder overseas, lying to a federal agent, and attempted identity theft. She faced a life sentence. She had been held in a federal detention center isolated from other prisoners in a special housing unit since October 2009. She spent twenty-three hours per day in her cell.

March 10, 2010—Pakistan—At 9:30 a.m., terrorists armed with assault rifles and a bomb attacked the Oghi, Mansehra district offices of the U.S.-based Christian humanitarian aid group World Vision, killing six Pakistani employees. The terrorists stole a computer and telephones. They spoke Urdu, Pashto, and the Pakistani dialect Hindko when telling the aid workers that they had been "forewarned to stop spreading immodesty." 10031001

March 10, 2010—Yemen—Authorities announced the arrest of Sharif Mobley, 26, a U.S. citizen born in New Jersey, in connection with terrorist activity. He had worked as a janitor at U.S. nuclear sites in New Jersey, Maryland, and Pennsylvania, but without access to sensitive information. Yemeni authorities suspected him of killing a hospital guard, whose weapon he seized during a medical visit the previous weekend after being arrested in a sweep of eleven al Qaeda suspects in Sana'a. He attacked guards at the hospital after asking them to join him in prayer, killed one and wounded another, and barricaded himself in a hospital room. He got into a shootout with the guards as he made his way from the fifth to the ground floor, where he was apprehended. He was believed to have been in contact with Anwar al-Aulaqi. U.S. counterterrorist officials believed he had left the United States to contact al Qaeda. He was believed to have been in detention in Yemen for several weeks before the shooting. He had been under FBI investigation in Delaware and New Jersey for some time. His mother was of Somali origin. He had obtained a Yemeni visa to study Arabic.

Mobley had graduated from Buena Regional High School in New Jersey in 2002. He was a member of the school's wrestling team and had a black belt in karate. 10031002

March 11, 2010—Georgia—Armenians Sumbat Tonoyan, 63, who once ran a dairy business, and Hrant Ohanyan, 59, a scientist at the Yerevan Institute of Physics, were arrested while attempting to sell 18 grams of 89.4 percent enriched uranium at a hotel in the Georgian capital to a representative of an Islamist group. They claimed to have much more of the material. They were instead

dealing with an undercover officer. Details of their secret trial were reported by the *Guardian* on November 8, 2010. The duo confessed to smuggling the uranium in a lead-lined cigarette box on a train from Yerevan to Tblisi. They claimed they obtained their sample from Garik Dadayan, a smuggler involved in a 2003 Georgian smuggling case in which the stolen highly enriched uranium (HEU) was traced to a nuclear fuel plant in Novosibirsk, Siberia. He had tried to smuggle 200 grams of HEU into Georgia.

March 12, 2010—Pakistan—Seven Taliban explosions—four of them suicide bombings—killed at least forty-three people in Lahore.

March 13, 2010—Afghanistan—Four suicide bombers attacked Kandahar during the evening, killing thirty-one people and wounding forty-five at a hotel, police station, and the city's main prison, in a possible attempt to free Taliban terrorists. Two car bombers set off their explosives at 7:30 p.m. Another was carried on a motorcycle and the fourth on a bicycle. One bomb killed women and children at a wedding hall near the prison. Rockets were also fired near the prison. A Taliban Web site deemed it a "message" to the "enemies of the mujahedin."

March 13, 2010—India—Authorities arrested Abdul Lateef Rashid, 29, and Riyaz Ali, 23, for planning to conduct attacks in Mumbai, the country's financial capital. The Indian citizens, detained in Mumbai's suburb, were planning to hit an office of the Oil and Natural Gas Corporation and a cloth market in South Mumbai and the Thakkar Mall in Mumbai's western suburbs. No pleas were recorded. The duo were to be charged on March 18. Police said they were receiving directions from handlers in Pakistan.

March 14, 2010—Mexico—Three individuals associated with the U.S. Consulate in Ciudad Juarez were killed in two drive-by shootings. Lesley A. Enriquez, 25, a pregnant American employee at the consulate, and Arthur Hancock Redelfs, 30, her U.S. citizen husband, were found dead inside a white Toyota RAV4 with Texas license plates after they left a children's birthday party. She was shot in the neck and left arm; he was hit near his right eye. Authorities retrieved a 9-mm shell casing. The body of Jorge Alberto Salcido Ceniceros, 37, a Mexican state police officer and husband of a Mexican employee of the consulate, was found inside a 2003 Honda Pilot. Salcido's children, aged 4 and 7, were injured. Drug cartels were suspected. Authorities suspected the Barrio Azteca street gang and were searching for Eduardo "Tablas" Ravelo, 41, a leader of the group on Ciudad Juarez, who joined the FBI's Most Wanted list in 2009. A $100,000 reward was issued for Ravelo, who was believed to have ordered the killings and carried them out himself.

On March 26, Mexican soldiers arrested Ricardo Valles de la Rosa, alias El Chino, alias El 29, 42 (or 45), in the case. He was a leader of the Barrio Aztecas street gang, which is affiliated with the Juarez drug cartel and carries out extortion, murders, and drug trafficking. He was also sought in connection with the murder of Zapata Reyes, a member of the rival Mexicles gang. Valles de la Rosa reportedly was earlier charged with ten counts related to drug trafficking in the United States. He lived in la Colonia Partido Romero in Ciudad Juarez and possibly rented a residence in El Paso. He told authorities that the target was jail guard Arthur Redelfs and the others were collateral damage. The gang claimed Redelfs had abused and menaced gang member El Chano at the El Paso County Jail. De la Rosa had been arrested in October 1995 on charges of being a member of a drug trafficking ring. He served twelve and a half years in U.S. federal prisons, joining the Azteca gang after meeting its leader, David Almaraz. He was deported to Juarez in 2007 after his release from an Oklahoma prison.

Mexican officials on July 2, 2010, arrested Jesus Ernesto Chavez, 41, leader of the U.S.-Mexican Barrio Azteca drug gang, who ordered the hit on Lesley Ann Enriquez because he thought she was dealing visas to the rival Sinaloa gang. Chavez reportedly ran contract killers for the Juarez cartel. He had served five years in Louisiana for distribution of narcotics. The Mexican Army arrested him on June 1, 2008, but he was soon released. He was linked to the murder of fifteen high school athletes and neighbors at a party in a Juarez barrio in 2010. The Aztecas thought they were members of the Artistic Assassins gang.

Authorities arrested Jose Guadalupe Diaz Diaz, alias El Zorro, 32, leader of the Aztecas gang affiliated with the Juarez drug cartel, on November 18, 2010, in connection with the murders.

On November 27, 2010, Juarez authorities arrested the head of the Aztecas, Arturo Gallegos Castrellon, alias El Farmero, 32, who admitted to being behind 80 percent of all drug-related killings in Juarez in the last sixteen months, including the consulate attack. Police seized 2 assault rifles, 2 handguns, 228 cartridges for different weapons, 90 grams of marijuana, 2 cars and 2 trucks, including one that was armored. In 1996, Gallegos was arrested in the United States for drug trafficking.

March 14, 2010—Israel—Authorities arrested senior Hamas operative Maher U'dda, who had been wanted since the end of the 1990s, in a nighttime raid in Ramallah. Israel said he was wanted for the deaths of more than seventy Israelis in several attacks. The 40-something U'dda was a founder of Hamas in Ramallah.

March 14, 2010—Yemen—Yemeni authorities said that two senior al Qaeda militants planning attacks and possibly eighteen other people were killed in an air strike in southern Abyan Province.

March 15, 2010—Nigeria—Two car bombs exploded in the early morning outside a government building in Warri, minutes before state governors were to discuss a peace program aimed at the Movement for the Emancipation of the Niger Delta (MEND) militants. Several people were injured in the attack by MEND. The group threatened to attack the oil infrastructure, including facilities of France's Total SA.

March 16, 2010—France—A French policeman was killed in a clash with Basque Nation and Liberty (ETA) carjackers in a Paris suburb. Authorities arrested Spanish citizen Joseba Fernandez Aspurz, an ETA member. Police suggested that the cars were to be used for attacks in Spain. 10031601

March 18, 2010—Israel—The previously-unknown Ansar al-Sunna claimed credit for a rocket attack from the Gaza Strip that killed a Thai worker. A second strike caused no casualties. 10031801

March 20, 2010—Somalia—Sheik Daud Ali Hasan, a commander of al-Shabaab who had been leading fighting against rival insurgents in Dhobley, near Kenya, was fatally shot in Kismaayo, near al-Shabaab's military base during the night. The group's local chair said several suspects had been arrested. Hizbul Islam denied involvement.

March 24, 2010—Saudi Arabia—Saudi authorities arrested 113 militants with al Qaeda ties who were planning attacks against oil operations and security facilities in the east. The arrests had taken place during the previous five months against three terrorist groups linked to the Yemeni-based al Qaeda in the Arabian Peninsula. Most of the suspects had been captured near the Yemen border. Police seized weapons, ammunition, cameras, prepaid phone cards, and computers. Those arrested included 47 Saudis, 51 Yemenis, a Bangladeshi, a Somali, and an Eritrean. The arrests included 11 Saudis and a Yemeni from two al Qaeda cells planning suicide attacks on oil facilities.

March 24, 2010—Iraq—U.S. and Iraqi troops arrested twelve people, including three senior al Qaeda in Iraq leaders who ran an extortion and assassination network that targeted oil companies and small businesses.

March 25, 2010—Qatar—Al-Jazeera aired a seventy-four-second Osama bin Laden audiotape in which he threatened retaliation against the United States if 9/11 mastermind Khalid Sheikh Mohammed is executed. Addressing "the American people about our prisoners who you are holding," he observed,

> Your master in the White House is following his predecessor in many important issues, like escalating the war in Afghanistan and unfairly treating our prisoners—led by the hero jihadi Khalid Sheikh Mohammed. The White House declared that they will execute Khalid Sheikh Mohammed and his comrades in arms. The day America makes that decision will be the day it has issued a death sentence for any one of you who fall prisoner to us. We have been enduring your masters' oppression for a long time, especially by supporting Israel's occupation of our land in Palestine. Our reaction to that oppression was heard loudly on the 11th with God's help. Justice is to be treated in the same manner.... The politicians of the White House were and still are wronging us, especially by supporting Israel and occupying our land in Palestine. They think that America, behind oceans, is safe from the wrath of the oppressed, until the reaction was loud and strong in your homeland on the 9/11 with God's help. Equal treatment is only fair. War is a back-and-forth.

March 26, 2010—United States—The United States indicted Chicago cab driver Raja Lahrasib Khan, alias Kojak, 56, on two charges of providing material support to terrorists by trying to send money to al Qaeda and discussing an attack on a U.S. stadium. He did not enter a plea. The Pakistani-born U.S. citizen claimed to know Ilyas Kashmiri, a Pakistani extremist with al Qaeda ties. An undercover agent gave Khan $1,000 to send to Kashmiri. Court papers mentioned a March 11 phone call in which Khan talked about attacking a U.S. stadium in August with bombs that go "boom, boom, boom, boom." Khan had told an FBI undercover agent, "If ... every day, you know we are bombing somewhere... kill fifty people, one hundred people, seventy people here, other state, other state ... eventually they get the message." The resident of Chicago's Uptown neighborhood sent a money transfer of $950 to a contact in Pakistan in November 2009 and asked that $300 go to the leader of a Sunni extremist group with ties to al Qaeda. On March 23, authorities at O'Hare International Airport stopped Khan's son before he could board a flight to the United Kingdom

with $700 cash that had been given to his father by an undercover FBI agent. Khan was to meet his son in the United Kingdom and give the cash to Ilyas Kashmiri to buy weapons and other supplies.

Khan had told an undercover FBI agent on February 23 that Osama bin Laden was well, in charge, and giving orders regarding terrorist operations. He admitted he had never met bin Laden.

March 26, 2010—Gaza Strip—Two Israeli soldiers and two Palestinians died in a gun battle on the border with Israel after an Israeli Army patrol found the terrorists planning explosives. The military wing of Hamas—the Izzedine al-Qassam Brigades (also known as the al-Aqsa Brigades)—and the little-known Palestine Taliban all claimed credit.

March 28, 2010—Greece—A man was killed and a mother and her 10-year-old daughter injured when a bomb exploded during the night outside a government building in the Patissia neighborhood of Athens. No one claimed credit.

March 28, 2010—United States—Authorities arrested Khalil Ibrahim Zarou, 31, of Leesburg, Virginia, for providing a false report about planting a bomb after he said early in the morning that people should come see the explosion because there was a bomb on a Carnival Cruise Lines ship *Carnival Sensation* outside Port Canaveral, Florida. The threat was a hoax. The ship, with 3,470 passengers and crew, was cleared out of port at 10:45 a.m.

March 29, 2010—United States—A federal grand jury in Detroit, Michigan, indicted six Michigan residents, two Ohioans, and an Indiana resident on five counts of seditious conspiracy, attempted use of weapons of mass destruction, teaching the use of explosive materials, and possessing a firearm during a crime of violence in connection with a "Christian warrior" militia that planned to kill a Michigan law enforcement officer and then attack other police at the funeral. The charge sheet said that since August 2008, the Lenawee County, Michigan, militia group called the Hutaree conspired to oppose by force the authority of the U.S. government. The indictment noted that Hutaree members view local, state, and federal law enforcement authorities as the enemy and have been preparing to engage them in armed conflict. The group's Web site said that Hutaree means "Christian warrior" and it was "Preparing for the end time battles to keep the testimony of Jesus Christ alive." "We believe that one day, as prophecy says, there will be an Anti-Christ. All

Christians must know this and prepare, just as Christ commanded." Those indicted were David Brian Stone, 45; his wife, Tina Stone, 44; his son Joshua Matthew Stone, 21, of Clayton, Michigan; and another son, David Brian Stone, Jr., 19, of Adrian, Michigan; Joshua Clough, 28, of Blissfield, Michigan; Michael Meeks, 40, of Manchester, Michigan; Thomas Piatek, 46, of Whiting, Indiana; Kristopher Sickles, 27, of Sandusky, Ohio; and Jacob Ward, 33, of Huron, Ohio. Eight of the defendants were arrested; seven appeared before U.S. Magistrate Judge Donald A. Scheer on March 29. Joshua Stone was arrested 20 miles west of his family's home. A bond hearing was set for March 31.

On May 3, 2010, U.S. District Judge Victoria Roberts announced that the nine Hutaree could be released on bond until the criminal charges against them were resolved. A federal grand jury had indicted them on charges of seditious conspiracy, attempted use of weapons of mass destruction, teaching the use of explosive materials, and possessing a firearm during a crime of violence. On May 6, a three-judge panel of the U.S. Court of Appeals for the 6th Circuit in Cincinnati issued a stay of the lower court's decision to release them with electronic monitors and other restrictions. On June 22, 2010, an appeals court reversed a federal judge and ordered the Hutaree members to stay in detention while awaiting trial. Two judges of the tribunal said "no conditions of release will reasonably assure the safety of the community."

On March 29, 2012, David Stone, Sr., 47, and his son Joshua Stone, 23, pleaded guilty to federal charges of possessing illegal automatic firearms two days after Federal District Judge Victoria Roberts in Detroit dropped the charges of sedition and conspiracy to use weapons of mass destruction against the government. They faced up to ten years in prison and a fine of up to $250,000. The Stones "admitted that they possessed machine guns, specifically a Bushmaster .223 caliber rifle and a Double Star Corporation .223 caliber rifle respectively, knowing that the firearms would shoot and were designed to shoot automatically more than one shot, without manual reloading, by a single function of the trigger," the U.S. Attorney's office said. Tina Stone, 46; David Stone, Jr., 22, another son of the elder Stone; Thomas Piatek, 48; Michael Meeks, 40; and Kristopher Sickles, 29, were cleared of all charges. Defendant Joshua Clough, 30, awaited sentencing after pleading guilty to a weapons charge in December 2011. Jacob Ward, 35, will be tried separately.

March 29, 2010—United States—Norman Leboon, 33, was charged with threatening to kill U.S. House of Representatives member Eric Cantor (R–VA) and his family. Cantor, the second-ranking Republican in the House, is the only Jewish Republican in the House. Leboon posted a YouTube video threatening to shoot Cantor. Leboon was arrested at his Philadelphia home on March 27. A bullet had been fired at Cantor's office on March 23. Leboon had previously been arrested on charges of terrorist threats, assault, and reckless endangerment. He faces fifteen years in prison, three years of supervised release, a fine of $500,000, and a $200 special assessment.

March 29, 2010—Russia—Chechen rebels were suspected when two female suicide bombers attacked the Moscow subway, killing forty and wounding more than eighty others in a rush hour attack. One detonated her device at 7:56 a.m. on a train at the Lubyanka stop near the Kremlin and Federal Security Service headquarters, killing at least twenty-three. The second went off forty-five minutes later at Park Kultury station, four stops further on the same train line, killing at least twelve. The explosive belts were packed with bolts and iron bars that served as shrapnel. Police were searching for two suspected female accomplices and released photos of the suspected suicide bombers. The Moscow subway is one of the largest in the world, with seven million riders each day.

On March 31, Doku Umarov, who in 2009 had reestablished a suicide battalion, claimed credit. He said the attacks were retaliation for a raid in February 2010 in which twenty people were killed, charging that authorities used knives to execute innocent forest villagers.

Three St. Petersburg metro stations were shut following a bomb scare.

The first bomber was believed to be the 20-year-old widow of a terrorist leader who was killed in October 2009.

Investigators announced that the second bomber was Dzhanet Abdullayeva, 17, widow of an Islamist rebel leader. Authorities shared photos of her posing with a handgun and a grenade. She grew up in Khasavyurt, 40 miles from the site of the March 31, 2010, bombing in Dagestan. Her husband, Umulat Magomedov, 30, died in a New Year's Eve shootout with security forces in Khasavyurt. They met via the Internet.

A bus driver said the suicide bombers and a man traveled to Moscow from the North Caucasus with shuttle traders.

Authorities were investigating whether the duo were part of the thirty suicide bombers allegedly recruited by Alexander Tikhomirov before his death. They were to be trained at a madrassa in Turkey.

On April 4, Rasul Magomedov told authorities that his daughter, Maryam Sharilova, 28, a schoolteacher in Dagestan, was one of the bombers. He identified her from a photo of the severed head that had run in the Russian media and sent to him via a friend's cell phone. He said she earned a degree in math and psychology from the Dagestan Pedagogical University in 2005. Upon returning home, she taught computer science at a local school. Her brother had been jailed for six months on weapons and kidnapping charges.

Dzhanet Abdullayeva ("Paradise" in the local language) grew up without a father.

The male counterparts of the female suicide bombers set off the explosives via remote control.

On August 21, 2010, Russian security forces killed Magomed-Ali Vagabov, orchestrator of the suicide bombings, in a raid in Dagestan Province.

March 31, 2010—Russia—Two suicide bombers killed twelve people in Kizlyar, Dagestan. The first exploded in a parked car, killing two police officers who drove up in their vehicle. As first responders arrived, a man in a police uniform walked into the crowd and set off a suicide vest, killing the city's police chief and eight other police officers and wounding two dozen people.

April 4, 2010—Russia—A bomb went off before dawn on a railway track in Dagestan, derailing eight carriages of a freight train carrying construction materials on the line from Moscow to Azerbaijan. The bomb damaged 44 yards of track. A passenger train going from Siberia to Baku, Azerbaijan, was stranded.

April 4, 2010—India—Maoist Naxalite terrorists set off a landmine in Orissa state, killing ten and wounding sixteen.

April 4, 2010—Iraq—Al Qaeda in Mesopotamia was blamed for three suicide car bombings at diplomatic targets that killed 30 and wounded 242. The car bombers were also wearing explosive vests. An al Qaeda front group claimed credit. One bomb went off at the Iranian Embassy in the Sahiya District, killing 20, including children, and wounding 125. Another went off at the residence of the Egyptian chargé d'affaires, after a suicide bomber drove into security guards and police and killed 15 and wounded 45. A third exploded at the home of the German ambassador in Mansour district. The bomber at the German site talked his way through four checkpoints without being searched. Police speculated that one of the targets was the Mar Yosif Chaldean Catholic Church in

the Mansour area or perhaps the Syrian Embassy, which is near the German's home.

A fourth suicide bombing was foiled at the offices of the government's embassy protective services in the Karada neighborhood of Baghdad when policemen shot and wounded the driver of a minibus carrying a ton of explosives. The bomber was identified as Ahmed Jassim, 17, who was hospitalized with a leg wound. He was believed to have been on drugs at the time of the attack. The bomb was defused.

A fifth car bomb exploded while being assembled, killing two terrorists and wounding a third.

Two "sticky" bombs, limpeted on the underside of autos in the Dora neighborhood of southern Baghdad, wounded 2 people. 10040401-03

April 5, 2010—Russia—A suicide bomber set off his explosives next to a police car and killed two police officers in Karabulak, Ingushetia. Another police officer was hospitalized with blast trauma.

A half hour later, a second car bomb went off near a police headquarters nearby, causing several injuries.

April 6, 2010—Iraq—Seven bombs exploded in Shi'ite neighborhoods in Baghdad, killing 35 and wounding 140. Al Qaeda in Iraq was suspected. In five of the bombings, explosives went off in rented rooms or stores near apartment buildings. In the Chikook neighborhood two weeks earlier, two people rented a restaurant and a convenience store, rigged explosives, and set them off at 9:00 a.m. The same took place in the Shawaka district of the old city of central Baghdad at an apartment building, a video game store, and a traditional café.

April 6, 2010—Pakistan—A suicide bomber killed fifty-one people and injured eighty-nine at a pro-government Awami National Party rally in Timaragarah in the Lower Dir district of North West Frontier Province. The rally was celebrating parliament's change of the North West Frontier's name to Khyber-Pakhtoonkhwa Province.

April 6, 2010—Pakistan—Hours later, militants attacked the U.S. Consulate in Peshawar. A suicide bomber set off his vehicle at a security checkpoint blocking the road outside the consulate. Terrorists in paramilitary uniforms then threw grenades and fired at security forces, who repelled the attackers. The Pakistani Taliban's spokesman Azam Tariq claimed credit, saying it was avenging drone attacks. Bodies of four attackers were found; two were wearing unexploded suicide vests. Two consulate guards were killed.

The UN announced a two-day closure of its offices in Peshawar. 10040601

April 6, 2010—India—At 6:30 a.m., between five hundred and one thousand Maoist Naxalite insurgents killed seventy-three Indian paramilitary Central Reserve Police Force officers on patrol in an isolated forest region in the Dantewada region of Chhittisgarh State during Operation Green Hunt.

April 6, 2010—United States—The FBI arrested Charles Alan Wilson in Yakima, Washington, after he left a threatening voicemail at the office of Democratic Senator Patty Murray because of her support for health care reform. The message said she had a target on her back and "it only takes one piece of lead." He had left another message on March 22 that said, "Now that you've passed your health care bill, let the violence begin." He had a concealed carry permit for his .38 caliber revolver. He was scheduled to appear in federal court on one count of threatening a federal official.

April 7, 2010—United States—The FBI arrested Gregory Lee Giusti, 48, at his home in San Francisco's Tenderloin District for threatening House Speaker Nancy Pelosi over her support of health care reform. He was accused of making dozens of threatening phone calls to her homes and her husband's office.

April 10, 2010—Mexico—A bomb was thrown over the wall of the U.S. Consulate in Nueva Laredo. No injuries were reported. 10041001

April 10, 2010—Afghanistan—The government arrested nine people, including three Italian medical workers, affiliated with the Milan-based aid group Emergency in Lashkar Gah, in a Quetta Shura suicide bombing assassination plot against leaders of Helmand Province. Among those targeted was southern Helmand Governor Gulab Mangal. Investigators discovered ten suicide vests, two pistols, nine hand grenades, and other explosives hidden in medicine cartons at a clinic. The Pakistani Taliban had provided the group $500,000 for the attack, which was to occur in a crowded location. Two bombs were to go off in Lashkar Gah, one in a populated area or a picnic site in the suburbs and the second at a hospital when Mangal would have visited the injured.

The government said the three Italians were responsible for killing Afghan translator Ajmal Naqshbandi following the Taliban's kidnapping of Italian journalist Danielle Mastrogiacomo, whose release had been negotiated by an Emergency in Lashkar Gah staffer. The three Italians and five of the Afghans were cleared of charges and released on April 18. A sixth Afghan remained detained.

April 11, 2010—Sudan—Four African Union peacekeepers were missing in Darfur after they left Nyala, the capital of South Darfur state en route to their private quarters 7 kilometers away.

April 12, 2010—Northern Ireland—Irish Republican Army (IRA) dissidents set off a bomb at 12:24 a.m. outside the MI5 headquarters in Hollywood city, hours before Catholic and Protestant leaders were to elect a new justice minister. Gunmen kidnapped a Belfast taxi driver at his home and used his car to transport the bomb to the security walls of Palace Barracks, a former British Army base that houses the Northern Ireland MI5 office. One man was hospitalized for shock. Little damage resulted. British power for running the justice system had been transferred at midnight. The Real IRA claimed credit.

April 12, 2010—Afghanistan—Hosiy Sahibzada, 24, an Afghan who worked for the Bethesda, Maryland-based DAI, a global development company, was shot to death as she walked home from the DAI office in Kandahar City. 10041201

April 12, 2010—Afghanistan—An Afghan employee of the Arlington, Virginia-based International Relief and Development was shot to death in the Garmsir area of Helmand Province. 10041202

April 13, 2010—Philippines—At 10:50 a.m., a bomb went off in a motorcycle park between the Santa Isabela Cathedral and Isabela Park in Isabela City, Basilan. Other bombs were found near the city hall, a judge's home, and a local high school. Another bomb went off during rush hour in a van parked at a grandstand at a local sports center. Some twenty-five Abu Sayyaf terrorists disguised as police officers and soldiers conducted other attacks and bombings, killing twelve people, including three Marines, a policeman, five civilians, and three terrorists, including Abu Sayyaf commander Bensar Indama, who wore a police uniform. Nine people were injured, including two terrorists who were captured. The terrorists had split into three groups when confronted by authorities, who said the terrorists planned to set off additional bombs and take hostages. Witnesses said Abu Sayyaf commander, Puruji Indama, brother of Bensar Indama, escaped. Puruji was believed behind kidnappings and beheadings.

April 13, 2010—Israel—An Israeli counterterrorism unit warned Israeli citizens in Egypt's Sinai Peninsula that terrorists were planning kidnappings in the tourist destination.

April 13, 2010—Congo—Mai Mai Yakutumba rebels abducted eight Red Cross employees in eastern Kivu Province. The government accused the terrorists of planning to use them as human shields to prevent a planned army assault. The aid group said negotiations were under way to secure their release.

April 13, 2010—Gaza Strip—Israeli troops killed at least two Palestinian militants attempting to plant explosives near a crossing between Gaza and Israel. Gaza medics recovered only two bodies, although authorities claimed to have killed four terrorists. Israel brought in tanks and helicopters in the firefight. Islamic Jihad was blamed.

April 14, 2010—Iraq—Local authorities arrested two members of al Qaeda in Iraq planning to hijack planes and fly them into Shi'ite holy shrines.

April 14, 2010—Afghanistan—A suicide car bomb exploded at 9:30 p.m. outside a Kandahar City compound used by Western contractors. Four Afghan security guards were killed and sixteen other people were wounded, among them two Americans and South African and Nepalese employees. The compound's USAID contractors include workers from Chemonics International, the Louis Berger Group, and the Central Asia Development Group. Three buildings were damaged. 10041401

April 15, 2010—Myanmar—The government blamed terrorists for setting off three bombs at 3:00 p.m. that killed twenty people and wounded more than seventy others (according to hospital records) during a New Year's water festival in Yangon at Kandawgyi Lake. The government said eight died, ninety were wounded. No one claimed credit.

April 15, 2010—Switzerland—Authorities arrested two Italians and a Swiss national (two men and a woman) on suspicion of planning to bomb an IBM nanotechnology research facility near Rueschlikon, 6 miles south of Zurich. Police found "explosive and further items in their car" and a note referring to "a planned attack on the branch of an international company," according to the Federal Prosecutors Office. As of April 26, the trio was in custody. WTOP Radio reported on May 2 that the Italians were ecoterrorists.

April 16, 2010—Pakistan—A suicide bomber killed eight people in a hospital emergency room in Quetta where Shi'ites were mourning a bank manager who had been shot to death that morning. A journalist and two police officers were among the dead.

April 17, 2010—India—Two explosions went off at a crowded cricket stadium in Bangalore, injuring fifteen of the thousands of spectators an hour before the Premier League match between the Mumbai Indians and the Bangalore Royal Challenge. Officials were trying to determine if terrorists were involved.

April 17, 2010—Pakistan—At noon, burqa-wearing suicide bombers killed forty-one and injured sixty-one at a camp for displaced people in Kohat northwestern Pakistan. The second bomb went off as people rushed in to help the victims of the first bomb. Umar, a spokesman for Lashkar-e-Jhangvi Al almi, said that the group was retaliating for the conversions to Sunni of two Shi'ite women from Kachai village in Kohat district. He claimed the two women were killed by Shi'ite Muslims in their village. The Pakistani Taliban was also suspected.

April 18, 2010—Iraq—Al Qaeda in Iraq leaders Abu Ayyub al-Masri, alias Abu Hamza al-Muhajer, true name Yasif al-Dardiri, and Abu Omar al-Baghdadi, true name Hamid Dawud Muhammad Khalil al-Zawi, were killed in a joint U.S.-Iraqi operation against a safe house in al-Tharthar, 10 kilometers south of Tikrit. The Egyptian al-Masri was the group's military leader; Al-Baghdadi, alias "Prince of the Faithful," led the Islamic State of Iraq, an umbrella group that includes al Qaeda in Iraq. Al-Masri's assistant and al-Baghdadi's son were killed as well when a suicide bomb went off inside the house and American forces dropped another bomb on the facility. Another sixteen terrorists were arrested. One U.S. soldier died and three were injured in a helicopter crash during the operation. On April 25, the Islamic State of Iraq confirmed that the two leaders had died.

April 19, 2010—Pakistan—The Associated Press ran a story of a foiled suicide bombing orchestrated by Abdul Baseer, 25, who sent grenades and an explosives vest ahead before boarding a bus with Mohi-ud-Din, 14, who was to be the suicide bomber. The duo would have attacked the PC International luxury hotel in Lahore frequented by Americans. The duo was arrested at the house of another suspect days before they were to set off the explosives.

Baseer, born in 1985 near the Swat Valley, claimed to have attacked a U.S. patrol in Afghanistan. He was the eldest of seven children of a wheat farmer. He attended three Islamic boarding schools, memorizing the Quran. One of them was Jamia Faridia in Islamabad, which was believed to be a madrassa used to recruit terrorists. He claimed to have done three summer internships for the Taliban in Kunar Province in Afghanistan. He later made ten suicide vests for Nazir, a Pakistani Taliban commander.

April 22, 2010—Thailand—Five M-79 grenades were fired from a shoulder-mounted launcher at a pro-government demonstration in Bangkok's business district, killing three and wounding seventy-five. Four people, including two foreigners, were seriously wounded. Anti-government "red shirts" were suspected; the group's leaders denied responsibility. 10042201

April 22, 2010—Niger—Al Qaeda in the Islamic Maghreb (AQIM) kidnapped retired French engineer Michel Germaneau, 78. The group had threatened to kill him if several imprisoned AQIM members were not freed by July 26. In a May video, he asked the French president to find a solution. On July 22, 2010, French and Mauritanian commandos attacked an AQIM campsite, killing six terrorists. Four others escaped in the Sahara on the border with Mali. Authorities said they were trying to foil a planned attack on a military base in Mauritania. Others suggested that they were attempting to free Germaneau, who was not at the raid site.

On July 25, AQIM leader Abdelmalek Droukdel sent an audio message to al-Jazeera in which he said that the group had killed Germaneau in retaliation for the July 22 raid. Droukdel observed, "Sarkozy has failed to free his compatriot in this failed operation ... he opened the doors of hell for himself and his people. As a quick response to the despicable French act, we confirm that we have killed hostage Germaneau in revenge for our six brothers who were killed in the treacherous operation." French Prime Minister Francois Fillon announced, "We are at war with al Qaeda." 10042202

April 23, 2010—Iraq—Ten morning car bombs went off at Shi'ite mosques in Baghdad, killing fifty-eight people. At least thirty-nine people died in two explosions in Sadr City. Residents threw bricks at arriving soldiers, who responded by opening fire, killing and injuring several. Another three car bombs killed nineteen in Hurriyah, Ameen, and Zafraniya, also Moqtada al-Sadr strongholds. The government blamed al Qaeda in Iraq.

Six bombs went off in Khaldiyah in Anbar Province, killing nine people. Targets included a contractor who worked with the U.S. military, a member of a Sunni paramilitary group, and an investigative judge.

April 25, 2010—Afghanistan—CNN reported that the Taliban was suspected of poison gas attacks against three girls' schools that sickened eighty-eight students and teachers in northern Kunduz Province.

April 26, 2010—Yemen—At 8:00 a.m., Othman Ali al-Salwi, 22, a student from Taiz Province, died when he set off his suicide vest next to the British ambassador's vehicle in a failed attempt to assassinate British Ambassador to Yemen Tim Torlot, 52. Three Yemeni bystanders, including at least one man and one woman, were hospitalized. No Britons were harmed by the blast, which took place a short distance from the U.K. Embassy in Noqom in eastern Sana'a. Al-Salwi was wearing sports gear with explosives strapped to his body. Torlot arrived in July 2007. Al Qaeda in the Arabian Peninsula was suspected. Al-Salwi's father said that his son had disappeared six weeks earlier. He condemned his son's actions and said he had tried to get him to marry and find a job. The terrorist had lived in Sana'a. The next day, the government arrested dozens of al Qaeda members, including seven Yemenis with close relations to al-Salwi. 10042601

April 27, 2010—France/United States—Passenger Derek Stansberry of Florida was restrained by federal air marshals after telling a flight attendant that he had a bomb in his luggage on Delta flight 273 from Paris Charles de Gaulle International Airport. The plane was diverted from its flight to Atlanta and landed safely at the Bangor, Maine, airport around 3:30 p.m. Stansberry had served as a U.S. Air Force intelligence officer until 2009. No explosives were found. The Airbus 330 had left Paris at 1:39 p.m. Paris time and was due to arrive in Atlanta at 5:25 p.m.

April 28, 2010—Egypt—A court convicted twenty-six men of membership in a Hizballah cell that planned to attack Israeli tourists in the Sinai Peninsula, fire on ships passing through the Suez Canal, and smuggle weapons, supplies, and people through tunnels to the Gaza Strip. Sentences ranged from six months to life in prison. Prosecutors had requested the death penalty for several defendants, including Muhammad Youssef Mansour, alias Sami Shehab, who had been sent by Hizballah to organize the cell in Egypt. Four of the defendants were tried in absentia. They included Mohammed Qublan and two others at large who were given life sentences.

April 30, 2010—United States—A Manhattan federal court charged Brooklyn-born Wesam el-Hanafi, 33, of traveling to Yemen to meet with al Qaida members in February 2008. He and a former accountant were charged with conspiracy to give computer advice, purchase wrist watches, and otherwise help the terrorist group to "modernize." The indictment said the terrorists "instructed him on operational security measures and directed him to perform tasks for al-Qaida." He also "took an oath of allegiance to al-Qaeda." After purchasing computer software that let him securely communicate with al Qaeda, he met in the summer with an unnamed co-conspirator and the second defendant, Sabirhan Hasanoff, 34, in Brooklyn to discuss joining the group. The third person gave $50,000 to Hasanoff, who later traveled to New York City and performed unspecified "tasks for al-Qaeda." The indictment said that El-Hanafi bought seven Casio digital watches in 2009. Prosecutors described Hasanoff as a dual citizen of the United States and Australia who has lived in Brooklyn. He has a Queens address and is a certified public accountant. A professional networking site says a Sabir Hasanoff was a senior manager at PricewaterhouseCoopers (PwC) who graduated from Baruch College in Manhattan. A PwC spokesman said Hasanoff worked there from 2003 to 2006. At an initial court appearance in Alexandria, Virginia, the duo waived their rights to a hearing. They were detained and ordered transferred to New York for a bail hearing. They faced fifteen years in prison. El-Hanafi was represented by attorney Victor Knapp; Hasanoff by Anthony L. Ricco. Federal Magistrate Judge James C. Francis, IV, refused to grant bail to Hasanoff on May 17. Hasanoff pleaded not guilty.

May 2010—Morocco—Authorities arrested twenty-four members of an al Qaeda–linked cell and were looking for another in France.

May 1, 2010—United States—A bomb threat was found on a lavatory mirror on United Airlines flight 148 from Chicago, Illinois, to Philadelphia, Pennsylvania. The plane landed shortly before 7:00 p.m. The threat was a hoax.

May 1, 2010—United States—Explosives were found in a tinted, dark green sport utility vehicle parked on 45th Street and Broadway near 7th Avenue in Times Square in New York City after street vendors Lance Horton and Duane M. Jackson noticed smoke pouring out of a 1993 Nissan Pathfinder with its engine running and hazard lights flashing shortly after 6:00 p.m. A firefighter reported a "mini explosion" in the back of the vehicle. Police seized three propane tanks, two filled five-gallon gas containers, two alarm clocks with batteries, 152 consumer-grade M-88 fireworks containing black powder, and 100 pounds of fertilizer in plastic bags bearing a store's logo and held in a 78-pound GC-14P gun steel security cabinet manufactured by Stack-On. Police also found three keys, including one to the apartment of Faisal Shahzad and one to his getaway car. The

SUV's Connecticut license plate was stolen from another truck parked at an automobile junkyard near Bridgeport, Connecticut. The vehicle's Vehicle Identification Number (VIN) had been scratched out from some of the car's parts; police found the VIN on its engine block. Police believed the car was parked at 6:28 p.m. and discovered minutes later.

In a seventy-one-second video, the Pakistani Taliban said it was retaliating for the deaths of Abu Omar al-Baghdadi and Abu Ayyub al-Masri (two al Qaeda in Iraq leaders) and of Pakistani Taliban leader Baitullah Mehsud. The video, in Urdu, said the group took "full responsibility for the recent attack in the USA" in response to "interference and terrorism in Muslim countries, especially in Pakistan for the Lalmasjid operation" in which the Pakistani Army in 2007 stormed the Red Mosque in Islamabad. The group complained about drone strikes and the "abduction, torture, and humiliation" of Aafia Siddiqui. Spokesman Qari Hussain, a Pakistani Taliban suicide bomber trainer, claimed credit. New York Police Department sources said there was no further evidence of Taliban involvement.

Police searched for a man on a security video seen leaving the area and taking off his shirt.

On May 3—within fifty-three hours and seventeen minutes of the discovery of the vehicle—police arrested Faisal Shahzad, 30, a naturalized U.S. citizen from Pabbi, Pakistan, residing in Connecticut, as he was boarding Emirates Airlines flight 202 from New York's John F. Kennedy International Airport to Dubai. He had used cash to purchase his ticket. Police were determining why he was let onto the plane although he was on a no-fly list. Authorities arrived after the plane's door had closed. After the plane's doors were closed following Shahzad's arrest, authorities had them opened a second time so that they could deplane two other persons of interest. The FBI said that it had him under surveillance before he boarded the plane but had lost him for a time.

He had purchased the Pathfinder with cash from a woman in Bridgeport, Connecticut, who advertised it for sale on Web sites. The SUV had 141,000 miles on the odometer and was available for $1,300, according to nothingbutcars.net and Craigslist.

Shahzad had also purchased a 9-mm Kel-Tec rifle from a gun shop in Shelton, Connecticut in March 2010. Investigators found the gun and ammunition magazines in an Isuzu Trooper he left at the airport.

Shahzad purchased the fireworks at Phantom Fireworks in Matamoras, Pennsylvania, on March 8.

He apparently did not know the difference between the consumer-grade M-88s, which do not jointly detonate, and M-80s, which would have caused a significant explosion.

Shahzad admitted setting the bomb and to having trained in bomb-making in Waziristan, Pakistan, by the Pakistani Taliban. He had family ties in Karachi. He had no history of violence or connection to militant Islam. His family often hosted barbecues on their back deck. His wife, Colorado-born Huma Mian, often wore a veil and robe. He wore suits or khakis.

Police read Shahzad his Miranda rights several hours after his arrest. He waived his rights and continued to cooperate with investigators.

Shahzad's father was Bahar ul–Haq, a retired vice air marshal living in Peshawar.

He had lived in the United States since January 16, 1999, after receiving a student visa at age 19. He earned a bachelor of science degree in computer science from the University of Bridgeport in 2000, and a master of business administration from the school in 2005. He earned Ds in English Composition and Microeconomics, Bs in Introduction to Accounting and Introduction to Humanities, and a C in Statistics. He had transferred from now-defunct Southeastern University in Washington. Professors called him an unremarkable student. He had worked at the Connecticut-based marketing company Affinion Group for three years as a financial analyst making $50,000 per year before leaving in June 2009. The couple had purchased a gray two story home in Shelton, Connecticut, for $273,000 and failed to sell it in 2008, defaulting on their mortgage. He did not attend the town's main mosque. The family—he, his wife, and two daughters—moved to Pakistan in 2009. He returned to the United States in February 2010. On April 16, he activated a prepaid cell phone that would expire within two weeks. He called the car seller, a Pennsylvania fireworks dealer, and Pakistan.

He had intended to take a connecting flight from Dubai to Pakistan.

Two people in Karachi, Pakistan were arrested in the case initially; five were in custody by May 4. Pakistani authorities said he might have had contact with Ilyas Kashmiri. Among those arrested was Tauhid Ahmed, who was in touch with Shahzad via e-mail and had met him either in the United States or Karachi. Detainee Muhammad Rehan had met with Shahzad during the latter's visit to Pakistan. Rehan was arrested in Karachi following morning prayers at a mosque frequented by Jaish-e-Muhammad. Rehan said he had rented a pickup truck and driven with Shahzad to Peshawar, where they stayed from July 7 to July 29, 2009.

The government charged Shahzad with five felony counts in a federal court in Manhattan.

On May 6, Taliban spokesman Azam Tariq denied responsibility.

FBI investigators arrived in Islamabad on May 7, tracking Shahzad's sources of funding for the attack. Shahzad brought $80,000 in cash into the United States when he returned from trips overseas between 1999 and 2008. Authorities believed he was in touch with Jaish-e-Muhammad. Shahzad said he was inspired by Anwar al-Aulaqi.

On May 9, the Obama administration said the Tehrik-e-Taliban had directed and probably financed Shahzad's efforts.

On May 13, federal authorities conducted raids in four northeastern states and arrested three people (two in the Boston area and one in Maine) in connection with—perhaps unknowingly—moving money to Shahzad via hawalas. The trio was charged with immigration violations. Authorities carried boxes of evidence from a house in Watertown, Massachusetts, and searched a car at a service station in Brookline, Massachusetts. Mohammad Shafiq Rahman, 33, a computer programmer, was arrested in Maine. The Bostonians were identified as Pir Khan, 43, a taxi driver, and his nephew Aftab Ali Khan, alias Aftab Ali, a 20-something gas station attendant, who were held on immigration violations. Authorities believed they had given money to Shahzad. They lived in a 39 Waverley Avenue apartment in Watertown, Massachusetts. Pakistani authorities arrested a suspect with connections to the Pakistani Taliban who was believed to be an accomplice. The next day, Pakistani authorities questioned five people from a Karachi mosque affiliated with Jaish-e-Muhammad. On May 29, Aftab Khan was ordered to return to Pakistan by immigration Judge Robin Feder. The Khans were represented by attorneys Mary Attia and Saher Macarius.

On May 10, Pakistani authorities arrested Salman Ashraf Khan, 35, an executive with Hanif Rajput Caterers, a firm that organized functions for the U.S. Embassy. Khan attended the University of Houston in 2000, majoring in computer science. He was believed to have been a member of a group in Islamabad who assisted Shahzad. Authorities also arrested his close friend, Ahmed Raza Khan.

The Associated Press reported on May 19 that Shahzad had told authorities he had also considered attacks on Grand Central Terminal, Rockefeller Center, the World Financial Center, and Sikorsky, Inc. He asked his questioners why his bomb failed.

On May 18, Shahzad was ordered held without bail.

On May 21, Pakistan arrested an army major in Rawalpindi.

On May 31, Pakistani authorities released former Pakistani Army Maj. Adnan Ahmad, who had been detained in mid–May for having links with Shahzad, including meeting and exchanging cell phone calls. He was cleared of the allegations. His brother, Qamar Ahmad, a computer engineer, was also expected to be released.

As of May 31, Shoaib Mughal, a Pakistani computer sales business owner from Islamabad, remained in custody. He was suspected of sending $11,000 to $15,000 from the Taliban to Shahzad with the help of Shahid Hussain, Shahzad's friend who had lived in Pakistan and the United States and who was also in Pakistani custody.

Shahzad's indictment by a federal grand jury in the Southern District of New York was released on June 17. He was charged with ten counts; the five new charges included conspiracy to use a weapon of mass destruction, being armed with a 9-mm rifle, and committing an act of terrorism "transcending national boundaries." The indictment said he received $12,000 from the Pakistani Taliban, which trained him in explosives in Waziristan. He received $5,000 on February 25 in Massachusetts and $7,000 two weeks later in Ronkonkoma, New York. Six counts carried life terms; life was the minimum sentence for two counts.

On June 21, 2010, Shahzad pleaded, "one hundred times" guilty to the charges. He said more attacks would come because the United States is "terrorizing the Muslim nations and the Muslim people." He chose the warm Saturday night because more people would be potential targets. He had no plea agreement and faced a mandatory life sentence; sentencing was set for October 5, 2010, by Judge Miriam Goldman Cedarbaum.

On July 2, Mohammad Shafiq Rahman's wife said he would soon be freed on $10,000 bail. Rahman was represented by attorney Cynthia Arn. The computer programmer came to the United States legally in 1999 and had no criminal record. He married in March 2010. He knew Shahzad when he lived in Connecticut ten years earlier. Arn said he had not seen him for eight years. On August 24, 2010, federal immigration Judge Brenda O'Malley reinstated bail for Mohammad Shafiq Rahman.

On September 8, 2010, Pakistan charged three young Pakistanis—Shahid Hussain, Shoaib Mughal, and Humbal Akhtar—who were close friends with Faisal Shahzad with criminal conspiracy to commit terrorism. Prosecutors said the trio confessed to helping to prepare Shahzad for the attack by setting up meetings with senior Pakistani Taliban leaders—including Hakimullah Mehsud—facilitating his training at Pakistani Taliban boot camps, and sending him $13,000.

On September 15, 2010, the FBI-led Joint Terrorism Task Force arrested Mohammad Younis, 44, at his home in Long Island, New York, and indicted him on charges of operating an unlicensed hawala. In April 2010, he had met with Shahzad and provided him with thousands of dollars. Younis pleaded not guilty to federal charges of conducting an unlicensed money transfer business and conspiring to do so. He faced ten years in prison. Prosecutors said he unwittingly aided the terror plot.

On September 29 during the trial, prosecutors said Faisal Shahzad planted the car bomb, then e-mailed his Pakistani Taliban contacts to brag about the act. Shahzad told authorities he thought the bomb would kill at least forty people, because he had watched live video feeds of the area for three months to get an idea of when the largest crowds were present. He told interrogators that he planned a second bombing in the city two weeks later and planned to conduct additional attacks until captured or killed. Sentencing was scheduled for October 5. Prosecutors requested a life sentence.

On September 30, Pakistan arrested Faisal Abbasi, an employee of the Council of Islamic Ideology, who accompanied Shahzad while in Pakistan.

On October 5, 2010, the court sentenced Faisal to life in prison. Shahzad shot back, "Brace yourself, the war with Muslims has just begun. The defeat of the U.S. is imminent, inshallah.... We will terrorize you.... My sentence reflects life in this world, not life in the hereafter.... I'm happy with the deal that God has given me.... The Quran gives us the right to defend ourselves."

Reuters reported the next day that Abdul Jabbar, a Briton killed in an air strike in Pakistan on September 8, 2010, had links to Faisal Shahzad.

On May 21, 2011, U.S. Immigration and Customs Enforcement (ICE) agents deported Aftab Ali Khan, 28, to Islamabad, Pakistan. He had pleaded guilty to unlicensed money transmitting and immigration document fraud. U.S. District Court Judge Denise J. Casper sentenced him to time served (eleven months) with three years of supervised release. He was then released to ICE for deportation hearings.

On February 26, 2012, Duane Jackson, the Times Square vendor who alerted police to the

SUV, said he would run for office in New York's 19th Congressional District.

On June 2, 2012, a Pakistani antiterrorism court acquitted four men who had been charged with providing financial and logistical support to Faisal Shahzad. They were identified as Muhammad Shouaib Mughal, Shahid Hussain, Humbal Akhtar, and Faisal Abbasi. They had been arrested in Pakistan shortly after Shahzad tried to detonate an SUV in Times Square, New York City. Three of them were indicted in November 2010 in a Pakistani antiterrorism court. Three were released by that evening; Abbasi remained in custody to face charges in another case. 10050101

May 1, 2010—Somalia—Two bombs went off minutes apart near the Abdala Shideya Mosque in the Bakaro market in Mogadishu, killing at least thirty people and wounding scores. The area is an al-Shabaab stronghold. The first bomb went off at 12:45 p.m. when worshipers were getting ready to pray. The second went off when rescuers arrived. Abdul Qadir, director of an ambulance service, said his vehicles carried fifty-two patients to a hospital and at least forty people died. No one claimed credit. Senior al-Shabaab leader Fuad Shongole was believed to have been injured in the explosions.

May 1, 2010—India—Canada, New Zealand, the United Kingdom, Australia, and the United States issued warnings to its citizens that terrorists were planning imminent attacks in New Delhi.

May 2, 2010 United States Pakistani Taliban leader Hakimullah Mehsud, earlier thought dead, released a nine-minute video produced by Umar Studio in which he promised attacks on major U.S. cities. The video apparently was made in early April; he claimed the date was April 4. "God willing, very soon in some days or a month's time, the Muslim [community] will see the fruits of most successful attacks of our fedayeen in USA." The group had claimed credit for the unsuccessful Times Square attack of the previous day. A followup audio by Mehsud appeared to have been taped on April 19.

May 2, 2010—United States—A bomb scare interrupted the Pittsburgh Marathon while police searched an abandoned microwave oven believed to have contained explosives. Reports differed as to whether the device found near the finish line was a bomb. A police robot dismantled the device.

May 3, 2010—Afghanistan—A suicide car bomber killed an Afghan civilian and wounded two Afghan security guards outside Camp Chapman in Khost Province, the same site where seven CIA officers were killed in a December 30, 2009, bombing.

May 9, 2010—Pakistan—Local authorities arrested Faiz Mohammad, 30, as he was about to board a Thai Airways flight from Karachi to Muscat after a routine security check found that he had hidden two batteries and electrical circuits in his shoes. He claimed it was a foot massager.

May 10, 2010—United States—A pipe bomb went off at the Islamic Center of Northeast Florida in Jacksonville, Florida, causing no injuries but some damage. On May 4, 2011, state and federal agents shot and killed Sandlin Matthews Smith, 46, of St. Johns County, Florida, after he pulled a firearm when they approached him in a field at Glass Mountain State Park near Orienta, Oklahoma. They were trying to serve an arrest warrant on him for federal charges in connection with the bombing.

May 11, 2010—Chile—Local police arrested a Pakistani man after traces of explosives set off detectors at the U.S. Embassy. U.S. Ambassador Paul Simon said Mohammed Saif Ur-Rehman had scheduled an interview.

May 12, 2010—Germany—Two Russian male pilots were arrested at Berlin's Tegel Airport after a witness told police she believed they were planning a hijacking. They were scheduled on an Air Berlin flight to Moscow.

May 12, 2010—Indonesia—Antiterrorism teams killed five suspected Islamist militants in shootouts in and around the capital. Those killed included Ahmad Maulana and Saptono, who died in a raid in Cikampek, 45 miles each of Jakarta. Saptono was one of Indonesia's twenty-five most wanted fugitives. The duo was wanted for several attacks, including the 2004 suicide bombing at the Australian Embassy. Authorities later said the terrorists were planning several Mumbai-like attacks in which a hotel catering to foreigners would be attacked, Indonesia's President Susilo Bambang Yudhoyono would be assassinated at an Independence Day ceremony on August 17, and President Obama would be targeted during a visit in June. Some of the terrorists were believed affiliated with al Qaeda of the Verandah of Mecca; others were members of Lintas Tanzim.

May 12, 2010—United States—An individual suggested on a jihadi Web site that "invasions suspicious bags [sic]" be placed in "the heart of Washington and New York" to desensitize first responders to true bombs. Before the May 1 Times Square attempt, there had been 90 calls per day to the New York Police Department regarding suspicious packages; the following week, there were 140 such calls.

May 14, 2010—United Kingdom—British-born Roshonara Choudhry, 21, attacked then–Treasury Minister Stephen Timms, 55, with a kitchen knife in an area of east London with a large Muslim population. She stabbed Timms twice. He was hospitalized for a week. She was represented by attorney Jeremy Dein. The Bengali-descended woman was found guilty in the Old Bailey court in London on November 2, 2010, of attempted murder of the Labour Party parliament member. Timms had voted in favor of participation in the war in Iraq. She was believed influenced by Anwar al-Aulaqi. She was a student in English language and communications at King's College London from September 2007 through April 2010, when she dropped out. She said she wanted to punish Timms and "get revenge for the people of Iraq."

May 16, 2010—Yemen—Al Qaeda in the Arabian Peninsula issued an audiotape on Islamist Web sites in which group leader Nasser al-Wahayshi warned of attacks if the United States should harm U.S.-born radical cleric Anwar al-Aulaqi. He admitted the December 25, 2009, airline bombing attempt "was a failure, but tell me, what will success be like.... It will inevitably be a disaster for you [Americans], for we are enamored with the attacks of September 11.... The threats of the United States do not frighten us.... Muslims, do not worry about the sheikh (Aulaqi), he is in safe hands."

May 17, 2010—India—Maoist rebels set off a landmine under a bus carrying police and civilians in Chhattisgarh State, killing thirty-five people, including nineteen civilians and sixteen police.

May 18, 2010—Sudan—American aid worker Flavia Wagner, 35, was kidnapped in Darfur. She worked for the U.S. charity Samaritan's Purse. She was freed on August 31, 2010, after 105 days in captivity. 10051801

May 20, 2010—France—French police arrested Basque Nation and Liberty leader Mikel Kabikoitz Carrera Sarobe and his deputy.

May 23, 2010—Yemen—Anwar al-Aulaqi posted a forty-five-minute video on the Internet in which he called on Muslims to kill U.S. civilians. "The American people, in general, are taking part in this, and they elected this administration, and they are financing the war.... Those who might be killed in a plane are merely a drop of water in a sea.... No one should even ask us about targeting a bunch of Americans who would have been killed

in an airplane. Our unsettled account with America includes, at the very least, one million women and children. I'm not even talking about the men."

May 24, 2010—Yemen—Sharda tribesmen kidnapped two American tourists—a man and a woman—and their Yemeni driver and demanded the release of a jailed tribesman. The two Americans were freed unharmed the next day. 10052401

May 28, 2010—Pakistan—Seven members of the Punjab provincial chapter of the Pakistani Taliban attacked mosques in Lahore, killing at least ninety-eight worshipers of the Ahmadi community, an ostracized minority sect. Another seventy-eight were wounded. Some seventy-five people died in the Model Town neighborhood when four gunmen fired at them and threw grenades. A gun battle raged in Garhi Shahu for hours after a gunman climbed on top of a minaret, firing an assault rifle and throwing grenades. Two other gunmen fired on police officers and held hostages. The three attackers set off suicide vests when police stormed the mosque, killing scores. Police arrested a 17-year-old who said the attackers had trained in North Waziristan.

May 28, 2010—India—Maoists rebels were suspected of damaging a train track that led to derailment of an overnight Gyaneshwari Express passenger train. An oncoming red cargo train then plowed into the blue passenger train, killing sixty-five and injuring two hundred. Rescuers needed three hours to reach the rural location near the small town of Sardiha, about 90 miles west of Calcutta. The Gyaneshwari Express was traveling from Mumbai to Calcutta when the derailment occurred at 1:30 a.m.

May 28, 2010—Northern Ireland—Two masked gunmen shot Robert Moffett, 43, in the face at point blank range on Shankill Road in Belfast. Police arrested a 40-year-old man.

May 29, 2010—Northern Ireland—A car bomb exploded shortly after midnight in Derry, 70 miles northwest of Belfast, causing no injuries.

May 30, 2010—Afghanistan—A U.S. air strike killed Haji Amir, the senior Taliban commander in Kandahar, and several of his fighters when he stopped at a small mud hut in the morning. He had escaped from prison in June 2008, moved to Pakistan to plan attacks, and returned to Afghanistan in April to conduct the attacks.

May 31, 2010—Pakistan—Three gunmen in police uniforms attacked Lahore's Jinnah Hospital, killing a dozen people, including four police officers, wounding seven others, and taking several hostages. Dozens of people who were injured in the May 28 mosque attacks were being treated in the hospital. The gunmen had tried to rescue one of the terrorists from the mosque attack who was being treated in the intensive care unit. A police commando team stormed the hospital. The terrorists escaped but not with their wounded colleague.

May 31, 2010—Afghanistan—Al Qaeda admitted that on May 21, a U.S. missile had killed Mustafa Ahmed Mohammad Uthman Abu al-Yazid, alias Sheik Saeed al-Masri, 54, the number 3 leader of al Qaeda and its operational commander in Pakistan and Afghanistan.

June 2010—Indonesia—Police in central Java Province arrested Abdullah Sunata, 32, on charges of helping set up Al Qaida in Aceh, a militant network that was plotting Mumbai-style attacks on foreigners at luxury hotels and embassies in Jakarta. His trial began in the East Jakarta District Court on December 29, 2010. Prosecutors told the court that he helped set up a jihadi training camp in westernmost Aceh Province and procure M-16 assault rifles, revolvers, and other weapons for the group, which had ties to terrorists in the Middle East and Philippines. He had been released from prison in 2009 after serving time for other terrorism-related offenses. He admitted that members of his group had discussed killing President Susilo Bambang Yudhoyono for cracking down on Islamic militants and attacking Westerners in Jakarta, but "it wasn't our policy. We had never made any decisions on this."

June 2, 2010—Yemen—The government announced the detention of several foreigners, including Americans, Britons, and an Australian woman, Shyloh Giddins, 30, in connection with al Qaeda activity. They were also investigating French citizens, Africans, and Asians. Some of them were believed connected to underwear bomber Umar Farouk Abdulmutallab and radical cleric Anwar al-Aulaqi. Giddins and her two children moved to Sana'a, Yemen, in 2006 after she converted to Islam. She was arrested on May 15. She was represented by attorney Abdel-Rahman Berman. Her passport was canceled in April because she was considered a security threat. She had studied Arabic and Islam and taught English in private institutes in Yemen. Her two children were then 5 and 7 years old. By June 7, 2010, Yemeni authorities said that they had arrested thirty foreigners, including a dozen Americans, possibly in connection with a U.S.-Yemeni terrorism investigation.

June 3, 2010—United States—A federal grand jury in Houston indicted Barry Walter Bujol, 29, of Hempstead, Texas, on two counts for attempting to supply al Qaeda in the Arabian Peninsula (AQAP) with personnel, currency, and other items. Referring to AQAP, Bujol said he aimed to "die with the brothers for the cause of Allah, and to be in Heaven." He had e-mailed Anwar al-Aulaqi asking how to provide money to overseas mujahideen. Bujol had used fourteen e-mail addresses, calling for attacks on facilities where U.S. military weapons were manufactured. Al-Aulaqi gave him a document entitled *42 Ways of Supporting Jihad*. Bujol had unsuccessfully attempted thrice in February and March 2009 to depart the United States and travel to Yemen or elsewhere in the Middle East. Bujol faced fifteen years for attempting to provide support for the terrorist group and five years for aggravated ID theft by using a fake ID card, which had been provided by an FBI confidential informant. Bujol used the fraudulent Transportation Workers ID Card (TWIC) card to access a secure part of a Houston port, intending to board a ship sailing for the Middle East. The source gave him currency, prepaid phone cards, mobile phone SIM cards, GPS receivers, and public access-restricted U.S. military publications. He agreed to courier a military-issue compass to the terrorist group. The FBI arrested him when he boarded the ship with the material. He had used the alias Abu Abuadah to communicate via code with an FBI informant. Bujol used the aliases Abdul Bari, Abyu Najya, Pat Lex, and Abdul-Bari al-Ameriki al-Aswad. In February 2009, while attempting to fly to Yemen, he was arrested on an outstanding traffic warrant. He tried to leave the United States at the Canada border in March 2009 near Detroit, but was denied entry by the Canadians. Weeks later, he was arrested in New Jersey for driving on a suspended license. He was arrested on May 30, 2010, and claimed he was attempting to fly to Egypt. He attended Prairie View A&M University in Texas.

He was represented by attorney Joseph Varela. He was arraigned on June 8, 2010, in Houston, where he pleaded not guilty. U.S. Magistrate Judge Frances Stacey ordered him held without bond.

June 3, 2010—United States—American Lebanese dual citizens Hor Akl, 37, and his wife, Amera Akl, 37, were taken into custody after an FBI informant provided them with $200,000 in cash, which they were preparing to hide in a vehicle that was to be shipped to Lebanon for passage to Hizballah. Prosecutors said the Ohio residents planned to hide up to $500,000 from anonymous donors. Charges included conspiracy to provide material support to a designated foreign terrorist organization, which carries a maximum sentence of up fifteen years in prison and a fine of $500,000 upon conviction. Prosecutors said Hor went to Lebanon in March 2010 to set up the money transfer and planned to receive a commission for the deal. He worked at a Toledo bar with his brother-in-law. He told the FBI informant that his brother-in-law ran a Lebanon recreation club used frequently by Hizballah to conduct meetings.

June 5, 2010—United States—Authorities at New York's John F. Kennedy International Airport arrested two U.S. citizens, Mohamed Mahmoud Alessa, 20, of North Bergen, New Jersey, and Carlos Eduardo Almonte, 24, of Elmwood Park, New Jersey, who had planned to take separate flights to Egypt and then to go Somalia "to join designated foreign terrorist organization al-Shabaab and wage violent jihad," according to federal prosecutors. The duo also said they were willing to conduct attacks in the United States, according to a federal criminal complaint. They were charged with conspiring to kill, maim, and kidnap people outside the United States. The FBI was tipped off about the duo in October 2006, from an individual who warned, "Every time they access the Internet all they look for is all those terrorist videos.... They keep saying that Americans are their enemies, that everybody other than Islamic followers are their enemies ... and they all must be killed." An undercover New York Police Department officer recorded several meetings in which the duo planned to train via paintball, then obtain military gear for use overseas. Prosecutors noted that on April 25, Almonte said that, "there would soon only be American troops in Somalia, which was good because it would not be as gratifying to kill only Africans." Alessa said in November 2009,

> We'll start doing killing here, if I can't do it over there." Referring to the Fort Hood shooter, Alessa added, "I'm gonna get a gun. I'm the type of person to use it at any time.... I'll have more bodies in it than the hairs on my beard.... It's already enough, you don't worship Allah, so.... There's a reason for you to die. Freaking Maj. Nidal-shaved-faced-Palestinian-crazy guy, he's not better than me. I'll do twice what he did.

The duo visited Jordan in 2007, hoping to go to Iraq to fight, but did not get there. The duo showed the undercover officer numerous jihadi videos, including those of U.S.-born cleric Anwar al-Aulaqi and some showing attacks by al-Shabaab. The two were to appear before a U.S. magistrate judge on June 7 and faced life in prison. The arrests were part of a federal investigation

known as Operation Arabian Knight. Magistrate Judge Madeline Cox Arleo set a preliminary hearing for June 21. Both defendants had resisted arrest. On June 10, Judge Arleo denied bail to the duo. On March 3, 2011, Mohamed Mahmood Alessa, 21, and Carlos Eduardo Almonte, 24, pleaded guilty in a federal court in Newark, New Jersey, to conspiracy to murder people outside the United States by joining al-Shabaab.

June 7, 2010—Gaza Strip—Authorities killed four Palestinians in diving gear off the coast of the Gaza Strip. Israel said they were planning a terrorist attack. Two divers survived; another was missing. The group was affiliated with the al-Aqsa Martyrs Brigades, which said that they were on an unarmed training mission 250 meters from the coastline.

June 8, 2010—Turkey—A bomb injured fifteen police officers in Istanbul.

June 9, 2010—Russia—The Federal Security Service arrested Ali Taziyev, of Ingushetia Province, who it said was behind hundreds of deaths in the Muslim North Caucasus. He was a leader of a would-be independent Caucasus emirate.

June 12, 2010—Philippines—Thirty Abu Sayyaf gunmen attacked a logging camp, kidnapping three Christian men hauling timber in a rain forest near Maluso, Basilan Island. They beheaded the trio, apparently in retaliation for government offensives, during the 112th anniversary of the country's independence. Authorities said Puruji Indama led the beheaders.

June 19, 2010—Yemen—Four al Qaeda terrorists attacked Aden's intelligence headquarters, freeing several detainees while killing seven security officers, three women, and a 7-year-old boy. The gunmen were disguised in military uniforms and fired machine guns. The next day, the government said it had arrested the mastermind of the attack, who was a member of "terrorist groups" and had a criminal record, including a bank robbery in 2009 conducted by al Qaeda. A security official privately told the press that at least eighteen militants had been arrested after the attack and that a sedan used in the attack was found.

On June 26, Yemeni forces in Aden's Saada area arrested thirty people following a two-day manhunt for al Qaeda operatives suspected in the attack. Nine were charged with having al Qaeda ties; the other twenty-one were charged with rioting. One detainee died. Security officials attributed the death to asthma. Defense forces said al Qaeda detainee Ghodel Mohammed Saleh Nahi had tipped them off to the terrorists' meeting.

June 20, 2010—Qatar—U.S.-born al Qaeda spokesman Adam Gadahn released a twenty-four-minute video in which he called President Obama "a devious, evasive, and serpentine American president with a Muslim name.... You're no longer the popular man you once were, a year ago or so ... nothing more than another treacherous, blood-thirsty and narrow-minded American war President ... slithering snakelike." He noted that Republicans had beaten the Democrats for the Massachusetts Senate seat. He demanded that the United States end support to Israel and insufficiently Islamic regimes and withdraw from Afghanistan. He complained that the United States had created "Muslim-only concentration camps" worldwide. He observed that comparing the number of Muslims deaths "with the relatively small number of Americans we have killed so far, it becomes crystal clear that we haven't even begun to even the score.... That's why next time, we might not show the restraints and self control we have shown up until now.... Honestly, Barack, as a president who has proven himself to be incapable of keeping intruders out of [the White House], do you really expect anyone to believe that you will be successful in your attempts to keep the mujahideen away from an entire continent?" Even without al Qaeda, "hundreds of millions of Muslims" would turn against the United States.

June 21, 2010—United States—The U.S. Supreme Court voted 6–3 in *Holder v. Humanitarian Law Project* to uphold the federal law banning "material support" to foreign terrorist organizations. The prohibition extended to "expert advice or assistance" or "training" in international law. The majority included Chief Justice Roberts and Justices Scalia, Kennedy, Thomas, Alito, and Stevens.

June 22, 2010—Turkey—A fragmentation bomb went off under a bus carrying thirty to thirty-five military personnel near a military barracks in the Halkali district of Istanbul at 7:10 a.m., killing five and injuring eleven. The Kurdistan Freedom Falcons, believed to be a front for the outlawed Kurdistan Workers Party (PKK), claimed credit in a posting to its Web site.

June 23, 2010—Canada—Toronto police said a person with weapons and explosives was detained near the G-20 Summit and taken to court.

June 24, 2010—China—The Ministry of Public Security announced the arrest of ten members of an Islamic separatist terrorist group, including two ringleaders, who were planning attacks in northwestern Xinjiang Uyghur Autonomous region.

The group was also blamed for attacks on police and bombings in Xinjiang in 2008 and was tied to an individual "dispatched from abroad." Public security officials showed photos of confiscated knives, hatchets, bullets, and explosives that had been seized between July and October from the East Turkestan Islamic Movement.

June 24, 2010—Greece—A parcel bomb went off at the Ministry of Citizen Protection in Athens, near the office of Minister Michalis Chrysochoidis, killing one person. The parcel was delivered to the assistant to the secretary of the ministry. No one claimed credit.

June 24, 2010—Canada—Royal Canadian Mounted Police officers arrested a 53-year-old man who had five cans of gas, guns, a crossbow, gas tanks, and chemical products in his car near the G-20 Summit site in Toronto, security officials said. He had no explanation for why the items were in his car.

June 29, 2010—Qatar—*Inspire*, claiming to be an English-language online magazine published by al Qaeda on the Arabian Peninsula, appeared on the Internet. Various pundits questioned its provenance. Only three of its sixty-seven pages loaded properly; the PDF appeared corrupted, perhaps with a virus.

June 30, 2010—A suicide bomber failed to injure Chechen President Ramzan Kadyrov, who was waiting outside a Grozny theater for a concert to begin.

July 1, 2010—Pakistan—Three suicide bombers set off explosives at the gate, in the basement, and inside the country's most important Sufi shrine in Lahore before midnight, killing 37 and injuring 175. The shrine is dedicated to Persian Sufi saint Abdul Hassan Ali Hajvery, also known as Data Ganj Bakhsh.

July 2, 2010—Afghanistan—Six Taliban suicide bombers attacked a USAID compound in Kunduz at 3:30 a.m. One set off an SUV at the entrance, killing an Afghan security guard. The five others attacked the DAI, a global consulting firm, building, killing a Filipino, a German, and another person and wounding several others before they died in a gun battle. The firm had a USAID contract to work on local governance and community development issues. 10070201

July 4, 2010—Nigeria—Gunmen kidnapped and later released a Latvian, a Lithuanian, a Ukrainian, seven Russians, and two Germans, all sailors working the oil-rich delta area. 10070401

July 8, 2010—Norway—Authorities arrested Mikael Davud, 39, a Chinese Uighur with Norwegian citizenship, on charges of planning to blow up unknown targets using the same type of explosives used in the 7/7 attacks on the London transit system in 2005. He was believed to be the leader of a Norway-based al Qaeda terrorist cell in intercepted e-mail contact with an al Qaeda operative in Pakistan. Davud arrived in Norway in 1999 as part of a UN refugee program. He obtained Norwegian citizenship in 2007. Davud and his wife traveled to Turkey in the fall of 2008, where he met an al Qaeda facilitator. He then traveled to an al Qaeda training camp in Waziristan, Pakistan. In May 2009, he e-mailed Ahmad (e-name Ismail), a mid-level al Qaeda operative in Pakistan, before returning to Norway. Ahmad was also in touch with plotters in the United Kingdom and United States. Twelve plotters were detained in Manchester, United Kingdom, in April 2009 and three arrested in New York in 2009. When the three Norway-based plotters attempted to acquire peroxide and other materiel that could be used to create the explosive triacetone triperoxide (TATP), authorities directed a pharmacy to provide inert liquid instead. Davud was represented by attorney Arild Humlen.

Police found a bomb lab in the group's Oslo basement apartment. Police also arrested Shawan Sadek Saeed Bujak Bujak, 37, an Iraqi Kurd and permanent resident of Norway; and David Jakobsen, 31, an Uzbek permanent resident of Norway. Jakobsen was represented by attorney Kjell T. Dahl. The trio faced twelve years in prison.

On January 30, 2012, the Oslo District Court found two al Qaeda members—Mikael Davud and Shawan Sadek Saeed Bujak—guilty of plotting to attack *Jyllands Posten*, a Danish newspaper that caricatured the Prophet Mohammad. A third defendant, David Jakobsen, an Uzbek who changed his name after moving to Norway, was found not guilty of terrorism but convicted of helping the duo find chemicals to be used for making explosives and was sentenced to time served—four months in prison. He served as a police informant.

Investigators linked Davud and Bujak to the planners of the plots to attack the New York subway system and a shopping mall in Manchester, United Kingdom, in 2009. Davud was sentenced to seven years in prison; he was represented by attorney Carl Konow Rieber-Mohn. Bujak was sentenced to three and a half years in prison. Davud said he was not affiliated with al Qaeda and was rather planning a solo attack on the Chinese Embassy in Oslo in retaliation for Beijing's oppression of Uighurs. Davud had moved to Norway in 1999 and later obtained Norwegian citizenship.

He said his co-defendants did not know he was planning a bombing when they helped him obtain explosives.

July 9, 2010—Pakistan—A suicide bomber killed 102, including 4 police officers, and injured 110 people outside a government office and the Yaka Ghund prison in Mohmand Agency. Several disabled people were there to obtain wheelchairs in the northwestern Federally Administered Tribal Areas. Four insurgents were among the 25 prisoners who escaped when a prison barrier wall collapsed. Officials believed the target was the office of the deputy political administrator of Mohmand. The bomber rode a motorcycle; another bomb exploded nearly simultaneously.

July 10, 2010—Brazil—Air France flight 443 flying from Rio to Paris made an emergency landing in Recife at 8:00 p.m. after a woman phoned a bomb threat to Rio's airport thirty minutes after takeoff. The 405 passengers and 18 crew members were safely evacuated. No bomb was found.

July 11, 2010—Uganda—At 10:30 p.m. three bombs at two sites in Kampala killed seventy-six people and injured another eighty-five watching the World Cup soccer finale on television. The dead included twenty-eight Ugandans, one Irish citizen, one Indian, one American—Nate Henn, 25, of Wilmington, Delaware, who worked for the charity Invisible Children—and eleven people who are either Ethiopian or Eritrean. Five Americans were hospitalized; two were in serious condition. Among them were Kris Sledge, 18, of Selinsgrove, Pennsylvania, and Emily Kerstetter, 16, from Ellicott City, Maryland. Another was Betty Nbagire, 37. Those injured at the restaurant included six members of an American church mission who hailed from the Christ Community United Methodist Church in Selinsgrove, Pennsylvania, and were working with a local congregation. They suffered broken bones, flesh wounds, temporary blindness, and hearing problems. The first bomb went off at the Ethiopian Village restaurant; Ethiopia is al-Shabaab's enemy. Fifty minutes later, another two exploded at the Kyandondo Rugby Club restaurant, where at least fourteen people died. The larger, second, bomb killed many who were trying to help victims of the initial bomb. Al-Shabaab claimed credit. Spokesman Ali Mohamoud Raghe told a press conference,

> And the best of men have promised and they have delivered.... Blessed and exalted among men—(taking) full responsibility.... We wage war against the six thousand collaborators; they have received their response. [There are six thousand African Union peacekeepers in Soma-

lia.] We are behind the attack because we are at war with them.... We had given warning to the Ugandans to refrain from their involvement in our country. We spoke to the leaders and we spoke to the people and they never listened to us. May Allah accept these martyrs who carried out the blessed operation and exploded themselves in the middle of the infidels.

Sheikh Abu Al-Zubeir, self-described emir of al-Shabaab in Somalia, posted on an al Qaeda Web site, "My message to the Ugandan and Burundian nations is that you will be the target for our retribution to the massacres perpetrated against the Somali men, women, and children in Mogadishu by your forces." One of the group's commanders, Sheik Yusuf Sheik Issa, told the Associated Press in Mogadishu that "Uganda is one of our enemies. Whatever makes them cry, makes us happy. May Allah's anger be upon those who are against us." During the previous Friday's prayers, al-Shabaab commander Sheik Muktar Robow had called for attacks in Uganda and Burundi, which contribute troops to the African Union force in Mogadishu. On July 13, al-Shabaab spokesman Yonis said the bombings involved planted explosives, not suicide bombers.

By July 14, authorities had arrested six people, including four foreigners, among them two Somalis. Security officials suggested a local Muslim extremist group, Allied Democratic Forces, assisted the terrorists. Police said they are based in the mountains near the Democratic Republic of the Congo. By July 18, twenty people were in custody, including citizens of Uganda, Somalia, and Ethiopia. Some were caught near the borders with Sudan and Rwanda while trying to flee the country.

On August 11, 2010, Kenyan authorities announced that they had sent six suspects to Uganda and released another. They included suspected al-Shabaab members Idris Magondu, Hussein Hassan Agade, and Mohammed Adan Abdow. They were represented by attorney Mbugua Mureithi. Kenyan police said Abdow had made satellite phone calls to al-Shabaab members. Agade and Abdow were street traders; Magondu was a driver. Abdow, a Kenyan of Somali origin, lived in Tawa. Magondu and Agade lived in Nairobi. Suspect Salmin Mohammed Khamis, 34, was released on bail on August 9, 2010. He was accused of harboring some of the suspects. He was acquitted in the 2002 bombing of an Israeli-owned hotel in Mombasa. In 2003, he confessed to a failed plot to bomb the U.S. Embassy in Nairobi.

On September 15, 2010, Kampala authorities arrested Omar Awadh Omar, alias Abu Sahal, a Kenyan and deputy commander of al Qaeda in the region, and Hussein Hassan Agade, one of his aides, in connection with the attack. The Uganda Web site New Vision said the duo was planning a follow-up attack. Omar was a key logistics and intelligence link to al-Shabaab and was the deputy of Fazul Abdullah Mohammed, who was behind the August 7, 1998, bombings of the U.S. embassies in Tanzania and Kenya.

As of October 8, 2010, Ugandan authorities had detained thirty-six suspects from seven countries: Kenya, Rwanda, Tanzania, Uganda, Somalia, Yemen, and Pakistan. One individual admitted being recruited and trained by al Qaeda. The suspects included businessmen, university students, and leaders of small mosques. Attorney Ladislaus Rwakafuuzi represented eight Kenyan suspects. Among those detained was al-Amin Kimathi, an activist with the Muslim Human Rights Forum in Nairobi. Suspect Haruna Luyima allegedly was to set off a fourth bomb at a Kampala dance club but changed his mind; he told a press conference in August that he did not want to hurt innocent people. He claimed he had been recruited into the plot by his elder brother, Isa Luyima. Mohamood Mugisha told police he was given $4,000 by the al-Shabaab plotters to help plan the attacks, rent a house in Uganda, and drive the bombs in from Somalia via Kenya.

On November 27, 2012, three Kenyans and a Tanzanian held in the bombing in Kampala that killed seventy-six people watching a World Cup soccer match claimed that FBI interrogators had physically abused them in 2010 and 2011, according to a report by the Open Society Justice Initiative. The four were identified as Selemi Hijar Nyamandondo, the Tanzanian, and Kenyans Omar Awadh Omar, Yahya Suleiman Mbuthia, and Hussein Hassan Agade. 10071101

July 11, 2010—Yemen/United States—Anwar al-Aulaqi, clerical leader of al Qaeda in the Arabian Peninsula, issued a hit against Molly Norris, a Seattle-based cartoonist who launched an "Everybody Draw Muhammad Day" in April, scheduled for May 20. He said the "proper abode is hellfire" of this "prime target of assassination." He added, "This campaign is not a practice of freedom of speech, but is a nationwide mass movement of Americans ... going out of their way to offend Muslims worldwide." He also called for attacks against Swedish, Dutch, and British citizens in the English-language *Inspire* online al Qaeda magazine, observing, "The medicine prescribed by the Messenger of Allah is the execution of those involved.... A soul that is so debased, as to enjoy the ridicule of the Messenger of Allah, the mercy to mankind; a soul that is so ungrateful towards its lord that it defames the Prophet of the religion Allah has chosen for his creation does not deserve life, does not deserve to breath the air." This was the first time the entire sixty-seven pages of the first edition of *Inspire* were successfully posted to the Internet. Another article was entitled "Make a Bomb in the Kitchen of Your Mom," written by "The AQ Chef."

On July 18, 2010, U.S. authorities said that Saudi-born graphics specialist and blogger Samir Khan, 24, was the editor-in-chief of *Inspire*. He had posted radical sentiments on his jihadi blog Inshallahshaheed ("A martyr soon if God wills.") in 2007, when he was living in Charlotte, North Carolina. He fled to Yemen in October 2009. His family had moved to Queens when he was 7. When he turned 15, he attended a weeklong summer camp sponsored by the Islamic Organization of North America. He became a fundamentalist, joining the Islamic Thinkers Society while a student at John Adams High School in Queens. The family moved to New Jersey in 2000 and North Carolina in 2004. Fox News profiled him and his Web site in 2008. He had called for the death of U.S. soldiers serving in Iraq and ran videos of U.S. troops injured in combat.

July 12, 2010—Russia—Authorities arrested six would-be female suicide bombers who had written "farewell letters" and were ready for deployment in Muslim Dagestan. Authorities also detained two men, one of whom was behind the two female suicide bombers who killed forty people at two Moscow subway stations in March. The women's ages ranged from 15 to 29. Four were widows of terrorists who had died in battles with security forces. Police confiscated suicide belts and weapons.

July 13, 2010—Uganda—Police found an explosives-laden vest in a bag hidden in a Kampala nightclub. The vest was connected to a cell phone serving as a detonator. It was filled with ball bearings.

July 14, 2010—Yemen—Twenty al Qaeda gunmen attacked an intelligence and security headquarters in Zinjibar in Abyan Province. Five people—including a policeman and two terrorists—died in the gunfight. Seven suspects were arrested in Abyan.

July 15, 2010—Iran—Jundallah claimed credit for a double suicide bombing that killed twenty-eight people and wounded three hundred, including ten police officers, at the main Shi'ite mosque in Zahedan, capital of Sistan-Baluchistan Prov-

ince. Iran blamed the United States. Jundallah said it was retaliating for the June execution of Jundallah leader Abdul Malik Rigi. Among the dead were members of the Revolutionary Guards and two policemen. Jundallah identified the bombers as Abdulbaset Rigi and Muhammad Rigi, relatives of the late Abdul Malik Rigi. By July 17, local authorities had arrested forty people.

July 19, 2010—Greece—Sokratis Giolias, 37, news chief at the private radio station Thema and writer for the news blog Troktiko, was killed gangland-style outside his home in Iliopoli, an Athens suburb, at 5:30 a.m. The gunmen wore uniforms and bulletproof vests. One terrorist buzzed his intercom to say that criminals were breaking into his car. He left behind a pregnant wife and one child. Cartridges from the sixteen bullets fired from two 9-mm pistols were linked to the Sect of Revolutionaries terrorist group. The group was apparently formed in February 2009, when the group said journalists were "manufacturing news to keep the public docile and subservient."

July 19, 2010—Yemen—Anwar al-Aulaqi issued an online audio in which he said,

> Imperial hubris is leading America to its fate: a war of attrition, a continuous hemorrhage that would end with the fall and splintering of the United States of America.... I could not reconcile between living in the United States and being a Muslim, and I eventually came to the conclusion that jihad against America is binding upon myself, just as it is binding on every other able Muslim.... America refuses to admit that its foreign policies are the reason behind a man like Nidal Hasan, born and raised in the United States, turning his guns against American soldiers.... If George W. Bush is remembered as being the president who got America stuck in Afghanistan and Iraq, it's looking like Obama wants to be remembered as the president who got America stuck in Yemen.

July 19, 2010—Qatar—Ayman al-Zawahiri released a message in which he said U.S. troops would leave Afghanistan and Iraq in "defeat." He said the Taliban and al Qaeda are "moving from one victory to another." The Taliban will "enter Kabul in triumph and Obama will leave it in fear.... Oh Obama, whether you admit it or not, Muslims have defeated you in Afghanistan in Iraq and you will be defeated in Palestine, Somalia, and the Arab Maghreb. You will not only be defeated militarily and economically but most important you will be defeated morally."

July 21, 2010—Russia—Between three and five gunmen raided a hydroelectric power station in

Kabardino-Balkaria, in the North Caucasus, around 5:30 a.m., shooting two guards. The masked men broke into the engine room and tied up employees, two of whom were later hospitalized. The terrorists set off four bombs, destroying three generators, but did not breach the dam. No power failures were reported. Chechen terrorists were suspected.

July 21, 2010—United States—The U.S. Attorney's Office announced that Zachary Adam Chesser, alias Abu Talhah al-Amrikee, YouTube alias LearnTeachFightDie, YouTube alias Al-QuranWaAlaHadeeth, 20, of Fairfax County, Virginia, was prevented from boarding a flight from New York to Uganda on July 10. He was on a no-fly list. He had claimed he intended to travel from Uganda to Somalia. The U.S. Attorney's Office said he had used his 7-month-old son, who was traveling with him, as a cover for his intent to join al-Shabaab in Somalia. He was arrested on July 21 and charged with providing material support to a designated foreign terrorist organization. The Muslim convert in April had made threatening statements on RevolutionMuslim.com about the *South Park* television show after it lampooned Muhammad by showing him in a bear suit; he said creators Trey Parker and Matt Stone would suffer the same fate as Dutch filmmaker Theo Van Gogh, who was killed by an Islamist terrorist. He had been in e-contact with Anwar al-Aulaqi, who had replied twice. In a July 13, 2009, e-mail, he told al-Aulaqi about a dream he had about joining al-Shabaab. He posted al-Aulaqi's lectures online and wrote the blog mujahidblog.com. He married a Muslim woman in 2009. Federal authorities interviewed him in May 2009. He tried to go to Somalia via Kenya in November 2009, but his mother-in-law hid the passport of his wife, Proscovia Nzabanita. The Oakton High School and Kilmer Middle School graduate, who spent a semester at George Mason University, faced fifteen years in prison. He was scheduled for a July 22 court appearance in Alexandria, Virginia. He was represented by public defender Michel Nachmanoff. On July 26, U.S. Magistrate Judge Ivan D. Davis declared him a danger to the community and his family and ordered him jailed until his trial. Chesser claimed that he had offered his services to the FBI to report on al-Shabaab.

On October 20, 2010, Chesser pleaded guilty to three charges of supporting Somali terrorists and threatening the *South Park* creators. U.S. District Judge Liam O'Grady set a sentencing hearing for February 25, 2010. Chesser faced thirty years in prison. In the plea agreement, Chesser agreed to seek no less than twenty years, although his proffer did not limit what the judge could impose. On February 24, 2011, Judge O'Grady sentenced Zachary Adam Chesser to twenty-five years in prison.

July 21, 2010—United States—Muslim convert Paul G. Rockwood, Jr., 35, of King Salmon, Alaska, admitted being radicalized by reading Anwar al-Aulaqi's writings and had created a fifteen-person hit list of individuals who had "desecrated Islam." He pleaded guilty in a federal court in Anchorage and was sentenced to eight years for making false statements in a terrorism investigation. He had given the list to his wife, Nadia Piroska Maria Rockwood, who agreed to five years probation, to be served in her native United Kingdom, after she pleaded guilty to making false statements. The duo went no further to attack those listed. He had lived in Virginia before moving to Alaska in 2006.

July 23, 2010—Afghanistan—The Taliban abducted two U.S. Navy sailors following a firefight during an ambush of their armored SUV in the villages of Matinai and Dasht, in Charkh district. The Taliban and provincial government officials said that one of the hostages had been killed in the gun battle; the second was wounded and in Taliban hands. The duo vanished after driving off their Kabul base. Taliban spokesman Zabiullah Mujahid told Afghan reporters that fifteen Taliban members had kidnapped the sailors and killed one of them. The body of Petty Officer 2nd Class Justin McNeley, 30, of Wheatridge, Colorado, was found in a garden in the Patanak Mountains of Charkh district. NATO officials said that the sailors had taken a wrong turn. On July 28, authorities found the body of Petty Officer 3rd Class Jarod Newlove, 25, of Renton, Washington, in the Baraki Barak district of Logar Province. He had sustained five gunshot wounds, including one to the head.

July 25, 2010—Thailand—A bomb wounded nine people at a Bangkok bus stop shortly after parliamentary election polls closed.

July 27, 2010—Qatar—Ayman al-Zawahiri released an audio in which he mourned the recent death of al Qaeda number 3 Sheikh Mustafa Abu Yazid, observing that the death "marks the glad tidings of the coming victory in Afghanistan, and soon the banner of the victorious Islamic Emirate of Afghanistan will be flying all over this blessed land." He also mused about the failed Times Square car bombing, the Israeli commando flotilla strike on May 31, and the proposed burqa ban in France. He told people from the U.S. and NATO countries,

You are the ones who are paying the hefty price. Your governments rejected our call for peace with all arrogance and conceit. This is why the campaigns against you kept coming one after the other.... Your leaders are collecting the money and the wealth from their war trades, and you are nothing but the fuel and the victims. We did offer you a truce once. We can all benefit, but your governments rejected our call for peace with all arrogance and conceit. This is why the campaigns against you kept coming one after the other, everywhere from Indonesia to Times Square, throughout Madrid and London. These campaigns will continue, and the jihadi reinforcement is still coming."

The Turkish people "need to restore the dignity of the Ottoman Empire" and end all "deals and treaties" with Israel.

Regarding burqas in France, al-Zawahiri said, "Freedom in the West is selective, and it is a freedom that only guarantees their Western rights. I can say that France with all of its might and power doesn't dare to touch the headscarf of a nun, but they defy our faith and want to transgress against our veiled Muslim women.... Every single woman who defends her veil is a holy warrior ... in the face of the secular Western crusade."

July 28, 2010—Strait of Hormuz—On August 4, 2010, the al Qaeda-inspired Abdullah Azzam Brigades claimed responsibility for the suicide bombing aboard the Japanese-owned, Marshall Islands–flagged *M. Star* oil tanker in the Strait of Hormuz near Oman designed to "strike an economic blow to the infidels." The statement, dated August 2, was issued by the al-Fajr Media Center, an al Qaeda media wing, and posted to jihadi Web sites. The attack was the "conquest of Sheikh Omar Abdel-Rahman. In a blessed episode of our Jihad in the name of God and in order to weaken the global infidel network, a battalion from our Jihadi brethrens managed to carry out an operation in order to strike an economic blow to the infidels." The group said it was aiming to
weaken the global infidel order that has assumed authority over Muslim lands, looting their resources, and to lift the oppression of the Muslims.... After midnight on last Wednesday, the hero, the martyrdom seeker Ayoub Tayshan, blew himself up in the Japanese tanker *M. Star* in the Strait of Hormuz between the United Arab Emirates and Oman causing damages, that were reported all over the international media outlets. This heroic operation will have a major effect on the global economy and the oil prices.... The enemies of God wanted to hide the truth of what happened in this operation and some even tried to explain it by saying there

was a strong earthquake. But indeed, our martyrdom-seeker shook the grounds underneath them by reaching his precious goal, proving to the global infidels again that the guardians of God—the Mujahideen—will open the most difficult doors with God's blessing, and nothing will stop them—no security system nor the intelligence service.

The ship carried a crew of thirty-one people—sixteen from the Philippines and fifteen from India—en route to Chiba, Japan, and two million barrels of oil. The ship's owner, Mitsui O.S.K. Lines, Ltd., initially said that the ship was under attack. Other observers said it had a square dent that might have been the result of a collision. Others attributed the damage to a wave started by an earthquake. Still others suggested it was hit by an explosives-carrying dinghy. A crewman was injured in the incident. 10072801

July 29, 2010—Yemen—Al Qaeda in Yemen released an internet audio in which it threatened to conduct more attacks on Yemeni forces. "You are covering for American crimes to subjugate the people of this country to serve U.S. interests in the region. These crimes will be responded to harshly.... The Aden operation came in the context of these crimes and, God willing, we will strike again when the time is right.... A message to security and national forces: God willing our swords are ready and we are resolved to cleanse the earth."

July 29, 2010—Mexico—The United States shut down its consulate in Juarez after receipt of threats from the local drug cartel.

July 30, 2010—France—Two employees of the U.S. Embassy in France were hospitalized after handling a suspicious letter that contained tear gas. They were found to be healthy. The previously unknown Abu Dujanah al-Khorasani Brigade said in the jihadi Web site Fallujah Islamic Network,
Regarding the chemical letters that were sent to the fortress-like American Embassy in Paris, which the mujahedin were able to observe and monitor: the mujahedin were not able to target the embassy with an explosive-rigged car, so the mujahedin decided instead to send a number of chemical letters. [They] did not achieve their desired objective, due to the difficulty and complexity and the multitude of the substances involved ... glad tidings about these unique and powerful operations that will shake the security of the Americans, and we promise America and its allies that what is coming is even more devious and more bitter.

Al-Khorasani was the kunya of Jordanian doctor Humam al-Balawi, an al Qaeda operative who killed seven CIA officers in a suicide bombing in Khost, Afghanistan, on December 30, 2009. 1007 3001

August 2010—Jordan—A rocket fired from Egypt's Sinai Peninsula hit the center of Aqaba, Jordan, killing a Jordanian and wounding four. 10089901

August 2, 2010—Worldwide—The UN completed its review of 346 al Qaeda members and 142 Taliban individuals and entities on the sanctions blacklist and de-listed 45 of them (10 Taliban and 35 al Qaeda), including firms based in the United States, Germany, Austria, Yemen, Qatar, Switzerland, Sweden, the Bahamas, and Liechtenstein. Eight of the individuals had died. Five of the firms were related to al-Barakaat, a money transfer hawala that worked in the United States and Somalia.

August 3, 2010—United States—The Treasury Department blacklisted senior Iranian officials and twenty-one Iranian parastatal businesses that were assisting terrorist groups. The firms operated in Belarus, Germany, Italy, Japan, and Luxembourg, and included Ascotec Japan, Breyeller Stahl Technology, IFIC Holding AG, Bank Torgovoy Kapital ZAO, and Onerbank ZAO (owned by the previously designated Bank Saderat). Nine of the Iranian firms conducted business in Germany. Among the individuals listed were four senior Quds Force, part of the Islamic Revolutionary Guard Corps (IRGC). Quds Force chief financial officer Hushang Allahdad and Mohammad Reza Zahedi were named as Hizballah supporters; Gen. Hossein Musavi, head of the Quds Force's Ansar Corps, and Col. Hasan Mortezavi were alleged to provide "financial and material support" to the Taliban. Also named were Ali Zuraik, director of Imam Khomeini Relief Committee (IKRC) in Lebanon, and Razi Musavi, Syria-based Iranian official who provides financial and material support to Hizballah. Two foundations—the Iranian Committee for the Reconstruction of Lebanon and IKRC-Lebanon—were believed to aid the flow of money and arms to Hizballah in Lebanon. Treasury also listed the Reconstruction committee's director, Hessam Khoshnevis. The European Union the previous month had banned business with the IRGC's Khatam al-Anbiya conglomerate.

August 4, 2010—Iran—A handmade grenade was thrown at the motorcade of Iranian President Mahmoud Ahmadinejad in Hamedan en route from the airport to a sports arena. No injuries were reported. Iranian officials denied that it was an assassination attempt, saying that it was a celebratory firecracker thrown at a minibus carrying journalists 100 meters behind the presidential vehicle. One man was arrested.

August 4, 2010—United States—Shaker Masri, 26, was charged in Chicago with attempting to provide material support to al Qaeda and trying to hide that support. He faced fifteen years in prison for plotting to travel to Somalia and train with al-Shabaab. The New Jersey man had been accused in June 2010 of trying to join al-Shabaab.

August 5, 2010—United States—The Department of Justice, in four indictments unsealed in Minneapolis, San Diego, and Mobile, Alabama, charged fourteen people with being part of "a deadly pipeline" to Somalia that sent money, personnel, and services from the United States to al-Shabaab. Seven were U.S. citizens and ten, all from Minnesota, left the United States to join al-Shabaab. Seven of the ten were charged earlier.

A Minnesota indictment said that two Somali-origin naturalized U.S. citizens and others went door-to-door in Minneapolis; Rochester, Minnesota; and elsewhere in the United States and Canada to raise funds for al-Shabaab. The women indicted said the money would go to the poor and needy, and used fake names for recipients to conceal that the money was going to al-Shabaab. Amina Farah Ali, 33, and Hawo Mohamed Hassan, 63, raised money via teleconferences "in which they and other speakers encouraged financial contributions to support violent jihad in Somalia." During one teleconference, Ali told others "to forget about the other charities" and focus on "the Jihad." The indictment said Ali and others sent the funds to al-Shabaab through various hawalas. Ali was accused of sending $8,608 to al-Shabaab on twelve occasions between September 17, 2008, and July 5, 2009.

Ali and Hassan appeared in St. Paul, Minnesota, before a federal judge, who banned their travel outside Minnesota. Prosecutors did not seek their detention. Ali said, "Allah is my attorney." She claimed to work in home health care and had lived in Rochester for eleven years. Hassan said she was a self-employed day care worker. Hassan was charged with three counts of making false statements and one count of conspiracy to provide material support to al-Shabaab. Ali was charged with one count of conspiracy to provide material support to al-Shabaab and twelve substantive counts of providing material support to al-Shabaab. They faced fifteen years on the conspiracy count. Ali faced fifteen years on each material support count. Hassan faced eight years on each false statement count.

A Columbus, Ohio, resident helped collect donations for al-Shabaab.

A second Minnesota superseding indictment charged Abdikadir Ali Abdi, 19, a U.S. citizen; Abdisalan Hussein Ali, 21, a U.S. citizen; Cabdulaahi Ahmed Faarax, 33, a U.S. citizen; Farah Mohamed Beledi, 26; and Abdiweli Yassin Isse, 26, with, inter alia, conspiracy and providing material support to al-Shabaab and conspiring to kill, maim, and injure persons abroad. Faarax and Isse had been charged in a previous criminal complaint. Faarax was charged with soliciting Salah Osman Ahmed, Shirwa Ahmed (now deceased), and Kamal Said Hassan to provide support to al-Shabaab. Faraax was charged with making false statements to the FBI in a matter involving international terrorism. Beledi was charged with committing passport fraud in October 2009.

The Minnesota superseding indictment also charged Ahmed Ali Omar, 27; Khalid Mohamud Abshir, 27; Zakaria Maruf, 31; Mohamed Abdullahi Hassan, 22; and Mustafa Ali Salat, 20, with conspiracy to provide material support to terrorists and foreign terrorist organizations; conspiracy to kill, kidnap, maim, and injure persons abroad; possessing and discharging a firearm during a crime of violence; and solicitation to commit a crime of violence. The five traveled in Somalia in 2008 and 2009.

A Birmingham, Alabama, superseding indictment charged Omar Shafik Hammami, alias Abu Mansour al-Amriki, alias Farouk, with providing material support to al-Shabaab. The three-count indictment said he provided material support, including himself as personnel, to terrorists; conspired to provide material support to a designated foreign terrorist organization, al-Shabaab; and provided material support to al-Shabaab. He faced forty-five years in prison. He grew up in Daphne, Alabama, and attended the University of South Alabama in Mobile. He appeared in a jihadist video in May 2009.

In San Diego, California, prosecutors charged Jehad Serwan Mostafa, alias Ahmed, alias Emir Anwar, alias Awar, 28, a U.S. citizen and former resident of California, with conspiring to provide material support to al-Shabaab. Mostafa was believed to be in Somalia, where he had served as a top lieutenant to Saleh Nabhan, a senior al Qaeda and al-Shabaab operative killed in a 2009 air strike. The three-count indictment said he provided material support, including himself as personnel, to terrorists; conspired to provide material support to a designated foreign terrorist organization, al-Shabaab; and provided material support to al-Shabaab.

August 6, 2010—Afghanistan—The Taliban shot to death ten members of a medical team, including six Americans, who were returning from providing eye treatment and other health care in remote villages in the north. Taliban spokesman Zabiullah Mujahid said that the Christian medical aid group International Assistance Mission (IAM) was "spying for the Americans" and "preaching Christianity," which IAM denied. The six Americans, one German, one Briton, and four Afghans were on a three-week trip to Nuristan Province, driving and later hiking with pack horses to the Parun Valley. IAM lost contact with the aid workers on August 4. The team was killed in Badakhshan Province while they were returning to Kabul, unarmed and without security guards.

The dead included:

- Tom Little, 61, team leader and American optometrist from Delmar, New York, who had worked in Afghanistan for more than thirty years. Little was PNGd (labeled persona non grata) by the Taliban in August 2001 after the arrest of two U.S. and six German Christian aid workers for alleged proselytizing. He returned after the overthrow of the Taliban government in November 2001. Tom Little on February 15, 2011, was posthumously awarded the Presidential Medal of Freedom, the country's highest civilian award.
- Cheryl Beckett, 32, an American interpreter from Knoxville, Tennessee. She specialized in nutritional gardening and mother-child health.
- Brian Carderelli, 25, an American videographer from Harrisonburg, Virginia
- Dr. Thomas Grams, an American dentist from Durango, Colorado, who provided dental care to children in Afghanistan and Nepal
- Glen Lapp, 40, an American nurse from Lancaster, Pennsylvania, who arrived in 2008
- Dan Terry, 63, an American aid worker from Wisconsin who had lived in Afghanistan with his wife since 1980; they had three daughters.
- Dr. Karen Woo, 36, of London, United Kingdom, a surgeon affiliated with the Bridge Afghanistan relief organization, who was engaged to be married. She had blogged earlier that "the trek will not be easy. The expedition will require a lot of physical and mental resolve and will not be without risk but ultimately, I believe that the provision of medical treatment is of fundamental importance and

that the effort is worth it in order to assist those who need it most."

- Daniela Beyer, 35, of Germany
- two Afghan interpreters from Bamiyan and Panjshir provinces. They were identified only as Mahram Ali, 50, and Jawed, 24.

Saifullah, an Afghan member of the team, survived the attack and phoned to report the killing on August 6. He told the attackers that he was a Muslim and recited verses from the Quran. Some suggested that he fingered the rest of the team. A fourth Afghan team member survived because he took a different route home. The bodies were found next to three bullet-riddled Land Rovers in Kuran Wa Munjan district. Local police said ten gunmen robbed them, then killed them execution-style. 10080601

August 10, 2010—Afghanistan—Two suicide bombers carrying grenades set off suicide vests at a guesthouse for foreigners in central Kabul after shooting to death two Afghan employees of Hart Security, a British private security firm. Taliban spokesman Zabiullah Mujahid said four Taliban fighters had managed to kill twenty-three people. 10081001

August 11, 2010—Rwanda—Twenty people were hospitalized after a grenade was thrown out of a moving car in a taxi park in downtown Kigali. President Paul Kagame had been reelected with 93 percent of the vote two days earlier. Dissident leader Col. Patrick Karegeya said from exile in South Africa, "There cannot be any change through election but through violent means."

August 15, 2010—France—At least thirty thousand worshipers were evacuated at the shrine at Lourdes on the Feast of the Assumption after receipt of a bomb threat.

August 17, 2010—Iraq—At 6:30 a.m., a suicide bomber set off his explosives among a crowd of Iraqi Army applicants in front of an army recruiting facility in central Baghdad, killing 51 and wounding 104. The government blamed al Qaeda in Iraq.

August 17, 2010—Congo—Dozens of rebels attacked a UN peacekeeping base in Kirumba, North Kivu Province, at 2:00 a.m., killing three Indian soldiers and wounding seven other peacekeepers. 10081701

August 17, 2010—Israel—A Palestinian armed with a knife and a toy gun and carrying a container of gasoline broke a window to get into the Turkish Embassy in Tel Aviv, but security officers shot and injured him before he could take a diplomat hostage. He requested asylum. 10081702

August 19, 2010—China—At 10:30 a.m., a man riding an electric tricycle threw explosives into a crowd of security volunteers in Aksu in Yoganqi township, Xinjiang Province, killing seven and injuring fourteen. Authorities said a man at the site was a suspected Uighur. Most of the victims were Uighurs.

August 21, 2010—Somalia—Eleven bomb makers died when their bombs exploded prematurely in Mogadishu. Seven were foreigners—three Pakistanis, two Indians, an Afghan, and an Algerian. Ten died while preparing a car bomb at their safe house in southern Mogadishu; the eleventh died while planting a roadside bomb. 10082101-02

August 21, 2010—Belgium—Police arrested Basque Nation and Liberty suspect Luis Maria Zengotitabengoa as he checked into a hotel in Ostend. In January, Spanish police linked him to an explosives-laden van in Zamora, near the Spain-Portugal border. In March, his brother, Andoni Zengotitabengoa, was arrested at Lisbon's airport before he could fly to Venezuela with a faked Mexican passport.

August 24, 2010—Moldova—Police seized 4 pounds of radioactive uranium in Chisinau and arrested three people, including two former police officers, planning to sell the material abroad.

August 24, 2010—Somalia—At 9:45 a.m., between two and four al-Shabaab gunmen, including two suicide bombers, attacked the Hotel Muna in Mogadishu's Hamar Weyne enclave, killing at least thirty-three people, including twenty-two civilians, five Somali soldiers, and six lawmakers in the transitional government. Another sixteen people were wounded. The gunmen wore government military uniforms. They shot their way into the hotel, killing bodyguards. The terrorists went from room to room in the three-story hotel, opening doors and firing at anyone inside. The lawmakers pulled out their own guns and engaged in a battle with the terrorists. When surrounded by soldiers, two of the terrorists set off their suicide vests. The dead included hotel staff members, a woman selling tea near the hotel, an 11-year-old shoeshine boy, and three youths who were washing cars outside the hotel. Among the injured was Mohammed Ahmed Bile, who was hit by shrapnel while walking to his job at the prime minister's office. Bodyguard Abdi Wali Ahmed was also hospitalized with shrapnel wounds. Lawmaker Isaac Ibrahim Ali, 46, fractured his leg when he jumped out a window and landed on a pile of bodies. The government claimed to have captured an attacker.

August 25, 2010—Afghanistan—An Afghan driver shot to death two Spanish Civil Guards who were training local police forces in northwest Badghis Province. The driver had worked for the Spanish military for five months. Spanish forces returned fire, killing him. He was suspected of being a Taliban mole. 10082501

August 26, 2010—Pakistan—The Pakistani Taliban called the presence of foreign relief workers "unacceptable," leading authorities to suggest that attacks were planned.

August 26, 2010—Canada—Authorities arrested a trio involved in an alleged homegrown terrorist plot to conduct attacks in Canada and abroad, including attacks on Canadian power plants and electrical power lines that transmit electricity to the United States. The arrests followed a year-long investigation called Project Samosa of a plot that began in February 2008.

Khuram Syed Sher, 28, a Pakistani-origin Canadian citizen and pathologist at St. Thomas–Elgin General Hospital, who competed in the *Canadian Idol* television show in 2008, was arrested in London, Ontario. Sher was charged with conspiracy. Sher was represented by attorney Ian Carter. Sher had moved with his wife and three daughters to London, Ontario, in July 2010. Sher played in Montreal's Muslim Ball Hockey League and had an award named after him for the most aggressive player.

Two other Canadian citizens both from Ottawa—Hiva Mohammad Alizadeh, 30; and Indian Canadian dual nationality x-ray technician Misbahuddin Ahmed, 26—were arrested in Ottawa.

Alizadeh was charged with conspiracy, committing an act for a terrorist group and providing or making available property for terrorist purposes. He was believed to be in contact with an Afghanistan-based terrorist group and to have trained in bomb making abroad. The charges carry maximum sentences ranging from fourteen years to life in prison. He was represented by attorney Sean May. Alizadeh attended Red River College technical school in Winnipeg, Manitoba, studying English as a second language and electrical engineering.

Ahmed was charged with conspiracy. He was born in India and lived in Saudi Arabia before coming to Canada. Ahmed is married and has a 7-month-old daughter. He was a radiography technologist at Ottawa Hospital.

The Royal Canadian Mounted Police said the trio possessed schematics, videos, drawings, instructions, books, and electrical components designed specifically for the construction of improvised explosive devices. Authorities seized more than fifty circuit boards designed to remotely detonate IEDs. Police said they were working with an "ideologically inspired group" with links in Iran, Afghanistan, Dubai, and Pakistan and were driven by "violent Islamist ideology."

Officials said they were investigating three other suspects who worked with the trio outside Canada—James Lara, Zakaria Mamosta, and Rizgar Alizadeh. One of them was Hiva Alizadeh's wife.

Police arrested a fourth man on August 27 on suspicion of terrorist activities but released him for lack of evidence. The prosecutor's office gave conflicting information to the press as to whether the fourth arrest was related to that of the other three in custody.

August 29, 2010—Russia—At 3:00 a.m., between fifteen and thirty Islamist terrorists attacked a construction site in Tsenteroi village, 150 yards from the residence of Chechnya's regional leader, Ramzan Kadryrov, setting off a three-hour gun battle that killed five police officers and twelve terrorists and injured seventeen police officers. One of the terrorists set off a grenade in a house, killing himself and a 30-year-old resident.

August 30, 2010—United States/Netherlands—Amsterdam police arrested two Yemeni men who had arrived on United flight 908 from Chicago after "suspicious items" were found inside their checked baggage. Permanent U.S. resident Ahmed Mohammed Nasser al-Soofi, 48, had come to Chicago from Birmingham, Alabama, where he was subjected to extra screening after security screeners determined that his baggy clothes contained $7,000 in cash. Hezem Abdullah Thabi al-Murisi, 37, a Yemeni in the United States on a visa, came from Memphis, Tennessee. Al-Soofi checked luggage on a flight going from Chicago to Washington's Dulles Airport and then to Dubai. Instead of getting on that flight, he joined the Chicago-Amsterdam flight. The luggage contained several cell phones strapped to bottles of Pepto Bismol, several watches taped together, a box cutter, and three large knives. Dutch authorities arrested them for "preparation of a terrorist attack." The media speculated that this was a dry run for an attack. Authorities removed the checked luggage when it was determined that the man did not get on that flight. Further screening established that explosives were not involved. Investigators later suggested that the two men did not know each other before boarding the plane and that the baggage items were not illegal, albeit odd.

Their abrupt changes of flights apparently were due to them missing their earlier flights. They were released without charge on September 1 after questioning.

August 30, 2010—Sudan—Two Russian pilots flying for Badr Airlines were kidnapped in Nyala in Darfur Province. 10083001

August 31, 2010—West Bank— In an attack on a car, Palestinian Hamas gunmen shot to death a couple, including Tali Ames, 45, pregnant and a grandmother; a married man, in his 20s; and a pregnant married mother of one, in her 30s. The couple leaves behind six children. The victims lived in Beit Hagai settlement in the south Hebron hills. They were pulled from their car and shot again to make sure they were dead. Palestinian Authority troops rounded up dozens of male suspects and Israeli soldiers conducted house-to-house searches. Hamas claimed credit and vowed to conduct more attacks during the peace talks with Israel in Washington.

September 2010—Cameroon—Gunmen kidnapped four Ukrainians, a Croatian, and a Filipino working in oil fields off the country's coast. They were released in October. 10099901

September 1, 2010—United States/Pakistan—The U.S. Department of State designated the Pakistani Taliban a terrorist group, allowing the U.S. government to pursue financial sanctions against the group's affiliates. The State Department offered a $5 million reward for the capture of the group's leader, Hakimullah Mehsud.

September 1, 2010—West Bank—Hamas gunmen fired on an Israeli car near Ramallah, injuring two Israelis, one seriously.

September 2, 2010—West Bank—Hamas conducted another drive-by shooting at Israelis.

September 3, 2010—Pakistan—A suicide bomber set off his explosives at a Shi'ite demonstration for Palestinians in Quetta, killing 73 and injuring 206.

September 3, 2010—Yemen—Authorities arrested fourteen al Qaeda members in a nighttime raid in Lawder, Abyan Province, 155 miles southwest of Sana'a.

September 3, 2010—Dubai—In early November 2010, authorities were investigating possible connections of the recent package bomb attempts to the September 3, 2010, crash of a UPS B747-400 shortly after takeoff from Dubai International Airport that killed Capt. Doug Lampe, 48, of Louisville, Kentucky, and First Officer Matthew Bell, 38, of Sanford, Florida. Initial reports said a fire had broken out in the plane shortly after takeoff en route to Cologne, Germany. Investigators had earlier said that there was no evidence of terrorism involved in the crash. Some forty minutes into the flight, the crew declared an emergency due to smoke in the cockpit. No explosion could be heard on the cockpit voice recorder. Al Qaeda in the Arabian Peninsula in its November 20, 2010, edition of *Inspire* claimed that it had bombed the airliner, but observers noted that the group did not provide any details on the operation. Authorities stood by their view that the plane crash was an accident.

September 4, 2010—Bahrain—The government charged twenty-three Shi'ite activists with forming a "terror network ... to change the political regime through illegal means" by holding secret meetings in Bahrain and abroad. Ten suspects, including eight opposition leaders arrested in mid–August, were charged with "undermining national security." Abduljalil al-Singace, a leader of the Haq (Movement of Liberties and Democracy, a splinter group of the Shi'ite Islamic National Accord Association) opposition group, was arrested on August 14 and charged with "running an illegitimate network" and "leading sabotage cells ... contacting foreign organizations and providing them with false and misleading information about the kingdom." Also named were Mohammed Saeed, a board member of the Bahrain Center for Human Rights, and Sheikh Mohammed al-Moqdad, alias Mohammed al-Saffaf. Also named were Sheikh Saeed al-Nuri, Abdulghani Ali Issa Khanjar, Jaffar al-Hessabi, Abdulhadi al-Mokhaider, and Abdulla Isa Abdulla Moqdad. Saeed was charged with receiving "financial support from foreign parties to achieve his illegitimate goals." Also charged were exiles Husain Mashaima, secretary general of Haq, and Saeed al-Sheehabi, secretary general of the Bahrain Freedom Islamic Movement.

September 5, 2010—Spain—Three Basque Nation and Liberty (ETA) leaders announced a cease-fire in a video released to several news media outlets, including the Basque newspaper *Gara*. The group called on the Madrid government to "agree to the minimum democratic solutions necessary to start a democratic process." The government noted that ETA did not indicate that the truce was permanent and did not renounce recruiting, shaking down businesses, or violence and did not suggest disarming or disbanding.

September 5, 2010—Russia—At 1:00 p.m., a suicide car bomber crashed his Zhiguli auto through the gate of a military base in Buinaksk, Dagestan, and killed five soldiers and wounded forty other people. Soldiers fired on him before he could reach the center of the base, where soldiers were quartered in tents.

September 6, 2010—Pakistan—A suicide car bomber crashed into a police building and killed nine police officers and eight civilians—including four children going to school—and wounded forty others in Lakki Marwat district in the North West Frontier Province.

September 8, 2010—Iraq—Four al Qaeda in Iraq detainees facing the death penalty escaped from U.S. custody at a Baghdad detention facility during the night. Two other detainees were caught trying to escape.

September 9, 2010—United States—A federal jury needed thirteen hours to deliberate before convicting Prouz Sedaghaty, alias Pete Seda, the co-founder of the U.S. chapter of the al-Haramain Islamic Foundation in Ashland, Oregon, of helping to smuggle $150,000 to Muslim terrorists in Chechnya. The United States had declared the Foundation a terrorist organization. He was convicted of one count of conspiracy to defraud the government and one count of filing a false tax return. His attorney vowed an appeal.

September 9, 2010—Russia—A suicide car bomber set off his explosives at a busy market in Vladikavkaz, capital of North Ossetia Province, killing 16 and wounding 133. About 98 people were hospitalized, many in grave condition.

September 9, 2010—Somalia—A suicide car bomber set off his explosives at the gate to the Mogadishu airport. Terrorists in a second vehicle crashed through and drove toward the terminal. Their bombs exploded before reaching the terminal. Five terrorists and nine people were killed. The attack occurred forty minutes after the Somali president flew out of the country.

September 10, 2010—Somalia—Dahir Gurey, a Somali American al-Shabaab commander, was killed in shelling in Mogadishu.

September 15, 2010—Niger—Five French citizens, a Togolese, and a Madagascar national were kidnapped while they were sleeping in their villas in the uranium mining town of Arlit. The hostages worked for the French nuclear group Areva and Sogea-Satom, a subsidiary of the Vinci construction group. Al Qaeda in the Islamic Maghreb (AQIM) claimed credit.

On November 18, 2010, Abu Mossab Abdelouadoud, alias Abdelmalek Droukdel, a leader of al Qaeda in the Islamic Maghreb, said in an audiotape broadcast by al-Jazeera that negotiations

for the release of five French hostages "must be done with Osama bin Laden and according to his conditions" and that French troops must withdraw from Afghanistan. "Unless you stop interfering in our affairs and committing your injustices to Muslims, and if you want the safety for the French people, then you should to quickly pull your forces from Afghanistan." Authorities believed the terrorists moved the hostages to Mali.

The French citizens included Francoise Larribe and her husband, Daniel, who was working at a uranium mine operated by the French firm Areva. He remained a captive as of December 13, 2012.

In February 2011, Francoise Larribe, a Togolese, and a Malagasy man were freed. The kidnappers demanded a 90 million Euro ($118 million) ransom.

In September 2012, the Sahara Media Web site ran a video of the four French hostages.

On September 19, 2012, AQIM threatened to kill the French hostages if Paris conducted a military intervention against it in northern Mali, which is controlled by AQIM and its Islamist allies. France would be "mad and provoke not only the death of the hostages, but that France would be dragged into the Azawad region which would bring France more tragedies and catastrophes." By October 2012, AQIM was demanding 90 million Euros ($118 million) for the release of four French workers. AQIM released a video on December 26, 2012, in which Abdelhamid Abu Zeid said the hostages were alive "for the time being." 10091501

September 15, 2010—Jordan/Israel—U.S. embassies in Jordan and Israel warned Americans of a "possible imminent threat" in the Red Sea port of Aqaba and recommended avoiding the resort town for the next forty-eight hours.

September 16, 2010—Turkey—The Kurdistan Workers' Party (PKK) denied responsibility for a landmine that exploded under a tour bus in a Hakkari Province village, killing nine and injuring four.

September 17, 2010—United Kingdom—London police arrested six men, aged 26 to 50, under the Terrorism Act in connection with a suspected threat to Pope Benedict XVI, who was in the United Kingdom on a four-day visit. Five were detained at a garbage depot in central London. A sixth was arrested at his home. The five were held in a predawn raid on suspicion of "the commission, preparation, or instigation of acts of terrorism." The BBC said they were from North Africa and not U.K. citizens. Some were subcontracted street cleaners.

September 18, 2010—Mauritania—Soldiers killed a dozen members of al Qaeda in the Islamic

Maghreb in a battle along the border with Mali. Two soldiers were killed.

September 19, 2010—India—Two Taiwanese nationals were injured when gunmen on a motorcycle fired at their tour bus at a mosque near a popular tourist site in Old Delhi. One tourist was hit in the head and another in the stomach in the 11:30 a.m. attack. Authorities were investigating a call to an Indian news service claiming credit, suggesting that criminals, not terrorists, were involved. 10091901

September 19, 2010—Germany—An afternoon explosion in a Loerrach apartment building apparently killed a woman and child. The apartment burst into flames. Soon after, a woman armed with a weapon was seen running from the explosion into nearby St. Elisabeth Hospital, where she killed a member of the hospital staff. She then fired on responding police, seriously wounding one police officer before she was killed in the gun battle. Loerrach is near the Switzerland-France border.

September 19, 2010—Netherlands—Acting on a tip from British authorities, Schipol Airport police arrested a British man of Somali ancestry for possible links to al-Shabaab. He was en route from Liverpool's John Lennon Airport to Uganda.

September 19, 2010—Iraq—Three car bombs in Baghdad and Fallujah killed at least 37 people and wounded more than 100. The worst bombing was in Baghdad's northern Kazimiyah neighborhood, where a car bomb went off near a local office of the National Security Ministry in Adan Square, killing at least 29 people and wounding 111. Three rockets were fired at the U.S. Embassy. 10091903

September 19, 2010—Colombia—Government troops killed Sixto Antonio Cabana, alias Domingo Biojo, a leader of the Revolutionary Armed Forces of Colombia, in a raid on his jungle hideout near the Ecuadoran frontier. The United States had offered a $2.5 million reward for the drug trafficker.

September 19, 2010—United States—Federal authorities arrested and charged Sami Samir Hassoun, 22, a Lebanese citizen and permanent resident alien of the United States, with attempted use of a weapon of mass destruction when he placed a backpack he thought contained explosives in a trash can outside a sports bar near Wrigley Field, Chicago. The bomb was placed after midnight, when the Dave Matthews Band concert crowd was exiting. Hassoun was charged with one count each of attempted use of a weapon of mass destruction and of an explosive device, both felonies. He faced a mandatory minimum

sentence of five years and a maximum of life in prison.

Hassoun's associate had cooperated with the FBI for months. Hassoun had talked about conducting a biological attack, poisoning Lake Michigan, attacking police officers, bombing the Willis Tower, and assassinating Chicago Mayor Richard M. Daley.

On April 23, 2012, he pleaded guilty to placing the backpack. He faced a thirty-year prison term. Sentencing was scheduled for August 15.

September 19, 2010—Philippines—Soldiers killed Abdukarim Sali, a leader of Abu Sayyaf, who had planned and conducted the kidnapping of three Americans and seventeen Filipinos from a resort in Basilan in May 2001. Sali was involved in beheading U.S. hostage Guillermo Sobero of California as an "Independence Day gift" to then-president Gloria Macapagal Arroyo. Sali died in a ten-minute firefight in Lantawan, Basilan Island. There was a $7,000 reward for Sali's capture.

September 19, 2010—Pakistan—Al Qaeda senior operational commander Sheikh Mohammad Fateh al-Masri—its third-ranking member—was killed in an air strike in Doga Macha Madakhel village in North Waziristan. The Egyptian was the emir of Qaidat al-Jihad fi Khorasan, the base of the jihad in the Khorasan which includes parts of Afghanistan, Pakistan, Uzbekistan, Tajikistan, and Iran. He had led attacks in Afghanistan and Pakistan. The *Asia Times* said that he was not a formal member of al Qaeda. He might have been a member of Al-Gama'a al-Islamiyya (Egyptian Islamic Group), a rival to Ayman al-Zawahiri's Egyptian Islamic Jihad.

September 19, 2010—Afghanistan—A British woman and three Afghans, all working for Development Alternatives, which works on projects for the U.S. Agency for International Development, were ambushed and kidnapped as they traveled in two vehicles in Kunar Province. Police and the kidnappers engaged in a gun battle before the attackers escaped. 10091902

September 22, 2010—Colombia—Air strikes killed Victor Julio Suarez, alias Jorge Briceno, alias El Mono Jojoy, 57, field marshal of the Revolutionary Armed Forces of Colombia, and twenty other rebels.

September 22, 2010—Nigeria—Three French citizens were taken hostage from the Bourbon Alexandre boat belonging to the oil services company Bourbon. It was not clear who captured them. The other thirteen were unharmed. Sixteen crew were on the ship when it was attacked by speedboats. The next day they were found by the Movement for the Emancipation of the Niger Delta (MEND). The group's spokesman, Jomo Gbono, said it had "located the three abducted French nationals and another individual abducted in a separate incident on the same night. We are in negotiations with the abductors towards effecting a transfer of the men to the custody of MEND." The trio was freed on November 10. It is not clear who the fourth hostage was. 10092201

September 24, 2010—Northern Ireland—The United Kingdom raised the terrorist threat level posed by Irish Republican Army dissidents to "substantial," the middle rung on a five-point scale. The al Qaeda threat level remained at "severe," one below "critical," which indicates an attack is imminent.

September 25, 2010—Afghanistan—A NATO air strike in the Korengal Valley in the east killed Abdallah Umar al-Qurayshi, a senior Saudi-born al Qaeda commander who coordinated attacks by Arab fighters in Kunar and Nuristan provinces near the Pakistan border, and Abu Atta Kuwaiti, an explosives expert.

September 26, 2010—Afghanistan—The Taliban kidnapped British citizen Linda Norgrove, 36, who worked for the Bethesda, Maryland-based aid organization DAI that does work for the U.S. Agency for International Development, and her three Afghan colleagues—two drivers and a security guard—in the Chawkay district of eastern Kunar Province. The three Afghans were released by October 2. Provincial officials organized district elders, religious scholars, and provincial council members to negotiate with the terrorists. She was killed in a rescue attempt on October 8 when her captors set off a bomb. Six terrorists were killed; no NATO troops were injured. An Afghan official said she was held by two Taliban commanders, Mullah Basir and Mullah Keftan, who were both killed in the raid.

Norgrove worked in projects in Afghanistan, Laos, Mexico, Uganda, and Peru and was involved in projects for the United Nations. She joined DAI in January as a senior manager on a program to create jobs, improve local economies, and help local leaders "reduce reliance on the opium economy," according to DAI.

Two days after the failed rescue, U.S. and British officials suggested that Norgrove might have been killed by a grenade thrown by U.S. Special Operations troops during the pre-dawn raid. 10092601

September 28, 2010—Europe—The news media, led by the *Wall Street Journal*, reported that al Qaeda central was planning armed attacks similar to the November 2008 Mumbai siege against London, Paris, and Berlin. The leader of the group was known only as Mauritani. ABC News reported that Ahmad Sidiqi, 36, a German of Afghan descent held in U.S. custody at Bagram Air Base in Afghanistan since his arrest in Kabul in July 2010, had provided a tipoff that several groups of attackers, all with European passports, had been trained and sent from camps in Waziristan. He said Osama bin Laden had approved the attack. Sidiqi reportedly had ties to Hamburg, living there until 2009, and the 9/11 plotters. He drove the father of Mounir al-Motassadeq, who had been convicted in Germany for his role in 9/11, to visit his son in prison and vacationed with the Motassadeq family. French authorities twice evacuated the Eiffel Tower. The Associated Press quoted a Pakistani intelligence official as claiming that two British brothers of Pakistani descent and eight Germans were involved in the plot. Abdul Jabbar, 20-something, one of the Britons from Pakistan's Jhelum district, had died in an air strike on September 8 in North Waziristan.

September 28, 2010—Spain—Authorities in Esplugues de Llobregat, a Catalan town near Barcelona, arrested Mohamed Omar Debhi, 43, a U.S. citizen of Algerian origin, on suspicion of transferring and laundering more than $81,000 for al Qaeda in the Islamic Maghreb. He was also suspected of document forgery and tax fraud. He was sent to Madrid for questioning. Police seized a luxury car, a boat docked in Badalona, laptops, hard disks, bank records, and business incorporation documents of companies used as fronts. Authorities said Debhi used bank and human couriers to send money to Toufik Mizi in Algeria, who in turn sent the money to terrorist cells. Mizi was wanted on terrorism charges by Spain's National Court. He had been a fugitive since 2008, escaping a police raid on a Spain-based cell that trained, provided logistic support, and funded al Qaeda in the Islamic Mahgreb. Debhi had at one time resided in Katy, Texas, and traveled between the United States and Spain between 2003 and 2006. National Court investigative Judge Santiago Pedraz ordered Debhi released on September 30 due to lack of evidence.

September 29, 2010—Dubai—Jihadi Web sites ran a video by American al Qaeda propagandist Adam Gadahn regarding the Pakistan floods.

September 29, 2010—Yemen—ABCNews.com reported that al Qaeda in the Arabia Peninsula posted a Web video from Anwar al-Aulaqi.

September 30, 2010—Dubai—Jihadi Web sites ran a purported As-Sahab video by Osama bin Laden, lasting eleven minutes and thirty-nine seconds, entitled *Pauses with the Method of Relief Work*, in which he called on Muslims to invest in infrastructure and awareness programs to deal with famine, flood relief, climate change, and water pollution in Pakistan, Sudan, Yemen, Chad, and Somalia. "Sending tents and medicine is necessary, but the catastrophe is bigger and way more than what is being offered in terms of quantity, quality, and timing. We need a big transitional change in the way we act in the relief effort." He said too much is spent on the armed forces, and added,

> If they had spent one percent of what they had allocated as their budget, in a wise and honest way, we would have witnessed a change in the areas where the poor people live, and their situation would have improved accordingly.... Several studies say that if anything happens to one of the major countries producing wheat and stopped the country from exporting it a lot of people in the world and especially in our region will enter a famine and therefore, the money will not help in lifting or stopping the starvation between the people, because the bread is not available.

September 30, 2010—Nigeria—A dozen people were killed and thirty-eight injured when the Movement for the Emancipation of the Niger Delta (MEND) set off two car bombs outside the Justice Ministry in Abuja during celebrations of the country's fiftieth anniversary. In claiming credit, MEND said, "There is nothing worth celebrating after fifty years of failure. For fifty years, the people of the Niger Delta have had their land and resources stolen from them. The constitution before independence which offered resource control was mutilated by illegal military governments and this injustice is yet to be addressed." The media reported that the group had sent a threat an hour before the bomb went off and that British intelligence had warned the government of a plot.

By October 6, 2010, South African prosecutors had charged alleged MEND member Henry Okah with terrorism-related offenses in connection with the bombings. Okah had been living in South Africa under amnesty granted in 2009. He was represented by South African attorney Rudi Krause.

October 2010—Nigeria—Gunmen attacked two pipelines belonging to Italian oil company Eni SpA. 10109901-02

October 2, 2010—Italy—Police in Naples arrested Ryan Hannouni, 28, a French citizen of Algerian origin, near the central train station. He was carrying bomb-making materials. He was suspected of having ties with a recruiting network that would send Europe-based radicals to Afghanistan and Pakistan. France requested his extradition. He had been living in Naples since early August. The next day, French authorities arrested three people whose names were in his cell phone.

October 3, 2010—Russia—A civilian Yakovlev Yak-42 carrying seventy-three passengers from Moscow's Vnukovo International Airport to Grozny was diverted to Volgograd after a telephoned bomb threat.

October 3, 2010—Europe—The U.S. Department of State issued a travel alert saying that al Qaeda and affiliated organizations were planning terrorist attacks.

October 3, 2010—Pakistan—A U.S. drone strike killed five to eight German terrorists among eleven suspected foreign militants and Pakistanis in the Mir Ali area of North Waziristan. They were members of Jehad al-Islami.

CNN reported that Naamen Meziche, 40, a French citizen of Algerian descent, recruited young men praying at the Taiba Mosque in Hamburg, Germany, to join in jihad. He was believed to be in the Afghanistan-Pakistan border area. Meziche's wife told CNN that he was overseas. Meziche had connections to al Qaeda dating to the 1990s. One European counterterrorism official said detainee Ahmed Sidiqi told his interrogators that Meziche was a planner, assisted by Asadullah M., in the new reported plot which Osama Bin Laden had approved.

CNN said the logistics arranger for the group was Asadullah M., 52, a Hamburg resident of Afghan origin thought to be in the Pakistani tribal area along the Afghanistan border.

One member of the group was Rami Makanesi, 25, a German of Syrian descent. Another was Shahab Dashti, a German citizen of Iranian descent. He appeared in an Islamic Movement of Uzbekistan video in late 2009. Brandishing a knife and gun, he urged other Germans to join in jihad against the United States in Afghanistan. Several other Germans in the video were firing weapons. Sidiqi said that Dashti was to be a "foot-soldier" in the plot against Europe. CNN reported that Dashti was at large in the tribal areas of Pakistan. Dashti began attending the Taiba Mosque after converting from Shi'ite to Sunni Islam to distance himself from a domineering father. Family members told CNN that he was tricked by extremists into going to Pakistan. His wife traveled with him to Pakistan and is still believed to be in the Afghanistan-Pakistan border region.

October 5, 2010—France—Police arrested three suspects—two in Marseille and one in Bordeaux—as part of a probe into a jihadi recruiting network to send European-based fighters to Afghanistan and Pakistan. The trio's names were found in the cell phone of Ryan Hannouni, who was arrested on October 2 in Naples, Italy. Hannouni was suspected of having ties with the recruiting network. France requested his extradition. He had been living in Naples since early August. Some thought the trio offered housing and false ID papers.

French police in Marseille and Avignon arrested nine other people in a separate probe into radical jihadi groups. They were held on suspicion of involvement in trafficking arms and explosives. Police found a Kalashnikov automatic rifle, a pump-action shotgun, two knives, and ammunition.

It was the first time al Qaeda in the Islamic Maghreb (AQIM) and al Qaeda in the Arabian Peninsula (AQAP) were believed to have collaborated. A year and a half earlier, a Yemeni AQAP emissary to AQIM was found beheaded in Algeria.

October 5, 2010—Thailand—A bomb exploded in Nonthaburi Province, 25 miles north of Bangkok, killing four people, including electrician Samai Wongsuwan, a known Red Shirt activist from Chiang Mai. He was making a 22-pound TNT bomb when it accidentally detonated in his apartment. Nine others were injured in the explosion.

October 6, 2010—United Kingdom—The French Foreign Ministry issued a travel alert regarding a high terrorism risk in the United Kingdom, particularly in public transport and tourist areas.

October 6, 2010—Yemen—At 8:15 a.m., gunmen fired a rocket-propelled grenade at an armored vehicle carrying five U.K. diplomats in Sana'a, slightly injuring one Briton and two local bystanders. The terrorists escaped. The vehicle was carrying Fionna Gibb, the deputy chief of mission. 10100601

October 6, 2010—Yemen—A Yemeni security guard shot to death a French contractor at a compound near Sana'a for staff members of OMV, an Austrian oil and gas company. Security guards overpowered the gunman. It was not clear if he was affiliated with a terrorist group; colleagues said he had an acrimonious relationship with his boss and was about to be fired. On November 2, Yemeni officials charged Hesham Mohammed Asem, 19, with "forming an armed group to carry out criminal acts targeting foreigners" as part of al Qaeda in the death of the contractor. Prosecutors said he had links with al Qaeda cells and had been offered money by Anwar al-Aulaqi to kill foreigners. 10100602

October 8, 2010—United States/Canada—The United States deported to Canada Mohammed Abdullah Warsame, 37, a Somali-born Canadian who admitted attending al Qaeda training camps and lectures by Osama bin Laden.

October 10, 2010—Yemen—A seventy-four-page second edition of the al Qaeda in the Arabian Peninsula's e-magazine *Inspire* appeared on the Internet. The edition featured suggestions on how to use a pickup truck as a vehicle bomb and how to shoot up a Washington restaurant. "The Ultimate Mowing Machine" suggested attaching a steel blade on the front of a four-wheel-drive truck and driving into a crowd of pedestrians. *Inspire* was released in time for the tenth anniversary of the attack in Yemen on the USS *Cole*.

October 13, 2010—Pakistan—Authorities interrogating seven newly-arrested Islamist detainees announced discovery of a plot by Laskkar-e-Jhangvi to assassinate the prime minister and foreign minister in a gun and suicide bomb attack in Multan. The seven were arrested when the terrorists fired on them during a routine police check of vehicles near Bahawalpur. The seven were also involved in a robbery. A hearing was scheduled for October 27. Police seized arms and ammunition from the detainees.

October 15, 2010—Thailand—Government officials warned that more bombings were expected to take place during October. Bangkok averaged two bombings per week in 2010. At least 71 bombs had exploded in Bangkok, with another 43 bombs defused. Authorities noted that 32 rocket-propelled grenades, 8,000 rounds of M-16 assault rifle ammunition, and other weaponry had been stolen from an army arsenal in September. Another 69 hand grenades and 3,100 assault rifle rounds were stolen from another army depot in March. Neither theft had been solved.

October 15, 2010—Yemen—Al Qaeda in the Arabian Peninsula fired at Yemeni Intelligence Col. Riyadh al-Katabi in Sayoun, Hadramut Province, seriously wounding him. He remained in intensive care in the hospital a week later.

October 16, 2010—United States—On June 17, 2011, authorities arrested Yonathan Melaku, 22, a Marine Reservist, at Arlington National Cemetery, after he fled Fort Myer. His backpack contained 9-mm shell casings, plastic baggies with ammonium nitrate—a bomb-making material, work gloves, a headlamp, and a notebook that included references to Osama bin Laden and *The Path to Jihad*. The notebook included a call to "defeat coalition and allies and America" and a list of foreign terrorists. In his bedroom, authorities found a video of him driving by the Marine Corps Museum and firing several shots out of the passenger window. In the video, he said, "all right next time this video turns on, I will be shooting.... That's what they get. That's my target. That's the military building. It's going to be attacked." On June 22, authorities charged him with three counts of causing injury to U.S. property by shooting with a firearm and causing damage in excess of $1,000, and one count of discharging a firearm during a crime of violence, citing the shootings at five military sites on October 16, October 17, October 19, October 25, October 28, October 29, November 1, and November 2, 2010. He was specifically charged in the shootings at the Marine Corps museum and the Pentagon. He was also charged by the Leesburg Police Department on May 27 with four counts of grand larceny for stealing items from several cars. He faced a minimum of thirty-five years in prison and a maximum life sentence.

Melaku joined the Marine Corps Reserve on September 4, 2007. He had received the National Defense Service Medal and the Selected Marine Corps Reserve Medal. The high school graduate lived with his parents. He was a naturalized U.S. citizen who moved to the United States from Ethiopia in 2005. He graduated from Edison High School in Franconia in 2006. He lived on Sage Drive in Alexandria, Virginia.

On January 26, 2012, Yonathan Melaku pleaded guilty to three counts, including the October 19, 2010, shooting at the Pentagon and attempting to damage veterans' memorials on U.S. property. He admitted to using his 9-mm to shoot at the National Museum of the Marine Corps, the Pentagon, and two military recruiting offices. The plea agreement called for him to serve twenty-five years in prison. Sentencing was set for April 27, 2012. Melaku was represented by attorney Gregory English, who said Melaku would otherwise have been sentenced to a mandatory eighty-five years. On January 11, 2013, U.S. District Judge Gerald Bruce Lee sentenced Yonathan Melaku to twenty-five years in prison for the shootings. Melaku planned to deface 2,379 graves at Arlington National Cemetery by scrawling Arabic phrases on the tombstones of those who served in Iraq and Afghanistan, shooting at more buildings, and blowing up a military fuel tanker truck.

October 17, 2010—United States—Bullet holes were found in the windows of the National Museum of the Marine Corps in Triangle, Virginia, 30 miles south of the Pentagon.

October 19, 2010—Russia—Three people, including two guards, were killed and seventeen injured when a suicide bomber set off explosives at the gates of the Chechen parliament. Gunmen then fired on nearby guards for twenty minutes. Three terrorists and a civilian died when guards returned fire in Grozny.

October 19, 2010—France—The French Court of Cassation (Supreme Court) ruled that police cannot interrogate suspected terrorists without their lawyer present.

October 19, 2010—Iraq—At 4:00 p.m., a roadside bomb went off next to a convoy transporting UN Special Representative Ad Melkert, a Dutch citizen, killing an Iraqi policeman and seriously wounding three others. The convoy was going to the Najaf airport after Melkert had met with Grand Ayatollah Ali Sistani regarding the seven-month impasse in forming a government. The Shi'ite group Asaib Ahl al-Haq was suspected. 10101901

October 19, 2010—United States—At 5:00 a.m., a gunman fired shots at the Pentagon, possibly using a high-powered rifle. No one was injured when the bullets hit two windows on the third and fourth floors. The FBI offered a $20,000 reward on November 15, 2010, for information about the series of shootings. Tipsters were to call 202-278-2000 or e-mail WashingtonField@ic.fbi.gov.

October 22, 2010—United States—The FBI arrested Abdel Hameed Shehadeh, a 21-year-old born and raised in New York who created Islamist Web sites and posted threats of Islamist terrorist violence, including one by Anwar al-Aulaqi. He was detained in Honolulu, where he was taking target practice. He was turned away by Pakistan and Jordan. He tried to get into Somalia but was on the U.S. no-fly list. He was turned down by the U.S. Army recruiting station in Times Square; he had hoped to go to Iraq. The FBI said he wanted to learn "guerrilla warfare and bomb making" by joining a radical Islamist group. A federal criminal complaint was unsealed on October 25, 2010, in which he was accused of making false statements in an international terrorism case. He faced eight years in prison. He was represented by attorney Matthew Winter.

Shehadeh had purchased a one-way ticket to Pakistan in June 2008 on Expedia; he told a New York detective that he was going to attend an Islamic school. In June 2009, he purchased a ticket to Dubai, hoping to go to Somalia, but was already on the no-fly list. He had posted to revolution-muslim.com under the name Abul-Qasim. During his November 2, 2010, court appearance, prosecutors opposed bail. He was represented by attorney Jeffrey Pittell.

October 22, 2010—Yemen—Al Qaeda in the Arabian Peninsula gunned down Yemeni Intelligence Lt. Col. Abdul-Aziz Abu Abed outside his house in Mukalla in eastern Hadramut Province. The terrorists escaped.

October 22, 2010—Turkey—The government arraigned Abdulkadir Kucuk, 23, a student in e-mail contact with Zekeriya, suspected al Qaeda leader on the Aegean coast, in a court in Izmir. He was ordered into custody; his four colleagues were released on bail. Authorities found software designed to help shoot down surveillance drones in Afghanistan; CDs with video of him setting off homemade bombs in a field; and bomb-making materials, including hydrogen peroxide, nails, and gunpowder at his Kayseri home. He was a math student who was calculating angles of fire and coordinates of Israeli-made Heron drones. The four other suspects, ages 19 to 39, were arrested on October 20 on suspicion of fund-raising for the group. Turkey later detained a dozen more suspects. Authorities said the group was named Taifatul Mansura (Assembly of the Victorious).

A senior Turkish official said the Turkish al Qaeda cell was run by Zekeriya. The overall Turkish group was lead by Ebuzer, alias Serdar Erbashi, who had fought in the second Chechen war and ran al Qaeda's Ankara cell.

October 23, 2010—Afghanistan—Three or four gunmen wearing suicide vests and firing RPGs were killed when they attacked a UN compound in Herat. Two Afghan guards were injured in the noon attack when a terrorist crashed a car bomb into a compound gate, making a hole for suicide bombers who were disguised as women wearing burqas. No UN personnel were hurt. 10102301

October 23, 2010—Dubai—Adam Gadahn, an American-born al Qaeda propagandist, released a forty-eight-minute Internet video to "to my Muslim brothers residing in the states of the Zio-Crusader coalition ... from the emigrant communities, like those which live on the margins of society in the miserable suburbs of Paris, London, Detroit," and those "arriving in America or Europe to study in its universities or seek their daily bread in the streets of its cities." He called on them to attack Americans. He told Detroiters, "Know that jihad is your duty as well, and you have an opportunity to strike the leaders of unbelief and retaliate against them on their own soil. As long as there is no covenant between you and them, here you are in the battlefield just like heroes before you." He

praised 9/11 leader Muhammad Atta; would-be Christmas underwear bomber Umar Farouk Abdulmutallab; and Fort Hood shooter Nidal Hasan. The As-Sahab video was entitled *The Arabs and Muslims: Between the Conferences of Desertion ... and the Individual Duty of Jihad*, and included video of Anwar al-Aulaqi.

October 23, 2010—Russia—A car bomber killed himself and a police officer in a failed attempt to attack a police dormitory in Khasavyurt, North Caucasus.

In Komsomolskoye, Dagestan, police attacked a militant hideout, killing two terrorists.

A car chase in Ingushetia ended with the deaths of two wanted terrorists.

October 24, 2010—Yemen—Authorities foiled an attempt to place 1,800 grams of dynamite near Al-Wahdah Stadium that was to be used at the Gulf Cup soccer tournament in November.

October 25, 2010—United States—Shots were fired at a Marine Corps recruiting station at 13881 MetroTech Drive in Chantilly, Virginia, that had been closed for renovations. The FBI said that the gun used in this shooting was also used in the Pentagon and military museum shootings. Authorities noted that all three shootings took place at night, at buildings—apparently to avoid casualties. They believed the shooter(s) used a high-velocity rifle.

October 25, 2010—Pakistan—Explosives hidden in milk canisters attached to a motorcycle exploded at the Sufi Islam Baba Farid shrine in Pakpattan in Punjab Province, killing seven and injuring fourteen.

October 25, 2010—United States—Omar Ahmed Khadr pleaded guilty to five separate war crimes in exchange for a sentence of eight years, one to be served in Guantanamo Bay military prison. On October 31, he was sentenced to forty years, but was to serve only eight years. On November 1, 2010, Canada agreed to repatriate him.

October 27, 2010—France—Osama Bin Laden released an audiotape in which he warned France to get its troops out of Afghanistan and not to oppress Muslims at home. Complaining about September legislation banning full-face veils, he said, "If you want to tyrannize and think that it is your right to ban the fair women from wearing the burqa, isn't it our right to expel your occupying forces, your men from our lands by striking them by the neck? ... The only way to safeguard your nation and maintain your security is to lift all your injustice and its extensions off our people and most importantly to withdraw your forces from

Bush's despicable war in Afghanistan" He said al Qaeda in the Islamic Maghreb's kidnapping of five French citizens in Niger on September 16 was justified. "How is it right for you to occupy our countries and kill our women and children and expect to live in peace and security? As you kill us, you will be killed. As you imprison us, you will be imprisoned, and as you threaten our security, we will threaten your security and the initiator of the injustice is the true aggressor." [A different interpretation is "The equation is clear: you are killed as you kill and abducted as you abduct, and as you damage our security we damage your security."]

October 27, 2010—Somalia—Ten al-Shabaab terrorists publicly shot to death two blindfolded teenage girls tied to a tree in Beledweyne. Sheikh Yusuf Ali Ugas, commander of Al-Shabaab, said, "Those two girls were evil and they were spies for the enemy [the Somali government], but the mujahideen caught them and after investigation, they admitted their crime, so they have been executed." Ayan Mohamed Jama, variously reported as 16 or 18, and Huriyo Ibrahim, 15, wore veils and blindfolds. Hundreds of local residents were forced to watch the massacre. Sheik Mohamed Ibrahim had sentenced the girls to death.

October 27, 2010—United States—The FBI announced the arrest of Farooque Ahmed, 34, a naturalized U.S. citizen born in Lahore, Pakistan, now living in Ashburn in Loudoun County, Virginia. Ahmed suggested to undercover FBI agents how to bomb the Washington Metro's Orange line stations in northern Virginia. He provided surveillance to the plotters and made suggestions on how to kill the most people. He said he was ready to "go operational" after a November hajj. He then planned to martyr himself in battle with U.S. troops in Afghanistan and Pakistan. He was self-taught in martial arts, use of firearms, and knife and gun tactics and offered to train two undercover operatives in those skills. He also offered to purchase firearms for jihad. Federal officials removed guns and ammunition from his townhouse. He faced fifty years in prison on charges of conspiracy to support a designated foreign terrorist organization (al Qaeda), collecting information to assist in planning a terrorist attack on a transit facility, and attempting to provide material support to terrorists. He did not enter a plea. He was represented by federal public defenders Todd Richman and Kenneth Troccoli.

He had immigrated to the United States with his family in 1993. They settled in Staten Island, New York. In 2003, he graduated from the College of Staten Island with a degree in computer science. He moved to Virginia in 2005—the year he became a U.S. citizen—working in telecommunications, according to his LinkedIn profile. He was working on an online graduate degree in risk management and data security with Aspen University. When arrested, he was working as a Reston-based contractor for Ericsson telecommunications.

The FBI spotted him in January 2010 and began the undercover operation that included clandestine hotel meetings near Dulles International Airport. He provided thumb drives with surveillance videos and suggested that placing bombs in rolling suitcases would be more effective than backpack bombs. In meetings with FBI operatives, he agreed to case the Arlington Cemetery Metro station, doing so on July 7 and 13. He was handed coded messages in a Quran. He was told his surveillance videos were helpful in preparing bomb attacks against the Arlington National Cemetery, courthouse, and Pentagon City Metro stops in Arlington, Virginia, which were used by military personnel. He also surveilled the Rosslyn and Pentagon City Metro stations and recommended bombing the Crystal City Metro station. He offered to provide Metro cards and other assistance to the plotters. He also offered $10,000 for jihadi causes in $1,000 increments "in order not to raise any red flags." He advocated setting the bombs off between 4:00 and 5:00 p.m. to cause the most casualties. He sketched diagrams of three Metro stations and had agreed to surveil a Washington hotel.

The media reported that the authorities were tipped off by a source from the local Muslim community. Ahmed had a colleague who also wanted to join a terrorist group and conducted the surveillance with Ahmed. The colleague had been cooperating with the authorities.

Ahmed had listened to sermons by Anwar al-Aulaqi but apparently never met him.

His wife, Sahar Mirza-Ahmed, of Birmingham, United Kingdom, had joined Hip Muslim Moms, a support group for mothers with children under 5 years old.

Farooque Ahmed pleaded not guilty on November 9, 2010, to charges of plotting to bomb four Northern Virginia Metro stations. U.S. District Judge Gerald Bruce Lee of the Eastern District of Virginia ordered him held for trial on April 11, 2011. He was charged with attempting to provide material support to terrorists and assisting in an attack on a transit facility. He faced fifty years in prison. Authorities seized a double-barreled shotgun, a .22-caliber rifle, a .40-caliber Smith and Wesson pistol, dozens of rounds of ammunition, $8,000 in cash, seven cell phones, four laptop computers, travel records for the family's upcoming Hajj, and several CDs of lectures and speeches and a pamphlet by Anwar al-Aulaqi. He was represented by Kenneth Troccoli and Todd Richman of the federal public defenders office.

On April 11, 2011, Farooque Ahmed, 35, pleaded guilty to two charges in U.S. District Court. U.S. District Judge Gerald Bruce Lee sentenced him to twenty-three years in prison and fifty years of supervised release. Changing his not guilty plea from 2010, he pleaded guilty to attempting to provide material support to a designated terrorist organization and to collecting information to assist in planning a terrorist attack on a transit facility.

October 28, 2010—Pakistan—Gunmen on a motorcycle fired on a Japanese consular vehicle in Karachi, wounding two local employees. Police suggested it could have been an attempted robbery. The three Pakistanis in the car had stopped by a bank to get cash. 10102801

October 28, 2010—United States—Several shots were fired during the night at the National Museum of the Marine Corps building in Triangle, Virginia, the second such attack in October. No injuries were reported.

October 29, 2010—United States/Europe/United Arab Emirates/Yemen—Two package bombs with out-of-date addresses of Chicago synagogues were found in cargo planes in Dubai and the United Kingdom. The Dubai package had transited via two commercial flights. The pentaerythritol trinitrate (PETN) filled bombs originated in Yemen.

The parcels were addressed to two historical figures. Diego Deza was a Grand Inquisitor during the Spanish Inquisition, succeeding Tomas de Torquemada. Reynald Krak, also known as Raynald of Châtillon, was a French knight of the Second Crusade who killed Muslim pilgrims. He was beheaded by Kurdish warrior Saladin during the defeat at the Battle of Hattin in 1187. The head was paraded around the streets of Damascus.

Yemeni authorities raided a Sana'a home and arrested Hanan al-Samawi, a woman suspected of mailing the packages; they said the United Arab Emirates and United States provided tipoff information about her. She was a medical student in her 20s who had left her phone number with a cargo company. Authorities released her when they determined it was a case of identity theft.

Authorities were searching for another two dozen Yemeni-originated packages.

Al Qaeda in the Arabian Peninsula was suspected. The bombs were believed to have been built by Ibrahim Hassan al-Asiri, 28, a Saudi based in Yemen. He had hidden a PETN-based bomb in the body cavity of his younger brother, Abdullah, who became a suicide bomber who wounded Saudi Prince Mohammed bin Nayef, a senior counterterrorism official, in August 2009. Ibrahim al-Asiri was also thought to have built the underwear bomb that Umar Farouk Abdulmutallab tried to use in the foiled Christmas Day 2009 bombing.

The packages had wires and a circuit board. They were designed to defeat detection systems at airports.

The package in the UPS plane at East Midlands Airport near Nottingham, England, was found at 3:30 a.m. It contained a toner cartridge with white powder on it. The U.K. package was to fly on a UPS plane, which would have crashed if the bomb exploded on it. German authorities said the bomb passed through Cologne-Bonn airport and contained 400 grams of PETN.

The package found at the FedEx facility in Dubai, United Arab Emirates, was to be shipped on a FedEx cargo plane to the United States. It was built inside a Hewlett Packard Laser Jet P2055 printer cartridge that contained lead azide (used in detonators), 10.58 ounces of PETN, an electric circuit, and a cell phone chip. It had flown on two Qatar Airways passenger flights before being discovered. Qatar Airways said the bombs were not detected by sniffer dogs or X-ray systems.

The United States and United Kingdom downplayed French Interior Minister Brice Hortefeux's claim that one bomb was disarmed only seventeen minutes before it was set to explode. Some authorities said the bombs were to explode in the air; they were not rigged to explode upon opening. They cited an apparent "dry run" in which clothing was shipped from the Middle East to Chicago to test whether materials could get through and the timing of when planes would be above specific cities.

Some observers suggested that an audiotape released by Osama bin Laden earlier in the month was a signal to begin the attacks.

Yemeni officials credited a tip from Saudi authorities for the discovery of the devices. On October 15, 2010, the Saudi government announced that Jabir Jubran Fayfi had surrendered in Yemen and had tipped off the Saudis about the package bomb plot. The Guantanamo Bay detainee had been released to the Saudi terrorist rehabilitation program. He rejoined al Qaeda in Yemen in 2006.

Authorities were investigating possible connections to the September 3, 2010, crash of a UPS

B747-400 shortly after takeoff from Dubai International Airport that killed Capt. Doug Lampe, 48, of Louisville, Kentucky, and First Officer Matthew Bell, 38, of Sanford, Florida. Initial reports said a fire had broken out in the plane shortly after takeoff en route to Cologne, Germany.

On November 5, al Qaeda in the Arabian Peninsula (AQAP) claimed credit, saying on a Web site, "We will continue to strike blows against American interests and the interest of America's allies." The group also claimed credit for the September 3 crash of a UPS cargo plane in Dubai, United Arab Emirates. "We decided not to announce it so we could carry on a similar operation. We did that this time using two devices, one of which was sent via the American UPS company and the other via the American FedEx company. Since both operations were successful, we intend to spread the idea to our mujahideen brothers in the world and enlarge the circle of its application to include civilian aircraft in the West as well as cargo aircraft." AQAP said the bombs' design "allow us the opportunity to detonate them in the air or after their arrival to their ultimate destination, and they are designed to pass through all detectors." The group complained about the Saudi tipoff, saying, "God has exposed you and showed the world that you are nothing but treacherous agents to the Jews because these bomb packages were headed to Jewish-Zionist temples, and you had to intervene with your treacherous ways to protect them, so may God curse you for being the oppressors."

On November 10, 2010, the London Metropolitan Police announced that "forensic examination has indicated that if the device had activated it would have been at 10:30 hours BST (5:30 a.m. EDT) on Friday, 29 October 2010," which would have put the plane over an unpopulated area of Canada.

On November 20, 2010, AQAP released a twenty-three-page special third edition of *Inspire*, in which it claimed credit for the foiled bombings and explained how it had conducted the attacks. The group said it cost only $4,200 to set up the bombs and mail them, listing "two Nokia mobiles, $150 each, two HP printers, $300 each, plus shipping, transportation and other miscellaneous expenses." It noted, "Operation Hemorrhage ... has succeeded in achieving its objectives. We thank Allah for His blessings." The group eschewed the grand attacks previously attributed to its namesake and suggested that "the strategy of a thousand cuts," that is, smaller attacks, were easier to conduct and tied up billions of dollars of Western economies. "It is more feasible to stage smaller attacks that involve less players and less time to launch and thus we may circumvent the security barriers America worked so hard to erect.... We have struck against your aircrafts twice within one year ... and we will continue directing our blows towards your interests and the interests of your allies.... This supposedly 'foiled plot' will without a doubt cost America and other Western countries billions of dollars in new security measures. That is what we call leverage."

The packages were sent to Chicago, "Obama's city," along with a copy of Charles Dickens's *Great Expectations*, reflecting the group's views "about the outcome of this operation.... We knew that cargo planes are staffed by only a pilot and a copilot, so our objective was not to cause maximum casualties but to cause maximum losses to the American economy." The group had determined that toner cartridges are carbon based, with a molecular composition close to PETN, so that it could not be detected. "We emptied the toner cartridge from its contents and filled it with 340 grams of PETN." 10102801-02

October 29, 2010—Hong Kong/Canada—A young passenger boarded Air Canada flight AC018 to Vancouver wearing a latex mask that made him look like an elderly Caucasian. Several hours into the flight, he went into the restroom, took off the mask, and emerged an Asian-looking male who appeared to be in his early 20s. Upon landing, Canadian Border Services Officers (BSOs) escorted the man off the plane where he requested refugee status.

October 30, 2010—Iraq—A suicide bomber killed twenty-six people and wounded sixty during the night at a Balad Ruz cafe in Diyala Province.

October 30, 2010—Sweden—Authorities arrested two individuals preparing to conduct terrorist attacks. Police had been tipped off about a potential bombing in central Gothenburg's Nordstan shopping mall. Several other people were arrested but released. Other arrests were expected.

October 31, 2010—Turkey—At 10:30 a.m., a suicide car bomber wounded thirty-two people, including fifteen police officers—five of them seriously—in central Istanbul's Taksim Square in the Beyoglu district. Only the male bomber was killed. A second unexploded device with a button detonator was found on his body. He was trying to get into a police bus when the bomb went off. The Kurdistan Workers' Party (PKK) was suspected of the National Day attack. This was the last day of a PKK-declared two-month cease-fire.

On November 3, Turkish officials identified the man as Vedat Acar, 24, born in 1986 from the Gurpinar district of Van. He had joined the PKK in 2004. He entered Turkey in August through a security post on the Iraq border.

The PKK denied involvement in the attack. PKK spokesman Roj Welat said the PKK would extend its unilateral cease-fire until after Turkey holds general elections, expected to take place in summer 2011.

October 31, 2010—Iraq—At 5:00 p.m., khaki-garbed terrorists parked a Dodge SUV at the back of Our Lady of Salvation Church (Sayidat al-Nejat) in Baghdad and began throwing sacks over the 7-foot wall. Guards at the nearby Baghdad Stock Market in the Karada neighborhood became alarmed and exchanged fire with the terrorists. Two security guards were killed and 4 wounded. The terrorists set off the explosives in the vehicle. They then set off a bomb at the church's rear door, ran inside, and took 120 hostages at the Assyrian rite Catholic Church. They conducted an hours-long siege before authorities stormed the building at 9:00 p.m. Priests shuttled the congregants to a room, but one of the terrorists caused casualties by throwing a grenade at them. At least 13 hostages, including 2 children, escaped. During a gun battle with the Golden Force antiterrorist unit, 58 people (among them 30 hostages and 7 security officers) were killed and 75 wounded (including at least 41 hostages and 15 security force members) when 2 terrorists set off explosive belts containing ball bearings. Father Thaer Abdullah and Father Wassim Sabih were killed, along with 17 security officers and 5 gunmen. Father Sabih had been pushed to the ground while grasping a crucifix, pleading with the gunmen to spare the worshipers. He was then shot. Police said most of the casualties were women and children. Among them were Radi Climis, 18, who was hit in the head by grenade shrapnel; and Marie Freij, shot in the right leg. Eight suspects were arrested.

Al Qaeda in Iraq was blamed; the Islamic State of Iraq claimed credit. The group posted on a Web site, "The Mujahideens raided a filthy nest of the nests of polytheism, which has been long taken by the Christians of Iraq as a headquarter for a war against the religion of Islam and they were able by the grace of God and His glory to capture those were gathered in and to take full control of all its entrances."

Police later found at the scene three Yemeni and two Egyptian passports, thought to belong to the suicide bombers. Many of the terrorists spoke with non–Iraqi accents.

The church was one of six that had been bombed in August 2004.

The next day the Iraqi Communication and Media Commission said al-Baghdadiya television had links to the terrorists and ordered the station closed. The government arrested two employees who were phoned by the terrorists, who demanded the release of female prisoners in Egypt and Iraqi prisoners in Iraq. The Iraqi-owned, Egypt-based station later broadcast the demand.

On November 3, the Islamic State of Iraq said its deadline for Egypt's Copts to release women who had converted to Islam had passed and it would attack Christians anywhere. "We will open upon them the doors of destruction and rivers of blood."

By November 27, Iraqi security forces had arrested twelve suspected al Qaeda members, including its Baghdad leader, Huthaifa al-Batawi, in connection with the case. 10103101

November 1, 2010—Greece—A parcel bomb exploded at a private courier company in Greece, injuring a woman's hands when she was moving packages. The bomb was in an envelope addressed to the Mexican Embassy. It was delivered by two men. Two suspects, both wearing wigs and carrying Glock 9-mm pistols, were soon arrested. One was wearing a bulletproof vest. The duo were carrying two other explosive parcels; one was addressed to French President Nikolas Sarkozy, the other to the Belgian Embassy. The packages were detonated by the bomb squad. Greek citizens Panagiotis Argyrou, 22, and Gerasimos Tsakalos, 24, an anarchist, were charged with terrorist offenses. Argyrou was charged with membership in the Greek leftist Conspiracy of the Cells of Fire and with involvement in three attacks on Greek targets in 2009 for which the group claimed credit. On November 25, 2010, the Conspiracy Nuclei of Fire posted a thirteen-page confessor letter on a Web site.

Another parcel bomb addressed to the Netherlands Embassy was found at a neighboring courier company. 10110101-04

November 1, 2010—Yemen—Authorities arrested fourteen suspected al Qaeda members.

November 2, 2010—Germany—A package containing explosives was found in the mail room of the office of German Chancellor Angela Merkel. A bomb squad detonated the package, which contained a pipe bomb in a hollowed-out book. The parcel had arrived on a flight from Athens. On November 25, 2010, the Conspiracy Nuclei of Fire posted a thirteen-page confessor letter on a Web site. 10110201

November 2, 2010—Italy—A package bomb addressed to Italian Prime Minister Silvio Berlusconi caught fire. A bomb squad detonated the package at an airport in Bologna. The bomb had arrived on a flight from Athens. On November 25, 2010, the Conspiracy Nuclei of Fire posted a thirteen-page confessor letter on a Web site. 10110202

November 2, 2010—Greece—Two parcel bombs were found in the cargo section of the Athens airport. They were addressed to the European Union law enforcement agency (Europol), based in The Hague, Netherlands, and the European Court of Justice in Luxembourg. Both parcels were detonated by police. On November 25, 2010, the Conspiracy Nuclei of Fire posted a thirteen-page confessor letter on a Web site. 10110203-04

November 2, 2010—Greece—A small bomb was thrown at the courtyard of the Swiss Embassy, causing no injuries. 10110205

November 2, 2010—Greece—A bomb exploded outside the Russian Embassy, causing no injuries. 10110206

November 2, 2010—Greece—Authorities detonated a package bomb at the Bulgarian Embassy and a suspicious package addressed to the Chilean Embassy, after a courier carrying the latter parcel thought it might contain an explosive device. A third parcel, addressed to the German Embassy, was detonated near a courier office because embassy officials thought it might be a parcel bomb and sent it back, police said. This was the same courier office used for the previous day's Mexican Embassy parcel bomb attack.

The next day, Greek government spokesman Giorgos Petalotis said the wave of parcel bombs was "not related to international terrorism and groups like al Qaeda." Greece instituted a forty-eight-hour ban on package deliveries abroad. On November 25, 2010, the Conspiracy Nuclei of Fire posted a thirteen-page confessor letter on a Web site. 10110207-09

November 2, 2010—Iraq—Twenty coordinated explosions in Baghdad during the night killed at least 63 people and wounded 285 others. The Associated Press said 76 were killed. The attacks involved fourteen car bombs, two roadside bombs and mortar attacks in at least seventeen neighborhoods of the capital, most of them in Shi'ite neighborhoods, such as Kadhimiya in the northwest; Amil, Bayaa, and Shulaa in the southwest; Ur and Zuhour in the northeast; Sadr City, Kamaliya, and Amin in the east; and Abu Dhsir in the south. Other blasts hit the mixed Sunni-Shi'ite neighborhoods of Waziriya, Yarmouk, Jihad, and Eghraiat. Al Qaeda in Iraq was suspected.

November 2, 2010—Yemen—Yemeni prosecutors charged Anwar al-Aulaqi with incitement to kill foreigners. The government later said he was wanted dead or alive. The government also charged in absentia Hisham Mohammed Asim, 19, of Taiz with al Qaeda links and the October murder of a French national who worked for an Austrian oil and gas company in Yemen. He denied all the charges. The government charged in absentia Othman al-Aulaqi, Anwar al-Aulaqi's cousin, with inciting violence against foreigners.

November 2, 2010—Yemen—Al Qaeda in the Arabian Peninsula was suspected of bombing a 204-kilometer oil pipeline in the volatile Shabwa Province of southern Yemen. The pipeline is operated by a South Korean state-owned Korea National Oil Corp (KNOC). The bomb caused a leak in an oil field that produces ten thousand barrels of oil per day. 10110210

November 2, 2010—Yemen—The government convicted sixteen men in the eastern province of Hadramout for supporting al Qaeda. They were sentenced to four years in prison.

November 2, 2010—United States—At least one rifle shot hit a Coast Guard recruiting office in a strip mall at 2721 Potomac Mills Circle in Woodbridge, Virginia. No one was injured. FBI ballistics tests linked the incident to four other shootings at military facilities in October.

November 2, 2010—United States—Federal prosecutors issued five counts of conspiracy to aid al-Shabaab against three San Diego residents arrested earlier in the week by the FBI. A grand jury indicted Basaaly Saeed Moalin, Mohamed Mohamed Mohamud, and Issa Doreh on October 22. The indictment was unsealed on November 2, when Moalin was arraigned. He was ordered held without bail. Charges included conspiracy to provide material support to terrorists, conspiracy to provide material support to a foreign terrorist organization, conspiracy to kill in a foreign country, and related offenses. Moalin was accused of coordinating fund-raising efforts and money transfers to al-Shabaab with Mohamud and Doreh at the behest of the late al-Shabaab military leader Hashi Ayrow. The indictment said Moalin and Ayrow were in telephone contact. After Ayrow's 2008 death, the trio continued to transfer money from San Diego to Somalia for weapons purchases.

November 3, 2010—United States—Federal prosecutors in St. Louis charged three men, two in the United States and one in Africa, for providing financial support to al-Shabaab. St. Louis–based Somali immigrant Mohamud Abdi Yusuf was charged with four counts of providing material support to a designated terrorist organization and one count of conspiracy to structure financial transactions. Minneapolis resident Abdi Mahdi Hussein was charged with conspiracy to structure financial transactions. Duane Mohamed Diriye, believed to be in Kenya or Somalia, was charged with three counts of providing material support to al-Shabaab. The transfers ranged from a few hundred dollars to $5,000 to purchase a car. The transfers occurred from February 2008 through July 2009.

November 3, 2010—United States/Iran—The United States designated the People's Resistance Movement of Iran (Jundallah) a foreign terrorist organization. The group operates primarily in the Iranian province of Sistan-Baluchestan, which borders Pakistan. The State Department said Jundallah "has engaged in numerous attacks resulting in the death and maiming of scores of Iranian civilians and government officials. Jundallah uses a variety of terrorist tactics, including suicide bombings, ambushes, kidnappings, and targeted assassinations." The group claimed credit for the July suicide bombings at the Shi'ite Zahedan Grand Mosque that killed twenty-seven people. The group is led by Al-Hajj Mohammed Dhahir Baluch. Individuals, property, and interests linked to Jundallah are prohibited in the United States. It is also illegal for Americans to provide any material support to the forty-six organizations on the terrorist list.

November 3, 2010—Philippines—U.S., U.K., and Australian authorities warned of possible imminent terrorist attacks by Muslim extremists in Manila and the south, saying citizens should stay away from airports, places of worship, shopping malls, convention centers, and places frequented by foreigners.

November 3, 2010—United Kingdom—Home Secretary Theresa May announced the arrest of an al Qaeda in the Arabian Peninsula member who was plotting an attack in the United Kingdom.

November 4, 2010—Qatar—Ayman al-Zawahiri posted an Internet recording in which he called for retaliation against the United States for sentencing Aafia Siddiqui to life in prison for shooting at FBI agents and soldiers in 2008. "The path is clear, whoever wants to free Aafia Siddiqui and retaliate against those who assaulted her and every Muslim woman should ... support the mujahideen and join them." He told Pakistanis, "The time for

action has come: your governments and army leaders have turned you into a people without dignity, without integrity ... and without even value."

November 4, 2010—Sudan—Eight militants in a vehicle kidnapped three Russian pilots who work for the United Nations World Food Program while walking in a neighborhood in the city of Nyala in south Darfur. 10110401

November 4, 2010—Greece—Police detonated a parcel bomb addressed to the French Embassy in Athens and were looking into other suspect packages at a courier company in an Athens suburb. On November 25, 2010, the Conspiracy Nuclei of Fire posted a thirteen-page confessor letter on a Web site. 10110402

November 4, 2010—Northern Ireland—A bicyclist threw a bomb at police who were investigating a robbery at a betting agent in Belfast during the night. The bomb went off on a sidewalk, hitting the officers with debris. One of the officers was hospitalized with injuries to his arm. Another was released from the hospital. A third suffered a hearing injury and shock.

November 5, 2010—Pakistan—Two mosques were attacked in the Khyber Pakhtunkhwa Province in the northwest. The first Pakistani Taliban suicide attack in Darra Adam Khel, about 40 kilometers south of Peshawar, killed at least sixty-seven people and wounded more than eighty others when a teen set off his explosives during Friday afternoon prayers. The roof collapsed on hundreds of worshipers. Tariq Afridi, a local Taliban chief of Darra Adam Khel, phoned to say that the Taliban warned members of local peace committees many times through letters and calls not to support the Pakistani military. "Whoever supports the military will see its results," Afridi said. Four hand grenades were thrown in the second attack, which killed four and injured eighteen at Salman Khel village on the outskirts of Peshawar.

November 5, 2010—United Kingdom—The Special Immigration Appeals Commission ruled that Abu Hamza al-Masri, a radical Muslim preacher wanted in the United States, could keep his passport. It said that he had lost his Egyptian citizenship and stripping him of his U.K. passport would make him stateless.

November 7, 2010—United States—At 9:00 a.m., a green laser was pointed at a plane bound for Seattle–Tacoma International Airport. The plane landed safely. This was the twelfth reported laser pointer incident involving planes landing at the airport.

November 8, 2010—Yemen—Anwar al-Aulaqi released a twenty-three-minute Arabic recording on Islamist sites in which he instructed would-be terrorists to go ahead with attacks without having to consult senior terrorist leaders. "One should not consult anyone in the matter of killing the Americans. Combatting the devil doesn't require a fatwa, nor consultation, nor does it require prayer to Allah. They are the party of Satan, and fighting them is the obligation of the time. We have reached with them to the point where it is either you or us. We are two opposites that do not meet. They want a situation that will come to pass only without removal." He said the jihadis versus the United States is "a fateful battle ... the battle of good and evil." He complained that Iran is attempting to dominate Sunni Muslims. "America and Israel control our ummah [community], and it will not be long before Iran comes in to take away its share of the pie.... Iranian political influence is increasing [in Yemen, spreading] a perverted creed that is alien to Yemen.... Iran today is the most developed country in the region in terms of military manufacturing ... is on the verge of joining the countries that possess nuclear weapons. The first victims of Iran will be the Sunni peoples of the Gulf."

Meanwhile, his father's American Civil Liberties Association attorney, Jameel Jaffer, argued before a U.S. judge that Washington could not order him killed.

November 8, 2010—Iraq—Two car bombs exploded at the Shi'ite holy cities of Najaf and Karbala, killing sixteen people and wounding more than fifty others. Buses carrying Iranian religious pilgrims appeared to be the targets. Most of the dead were Iraqis. The first bomb exploded at 8:30 a.m. in Karbala near a bus at one of the city's main entrances, killing nine and injuring thirty-four. Karbala is the site of the Shrine of Imam Hussein, grandson of the Prophet Muhammad. At 11:30 a.m., 50 miles to the south, a second bomb went off at a police checkpoint in Najaf, several hundred yards from the gold-domed Shrine of Imam Ali, son-in-law of the Prophet Muhammad. Seven died in that attack. 10110801

November 8–9, 2010—France—Police arrested five French citizens, some of Algerian descent, suspected of recruiting and transferring French citizens to the tribal zone on the Afghanistan-Pakistan border to train for war. Three were picked up the afternoon of November 8 in Paris. Two others were detained at Charles de Gaulle Airport on their morning return to France on November 9. The four men and one woman ranged in age from 25 to 30. One of them was questioned about a plot to attack the rector of the Grand Mosque of Paris, Dalil Boubakeur. Police later said the five were planning to conduct an attack in France and one was prepared to die. One had spent time in Afghanistan; the other four were planning to go to Pakistan. Interior Minister Brice Hortefeux said they "clearly belong to the radical Islamist sphere," but the cell had been "dismantled." On November 13, France charged the four men with "criminal association linked to a terrorist enterprise."

November 10, 2010—Iraq—Four Palestinian Jordanians in their 20s and 30s were killed while fighting U.S. troops. Three of them had served jail terms for plotting anti–U.S. terrorist attacks.

November 10, 2010—Pakistan—In a nighttime attack, five pedestrian gunmen fired on security personnel at a checkpoint, clearing the way for a Pakistani Taliban suicide car bomber to kill eighteen people and injure more than one hundred when he crashed the vehicle into the Karachi Police Crime Investigation Department facility. Pakistani Taliban spokesman Azam Tariq told CNN that "We will continue such attacks as long as military operations continue against us."

November 12, 2010—United States—Federal authorities arrested Nima Ali Yusuf, 24, a Somali female permanent resident in San Diego, California, of conspiring in southern California and elsewhere to aid al-Shabaab by providing money and recruits. She was arrested in San Diego. She was charged on November 15 with conspiracy to provide material support to terrorists, conspiracy to provide material support to a foreign terrorist organization, and making a false statement to an FBI agent and Customs and Border Protection officer by denying sending money to anyone in Somalia in the past year. She was held without bail pending a November 18 hearing.

November 12, 2010—United States—WAMU-FM radio reported that a leaked Metro security report warned its security guards about two men who were seen videotaping in trains and on a station platform. The previous week, a rider reported that the duo were filming in the L'Enfant Plaza Station and on an Orange Line train with their video cameras held closely to their chests and waists. The rider included a photo of the two men.

November 12, 2010—Lebanon—A Lebanese military court sentenced to life in prison with hard labor twenty-four individuals, including radical Salafist cleric Omar Bakri Mohammed, 52, a Lebanese Syrian national, in a terrorism case he claimed he knew nothing about. On November 12, 2010, he was found guilty in absentia of providing weapons training to Fatah al-Islam, an al Qaeda–inspired group that fought the Lebanese Army in a Palestinian refugee camp in the north. Other charges included incitement to murder, looting, vandalism, possession of explosive materials, and aiding criminals to escape justice.

In 2005, the former London resident had been banned from returning to the United Kingdom after giving a series of interviews in which he labeled the 9/11 hijackers "the magnificent 19." He was expelled from Saudi Arabia, then spent twenty years in the United Kingdom. He had developed Hizb-ut-Tahrir in the United Kingdom and led al Muhajiroun (Immigrants) until it was disbanded in 2004. He had lived in Tripoli, Lebanon, since arriving in the country in 2005. He said he would not give himself up. On November 14, he was arrested after a car chase and shootout. There were no casualties. He had two weeks to appeal the verdict. He was released on $3,333 bail on November 24, pending resumption of the trial on December 6.

Thirty other people received lesser sentences. The defendants included Saudis, Syrians, Palestinians, and Lebanese. Charges included belonging to an armed group with violent aims, provoking criminal acts, and supplying weapons to terrorists.

November 13, 2010—Bangladesh—A suicide bomber killed three people near Khustia, 190 miles west of Dhaka. Police were investigating whether the bombing was related to the eviction of former Prime Minister Begum Khaleda Zia from the home where she had lived for forty years. The eviction sparked violent demonstrations; more than one hundred protestors were injured.

November 13, 2010—Nigeria—The Movement for the Emancipation of the Niger Delta kidnapped seven expatriate workers from an offshore oil rig working for the London-based Afren PLC and a nearby support ship. 10111301

November 13, 2010—France—Authorities charged four men with belonging to a network sending French residents to the Pakistan-Afghanistan border tribal zones to train for combat. They were charged with "criminal association linked to a terrorist enterprise."

November 14, 2010—Nigeria—Gunmen in five skiffs attacked Exxon Mobil's Oso platform in the Niger Delta and kidnapped eight Nigerian crew members. The gunmen conducted a room-to-room search, beat and robbed crewmen and staff, cut the power supply, and damaged communica-

tions equipment. The field can produce 5 percent of the country's daily output, circa one hundred thousand barrels of oil per day. 10111401

November 16, 2010—Cameroon—Gunmen killed three Cameroonian soldiers and two private Cameroonian security contractors guarding a vessel at the Moudi oil field operated by the French firm Perenco SA. No group claimed credit, although the Movement for the Emancipation of the Niger Delta was suspected in the attack on the border of Nigeria. 10111601

November 16, 2010—United Kingdom—The British government agreed to pay millions of dollars in compensation to fifteen former Guantanamo Bay detainees and one man still held there who had accused MI5 and MI6 of colluding in their alleged torture. All of them were U.K. citizens or legal residents. The U.K. government did not concede liability with regard to the torture allegations and was said to be opting to "save public money"—some $50 million to $80 million—in likely years of litigation. Security services were facing having to review 250,000 documents. This was the first time any former Gitmo detainee had received any financial settlement. Both sides agreed not to reveal the financial sum paid out, although some pundits suggested it could be $1.6 million each. Those to be paid included:

- Jamal Malik al-Harith, a Briton captured in Afghanistan and released on March 9, 2004
- Shafiq Rasul, a Briton captured in Afghanistan and released on March 9, 2004
- Asif Iqbal, a Briton captured in Afghanistan and released on March 9, 2004
- Ruhal Ahmed, a Briton captured in Afghanistan and released on March 9, 2004
- Tarek Dergoul, a Moroccan Briton captured in Afghanistan and released on March 9, 2004
- Feroz Ali Abassi, a Briton captured in Afghanistan and released on January 25, 2005
- Moazzam Begg, a Briton captured in Pakistan and released on January 25, 2005
- Richard Dean Belmar, a Briton captured in Pakistan and released on January 25, 2005
- Martin John Mubanga, a Briton captured in Zambia and released on January 25, 2005
- Bisher Amin Khalil al-Rawi, an Iraqi captured in the Gambia and released on March 30, 2007
- Omar Amer Deghayes, a Libyan captured in Pakistan and released on December 19, 2007
- Jamil el-Banna, a Jordanian captured in the Gambia and released on December 19, 2007
- Sameur Abdenour, an Algerian captured on the Pakistan-Afghanistan border and released on December 19, 2007

- Binyam Mohamed, an Ethiopian captured in Pakistan and freed on February 23, 2009

The incarcerated Gitmo detainee to be compensated was Saudi-born Shaker Aamer, who was arrested in Afghanistan. He had yet to bring suit against the U.K. government. His release was not part of the settlement. He is married to a British citizen with whom he had four children in the United Kingdom. A U.S. interagency task force recommended against his release. He had rejected an offer of repatriation to Saudi Arabia.

Proceedings were being brought by others who were not taken to Guantanamo but were held in Pakistan, Bangladesh, and Ethiopia for the United Kingdom, according to the *Manchester Guardian*.

Among those reacting negatively were individuals who said that terrorists were being paid while victims and their families were being ignored during an economic downturn. Others wondered whether the United Kingdom was in contravention of treaties against financing terrorists.

November 17, 2010—Germany—Authorities announced that al Qaeda might be planning an attack in the country in the next fortnight. Security was increased at train stations and airports. One official said al Qaeda leader Younis al-Mauritani was planning an attack against Europe and the United States. Between two and four al Qaeda terrorists were expected to arrive in Germany on November 22. *Der Spiegel* suggested that another group involving six terrorists, included two who had already arrived in Berlin to be followed by four more. The additional four included a German, a Turk, and a North African. German police said there was no imminent threat to attack the Reichstag parliament building, despite a *Der Spiegel* report. Even so, the Reichstag was partly shut on November 22. Police closed off several tracks of the Hanover train station, Berlin police officers sealed off a post office to investigate a suspicious package, and a Kiel-to-Basel train was stopped for police to check another suspicious package.

November 17, 2010—Namibia—A suspect laptop bag was found in the luggage hall of Windhoek Airport. The bag was to fly on an Air Berlin plane to Germany. A scan found batteries attached by wires to a fuse and clock, although no explosives were in the bag. It was later determined to be a test of the airport security system, although no agency came forward to identify itself as the testing group. The device was assembled by an 80-year-old grandmother working at a U.S.-based mom-and-pop security firm run by Larry Copello of Sonora, California. Copello said he had sold the device four or five years earlier. On November 20, Namibian officials arrested a Windhoek International Airport official who had admitted having some involvement with placing the bag. He was identified from closed-circuit television footage. Namibian authorities said no one from Namibia, Germany, or the United States had been involved in conducting an authorized test.

November 17, 2010—United States—A federal jury convicted Ahmed Ghailani, 36, of one count of conspiracy to damage or destroy U.S. property. He was acquitted of 284 counts of murder and attempted murder in the August 7, 1998 bombings of the U.S. embassies in Kenya and Tanzania that killed 224 people, including 12 Americans. He was the first former Guantanamo Bay detainee to be tried in a federal criminal court. He faced twenty years to life. Sentencing was set for January 25, 2011. He was represented by Peter E. Quijano, Steve Zissou, Michael K. Bachrach, and Anna N. Sideris.

November 17, 2010—Nigeria—Authorities freed nineteen hostages—twelve Nigerians, two Americans, two Frenchmen, two Indonesians, and a Canadian—who had been held by rebels in the Niger Delta region. Authorities also seized an antiaircraft gun, rocket-propelled grenade launchers, thirty thousand rounds of ammunition, and dynamite. There were no casualties in the rescue operation. On November 20, Nigerian armed forces arrested Tamunotonye Kuna, alias Obese, 25, along with sixty-three of his gang members thought to be behind the kidnapping. 10111701

November 20, 2010—Yemen—Al Qaeda in the Arabian Peninsula released the third edition of *Inspire*, its twenty-three pages devoted to the attempted mail bombings via FedEx and UPS the previous month. "We will continue with similar operations and we do not mind at all in this stage if they are intercepted. It is such a good bargain for us to spread fear amongst the enemy ... in exchange for a few months of work and a few thousand bucks." Although destruction of a plane "would add to the element of fear and shock ... but that would have been an additional advantage ... not a determining factor of its success."

November 20, 2010—Colombia—Colombian President Juan Manuel Santos said Revolutionary Armed Forces of Colombia (FARC) commander Jose Benito Cabrera Cuevas, alias Fabian Ramirez, had likely been killed in a military raid on a FARC camp. Authorities discovered several items, including weapons, computers, and a backpack, believed to have belonged to Cabrera. Four or five other FARC members were killed in the early morning raid on a jungle camp near San Vicente del Caguan, in southern Caqueta Department. Cabrera was wanted in the United States on drug charges. He had claimed credit in 2002 for the kidnapping of Presidential candidate Ingrid Betancourt. He was part of FARC's twenty-person general staff and deputy chief of FARC's southern bloc. The United States had offered a $2.5 million reward for his arrest and accused him of cocaine trafficking. The U.S. Department of State noted that "he is responsible for over 1,000 tons of cocaine production" and was managing "all aspects of the drug trade for the southern bloc."

November 22, 2010—Israel—An audio message in Hebrew addressed to "the attacking Jews" by the Gaza-based Jemma Ansar al-Sunna (Community of Sunna Supporters) threatened further rocket attacks into Israel. The previous day a senior figure in another Gaza-based Islamist group was slain in an Israeli targeted killing. The Internet posting said, "The killing of our brothers will not stop us from continuing the Jihad ... and our rockets will continue if you do not leave the land of Palestine."

November 23, 2010—Belgium/Germany/Netherlands—Police arrested eleven people using the jihadist Ansar al-Mujahideen Web site to plan a terrorist attack on an unspecified target in Belgium. Seven people were arrested in Antwerp, three in Amsterdam, and one in Aachen, Germany (a 31-year-old Russian who was to be transferred to Belgium). They included Belgians, Dutch, Moroccans, and Russians (Chechens). They had talked about attacking Jews and NATO vehicles in Belgium. Authorities were looking into the group's possible links with Sharia4Belgium, a Belgian Islamist organization. The investigation began in late 2009 and included a look at financing of a Chechen terrorist group. Other arrests had earlier taken place in Spain, Morocco, and Saudi Arabia and involved "the recruiters, candidate jihadist, and financing of a Chechen terrorist organization (The Caucasus Emirate)."

Police said a separate terrorist investigation was under way in Brussels, including police searches of seventeen locations tied to a terrorist cell linked to Bassam Ayachi, who was charged in 2009 with preparing terrorist attacks.

November 23, 2010—United States—The Animal Liberation Front claimed it had sent AIDS-infected razors and a threatening note to the home of University of California, Los Angeles (UCLA) neuroscientist David Jentsch. It posted an unsigned communique on its Web site from the Justice Department at UCLA, saying that Jentsch used primates for National Institutes of Health–funded testing of drug addiction. "He has no business addicting primates to phencyclidine known on the streets as PCP and other street drugs using grant money from the federal government." The professor of psychology, psychiatry, and biobehavioral sciences had used vervet monkeys to study biochemical processes that contribute to methamphetamine addiction and tobacco dependence in teenagers, and the cognitive disabilities affecting schizophrenia patients. Similar protestors set his car on fire in March 2009. He said the package with razor blades had arrived a week earlier. "The letter inside contained quite specific and heinous acts of violence to kill me.... They said they were going to cut my throat, and they named one of my students."

November 26, 2010—Saudi Arabia—The government announced it had arrested 149 al Qaeda members, including 124 Saudis and several Yemenis and Egyptians, belonging to 19 terrorist cells during the previous eight months. One was a woman. The terrorists were planning to kill government officials, security forces, and the media. Gen. Mansour al-Turki, Interior Ministry spokesman, said, "Their general motives are spreading an ideology of hate by calling others disbelievers, collecting money to finance the deviant al Qaeda group inside and outside the kingdom, easing travel for some individuals for training in destabilized places, and executing criminal plots to spread chaos and insecurity." Officials seized 2.24 million riyals ($600,000). Authorities said the terrorists were financing terrorism, targeting oil refineries and government buildings, training in weapons, and making hand grenades. The terrorists were using the hajj as a cover for their operations. Some of their Internet recruiting efforts included using screen aliases, such as God's beloved, the killer, the immigrant lion, the newcomer, and the daughter of beloved Najid.

November 26, 2010—United States—Mohamed Osman Mohamud, a 19-year-old naturalized U.S. citizen born in Mogadishu, Somalia, in 1991, attempted to set off a car bomb at 5:42 p.m. at the Portland, Oregon, Christmas tree lighting in Pioneer Courthouse Square. He dialed a cell phone he believed would set off the van filled with explosives parked near a major light rail transit stop and across from a federal courthouse at the "city's living room," which can hold up to ten thousand people. But the bomb was a fake device fabricated by FBI experts, part of a sting operation begun the previous June. Mohamud yelled, "God is great" and kicked FBI agents arresting him. He was charged with attempted use of a weapon of mass destruction, which carries a sentence of life in prison and a $250,000 fine. A hearing in federal court was scheduled for November 29.

He was not bothered by killing hundreds of families with small children, telling an undercover agent, "Huge mass that will ... be attacked in their own element with their families celebrating the holidays.... I want whoever is attending that event [in Portland] to leave, to leave either dead or injured."

Mohamud graduated from a Portland high school and attended Oregon State University (OSU) as a non-degree student but had not been enrolled since October 6. He said he had been thinking about violent jihad since age 15.

The FBI said a tip from the Muslim community led them to Mohamud. Mohamud was in e-contact with a previous radicalized OSU student living in Pakistan on the Afghanistan border, but there was no immediate evidence that a foreign terrorist group or U.S. collaborators were involved. An FBI agent sent him an e-mail in June saying he was a colleague of the co-conspirator. He met with two FBI undercover operatives in July, saying he needed help to carry out an "explosion." At the second meeting, in August, he had picked out the squad. He later gave the agents a thumb drive with instructions for the attack. On November 4, he and the FBI agents set off a test bomb in a backpack in a remote Oregon location. That day he recorded a confessor video, saying, "Explode on these [infidels] ... alleviate our pain."

Mohamud mailed bomb components to undercover FBI operatives, who assembled the dud bomb. The afternoon of the would-be attack, he walked with two undercover FBI agents to a white van that carried six 55-gallon drums containing inert material, a detonation cord, blasting caps, and a gallon of diesel fuel. On the front seat was the cell phone. Five hours later, Mohamud and an operative drove to the target, where thousands of people were attending the tree-lighting ceremony serenaded by the musical group Pink Martini. The duo left the van and drove another vehicle to Union Station less than a mile away. Mohamud tried twice to call the cell phone to set off the bomb, then was arrested.

On November 28 at 2:15 a.m., the Salman Al-farisi Islamic Center in Corvallis, a mosque Mohamud had attended, was torched. Authorities offered a $10,000 reward for information leading to an arrest.

Mohamud pleaded not guilty in a Portland courtroom on November 29. His defense attorney claimed entrapment, which the attorney general denied. On January 31, 2013, Mohamud was found guilty of trying to blow up the ceremony. He faced a life term.

November 28, 2010—Iran—Two car bombs exploded at 7:40 a.m. in separate locations near Shahid Beheshti University, killing scientist Majid Shahriari. Fereydoun Abbasi, a senior Iranian Defense Ministry official involved with the country's nuclear program, was injured. The two were parking their cars. In each case, the victim's car was approached by men on motorcycles who attached explosives to the vehicles and detonated them seconds later. Both men were with their wives, who were also injured.

Abbasi had been under UN Security Council sanctions since 2007; he was believed to be involved in Iran's nuclear and ballistic missile program. Shahriari was involved in the Synchrotron-light for Experimental Science and Applications in the Middle East (SESAME) as well as Iranian nuclear research.

November 30, 2010—Ireland—Police arrested four men after discovering a car bomb near the border with Northern Ireland during the night. The car was heading north on the M1 motorway near Dundalk and contained a mortar and launch tube. Dissident Irish Republicans were suspected. Police removed the bomb.

December 1, 2010—Spain—Police arrested seven al Qaeda suspects in Barcelona. Six were from Pakistan; the other from Nigeria. Thai police arrested another three individuals who said they were directing the operation in Spain. The group stole travel documents, mostly passports, and sent them to Thailand to be reworked and given to groups with al Qaeda links, such as Lashkar-e-Taiba in Pakistan and the Tamil Tigers in Sri Lanka. Police seized nine passports that were to be shipped to Thailand, another that had been forged, a computer, and fifty cell phones in Raval.

December 1–2, 2010—Thailand—In arrests linked to those in Spain, Bangkok police arrested two Pakistanis and a Thai, including Muhammad Athar Butt, alias Tony, 42, a Pakistani who was suspected of directing a forging operation for al Qaeda. Butt also ran cells in Brussels and London.

December 2, 2010—United States—The U.S. Department of the Treasury listed three senior members of Pakistani terrorist groups as terrorists, imposing financial sanctions on Amanullah Afridi, senior leader of Lashkar-e-Jhangvi; Mati ur-Rehman, Lashkar-e-Jhangvi's chief operational commander; and Abdul Rauf Azhar, a senior leader in Jaish-e-Mohammed. The United States had earlier designated the groups as terrorist organizations.

December 4, 2010—Iraq—Bombs in Baghdad killed seven Iranian pilgrims and injured more than one hundred people in morning attacks. The initial bomb went off at a bus carrying Iranians going to the Imam Musa al-Kadhim shrine, killing two and wounding twenty-eight. A few minutes later, a car bomb and two roadside bombs exploded at a rest house popular with Iranian pilgrims in the Kadhimiya Shi'ite neighborhood, killing six people and wounding twenty-four.

Meanwhile, a car bomb exploded in an outdoor market in the Baiyaa Shi'ite neighborhood in southwestern Baghdad, killing six and injuring forty-two.

December 5, 2010—Greece—Police arrested six people linked to domestic terrorism, including Alexandros Mitrousias, 21, and Georgios Karagiannidis, 30, who had ties to the Conspiracy of the Cells of Fire, which had claimed responsibility for a recent letter bomb campaign. Raids in Athens and other cities found weapons and explosives.

December 6, 2010—Pakistan—Two Taliban suicide bombers in Ghalanai, Mohmand, killed 50 people and injured 120. The group had distributed pamphlets twenty days earlier warning members of peace committees to not aid the government in fighting the Taliban.

December 6, 2010—Indonesia—Authorities announced that an Islamist terrorist group in Pekanbaru, capital of Riau Province, on Sumatra Island had planned to attack buses carrying foreign workers at the Chevron installation and ambush tourist speedboats in Anak Krakatau. Authorities said the information was provided by Fadli Sadama, who was captured in Malaysia and taken to Indonesia during the weekend for trial. He had been in jail for more than four years in Indonesia for involvement in ferrying explosives for a car bomb at the J.W. Marriott Hotel in Jakarta in 2003. After he was released from prison, he rejoined the terrorist group, robbing banks in north Sumatra to fund terrorist attacks against foreigners. He also sent some of the funds to the treasurer of Jema'ah Ansharut Tauhid, an Islamist group in Java led by Abu Bakar Baaysir. Sadama was also linked to militants in southern Thailand who were to supply weapons for attacks in Indonesia.

December 6, 2010—United States—Awais Younis, 25, alias Mohhanme Khan, alias Sundullah "Sunny" Ghilzai, was arrested after threatening on his Facebook page to use explosives in the Washington, DC, area. The Arlington County, Virginia, resident said he could put pipe bombs on the third and fifth cars of Metro (subway) trains or in Georgetown at rush hour. He was charged in U.S. District Court in Alexandria, Virginia, with communicating threats via interstate communications. He told another Facebooker how to build a pipe bomb and what type of shrapnel would cause the most damage. A Facebook user from New Orleans contacted the FBI in late November and on December 5 regarding postings by Sundullah Ghilzai, aka Younis. Younis was detained on December 6; his case was unsealed on December 9. A judge ordered a mental health examination. Federal Magistrate Judge Ivan Davis denied him bail in U.S. District Court in Alexandria, Virginia, on December 22, 2010. Younis pleaded guilty on March 9, 2011, after the charge was lessened to making a threat against another person via interstate communications. He was represented by attorney Frank Salvato. Judge T. S. Ellis, III, sentenced Younis to two years of supervised release and credited him for three months of time served.

December 7, 2010—India—A bomb exploded at 6:35 p.m. in the Hindu holy city of Varanasi, killing a 2-year-old girl and injuring twenty others, some of whom were injured in the ensuing panic. Police found other unexploded bombs. The Indian Mujahideen claimed credit.

December 7, 2010—Georgia—The government announced the arrest of six people in connection with a series of bombings attributed to Russian Army Maj. Yevgeny Borisov, who is based in Abkhazia Province. The five explosions occurred over the previous several months and included one near the U.S. Embassy and two near the central Tbilisi rail station. One person died in the blasts, which involved metal cans packed with hexogen explosive. A search of one house yielded thirteen homemade bombs, including four packed with nails or bullets. Two more suspects were in Abkhazia. The Georgian Interior Ministry said Borisov was a Russian military intelligence (GRU) officer and had supplied the bombs, gave detailed instructions, and paid two suspects.

December 7, 2010—United States—A report made public by the Office of the Director of National Intelligence on the status of former Guantanamo Bay detainees indicated that 2 of the 66 detainees repatriated or resettled by the Obama administration had returned to terrorist activities; another three were suspected of recidivism. The

Bush administration had released 532 Gitmo detainees; 79 of them had returned to terrorism and 66 were suspected of rejoining groups. Thirteen Gitmo alumni were dead, 54 were in custody, and 83 remained at large.

December 7, 2010—United States—U.S. District Judge John D. Bates of the District of Columbia ruled in an eighty-three-page opinion that the Yemeni father of Anwar al-Aulaqi lacked standing to challenge in federal court the administration's kill-or-capture order for his son.

December 8, 2010—Pakistan—A teen suicide bomber killed eighteen people and wounded thirty-three others on a bus at the Tirah Bazar market in Kohat in the Khyber Pakhtunkhwa Province, formerly known as the North West Frontier Province.

December 8, 2010—United States—Baltimore construction worker and U.S. citizen Antonio Martinez, 21, a Muslim convert renamed Muhammad Hussain, was arrested for plotting to bomb a military recruiting station (Armed Forces Career Center in the 5400 block of Baltimore National Pike) in the Baltimore suburb of Catonsville, Maryland. He had posted on Facebook in October his anger that U.S. forces were killing "Muslim brothers and sisters" overseas. Three people rebuffed his efforts to recruit them for the plot. He was arrested after attempting to detonate an inert device supplied to him by an undercover FBI agent posing as "an Afghani brother." He and the undercover FBI agent placed the SUV bomb near the recruiting center, then walked away to a staging area. Martinez pressed what he thought was a button for a remotely-controlled detonator, then was arrested. Public defender Joseph Balter was assigned to his case. Charges included attempting to kill federal officers and attempting to use a weapon of mass destruction against U.S. property. He faced a life sentence plus twenty years.

The FBI had monitored him for months. The affidavit said he wanted to tell those joining the U.S. military that they would be killed. He also hoped to spark a Muslim uprising against U.S. forces. The FBI agent gave him numerous chances to back out, but he wanted to proceed. He initially wanted to shoot everyone in the recruiting center with a rifle, then moved on to the car bomb plot as the first of many he would perpetrate. Among the others would be an attack on Andrews Air Force Base using a truck filled with gasoline. He wanted to become a martyr, killing everyone in the recruiting center, climbing up to its roof, escaping, and making a last stand from a clandestine woodland camp. He was ordered held without

bond pending a December 14 detention hearing. He faced life in prison.

Martinez went to school in Prince George's County, Maryland. He said he was in the class of 2005 at Laurel High School. He had no fixed address, although some reports said he lived with his mother, who disapproved of his activities. He claimed to be married to a woman who was a senior at Pine Manor College outside of Boston. He was convicted of petty theft in Montgomery County in 2008 and placed on probation. WBAL-TV said he was originally from Nicaragua. A co-worker said he had been baptized as a Christian in 2009.

He was inspired by bin Laden and Anwar al-Aulaqi. He wrote on his Facebook wall, "IM just a yung brotha from the wrong side of the tracks who embraced Islam. We gotta rise up."

On December 21, 2010, a federal grand jury indicted him on charges of attempted murder of federal officers and attempted use of a weapon of mass destruction.

On January 26, 2012, Martinez pleaded guilty to attempted use of a weapon of mass destruction against federal property. Although he renounced terrorism, on January 31, authorities seized from his cell a hand-drawn banner depicting crossed swords and an AK-47 assault rifle. On April 6, 2012, he was sentenced to twenty-five years in prison, then five years of supervised release.

December 10, 2010—Pakistan—CNN reported that a drone strike killed two British militants and two other terrorist suspects sitting in a car in the Data Khel area of North Waziristan. They were identified as Gerry Smith, Islamic name Mansoor Ahmed, and Stephan, alias Abu Bakar.

December 11, 2010—Sweden—A white Audi 80 Vantage station wagon car bomb containing gas canisters exploded shortly before 5:00 p.m. in Olof Palmes Gatta in Drottninggatan, a busy shopping street in the center of Stockholm. Minutes later, a second bomb exploded 200 yards away in Bryggargatan. An injured man was found nearby and later pronounced dead at a local hospital. Two other people were hospitalized with less serious injuries. The Swedish news agency Tidningarnas Telegrambyra and the security service Sakerhetspolisen (SAPO) received a threatening e-mail, with a voice attachment in Arabic and Swedish, ten minutes before the explosions, from Taimour Abdulwahab al-Abdaly, 28, the suspected bomber, regarding the country's military presence in Afghanistan and the Muhammad cartoon caricatures by Swedish artist Lars Vilks, 64. In the audio, he said, "Now your children, daughters, and sisters shall die like our brothers and sisters and children are dying.... Our actions will talk for themselves. As long as you do not end your war against Islam and humiliation of the prophet and your stupid support for the pig Vilks.... Now it's time to act, don't wait any longer. Come forth with whatever you have, even if it is a knife, and I know that you can bring more than knives. Fear no one, don't fear prison, don't fear death." He asked his family for forgiveness for lying to them about his Middle East travel. "I didn't go to the Middle East to work. I went there for jihad."

Authorities suspected the suicide bomber was trying to get the bombs to a more populated area. Some reports said that he had twelve pipe bombs taped around him, but only one exploded, apparently early. He was carrying a backpack filled with nails.

On the evening of December 12, London's Metropolitan Police searched a property in Bedfordshire, north of London, in connection with the Stockholm attack. Al-Abdaly, a disaffected Iraqi Swede, had clashed with Qadeer Baksh, chairman of the Luton Islamic Centre, a mosque north of London, during the month of Ramadan in either 2006 or 2007. Baksh objected to al-Abdaly preaching violent jihad around the mosque and accusing other Muslim leaders of apostasy. Al-Abdaly attended college in the United Kingdom from 2001 to 2004.

In the profile he posted on the dating site www.muslima.com, al-Abdaly said he was born in Baghdad and moved to Sweden with his family, including an older sister, in 1992, when he was 10. He grew up in Tranas, three hours from Stockholm. His Facebook profile lists studying sports therapy at the University of Bedfordshire and a 2004 wedding. His wife and three children were believed to live in the United Kingdom. His e-mail to Tidningarnas Telegrambyra referred to "the Islamic state," which could have been a reference to al Qaeda in Iraq.

He had purchased the Audi in November for $1,500 from a used car dealer in Vadstena. 1012 1101

December 14, 2010—Iraq—Ten Shi'ite pilgrims were killed and twenty-one were wounded when a roadside bomb went off in western Baghdad's Ghazaliya neighborhood. Fourteen Shi'ite pilgrims were wounded by a roadside bomb near a procession in Khalis, Diyala Province.

December 14, 2010—Germany—Interior Ministry police raided Salafist safe houses in Bremen, Lower Saxony, and North Rhine-Westphalia, targeting Invitation to Paradise in Brunswick and Monchengladbach and the Islamic Culture Cen-

ter of Bremen. Police used statutes that had mainly been used against right-wing groups seeking to overthrow the government.

December 15, 2010—Iran—Two suicide bombers killed thirty-nine Shi'a worshipers outside the Imam Hussein Mosque in Chabahar in the southeast on the eve of the holy period of Ashura. Another ninety people were hospitalized. Among the dead was a newborn. Authorities arrested a suspect. The next day, nine suspects were in custody. Jundallah claimed credit.

December 16, 2010—Yemen—A bomb was thrown at a car carrying U.S. Embassy staffers outside a restaurant in Sana'a's Hadda neighborhood, causing no injuries but disabling the vehicle. Local authorities arrested several suspects, including a Jordanian in his 20s. Authorities arrested Jordanian engineer Maath Mohammed Kamal Alia, 45, on suspicion of throwing the bomb. 10121601

December 17, 2010—Ivory Coast—Six armed men in a car fired on a UN vehicle in Abidjan. 10121701

December 18, 2010—Ivory Coast—Masked gunmen fired at the UN base in Abidjan. No one from UN Côte d'Ivoire was injured. 10121801

December 18, 2010—Israel—Two Western tourists from CMJ United Kingdom (short for Christian Ministry Among Jewish People) were reported missing after going hiking in a forest near Beit Shemesh and Mata, west of Jerusalem. Two men attacked them, tied them up, and stabbed them. On the morning of December 19, the body of American female tourist Christine Logan (also spelled Kristine Luken), 40, was found in a forest outside Jerusalem. Her friend, Kaye Susan Wilson, a U.K. citizen living in Israel, showed up at a picnic area with her hands bound and multiple stab wounds, saying she and her friend had been attacked. Wilson managed to escape. Wilson was in stable condition at a Jerusalem hospital and told investigators that one of the men had a long serrated knife. They appeared to be Arabs. Wilson was wearing a Star of David necklace when attacked. Her attacker carefully removed it, then stabbed her where it had hung. She was the senior tour guide of the group; Luken was the administrator for tours. Authorities were investigating whether it was a "nationalist"-based attack and were treating it as a political attack. There was no evidence of sexual assault or robbery.

On January 26, 2011, Israeli police arrested four Palestinian men from the villages of Tarkumieh and Tzurif near Hebron in the southern West Bank in connection with the case. They were to be charged with murder in Luken's death, also with killing an Israeli woman, Neta Sorek, in February 2009, the attempted murder of Kay Susan Wilson, and the attempted murder of another couple. The four told police they were avenging the January 2009 killing of Hamas official Mahmoud al-Mabhouh in Dubai. 10121802

December 20, 2010—Iran—The government executed eleven Jundallah members.

December 20, 2010—United Kingdom—Police arrested twelve would-be terrorists, ages 17 to 28, in 5:00 a.m. raids in London, Cardiff in Wales, and Stoke and Birmingham in central England. Five were detained in Cardiff (three at a Victorian house in Riverside; two others at Ely); three in London; three in Stoke-on-Trent; and one in Birmingham. Some were believed to be of Pakistani descent; at least five were Bangladeshi. They were held on suspicion of "preparation or instigation of an act of terrorism in the United Kingdom." Eleven were arrested at their homes; the twelfth was grabbed at someone else's Birmingham residence. The *Times* reported that they were planning to bomb nightclubs, shopping centers, and landmarks and were in contact with terrorists overseas, possibly with al Qaeda connections. ABCNews.com later reported that targets included the U.S. Embassy, London Stock Exchange, and unnamed political and religious figures. Police seized computers and cell phones. The group reportedly planned to use parcel designs published in *Inspire*, an al Qaeda in the Arabia Peninsula newsletter. The operation was conducted by Scotland Yard's (Metropolitan Police) Counter-Terrorism Command, the West Midlands Police counterterrorism unit, and Staffordshire and South Wales police. The terrorist plot had begun on October 1.

On December 26, British police charged nine of the men in the City of Westminster Magistrates Court with conspiring to cause explosions, engaging in conduct in preparation for acts of terrorism with the intention of either committing acts of terrorism or assisting another to commit such acts, reconnoitering targets, downloading and researching terrorism-related material from the Internet, and testing incendiary material. The other three detainees were released without charge.

West Midlands Police identified the suspects charged as Gurukanth Desai, 28, Omar Sharif Latif, 26, and Abdul Malik Miah, 24, from Cardiff; Mohammed Moksudur Rahman Chowdhury, 20, and Shah Mohammed Lutfar Rahman, 28, from London; and Nazam Hussain, 25, Usman Khan, 19, Mohibur Rahman, 26, and Abul

Bosher Mohammed Shahjahan, 26, from Stoke-on-Trent. Judge Howard Riddle ordered them held in prison until a further hearing on January 14, 2011.

On February 1, 2012, four of the British citizens—Mohammed Chowdhury, 21, and Shah Rahman, 28, both of Bangladeshi descent from London, and Wales residents Gurukanth Desai, 30, and Abdul Miah, 25—pleaded guilty to planning to bomb toilets in the London Stock Exchange, saying they had been inspired by al-Aulaqi. They had also considered attacking the home of the London mayor, two rabbis, and the London Eye, a 440-foot Ferris wheel. Sentencing was set for the following week.

On February 9, 2012, the court sentenced Mohammed Shahjahan, 27, to a minimum term of eight years and ten months. Stoke-on-Trent Islamists Usman Khan, 20, and Nazam Hussain, 26, were sentenced to eight years. The trio planned to establish a terrorist camp in Kashmir on land owned by Khan's family. Khan and Hussain planned to receive military instruction there. Abdul Miah, 25, was sentenced to sixteen years and ten months for leading the group. His brother, Gurukanth Desai, 30, and Shah Rahman, 28, were jailed for twelve years. Mohammed Chowdhury, 22, linchpin of the group, was sentenced to thirteen years and eight months. Omar Latif, 28, was sentenced to ten years and four months. Mohibur Rahman was sentenced to five years. 10122001

December 20, 2010—Kenya—Al Shabaab was suspected of setting off a bomb at a downtown bus station in Nairobi as passengers boarded a bus, killing two people and wounding thirty-nine. The dead person was carrying luggage that contained the bomb. Police had not determined whether it was a suicide attack. Most of the wounded were Ugandans planning on going home for Christmas. Kenyan Police Commissioner Mathew Iteere said that the attacker had boarded a Kampala-bound bus carrying a Russian-made grenade in a plastic bag. When he thought he was about to face a security search, he dropped the bag, which detonated prematurely. Police said that the attacker was a Tanzanian. 10122002

December 21, 2010—Italy—At 10:00 a.m., a train engineer found a bomb-like device in a plastic bag under a seat at the Rebibbia stop on the outskirts of Rome. A bomb squad determined that it could not explode. The package contained a potentially explosive cylinder.

December 21, 2010—United States—CBS and CNN cited unnamed terrorism experts as saying that al Qaeda in the Arabian Peninsula had considered using ricin and cyanide to contaminate salad bars and buffets at U.S. hotels and restaurants. U.S. officials downplayed the threat, noting that the story was months old and only a discussion rather than a plot.

December 21, 2010—Iraq—The Islamic State of Iraq warned on a Web site that it would continue to attack Christians until Egypt's Coptic Church released two women the terrorists said the church was holding hostage until they renounced their conversion to Islam.

December 22, 2010—Pakistan—Pakistani authorities arrested Abdul-Rauf Rigi, leader of the Sunni Muslim ethnic Baluch group Jundallah, and eight accomplices along the Iran-Pakistan border. Iran and the United States consider Jundallah to be a terrorist group. Pakistan's *News* said authorities traced his cell phone call to the London-based *Asharq al-Awsat* newspaper and arrested him. Rigi is the younger brother of Abdulmalak Rigi, Jundallah's founder, who was hanged by Iran in June 2010.

December 23, 2010—Italy—The Informal Federation of Anarchists, a splinter of the Italian Anarchist Federation (FAI), claimed credit for two mail bombs that went off at the embassies of Chile and Switzerland. No warning was issued. The bomb at the Swiss embassy seriously injured a Swiss-born mailroom worker, age 53. Surgeons removed metal from the chest of Chilean embassy employee César Mella, who lost part of his hand, sustained face and abdomen injuries, and might lose sight in one eye. A second person was hospitalized when the Chilean Embassy bomb exploded at 2:27 p.m. Notes were included in the small boxes that contained the bombs, and read, "We have decided to make our voices heard again, in words and deeds. We will destroy the system of domination. Long live FAI. Long live anarchy." The notes mentioned Lambros Fountas, 35, who was shot dead in March while protesting in Athens. He had become a rallying point for anarchists in Greece, Spain, and Italy. A suspicious package found at the Ukrainian Embassy in Rome contained no bomb. False alarms were reported at the embassies of the Ukraine, Slovenia, and Estonia. Bomb threats were phoned to City Hall and another government office in Rome; no bombs were found. 10122301-02

December 23, 2010—Somalia—Hizbul Islam and al-Shabaab hosted a joint news conference in Mogadishu to announce their merger. They threatened to attack African Union (AU) peacekeepers in the city, as well as conduct attacks in

Uganda and Burundi, which contribute troops to the AU force. 10122303

December 24, 2010—Pakistan—Some 150 terrorists attacked five security checkpoints in Mohmand Agency, killing 11 soldiers. Security forces later killed 24 attackers and another 16 on Christmas.

December 24, 2010—Pakistan—Officials said that in recent days they had detained Nasiruddin Haqqani as he was driving from Peshawar to North Waziristan. He was believed based out of Miram Shah in North Waziristan. He is the son of Jalaluddin Haqqani, who leads a Taliban-affiliated tribal group.

December 24, 2010—India—Police in Mumbai issued a terrorist threat alert because four Lashkar-e-Tayyiba terrorists had entered Mumbai and were planning violence on Christmas and New Year's Day. Police named Abdul Kareem Moosa, Noor Abu Ilahi, Walid Jinnah, and Mahfooz Alam, all between ages 20 and 30. Their nationalities were unknown.

December 24, 2010—Nigeria—At 7:00 p.m., thirty-one people were killed and seventy-four others wounded when seven bombs went off in Jos as residents celebrated Christmas Eve. Some of the injuries included leg amputations. Four bombs went off in Kabong and three in Angwa Rubuka. Islamist terrorists were suspected.

December 24, 2010—Netherlands—Rotterdam police arrested a dozen Somalis, aged 19 to 48, planning terrorist attacks. No weapons or explosives were found in searches of a pawn shop, four homes, and two hotel rooms. Six of the suspects were Rotterdam residents; one was from Denmark; five had no permanent address. Some were Dutch citizens. By December 27, six of them had been released. By December 28, only one remained in custody, and he was to be held for only three more days. The other eleven were released outright or passed to immigration authorities. The final one was freed on December 30; three remained suspects. 10122401

December 25, 2010—Pakistan—A female suicide bomber, aged between 16 and 18, set off explosives at a security checkpoint 600 meters from a UN World Food Program distribution point in Khar, Bajaur Agency, that killed 46 people, including several women and children, and injured 105 others. Pakistani Taliban spokesman Azam Tariq claimed credit, saying it had targeted people who had formed a pro-government and anti–Taliban group. Authorities believed it was the first time a burqa-clad suicide bomber had attacked in Pakistan. Tariq denied it was a woman, saying, "We have thousands of male suicide bombers ready who are keenly waiting for their turns. Then why would we use a woman, which is against the traditions of Islam?" 10122501

December 25, 2010—Saudi Arabia—Authorities shot and killed Mohammed Essam Taher Baghdadi, a male terrorist disguised as a woman at a checkpoint 400 miles southeast of Riyadh. The man, who was wanted for al Qaeda ties, was one of two people who were stopped in their car. When the duo got out of the car to present their ID cards, the disguised man opened fire and was killed in the gun battle.

December 25, 2010—Philippines—A bomb exploded during Christmas Day Mass on Jolo Island, wounding a priest and ten parishioners. Al Qaeda-linked terrorists were suspected.

December 26, 2010—Afghanistan—Four Turkish engineers were kidnapped. The group was building an Afghan national police post in Shpola village in southeastern Paktia Province, one kilometer from the border with Pakistan, near Para Chinar and Korm Agency. The engineers had relied on six armed Afghan local guards. 10122601

December 27, 2010—Italy—A bomb was found in a small metal licorice box at the Greek Embassy in Rome. The Informal Anarchist Federation left a note with the package, an A4-sized padded envelope which went through the Italian mail system. The note read, "We're striking again, and we do so in response to the appeal sent by the Greek comrades of the Conspiracy of the Cells of Fire. That is why we are directing the new attack to one of the structures that represents the Greek state and its servants, in solidarity with the comrades arrested in Athens and the Conspiracy's project which, like ours, is based on the actions and methods of revolutionary violence." Suspicious packages, none of them containing bombs, were found at the embassies of Venezuela, Albania, Egypt, Finland, Slovenia, Sweden, Monaco, and Denmark. They were eventually determined to contain holiday packages. 10122701

December 27, 2010—Morocco—Authorities announced that they had wrapped up a six-man terrorist cell planning to attack "hot spots across the world." The men had "considerable experience in the manufacture of explosives," and planned to use car bombs against foreign interests in Morocco, several locations in its territory vital to national security interests, and in unspecified countries. The group was also involved in unspecified "cyberterrorism." 10122702

December 27, 2010—Somalia—Fuad Mohamed "Shongole" Qalaf, a senior member of al-Shabaab, said in a radio broadcast in Afgoye, "We tell the American President Barack Obama to embrace Islam before we come to his country." He was meeting with Sheik Hassan Dahir Aweys, former leader of Hizbul Islam, which had merged with al-Shabaab.

December 27, 2010—Iraq—Two seriatim suicide bombings killed nineteen people and wounded forty-five in Ramadi. The first bomber drove his car into the front gate of the Anbar provincial compound, where family members of thirteen police and security workers killed in a December 12 attack were arriving to receive promised government compensation. Three minutes later a second suicide bomber set off his suicide vest among the rescue workers. Many of the wounded lost body parts and were severely burned. Al Qaeda in Iraq was suspected.

December 28, 2010—Iran—The government hanged Ali Saremi, 63, for propagandizing for the Mujahideen e-Khalq (MEK) exile extremist group and "being an enemy of God." He had been arrested several times since 1982 and was finally arrested in 2007 and sentenced to death. His wife, daughter, and two others were arrested outside Evin Prison after his execution. The family said that Saremi's son was an MEK member living at the group's base at Camp Ashraf in Iraq. The father traveled to visit his son, but the family said he was not an MEK member.

December 29, 2010—Denmark/Sweden—Danish police arrested four militant Islamists believed planning an "imminent" terrorist attack; Swedish police arrested a fifth suspect—a 37-year-old Swedish citizen of Tunisian origin residing in Stockholm. The group was believed ready to enter the building housing *Jyllands-Posten*, a newspaper that ran a cartoon of Muhammad, and "kill as many of the people present as possible." Three of the four men were Swedish residents who had left Stockholm and entered Denmark on December 28 and 29. They included a 44-year-old Tunisian, a 29-year-old Lebanese-born man, a 26-year-old Iraqi asylum seeker living in Copenhagen, and a 30-year-old of unknown extraction. The four men were to appear in court on December 30, facing preliminary charges of attempting to carry out an act of terrorism. They were arrested in Greve, south of Copenhagen, and Herlev, to the west. Police seized an automatic weapon, a silencer, 122 rounds of ammunition, and plastic strips that could be used as handcuffs.

On June 4, the four Islamist terrorists were convicted in a courthouse in Glostrup, outside Copenhagen. The three Swedish nationals and one Tunisian resident of Sweden were each sentenced to twelve years in prison. They were identified as Mounir Dhahri, 46, a Tunisian citizen; Munir Awad, 31, of Lebanese descent; Sahbi Zalouti, 39, of Tunisian descent; and Omar Aboelazm, 32, of Egyptian descent. Counterterrorism officials in the United States and Scandinavia believe the plot was directed by al Qaeda operatives in Pakistan, who called for the terrorists to execute hostages. A prosecutor said that the terrorists might have been targeting a reception to be attended by the Danish crown prince in the same building as the newspaper.

Swedish and Danish security services had tracked the suspects in December 2010 as they drove from Sweden to Denmark with a submachine gun, a silencer, several dozen 9-mm submachine gun cartridges, $20,000 cash, and wrist strips that would be used to bind up to two hundred journalist hostages.

Dhahri, the ringleader, Awad, and Zalouti traveled to Pakistan in early 2010. Awad and Zalouti were arrested by Pakistani authorities in August 2010 before they could reach North Waziristan. Dhahri made it back from Pakistan via Athens and Brussels, from which Zalouti gave him a ride. Zalouti admitted to Swedish police he wired money from Sweden via Western Union to Dhahri in Bannu, a town bordering North Waziristan. The duo went to Copenhagen, where they cased targets. Dhahri and Awad were linked to Farid, a Stockholm-based militant of Moroccan descent suspected of being a facilitator for Ilyas Kashmiri's terrorist network. 10122901

December 29, 2010—Vatican—A suspicious package found at the U.S. Embassy to the Holy See was a false alarm.

December 29, 2010—Italy—Two small bombs exploded in front of the northern Italian headquarters of a right-wing party.

December 30, 2010—Greece—Anarchists were believed responsible for setting off a bomb outside an Athens administrative court, causing severe damage but no injuries. Police evacuated the area after receiving a telephoned warning.

December 31, 2010—Greece—A small bomb exploded just before 4:00 a.m. outside a closed nightclub in Athens. No injuries were reported. Authorities blamed extortionists.

December 31, 2010—Nigeria—At 7:00 p.m., a bomb exploded at the crowded Mammy market, within the grounds of the Sani Abacha barracks in Abuja, killing at least eleven people, including three women, and wounded thirteen, including six women.

2011

2011—Georgia—Authorities arrested two Georgian men who had cesium–137, firearms, and TNT. One detainee was a former Soviet officer in an army logistics unit who retired in the early 1990s. He had kept the cesium for years before he and a relative tried to sell it to a Georgian agent.

January 1, 2011—Egypt—Thirty minutes after midnight, a suicide bomber stepped out of his car and set off explosives at the entrance to the Coptic Christian Church of Two Saints in Alexandria, killing twenty-three worshipers and injuring ninety-seven, including four police officers, as nearly one thousand parishioners were exiting Mass. The homemade device contained nails and ball bearings. Authorities blamed al Qaeda, whose Iraqi affiliate had threatened to attack Christians. The newspaper *al-Masry al-Youm* reported that security services said several foreign "infiltrators" had entered the country, although the bomb seemed to have been locally made. Egyptian Interior Minister Habib al-Adly blamed the al Qaeda-linked Palestinian Islamic Army. Abu Musanna, a spokesman for the Army of Islam, denied the charge. 11010101

January 2, 2011—Israel—Authorities charged five Hamas members who were arrested in November 2010 with planning to fire a rocket into a Jerusalem stadium during a soccer game. The key suspects were Hamas and Muslim Brothers members Mussa Hamada of East Jerusalem, and Bassem Omri, an Israeli citizen living in Beit Tzafafa. The other three Palestinian defendants were charged with selling them pistols.

January 4, 2011—Turkey—The Supreme Court of Appeals ruled that detainees could be held for only ten years without sentencing. The government released eighteen members of Turkish Hizballah and five members of the Kurdish Workers Party after they had spent more than a decade in jail without having the sentences endorsed by that court. One of those released was Edip Gumus, a Turkish Hizballah member who was freed from Diyarbakir's jail. He was arrested in 2000 and sentenced to life in prison in December 2009 for membership in a terrorist organization and participating in more than one hundred murders. He admitted membership in the group but denied involvement in the murders.

January 4, 2011—Pakistan—Mumtaz Qadri, a bodyguard for Punjab Province's Governor Salman Taseer, fatally shot Taseer in Islamabad. Taseer had criticized the anti-blasphemy law. On October 1, a Pakistani court sentenced Qadri to two sentences of death for murder and terrorism. He had seven days to file an appeal.

January 5, 2011—Norway/Turkey—Cuma Yasar, 40, a man wearing a snow mask and claiming to have a bomb, tried to enter the cockpit of a Turkish Airlines B-737–800 about to land at Ataturk International Airport in Istanbul. He demanded that the captain fly back to Oslo. He was tackled by passengers Firat Faysal Ali and Dag Gjerstad; authorities then took him into custody. The hijacker was reportedly mentally ill. 11010501

January 5, 2011—Morocco—Morocco arrested a member of al Qaeda in the Islamic Maghreb (AQIM) and twenty-six other people planning to attack local and foreign security services and rob banks in Casablanca and Rabat. They had cached weapons, including thirty Kalashnikov rifles, two rocket-propelled grenade launchers, and several handguns at three sites in Amghala, an oasis in Western Sahara. The government said the group wanted to send recruits "to AQIM camps in Algeria and Mali to undergo paramilitary training before returning to Morocco to execute their destructive plans." Observers said it was the first evidence of links between AQIM and the Popular Front for the Liberation of Saguia el-Hamra and Rio de Oro (POLISARIO).

January 6, 2011—United States—Two Maryland state employees sustained burns to their fingers when they opened packages that flashed, caught fire, and gave off smoke and a sulfur smell. One package was addressed to Governor Martin O'Malley in Annapolis and was opened at 12:30 p.m.; the other to Maryland Secretary of Transportation Beverley K. Swaim-Staley near Hanover and went off fifteen minutes later. Suspicious packages at the Maryland Department of Health and Mental Hygiene and the federal courthouse in Baltimore were determined to be harmless. Both packages were the size of small books. One had five holiday stamps. Officials did not find explosives in the devices, which were 12 inches long, 4 to 8 inches wide, and one inch thick. A note that accompanied the package to O'Malley read, "Reports suspicious activity! Total bull[—]! You have created a self fulfilling prophecy. -X-" in all capital letters. The note referred to Maryland's 113 highway signs asking for drivers to assist in spotting terrorist activities.

January 7, 2011—Niger—In a nighttime attack on Le Toulousain, a restaurant owned by a French citizen, in Niamey, al Qaeda in the Islamic Maghreb kidnapped two French citizens. The next day, the terrorists executed them during a French rescue attempt at Ouallam, 60 miles northwest of Niamey. The duo was found dead at the Niger-Mali border. 11010701

January 7, 2011—United States—A package addressed to Secretary of Homeland Security Janet Napolitano ignited at 2:45 p.m. when a mail sorter threw it into a bin at a U.S. Postal Service annex on V Street Northeast in Washington, DC, causing no injuries.

January 8, 2011—United States—At least six people, including a 9-year-old and U.S. District Court Judge John M. Roll, 63, the chief judge in Arizona, were killed and fourteen wounded when gunman Jared Lee Loughner, 22, fired a Glock 19 pistol at Arizona Member of the U.S. House of Representatives Gabrielle Giffords, 40, outside a Safeway grocery store in Tucson, Arizona, as the Democratic leader met with constituents. Giffords, a "blue dog" Democrat, sustained a bullet to the head and was sent to surgery; she was able to communicate, but not talk, within a few hours. Gabe Zimmerman, her local director of community outreach, died. Giffords's district director Ron Barber, 65, a lifelong social worker with four grandchildren, and Pamela Simon, her community outreach aide, were wounded.

The 9-year-old was identified as Christina Taylor Green, who was born on September 11, 2001. She was a member of her school's student council. She was the only girl on her Little League baseball team. She was the granddaughter of Dallas Green, the Philadelphia Phillies former manager. Susan Hileman, the neighbor who brought her to the event so that she could learn more about the political process, was shot four times.

Loughner's Glock was fully loaded with thirty rounds. He had another magazine with thirty rounds, and two others that had fifteen bullets. He also carried a knife. He purchased the Glock on November 30 at Sportsman's Warehouse in Tucson, where he immediately passed a background check despite a history of bizarre behavior in his community college. He could conceal and carry the pistol without a permit under Arizona law.

President George H. W. Bush had appointed Roll in 1991; Roll became chief judge in 2006. He received hundreds of threats in February 2009 when he permitted a lawsuit filed by illegal immigrants to continue. He was put under twenty-four-hour protection for a month.

Giffords was beginning her third term having served earlier as a member of the Arizona House and Senate. She is married to astronaut Mark E. Kelly, who piloted space shuttles *Endeavour* and *Discovery*. The two met in China in 2003 and were married in January 2007. She had been subjected to threats. In August 2009, during a similar Congress on Your Corner event, a protester shouted invective and dropped a handgun. On March 22, 2010, the glass door to her Tucson office was shattered after she voted in favor of the health care bill.

Loughner posted several incoherent anti-government messages on the Internet, complaining about low educational attainment in Giffords's district. Authorities were looking at his possible links to anti-government groups. He was rejected when he applied to the army. He posted a video attacking police at Tucson's Pima Community College where he entered as a student in 2005. He withdrew in fall 2010 after disciplinary issues. Between February and September 2010, campus police were called five times to deal with his disruptive behavior in classrooms and libraries. His rap sheet included a drug arrest.

Loughner was represented by Judy Clarke, a San Diego public defender who defended Unabomber Theodore Kaczynski and assisted in the defense of would-be twentieth 9/11 hijacker Zacarias Moussaoui. She was joined by San Diego defender Mark Fleming. Loughner was charged with five federal offenses, including two capital murder counts, as well as attempted murder of Giffords and two others.

Authorities believed he acted alone and had planned the attack for some time. He had met Giffords at a similar Tucson mall public event in 2007.

A federal grand jury indicted Loughner on January 19, 2011, on three counts of attempting to assassinate Giffords and two counts of attempted murder of Ron Barber and Pam Simon. He faced life in prison and twenty years, respectively, on the charges. On January 24, a federal judge entered a plea of not guilty on behalf of Loughner to three counts of attempted murder.

On March 4, 2011, federal authorities charged Loughner with forty-nine counts of murder and attempted murder. The superseding indictment still charged him with the murder of two federal officials—Judge Roll and Gabriel Zimmerman—and added causing the deaths of Dorothy Morris, Phyllis Schneck, Dorwan Stoddard, and Christina Taylor. He was also charged with injuring ten others and with numerous weapons infractions. The prosecutors argued that everyone was in a feder-ally protected area, exercising their constitutional right of free assembly, and that their civil rights had been violated by the attack. On March 9, he pleaded not guilty. On May 25, 2011, U.S. District Judge Larry A. Burns declared Loughner mentally unfit to stand trial and remanded him to a federal facility in Springfield, Missouri, to receive treatment for up to four months.

Representative Giffords attended the 2012 State of the Union address, finished the Congress on Your Corner event that had been halted by Loughner's attack, and announced that she was resigning so that she could devote her time to her rehabilitation.

On August 7, 2012, Loughner agreed to a plea bargain accepted by Judge Larry A. Burns under which the gunman would spend the rest of his life in prison. Court-appointed psychiatrist Christina Pietz testified that he was able to understand the criminal charges, but was still seriously mentally ill with schizophrenia and his condition could deteriorate during a trial. He had been forcibly medicated with psychotropic drugs for more than a year. On November 8, 2012, U.S. District Judge Larry A. Burns sentenced Loughner to seven consecutive life terms without parole plus 140 years.

January 9, 2011—Philippines—Government troops killed two Abu Sayyaf gunmen and captured a third following a forty-five-minute gun battle in the mountains outside Tipi Tipo on Basilan Island. The soldiers seived two M-16 rifles with ammunition and a rocket-propelled grenade.

January 10, 2011—Spain—The Basque Nation and Liberty (ETA) announced a permanent cease-fire as:

> a firm commitment towards a process to achieve a lasting resolution and toward an end to the armed confrontation.... It is time to act with historical responsibility. ETA calls upon those governing Spain and France to end all repressive measures and to leave aside for once and for all their position of denial towards the Basque Country.... The solution will come through the democratic process with dialogue and negotiation as its tools and with its compass pointed towards the will of the Basque people ... ETA will continue its indefatigable struggle and efforts to promote and to bring to a conclusion the democratic process until there is a truly democratic situation in the Basque Country.

The group did not mention a surrender of its weapons.

January 11, 2011—France/Spain—Police arrested Basque Nation and Liberty (ETA) member Iraitz Guesalaga in the southern town of Ciboure. He was believed to be one of the group's technology experts, handling encryption. Spanish police arrested his girlfriend, Ixaso Urriaga, in Zarautz, for aiding the ETA.

January 11, 2011—Egypt—Yelling "There is no God but God," a deputy policeman killed a Christian man and wounded five other Christians on a train.

January 13, 2011—Ireland—Irish police detained five suspected Irish Republican Army dissidents under Section 30 of the Offenses Against the State Act after finding a bomb-making factory with metal tubes and other components at a remote farm 40 miles from Dublin in County Kildare. Police later released one man but held the others for questioning. Police suspected the dissident group Óglaigh na hÉireann (Irish Volunteers) was making mortar bombs to be used in Northern Ireland.

January 16, 2011—Pakistan—Gunmen in Dera Murad Jamali in Baluchistan Province torched ten parked oil tankers carrying fuel for NATO troops in Afghanistan. One person was injured. 11011601

January 17, 2011—Yemen—A Yemeni court sentenced Anwar al-Aulaqi in absentia to ten years in prison on charges of inciting to kill foreigners. The court sentenced Hisham Asim, 19, to death; prosecutors said al-Aulaqi incited him to kill a Frenchman in an October shooting. The court sentenced in absentia Anwar al-Aulaqi's cousin, Othman al-Aulaqi, to eight years in prison on charges of inciting to kill foreigners.

January 17, 2011—Paraguay—The leftist Paraguayan People's Army claimed credit for a bombing that injured five people when a backpack bomb exploded outside a police station in Horqueta. It was the third bombing in a week. The group left a handwritten note saying it would keep up the anti-government attacks.

January 17, 2011—Iraq—A suicide bomber driving a car killed one person when he attacked the convoy of the governor of Anbar Province.

January 18, 2011—Iraq—A suicide bomber set off his explosive vest at a line of recruits at a police station in Tikrit, killing 67 and wounding 160 others.

January 18, 2011—Spain—The government arrested ten suspected members, including two women, of the Basque Nation and Liberty (ETA). Nine were arrested in Navarra, the other in Alava. Six suspects were linked to Ekin, a group which Spain's National Court in 2007 ruled was "part of the heart" of ETA. The other four were linked to Askatasuna, a pro–ETA propaganda group.

January 18, 2011—United States—Three city employees found a Swiss Army backpack containing a bomb on a park bench in Spokane, Washington, an hour before a Martin Luther King, Jr., Day parade was to begin. Police defused the device, which they said could have caused multiple casualties. It contained metal pellets and a chemical found in rat poison. Authorities said it had a remote detonator. Officials noted that there are white supremacist and militia groups in the area. On April 22, 2011, a superseding indictment accused Kevin Harpham, 36, of Colville, Washington, with a hate crime—planting the bomb "because of actual or perceived race, color, and national origin" of march participants. On March 9, federal authorities had arrested Harpham. He pleaded not guilty in federal court to attempting to use a weapon of mass destruction and for possessing an unregistered explosive device. He often posted on white supremacist Web sites, including the Vanguard News Network. He observed, "Those who say you can't win a war by bombing have never tried."

January 19, 2011—Iraq—Fifteen people were killed in two suicide bombings in Diyala Province. A suicide bomber crashed an explosives-laden ambulance into a police training center in Baqubah, 35 miles northeast of Baghdad, killing thirteen and wounding seventy, many of them training with the Facilities Protection Service. Two people died and fifteen were injured when a man set off his explosive vest near the convoy of a senior provincial official during a gathering of Shi'ite pilgrims in Khalis district, north of Baqubah.

January 20, 2011—Iraq—Three bombs killed 50 Shi'ite pilgrims and injured at least 150 in attacks in Karbala in the runup to the Arbaeen religious commemoration. Two parked cars and a motorcycle had been rigged with the explosives.

January 21, 2011—Qatar—Al-Jazeera ran an Osama bin Laden audio in which he said that the release of two kidnapped French journalists depended on changes in France's military role in Afghanistan.

> We repeat the same message to you. The release of your prisoners from the hands of our brethren depends on the withdrawal of your soldiers from our countries.... The dismissal of your President [Nicholas] Sarkozy to get out of Afghanistan is the result of his subservience to the United States and this [dismissal] is considered to be the green signal to kill your prisoners without delay.... We will not do that at the time that suits him [Sarkozy] and this position will cost you dearly on all fronts, in France and

abroad ... [France] with its debt and budget deficit does not need new fronts.

The Taliban had kidnapped France 3 Television reporter Herve Ghesquiere and cameraman Stephane Taponier in December 2009.

January 21, 2011—United States/Pakistan—The United States imposed sanctions on Tehrik-e-Taliban Pakistan leader Qari Hussain Mehsud, who had recruited children as suicide bombers. The United States blocked all property "subject to U.S. jurisdiction in which Hussain has an interest" and prohibited all transactions by U.S. persons with him.

January 24, 2011—Russia—A suicide bomber set off explosives at 4:32 p.m. at the entrance of the international arrivals section of Moscow's Domodedovo Airport, killing thirty-five people and wounding more than two hundred. The bomb included small metal objects that served as shrapnel. WTOP reported that eight foreigners, including two Britons and several French and Italian citizens, were among the dead. Passengers from Italy, Tajikistan, and Germany were coming through the unsecured customs area when the bomb exploded. North Caucasus Muslim separatists were suspected. A witness said the bomber was a short, dark man with a suitcase. Authorities said on January 29 that the bomber was a 20-year-old male but did not release his name. The *Kommersant* newspaper reported that authorities were searching for a Russian from Stavropol who was a member of the radical Islamist group Nogai Jamaat. The individual was believed involved in an August 17, 2010, terrorist attack.

In a Webcast on Kavkazcenter.com on February 7, Islamic leader Doku Umarov said he had ordered the suicide bombing and vowed further attacks. On February 9, Russian officials said the bomber was Magomed Yevloyev, 20, from Ingushetia. They arrested his teenage brother and sister on suspicion of involvement in the attack. On March 29, Russian authorities arrested two suspects in the attack. Investigators charged Chechen warlord Doku Umarov and another terrorist with organizing the bombing. Russian media reports suggested that Umarov might have been killed in a March 29 law enforcement raid in Ingushetia Province in which seventeen militants were killed. 11012401

January 24, 2011—United States—Police in Dearborn, Michigan, arrested southern California resident Roger Stockham, 63, for having explosives in his vehicle in the parking lot outside the Islamic Center of America, one of the nation's largest mosques. He was arraigned on January 27 on one count of making a false report or threat of terrorism and one count of possessing explosives with an unlawful intent. He had a large quantity of class–C fireworks including M-80s, which are outlawed in Michigan. Stockham was jailed on a $500,000 bond.

January 25, 2011—Thailand—At 5:25 p.m., a bomb exploded in the Yaha district of Yala Province, killing nine civilians and wounding two others. Muslim separatists were suspected.

January 25, 2011—Philippines—Four were killed and fifteen injured when a bomb exploded at 2:00 p.m. under a seat in a bus in Manila's financial district. The Newman Bus Lines bus was approaching a Metro Rail Transit station on Buendia Avenue in Makati City.

January 25, 2011—Pakistan—Suicide bombers killed sixteen Shi'ite Muslims—thirteen in Lahore and three in Karachi. In Lahore, a bomb went off in front of a market near a procession of Shi'ite mourners observing the fortieth day of Ashura. In Karachi, a motorcyclist set off his bomb next to his police van at a security checkpoint outside another Shi'ite festival, killing two police officers. At least fifty-two people were hospitalized in Lahore; fifteen were in critical condition. Shakir Ullah Shakir, a spokesman for the Fedayeen-e-Islam, an offshoot of the Pakistani Taliban and Laskhar-e-Jangvi Sunni terrorist groups, claimed credit for the Lahore attack, observing that Shi'ites are enemies of Islam. Police said the Lahore bomber was a boy between 13 and 15 years old, carrying a bag. He set off the bomb after police stopped him.

January 27, 2011—Iraq—A parked car bomb went off near a funeral tent in the Shi'ite neighborhood of Shula in northwestern Baghdad, killing 48 and injuring 121.

January 27, 2011—United States—Secretary for the Department of Homeland Security (DHS) Janet Napolitano announced the five-color terrorist warning system would be phased out over ninety days and said DHS would use a two-tier warning system that provided more specific information on threats and how to respond to them.

January 28, 2011—Pakistan—A car bomb exploded in the Kohat Tunnel in Khyber Pakhtunkhwa Province, killing seven and wounding fifteen.

January 28, 2011—Afghanistan—After firing a weapon, a suicide bomber set off his explosive vest in the Finest supermarket in Kabul's diplomatic quarter, killing eight people, including three foreign women, and injuring six. Taliban spokesman

Zabiullah Mujahid claimed credit, saying it was targeting the chief of Xe Services.

The Afghan National Security (ANS) Directorate revealed on February 10, 2011, that Talib Jan, 45, an imprisoned Taliban fighter, planned the suicide bombing from Pul-i-Charkhi prison outside Kabul. He had been held there for three years. ANS spokesman Lutfullah Mashal said the group planned to assassinate two French diplomats; earlier reports had incorrectly said that the group was trying to kill the head of U.S. security contractor Xe Corporation. The ANS arrested Muhammad Khan, 33, a Kabul resident who told a news conference that he drove the bomber from Pakistan into Afghanistan. He also said he had earlier planted explosives along a road and bridge used by coalition troops. He said he did not know that his passenger, Muhammad Shoib, was a suicide bomber. 11012801

February 2011—South Sudan—Rebel leader George Athor killed 211 southern civilians and security troops in an attack in Jonglei State. Minister for Humanitarian Affairs and Disaster Management James Kok Ruea said that circa 160 were civilians, including children, elderly, and refugees. Thirty of the attackers died. The ruling party said that Khartoum armed and financed rebel leaders.

February 2011—Yemen—*Sada al-Malahim*, al Qaeda in the Arabian Peninsula's online magazine, called for the Tunisian people to implement "God's Law" rather than following democracy, which it deemed the road to hell.

February 2011—Georgia—Authorities arrested two men in Kutaisi with a small quantity of two radioactive materials stolen from an abandoned Soviet helicopter factory. Businessman Soslan Oniani was linked to the case. His cousin, Tariel Oniani, was an organized crime boss convicted in Russia of kidnapping. Police surveillance in 2012 established that Soslan was involved in a deal for radioactive materials.

February 2011—Algeria—Armed al Qaeda in the Islamic Maghreb gunmen seized Italian tourist Maria Sandra Mariani, 54, near the Niger border. They freed her on April 17, 2012. 11029901

February 1, 2011—Mauritania—Three al Qaeda suspects died when their vehicle exploded during a shootout with local soldiers. The trio planned to attack the French Embassy and an army base. The vehicle was one of a three-car convoy that crossed the Mali border the previous weekend. Authorities captured a driver and his vehicle that contained 1.5 tons of explosives. The second vehicle exploded; one of the suspects set off his ex-

plosive belt. The third vehicle eluded capture. A suspect was arrested on February 5. 11020101

February 2, 2011—Pakistan—Nine people, including three children, died and another twenty people were injured when a car bomb exploded near Peshawar on a road leading to the Afghanistan border.

February 3, 2011—Belgium—Police in Brussels announced the arrest on a Spanish National Court warrant of two Pakistani brothers connected to a cell that forged passports for al Qaeda supporters.

February 5, 2011—Egypt—An armed gang attacked a natural gas terminal near el-Arish in the northern Sinai Peninsula, disrupting supplies to Israel and Jordan for a month. 11020501

February 10, 2011—Pakistan—A 14-year-old Pakistani Taliban suicide bomber wearing a school uniform killed twenty-seven army recruits and wounded another forty-two during morning calisthenics at a military training center in Mardan, 50 kilometers north of Peshawar in Khyber-Pakhtunkhwa Province. A school for children of the recruits is inside the training facility. Pakistani Taliban spokesman Azam Tariq said it was a "message for those who wish to join pro–American military.... We will continue targeting Pakistan military until it stops supporting the United States."

February 10, 2011—United States—The U.S. Department of the Treasury (DOT) and the U.S. Drug Enforcement Administration (DEA) accused the Beirut-based Lebanese Canadian Bank SAL of laundering $200 million per month in drug profits for a smuggling group tied to Hizballah. The Bank was designated a "primary money laundering concern" under terms of the U.S. Patriot Act. DOT and DEA said the ring was run by Ayman Joumaa, whose group smuggled drugs from South America to Europe and the Middle East via West Africa. The money was laundered via trading consumer goods throughout the world, including via U.S. used car dealerships. As of 2009, the bank had assets of more than $5 billion.

February 11, 2011—Iraq—A suicide car bomber set off his explosives among a group of Shi'ite pilgrims in Samarra, killing eight and wounding thirty.

February 12, 2011—Iraq—A suicide bomber set off his explosives vest at a bus terminal for Shi'ite pilgrims in Samarra, killing thirty-eight and wounding seventy-four people. The vest contained 22 pounds of explosives.

February 14, 2011—United States—Prosecutors accused seven men of trying to sell surface-to-air missiles and smuggle drugs to informants they had believed were Taliban operatives. They agreed in meetings in Benin, Romania, Ghana, and the Ukraine to transport and sell heroin for the Taliban and tried to sell cocaine to the informants. Five of the men were arrested in Liberia on February 10 and 11 and were to be extradited to the United States.

February 18, 2011—Egypt—Ayman al-Zawahiri issued a thirty-four-minute taped message to the Egyptian people, entitled *A Message of Hope and Glad Tidings to Our People in Egypt*, in which he said that their government had "deviated from Islam" and that democracy "can only be nonreligious." He asked, "What is the reality through which Egypt is living? The reality of Egypt is the reality of deviation from Islam." Mubarak's rule was "a regime that rules the people through the use of torture, rigged elections, corrupt media, and an unjust justice system." He said democracy "means that sovereignty is to the desires of the majority, without committing to any quality, value, or creed. A democratic state can only be secular, meaning nonreligious." He then traced the history of Egypt's move toward secularism. A second part of the video was to answer the question, "How do we change this reality to what Islam wanted us to have?"

February 19, 2011—Russia—Masked gunmen killed three Moscow-area vacationers on a road in Kabardino-Balkaria in the North Caucasus. Islamist terrorists were suspected.

February 20, 2011—Russia—Police discovered and defused three bombs, containing 154 pounds of TNT, in a car parked near a hotel in the Kabardino-Balkaria region in the North Caucasus. A few days earlier, terrorists had shot five people.

February 21, 2011—Afghanistan—A suicide bomber killed thirty people and injured thirty-six in a noon attack on the office of the Imam Sahib district governor in northern Kunduz Province where people were lining up to collect ID cards.

February 23, 2011—United States—The FBI in Lubbock, Texas, arrested Saudi citizen Khalid Ali-M Aldawsari, 20, a student at a Texas college, for "attempted use of a weapon of mass destruction" in connection with his alleged purchase of chemicals and equipment necessary to make an improvised explosive device (IED). His "research of potential U.S. targets," included getting the address of former President George W. Bush's home in Dallas. The Department of Justice (DOJ) said Aldawsari had "purchased ingredients to construct an explosive device and was actively researching potential targets in the United States." This included purchasing "concentrated nitric and sulfuric acids" and trying to purchase phenol, a precursor of "the explosive trinitrophenol, also known as T.N.P., or picric acid." DOJ said, "Legally authorized electronic surveillance revealed that Aldawsari used various e-mail accounts in researching explosives and targets, and often sent emails to himself as part of this process.... Aldawsari sent himself an e-mail titled 'Tyrant's House,' in which he listed the Dallas address for former President George W. Bush." Another e-mail said, "One operation in the land of the infidels is equal to ten operations against occupying forces in the land of the Muslims." He wrote in his journal, "And now, after mastering the English language, learning how to build explosives, and continuous planning to target the infidel American, it is time for Jihad." He referred to the Saudi royal family derisively as "Saululi" and said the king was the "Traitor to the Two Holy Places." In a March 2010 blog entry, he wrote, "Grant me martyrdom for Your sake and make Jihad easy for me." Other targets included three soldiers who had served at Abu Ghraib prison in Iraq, a dozen dams and reservoirs in California and Colorado, and nuclear power plants. He considered hiding the explosives in realistic-looking baby dolls nestled in baby carriages and bringing an explosive backpack into a nightclub. Authorities said he acted alone. He faced a maximum sentence of life in prison and a $250,000 fine.

Aldawsari arrived in the United States in September 2008 on a student visa. He initially studied English as a second language at Vanderbilt University, then moved on to Texas Tech University in August 2009 to study chemical engineering. His wandering continued with a transfer to study business at South Plains College in Lubbock in January 2011. A Saudi firm had financed his education.

On March 9, 2011, a federal grand jury in Texas indicted Aldawsari on one count of attempting to use a weapon of mass destruction. He pleaded not guilty on March 28. His trial was scheduled for May 2.

The chemical company Carolina Biological Supply of Burlington, North Carolina, notified the FBI when he made a suspicious $435 online purchase of phenol. Shipping company Con-way Freight alerted the Lubbock police and the FBI, saying the order did not appear to be for commercial use.

During his trial, prosecutors played a recording from his apartment made on the night before his arrest in which he said he would get "maximum satisfaction" and would be "smiling" after attacking Americans. Closing arguments were heard on June 27, 2012. Later that day, he was found guilty in federal court in Amarillo, Texas. He was represented by attorney Dan Cogdell, who presented no testimony or evidence.

February 24, 2011—Internet—Ayman al-Zawahiri posted an audio on the Internet cautioning against attacking civilians, observing, "I and my brothers in al Qaeda distance themselves ... from such operations and condemn them." He claimed Osama bin Laden was behind the reminder.

February 27, 2011—Afghanistan—Taliban gunmen in Ghazni Province kidnapped a Canadian man from Toronto, identifying him on its Web site as a "secret agent" who had "been involved in some clandestine activities to get some secret information especially to learn the whereabouts of the mujahideen." The group said the Canadian government did not respond positively to its conditions for his release and would post a video of him online. 11022701

March 2011—Israel—Early in the month, a pipe bomb exploded in a trash can in Jerusalem, tearing off the hand of an Israeli municipal worker. A fortnight later, no arrests had been announced.

March 2, 2011—Germany—At 3:30 p.m., Arid Uka, a 21-year-old from Mitrovica, Kosovo, walked up to a U.S. military bus parked outside Frankfurt Airport's Terminal 2, started arguing with U.S. service members, a group of thirteen who had arrived from London and were on their way to Ramstein military base. Uka pulled out a handgun and began firing outside then inside the bus. He killed two U.S. airmen from Lakenheath base in Britain, including the bus driver, and wounded two security forces members on their way to deployment to Afghanistan. The dead were Airman 1st Class Zachary Cuddeback, 21, of Virginia, and Staff Sgt. Nicholas Alden, 25, of South Carolina. Uka held his gun to the head of a fifth serviceman and pressed the trigger twice, but the gun jammed. Uka fled into the terminal but was captured by the uninjured U.S. airman and two German federal police officers.

Uka had passports from former Yugoslavia and Germany. He was in the process of obtaining German citizenship. He had links to radical Islamists in Germany but was believed to have acted alone. He had attended Eduard Spranger School until 2007. Two years before the attack he had befriended Syrian German Rami Makanesi, who was at this time in a German jail on charges of aiding terrorists in Pakistan. Uka also had Facebook connections with several radical Islamists. In January 2011, he started as a temp at the international letter-sorting office of Deutsche Post AG at Frankfurt Airport. Uka told investigators that he was seeking revenge for the deployment of U.S. troops in Afghanistan. Authorities were expected to charge Uka with murder, attempted murder, and aggravated assault.

On August 31, 2011, Uka confessed to the attack in a court hearing saying he had been influenced by online Islamist propaganda. He faced two counts of murder and three counts of attempted murder for wounding two more airmen and aiming at a third. On February 20, 2012, Uka was convicted of murder, attempted murder, and serious bodily harm and sentenced to life in prison. The judge said Uka would not be immediately eligible for parole in fifteen years; he would have to wait several more years for a review of his sentence. 11030201

March 2, 2011—Pakistan—Gunmen shot to death Shahbaz Bhatti as he left for work from his mother's home in Islamabad. Bhatti was serving as the federal minorities minister and was the lone Christian in the government's cabinet. The attackers left leaflets from the Punjabi Taliban and al Qaeda. Bhatti had criticized the government's tough anti-blasphemy laws.

March 2, 2011—Gaza Strip—Hamas officials arrested Hisham al-Suaydani, alias Sheikh Abu Walid-al-Maqdasi, spiritual leader of Monotheism and Holy War, a Salafist faction in Gaza inspired by al Qaeda. Al-Suaydani is a Palestinian with Egyptian citizenship. The group claimed responsibility for firing rockets at Israel in contravention of a two-year-old truce.

March 4, 2011—Madagascar—A bomb exploded next to the car of President Andry Rajoelina, causing no injuries. His car had been fired on in December 2009.

March 8, 2011—Pakistan—The Pakistani Taliban set off a car bomb at a gas station near an office of the country's main intelligence agency, killing twenty-five and injuring one hundred. Natural gas cylinders also exploded, destroying an office of the national airline and several other business offices in Faisalabad.

March 9, 2011—Pakistan—A Pakistani Taliban suicide bomber killed thirty-six and injured dozens in the Peshawar suburbs at a funeral for the wife of an anti–Taliban Adezai tribal militia member. The militia is led by Dilawar Khan. The bomber was a teen pretending to attend the funeral.

March 11, 2011—West Bank—A Palestinian broke into Itamar, a West Bank settlement near Nablus, and killed two parents and their three children, stabbing them in their sleep. Two other children, also asleep, were untouched. The dead were Ruth, 36, and Ehud Fogel, 37, and their children Yoav, 11, Elad, 4, and Hadas, 3 months. On April 17, the Israeli Defense Forces announced the arrests of Amjad Awad, 19, and Hakim Awad, 18, in the nearby Palestinian village of Awarta. The duo were accused of conducting the attack. Hakim was arrested on April 5; Amjad on April 10. Six others were arrested for aiding them. The two members of the Popular Front for the Liberation of Palestine apparently acted independently of the group.

March 14, 2011—Afghanistan—A Taliban suicide bomber killed thirty-seven people and wounded another forty at an Afghan National Army recruiting center in Kunduz Province. Among the dead were four children playing outside the base.

March 15, 2011—Indonesia—A mail bomb addressed to the Jakarta offices of the U.S.-funded Islamic Liberal Network injured four people while police were trying to defuse it. The bomb was secreted inside a hole in a heavy book entitled *They Should Be Killed for the Sins Against Islam and the Muslims.*

March 23, 2011—Israel—A rolling suitcase with a 2 to 4 pound bomb hidden near a public telephone exploded at 3:00 p.m. at Jerusalem's central bus station, killing a 59-year-old woman and injuring more than fifty people, including two pregnant women. Ball bearings had been hidden in the device. Palestinian Prime Minister Salam Fayyad condemned the attack. No group claimed credit, but the Islamic Jihad and the Popular Resistance Committees praised the attack. Police said they were searching for a car seen fleeing the scene.

Meanwhile, two Katusha rockets landed in Beer Sheva, injuring a man and damaging buildings, including a synagogue. A third rocket crashed near Ashdod.

March 24, 2011—Pakistan—A Taliban suicide bomber's car exploded at a police station in Hangu District in Khyber Pakhtunkhwa Province, killing five people and wounding more than two dozen.

March 27, 2011—Egypt—An armed gang planted explosives at a natural gas terminal near el-Arish in the northern Sinai Peninsula, but the detonator fizzled. 11032701

March 29, 2011—Yemen—Al Qaeda in the Arabian Peninsula released a fifth edition of *Inspire*, featuring Anwar al-Aulaqi's "The Tsunami of Change" broadside against Peter Bergen's coverage of al Qaeda. Al-Aulaqi argued against CNN's Fareed Zakaria, who has said, "The Arab revolts of 2011 represent a total repudiation of al Qaeda's founding ideology," rather the world should "know very well that the opposite is the case." Al-Aulaqi also observed, "For a so-called 'terrorism expert' such as Peter Bergen, it is interesting to see how even he doesn't get it right this time. For him to think that because a Taliban-style regime is not going to take over following the revolutions is a too short-term way of viewing the unfolding events.... The Mujahideen around the world are going through a moment of elation and I wonder whether the West is aware of the upsurge in Mujahideen activity in Egypt, Tunisia, Libya, Yemen, Arabia, Algeria, and Morocco?"

March 29, 2011—Russia—A joint team of Russia's Investigative Committee, the Federal Security Service (FSB), and the Interior and Defense ministries killed seventeen militants in two special law enforcement operations in Ingushetia. Two FSB servicemen and one police officer were also killed in the raids. Meanwhile, authorities detained two suspected accomplices in the January 24, 2011, bombing at Moscow's Domodedovo International Airport.

March 31, 2011—Switzerland—A parcel bomb exploded in the Olten offices of Swissnuclear, an umbrella group for the nuclear industry, injuring two people.

April 2, 2011—Egypt—Israel issued a warning to its citizens to evacuate the Egyptian Sinai Peninsula, citing "terrorist plans to kidnap Israelis and use them as bargaining chips." Earlier that day an Israeli aircraft fired on a group of Hamas members "planning to carry out kidnappings" during Passover, and three would-be terrorists died in a car near Gaza City around 2:00 a.m. Meanwhile, the Democratic Front for the Liberation of Palestine revoked its cease-fire with Israel.

April 2, 2011—Northern Ireland—A booby-trapped bomb exploded under the car of Police Constable Ronan Kerr, 25, outside his Omagh home, killing him. Irish Republican Army dissidents were suspected. This was the first lethal bombing in the current campaign. Several thousand mourners attended his Catholic funeral. By July 27, authorities had arrested ten people, including a 23-year-old woman. A 33-year-old man from Omagh was charged after arms and explosives were found in Coalisland, County Tyrone.

April 3, 2011—Pakistan—Two suicide bombers killed forty-two people (nineteen men, fourteen women, and nine children) and wounded more than one hundred at the entrance to the Sufi Sakhi Sarkar shrine in Punjab Province's Dera Ghazi Khan district. Police arrested a third would-be suicide bomber wearing an explosive jacket that partially detonated, wounding him, and arrested a fourth wannabe suicide bomber before he could set off his explosives. Taliban spokesman Ahsanullah Ahsan claimed credit in a call to the Associated Press. The Sufis were celebrating the 942nd feastday of saint Hazrat Syed Ahmad Sultan, also known as Sakhi Sarwar.

April 4, 2011—Israel—Israel charged Dirar Abu Sisi, 42, operations manager at Gaza's power plant, with developing rockets, increasing their range, and making them penetrate tank armor for Hamas. The engineer had disappeared from a train in the Ukraine on February 19 but reappeared a few days later in an Israeli jail. His Ukrainian wife claimed Mossad kidnapped him. He was also charged with setting up a military academy in Gaza to train Hamas.

April 4, 2011—West Bank—A masked gunman shot to death Juliano Mer Khamis, 52, a prominent Israeli actor and doctor who founded the Freedom Theater in Jenin's refugee camp in 2006 with Zakaria Zubeidi, a former Palestinian military leader. Khamis was born to a Jewish mother and a Christian Arab father and had supported Palestinian causes. Khamis was walked to his car near the theater and then shot five times. He had appeared in nearly thirty movies.

April 6, 2011—Pakistan—Four gunmen on two motorcycles in Balochistan Province's Bolan district fired on two tankers carrying fuel headed for U.S. and NATO troops in Afghanistan. The gunmen then set the tankers alight before escaping. No one was injured, but the tankers were destroyed. No one claimed credit. 11040601

April 7, 2011—Israel—Izzedine al-Qassam Brigades gunmen fired a Russian-made Kornet anti-tank missile from Gaza into Israel, hitting a school bus. A 16-year-old boy was critically wounded and the driver was injured. The terrorists said they were retaliating for an Israeli air strike on April 1 that killed three senior Hamas operatives. The boy died on April 17.

April 9, 2011—Northern Ireland—Police defused a 500-pound bomb hidden in an abandoned van outside Newry on the main road between Dublin and Belfast. Authorities suspected the Provisional Irish Republican Army dissidents who had killed a police officer in Omagh on April 2.

April 11, 2011—Belarus—An explosion in the Minsk Oktyabrskaya subway station during the 6:00 p.m. rush hour killed fifteen and wounded two hundred to three hundred, including Lyudmila Zhechko. The bomb, which went off at 5:55 p.m., was packed with nails and metal balls and wired to a remote detonator. Officials blamed unnamed terrorists and rounded up dissidents for questioning. The station is close to government offices and the official residence of President Aleksandr G. Lukashenko. Later that night, police arrested two suspects described as Belarus citizens who had known each other for a long time. Surveillance video indicated that one of the men left a bag at a bench and then left. One individual was born in 1986. President Lukashenko said the duo confessed to committing terrorist attacks on Independence Day in Minsk on July 3, 2008, and in Vitebsk in September 2005. Two days later, authorities said one of the detainees had confessed to the subway bombing. By April 15, authorities had five suspects in custody, including an electrician and a lathe operator. Authorities said the bomb was remotely detonated by radio, contained nails and small metal balls, and had the equivalent of 5 kilograms of TNT.

Vladislav Kovalyov and Dmitry Konovalov, a lathe operator, both 26-year-old childhood friends, were convicted in the Supreme Court of the Republic of Belarus on November 30, 2011, of the bombing. Neither man had a previous criminal record; many questioned the evidence offered at trial. Konovalov admitted his guilt in building and detonating the bomb. Kovalyov, an electrician, pleaded not guilty to aiding Konovalov, saying he did not take part in the attack. He retracted his confession, saying he was beaten. They were sentenced to death on March 17, 2012. They were also charged and convicted of two bombings in 2005 and 2008 that caused injuries. On March 18, 2012, Belarus announced that the two had been executed with a shot to the back of the head. Human rights activists protested the quick execution. No motive was ever given.

April 13, 2011—Gaza Strip—Gunmen kidnapped Vittorio Arrigoni, 36, Italian freelance journalist and pro–Palestinian humanitarian activist for the International Solidarity Movement. On April 15, Hamas security forces found his body in an empty house in Gaza City after a detained kidnapper had revealed the hideout following Hamas's interrogation. He had been strangled with a plastic handcuff strip. He had been beaten about the head before he died. One person was detained for questioning. Arrigoni was killed just a few hours before police found the hideout. A few hours before the murder, a video was posted on YouTube that showed a blindfolded Arrigoni, whose right cheek appeared to have been bruised. His hands were tied behind his back and someone was grasping his hair to point his head toward the camera. Arabic writing indicated that he would be murdered if Hesham al-Saeedni, who had been held for nearly a year by Hamas, and Salafist leader Abu Walid al-Maqdisi, were not released within thirty hours of 11:00 a.m. Thursday. Al-Saeedni led an al Qaeda-inspired group. The text said Italy was an "infidel nation whose armies are still present in Muslim lands." Al-Tawhid wal–Jihad (Monotheism and Holy War) claimed credit. Hamas had arrested its leader, Abu Walid al-Maqdisi, in March. On April 19, 2011, Hamas announced the deaths of two of the suspects and the arrest of a third in a raid. A Jordanian suspect shot himself after throwing a grenade that killed a second suspect. 11041301

April 13, 2011—Afghanistan—A 13-year-old suicide bomber set off his explosive vest at a meeting of tribal elders in the Asmar district of Kunar Province, killing ten people, including five school boys and tribal elder Malik Zareen, a former military commander who had battled the Soviet occupation and who supported the government.

April 14, 2011—Pakistan—Al Qaeda deputy Ayman al-Zawahiri released a sixty-nine-minute video, the fifth part of the series entitled *A Message of Hope and Glad Tidings to Our People in Egypt,* recorded before the intervention in Libya, in which he called upon Muslims to rise up against NATO and Muammar Qadhafi in Libya. "I want to direct the attention of our Muslim brothers in Libya, Tunisia, Algeria, and the rest of the Muslim countries, that if the Americans and the NATO forces enter Libya then their neighbors in Egypt and Tunisia and Algeria and the rest of the Muslim countries should rise up and fight both the mercenaries of Qadhafi and the rest of NATO." He warned that Qadhafi should be ousted before "Western aid ... turns into invasions." He said the Egyptian government had shown "separation from Islam" and "subservience to the West." The video included a clip from an earlier message by Anwar al-Aulaqi.

April 15, 2011—Indonesia—A suicide bomber in Cirebon, West Java killed himself at a mosque where police were praying, wounding twenty-eight people. The bomb contained nails, nuts, and bolts. It was the first time a house of worship had been targeted in the latest wave of violence.

April 15, 2011—Jordan—Counterterrorism authorities arrested 103 Salafists, among them Ayman al-Balawi, 38, the brother of Humam al-Balawi, the al Qaeda terrorist who killed seven CIA officers in Khost, Afghanistan, on December 30, 2009.

April 18, 2011—Afghanistan—Between seven and twelve Iranian engineers and five Afghani citizens were kidnapped in western Afghanistan, according to conflicting Iranian media reports. They worked for a construction company that was building a police training center in the Hassan-Abad region of Farah Province. The kidnappers also stole the hostages' two cars. 11041801

April 20, 2011—United States—A pipe bomb with propane tanks failed to detonate in a back hallway at the Southwest Plaza Mall in Littleton, Colorado, on the twelfth anniversary of the attack at Columbine High School. A small fire was quickly put out. On April 26, 2011, authorities arrested Earl Albert Moore, 65, at King Soopers grocery store in Boulder after customers and employees told police that he was acting suspiciously. Moore had been released on April 13 from the medium-security Federal Correctional Institution in Estill, South Carolina, after serving time for bank robbery. He had been sentenced to eighteen years in prison for a March 2005 robbery of $2,546 at the Whitesville State Bank in Crab Orchard, West Virginia.

April 22, 2011—Northern Ireland—Police arrested three men and seized weapons and explosives from an Omagh storage facility.

April 23, 2011—Northern Ireland—Authorities found bomb-making equipment in South Armagh.

April 24, 2011—Iraq—A bomb exploded outside the Sacred Heart church in Baghdad's Karrada neighborhood as a police pickup truck pulled away, injuring two Iraqi policemen and two passersby.

Elsewhere, four Iraqi police officers were wounded in a firefight with gunmen outside Mary the Virgin Catholic Church in Baghdad.

April 25, 2011—Northern Ireland—Provisional Irish Republican Army (IRA) dissidents warned that they would oppose the May 17 to 20 visit to Ireland of Queen Elizabeth II and that they would continue to kill local police officers, particularly those from the Catholic regions. A masked Real IRA speaker in Londonderry said, "The Queen of England is wanted for war crimes in Ireland and not wanted on Irish soil." The visit was the first by a British monarch to Ireland since 1911.

April 27, 2011—Egypt—An armed gang set off explosives at a natural gas terminal near el-Arish in the northern Sinai Peninsula. The pipeline supplying gas from the main terminal at Port Said to Israel and Jordan was shut down to quench the fire. The pipeline supplies small quantities of gas to Syria and Lebanon. Anti-regime Bedouin tribesmen were suspected. 11042701

April 27, 2011—Afghanistan—Ahmad Gul, a portly Afghan Air Force helicopter pilot, pulled a 9-mm pistol from his flight suit and opened fire with no warning inside a NATO military base in Kabul, killing eight U.S. service members, a U.S. civilian contractor, and an Afghan soldier and wounding five following an argument at a morning meeting. He then turned the gun on himself. Gul had served for two decades in the air force. On January 17, 2012, the U.S. Air Force concluded that Gul had acted alone. He had become radicalized while attending a mosque in Pakistan and told relatives that he wanted to kill Americans. He yelled, "Good Muslims—please stay away! Muslims, don't come close or you will be killed," outside the window of the Air Command and Control Center at the Kabul Airport. He dipped his finger in blood, and wrote, "Allah is one" on a wall in Dari and "Allah in your name" on the facing wall. The dead Americans were identified as Maj. Philip D. Ambard, Maj. Jeffrey O. Ausborn, Maj. David L. Brodeur, Lt. Col. Frank D. Bryant, Jr., Maj. Raymond G. Estelle, II, Capt. Nathan J. Nylander, Maj. Charles A. Ransom, M. Sgt. Tara R. Brown, and private contractor James McLaughlin, Jr., a retired U.S. Army lieutenant colonel. Some 1,500 attended Gul's funeral, praising him as a martyr. 11042702

April 28, 2011—Morocco—At 11:00 a.m., two bombs exploded at the Café Argana, which overlooks the Jama el-Fnaa Square in Marrakesh, killing seventeen people, including six French citizens, two Canadians, a Briton, a Dutch tourist, two Russians, a Portuguese citizen, a Swiss citizen, and four Moroccans (several were dual nationals), and injuring twenty-five others. Among the dead were Michael Zekry, 29, a pregnant Israeli Canadian, and her husband, Messod Wizman, 30, a Moroccan Canadian. They had been married for three years and had a 2-year-old boy. The duo had come from Shanghai to visit his parents, who live in Casablanca. Eric, the son of Nadine Asnar, died. Initial reports said a suicide bomber was involved, but the government later said the bombs were remotely detonated and packed with nails, triacetone triperoxide (TATP), and ammonium nitrate. Al Qaeda in the Islamic Maghreb was sus-

pected. No one claimed credit. The café was designated a World Heritage Site by the United Nations.

On May 7, 2011, Moroccan authorities arrested three Moroccan suspects with al Qaeda contacts. On June 30, 2011, the Rabat trial began of seven people accused in the attack. The hearing was to continue on August 18. On September 22, 2011, the chief suspect, Adel Othmani, recanted his confession. He had been charged with premeditated murder and bomb making. He claimed, "I have never set foot in Marrakech." He was arrested three days after the bombing. A mobile SIM card that he owned was used in the bombing. The others were charged with membership in a banned group. 11042801

April 28, 2011—Pakistan—A roadside bomb went off under a bus ferrying Pakistani Navy employees to work in Karachi, killing four sailors and a passerby. Pakistani Taliban spokesman Ahsanullah Ahsan said the group attacked the navy because it is part of the Pakistani Army.

April 29, 2011—Germany—At 6:30 a.m., authorities in Duesseldorf and Bochum arrested three young Moroccans suspected of planning an al Qaeda attack. Police seized large amounts of explosives. One of the suspects, Abdeladim El-K., 29, had lived for a decade in Germany. He visited an al Qaeda training camp in 2010 near the Afghanistan-Pakistan border, training in weapons and explosives, and was ordered to conduct an attack in Germany. He reentered Germany illegally in May 2010, recruiting longtime friends Jamil S., 32, who has joint German-Moroccan citizenship, and Amid C. (also identified as Ahmed Sh.), 29, who is a dual citizen of Germany and Iran. German authorities said the trio appeared to have been inspired by the attack in Morocco the previous day, but there did not seem to be any connection to that attack. The trio was obtaining hydrogen peroxide and acetone for bomb making. Some observers suggested that they planned to attack the Eurovision Song Contest in Dusseldorf, scheduled to run May 10–14; others said transportation hubs were targeted. One other suspect remained at large. The trio had been under surveillance for seven months.

May 2011—Pakistan—Two hand grenades were thrown at the Karachi consulate of Saudi Arabia, causing some damage but no injuries. 11059901

May 2011—Nigeria—Chris McManus of the United Kingdom and Franco Lamolinara of Italy were kidnapped by what were believed to be Boko Haram terrorists. The duo were grabbed from their homes in the northwest. They worked for an Italian construction firm in Nigeria. Their kidnappers killed them on March 8, 2012, just before rescuers arrived. 11059902

May 2011—China—A bomb exploded outside a rural bank in Gansu Province, injuring more than forty people. Local media said an embezzlement case was involved.

May 2011—China—Qian Mingqi, 52, set off three bombs in Fuzhou, Jiangxi Province. He was killed in the third bombing. He was frustrated at not being able to get satisfaction of an "illegally removed" building in 2002. He had threatened, "I could take action I don't want to take."

May 1, 2011—Afghanistan—A 12-year-old suicide bomber set off his explosives in a bazaar in the Barmal district of Paktika Province, killing four people and injuring a dozen others. Among those killed was Sher Nawaz, head of a district council in the Shakeen area of Paktika Province.

May 1, 2011—Pakistan—President Barack Obama announced that a U.S. Navy SEAL team had killed Osama bin Laden in a mansion in Pakistan. The following is a transcript of his remarks made from the East Room at 11:35 p.m. EDT.

Good evening. Tonight, I can report to the American people and to the world that the United States has conducted an operation that killed Osama bin Laden, the leader of al Qaeda, and a terrorist who's responsible for the murder of thousands of innocent men, women, and children.

It was nearly ten years ago that a bright September day was darkened by the worst attack on the American people in our history. The images of 9/11 are seared into our national memory—hijacked planes cutting through a cloudless September sky; the Twin Towers collapsing to the ground; black smoke billowing up from the Pentagon; the wreckage of Flight 93 in Shanksville, Pennsylvania, where the actions of heroic citizens saved even more heartbreak and destruction.

And yet we know that the worst images are those that were unseen to the world. The empty seat at the dinner table. Children who were forced to grow up without their mother or their father. Parents who would never know the feeling of their child's embrace. Nearly three thousand citizens taken from us, leaving a gaping hole in our hearts.

On September 11, 2001, in our time of grief, the American people came together. We offered our neighbors a hand, and we offered the wounded our blood. We reaffirmed our ties to each other, and our love of community and country. On that day, no matter where we came from, what God we prayed to, or what race or

ethnicity we were, we were united as one American family.

We were also united in our resolve to protect our nation and to bring those who committed this vicious attack to justice. We quickly learned that the 9/11 attacks were carried out by al Qaeda—an organization headed by Osama bin Laden, which had openly declared war on the United States and was committed to killing innocents in our country and around the globe. And so we went to war against al Qaeda to protect our citizens, our friends, and our allies.

Over the last ten years, thanks to the tireless and heroic work of our military and our counterterrorism professionals, we've made great strides in that effort. We've disrupted terrorist attacks and strengthened our homeland defense. In Afghanistan, we removed the Taliban government, which had given bin Laden and al Qaeda safe haven and support. And around the globe, we worked with our friends and allies to capture or kill scores of al Qaeda terrorists, including several who were a part of the 9/11 plot.

Yet Osama bin Laden avoided capture and escaped across the Afghanistan border into Pakistan. Meanwhile, al Qaeda continued to operate from along that border and operate through its affiliates across the world.

And so shortly after taking office, I directed Leon Panetta, the director of the CIA, to make the killing or capture of bin Laden the top priority of our war against al Qaeda, even as we continued our broader efforts to disrupt, dismantle, and defeat his network.

Then, last August, after years of painstaking work by our Intelligence Community, I was briefed on a possible lead to bin Laden. It was far from certain, and it took many months to run this thread to ground. I met repeatedly with my national security team as we developed more information about the possibility that we had located bin Laden hiding within a compound deep inside of Pakistan. And finally, last week, I determined that we had enough intelligence to take action, and authorized an operation to get Osama bin Laden and bring him to justice.

Today, at my direction, the United States launched a targeted operation against that compound in Abbottabad, Pakistan. A small team of Americans carried out the operation with extraordinary courage and capability. No Americans were harmed. They took care to avoid civilian casualties. After a firefight, they killed Osama bin Laden and took custody of his body.

For over two decades, bin Laden has been al Qaeda's leader and symbol, and has continued to plot attacks against our country and our friends and allies. The death of bin Laden marks the most significant achievement to date in our nation's effort to defeat al Qaeda.

Yet his death does not mark the end of our effort. There's no doubt that al Qaeda will continue to pursue attacks against us. We must— and we will—remain vigilant at home and abroad.

As we do, we must also reaffirm that the United States is not—and never will be—at war with Islam. I've made clear, just as President Bush did shortly after 9/11 that our war is not against Islam. Bin Laden was not a Muslim leader; he was a mass murderer of Muslims. Indeed, al Qaeda has slaughtered scores of Muslims in many countries, including our own. So his demise should be welcomed by all who believe in peace and human dignity.

Over the years, I've repeatedly made clear that we would take action within Pakistan if we knew where bin Laden was. That is what we've done. But it's important to note that our counterterrorism cooperation with Pakistan helped lead us to bin Laden and the compound where he was hiding. Indeed, bin Laden had declared war against Pakistan as well, and ordered attacks against the Pakistani people.

Tonight, I called President Zardari, and my team has also spoken with their Pakistani counterparts. They agree that this is a good and historic day for both of our nations. And going forward, it is essential that Pakistan continue to join us in the fight against al Qaeda and its affiliates.

The American people did not choose this fight. It came to our shores, and started with the senseless slaughter of our citizens. After nearly ten years of service, struggle, and sacrifice, we know well the costs of war. These efforts weigh on me every time I, as Commander-in-Chief, have to sign a letter to a family that has lost a loved one, or look into the eyes of a service member who's been gravely wounded.

So Americans understand the costs of war. Yet as a country, we will never tolerate our security being threatened, nor stand idly by when our people have been killed. We will be relentless in defense of our citizens and our friends and allies. We will be true to the values that make us who we are. And on nights like this one, we can say to those families who have lost loved ones to al Qaeda's terror: Justice has been done.

Tonight, we give thanks to the countless intelligence and counterterrorism professionals who've worked tirelessly to achieve this outcome. The American people do not see their work, nor know their names. But tonight, they feel the satisfaction of their work and the result of their pursuit of justice.

We give thanks for the men who carried out this operation, for they exemplify the professionalism, patriotism, and unparalleled courage of those who serve our country. And they are part of a generation that has borne the heaviest share of the burden since that September day.

Finally, let me say to the families who lost loved ones on 9/11 that we have never forgotten your loss, nor wavered in our commitment to see that we do whatever it takes to prevent another attack on our shores.

And tonight, let us think back to the sense of unity that prevailed on 9/11. I know that it has, at times, frayed. Yet today's achievement is a testament to the greatness of our country and the determination of the American people.

The cause of securing our country is not complete. But tonight, we are once again reminded that America can do whatever we set our mind to. That is the story of our history, whether it's the pursuit of prosperity for our people, or the struggle for equality for all our citizens; our commitment to stand up for our values abroad, and our sacrifices to make the world a safer place.

Let us remember that we can do these things not just because of wealth or power, but because of who we are: one nation, under God, indivisible, with liberty and justice for all.

Thank you. May God bless you. And may God bless the United States of America.

On May 20, 2011, President Obama addressed intelligence officers in the lobby of the CIA Original Headquarters Building:

That's why I came here. I wanted every single one of you to know, whether you work at the CIA or across the community, at every step of our effort to take out bin Laden, the work you did and the quality of the intelligence that you provided made the critical difference—to me, to our team on those helicopters, to our nation.

After I directed that getting bin Laden be the priority, you hunkered down even more, building on years of painstaking work; pulling together, in some cases, the slenderest of intelligence streams, running those threads to ground until you found that courier and you tracked him to that compound. And when I was briefed last summer, you had built the strongest intelligence case against—in terms of where bin Laden was since Tora Bora.

In the months that followed, including all those meetings in the Situation Room, we did what sound intelligence demands: We pushed for more collection. We pushed for more evidence. We questioned our assumptions. You strengthened your analysis. You didn't bite your tongue and try to spin the ball, but you gave it to me straight each and every time.

And we did something really remarkable in Washington—we kept it a secret. (Laughter and applause.) That's how it should be.

Of course, when the time came to actually make the decision, we didn't know for sure that bin Laden was there. The evidence was circumstantial and the risks, especially to the lives of our special operations forces, were huge. And I knew that the consequences of failure could be enormous. But I made the decision that I did because I had absolute confidence in the skill of our military personnel and I had confidence in you. I put my bet on you. And now the whole world knows that that faith in you was justified.

So just as impressive as what you did was how you did it. It was a tribute to your perseverance, your relentless focus and determination over many years. For the fight against al Qaeda did not begin on 9/11. Among you are veterans who've been pursuing these murderers for many years, even before they attacked our embassies in Africa and struck the *Cole* in Yemen. Among you are young men and women for whom 9/11 was a call to service. This fight has defined your generation. And on this wall are stars honoring all your colleagues and friends, more than a dozen who have given their lives in the fight against al Qaeda and its violent allies.

As the years wore on, others began to think that this terrorist might never be brought to justice. But you never quit. You never gave up. You pulled together across this Agency and across the Community.

No one piece of information and no one agency made this possible. You did it together—CIA, National Security Agency, National Reconnaissance Office, the National Geospatial Intelligence Agency, everyone at ODNI [Office of the Director of National Intelligence] and the National Counterterrorism Center. Folks across the country, civilian and military, so many of you here today.

And that's exactly how our Intelligence Community is supposed to work, using every capability—human, technical—collecting, analyzing, sharing, integrating intelligence, and then acting on it.

That's what made this one of the greatest intelligence successes in American history, and that's why intelligence professionals are going to study and be inspired by your achievement for generations to come.

An interagency team had been planning the pre-dawn operation since August 2010 when a trusted bin Laden courier, Abu Ahmed al-Kuwaiti, was detected making a cell phone call to a friend. Most of bin Laden's couriers made calls at least 90 miles away from his walled compound. Al-Kuwaiti was tracked to bin Laden's hideout in Ab-

botabad, Pakistan. A U.S. Navy SEAL Team 6 strike team helicoptered to the mansion built in 2005 for bin Laden. One of the Black Hawk helicopters stalled, but the pilot landed safely. The team worked its way up three floors strewn with barricades intended to impede their progress. The team reported that bin Laden put up resistance, and they shot him twice. Also killed was son Khalid bin Laden, 20; Abu Ahmed al-Kuwaiti, the Pakistani-born Pashtun courier; the courier's wife, Bushra; and the courier's brother, Abrar. One of bin Laden's wives was shot in the leg. After DNA testing in Afghanistan proved his identity, bin Laden was buried at sea in an Islamic service aboard the USS *Carl Vinson*. The assault team seized numerous computers, thumb drives, and hard drives. The Taliban announced his death within twenty-four hours. The White House announced that it would not release death photos.

The three-story compound was eight times the size of surrounding houses and was a few hundred feet away from a Pakistani military academy, leading many observers to speculate on how much the Pakistani government really knew about bin Laden's hideout. Pakistani authorities said that the house was registered in the name of Arshad Khan, which may have been fake.

Word of the contents of the materials that were taken out of the compound quickly was released to the media, which eagerly reported the presence of a trove of pornography. Also found were notes on plans as of February 2010 to attack the U.S. commuter rail network and cause mass casualties on the tenth anniversary of 9/11. One operation was to tamper with the rails so that the train would fall off a track at a valley or bridge.

Reaction to the Operation Geronimo raid in Pakistan was mixed, with many criticizing the United States for a breach of sovereignty and the Pakistani government for either incompetence in not spotting bin Laden, dereliction of duty in not stopping the U.S. raid, or complicity in hiding bin Laden. The Pakistani government was suspected of leaking to the local news media the name of the U.S. chief of station (COS) in Islamabad; this was the second time in a year that a COS/Islamabad's name appeared in the press.

Pakistan permitted the United States to interview bin Laden's three wives, who had been living with him at the compound. Two were Saudis; one Yemeni. Pakistan agreed on May 26 to allow U.S. intelligence officers to examine the contents of the safe house.

On December 9, 2011, Pakistan announced that two of bin Laden's widows, Khairiah Sabar and Siham Sabar, would be allowed to return to their native Saudi Arabia, which had restored their citizenship. Yemen rejected a return by bin Laden's third wife, Amal Ahmed al-Sadah, whom he married in 2000. She might be offered a new home in Qatar. Bin Laden married Kairiah in 1985 and Siham in 1987. The two college graduates lost their citizenship when Saudi Arabia pulled his citizenship in 1994. Eight of bin Laden's children would accompany the duo to Saudi Arabia. Bin Laden's first wife, a Syrian, deserted in Afghanistan a few weeks before 9/11 to return to Syria. His second marriage ended in divorce in the early 1990s. One of his daughters, Safiya, 12, remained in Pakistani custody.

Three of Osama bin Laden's widows—Amal Ahmed al-Sadah, Siham Saber, and Khairiah Saber—who were taken into custody the night he was killed, were reported on March 8, 2012, with having been charged with illegally entering the country. On April 26, 2012, Pakistan deported bin Laden's three widows and several children and grandchildren to Saudi Arabia.

May 2, 2011—United Kingdom—Police officers from the Civil Nuclear Constabulary and Cumbria Constabulary arrested five London men in their 20s on suspicion of terrorism near a nuclear waste processing plant in Sellafield in northwestern England. Metropolitan Police officers searched four homes in east London.

May 7, 2011—Iraq—Huthaifa al-Batawi, a senior al Qaeda in Iraq operative, grabbed a gun from a Baghdad prison guard on May 7, 2011, on his way to a nighttime interrogation, fired on his guards, freed inmates, and conducted a gun battle that killed eleven inmates and six Iraqi counterterrorism officers, including the senior counterterrorist official for an affluent Baghdad neighborhood. Al-Batawi was believed to have organized an October 2010 attack on a church that killed dozens and to have been involved in several car bombings against government officials and security forces.

May 8, 2011—Afghanistan—Afghan and the International Security Assistance Force coalition captured an al Qaeda Moroccan facilitator who recruited foreign fighters. The individual was captured in southern Zabul Province following a gun battle that left ten insurgents dead. Authorities found passports and ID cards from France, Pakistan, and Saudi Arabia on the bodies.

May 9, 2011—France—Authorities arrested five men, including some French citizens, during police raids in Paris and two heavily immigrant suburbs; a sixth was arrested on May 10 at Charles de Gaulle Airport as he arrived from Algeria. The group was planning to train in Pakistan with Islamic militants. French Interior Ministry Claude Gueant said, "Nothing indicates that those people were planning an attack in France." Gueant said the sixth man, an Indian engineer, was the group's leader and had "a high level of technical training." The group had been in contact with two French citizens who had been arrested in Lahore, Pakistan, in January 2011 and were members of the group that conducted the Bali bombing attack in 2002 that killed two hundred people.

May 12, 2011—United States—New York City police arrested Ahmed Ferhani, 26, an Algerian, and Mohamed Mamdouh, 20, a Moroccan-born U.S. citizen, after they purchased three pistols, ammunition, and an inert grenade from an undercover officer. The arrests ended a seven-month operation designed to foil a plan to attack synagogues, kill Jews, and blow up the Empire State Building. They were charged under state terrorism statutes that carry a life sentence. They were also charged with hate crimes. On June 15, 2011, authorities dropped the charge of second degree conspiracy as a terror crime, which carried a life sentence. The duo pleaded not guilty to lesser state charges, including criminal possession of a weapon as a terror crime, in the plot to blow up New York City synagogues. They were also charged with terror conspiracy and hate crimes. The duo faced thirty-two years in prison if convicted. Mamdouh was represented by attorney Aaron Mysliwiec.

May 13, 2011—Pakistan—A Pakistani Taliban suicide bomber set off his explosives at 6:00 a.m. at a military training center, killing eighty members of the Frontier Constabulary at Shabqadar Fort in Charsadda as they were preparing for their graduation ceremony. Another eighty people were injured. A second bomber was believed involved.

May 14, 2011—United States—Authorities arrested three people on charges of providing $50,000 to the Pakistani Taliban. Hafiz Muhammad Sher Ali Khan, 76, was arrested after morning services at Miami's Flagler Mosque, where he serves as imam. Police arrested one of his sons, Izhar Khan, 24, imam at the Jamaat al-Mu'mineen Mosque in Margate, Florida, following their morning services. Los Angeles police detained the other son, Irfan Khan, 37, at his hotel room. Three other people were charged in the indictment for handling the distribution of funds and remained at large in Pakistan, including Hafiz's daughter, grandson, and an unrelated man. The funds were used to purchase guns, support militants' families, and promote the Pakistani Taliban cause. The Florida residents faced fifteen years in prison for each of four counts listed in the indictment. Khurrum Wahid, attorney for the imam, said that his client would plead not guilty to providing material assistance to the terrorist group from 2008 to 2010, and conspiracy to provide material support to a conspiracy to murder, maim, and kidnap people overseas. The trial was heard in Miami's Federal District Court by Magistrate Judge Barry L. Garber.

May 16, 2011—Pakistan—Two gunmen on two motorbikes shot to death Hassan M. al-Kahtani, a Saudi diplomat who was driving a silver Toyota Corona by himself in Karachi. Police said a 9-mm pistol was used. The diplomat appeared to be on his way from his home to work as a member of the consulate's security staff. The *New York Times* quoted an unnamed Pakistani security official who said that al-Khatani was an intelligence officer. No group claimed credit. 11051601

May 16, 2011—United Kingdom—Irish Republican Army dissidents were suspected of making a bomb threat against central London the day before Queen Elizabeth II was due to visit Ireland, the first by a British monarch in one hundred years. No bomb was found.

May 17, 2011—Ireland—Police detonated a pipe bomb found on a bus in County Kildare that was on its way to Dublin, where the British Queen was to visit.

May 17, 2011—Pakistan—Pakistani military authorities announced the arrest in Karachi of Muhammad Ali Qasim Yaqub, alias Abu Sohaib al-Makki, a Yemeni who has been working directly under al Qaeda leaders along the Afghanistan-Pakistan border.

May 18, 2011—Afghanistan—Noman Benotman, former leader of the Libyan Islamic Fighting Group, told the news media that Saif al-Adel, alias Muhamad Ibrahim Makkawi, was named interim leader of al Qaeda.

May 18, 2011—Russia—Reuters reported that the al Qaeda magazine *Inspire* had been translated into Russian in an attempt to reach out to Islamists in the North Caucasus. The magazine was posted on the Web site Ansar al-Mujahideen, a Russian-language forum.

May 18, 2011—Pakistan—Al Qaeda released a thirteen-minute audiotape entitled *Speech from the Martyr of Islam—As We Think of Him—To the Islamic Ummah* from the now-late Osama bin Laden, apparently recorded after February 17. Navy SEALs found a copy of the tape in the Abbottabad safe house where he was killed. He mentions the Arab Spring in Tunisia and Egypt, observing,

[It would be a sin] to lose this opportunity.... What are you waiting for? Save yourselves and your children, because the opportunity is here.... The winds of change flew to the square of Tahrir and a great revolution was begun. This wasn't a revolution of starving and pain, but a revolution of giving and peace. The great oppression in our countries has reached great levels, and we have delayed enough the wave of change. Let the truth ring out. Remember those that go out with a sword are true believers, those that go fight with the tongue are true believers, and those that fight in their hearts are true believers. Oh, Muslims, you have seen many revolutions in your past. Those that the people have been so happy about, but then have turned into nothing. And the way to keep these revolutions from having the same problem is fighting ignorance. And some of the most important information is Islam. For this is the true crisis that has hit our nations.... The sun of the revolution has risen from the Maghreb. The light of the revolution came from Tunisia. It has given the nation tranquility and made the faces of the people happy.

He said his supporters should

set up an operations room that follows up events and works in parallel ... to save the people that are struggling to bring down their tyrants.... A delay may cause the opportunity to be lost, and carrying it out before the right time will increase the number of casualties. I believe that the winds of change will envelop the entire Muslim world. The youth must prepare what is necessary and must not make any decision without consulting those of experience and honesty who avoid half solutions.... Tunisia was the first but swiftly the knights of Egypt have taken a spark from the free people of Tunisia to Tahrir Square. It has made the rulers worried.... We watch with you this great historic event and we share with you joy and happiness and delight and felicity. We are happy for what makes you happy, and we are sad for what makes you sad. So congratulations to you for your victories.

Bin Laden said the Arab Spring put the region at a "serious crossroads ... a great and rare historic opportunity to rise with the Ummah and to free yourselves from servitude to the desires of the rulers, man-made law, and Western dominance." Officials suggested the likelihood of the airing of other posthumous bin Laden tapes as others were found at the Abbottabad compound.

May 20, 2011—Pakistan—Nine NATO oil tankers were set alight after a remote-controlled bomb went off under the lead vehicle at Torkham, at the Pakistan-Afghanistan border.

May 20, 2011—Pakistan—A remote-controlled bomb exploded under a NATO oil tanker during the morning in Khyber Agency about 8 kilometers east of the Afghanistan border. When local residents gathered to collect oil leaked from the tank, it caught fire and killed sixteen, including five children.

May 20, 2011—Internet—A jihadi Web site posted an audio message from Ayman al-Zawahiri that was recorded prior to bin Laden's death. He called the United States the leader of "crusader enemies ... NATO is not a goodwill organization. It is an aid to the hegemonic powers in this world. They aim to end the corrupt Qadhafi regime but then install their own ideals. They want to steal Libya's resources and relics because of their greed and politics." He called on Egyptians to aid Libyans, observing "the fight in Libya today is the fight of the Muslim nation after the governments failed to protect the Libyan people from the crimes of Qadhafi." He also praised the fall of Hosni Mubarak in Egypt.

May 21, 2011—Northern Ireland—Masked men claiming to be members of the Irish Republican Army left a small bomb at the office of the Santander bank on Shipquay Street in a Londonderry commercial area. The bomb exploded an hour later, causing no injuries and little damage.

May 22, 2011—Pakistan—Militants attacked a Pakistani naval base in Karachi, taking several Chinese technicians hostage during a sixteen-hour siege. Ten Pakistani security officers were killed in the attack. 11052201

May 25, 2011—United States—Federal authorities arrested Waad Ramadan Alwan, 30, and Mohanad Shareef Hammadi, 23, in Bowling Green, Kentucky on a twenty-three-count federal indictment. Terrorism charges included trying to ship Stinger missiles and explosives to al Qaeda in Iraq. The duo had been admitted into the United States as refugees in 2009. Alwan was charged with conspiracy to kill U.S. nationals abroad, conspiring to use explosives against U.S. nationals abroad, and conspiracy to export Stinger missiles. Hammadi was charged with attempting to provide material support to terrorists and al Qaeda in Iraq (AQI). James Earhart represented Hammadi. Alwan was assigned a public defender.

The FBI began its investigation of Alwan in September 2009, five months after he entered the United States. They used an undercover informant, who learned that Alwan had been an AQI insurgent who attacked U.S. troops from 2003 until his capture by Iraqi authorities. In 2010 the FBI matched his fingerprints with two prints found on an unexploded bomb in Iraq in 2005. The FBI began a sting in September 2010 when the inform-

ant claimed he was supporting AQI. The duo delivered money, inert explosives, and weapons, including the Stingers, to a tractor-trailer.

On December 16, 2011, Alwan pleaded guilty in federal court in Kentucky to trying to send weapons and cash to AQI, conspiring to attack U.S. soldiers in Iraq, conspiracy to use a weapon of mass destruction, and attempting to provide material support to terrorists. On January 29, 2013, U.S. District Judge Thomas B. Russell sentenced Hammadi to life in prison without parole and Alwan to a forty-year sentence. Alwan was represented by attorney Scott Wendelsdorf. Hammadi was represented by attorney James Earhart of Louisville, Kentucky; he planned to appeal the sentence. Among the wounded from explosives planted by the duo was former Pennsylvania National Guard Sgt. Brandon Miller of Chadds Ford, Pennsylvania, who suffered burn injuries when his Humvee hit a roadside bomb near Bayji. Prosecutors said Alwan worked with the Mujahideen Shura Council who had claimed credit for the kidnapping, torture, and deaths of two soldiers with the 101st Airborne Division and the death of a third soldier. Hammadi was linked to Jaish al-Mujahideen, alias the Mujahideen Army, which said it shot down U.S. helicopters in 2006 and 2007. Hammadi had told a confidential informant that he was involved in eleven bomb attacks against U.S. soldiers.

May 26, 2011—Pakistan—A Pakistani Taliban suicide bomber set off explosives in his pickup truck near several government offices in Hangu, killing twenty-six people.

May 26, 2011—China—Three bombs, including two car bombs, exploded within an hour outside government offices in Fuzhou city. Observers suggested it was the work of a farmer displeased with the legal system. Two people were killed and six injured. One bomb went off at a local prosecutor's office, another at a government building, and the last at a food and drug administration office. The Chinese government attempted to cover up the incidents, according to the *Washington Post*.

May 27, 2011—Lebanon—A bomb exploded beneath a UN Interim Force in Lebanon convoy, injuring six Italian UN peacekeepers. No one claimed credit for attacking the logistics convoy on the highway outside Sidon. 11052701

May 27, 2011—Pakistan—A Pakistani Taliban suicide bomber set off explosives in his car that killed twenty-five and injured fifty-six near local law enforcement and court buildings in Hangu District in Khyber Pakhtunkhwa Province.

May 28, 2011—Afghanistan—A Taliban suicide bomber garbed as a policeman opened fire and set off his explosives in a meeting of Afghan and NATO officials, killing Gen. Daud Daud, the north's senior police official; senior Takhar Province Police Chief Shah Jan Noori; the governor's secretary; and two German soldiers. The attack wounded ten others, including Maj. Gen. Markus Kneip, the seniormost German commander in the country, and Abdul Jabar, the provincial governor. Daud had earlier served as Deputy Interior Minister for Counter-Narcotics Affairs. He had also been an aide to Northern Alliance Cdr. Ahmed Shah Massoud, who was assassinated by al Qaeda two days before 9/11. 11052801

May 29, 2011—Nigeria—Following the inauguration of the southern Christian Goodluck Jonathan as the country's president, several bombs went off in the country's Muslim north and a city near Abuja, killing fifteen people. One explosive at a Bauchi bar went off at 8:00 p.m., killing between ten and fifteen people and injuring thirty-five. Another bomb went off at a beer garden in Zuba, near Abuja, killing two and wounding eleven. Several people were injured in a bombing of a bar in Zaria. No one claimed credit.

May 29, 2011—United States—A Florida man was arrested after firing an AK-47 in a market. He claimed membership in a "sovereign citizen movement."

May 30, 2011—Nigeria—Two teens were injured when they stepped on explosives in Zaria. A bomb went off near an army patrol vehicle in Maiduguri, causing no casualties. Five people were arrested. No one claimed credit.

May 30, 2011—Turkey—A small bicycle bomb exploded near an overpass in the Etiler district of Istanbul during 9:00 a.m. rush hour, injuring seven people and damaging five vehicles.

May 30, 2011—Somalia—Suicide bombers drove their minivan up to an African Union (AU) peacekeeping base in Mogadishu and fired on guards. Three attackers were shot, but explosives on one of the bodies went off, killing two AU soldiers and a member of a government-allied militia and wounding five other AU peacekeepers. A fourth terrorist was captured. Al-Shabaab claimed that the bomber was Abdullahi Ahmed, 25, a Somali American.

May 31, 2011—United States—The Department of Justice refiled capital charges of conspiracy, murder in violation of the law of war, attacking civilians, attacking civilian objects, intentionally causing serious bodily injury, destruction of property in violation of the law of war, hijacking aircraft, and terrorism against 9/11 plotters Khalid Sheikh Mohammed, Walid bin Attash, Ramzi bin al-Shibh, Ali Abdul Aziz Ali, and Mustafa Ahmed al-Hawsawi to allow prosecution before a military commission at Guantanamo Bay.

May 31, 2011—Netherlands/France/Belgium—Package bombs set off by alarm clocks ignited gunpowder at IKEA stores in Ghent, Belgium; Lille, France; and Eindhoven, the Netherlands. Two workers in Belgium were slightly injured. 11053101-03

June 1, 2011—Libya—A timer-activated car bomb exploded at 7:00 p.m. in the parking lot of the fourteen-story Tibesty Hotel, which is used by foreign diplomats, including the U.S. ambassador, security, and Qatari military advisors, UN officials, and Western media outlets in rebel-held Benghazi. Rebel leaders blamed Qadhafi "sleeper cells." No casualties were reported. The previous day, Italy Foreign Minister Franco Frattini had met with rebel leaders at the same hotel. 11060101

June 2, 2011—Internet—Al Qaeda spokesman Adam Gadahn released a one hundred-minute video, entitled *You Are Only Responsible for Yourself* (alternative title, *Do Not Rely on Others, Take the Task Upon Yourself*), that included clips from six other al Qaeda leaders, including bin Laden, al-Zawahiri, Abu Laith al-Libi, and Attiya. Gadahn observed,

> Muslims in the West have to remember that they are perfectly placed to play an important and decisive part in the jihad against the Zionists and Crusaders and to do major damage to the enemies of Islam, waging war on their religion, sacred places, and things, and brethren. This is a golden opportunity and a blessing. Let's take America as an example. America is absolutely awash with easily obtainable firearms. You can go down to a gun show at the local convention center and come away with a fully automatic assault rifle, without a background check, and most likely without having to show an identification card. So what are you waiting for? ...
> It's important that we weaken our cowardly enemies' will to fight by targeting influential public figures in Crusader and Zionist government, industry, and media.

He suggested that Western-born or Western-raised jihadis, the "brothers who came from abroad," are ready to return to their "Crusader" countries to "discharge their duty of jihad." Imprisonment is not a concern, because "over these past few years, I've seen the release of many, many mujahideen who I had never even dreamed would regain their freedom." Many former detainees "are now back home with their families, or back on the frontlines, fighting the enemies." "If it's Allah's will that you be captured, then it's not the end of the world, and it doesn't necessarily mean that you're going to spend the rest of your life in prison." Showing the logos of Exxon, Merrill Lynch, and Bank of America, he suggested attacking "influential public figures. Getting to these criminals isn't as hard as you might think. I mean we've seen how a woman knocked the Pope to the floor during Christmas mass, and how Italian leader Berlusconi's face was smashed during a public appearance. So it's just a matter of entrusting the matter to Allah and choosing the right place, the right time, and the right method." The video includes references to bin Laden, followed by, "May Allah have mercy on him," suggesting the video was made after his death. The narrator cited several Muslims who carried out individual attacks.

June 3, 2011—Pakistan—Al Qaeda military operations chief Mohammed Ilyas Kashmiri, 47, and eight other terrorists were killed by a drone strike on an apple orchard in Ghwa Khwa/Laman village near Wana in South Waziristan. The compound belonged to Mir Ajam Khan, a tribesman with radical links. Kashmiri had reportedly been killed in September 2009; verification of terrorist deaths is difficult. His Harakat-ul-Jihad al-Islami's 313 Brigade announced that he had been "martyred" in the 11:15 p.m. strike. The Pakistani was believed to have planned the November 26–28, 2008, siege of Mumbai, India, and to have killed several Pakistanis. He was also believed to have plotted an attack on the Danish *Jyllands Posten* newspaper that published the Muhammad cartoons in 2005. Pakistan blamed him for the May 22, 2011, assault on the Mehran naval base in Karachi.

Abu Hanzla Kashir, who claimed to be a spokesman for Kashmiri's Harbat-ul-Jihad-e-Islami group, said in a fax to a Pakistani TV station, "God willing ... America will very soon see our full revenge. Our only target is America."

June 7, 2011—Pakistan—Islamic militants were suspected of setting off a blast that burned five NATO oil tankers at the Torkham crossing into Afghanistan.

June 7, 2011—West Bank—Arsonists desecrated a mosque in the Palestinian village of al-Mughayyir, near Ramallah. They sprayed Hebrew messages ("price tag" and "Alei Ayin") on the walls. Jewish settler extremists were suspected of having thrown a burning tire through a window, setting off a fire on a carpet. Price tag refers to a settlement response to Israeli military attempts to stop

their building via attacks on Palestinians. Alei Ayin is an unauthorized Jewish settlement.

June 8, 2011—Internet—Al Qaeda deputy chief Ayman al-Zawahiri released a twenty-eight-minute video eulogy of Osama bin Laden, entitled *The Noble Knight Dismounted*. Al-Zawahiri said bin Laden continued to be a source of inspiration for Muslims, and that the United States would face reprisals, "blood for blood."

> The Sheikh has departed, may God have mercy on him, to his God as a martyr, and we must continue on his path of jihad to expel the invaders from the land of Muslims and to purify it from injustice.... He terrified America when he was alive and is terrifying it as a dead man, to the point that they shudder at the prospect of giving him a grave because of what they know of the love of tens of millions for him ... [Osama bin Laden] haunt America and Israel and their Crusader allies, their corrupt agents.... His famous pledge that "you don't dream of security until we live it as a reality and until you depart the land of Islam" will continue to deprive them of sleep.... Today, and thanks be to God, America is not facing an individual or a group ... but a rebelling nation which has awoken from its sleep in a jihadist renaissance challenging it wherever it is.

He warned the United States, "You should await what will befall you after every celebration." He criticized Osama bin Laden's Islamic burial at sea, complaining, "What Islam is this? The Islam of America, or the Islam of Obama, who sold his father's religion, became a Christian, and prayed like the Jews to gain favor with the rich and powerful." He said 9/11 "destroyed the symbol of American economy in New York and the symbol of American military might in the Pentagon." He called on Pakistani youth to overthrow the regime, to "shake off the dust of humiliation and overthrow those who have sold you in the slave market to the United States ... just as your brothers in Tunisia, Egypt, Libya, and Syria have done." Unrest in Yemen will lead to "a good regime that rules in accordance with Shariah" and "expels the Americans and their henchmen."

June 8, 2011—Colombia—Seven Revolutionary Armed Forces of Colombia (FARC) rebels kidnapped three Chinese contractors and a translator who were working for the British Emerald Energy company, part of the China-based Sinochem Group, while engaged in oil exploration in San Vicente del Caguan. Their driver was released with their vehicle. The International Committee of the Red Cross and the Chinese Embassy were involved in the negotiations for their release. No proof-of-life was ever received. Translator Jian Mingfu, 46, and contractors Tang Guofu, 28, Zhao Hongwei, 36, and Jiang Shang, 24, were freed on November 22, 2012. They were FARC's last foreign hostages. 11060801

June 9, 2011—China—An explosion possibly due to a bomb destroyed most of a multi-story police station and killed a police driver in Huangshi township, southern Hunan Province. Some observers suggested it was a revenge attack against corrupt police.

June 10, 2011—Somalia—Interior Minister Abdishakur Sheik Hassan, who also served as Ministry for National Security, was killed when a female suicide bomber set off her explosives at his home. A relative said the bomber was his niece, who had joined al-Shabaab. The group's spokesman, Sheik Ali Mohamud Rage, claimed credit at a press conference in Mogadishu on June 11.

June 10, 2011—China—A bomb exploded outside a local government headquarters in Tianjin, slightly injuring two people. The male bomber, Lin, wanted revenge on society, according to state-run media. News media said he was carrying twenty homemade bombs the shape of a soda can and had thrown four of them in the Hexi district of Tianjin. It was the third bombing at government facilities in the past three weeks.

June 12, 2011—Pakistan—Just after midnight, two bombs, one by a suicide bomber, killed thirty-four people and injured ninety-eight, eighteen critically, in Peshawar. The first small bomb drew rescue workers to the site. A suicide bomber on a motorcycle set off 22 pounds of explosives, causing the casualties.

June 16, 2011—Internet—Al Qaeda's (AQ) general command announced that Ayman al-Zawahiri had succeeded Osama bin Laden as the group's leader. "The general leadership of al Qaeda group, after the completion of consultations, announces that Sheikh Dr. Ayman al-Zawahiri, may God give him success, has assumed responsibility for command of the group... We seek with the aid of God to call for the religion of truth and incite our nation to fight ... by carrying out jihad against the apostate invaders ... with their head being crusader America and its servant Israel, and whoever supports them." The announcement noted that AQ wanted to "assure our affirmation and support of everyone who carries out jihad ... We do not differentiate between an Arab and a foreigner except in piety and righteous deeds." The group referred to the Guantanamo prisoners, saying, "The lions in the chains who have to be patient ... sac-

rificed and suffered for the cause of supporting Islam and the Muslims." Al-Zawahiri called on "lone wolf" terrorists to attack those named on a forty-person hit list posted on Ansar al-Mujahideen's Web site. The list includes U.S. government, military, and media figures. Among them were a member of Congress, Pentagon officials, a conservative pundit, executives of a U.S. company making drones, and two prominent French executives. The site includes photos of twenty-six of the targeted individuals. Al-Zawahiri turned 60 on June 19, 2011.

June 16, 2011—Nigeria—At 8:45 p.m., a Boko Haram suicide bomber killed two people in the parking lot of the Abuja police headquarters. A second Boko Haram bomb in the northeast killed three children. Abu Zaid, the group's spokesman, and senior leader Usman al-Zawahiri claimed credit for the police blast. Boko Haram in Hausa means, "Western education is sacrilege." Some observers said Boko Haram was seeking ties to al Qaeda in the Islamic Maghreb. Boko Haram leaflets said that its members had trained in Somalia with al-Shabaab.

June 18, 2011—Iraq—On March 17, 2012, an Iraqi Shi'ite militia loyal to radical cleric Muqtada al-Sadr announced at a pre-taped news conference that it was releasing U.S. soldier Rand Michael Hultz, who it had kidnapped and held for nine months. He said he was a former soldier who was working as a civilian when he was abducted on June 18, 2011, in Baghdad by "Yom al-Maoud under the direction of Sayyed Muqtada al-Sadr," also known as the Promised Day Brigade. U.S. officials said all American soldiers had been accounted for and no civilian was reported missing. His ex-wife did not know he was missing. A Rand Michael Hultz had served in Iraq shortly after the 2003 invasion. The UN Assistance Mission for Iraq said Iraqi lawmakers Maha al-Douri and Quasay al-Suhail handed over Hultz, who was transferred to the U.S. Embassy.

June 22, 2011—Yemen—Some sixty-two male Islamist terrorists escaped through a 50-yard tunnel from a prison in Mukalla. The terrorists used daggers to attack a guard, grabbed his gun, and fired it. One guard died, another was wounded. Terrorists outside the prison fired at other guards for thirty minutes, offering covering fire for the escaping prisoners. Three escapees were killed; two were captured. At least fifty-seven of the escapees had been convicted on terrorism charges; some had been given a death sentence. Among the escapees were members of an al Qaeda cell that had killed foreign tourists and tried to attack the U.S.

Embassy and other Western targets. Two Saudis and two Syrians were among the escapees. Al Qaeda in the Arabian Peninsula had used the same tactic in a prison escape in Aden the previous summer.

June 22, 2011—United States—Islamic converts Abu Khalid Abdul-Latif, 33, born Joseph Anthony Davis, of Seattle, and Walli Mujahidh, 32, born Frederick Domingue, Jr., of Los Angeles, were arrested at a Seattle warehouse for planning to use grenades and machine guns to attack the Military Entrance Processing Station on East Marginal Way in Seattle on July 5. Prosecutors said the duo had purchased two inerted automatic weapons for $800 from an informant and discussed getting pistols. They had planned to deter U.S. military action in Islamic countries. They initially targeted the Joint Base Lewis-McChord outside Seattle. Abdul-Latif told an informant that "if one person (Nidal Hasan) could kill so many people, three attackers could kill many more" and that his son would be proud if Latif died while fighting "nonbelievers." The prosecution said Abdul-Latif told Mujahidh that he would drive a "truck that looks like the Titanic" through the "front gate" and that he wanted to use fragmentation grenades in the facility's cafeteria to deter pursuers and kill or maim others. He observed, "Imagine how many young Muslims, if we're successful, will try to hit these kinds of centers. Imagine how fearful America will be." "If we gonna die," Abdul-Latif said, "we gotta die taking some kafirs with us. I'm not trying to run out of ammunition ... We're not only trying to kill people ... We're trying to send a message. We're trying to get something that's gonna be on CNN and all over the world." Mujahidh took a bus from Los Angeles to Seattle on June 21. The charge sheet said that Mujahidh expected a headline to read, "Three Muslim Males Walk Into MEPS Building, Seattle, Washington, and Gun Down Everybody." "That's what it's going to come down to," Mujahidh said, "because if they surround the building, the only way out is through them ... and guns blazing man, guns blazing ... We're not walking out of there alive." Authorities said they converted to Islam in prison, where they met. Abdul-Latif served in the U.S. Navy in 1995. He was convicted of felony robbery in the first degree in 2002 and assault in 2003 while serving time in Washington State for the robbery. The duo faced life in prison. On December 8, 2011, Mujahidh pleaded guilty to charges that he joined Abu Khalid Abdul-Latif in planning the attack. Mujahidh faced twenty-seven to thirty-two years in prison on pleading guilty to

weapons and conspiracy charges. The petty thief had a long history of mental illness and had logged twelve stays at psychiatric hospitals, according to defense attorney Michele Shaw.

June 23, 2011—Iraq—Several men wheeled in explosives on produce carts around 7:00 p.m., then exploded their three bombs in the Shi'ite al-Shurta neighborhood market in Baghdad, killing 21 people and injuring 107.

June 23, 2011—Iraq—Stephen Everhart, an international finance expert working for the U.S. Agency for International Development, died when a bomb exploded under his diplomatic convoy while leaving a Baghdad university. Three other people, including one U.S. citizen, were injured. Everhart was working with the Iraqi Ministry of Higher Education. He was an associate dean at the American University in Cairo. He had been managing director of the Overseas Private Investment Corporation (OPIC). He was married and had two daughters and a son. 11062301

June 24, 2011—Myanmar—Four bombs exploded in three Burmese cities, wounding two people. The first explosion went off in a house near a market in Naypyidaw, the administrative capital, near a zone featuring hotels and near the Gems Museum. A second bomb went off at noon, destroying a car and wounding a traffic cop and another person. A third bomb went off in Mandalay at 3:00 p.m., three blocks away, but caused no injuries. Twenty miles away, a bomb went off in Pyinoolwin, where a defense academy is located.

June 25, 2011—Afghanistan—Just after noon, a suicide bomber drove a vehicle bomb into the front entrance of a public hospital in the Azra district of rural Lugar Province, killing at least twenty-five people, including patients, staff, and children, many of them in the maternity ward. Some news reports said sixty people had died.

June 25, 2011—United States—Two explosive devices were found in a Borders Bookstore in the suburban Colorado Mills Mall in Golden, Colorado, a Denver suburb. The crude devices caused minimal damage inside the store. No one was injured.

June 25, 2011—Pakistan—A married Uzbek couple conducted a five-hour gun battle at a police station in Dera Ismail Khan, killing ten officers before setting off three explosions that killed themselves. The Pakistani Taliban said it was avenging the death of Osama bin Laden. 11062501

June 26, 2011—Nigeria—Motorcyclists threw bombs into three outdoor beer gardens in Maiduguri, killing twenty-five people. Boko Haram was suspected in the 5:00 p.m. attacks.

June 27, 2011—Afghanistan—At 10:00 p.m. three Taliban gunmen and five or six suicide bombers attacked Kabul's Hotel Inter-Continental, which frequently has foreign guests. Gunmen wearing police uniforms shot two guards, set off a truck bomb, then stormed the building. Taliban spokesman Zabiullah Mujahid said in an e-mail to CNN that "one of the suicide attackers told us on the phone that they are in the lobby and chasing guests into their rooms by smashing the doors of the rooms and he added that they have killed about fifty guests of this hotel." Four hours later, NATO/International Security Assistance Force helicopters killed three gunmen who were firing rocket-propelled grenades from the roof at the first vice president's house. Twenty Afghan troops entered the hotel and did a floor-by-floor search, killing two of the would-be suicide bombers. Two others ran upstairs. All of the suicide bombers eventually set off their explosives. Soon afterwards, three bombs went off. At the end of the siege, the government announced that all nine terrorists had died, as had a dozen other people, including nine Afghans, a Turkish pilot, a French tourist, and a Spaniard. The Canadian Embassy denied an early report that one of its diplomats was killed. The U.S. Embassy said all Americans were accounted for. Another dozen people were wounded.

At the time of the attack, the hotel was hosting a wedding and was preparing to host a meeting of provincial governors.

A Taliban spokesman said seven of the group's members hailed from Konar, Khost, Kunduz, Paktia, Wardak, and Zabul provinces.

On June 28, an air strike killed Haqqani network member Ismail Jan, commander in the Khost-Gardez Pass area and deputy to the senior Haqqani commander, in Paktiya Province. Jan was believed to have organized the hotel attack. 11062701

July 2011—Algeria—An al Qaeda in the Islamic Maghreb suicide bomber killed two people at a police headquarters in Bordj Maniel, west of Tizi Ouzou.

July 2011—United States—Ulugbek Kodirov, an Uzbek illegally in the United States, was arrested on charges of plotting to kill President Obama with an automatic rifle, acting on instructions of the Islamic Movement of Uzbekistan (IMU). He pleaded guilty on February 20, 2012, in a hearing in Birmingham, Alabama, before U.S. District Judge Abdul K. Kallon; the charges were threatening to kill the president, possession of an automatic weapon, and providing material support to terrorists; four other charges were dropped. The 22-year-old was represented by attorney Lance Bell, who said the plea bargain dropped the sentence from life in prison to a possible fifteen to thirty years to be followed by deportation.

Kodirov said he had been communicating with "the Emir," a member of the IMU. He approached an individual to obtain a Sendra M-115A1 automatic rifle for the assassination; the friend became a confidential source for the government. Kodirov bought the gun from an undercover agent at a Birmingham motel on July 13, 2011, and threatened the president a fourth time. The agent also gave Kodirov four inerted hand grenades. 11079901

July 2011—United Kingdom—Manchester authorities arrested Mohammed Sajid Khan, 33, and his wife, Shasta, 38, after the duo got into an argument. Family members were drawn into the fight; her brother told police that Mohammed was a "home-grown terrorist." Shasta then admitted that her husband was planning an attack but denied that she was involved. Police discovered a plan to bomb Jewish sites in Manchester and found beheading videos, al Qaeda propaganda, bomb-making guides, hydrogen peroxide, and addresses in the town's Jewish community. She was convicted on three terrorism-related counts on July 19, 2012, at Manchester Crown Court. He had earlier pleaded guilty.

July 1, 2011—Pakistan—A Swiss married couple were kidnapped while traveling by car in Loralai in southwestern Baluchistan Province. The tourists were on their way to Quetta. 11070101

July 5, 2011—Gaza Strip—Israeli forces killed two Palestinian gunmen and wounded a third who were affiliated with Tawheed and Jihad, a group with links to al Qaeda. The trio were approaching a boundary fence and were believed preparing to fire a rocket into Israel.

July 12, 2011—Egypt—Masked gunmen bombed a terminal of the Egyptian natural gas pipeline to Israel and Jordan. No casualties were reported. No one claimed credit. 11071201

July 12, 2011—Afghanistan—Sardar Mohammad, 35, a police commandant and longtime confidant of President Hamid Karzai's half brother, Ahmed Wali Karzai, 48, fired three shots that killed Ahmed Wali Karzai before bodyguards killed Mohammad. Ahmed Karzai was meeting with tribal elders and politicians in his home in Kandahar. Ahmed Karzai was the most powerful man in southern Afghanistan but was also reputedly involved in extensive corruption. The Taliban claimed credit. It was not clear why Mohammad killed Karzai; he had worked against the Taliban during his career. The press claimed that Mohammad had met with Taliban insurgents in Quetta, Pakistan, within the previous three months. On October 15, 2011, a senior NATO official said that he was not a Taliban member and had shot Karzai because he had learned that he was to be disciplined and wanted to avoid being publicly shamed.

On July 14, a suicide bomber set off a bomb hidden in his turban, killing four people and injuring fifteen at a morning memorial service for Karzai in Kandahar's Red Mosque. The dead included Maulvi Hekmatullah Hekmat, chief cleric of Kandahar. Karzai family members and the cabinet ministers in attendance were not harmed.

July 12, 2011—Philippines—More than a dozen Abu Sayyaf gunmen kidnapped Gerfa Yeatts Lunsman, 41, a Filipina American vet, and her son and nephew on the resort island of Tictabon, near Zamboanga. The group fled in motorboats. A large ransom was demanded. She was dropped off by boat at a wharf in an isolated area of Basilan Island the evening of October 3, 2011, and walked to nearby Maluso township. Her American son Kevin, 14, and Filipino nephew Romnick Jakaria, 19, remained as hostages. It is not known whether a ransom was paid. Lunsmann was born near Zamboanga city but was adopted by a U.S. family and grew up in the United States. She lives in Virginia. Kevin Lunsman was freed on December 10, 2011; there was no indication regarding a ransom payment. 11071202

July 12, 2011—Turkey—Authorities announced they arrested fifteen suspected al Qaeda terrorists in Ankara, Bursa, and Yalova who were planning attacks on foreign targets, including the U.S. Embassy in Ankara. Police seized 700 kilograms of chemicals that could be used in bomb making, two assault rifles, ammunition, and maps of Ankara. Authorities had surveilled a suspect, C.I., for six months. C.I. had al Qaeda contacts. Authorities believed he was trained in arms and explosives, and rented a two-story house in Sincan, near Ankara. He was arrested on a Sincan street earlier in the week. C.I. had led to the arrest of nine suspects in Ankara, three in Bursa, and two in Yalova. 11071302

July 13, 2011—India—Terrorists set off three bombs at 6:45 p.m. in the Dadar, Opera House, and Zaveri Bazar commercial hubs in Mumbai, killing 18 people (originally reported as 21) and wounding 133. The Zaveri bomb was hidden in

an umbrella near a motorcycle; the others were in trash under a cart and on top of a bus stop billboard. Lashkar-i-Taiba, radical Hindus, and Indian Mujahideen were suspected, although no group claimed credit immediately. On July 26, Nepalese media reported that over the weekend police had arrested Muhammad Zahir, a man in his 40s, on suspicion of involvement in the attack. Authorities said he spoke on a cell phone and texted about the explosions. 11071303

July 18, 2011—China—Muslim Uighur gunmen attacked a police station in the grand bazaar section of Hotan, Xinjiang Province, near the Pakistan border. Police killed fourteen gunmen but lost an armed policeman, a security guard, and a woman and a teen girl; the latter two had been taken hostage. Another three civilians were injured. Six hostages were freed. Police arrested four gunmen. State news services said the Uighur "rioters" were armed with axes, knives, daggers, Molotov cocktails, and explosives and that they had hacked to death the security guard.

The German-based World Uighur Congress claimed that Uighurs were protesting in front of the police station and were fired on by police.

July 19, 2011—Internet—Al Qaeda in the Arabian Peninsula released the sixth edition of *Inspire*, which cited the death of Osama bin Laden and succession by Ayman al-Zawahiri. *Inspire* claimed that bin Laden fought back against U.S. Navy SEALS in a "vicious battle" on May 2, 2011, before he was killed. "He confronted them, his weapons against theirs, and his strength against theirs, and he accepted the challenge of those who came out with their fancy equipment, machinery, weapons, aircrafts, and troops, all haughty and pompous. His determination did not weaken in front of them, nor was he sapped of strength. Rather, he stood and confronted them face to face like a firm mountain, and continued to engage them in a fierce battle ... after which he excused himself and fulfilled the trust, receiving bullets of treachery and infidelity." It was unclear how the *Inspire* writer could know this directly. Other articles in the magazine showed how to fire an AK-47 and how to form acetone peroxide explosives.

July 20, 2011—Yemen—A bomb placed under the driver's seat of a British man in Aden killed him. The ship surveyor worked in Aden for the Arab Company for Inspection and Marine Consulting. No group claimed credit for killing the longtime resident. 11072001

July 22, 2011—Norway—Norwegian citizen Anders Behring Breivik, 32, set off a car bomb at 3:26 p.m. in Oslo, killing eight people and injuring thirty, before conducting a shooting spree at a youth Labor Party political conference on Utoya Island, 25 miles to the northwest, killing at least sixty-eight people (initial reports said eighty-five people) and injuring another sixty-six in a ninety-minute rampage. More than sixty of the victims were teens. The Oslo bomb went off near the seventeen-story building that houses the prime minister's office, setting off a fire at the neighboring Oil Ministry. Two hours later, dressed in a police uniform, he herded the students together before opening fire. Several tried to swim away, but were shot in the water. Four people were missing two days after the attack. Residents near the island called police at 5:27 p.m. The first police patrol arrived at 5:52 p.m.; an emergency team from Oslo joined them at 6:09 p.m. They had to use motorboats from local residents to get to the island at 6:25 p.m. Breivik had no getaway plans.

Breivik soon confessed. He was carrying a Glock pistol and an automatic weapon. Police Directorate spokesman Runar Kvernen said that he was "suspected of having some right-wing sympathies," which were amply demonstrated in Breivik's Internet postings. If convicted of terrorism charges, he faced twenty-one years in prison. His lawyer, Geir Lippestad, said his client called the attacks "atrocious" but "necessary." Lippestad said his client was insane. The fundamentalist Christian belonged to an anti-immigrant party and opposed Islam, multi-culturalism, and "cultural Marxists." He had recently bought tons of fertilizer that could be used in bomb making. In his fifteen-hundred-page English-language manifesto, *2083: A European Declaration of Independence*, he called for a civil war and detailed how he made the explosives. Symbols of Knights Templar appeared in the document. A Norwegian newspaper reported that some sections came from Unabomber Ted Kaczynski's manifesto. He appeared in a video in which he was wearing quasi-military uniforms. He considered using anthrax in attacks, but there was no evidence that he knew how to use it or had obtained it.

A little-known jihadist group claimed credit, and jihadi Internet fora praised the attacks.

Breivik told an Oslo court that he acted alone. He later said that there were two cells at large in Norway and possibly others elsewhere in Europe. He entered a plea of not guilty.

Jens David Breivik, a former Norwegian diplomat, said he wished his son had committed suicide. He cut off contact with his son in 1995.

On July 26, police were investigating a Polish chemist who sold chemicals to Breivik online that the latter used to make bombs.

In November, during the first public hearing since the attack, District Court Judge Torkjel Nesheim said there was no reason to believe that Breivik is insane and no reason to believe he had accomplices. Breivik was ordered held in custody for another twelve weeks.

On November 29, 2011, psychiatrists declared that Breivik was a psychotic paranoid schizophrenic at the time of the attacks and during the thirteen interviews they conducted with him. He thus could not be sentenced to prison or preventive detention, but he could be confined to a mental hospital for the rest of his life. Courts would review the compulsory mental health care order every three years.

On February 6, 2012, Breivik defended his act during a custody hearing, saying, "people subjected to genocide" may legally defend themselves. He said, "The attacks on the government headquarters were preventive attacks on traitors to the nation, people committing or planning to commit cultural destruction, including destruction of Norwegian culture and Norwegian ethnicity."

On March 7, 2012, Breivik was indicted on terrorism and murder charges. He was expected to be involuntarily committed to psychiatric care.

On June 21, 2012, Norwegian prosecutors asked that Breivik be transferred to a psychiatric institution, calling him mentally ill. Failing that, they would ask for a sentence of twenty-one years in prison. The trial ended on June 22, 2012. He was represented by defense lawyer Geir Lippestad, who argued that Breivik acted out of necessity, not insanity. Judges scheduled an August 24 verdict announcement. Brieivik was deemed sane and on August 24, 2012, sentenced to twenty-one years in prison. He gave the court a clenched-fist salute.

July 23, 2011—Iran—On July 24, 2012, Iran announced the arrests of suspects in the July 2011 murder of 35-year-old nuclear physicist Daryoush Rezaie outside his Tehran home. Tehran said, "Two groups in charge of training terrorists were arrested inside and outside Iran."

July 24, 2011—Yemen—A suicide bomber rammed into an army checkpoint outside Aden, killing nine soldiers and wounding twenty-one others. The government blamed al Qaeda in the Arabian Peninsula.

July 26, 2011—Afghanistan—A Taliban suicide bomber hid his explosives in his turban, snuck into a city hall meeting, and killed Kandahar's mayor, Ghulam Haidar Hamidi, 65.

July 26, 2011—Yemen—Nasser al-Wahishi, leader of al Qaeda in the Arabian Peninsula, posted a ten-minute audio to Islamist Web sites in which he vowed loyalty to Ayman al-Zawahiri as bin Laden's successor. "I give you allegiance of obedience in good and hard times, in ease and difficult, and in fighting the enemies of Allah as much as I can—myself and your loyal soldiers who are with me on the Arabian Peninsula." He said that the group would continue seeking to overthrow President Ali Abdullah Saleh. "My soldiers and those soldiers with me in the Arab Gulf will not give up nor give in until Islam is ruling by God's will and strength." The Arab Spring has "blown America's dreams to the winds" and provided Muslims "a natural chance to rid themselves of the West's cross—its plots and its plans—to chisel its own course for a return to the glory days ... Our war against the Zionist Crusaders remains for they have chosen this war. We are people of war; we were born from its womb and we grew up in its midst. It is as if we were only created to fight them and bother them."

July 26, 2011—Iraq—The Islamic State of Iraq posted an online plea for funds, saying it needed money to help thousands of widows and children of martyrs. Webmaster Seif Saad said, "A few days ago a brother was martyred, leaving behind a wife and children. There is no need to explain how we were running here and there to collect money for their minimum requirements of life." He suggested that al Qaeda in Iraq members extort foreign oil, construction, transport, and cell phone firms, along with international media services. Web site administrator Mohamed Abdel-Hadi suggested shaking down wealthy Shi'ites, because "all the Shi'ites, including merchants or government officials, are infidels and confiscating their money is part of jihad."

July 26, 2011—Lebanon—A roadside bomb went off next to a UN Interim Force in Lebanon convoy carrying French peacekeepers at the southern entrance of Sidon, wounding six of them. One sustained injuries to the face and chest. No group claimed responsibility, although Hizballah was suspected. Investigators said the bomb contained two kilograms of explosives. 11072601

July 26, 2011—United States—Federal prosecutors in New York unsealed two indictments that charged four men as part of two undercover heroin stings in Romania and Afghanistan. The undercover operatives said that the profits would fund Hizballah. A Drug Enforcement Administration (DEA)-sourced indictment said that Afghan citizen Taza Gul Alizai sold six AK-47 assault rifles and 15 kilograms of heroin during two years to a DEA informant. Alizai faced life in prison on

charges of narcoterrorism conspiracy, narcoterrorism, and narcotics importation. He was arrested in the Maldives on July 25; he pleaded not guilty the next day in a Manhattan court.

In the second indictment, three men were charged with conspiracy to import heroin and provide material support to Hizballah. The charge sheet said that Sioavosh Henareh, alias The Doctor, agreed to import heroin to the United States so that profits could go to Hizballah. Informants were introduced to Cetin Aksu and Bachar Wehbe, a Lebanese; the duo tried to buy Stinger antiaircraft missiles, AK-47s, and Glock handguns from the informants. Wehbe said he was purchasing them for Hizballah. Aksu and Henareh faced life in prison on charges of conspiracy to distribute heroin. Aksu and Wehbe were charged with conspiracy to acquire antiaircraft missiles, which also carries a life sentence. Wehbe was arrested in the Maldives on July 25; he pleaded not guilty the next day in a Manhattan court. Aksu and Henareh were arrested in Romania on July 25; extradition was expected to be requested.

July 27, 2011—Internet—Ayman al-Zawahiri praised Syria's pro-democracy movement in a seven-minute As-Sahab video posted to jihadi Web sites. "The time of humiliation is gone, the time of deceit is over, and the rule of the thieves is finished." He said the protestors were part of a broader revolution in the Muslim world. He called Syrian President Bashar al-Assad "the leader of criminal gangs, the protector of traitors," and a corrupt tyrant who was "America's partner in the war on Islam." He said al-Assad "abandoned" the Golan Heights after the 1967 Arab-Israeli war and that he now serves as "Israel's border guard."

> Oh free people of Syria and its mujahideen, it is better for you not to ally yourself with the colonialist powers of the world and the new crusades. America, which had committed itself to Bashar for the length of his rule, announces today that it stands with you. After what it saw and the ground shook from the thunder of your rage and after it was devastated by the loss of its two biggest agents in Egypt and Tunisia ... Washington today seeks to replace Assad, who sincerely protected the borders of the Zionist entity, with another regime that squanders your revolution and jihad in a new regime that follows America, takes care of Israel's interests, and grants the Muslims some freedoms ... I would have been amongst you and with you, [but] there are enough and more mujahideen and garrisoned ones.

July 28, 2011—United States—U.S. Army Pfc. Naser Jason Abdo, 21, was arrested while AWOL by Killeen, Texas, police at a traffic stop near Fort Hood. The Muslim told investigators that he wanted to attack his colleagues at the base in support of Maj. Nidal Hasan, who had shot to death thirteen people at the base in 2009. Police said he had no accomplices. FBI agents found bomb-making materials in his hotel room. Guns Galore, a Texas gun dealer that had sold Nidal Hasan his weapons used in the earlier attack on Fort Hood, alerted police to Abdo's suspicious behavior. Abdo bought gunpowder, shotgun ammunition, and a magazine for a semiautomatic handgun. Abdo set aside six one-pound canisters of smokeless gunpowder, but then asked about the powder, raising suspicions. Abdo also bought uniforms with Fort Hood unit patches from a local military surplus store. A search of Abdo's hotel room and backpack turned up the six pounds of smokeless powder, Christmas lights, and battery-operated clocks—which could be used for a timing and triggering device—sugar, shrapnel, a pressure cooker, shotgun shells that were being dismantled for their raw explosives, a .40-caliber pistol, and Islamic extremist literature, including an article from the al Qaeda magazine *Inspire*. He was to be charged with possession of bomb-making materials. On August 9, he was indicted on charges of possession of an unregistered destructive device, possession of a firearm, and possession of ammunition by a fugitive from justice.

Abdo had been a member of Company E of the 101st Airborne Division's 1st Brigade Combat Team. He joined the infantry in 2009. Abdo had refused to deploy to Afghanistan on religious grounds. The army approved his request to be discharged as a conscientious objector. Soon after, he went AWOL from Fort Campbell, Kentucky, after he was charged with possession of child pornography on his computer on May 13. At a military hearing on June 15, he was recommended for court-martial. His father, Jamal, was deported to Jordan in February 2010 after conviction of solicitation of sex online from a police officer posing as a 15-year-old girl.

He was charged on July 29 in U.S. District Court in Waco, Texas, with possession of an unregistered destructive device in connection with a bomb plot. He faced a ten-year sentence.

On November 8, 2011, Abdo was indicted on charges of attempted use of a weapon of mass destruction. He faced a life sentence.

On May 22, 2012, Abdo's civil murder trial opened in U.S. District Court. He was represented by defense lawyer Zachary Boyd. FBI agent Charles Owens said Abdo planned to bomb a Chinese restaurant because he said buffets were popular with soldiers; he would then shoot survivors. On May 24, 2012, a federal jury convicted him of attempting to use a weapon of mass destruction, which carried a life sentence. He was also convicted of attempted murder of U.S. officers or employees and four counts of possession of a weapon in furtherance of a federal crime of violence. Abdo was also to be tried for murder in a military court on August 20, 2012.

On August 10, 2012, U.S. District Judge Walter Smith sentenced Abdo to two consecutive life sentences, plus sixty years in prison. Abdo represented himself in the hearing and said he remained committed to jihad. "I don't ask the court for mercy because Allah is the one who gives me mercy."

July 30, 2011—Egypt—At dawn, gunmen did little damage when they fired rocket-propelled grenades at the pipeline terminal at al-Shuluq in northern Sinai. No injuries were reported. The pipeline carries natural gas from Egypt across the Sinai Peninsula to Israel and Jordan. The pipeline had been shut down after a previous attack.

August 2011—Spain—Spain arrested a terrorist of Moroccan descent "planning to poison the water supplies of tourist locations in Spain, in retaliation for the death of bin Laden," according to the *European Union Terrorist Situation and Trend Report*.

August 2011—China—Late in August, the Turkestan Islamic Party (TIP) released a ten-minute video claiming credit for attacks in July in the West that killed three dozen people. The Islamist Uighur group was believed to be based in Pakistan and had links to al Qaeda. TIP leader Abdul Shakoor Damla said the attacks were revenge against the Chinese government. In 2008, the group had claimed credit for several bus bombings in China. The video included footage of TIP member Memtieli Tiliwaldi, a suspect in the July attacks who was fatally shot by Chinese authorities in a cornfield in July.

August 2, 2011—Iraq—A car bomb exploded outside the Holy Family Catholic church in Kirkuk's Shatterlo neighborhood at 5:30 a.m., wounding twenty-three people.

August 12, 2011—United States—Daniel Wells Herriman, 40, of Konawa, Oklahoma, phoned Seminole County 911 to say that he had placed a homemade time bomb under a natural gas pipeline 75 miles east of Oklahoma City. Hours earlier, employees of Enerfin Resources had found the device, which did not explode. Herriman had no connection to the company. The bomb consisted of sealed white pipes containing black powder, a propane tank, two batteries, wires, broken light bulbs, and a wind-up alarm clock.

August 13, 2011—Pakistan—At 3:10 a.m., circa eight to ten gunmen kidnapped Warren Weinstein, 70, an American, from his Lahore home in the Model Town neighborhood. He was working as J.E. Austin Associates, Inc., country director on a development project. He had planned to finish his work that weekend and move out of the country by August 15, possibly to return to his home in Rockville, Maryland. The gunmen had told guards that they wanted to give them food during Ramadan. After the guards opened the gate, two of the assailants ran through the gate while six others used the back door. Police claimed that the gunmen tortured the guards, then escaped with the American. As of August 14, police had developed no leads and were not sure whether the attackers were terrorists or criminals seeking ransom.

Weinstein had twenty-five years of experience in international development projects. He earned his doctorate in international law and economics at Columbia University. He speaks six languages, including Urdu. The company said he was an expert in governance, microfinance, small and medium-size business development, and institutional development. The firm said he was in poor health and posted a list of medications, including those for heart problems, that it hoped the kidnappers would give him.

On August 18, Pakistani police released a sketch of a possible suspect, a thin youth with short dark hair and a stubbly beard.

On August 25, Pakistani police retracted the day's earlier announcement that Weinstein had been found 120 miles from Lahore in the Khushab district. The kidnappers had fled a safe house before the police raid.

Pakistani police arrested three men in connection with the kidnapping. The trio were from the province in which Weinstein had lived for seven years. Police had tracked their cell phone numbers.

On December 1, 2011, Ayman al-Zawahiri said via a thirty-minute audio posting on Islamist Web sites that al Qaeda was responsible and demanded the release of al Qaeda and Taliban terrorists from several prisons around the world, including everyone held at Guantanamo. He also demanded the end of U.S. air attacks against Islamists in Afghanistan, Pakistan, Somalia, Gaza, and Yemen; the free movement of people and goods between Egypt and Gaza; and closure of Guantanamo. He

said Weinstein's family should not trust U.S. President Obama. "Your government tortures our prisoners, but we have not tortured your prisoner ... Your problem is not with us but with Obama. We have raised fair demands ... So continue to pressure Obama, if you want your relative to be handed back." He said that Obama wished Weinstein "would be killed to get rid of his problem." He demanded the release of six prominent members of al Qaeda in the West, including Ramzi Yousef, Sheikh Omar Abdel Rahman, and members of bin Laden's family. "Obama has the power, capacity, and authority to free [Weinstein]. He could also leave him in captivity for years and, if he does something stupid, kill him." Al-Zawahiri said, "Just as the Americans detain all who they suspect of links to al Qaeda and the Taliban, even remotely, we detained this man who is neck deep in American aid to Pakistan since the 1970s." He noted that Libyan terrorist Jamal Ibrahim Ashtiwi al-Misrati, alias Attiyatullah, alias Atiyah Abd al Rahman, survived an initial air strike but died with his son Issam in a second attack on August 23, 2011. "He was martyred, may God have mercy on him ... by bombing by a crusader spy plane." Al-Zawahiri added, "I tell the captive soldiers of al Qaeda and the Taliban and our female prisoners held in the prisons of the crusaders and their collaborators, we have not forgotten you and in order to free you we have taken hostage the Jewish American Warren Weinstein."

NBC News reported on December 2, 2011, that Tehrik-e-Taliban was responsible for the kidnapping of Weinstein, who was shifted to various locations.

McClatchyDC.com reported that Weinstein was alive and in good health as of January 25, 2012. He was being held by Lashkar-e-Jhangvi militants in North Waziristan. In December 2011, Ayman al-Zawahiri had said in a video that al Qaeda was holding Weinstein.

On March 16, 2012, al-Zawahiri released an eleven-minute As-Sahab Internet video in which he said, "By the grace of Allah, we, on our part, have captured the American Jew Warren Weinstein." He demanded the release of al Qaeda prisoners, including blind sheik Omar Abdel Rahman, Aafia Siddiqui, Osama bin Laden's family, and "every single person arrested on allegations of links with al Qaeda and Taliban" for the release of Weinstein. Al-Zawahiri said the Pakistani Army "slaves of America" were taking bribes, and that the populace should,

Rise up in the face of these treacherous generals! Take to the streets! Revolt! Rise and step forward to face death so that you may be given life once again! ... Cannot a million free and noble people rise from amongst the Muslims of Pakistan to stage a protest against the generals of Pakistan Army so as to force them to stop their treachery ... by participating with America in its war against Islam, compel them to stop drone strikes and pressurize them to bring an end to army operations in the tribal areas [in the Swat border region] ... Partnership with America only leads to loss in this world and the hereafter ... O our people in Pakistan! The Arab world around you is surging in a wave of revolution. Tyrants and oppressive rulers are falling. Why are you not making any move? Why are you not deposing these tyrants? Why are you not toppling these treacherous bribe-takers?

He mentioned a U.S. air strike in November 2011 that killed twenty-four Pakistani soldiers on the Afghanistan border.

On May 5, 2012, the kidnappers released a three minute and forty seconds video in which Weinstein said, "My life is in your hands, Mr. President. If you accept the demands, I live. If you don't accept the demands, then I die. It's important you accept the demands and act quickly and don't delay. There'll be no benefit in delaying, it will just make things more difficult for me." He said if Obama accepted the demands, "then I will live and hopefully rejoin my family and also enjoy my children, my two daughters, like you enjoy your two daughters." He said he wanted his wife to know, "I'm fine, I'm well. I'm getting all my medications. I'm being taken care of."

On September 12, 2012, Weinstein appeared in a ninety-second As-Sahab video in which he asked Israeli Prime Minister Benjamin Netanyahu to negotiate with the terrorists. "Unfortunately President Obama and the American government have shown no interest in my case. Therefore, as a Jew, I am appealing to you, Prime Minister Netanyahu, the head of the Jewish State of Israel, as one Jew to another, to please intervene on my behalf, to work with the mujahideen and to accept their demands so that I can be released and returned to my family, my wife, my children and my grandchildren again." He asked his wife "Please make as many contacts as you can with Jewish communities in the United States in order to put pressure on the American government and President Obama to work with and accept the demands of the mujahideen in order for me to get my freedom." He also asked Elaine Weinstein to appeal to the "Republican candidate." He said he was taking his medication and was "being taken care of." 11081301

August 13, 2011—Yemen—The *New York Times* reported that al Qaeda in the Arabian Peninsula

was trying to obtain castor beans to produce ricin, which it would pack around explosives to be used in attacks against U.S. subway stations, malls, and an airport. The group mentioned ricin in a fall 2010 edition of its online magazine *Inspire* in an article entitled "Tips for Our Brothers in the United States of America."

August 13, 2011—Algeria—At 4:30 a.m., Anes Abu El-Nadr, an al Qaeda in the Islamic Maghreb (AQIM) suicide bomber, injured twenty-nine people when he tried to drive his Toyota Hilux pickup truck bomb into police headquarters in Tizi Ouszou. AQIM in a posting to an Islamist Web site claimed thirty-five people were killed or wounded.

August 14, 2011—Afghanistan—Six Taliban suicide bombers attacked a provincial governor's compound in Chaikar, Parwan Province, killing twenty-two people. Governor Abdul Basir Salangi, his police chief and intelligence director, a local army commander, and two NATO advisors were meeting in the home. Salangi survived. The first explosion was a car bomb outside the front gate. Five other terrorists ran through the subsequent hole in the wall, bringing with them suicide vests, automatic weapons, and rocket-propelled grenades. Police killed three of the attackers before they could make it to the house.

August 15, 2011—Internet—Al Qaeda leader Ayman al-Zawahiri released a twelve-minute video on an Islamist Web site addressed to "Muslim brothers everywhere" in which he observed, "America today is staggering. Hunt her down wherever you may encounter her. Hunt her down to cut what is left of her corruption's tail. Pursue America, which killed the Imam of the Mujahideen and threw his body into the sea, and then captured his women and sons. Hunt her down until history says that a murderous country spread corruption in the earth so God sent his faithful to her to make an example out of her."

August 18, 2011—Israel—Terrorists crossed from the Egyptian Sinai Peninsula into Israel and conducted several attacks on vehicles and soldiers near the Eilat resort, killing eight and wounding more than twenty-four. In the first attack at noon, gunmen on a road several miles outside Eilat fired on an intercity bus carrying soldiers. Driver Benny Bilbaski saw "two men in fatigues shooting at me" and quickly drove out of range. The injured were treated. A simultaneous attack on a bus and two cars, plus a bombing of a military vehicle carrying troops responding to the scene, resulted in a soldier being killed by the blast and ensuing gun battle. One car was hit by an antitank rocket. Two attacks set off suicide belts. Terrorists also fired mortars from Gaza at troops conducting maintenance on the border fence. Israeli helicopter gunships killed seven attackers.

A retaliatory Israeli air strike on Rafah town in the Gaza Strip killed eight Palestinians, including Kamal al-Neirab, the leader of the Popular Resistance Committees; Imad Hamad, the leader of the group's armed wing; the group's rocket expert; his two-year-old son; along with the leader of the armed wing of the Islamic Jihad group and his son and brother. Another forty people were injured. The group retaliated by firing a Grad rocket at Ashkelon town. The Iron Dome missile defense system knocked down the rocket.

An Egyptian military officer and two police officers were killed in border skirmishes after the attacks.

On September 21, 2012, three gunmen wearing sand-colored camouflage uniforms crossed the Sinai border with Israel at Har Harif in a mountainous area but were shot to death in a firefight with Israeli troops, who lost one soldier; a second soldier was wounded. The terrorists had fired on Israeli soldiers who were bringing water to African migrants and securing a construction zone for a security fence at Mount Harif between the Gaza Strip and Eilat. An explosives belt worn by one of the terrorists detonated. The gunmen had three rocket-propelled grenade launchers and a machine gun hidden in a nearby pit. The Supporters of the Holy Places claimed credit, saying it was retaliating for the anti–Muhammad video. The group also claimed credit for the August 18, 2011, attack near Eilat that killed eight and wounded more than thirty people. The group said one of its leaders, Ibrahim Aweida, helped lead the Eilat attack and that he died in an Israeli attack in the Sinai village of Khreiza in August 2012. The most recent attack was also to avenge his death.

August 19, 2011—Pakistan—A suicide bomber killed forty-eight worshipers and wounded more than one hundred at a Sunni mosque in Ghundi in the Khyber region near the Afghanistan border. A boy believed to be about 15 or 16 years old set off a suicide vest packed with ball bearings. The roof of the mosque collapsed on the worshipers, who were engaged in Friday prayers during Ramadan.

August 19, 2011—India—Maoist rebels were blamed for an attack on a police patrol in the Bijapur district of Chhattisgarh State. The terrorists shot to death nine officers and a civilian.

August 19, 2011—Afghanistan—Taliban gunmen attacked the British Council in the Karte

Parwan residential neighborhood in Kabul, initially killing at least four people, including three Afghan police officers and a civilian municipality worker. The attack came on the day Afghans mark their 1919 independence from the British. After a truck bomb exploded at the entrance to the compound at 5:30 a.m., gunmen stormed the building. A second bomb went off ten minutes later. A grenade went off at 7:45 a.m., as the gun battle with hundreds of police officers continued. At least five wounded people, four of them police officers and one a Nepalese guard wearing a U.K. Embassy guard force hat, were rushed to hospitals during the eight-hour gun battle. Two Britons and a South African survived by hiding in a safe room. At least eight people, including a New Zealand Special Forces soldier, five police officers, and two Afghan guards, were later reported killed, as were the terrorists. Another twenty-two people were injured. 11081901

August 22, 2011—Pakistan—An air strike against a vehicle and a guest house in Nork in Pakistan's northwest tribal area killed five people, including al Qaeda deputy chief and operational planner Atiyah Abd-al-Rahman. The Libyan was believed to have met Osama bin Laden while still a teen. He was the group's principal operational planner, served as liaison between the group's senior leaders and its foot soldiers, and ran the group's financial operations after the death of Saeed al-Masri in May 2010. He sent a letter to al Qaeda in Iraq leader Abu Musab al-Zarqawi in 2006 telling him to back off from attacks on Shi'ites. He was linked to the December 2009 bombing of the CIA base in Khost, Afghanistan. He tried to be the liaison between al Qaeda and Algerian terrorists in 1993, having earlier fought against the Algerian government, but the Armed Islamic Group detained him and threatened to kill him. He escaped after five months and fled the country. He became the liaison between al Qaeda-linked groups in Iraq, Iran, and Algeria.

August 26, 2011—Nigeria—A Boko Haram suicide car bomber crashed into the main UN building in Abuja, killing twenty-three and wounding eighty-one. It was the first suicide bombing against foreigners in Nigeria. Nigerian authorities claimed the terrorists had al Qaeda links. The State Security Service said it had arrested two men—Babagana Ismail Kwaljima and Babagan Mali—suspected of planning the attack on August 21. The Service said it had a tipoff of the bombing on August 18. Mamman Nur, a third suspect, remained at large as of August 31. Local authorities offered a $160,000 reward for information leading to the arrest of Mamman Nur, believed to be the mastermind of the bombing. On December 28, 2011, UN Childrens' Fund (UNICEF) worker Fred Willis died from his wounds, bringing the death toll to twenty-five. 11082601

September 2011—Niger—Al Qaeda in the Islamic Maghreb kidnapped seven French citizens from Arlit, a mining town. 11099901

September 1, 2011—Afghanistan—Taliban gunmen kidnapped forty boys who were lured across the border from Bajaur Agency along Pakistan's tribal region during an outing. The Taliban freed those younger than 12 years old, but kept thirty teens. The group said it was punishing the boys' tribe for forming a pro-government militia. The boys were walking to a picnic area along a river to mark the end of Ramadan when a man coaxed them across the border. Local elders were negotiating with the terrorists. 11090101

September 2, 2011—United States—Federal authorities arraigned Jubair Ahmad, 24, a native of Pakistan and resident of Woodbridge, Virginia, after he produced a violent jihadist video in September 2010 with the help of the son of a leader of Lashkar-i-Taiba, a Pakistani terrorist group. Charges in U.S. District Court in Alexandria, Virginia, included providing material support to terrorists and making false statements to the FBI during a terrorism investigation. The five-minute video was posted to YouTube. It included images of Lashkar leader Hafiz Mohammed Saeed and showed the bombing of armored trucks. Authorities said Ahmad consulted with Saeed's son, Talha, on what photos, videos, and music to use. Talha gave him editing suggestions in October 2010. Authorities said that while Ahmad was a teen in Pakistan, he received religious and weapons training from Lashkar. He faced fifteen years in prison for material support and another eight for the false statement.

September 3, 2011—Iraq—*Lancet*, a British medical journal, reported that 12,284 Iraqi civilians had died in 1,003 suicide bomb attacks from March 2003 through December 2010. The 79 suicide attacks against coalition forces killed 200 troops, according to iCasualties.org.

September 5, 2011—Pakistan—The Inter-Services Intelligence arrested Younis al-Mauritani and two al Qaeda associates—Abdul Ghaffar al-Shami and Messara al-Shami—in the suburbs of Quetta. Pakistani authorities said Osama bin Laden had tasked him with focusing "on hitting targets of economic importance in United States of America, Europe, and Australia." U.S. targets included gas and oil pipelines, dams, and oil tankers.

September 6, 2011—United States—The FBI arrested Agron Hasbajrami, an Albanian immigrant, at John F. Kennedy Airport before boarding a plane to Turkey after they intercepted messages supporting terrorists in Pakistan. An FBI informant offered to help him join an overseas radical group. Hasbajrami, 27, had lived legally in Brooklyn since 2008. He was accused of sending more than $1,000 to a contact in Pakistan to fund terrorism and joining a jihadi group. On April 12, 2012, as part of a plea bargain, he admitted in court to providing the money and pleaded guilty before Judge John Gleeson in Federal District Court in Brooklyn to one count of attempting to provide material support to terrorists. He faced fifteen years in prison upon his September 14 sentencing. He would have faced sixty years if convicted. The government dropped three other counts of providing material support to terrorists. He agreed to be deported after serving prison time.

September 7, 2011—India—A bomb hidden in a briefcase exploded at 10:15 a.m. in front of gate 5 of the Delhi High Court, killing thirteen people and wounding seventy-four. Police released sketches of two suspects. Harkat-ul-Jihar-al-Islami in Kashmir took credit, as did the Indian Mujahideen. Police said the bomb contained ammonium nitrate. Police detained six men for questioning on September 8. They included the owners, a manager, and two patrons of an Internet café that was used for sending a message claiming credit by the Kashmiri group. Police also detained an 8-year-old laborer at a bus station in Uttar Pradesh.

September 7, 2011—Pakistan—Two Pakistani Taliban suicide bombers attacked the Quetta residence of Brig. Gen. Farrukh Shahzad, deputy chief of the Frontier Corps paramilitary force that combats terrorist groups. At least twenty-three people, among them Shahzad's wife and six security personnel, were killed and fifty-two wounded, including the general. The first terrorist set off his car bomb among security vehicles parked outside. The second attacker ran into the house, was shot at, and set off his explosives. A spokesman for Tehrik-e-Taliban, Ihsanullah Ihsan, said Shahzad was targeted in retaliation for Shahzad's involvement in an operation against the group on the Pakistan-Afghanistan border in May. Police found an Afghan refugee card at the site; a picture on the card matched the description of one of the bombers. The card belonged to a 21-year-old man from Afghanistan's Kunduz Province who was living in Peshawar, Pakistan. The two bombs contained 60 kilograms of explosives. 11090701

September 8, 2011—Germany—Police in the Kreuzberg and Neukoelln districts of Berlin arrested two bomb plotters—a 24-year-old German of Lebanese descent and a 28-year-old man from Gaza. The duo had tried to obtain bomb-making chemicals. Police did not determine whether the terrorists had a specific target and did not find any links to terrorist groups. The duo had been surveilled for months after attempting to acquire a large amount of cooling agent.

September 8, 2011—United States—The news media reported that intelligence agencies alerted the president to "specific, credible but unconfirmed" information regarding a possible Pakistan-based terrorist threat to New York and Washington, DC, tunnels and bridges during the 9/11 tenth anniversary period. The plot involved three individuals, including one U.S.-born person, who possibly had already entered the United States in the past few weeks, driving an explosives-laden vehicle. Two of them might have used U.S. documents such as green cards to enter the country. Authorities believed they had traveled from Afghanistan or Pakistan, possibly transiting through Dubai on their way to the United States. Officials suggested that al Qaeda leader Ayman al-Zawahiri had ordered the attack.

September 9, 2011—United States—Reed S. Berry, 26, of St. Joseph, Michigan, who was under FBI surveillance because of his suspected links to terrorists, put his car in reverse and sped toward FBI special agent Samuel Moore, who avoided the collision. On October 2, 2011, a federal judge ordered Berry held for attempting the crash.

September 9, 2011—Pakistan—The government warned that the Taliban was planning to kidnap a senior government official to barter for the release of Osama bin Laden's wives and children. The Interior Ministry sent the warning on August 23 to senior security officials, three days before the kidnapping of Shahbaz Taseer, son of a wealthy provincial governor.

September 10, 2011—Kenya—At 12:30 p.m., gunmen attacked the Kiwayu Safari Village beach resort north of Lamu near the Somalia border, killing British citizen David Tebbut and kidnapping Judith, his wife. They escaped by boat. The couple had arrived after visiting the Maasai Mara reserve. They were the sole guests in the cloth-doored hotel. Somalia militia were suspected of taking her toward Ras Kamboni in Somalia. On

September 13, Kenyan police arrested a suspect. Somali pirates freed Judith Tebbut on March 21, 2012. The Kenya government blamed al-Shabaab. A pirate told the press that a ransom was air-dropped. 11091001

September 10, 2011—Sweden—Swedish police arrested four people in Goteborg on suspicion of preparing a terror attack. They also evacuated the Roda Sten arts center under the city's Alvsborg Bridge. Swedish prosecutors on September 12 told a judge that the four were "planning to commit murder." The four, ages 23 to 26, included three Somali men and an Iraqi. They were identified as Kulan Mohamud Abel, Mahamud Abdi Aziz, Mahmood Salar Sami, and Mohamud Abdi Weli.

The Somalia-born Weli was represented by attorney Eva Henriksson. Weli obtained Swedish citizenship in 2000. In 2009 he had received a suspended sentence and was fined for assault. Sami was born in Iraq and obtained Swedish citizenship. He had earlier been charged with multiple counts of theft, assault, and making threats, among other crimes, and had served several years in prison. Somali-born Aziz had lived in Sweden since 1999, but retained Somali citizenship. He had been fined for minor driving offenses. Somali-born Abel obtained Swedish citizenship and had no prior criminal record. Swedish media said they were suspected of al-Shabaab links.

September 12, 2011—Iraq—Local authorities believed foreigners were among the gunmen who hijacked a bus filled with Shi'ite pilgrims in a Sunni-dominated section of Anbar Province. The gunmen forced the men out of the bus and shot to death twenty-two of them. Four suspects were released for lack of evidence; as of September 18, another four were being held.

September 13, 2011—Pakistan—The Tehrik-e-Taliban Pakistan attacked a school bus with rocket and small arms fire near Peshawar Tuesday, killing the driver and three children and injuring sixteen others. The group's spokesman, Mohammad Talha, said it was responding to growing anti–Taliban resistance groups.

September 13, 2011—Pakistan—Seven members of the Taliban-affiliated Haqqani network conducted a twenty-hour gun battle against the U.S. Embassy and other targets. Afghan and NATO troops killed the last gunman around 9:30 a.m. on September 14. The terrorists threw grenades and fired automatic weapons from a neighboring building that was under construction. They wore burqas to hide weapons but not suicide vests. During the battle, four suicide bombers attacked other targets in Kabul. The day's attacks killed eleven

Afghan civilians, including five children, and five policemen, and wounded another twenty Afghan civilians. Three NATO troops were wounded while clearing their building; another three were hurt when grenades exploded at a military base. The Taliban claimed credit saying it wanted to expel foreign troops from the country.

September 16–17, 2011—Ivory Coast—Gunmen from neighboring Liberia conducted attacks on southwestern border villages over two days, killing at least fifteen people. 11091601, 11091701

September 19, 2011—United Kingdom—Police arrested six people in Birmingham and another in West Midlands on suspicion of "commission, preparation or instigation" of an act of terrorism. A woman was held for failing to disclose information that might prevent an act of terror. The suspected Islamic extremists were aged 22 to 32; all were British residents. Police raided more than a dozen homes and businesses in the sweep. Police said the plot was in its early stages but significant. On September 26, the government charged the six men from Birmingham. Irfan Nasser, 30, and Irfan Khalid, 26, faced twelve counts, including planning a suicide bombing event, making a martyrdom film, traveling to Pakistan for training in terrorism, including bomb making, weapons, and poison making. Four were charged with preparing for an act of terrorism in the United Kingdom. Two were charged with failing to disclose information. The six were denied bail at their court hearing. The Midlands man was still being questioned.

On October 22, 2012, the trial in London's Woolwich Crown Court began of Irfan Khalid, 27, Ahik Ali, 27, and Irfan Naseer, 31, who were inspired by the sermons of Anwar al-Aulaqi. Authorities said they were planning to set off eight knapsack bombs in a suicide attack or to set off time-delay bombs in crowded areas "in order to cause mass deaths and casualties." They were charged with preparing for terrorism by plotting a bombing campaign, recruiting others, and fundraising. Khalid and Naseer were also charged with traveling to Pakistan for terrorism training. The trio pleaded not guilty. Naseer had a degree in pharmacy, which prosecutors said helped him in designing chemical compounds suitable for bomb making. Rahim Ahmed was named as a co-conspirator and the group's chief financier, using fake charities on financial markets to raise money. He lost most of the terrorists' money through inept trading. He pleaded guilty to supporting terrorism. Prosecutors said the group also discussed strapping blades on the front of a truck and driv-ing it into a crowd, a tip offered in al Qaeda in the Arabian Peninsula's *Inspire* magazine.

September 20, 2011—Turkey—An explosion in a car parked in front of the Cankaya municipal building on Kumrular Street near Ankara's Kizilay metro station and a school killed three people and wounded fifteen. The Kurdistan Freedom Falcons claimed credit, saying it was retaliating for the government's "War" against them.

September 20, 2011—Afghanistan—Former Afghan President Burhanuddin Rabbani, who was leading government attempts to negotiate with the Taliban, was killed in his home in Kabul by Esmatullah, a Taliban suicide bomber. Rabbani was president from 1992 to 1996. The suicide bomber hid explosives in his turban. Two other peace council members were wounded in the murder of the Tajik leader of the Northern Alliance. One of them was Rahmatullah Wahidyar, who brought the killer to the home. The bomber had obtained access by sending an audio recording that he said included messages from Taliban leaders and that he was going to bring a second audio that could go only to Rabbani. On September 25, Afghan authorities announced the arrest in Kabul of Hamidullah Akhund, who had delivered a message from Rabbani to the Taliban. On October 2, an investigative delegation established by Afghan President Hamid Karzai said the evidence and a confession from a man involved in the killing established that the bomber was from Chaman, Pakistan, and that the bombing had been plotted in Quetta, Pakistan.

September 20, 2011—Pakistan—Eight to ten gunmen in a pickup truck stopped a bus of Shi'ite Muslim pilgrims, pulled them outside, and fired Kalashnikov automatic rifles and rocket launchers, killing twenty-six and wounding six. Lashkar-e-Jhangvi claimed credit. Later that day, two other Shi'ites died when gunmen attacked their vehicles. The victims were relatives of bus victims.

September 21, 2011—Russia—A bomb exploded in Makhachkala, capital of Dagestan, killing three people in a car that was transporting a bomb. Several bystanders were wounded.

September 22, 2011—Russia—Two bombs exploded in Makhachkala, capital of Dagestan, killing one person and wounding sixty. One bomb hit a police car and injured four police officers. A second bomb, hidden inside or beneath a car, wounded police officers and other first responders.

September 25, 2011—Afghanistan—A Taliban gunman attacked the U.S. Embassy in Kabul, killing at least one American and injuring another at the Ariana Hotel annex in the compound before he was killed. The news media said the annex was used by the CIA. Federal News Radio reported that the family of Jay Henigan, 61, a plumber from Sycamore, Illinois, was shot by an Afghan worker providing security to the facility. 11092601

September 25, 2011—Indonesia—A suicide bomber wounded twenty-two people at a Protestant church in Solo, Java. Hundreds of worshipers were leaving at the end of the service when the bomb went off. It was strapped to the terrorist's stomach and was packed with nails, nuts, and bolts.

On October 8, 2001, authorities arrested three men suspected of planning a suicide bombing in April at a mosque in a police compound in Cirebon, West Java, and another on September 25. The April bomber died and injured several dozen police officers when he set off the bomb, spewing nails, nuts, and bolts into the crowd. One of the planners was Heru Komarudin, 31, detained at a market in central Jakarta. Two others with links to him were arrested in Bekasi, a Jakarta suburb, where police confiscated two boxes of suspicious materials. One of the men was a computer repairman. The September 25 bomber, Achmad Yosepa Hayat, was a member of Jamaah Ansharut Tauhid, which was founded by Abu Bakar Baasyir, spiritual leader of Jemaah Islamiyah.

September 27, 2011—Yemen—An al Qaeda suicide bomber attacked the convoy of Defense Minister Mohammed Nasser Ahmed in Aden by driving his car next to the convoy on a coastal highway. Several security officers were injured but Ahmed was unharmed. The previous month his car hit a landmine in Abyan Province, killing two guards.

September 27, 2011—Internet—The seventh edition of al Qaeda in the Arabian Peninsula–sponsored *Inspire* magazine was posted. The group noted 9/11 by devoting the edition to "The Greatest Special Operations of All Time." The edition complained that Iranian President Mahmoud Ahmadinejad was stirring conspiracy theories by crediting the U.S. government rather than al Qaeda with 9/11. Abu Suhail wrote, "The Iranian government has professed on the tongue of its president Ahmadinejad that it does not believe al Qaeda was behind 9/11 but rather, the U.S. government. So we may ask the question: why would Iran ascribe to such a ridiculous belief that stands in the face of all logic and evidence?" An article attributed to the late Osama bin Laden counseled, "Do not let America's front and its troops seem

hard and become great in your eyes." Samir Khan wrote the main article, "The Media Conflict." *Inspire* noted, "While America was focused on battling our mujahideen in the mountains of Afghanistan and the streets of Iraq, the jihadi media and its supporters were in fifth gear. Thousands of productions were produced and dispersed to both the net and real world. Something that was produced thousands of feet above in the mountains of Afghanistan was found distributed in the streets of London and California. Ideas that disseminated from the lips of the mujahideen's leaders were carried out in Madrid and Times Square." The edition included an article by Anwar al-Aulaqi entitled "Targeting the Populations of Countries That Are at War with the Muslims." These were the last articles written by Khan and al-Aulaqi.

September 28, 2011—United States—Authorities arrested U.S. citizen Rezwan Ferdaus, 26, on charges of planning to fly seven remote-controlled aircraft filled with C-4 explosives into the Pentagon and the U.S. Capitol to "kill as many people as possible." He had told FBI undercover agents purporting to be al Qaeda operatives that "I just can't stop. There is no other choice for me. This is what we have to do. This is the righteous way ... to terrorize enemies of Allah." Ferdaus rigged mobile phones to serve as electrical switches to set off the explosives and gave eight of them to the FBI agents. They later told him that the devices had killed three U.S. soldiers and injured four others in Iraq, to which he replied, "That was exactly what I wanted." He told FBI agents he had been inspired by videos and literature promoted by al Qaeda, which showed him "how evil America is and that jihad is the solution." He had earlier planned to attack federal buildings before he met the undercover operatives, taking pictures of the Capitol and Pentagon. He was working with a former felon who introduced him to the FBI agents in March. The FBI gave him $7,000 to purchase a remote-controlled plane, and gave him 25 pounds of C-4, three grenades, and six AK-47 rifles, all of which remained under the control of the FBI. He had kept a model plane to be used in the attack in a storage locker in suburban Boston rented under the name Dave Winfield. He gave the FBI two thumb drives with details of his plan. He planned to recruit six snipers to attack people fleeing the bombed Pentagon. He bought the plane in August. The FBI delivered the explosives to a storage facility in Framingham, Massachusetts, where they arrested him after he took possession.

The planes were more than 5 feet long, with a 4-foot wing span, and could carry 10 to 12 pounds of explosives. They were models of the F-4 Phantom and F-86 Sabre.

He was arraigned in U.S. District Court in Worcester, Massachusetts, and ordered held without bail. A dangerousness hearing was scheduled for October 3, 2011.

He lived in the basement of his parents' home in Ashland, Massachusetts. He played with the psychedelic Latin/funk band Goosepimp Orchestra and the Slik Road band. In 2003, he and two Ashland High School classmates were charged for pouring concrete in front of ten school doors. He was placed on probation and ordered to pay $406 in restitution. He earned a bachelor of science degree in physics in 2008 from Northeastern University.

Ferdaus pleaded not guilty in a court in Worcester, Massachusetts, on October 3, 2011. On July 10, 2012, his lawyers and prosecutors agreed to a plea deal in which he would plead guilty to two charges—attempting to provide material support to terrorists and attempting to damage and destroy federal buildings by means of explosives. The charges carried a thirty-five-year maximum sentence, but the attorneys agreed to request a seventeen-year sentence followed by ten years of supervised release. Ferdaus pleaded guilty on July 20, 2012, in a Boston federal court. He was sentenced on November 1, 2012, to seventeen years in prison. His attorney, Miriam Conrad, claimed he was mentally ill.

September 29, 2011—United States—The U.S. Department of the Treasury (DOT) listed Lashkar-e-Taiba leaders Zafar Iqbal and Hafiz Abdul Salam Bhuttavi as specially designated global terrorists. Iqbal was a co-founder and key fund-raiser for the group. Bhuttavi is its deputy emir and main ideologue. DOT also designated Hajji Faizullah Khan Noorzai, Hajji Malik Noorzai, Abdur Rehman, Abdul Aziz Abbasin, and Fazal Rahim for supporting al Qaeda, the Taliban, or the Haqqani network. Faizullah is a prominent Taliban financier who collected more than $100,000 from Gulf donors and invested funds for senior Taliban leaders. The money went toward training Taliban and al Qaeda terrorists to attack Afghan military forces. Pakistani-based businessman Malik was accused of investing "millions of dollars" for the Taliban. He also managed a madrassa on the Afghanistan-Pakistan border. He stored vehicles later used as car bombs. Rehman was a Taliban terrorist facilitator for three years; his Karachi madrassa supported the Tal-

iban. He also funded al Qaeda and helped other terrorist groups. Abbasin, a key Haqqani commander, was behind ambushes of Afghan supply vehicles and trained fighters. Pakistan authorities arrested Rahim in 2010. He had been a financier for al Qaeda and the Islamic Movement of Uzbekistan, distributing funds to terrorists and recruiting terrorists. The United States froze their assets, prevented them from using financial institutions, and could prosecute them for terrorist activities.

September 30, 2011—Yemen—Sunni cleric and al Qaeda in the Arabian Peninsula (AQAP) operations chief Anwar al-Aulaqi, 40, and AQAP-sponsored *Inspire* magazine editor Samir Khan, 25, were killed in a 9:55 a.m. air strike on their Toyota pickup truck in Khashef, northern Yemen, 87 miles east of Sana'a. Tribal leaders said seven people were killed in the strike. Al-Aulaqi was staying in the house of Khamis bin Arfaaj, a prominent Islamist who had run for the country's parliament for the Islah Party, which has AQAP ties, according to the government. Authorities were attempting to determine whether they had also killed Ibrahim Hassan al-Asiri, a Saudi bomb maker who had created the explosive devices used in the Christmas 2009 underwear bomber plot and the October 2010 AQAP cargo plane plot.

September 30, 2011—Turkey—A suicide bomber set off his explosives at a paramilitary police station in Kemer, killing one person and wounding two others.

October 2011—Somalia—UN Childrens' Fund (UNICEF) reported that twenty-four children were killed and fifty-eight injured during conflicts that month.

October 1, 2011—Kenya—Ten al-Shabaab terrorists kidnapped Marie Dedieu, 66, a French woman, from her vacation home in Manda Island in the north and sped off with her on a boat towards Somalia. Kenyan navy units failed to stop the getaway despite injuring several of the abductors in a shootout. Officials said the terrorists were operating from Ras Kamboni, Somalia. The wheelchair-using Frenchwoman lives in Kenya six months each year. The woman, a quadriplegic suffering from cancer, died in captivity in Somalia. Her death was reported by the press on October 19, 2011. 11100101

October 4, 2011—Pakistan—Sunni extremists riding motorcycles shot to death thirteen Shi'ites and one Sunni after ordering them off a bus and lining them up in southwest Pakistan. Another four Shi'ites and two Sunnis were injured. The victims had been headed to work in a vegetable market in the Quetta suburbs.

October 4, 2011—Somalia—A suicide bomber killed seventy-two people in Mogadishu by setting off a truck bomb loaded with drums of fuel outside the Education Ministry. Students accompanied by their parents were registering for scholarships offered by the Turkish government. Another forty-two were wounded; many suffered amputated limbs and burns. The group claimed credit via an Internet posting. "Our mujahideen fighters have entered a place where ministers and AMISOM foreigners stay." AMISOM is the African Union peacekeeping team consisting of Ugandan and Burundian forces. The next day, al-Shabaab spokesman Ali Mohamud Rage promised further attacks. He said the group was warning those who thought the group had fled from Mogadishu for good in August. "We wish to inform the Muslim people that the campaign against infidels will be back-to-back, and by God's grace, will increase day by day and will increase in the coming hours."

October 5, 2011—Afghanistan—Authorities announced the arrests of six people planning to assassinate President Hamid Karzai. The duo confessed to working with an Egyptian and a Bangladeshi operating out of Pakistan who had links to al Qaeda and the Haqqani network, a Taliban affiliate. The group included Emal Habib, chairman of the microbiology department at Kabul University's medical school, three students including a fourth-year medical student, and Mohibullah Ahmady, a security guard at the presidential palace who was to kill Karzai during a trip to the provinces. Ahmady was from Karzai's home village of Karz. The plotters had worked with the Pakistan-based duo for a year. They had traveled to Pakistan to learn bomb making and how to fire guns. The president's office clarified on October 8 that Ahmady was not a presidential bodyguard, but rather a member of the palace protection unit assigned to an outer gate, with no access to the palace.

October 10, 2011—Sudan—In a late night attack, gunmen killed three UN African Union peacekeepers and injured another six who were guarding the Zam Zam camp for displaced people in North Darfur. 11101001

October 11, 2011—United States—Authorities announced that they had disrupted an Iran-backed assassination plot against Saudi Ambassador to the United States Adel A. al-Jubeir, 49, by Manssor Arbabsiar, 56, a naturalized U.S. citizen of Iranian descent who was a used-car salesman living in Round Rock, Texas, and Gholam Sha-

kuri, an Iran-based member of Iran's elite covert action Quds Force unit of the Revolutionary Guards Corps. Authorities arrested Arbabsiar on September 29 in New York's John F. Kennedy Airport after being denied entry to Mexico to contact Los Zetas. Shakuri remained at large. The duo had referred to the plot as "buying a Chevrolet." They were charged with conspiracy to murder a foreign official, conspiracy to use a weapon of mass destruction, and conspiracy to commit an act of international terrorism. Arbabsiar told authorities he had been recruited and funded by members of the Quds Force. The news media said the plotters hoped to strike other targets, including the Saudi and Israeli embassies, after the assassination. The plan was to blow up a restaurant frequented by the ambassador. The U.S. government imposed financial sanctions on five Iranians, including the two suspects and Quds Force leader Qassem Soleimani. Arbabsiar was arraigned on October 11 in U.S. District Court in Manhattan and ordered held without bail. His court-appointed attorney was Sabrina Shroff.

The complaint indicated that Arbabsiar was approached by his cousin—Abdul Reza Shahlai, 54, a senior commander in the Quds Force—in Iran in the spring regarding a plot to kidnap Jubeir. Arbabsiar replied that he knew Mexican drug traffickers who "are willing to undertake criminal activity in exchange for money." Arbabsiar told a Drug Enforcement Administration informant who was posing as a member of a Mexican drug cartel that he would need four men to carry out the attack and would pay $1.5 million. He wired a $100,000 down payment to an account monitored by the FBI. He dismissed as "no big deal" that U.S. senators and others could be killed in the restaurant bombing. "They want that guy done. If the hundred go with him, [blank] them."

On October 24, 2011, Arbabsiar pleaded not guilty to a five-count indictment in the U.S. District Court in Manhattan.

On October 3, 2012, U.S. prosecutors told the court that Dr. Gregory B. Saathoff, a University of Virginia psychiatrist who had examined Arbabsiar for more than thirty hours, had determined that he was not mentally ill and had not experienced manic episodes when questioned by federal agents. On October 17, 2012, Arbabsiar pleaded guilty to plotting to assassinate the ambassador. Sentencing was set for January 23, 2013. Gholam Shakuri, also charged in the plot, remained at large in Iran. 11101101

October 12, 2011—Internet—Ayman al-Zawahiri issued a video on Islamist Web sites in which

he called on Algerians to mimic Libyans in over-
throwing their government. He also attacked
Egypt's military leadership for maintaining ties to
Israel and not backing the Arab Spring uprisings
against Tunisian leader Zine al-Abidine Ben Ali
and Egyptian President Hosni Mubarak. "Oh
lions of Algeria! Look at your brothers in Tunisia
and Libya when they cast their leaders into the
dustbin of history. So, why don't you revolt
against your despot [President Abdelaziz Boute-
flika]? ... The Muslim nation across the world ex-
pects you to deliver a model of jihad and struggle
by opposing the corrupt dictators." He called the
Libyan rebels "our people." "I congratulate our
brothers, the mujahideen who carried out the two
operations in Eilat [southern Israel] and I pray for
God to shower them with rewards ... The military
council did not move when Qadhafi's forces
crushed our people in Libya, the military council
did not move when Israel bombed Gaza." He
called on Egyptian protestors to continue to ha-
rass the Israeli Embassy, saying, "You have stormed
the Israeli Embassy and expelled the Israeli ambassador. Don't allow him to return. You should
continue with this popular uprising until the Israeli Embassy is closed and the peace treaty revoked."

October 13, 2011—Kenya—Suspected al-Shabaab terrorists kidnapped two Spanish women
working for Doctors Without Borders at the
Dadaab refugee camp in North Eastern Province.
A driver was wounded in the attack. Security
forces chased the kidnappers toward the border
with Somalia. Dadaab is 60 miles from the border.
It is the world's largest refugee camp, hosting four
hundred thousand people. The next day, security
forces found the aid workers' abandoned vehicle
in a desert. 11101301

October 13, 2011—Pakistan—The *Washington
Post* reported that U.S. missile strikes killed terrorist leaders in North Waziristan. Among the
dead was Ahmed Omar Abdul Rahman, alias Saifullah, 45, son of the blind cleric who was jailed
in connection with the bombing of the New York
City World Trade Center on February 26, 1993.
A separate strike killed Janbaz Zadran, a deputy
of Haqqani network leader Sirajuddin Haqqani
and close aide to Haqqani's brother Badruddin.
He was killed in a drone strike in Dane Darpa
Khel, Pakistan. He had handled the group's fi-
nances and arms shipments. Pakistani authorities
said the dead also included Khan Mohammad,
deputy of Taliban commander Maulvi Nazir.

October 14, 2011—Pakistan—The *Washington
Post* reported that U.S. missile strikes killed Abu

Miqdad al-Masri and Abd al-Rahman al-Yemeni,
two al Qaeda terrorists with ties to the group's
senior leadership, in Pakistan's tribal areas. Al-
Masri was a bin Laden associate.

October 15, 2011—Yemen—A U.S. missile strike
killed nine al Qaeda terrorists, including Abdul-
Rahman al-Aulaqi—16-year-old son of Anwar al-
Aulaqi—and his 17-year-old cousin and Egyptian-
born Ibrahim al-Bana, propaganda chief of al
Qaeda in the Arabian Peninsula, in Azzan. Tribal
elders said four other members of the al-Aulaqi
clan were killed, along with local militant Maulana Iftikhar. U.S. officials privately told the media
that they were not aware that al-Aulaqi was in the
area when the order to fire the missiles came.

October 20, 2011—Libya—Libyan dictator
Mo'ammar Qadhafi, fleeing his hometown of Sirte
in a one hundred–SUV convoy, was wounded and
captured by supporters of the Transitional National Government. He was pulled out of a cul-
vert, beaten, and shot in the head. His body was
shown on worldwide television.

October 20, 2011—Spain—The Basque Nation
and Liberty announced that it was ending its
forty-three-year armed struggle for independence
and said it wanted to open talks with Spain and
France. It had earlier announced a cease-fire.

October 21, 2011—Philippines—Three South
Koreans scouting for mining opportunities were
kidnapped from their hotel in Cagayan de Oro
and taken to Lanao del Sur. The kidnappers contacted the hostages' relatives via the hostages' cell
phones. One—Choi Inn So—was found on Mindanao Island on November 26. The military rescued the other two—Wu Seok-Bung and Kim
Nam-Du—on November 27, 2011. Choi was treated
in a local hospital for an ulcer. 11102101

October 23, 2011—Algeria—The jihadi Movement for Unity and Jihad in West Africa (MUJAO)
kidnapped three aid workers—Italian Rossella
Urru and Spaniards Enric Gonyalons and Ainhoa
Fernandez del Rincon—from a southern refugee
camp in Tindouf, near the border with Mauritania, and spirited them to northern Mali. On December 9, 2011, al Qaeda in the Islamic Maghreb
denied involvement in the kidnapping. They were
freed on July 19, 2012, and reunited with their
families in Europe. The group claimed that they
received a ransom of 15 million Euros ($18.4 mil-
lion) and obtained the release of two imprisoned
MUJAO members. MUJAO spokesman Adnan
Abu Elwalid Sahraoui threatened to stage more
kidnappings, observing, "We will take them as
soon as they enter the territories of Mauritania,

Mali, Algeria, or Niger." Gen. Gilbert Diendere, a senior security aide to Burkina Faso President Blaise Compaore, was one of the mediators. 1110 2301

October 24, 2011—Kenya—Two grenades went off in Nairobi, killing one person and injuring twenty. The first bomb went off at a blue-collar nightclub, injuring a dozen people. The second bomb, at a downtown bus station, killed one person and injured eight. Two days earlier, the U.S. Embassy had warned of credible information of an imminent terrorist attack. The bombs targeted Kenyans rather than foreigners. Kenyan police arrested a man with thirteen grenades, four revolvers, an assault rifle, a machine gun, and seven hundred rounds of ammunition. Later that month, a Kenyan court sentenced to life Elgiva Bwire Oliacha, 28, a non–Somali Kenyan citizen, after he pleaded guilty to charges of throwing the grenade at the bus stop.

October 25, 2011—Somalia—Three staffers from the Danish Refugee Council—American Jessica Buchanan, 32, Dane Poul Thisted, 60, and a Somali man—were kidnapped near Galkayo at 3:00 p.m. in the semi-autonomous Puntland area. The trio worked for the Council's Danish Demining Group. Some of the aid workers' bodyguards were arrested. Several Somali leaders were assisting in resolving the case. The Habargedir clan condemned the kidnapping by al-Shabaab terrorists; other sources attributed the attack to pirates. The gunmen demanded $10 million ransom and rejected an offer of $1.5 million.

In November 2011, the captors permitted a physician to examine Buchanan for a kidney ailment.

On January 25, 2012, two dozen U.S. Navy SEAL Team 6 members rescued Buchanan and Thisted. One dozen parachuted from an Air Force Special Operations plane to a place 2 miles from the hideout in Hiimo Gaabo, south of Galkayo. The SEALs killed nine terrorists, then whisked away the hostages in helicopters. No SEALs were harmed. The rescued hostages were flown to a U.S. air base in Djibouti. 11102501

October 25, 2011—Thailand—Islamic militants were suspected of setting off bombs in twenty-three places in Yala city, killing three and injuring forty-four.

October 27, 2011—Somalia—Al-Shabaab gunmen ambushed Kenyan soldiers, killing one and injuring another. This was the first Kenyan battlefield casualty in its thirteen days of operations against al-Shabaab, which had been crossing the Kenya border to conduct attacks. 11102701

October 28, 2011—Kenya—Al-Shabaab set off a bomb against a Kenyan security forces vehicle, wounding four police officers. 11102801

October 28, 2011—Bosnia—A radical Islamist gunman opened fire with an automatic rifle at the front of the U.S. Embassy in Sarajevo during rush hour, wounding a guard. Authorities said he was targeting the building in a terrorist attack. A police SWAT team shot and arrested the bearded gunman, who was wearing a long brown camouflage coat. The *Dnevni Avaz* newspaper said he was Mevlid Jasarevic, 23, from Novi Pazar in Sandzak region in southwest Serbia. He was reportedly a follower of Wahhabism. He had a police record which included an arrest in November 2010 for carrying a large knife outside a visit by the U.S. Ambassador to Serbia to Novi Pazar. Jasarevic had been deported in 2008 from Austria after a robbery in Vienna. Serbia police briefly detained seventeen of his associates in Sandzak. 11102802

October 28, 2011—Yemen—A car bomb exploded beneath the car of Maj. Ali al-Haji, battalion commander in the Central Security Forces (CSF), as he was driving from his office to his home via a market near the Arish area of Aden. He was the head of counterterrorism for the CSF. Two bystander children were wounded. Al Qaeda was suspected.

October 29, 2011—Afghanistan—A suicide car bomber hit an armored Rhino bus in a NATO military convoy as it passed the private American University near the Darul Aman Palace, killing thirteen NATO personnel (five soldiers and eight civilians), two British civilians working for a building contractor, a Canadian, and four Afghans, including two students. Among the dead was Canadian Master Cpl. Byron Greff. The injured included Afghan citizen Ahmad Fawad, 20, who sustained wounds to the face and left arm. A Taliban spokesman texted that the group had killed "Sixteen foreign soldiers, one civilian" and injured many others. The group claimed that 1,500 pounds of explosives were used. 11102901

October 29, 2011—Somalia—Two al-Shabaab suicide bombers and ten gunmen attacked an African Union peacekeepers' base in Mogadishu, setting off a two-hour gun battle. One of the bombers was Abdisalan Hussein Ali, 22, a Somali American born in Somalia but who had lived in Minneapolis, according to the terrorists' posting of his suicide message on a Web site. He had been a pre-med student at the University of Minnesota before he disappeared in November 2008. 1110 2902

October 29, 2011—Turkey—Two people died and twenty were injured when a female suicide bomber set off her explosives in the primarily Kurdish town of Bingol, near the local headquarters of the governing Justice and Development Party. Turkey was celebrating the eighty-eighth anniversary of the founding of the republic. Kurdish PKK rebels were suspected, although no one claimed credit.

October 30, 2011—Thailand—Muslim insurgents were suspected of killing four people when four gunmen riding two motorcycles shot dead two men and a woman at a grocery store in Narathiwat during the morning. Gunmen on a pickup truck shot dead another man in neighboring Songkhla Province. Terrorists also set off ten homemade bombs at grocery stores, shops, and residences in five of the thirteen districts in Narathiwat Province during the evening, causing no casualties.

October 31, 2011—Afghanistan—At 6:10 a.m., a Taliban terrorist crashed his pickup truck into a checkpoint at a nongovernmental organization's facility near the offices of the UN High Commissioner for Refugees (UNHCR) in Kandahar, then set off explosives. Three terrorists ran through the hole in the security wall and seized the building. The gun battle lasted until 1:00 p.m. Three UNHCR staffers were killed and two wounded in the attack. A total of five people died, including two security contractors; six people, including a police officer, were wounded. 11103101

October 31, 2011—Kazakhstan—Jund al-Khilafah (Soldiers of the Caliphate) claimed credit for a suicide bombing in Atyrau. They released a video demanding the repeal of new laws requiring official registration of religious groups and banning state employees from praying at work.

November 2011—Venezuela—A Chilean official was kidnapped. He escaped soon after but was shot in the leg. 11119901

November 2011—Azerbaijan—The *Washington Post* reported on May 28, 2012, that Iran was behind a plot to attack U.S. Embassy officials and their families with snipers with noise-suppressed rifles and a car bomb. Azerbaijan authorities detained nearly two dozen people in January and March 2012. It was unclear whether Hizballah was to provide the muscle. Intercepted messages, according to the *Post*, were traced to Azerbaijan criminal Balagardash Dashdev who had links to Iranian militants. In October 2011, he had coordinated the shipment of explosives, weapons, and cash to local contacts. Potential targets were to include the country's small Jewish community, diplomats, and foreign-owned businesses in Baku. At least ten Iranians snuck into the country. Locals conducted surveillance against potential targets, including a Jewish elementary school, a U.S.-owned fast food restaurant, and an oil company office, according to the Azerbaijan government. Dashdev told investigators that he planned to avenge the deaths of Iranian nuclear scientists. His confession ran on local television.

November 1, 2011—United States—Authorities arrested four Georgia men plotting to conduct an attack with explosives and ricin against U.S. government buildings in Atlanta, Washington, DC, and other U.S. cities. They also planned to attack officials with firearms, explosives, and ricin. They were inspired by *Absolved*, an online novel written by a former Alabama militiaman, according to prosecutors. The ricin would be blown out of a moving car on a highway. One of the men was a former lab technician at the Agriculture Department and allegedly had obtained castor beans, from which ricin can be made. Defendant Frederick Thomas created a "bucket list" of targets, government workers, politicians, corporate leaders, and members of the news media, telling an undercover FBI informant that a politician and others needed to be "taken out" to "make the country right again." "When it comes to saving the Constitution, that means some people gotta die." The four, aged 65 to 73, appeared in U.S. District Court in Gainesville, Georgia, on November 2. They were identified as Thomas, Dan Roberts, Ray H. Adams, and Samuel J. Crump, members of a fringe group of a militia organization called the "covert group" which met in the Georgia foothills. They met with an FBI informant, who recorded their meetings, and by a federal agent undercover as an arms dealer. Thomas and Roberts were charged with conspiracy to receive unregistered firearms. Crump and Adams were charged with attempting to produce a biological agent for use as a weapon.

On April 10, 2012, Thomas and Roberts pleaded guilty in federal court in Gainesville, Georgia, to conspiring to obtain an unregistered explosive and an illegal gun silencer. Thomas, 73, and Roberts, 67, faced five years in prison and a $250,000 fine. Adams, 55, and Crump, 68, were charged with conspiring and attempting to make ricin. On August 22, 2012, U.S. District Judge Richard Story sentenced the duo to five years in prison. Thomas was represented by attorney Jeffrey Ertel.

November 2, 2011—France—A firebomb gutted the headquarters of the satirical magazine *Charlie*

Hebdo after it ran a cartoon image of the prophet Muhammad on its cover with the words "100 lashes if you don't die of laughter." It said Muhammad had guest-edited the edition. The magazine's Web site was hacked and showed images of a mosque with the words "No God but Allah."

November 3, 2011—Afghanistan—At 10:00 a.m., a suicide bomber set off his vehicle at a logistics company that works with Italian NATO troops near Herat Airport. A second vehicle crashed into a second checkpoint and exploded. The two drivers wore Afghan Army uniforms. Three terrorists, also in army uniforms, ran into the building and fired on guards. The three-hour gun battle killed two Afghan security guards and five terrorists. Four people were wounded. 11110301

November 4, 2011—Nigeria—A car bomb exploded at a three-story building used as a military office and barracks in Damaturu, injuring two soldiers.

Four bombs exploded in Maiduguri. Boko Haram was suspected.

November 5, 2011—Nigeria—Bombings and armed attacks in the northeast Yobe State city of Damaturu against three police stations, a bank, mosques, and churches killed sixty-seven and injured more than one hundred. During the three hours of attacks, the gunmen fired on the police headquarters and the antiterrorism office before moving to churches and mosques. Three suicide bombers drove a stolen black SUV toward the three-story Joint Task Force headquarters but could not get through the gate. They set off their explosives, damaging roofs and walls. Two other bombs went off at other military facilities, injuring several soldiers. Other gunmen raided nearby Potiskum village, killing two people. Boko Haram ("Western education is sinful.") claimed credit and said it would continue its attacks.

November 5, 2011—Nigeria—The U.S. Embassy warned that Boko Haram could bomb the Hilton, Nicon Luxury, and Sheraton hotels in Abuja. The hotels are frequented by diplomats, politicians, and local business leaders. The attacks could occur during Eid al-Adha celebrations.

November 7, 2011—Sudan—Armed gunmen killed a Sierra Leonean member of an African Union-United Nations Mission in Darfur patrol near Nyala. Two other Sierra Leonean soldiers were wounded. UN peacekeepers arrested a suspect and turned him over to Sudanese police. 11110701

November 7, 2011—Afghanistan—An Afghan soldier fired on his Australian trainers in Oruzgan Province, wounding three Australian soldiers and two Afghan soldiers. The gunmen stole a Humvee and escaped. The vehicle was later found abandoned and on fire. 11110702

November 9, 2011—Venezuela—Three gunmen in an SUV pulled up to the Valencia home of the parents of Washington Nationals catcher Wilson Ramos, 24, and kidnapped him. The next day, authorities found the SUV in Bejuma. Police later found a car in Aguas Claras that was used to transport Ramos after the SUV was abandoned. They also found a house containing provisions for the kidnapping. No ransom demand was made.

He was freed by security authorities, including the National Guard and the judicial police, fifty-one hours later in a raid on a remote cabin in Montalban. Ramos hid under a bed while the kidnappers responded with heavy gunfire. Four Venezuelan kidnappers were taken into custody; authorities were searching for four Colombians. Media reports suggested that either common criminals or leftist rebels were behind the kidnapping. Ramos said that the men in the cabin had Colombian accents and often talked "about the guerrilla" in Colombia. As of the Ramos kidnapping, there had been 1,050 kidnappings in Venezuela in 2011. Venezuela logged more than 17,000 murders in 2010, a rate higher than Iraq's. Ramos stayed in the country so that he could play in Venezuela's winter baseball league. He told reporters that the kidnappers "did not tie me up, they did not tape my mouth, they did not have a hood on me. They did not mistreat me physically, but psychologically the damage was very big." Some said if "there is no collaboration things will get difficult." He said it appeared that the kidnappers had watched his movements for some time.

November 10, 2011—Egypt—Bombers set off remote-controlled explosives, shutting down the gas pipeline between Egypt, Israel, and Jordan on the Northern Sinai. The first bomb went off near Mazar, 18 miles west of al-Arish. A second bomb went off west of al-Arish near a pumping station. Extended wires were found at the scene. Authorities said the saboteurs used two trucks. The pipeline is run by Gasco, an Egyptian gas transport company that is a subsidiary of EGAS, the national gas company. 11111001

November 10, 2011—United States—The Illinois Statewide Terrorism and Intelligence Center initially claimed that foreign-based hackers using an address in Russia had caused a pump at a Curran-Gardner Townships Public Water District water plant, outside Springfield, Illinois, to fail. It would have been the first known cyberattack to damage U.S. infrastructure. Authorities later said it was not a foreign cyberattack. By November 23, federal officials said there was no evidence that foreign hackers were involved.

November 11, 2011—Turkey—At 5:00 p.m., a lone Kurdish gunman seajacked the ferry *Kartepe*, which was carrying twenty-four passengers and crew near Izmit on the Marmara Sea. The gunman, who demanded that the attack be televised live, was later killed by security forces.

November 11, 2011—United States—A single bullet hit a White House window at 9:30 p.m.; several others hit an exterior wall. Authorities said the bullet was fired by Oscar Ramiro Ortega-Hernandez, celebrating his 21st birthday. The Idaho man drove from his home in Idaho Falls and stopped his 1998 black Honda Accord near 17th Street and Constitution Avenue Northwest. He was 750 yards from the south face of the White House. He abandoned the car, which had stalled, on the lawn of the U.S. Institute of Peace in the 2300 block of Constitution Avenue and ran away. He apparently crossed the Theodore Roosevelt Memorial Bridge into Virginia. Police found a loaded Romanian-made Cugir SA semiautomatic rifle with a telescopic sight, three spare magazines of 7.62 × 39-mm ammunition, several boxes of bullets, brass knuckles, nine spent shell casings, and an aluminum baseball bat in his car. State police arrested him on November 16 at 12:30 p.m. at a Hampton Inn hotel in Indiana, Pennsylvania.

He was initially charged with felony possession of a dangerous weapon. After he told authorities that he "needed to kill" President Obama—who was in San Diego at the time—he was charged with attempted assassination. He had earlier been arrested on minor counts in Idaho, Texas, and Utah. He did not appear to have any ties to radical organizations nor the Occupy Washington protestors. He told investigators that Obama was "the devil" and "the antichrist" and he "will not stop until it's done." He told authorities that he was the second coming of Jesus. He faced life in prison. He was initially arraigned before a federal magistrate in Pittsburgh. Bond was denied. He was to appear in U.S. District Court in Washington, DC; a full hearing was postponed until December 12. Prosecutors on November 28 asked for a more extensive psychiatric examination. He was on probation for resisting arrest and obstructing justice stemming from his arrest for possession of drug paraphernalia. Three Idaho witnesses had known of his intention to harm the President.

On January 17, 2012, a federal grand jury indicted Oscar Ramiro Ortega-Hernandez with attempting to assassinate the president, three counts each of assaulting a federal officer, assault with a dangerous weapon, and possessing a gun during a violent crime. There had been three Secret Service officers in the line of fire when the shots were fired at the White House. He was indicted on five counts of using a firearm during a violent crime, one count of illegally transporting a gun across state lines, and one count of damaging federal property. The indictment followed his initial appearance before a federal magistrate in Pittsburgh, who ordered him to remain in custody. He faced life in prison. He was charged On May 11, 2012, with two additional offenses, "injury to a dwelling" and "placing lives in jeopardy," each punishable by up to twenty years. He was scheduled to appear in U.S. District Court in Washington on July 20 for a status hearing.

November 12, 2011—Kazakhstan—M. K. Kariyev, a jihadi gunman, shot to death at least seven people before blowing himself up in Taraz. He initially shot two members of the Kazakh security service, then broke into a weapons store at 11:30 a.m., killing a guard and a customer, then stole two semiautomatic rifles and ammunition. He then shot to death two pursuing police officers and took their weapons, including an assault rifle. He took over a car, which he drove home, where he picked up a grenade launcher. He then attacked the regional headquarters of the National Security Committee, but was wounded. When the police moved to arrest him, he blew himself up, killing police commander Capt. G. Baitasov. Witnesses said he was an ethnic Kazakh.

The previous week, the newly-formed Jund al-Khilafah was believed responsible for a suicide bombing in Atyrau that killed only the terrorist. Two similar bombings in May left only the attackers dead.

November 12, 2011—Qatar—Authorities discovered an Iran-linked, four-person Bahraini terrorist cell plotting attacks in Bahrain. Authorities seized a laptop with information about the Saudi Embassy and Interior Ministry building in Manama. The four were extradited to Bahrain.

November 12, 2011—Yemen—Soldiers killed six al Qaeda-linked fighters in Zinjibar; six soldiers were wounded.

November 12, 2011—Egypt—Authorities arrested Abdel-Halim Hassan Heneidi, a terrorist leader in el-Arish. He was part of al Qaeda in the Sinai, which calls for an Islamic emirate.

November 13, 2011—Egypt—At dawn, authorities arrested Mohammed Eid Muslih Hamad, alias El-Hiti, at a seaside vacation house in el-Arish in the northern Sinai. He ran an al Qaeda-inspired group in the Sinai that was responsible for attacks on police and a gas pipeline that transports fuel to Jordan and Israel. He was being questioned regarding a series of attacks in August in southern Israel. He was part of al Qaeda in the Sinai, which calls for an Islamic emirate.

November 14, 2011—Germany—German prosecutors announced the arrests of two neo–Nazi terrorist cell members linked with ten murders, mostly of individuals of Turkish and Greek origin. Authorities seized a confessor video in which the terrorists claimed credit for killing eight Turks and a Greek from 2000 to 2006 and a female police officer in 2007 during the "Doener Murder Series." The name came from the workplace of some of the victims, who sold doener kabobs. Some were shot in the face at point-blank range. The video also claimed the group was behind more than a dozen bank robberies and a nail-bomb attack in Cologne in 2004 on a street with mostly Turkish and Kurdish residents. The Prosecutor General's Office announced that two of the terrorists, Uwe Boehnhardt and Uwe Mundlos, were found dead in a burning motor home in Eisenach on November 4, 2011. Flatmate Beate Zschaepe, 36, set off a bomb in Zwickau in an apparent attempt to destroy evidence and then fled. She surrendered to local police on November 8 and was charged with co-founding and belonging to a terrorist organization. Investigators found weapons used in the attacks, along with pro–Nazi materials. On November 13, authorities arrested Holger G. (or Holger Z.) near Hannover on suspicion of involvement in terrorist activities by the National Socialist Underground (NSU). He appeared before a judge on November 14, detained as a suspected accomplice in the killings. *Der Spiegel* called the group the Brown Army Faction.

Three of the attackers had previous criminal records. In 1998, Beate Zschaepe, Uwe Mundlos, and Uwe Boehnhardt were arrested after preparing a bomb attack but were not kept under surveillance following their release.

November 15, 2011—Kenya—A landmine exploded at the Dadaab refugee camp—the world's largest—injuring two guards. A UN official said the bomb targeted a passing police convoy. Somali militants were believed responsible. They had set off a bomb at the same camp earlier in the month. 11119901, 11111501

November 15, 2011—Internet—Ayman al-Zawahiri released a thirty-minute Internet video entitled *Days with the Imam, Part One*, in which he cited Osama bin Laden's "superior morals" and loyalty, noting his "delicate ... human side," and describing him as noble, generous, and good. He wanted to "shed light on the human side of Osama bin Laden—his noble, refined side."

> People probably don't know, they remember the lion of Islam threatening America and Bush, but people don't know that he was a very delicate, nice, shy man ... No one has ever met with him, friend or foe, and not spoken of his nobility and his modesty ... He was known for crying and tearing up very easily. He would tell me that certain brothers would tell him to try and hold them back a bit and I told him that it was a blessing he had ... I had the honor of the companionship of that man for long periods in travel and in different circumstances ... Sheikh Osama would feel great sadness if he felt that his brothers in the path of jihad had been oppressed or had not reached their rightful goal. That man was very loyal to his brothers and he was intent on remembering them in virtue and praising their way ... He used to remember the nineteen who attacked the idiot of the age, America, in the Pentagon, the seat of its military leadership, and in New York, the symbol of its economic power.

He promised that other bin Laden tribute videos would follow.

November 15, 2011—Colombia—Rodrigo Londono, 52, alias Timochenko, alias Timoleon Jimenez, was named head of the Revolutionary Armed Forces of Colombia (FARC) on November 15, 2011, when he was 52 years old. He had joined the FARC in 1982 and had risen to become a member of its Secretariat in 1989. He was believed to be a senior FARC liaison with the Venezuelan government. He faced more than one hundred arrest warrants on charges of terrorism, kidnapping, and aggravated homicide.

November 19, 2011—United States—NYPD police arrested unemployed al Qaeda sympathizer Jose Pimental Sosa, alias Muhammad Yusuf, 27, a Dominican Republic-born naturalized U.S. citizen living in Manhattan, who plotted to bomb a police station in Bayonne, New Jersey, police and post offices in New York City, and U.S. troops returning home. Mayor Michael R. Bloomberg said he was motivated by terrorist propaganda and opposition to U.S. military presence in Iraq and Afghanistan. He had decided to build bombs in August and was further spurred on by the killing of Anwar al-Aulaqi on September 30. He appeared to be working alone. He was accused of having an explosive substance that he planned to use against people and property to terrorize the public. The bombs were to be studded with nails to increase injuries. He faced twenty-five years to life if convicted of criminal possession of a weapon in the first degree as a crime of terrorism and of conspiracy as a crime of terrorism. He was represented by attorneys Lori Cohen and Joseph Zablocki. Sosa pleaded not guilty and was denied bail.

Sosa had sought assistance from a New York Police Department (NYPD) informant in drilling holes in metal tubes to be used for the three pipe bombs. The FBI had a separate investigation into Sosa's activities. He had lived with his uncle on West 137th Street in the Hamilton Heights neighborhood in New York City after his mother had recently thrown him out. Witnesses said he appeared to be unstable and had tried to circumcise himself. Dominican authorities said he had left the country at an early age and had no criminal record in that country. He lived mostly in Manhattan but spent five years in Schenectady, where he was arrested for credit card fraud. U.S. authorities said he converted from Roman Catholicism to Islam in 2004. He had been under surveillance for more than two years. In May 2009, an Albany police department discovered that he had talked about going to Yemen to obtain terrorist training before returning to the United States. NYPD officers made more than four hundred hours of secret recordings. In October 2010, he began to maintain trueislam1.com, a radical Islamist Web site that included al Qaeda propaganda and instructional materials from *Inspire*. He had been unsuccessful in contacting al-Aulaqi. Federal officials believed he was not prosecutable under federal laws for unilateral conspiracy. NYPD said police had used at least four confidential informants in the case.

November 21, 2011—Lebanon—The news media reported that earlier in the year, Hizballah had captured six CIA informants by combing telephone records. In June, Hizballah leader Hassan Nasrallah said on television that his group had identified at least two CIA assets. In a December 9 al-Manar Television broadcast, the group released what it claimed were the names of several CIA officers working in Lebanon.

November 22, 2011—Somalia—A roadside bomb exploded in the Medina neighborhood of Mogadishu, killing eleven civilians and wounding many others. Al-Shabaab was suspected.

November 24, 2011—Mali—Gunmen kidnapped two French citizens from their hotel in Hombori

during the night. Al Qaeda in the Islamic Maghreb (AQIM) later claimed credit, saying Serge Lazarevic and Philippe Verdon were French intelligence agents. Reuters quoted French media reports indicating that Lazarevic, of Hungarian extraction, "took part during the 1990s in the recruitment of Yugoslav mercenaries to fight in then Zaire." The press also claimed that Verdon was arrested in September 2003 in Comoros for involvement in a coup attempt. The group said the attack was to avenge Malian attacks against AQIM and French aggression in the Sahel. Addressing the Malian government, the group said, "It is time you learned your lesson and stop killing mujahideen and their families to please the impious crusaders." 11112401

November 24, 2011—Kenya—Al-Shabaab was suspected of setting off a landmine under a large military truck carrying several soldiers near Mandera on the Kenya-Somalia border. The blast killed one soldier and seriously wounded five others.

At 7:30 p.m., terrorists threw hand grenades at a hotel and shopping center in Garissa, killing three and wounding six. Authorities detained hundreds of ethnic Somalis.

November 25, 2011—Mali—At 2:30 p.m., gunmen broke into Timbuktu's Amanar restaurant, grabbed four European tourists, and shot one—a German citizen—to death when he refused to get into their truck. Al Qaeda in the Islamic Maghreb (AQIM) was suspected. On April 30, 2012, AQIM offered to release British citizen Stephen Malcolm if the United Kingdom freed Abu Qatada. The group said on a jihadi Web site, "The initiative to the British government is to release its citizen Stephen Malcolm, who also has South African nationality, if it deports Abu Qatada to one of the 'Arab Spring' countries ... If Britain ignores this offer it will bear the consequences of handing Abu Qatada to the Jordanian government." The other hostages were identified as Swiss national Nils Joan Viktor Gustafson and Dutch national Jacobus Nicolo Ruke. AQIM released a photo of the three hostages in December 2011. 11112501

November 26, 2011—Colombia—The Revolutionary Armed Forces of Colombia (FARC) shot and killed four hostages, all of them security force members, held for more than a decade. Three hostages were shot in the head; the fourth sustained two shots in the back. Authorities found a fifth hostage, policeman Luis Alberto Erazo, 48, alive after he had fled from the group; he had been held for twelve years. FARC chased him, throwing grenades. He was wounded in the face. Police also found chains near the bodies, which were discovered in Caqueta during military operations against the group. Some of the hostages had been kidnapped twelve to thirteen years earlier. FARC routinely kills hostages to prevent rescue attempts.

November 27, 2011—Philippines—A 10-kilogram TNT bomb went off in room 226 at the two-story Atilano Pension House budget hotel in Zamboanga City in the southern Philippines, killing three people and wounding twenty-seven, including several wedding guests. Two people were in serious condition and another dozen were in a hospital the next day. The ensuing fire gutted the hotel, collapsed much of the second floor, blew off the roof, and shattered windows in nearby buildings. Abu Sayyaf was suspected. Three of its bomb makers died in one of the hotel's rooms in January 2000 while they were assembling a bomb.

November 27, 2011—Philippines—Authorities in Isabela City on Basilan Island found and defused two explosives.

November 27, 2011—Philippines—Authorities arrested three men and a woman for hacking into AT&T customer phones in an attempt to send money to Jemaah Islamiyah. The hackers had worked with a group that financed the 2008 attacks in Mumbai, India. The group began its hacking in 2009. Local police said the "remote toll fraud" scheme cost $2 million.

November 28, 2011—Somalia—Al-Shabaab announced that it had banned sixteen aid groups, including six UN agencies, from central and southern Somalia. Masked gunmen seized equipment from aid offices in Beldweyne and Baidoa towns.

November 28, 2011—Iraq—At 8:00 a.m., a suicide bomber crashed his car into the gate of al-Hout prison in Taji, north of Baghdad, killing nineteen people, including ten policemen and nine civilians, and injuring twenty-two people. Al Qaeda in Iraq was suspected.

November 30, 2011—Somalia—A suicide bomber in a military uniform feigned a stomach ache to draw people to him, then set off his explosives at army headquarters, killing four soldiers and wounding twelve others, four seriously. Somali soldiers shot the terrorist to death. Gen. Abdikarim Yusuf Dhagabadan, head of the country's armed forces, said he believed the terrorist was trying to assassinate him as he arrived at the office. Al-Shabaab was suspected.

December 4, 2011—Bahrain—After midnight, a canister placed under a minibus's front tire ex-

ploded near the fence of the U.K. Embassy, causing no casualties. 11120401

December 6, 2011—Afghanistan—Suicide bombers killed at least sixty minority Hazara Shi'ite worshipers during Ashura observances in Kabul and Mazar-e Sharif. The Pakistani group Lashkar-i-Jhangvi called Radio Free Europe to claim credit. Lashkar spokesman Ali Sher-e-Khuda told the BBC that the group was battling discrimination by "Afghanistan's ruling Shi'ite elite." The Taliban and the Pakistani intelligence service denied involvement. In the Kabul attack, at noon, a suicide bomber walked to the Abul Fazal Abbas shrine in the Murad Khani district, set off his explosives, and killed fifty-six people. Later that day, a bicycle bomb killed four Shi'ite pilgrims in Mazar-e Sharif.

December 7, 2011—Germany—A package bomb was sent to Josef Ackermann, chief executive of Deutsche Bank, at the bank's headquarters in Frankfurt. The bomb was discovered in the mail room and caused no injuries. Its return address was European Central Bank, also in Germany.

December 8, 2011—Pakistan—Gunmen fired rocket-propelled grenades and automatic weapons, destroying more than twenty NATO-bound oil tankers just outside Quetta. 11120801

December 8, 2011—Germany—A police special operations team in Bochum arrested Halil S., a 27-year-old German man, who was believed to be a member of the Duesseldorf cell, which was believed to be plotting to conduct a bombing in Europe for al Qaeda. Three of its members were arrested in April when they were making a shrapnel bomb to attack a bus or crowded place in Germany. Halil S. was accused of supporting the trio with financial and logistical help, then conducting the attack after their arrest. Police found no weapons or explosives in his apartment.

December 11, 2011—Pakistan—During the night, gunmen on motorcycles fired on a convoy of eight civilian tankers bringing oil for NATO forces in Afghanistan, killing one of the truck drivers in an attack 55 miles southwest of Quetta. 11121101

December 11, 2011—Kenya—A bomb killed a police officer and wounded three others in Mandera, on the Somalia border. A second bomb killed nine soldiers.

December 12, 2011—Yemen—Fifteen members of al Qaeda in the Arabian Peninsula dug a 130-foot tunnel and escaped from the Central Security prison in Aden. Twelve of the escapees had been convicted in the killing of security officials and of a bank robbery. Three were captured within twenty-four hours.

December 12, 2011—Kenya—A bomb killed six people, including the district head of intelligence and his driver, and wounded four civilian bystanders, including two women, in Wajir during Kenyan Independence Day celebrations. The bomb exploded beneath a car carrying intelligence officers out of a stadium following a parade.

December 12, 2011—France—Authorities discovered and defused a package bomb that was sent to the Greek Embassy in Paris. The package had no external markings and contained a low-power explosive device. 11121201

December 13, 2011—Belgium—WNRN reported that Nordine Amrani, 33, of Liege threw three grenades and fired from a rooftop elevated walkway into the crowded Christmas market at a city center square near a court building on shoppers in Place St. Lambert in Liege, killing 4 and wounding 123. He died in the incident, but it was unclear how, as police did not kill him. The dead included a 23-month-old child, two teen boys aged 15 and 17, and a 75-year-old woman. At least 52 people were treated for their injuries at a makeshift field hospital at the scene. Another 31 people were admitted for treatment at the Citadelle Hospital. Police said that the gunman was not a terrorist, as he had acted alone. He was carrying a pistol, a semiautomatic rifle, and grenades in his bag. Amrani had earlier been convicted on sexual abuse, drugs, and arms racketeering offenses and was on conditional parole. He had served forty months in jail. He had been cultivating several thousand cannabis plants. He was scheduled to meet with police that day regarding a suspected rape.

December 13, 2011—Yemen—Yemeni security forces captured six al Qaeda in the Arabian Peninsula members, including Musaed al-Barbari, who attacked the Sana'a International Airport in 2009. The Yemeni Embassy in Washington reported, "The terrorism suspects have been carrying out surveillance, and planning missions aimed at targeting government and high ranking security officials. Furthermore, the cell was planning on orchestrating attacks on foreign missions and critical state installations." Al-Barbari had weapons, explosives, and training and recruiting material.

December 13, 2011—Italy—Right-wing extremist Gianluca Casseri, 50, fired in an outdoor Florence market, killing two Senegalese vendors and wounding three other Senegalese immigrants in a second Florence market before shooting himself to death. He had earlier participated in racist marches. 11121301

December 15, 2011—United States—An elderly Chinese man turned himself in to police after firing nine shots at the Chinese Consulate in Los Angeles. A police spokesman said, "He was protesting their human rights record or lack thereof." 11121501

December 17, 2011—Nigeria—The joint military task force for Borno State raided a house that contained a Boko Haram bomb factory in the Bolori ward of Maiduguri. Authorities seized IEDs, AK47s, ammunition, and other items. Gun and bomb attacks in the north during the previous four days had left seven dead.

December 17, 2011—Indonesia—A helicopter carrying twenty-nine workers and family members for the Phoenix-based Freeport-McMoRan mining firm was hit by six shots near the firm's Grasburg gold and copper mine in the east. The wife of a Freeport employee was injured by shrapnel. The helicopter landed 55 miles away from the attack. 11121701

December 18, 2011—Iraq—The last U.S. troops departed the country.

December 20, 2011—Yemen—Al Qaeda in the Arabian Peninsula (AQAP) released a video that included Abu Yazeed, an English speaker who might become the replacement for Anwar al-Aulaqi, who was commemorated in the video. In referring to the deaths of al-Aulaqi and Samir Khan in an air strike, he noted, "Their willingness to exceed all limits is just unthinkable and by assassinating three of its own citizens far away from combat zones and with no judicial process." It was the first time an Anglophone besides al-Aulaqi had appeared in an AQAP video. The video included a posthumous use of al-Aulaqi footage in which he said, "You have two choices: either hijra (emigration) or jihad (holy war) ... I specifically invite the youth to either fight in the West or join their brothers in the fronts of jihad: Afghanistan, Iraq, and Somalia. I invite them to join us in our new front, Yemen, the base from which the great jihad of the Arabian Peninsula will begin, the base from which the greatest army of Islam will march forth." The video included a eulogy for al-Aulaqi by Gitmo alumnus Ibrahim al-Rubaish, an AQAP leader. "As a result, the mujaheed brother Nidal Hasan ... executed a heroic slaughter in Fort Hood military base, killing those soldiers who were preparing to go to Iraq."

December 22, 2011—United States—The U.S. Department of the Treasury announced that information leading to the location of Syria-born al Qaeda (AQ) financier Yasin al-Suri, alias Ezedin

Abdel Aziz Khalil, alias Izz al-Din Abd al-Farid Khalil, alias Zayn al-Abadin, who was believed to be in Iran, would net $10 million from the Rewards for Justice program. He was one of six individuals upon whom sanctions were imposed in July 2011. Robert A. Hartung, assistant director for Threat Investigations and Analysis at the U.S. Department of State's Bureau of Diplomatic Security, told the press, "From his sanctuary inside Iran, he has moved terrorist recruits through Iran to al Qaeda leaders in Pakistan and Afghanistan. He has also arranged for the release of al Qaeda operatives from Iranian prisons and their transfer to Pakistan. And he has funneled significant amounts of money through Iran to AQ leadership in Afghanistan and Iraq."

December 22, 2011—Iraq—Seventeen bombs exploded in eleven Baghdad neighborhoods, most of them Shi'ite, killing 69 and injuring 207, in the worst day of violence since U.S. troops left. Unlike the most recent bombing campaigns which targeted police and other government facilities, the attacks aimed at civilian casualties. Al Qaeda in Iraq, using the name Islamic State of Iraq, eventually claimed credit. Among the dead was Fadil Ahmed, 31. One of the bombs was hidden in a minibus disguised as an ambulance, which was permitted to get close to a government building. In another bomb attack, an SUV picked up day laborers before the driver set off its explosives. Two other bombs went off as rescuers arrived. Other bombs targeted an elementary school, a vegetable market, and the convoy of a senior bank official. Fifteen of the attacks occurred between 6:30 and 8:30 a.m. Two other bombs went off in the evening; one car bomb injured three civilians and another damaged houses and shops. Four of the bombings used car bombs, including two suicide drivers. Police defused another five car bombs. A Katyusha rocket killed one person and injured another in a western Baghdad neighborhood.

December 22, 2011—Egypt—The Ansar al Jihad in the Sinai Peninsula posted its mission statement on jihadi Internet sites, saying, "With this message we send you the good tidings of the birth of the group Ansar al-Jihad in the Sinai Peninsula and we pledge unto Allah the Great and Almighty to do our best to fight the corrupt regime and its henchmen among the Jews, the Americans, and those around them." It pledged an oath to the late Osama bin Laden, and said that the United States "nor those who live in America will ever enjoy security as long as we don't live it in reality in Palestine."

December 23, 2011—Syria—The government blamed al Qaeda when two suicide car bombs exploded outside buildings of the General Security Directorate and a military intelligence service branch in the Kfar Sousa area of Damascus, killing 44 people and wounding 166. Oppositionists said the government had set off the bombs, killing detained protestors. The UN Security Council condemned the bombings.

December 24, 2011—Nigeria—Paramilitary forces battled Boko Haram in Yobe and Borno states, killing sixty-one people. Three bombs went off at churches in Maiduguri, capital of Borno, killing eleven.

December 25, 2011—Nigeria—A series of Boko Haram bombings and shootings hit churches in Madalla, Jos, Kano, Damaturu, and Gadaka, killing forty-two people. At 8:00 a.m., a bomb exploded at St. Theresa Catholic Church in Madalla, killing thirty-five and wounding fifty-two. A second bomb went off in Jos near the Mountain of Fire and Miracles Church, causing no deaths. Gunmen fired on police guarding a second church that had been bombed, wounding one officer who later died. A suicide car bomber killed three people in Damaturu, capital of Yobe State, at the state headquarters of the Nigerian secret police. The target, a senior military commander, survived. A Damaturu police station was also bombed. Police arrested four people and recovered four unexploded bombs. On January 17, 2012, police arrested Kabiru Sokoto at the mansion of the Borno State governor in Abuja, charging him with being the mastermind of the bombing of St. Theresa's. He escaped later that day when Boko Haram attacked his police convoy that was transferring him to a police station in Abaji, outside Abuja.

December 25, 2011—Afghanistan—A suicide bomber killed twenty people, including parliamentarian Abdu Mutalib Baig and an 8-year-old boy, at a 2:00 p.m. funeral in Taloqan, capital of Takhar Province. Dozens were wounded.

December 29, 2011—Afghanistan—An individual wearing an Afghan National Army uniform opened fire on his French instructors, killing two French Foreign Legionnaires, before he was shot to death. The Taliban claimed credit for the attack in the Kapisa valley by a man named Ibrahim. 11122901

2012

January 2012—South Korea—Liu Qiang, a Chinese citizen, conducted an arson attack at the Japanese Embassy in Seoul. He had conducted an arson attack on Tokyo's Yasukuni Shrine for Japan's World War II dead in December 2011. He served ten months in a South Korean prison for the embassy attack. A Seoul court rejected a prosecution effort to extradite him to Tokyo. On January 4, 2013, he flew home to China. 12019901

January 2012—Azerbaijan—The Ministry of National Security announced it had stopped "preparations" by Iran-backed terrorists to attack "foreign public figures in Baku," including Israeli Ambassador Michael Lotem, a rabbi, and a teacher at a local Jewish school. The ministry said the Iranians had budgeted $150,000 for the attack and that by living in Iran, the terrorists' leader could meet "with Iranian special services."

January 2012—United States—The Ohio-based King Hearts for Charitable Humanitarian Development disbanded. Six years earlier, the U.S. Treasury Department had ordered U.S. banks to freeze the group's assets because it suspected that the group was funding Hamas.

January 2012—Algeria—The Algerian Direction de la Sécurité Interieure arrested three members of al Qaeda in the Islamic Maghreb who were planning suicide attacks against U.S. and European ships in the western Mediterranean. The trio had purchased a boat that they planned to pack with explosives.

January 1, 2012—United States—At 8:44 p.m., a Molotov cocktail exploded at the main entrance of the Imam al-Khoei Foundation's mosque in Queens, New York, while about eighty worshipers were in the building. A second firebomb was thrown at the sign for the center's school. Molotov cocktails went off at a convenience store and three homes that evening. Structural damage was minimal. The foundation has branches around the world, promoting development, human rights, and minority rights as a consultant to the UN's Economic and Social Council (ECOSOC).

Ray Lazier Lengend, 40, a Queens resident of Guyanese descent, said he threw the firebombs in part because he was not permitted to use the mosque's bathrooms. Police found him after tracking a stolen car with Virginia license plates that was spotted at two sites. He was arrested on January 3 and charged with one count of arson as a hate crime, four counts of arson, and five counts of criminal possession of a weapon. He was given a psychiatric examination. Authorities said he was believed to have been kicked out of the store on December 27 for stealing milk and coffee in a glass bottle.

January 4, 2012—Ukraine—On February 27, 2012, Russian Channel One television reported that Ukrainian and Russian intelligence services had foiled a plot to assassinate Russian Prime Minister Vladimir Putin in Odessa. Authorities learned of the plot after a bomb went off on January 4 inside an Odessa apartment, killing Ruslan Madayev, 26. Adam Osmayev, 31, and Ilya Pyanzin, 28, a Kazakh citizen, survived. Several of the inhabitants had been sent by Doku Umarov, Chechen terrorist leader. Pyanzin said the group planned to first attack strategic sites in Moscow, then attack Putin. Pyanzin had traveled to the Ukraine from the Arab Emirates via Turkey. Osmayev, who lived in London for several years, said the group had surveilled Moscow routes taken by Putin's drivers. The group was to conduct the attack in the days leading up to the March 4 presidential elections. The bomb would go off on Kutuzovsky Prospect, a wide avenue. Opposition party leaders suggested the story was a hoax.

January 5, 2012—Pakistan—Pakistani Taliban gunmen kidnapped Khalil Rasjed Dale, 60, a British doctor working for the International Committee of the Red Cross (ICRC), while on his way home from work. On April 29, 2012, Dale's beheaded body, wrapped in plastic, was found by the roadside in Quetta. Dale's name was written with black marker on the white plastic bag. The Taliban said a ransom had not been paid. A doctor said he had been killed twelve hours before being found; a sharp knife had been used to cut his head off. He had worked for the ICRC and the British Red Cross in Somalia, Afghanistan, Iraq, and Pakistan. He had been managing a health program for Baluchistan for the past year. 12010501

January 5, 2012—United States—A federal court in the District of Columbia sentenced Pakistani citizen Irfan ul-Haq, 37, to four years in prison for conspiring to smuggle a member of the Pakistani Taliban into the United States. He and two other Pakistanis had pleaded guilty in September 2010 to conspiring to provide material support to a foreign terrorist organization. Qasim Ali, 32, and Zahid Yousaf, 43, in December 2010 were sentenced to three years in prison as part of their plea bargains. They were to return to Pakistan after their release. Federal agents ran a sting operation in Ecuador against them in January 2011, sending informants to ask them to smuggle the individual to the United States. The individual would journey from Pakistan to Dubai, Cuba, the Dominican Republic, then on to the United States. One of the smugglers said the normal rate for such a job was between $50,000 and $60,000. The trio was arrested in Miami on March 13, 2011, after accepting partial payment and obtaining a fake Pakistani passport.

January 5, 2012—Iraq—A suicide bomber set off his explosives near Shi'ite pilgrims near Nasiriyah, killing forty-eight and wounding eighty-one. An Iraqi security officer tried to stop him by wrapping his arms around him. The Sunni officer was killed in the blast and became a local hero. On February 6, 2012, the al Qaeda affiliate Islamic State of Iraq said, "Sunni heroes of heroes" killed "nonbelievers and Iranian agents" in the attack.

January 6, 2012—Syria—A suicide bomber set off his explosive device at a busy intersection in the center Midan neighborhood of Damascus, when many people were heading to Friday prayers. The blast killed twenty-six, including eleven police officers, and wounded sixty-three. The government blamed terrorists; the opposition blamed the government. Col. Malik Kurdi, an assistant commander of the Free Syrian Army opposition group, denied involvement.

January 6, 2012—United States—Authorities arrested Craig Benedict Baxam, 24, of Laurel, Maryland, at Baltimore-Washington International Airport as he returned to the United States after trying to get to Somalia to join al-Shabaab. He secretly converted to Islam in July, days before leaving the army. He was charged with attempting to provide material support to a terrorist group. He left the United States on December 20 on a flight to Kenya, en route to Somalia. He was arrested by the Kenyans on a bus to Garissa on December 23. The FBI interviewed him twice in Kenya. He had served in Baghdad and South Korea, and had been trained in cryptology and intelligence. He faced fifteen years in prison followed by three years of supervised release.

January 6, 2012—Kenya—The Kenya-based Muslim Youth Center claimed that its leader had been named to represent al-Shabaab in Kenya. In 2011, the UN said the group had recruited, funded, and run training and orientation events for al-Shabaab. Amiir Ahmad Iman Ali, alias Abdul Fatah of Kismayo, issued a fifty-minute video lecture produced by al-Kataib, al-Shabaab's media foundation. He noted wars in Yemen, Afghanistan, Iraq, and Chechnya. Ali said, "If you are unable to reach the land of jihad ... then raise your sword against the enemy that is closest to you. Jihad should be now waged inside Kenya, which is legally a war zone. You don't have to get permission from your parents." In a separate statement, he said, "The Muslim lands will once again rule with Shari'ah and your kufr democracy will be dumped in the sewage." Ali, a Kenyan, had been based in Somalia since 2009. He was believed to command between two hundred and five hundred

fighters. He speaks Swahili, English, Arabic, and Somali.

January 6, 2012—Georgia—Police arrested a man in Tbilisi and confiscated thirty-six vials of cesium–135, a radioactive isotope. He claimed he obtained the material in Abkhazia.

January 7, 2012—United States—The FBI arrested Sami Osmakac, 25, a naturalized American born in Kosovo who was planning on conducting a car bombing, hostage-taking, and suicide bombing in the Tampa, Florida, area. The Florida resident intended to use explosives and weapons "to create mayhem" in Tampa, but the Muslim community tipped off authorities, who conducted a sting operation. On January 9, he was charged with one count of attempted use of a weapon of mass destruction.

Osmakac recorded a martyrdom video in which he said he would "pay back for wrongs he felt were done to Muslims," according to prosecutors. He had posted anti–Jewish and anti–Christian videos on the Internet. The FBI was tipped off in September 2011 that the resident of Pinellas Park, Florida, "asked for al Qaeda flags." He went on to discuss potential targets, and asked for an informant's assistance in obtaining guns and explosives. An undercover FBI employee met him on December 21, when Osmakac said he wanted an AK-47-style machine gun, Uzi submachine guns, high capacity magazines, grenades, and an explosive belt. Prosecutors said he gave the FBI employee a $500 down payment. The FBI inerted the weapons, which were to be used in night clubs in the Ybor City area of Tampa, the operations center of the Hillsborough County Sheriff's Office in Ybor City, a business in the South Tampa area, and an Irish bar in south Tampa—all places where there would be large crowds. In a follow-up hostage-taking, he planned to demand prison release, then set off an explosive belt. He faced life in prison.

Osmakac was born in Lubizde, near the Prokletije Mountains of Kosovo on the Albania border. His family, followers of a Sufi sect, immigrated to the United States when he was 13. Locals said he was a loner in high school who rapped about bombs and killing. Osmakac was jailed for head-butting a Christian preacher outside a Lady Gaga concert. He had also physically threatened a Tampa area activist. He had tried to travel to Saudi Arabia to study Islam but had visa problems and only made it to Turkey.

January 7, 2012—Afghanistan—An Afghan soldier shot to death a member of NATO.

January 10, 2012—Pakistan—A bomb exploded at a Jamrud bus station, killing thirty people and injuring dozens in what was believed to be an attack on a pro-government militia. Some members of the Zakakhel tribe were among those waiting in the passenger pickup area. At least six tribal police officers were killed. The Pakistani Taliban was suspected.

January 10, 2012—Pakistan—Aslam Awan, alias Abdullah Khorasani, 29, a Pakistani from Abbottabad who was a senior operations organizer for al Qaeda, was killed in a drone strike at a compound near Miran Shah in North Waziristan. He was close to the group's chief of external operations. He had lived for several years in the Cheetham Hill area of Manchester, United Kingdom. He arrived in the United Kingdom in 2002 on a student visa, moving into an apartment with Abdul Rahman, a school friend from Pakistan. They were joined by Murad Iqbal, a Pakistani from Karachi. The trio recruited other youths in Manchester, going camping in the Lake District in March 2006 and June 23, 2006, and simulating suicide bombing exercises. Awan went to the Afghanistan-Pakistan border area in late 2006. He wrote to Rahman to have him and his colleagues join him. He noted terrorist training and participation in fighting. One of the recruits was Omar Arshad, who had dropped out of pharmacy studies at Manchester University and went missing. In January 2007, Arshad's father had tracked him down and obtained a British control order, which limited his movements and communications. The group planned to help him escape. He shaved his beard, a colleague drove him to Birmingham Airport, and he flew to Iran then Lahore, Pakistan, the next day on a ticket Rahman bought for him. U.K. authorities believed Arshad joined militants in Pakistan. Iqbal went to the border region to join his friends.

In November 2007, Rahman pleaded guilty to dissemination of terrorist literature and aiding and abetting a breach of a control order. Rahman had arrived in the United Kingdom from the Pakistan border area to study biotechnology at Abertay University in Dundee, United Kingdom, but quit on his first day and moved to Manchester, working as a mobile phone salesman. The Cheetham Hill team was linked to Rangzieb Ahmed, a senior al Qaeda facilitator in Manchester who was arrested in Pakistan and convicted in the United Kingdom in 2008 of directing terrorism.

January 11, 2012—Iran—A bomb magnetically attached by a passing motorcyclist to a Peugeot 405 killed Mostafa Ahmadi Roshan, 32, a chemical engineer at the Natanz uranium enrichment plant, and his bodyguard. Roshan was deputy director of the facility. Tehran blamed Israel for the rush-hour attack. No one claimed credit for the fourth attack on an Iranian nuclear scientist in the past two years. On February 9, 2012, MSN.com said Iranian officials claimed that Mossad had financed, trained, and armed the People's Mujahedin of Iran (MEK), a group designated as terrorists by the United States, to carry out attacks on Iranian nuclear scientists.

January 11, 2012—Kenya—Al-Shabaab took several hostages in an attack on Gerille, killing six people, including three police officers, a civilian servant, and a primary-school teacher. At least four government officials were missing.

January 12, 2012—Pakistan—The Associated Press said that intercepted militant radio communications suggested that Hakimullah Mehsud, head of the Pakistani Taliban, was killed in an air strike in North Waziristan.

January 14, 2012—Iraq—A suicide bomber killed 53 Shi'ite pilgrims, including 3 children, and wounded 137 near Basra. He was wearing a military uniform. On February 6, 2012, the al Qaeda affiliate Islamic State of Iraq said, "Sunni heroes of heroes" killed "nonbelievers and Iranian agents" in the attack.

January 15, 2012—Yemen—Armed Obeyid Marib tribesmen kidnapped a 34-year-old Norwegian man working for the UN in Sana'a, then transferred him to central Marib Province, 110 miles east. The group demanded the release of a fellow tribesman arrested for killing four soldiers guarding oil tankers. 12011501

January 15, 2012—Yemen—Al Qaeda in the Arabian Peninsula announced it had murdered two soldiers who had been kidnapped two months earlier near Zinjibar, capital of Abyan Province. The bodies were found in southern Yemen.

January 16, 2012—Nigeria—Boko Haram gunmen shot and killed three Chadians in Kamaturu in Yobe State. 12011601

January 16, 2012—Thailand—Thai police detained Hussein Atris (variant Atris Hussein), a former hairdresser born in Lebanon, who held a Swedish passport and was alleged to have links to Hizballah. He led police to a warehouse containing more than 8,800 pounds of urea fertilizer and several gallons of liquid ammonium nitrate. Police said he had distilled the materials into crystal form, one step toward making a bomb. Police charged Atris Hussein after finding "initial chemical materials that could produce bombs." Authorities said he wanted to attack popular Western tourist spots in Bangkok. Police said they had foiled a bombing but that another suspect was at large.

January 17, 2012—Ethiopia—Gunmen from Eritrea attacked a group of twenty-two European tourists before dawn in the volcanic northern Afar region, killing five—including two Germans, two Hungarians, and an Austrian—and seriously hurting two Belgians before kidnapping two Ethiopians and two Germans. Two Italians escaped unharmed. The tourists were traveling with the Addis Ababa-based Green Land Tours and Travel, according to local observers. The Eritrean government denied involvement. In February, a rebel group in the Afar region claimed it had freed the two Germans, although by mid–April, there had been no official confirmation of the release. 1201 1701

January 19, 2012—Somalia—A bomb went off at a police checkpoint to a refugee camp near Mogadishu, killing two Somali policemen and four refugees.

January 19, 2012—Somalia—A hand grenade was thrown at a UN compound in Mogadishu, causing no casualties. 12011901

January 19, 2012—Northern Ireland—Irish Republican Army dissidents set off two bombs within ten minutes in Londonderry during the night, causing no injuries. Police had evacuated the areas after received phoned warnings. One bomb went off outside Londonderry's main tourist office while seventy-five residents of a nursing home were being evacuated 25 yards away. A bomb was hidden in a gym bag.

January 19, 2012—Pakistan—Gunmen broke into a home in Multan and kidnapped Italian citizen Giovanni Lo Porto and a German man who worked for Welthungerhilfe, an international aid group based in Bonn. The kidnappers overpowered the private guard who watched over the rented house. The gunmen threw the duo into a car and sped away. The group was providing aid to victims of the 2010 floods and had returned after a visit to nearby Kot Addu town. No one claimed credit. It was unclear whether the Taliban or criminals were responsible. 12011902

January 20, 2012—India—Indian-born British author Salman Rushdie, 64, called off his visit to the Jaipur Literature Festival after learning that he was a target for assassination by Muslim protestors. Muslim clerics and lawmakers had called for him to be banned from entering India. Rushdie said that paid assassins from the Mumbai underworld had been hired to kill him. On January 24, he was prevented from speaking to the convention via video link when William Dalrymple, the event's organizer, received a death threat and police warned of likely violent protests.

January 20, 2012—Nigeria—Boko Haram conducted a series of bombings and gun attacks on police stations, immigration offices, and the local headquarters of the secret police in Kano, killing 186 people, including 150 civilians, 29 police officers, 3 secret police officers, 2 immigration officers, and a customs officer. A suicide car bomber set off explosives outside a regional police headquarters, freeing many Boko Haram prisoners. Spokesman Abul Qaqa took credit for the group, saying the state government had refused to release the prisoners. Authorities announced on January 23 that they had discovered ten unexploded car bombs in Kano.

January 20, 2012—Nigeria—Gunmen in the Niger Delta kidnapped William Gregory, 50, a U.S. citizen working for Marubeni Corporation, in the southeastern town of Warri. The group killed his driver and demanded a ransom. He was released on January 27. Marubeni said it had not paid a ransom. 12012001

January 20, 2012—Afghanistan—Abdul Basir, an Afghan soldier belonging to the 201 Army Corps, turned his gun on allied forces, killing five French soldiers and wounding fourteen in Kapisa Province, east of Kabul, on a joint French-Afghan base. On July 17, 2012, an Afghan military court sentenced the gunman to death. 12072002

January 21, 2012—Somalia—Gunmen surrounded the car of Michael Scott Moore, a German American journalist who had just left the airport after dropping off an Indian colleague, threw him into another vehicle, and kidnapped him in the northern town of Galkayo, Adado, on the border between Puntland and Galmudug. The gunmen severely beat his Somali companion. The American engineer came to Somalia to look into building a deep water port in the town of Hobyo, a coastal pirate base. Local officials said the attackers might have been his guards who had links to pirates. They were believed to have driven to Hobyo. The group moved him at least three times within twenty-four hours and on January 26 threatened to kill him after the U.S. Navy SEALs rescued an American and a Danish hostage the previous night. Hassan Abdi, a pirate connected to the kidnappers, said, "If they try again, we will all die together ... It's difficult to hold U.S. hostages, cause it's a game of chance: die or get huge money. But we shall stick with our plans and will never release him until we get a ransom." 12012101

January 21, 2012—Sudan—A gunman shot a UN–African Union peacekeeper and wounded three others in an ambush on a patrol in eastern Darfur. 12012102

January 21, 2012—United States—The FBI's Denver and Chicago Joint Terrorism Task Forces arrested Jamshid Muhtorov, 35, an Uzbek refugee living in Aurora, Colorado, at Chicago's O'Hare Airport on charges that he planned to travel overseas to fight for a terrorist group. There was no evidence that he was plotting attacks in the United States. Muhtorov was charged with providing and attempting to provide material support to the Islamic Jihad Union in Uzbekistan. He was detained before boarding a flight to Istanbul, Turkey. Judge Morton Denlow in Chicago ordered him transferred to Denver. Neighbors said Muhtorov worked as a truck driver. The FBI said intercepted phone calls with his wife indicated that they argued about his plans. He told his daughter he would never see her again, but "if she was a good Muslim girl, he will see her in heaven." He faced fifteen years in prison and a $250,000 fine. He was represented by a court-appointed attorney. In his February two court appearance in Denver, he denied the allegations, saying, "I swear to Allah I never did anything like that."

January 22, 2012—United States—Authorities arrested North Carolina teacher Nevine Aly Elsheikh and Shkumbin Sherifi on charges of plotting to behead three witnesses who testified against Shkumbin's brother, Hysen Sherifi, who on January 13 was sentenced to forty-five years in prison for conspiracy to kill people overseas and kill a federal officer. Elsheikh was scheduled to appear in federal court on February 3 on charges of conspiracy to commit murder. Elshiekh was on leave as director of special education at the Sterling Montessori Academy in Morrisville, North Carolina. She was represented by attorney Charles Swift.

Hysen Sherifi is a native of Kosovo and a U.S. legal permanent resident in North Carolina. Prosecutors quoted FBI informants as saying that Hysen wanted to hire someone to kill the witnesses and to attack an inmate who "defrauded" him out of money concerning his federal charges. He wanted photos of their corpses as proof. Prosecutors said Elsheikh had visited him in a North Carolina jail in December 2011, when she learned of his plans. In January 2012, she handed $750 to an informant to kill one witness. Shkumbin Sherifi gave the same informant the other $4,250.

January 24, 2012—Somalia—Al-Shabaab set off a truck bomb at an Ethiopian military base in Beledweyne. The group claimed thirty-three Ethiopian troops were killed.

January 26, 2012—Afghanistan—A suicide car bomber killed three people and wounded thirty-one outside the gates of a NATO-sponsored Provincial Reconstruction Team aid office in Lashkar Gah, capital of Helmand Province. The bomber appeared to be targeting vehicles that held foreigners. It was not clear whether foreigners were among the casualties. 12012601

January 26, 2012—United States—The Department of State designated a trio as terrorists for targeting Americans overseas. Brothers Yassin Chouka and Monir Chouka were involved in 2010 and 2011 attacks on civilians in Afghanistan. State said they were "fighters, recruiters, facilitators and propagandists for the Islamic Movement of Uzbekistan." Mevlu Kar had tried to set up an al Qaeda branch in Lebanon where he was a wanted man and subject of an Interpol Red Notice. State said he was involved in a 2007 bomb plot against U.S. military installations in Germany to be conducted by the Islamic Jihad Union. Their U.S.-based financial assets were frozen.

January 27, 2012—Nigeria—Al Qaeda kidnapped German engineer Edgar Fritz Raupach in Kano. Raupach worked for Dantata and Sawoe Construction Co., Ltd. He appeared in an online video in March, wearing a tank top and guarded by two rifle-toting masked terrorists. He said in German and English, "I beg my government to save my life. They will kill me here." The group demanded the release of Umm Sayf Allah al-Ansariya, also known as Filiz Gelowicz, who had been sentenced in March 2011 to thirty months in prison on five counts of supporting a terrorist organization and six counts of recruiting for a terrorist group. Prosecutors said she had collected money and posted Internet text and video for al Qaeda, the Islamic Jihad Union, and the German Taliban Mujahideen. Her husband was arrested in 2007 as the leader of the Sauerland Group, a German terrorist organization. In April 2012, the Berliner Kammergericht ordered her released after she served two thirds of her sentence. He attorney, Mutlu Gunal, said she did not want to be released as part of al Qaeda in the Islamic Maghreb's (AQIM) demands.

Raupach's kidnappers stabbed him to death when Nigerian soldiers attacked their hideout on May 31. The soldiers killed all four kidnappers, then found his body.

It was believed to be the first AQIM operation on Nigerian soil.

On June 11, 2012, AQIM blamed the German

government for Raupach's death, even though Berlin had complied with their demand for Gelowicz's release. The group posted a note on the Internet, saying, "Your government gave the green light for the operation" to rescue Raupach. AQIM warned European governments to not be "dealing in foolishness" during hostage negotiations. A German official told the press that the government was not aware beforehand that Nigerian troops were going to attack the hideout and that the troops were trying to arrest terrorists and did not know that Raupach was being held at that location. 12012701

January 27, 2012—Nigeria—Boko Haram leader Abubakar Shekau released a forty-five-minute Hausa-language tape in which he threatened to kill more security personnel and kidnap their families. He claimed U.S. President Barack Obama was conducting war against Islam. He said that Nigerian President Goodluck Jonathan could not stop the group. He claimed credit for the recent attacks in Kano that killed 186 people. "We attacked the securities base because they were arresting our members and torturing our wives and children. They should know they have families, too, we can abduct them. We have what it takes to do anything we want." But he also said the group was not responsible for civilian casualties. "We never kill ordinary people. Rather, we protect them. It is the army that rushed to the press to say we are the ones killing civilians. We are not fighting civilians. We only kill soldiers, police, and other security agencies." Turning to the United States, he observed, "In America, from former President George Bush to Obama, the Americans have always been fighting and destroying Islam. They have tagged us terrorists, and they are paying for it. It is the same in Nigeria, and we will resist."

January 28, 2012—Sudan—Gunmen from the Sudan People's Liberation Movement–North (SPLM-N) kidnapped forty-seven Chinese workers near Abbasiya in the South Kordofan region, 390 miles south of Khartoum. At least eighteen escaped but one was missing. China announced on February 2 that a worker shot by rebels during a Sudanese government rescue attempt probably had died; he remained missing. The hostages were employed by Sino-hydro, a state-controlled engineering and construction company. Beijing sent a hostage negotiation team to Sudan and approached the new government of South Sudan to mediate. The rebels demanded that Beijing include the government to get them to stop military attacks and let aid reach South Kordofan and suggested that Beijing move its nationals out of the

war zones. Yasir Arman, SPLM-N General Secretary, said, "The SPLM-N calls upon China to contribute to the humanitarian operation and to ask Khartoum government to open safe corridors for humanitarian operations. SPLM-N calls again upon China to support the demand of an international investigation on the war crimes against Sudanese people." Authorities believed the hostages were held in the mountainous Nuba region of South Kordofan. The Chinese public expressed outrage at the lack of a strong Chinese strike against the hostage takers. Arman said China's Ambassador to Ethiopia Xie Xiaoyan had held talks with his group. The rebels released the twenty-nine Chinese workers on February 7, 2012. The Sudanese government suggested that the government of South Sudan had intervened. The Red Cross transferred the freed hostages to Nairobi. One of the missing workers was found dead. 12012801

January 29, 2012—Venezuela—Four gunmen kidnapped Mexican Ambassador Carlos Pujalte Pineiro, 58, and his wife, Paloma Ojeda, from their BMW following a reception in the "country club" section of Chacao in Caracas, holding them for four hours before police forced the kidnappers to release them unharmed in a slum the next morning. This was the second time in two months Pineiro had been taken hostage. Police suspected criminals interested in quick money via an "express kidnapping."

January 31, 2012—Yemen—An air strike killed a dozen al Qaeda in the Arabian Peninsula (AQAP) terrorists, including Abdul Monem al-Fahtani, a mid-level AQAP leader believed to have participated in the 2000 USS *Cole* attack. Yemeni forces had attacked him in late 2010; his death was never confirmed.

January 31, 2012—Egypt—Bedouins blocked a road and kidnapped twenty-four Chinese workers and a translator who were on their way to a military-owned cement factory. The kidnappers demanded the release of prisoners but freed the hostages a day later. 12013101

January 31, 2012—Yemen—Armed tribesmen kidnapped a German, a Colombian, an Iraqi, a Palestinian, and two Yemenis, all of whom worked for the UN Humanitarian Office, near Sana'a. They were released unharmed on February 2. 12013102

February 2012—Colombia—The Colombian National Liberation Army kidnapped eleven oil workers in Arauca Province from a bus on the way to the Bicentennial pipeline. They were freed at the request of the families on March 6, 2012.

February 1, 2012—Philippines—Abu Sayyaf was believed responsible for kidnapping two tourists—a Dutch citizen and a Swiss citizen—in southern Tawi-Tawi Province. 12020101

February 1, 2012—Nigeria—A member of the State Security Service announced the arrest of Boko Haram spokesman Abul-Qaqa after tracking his cell phone. He was flown to Abuja for questioning.

February 2, 2012—Philippines—The military announced that in a 3:00 a.m. air strike on a terrorist safe house in Parang on Jolo Island, it had killed Malaysian citizen Zulkifli bin Hir, alias Marwan, senior leader of Jemaah Islamiyah; Umbra Jumdail, a leader of Abu Sayyaf; and Abdullah Ali, alias Muawiyah, a Singaporean leader of Jemaah Islamiyah. The United States had offered a $5 million reward for Marwan's capture. The U.S.-trained engineer was accused of involvement in several bombings in the Philippines and training new terrorists. The military said thirty terrorists were at the camp. Fifteen of them were killed.

February 3, 2012—Egypt—Masked Bedouin gunmen kidnapped two American tourists and their local tour guide from a minibus on the way from St. Catherine's Monastery on the Sinai Peninsula to the Red Sea resort of Sharm el-Sheikh on the heels of major soccer rioting following the one-year anniversary of the kickoff of the Arab Spring. The kidnappers left behind three other people. The Bedouins demanded the release and retrial of thirty-three detained Bedouins, some of whom were believed responsible for the shooting of a French tourist during an armed robbery of a Sharm el-Sheikh currency exchange shop the previous week. The hostages were freed the same day into the custody of the military. One of the freed Americans, E. P., said that she was not afraid and that the Bedouins were "very nice ... They kept on reassuring us that we will be fine ... They treated us like family." 12020301

February 5, 2012—Egypt—An explosion went off at the Egyptian pipeline carrying gas to Israel and Jordan in the northern Sinai at the entrance of the town of al-Arish. No group claimed credit. The pipeline was shut down for at least two months. The pipeline is run by Gasco, a subsidiary of the national gas company EGAS.

February 5, 2012—Nigeria—The Movement for the Emancipation of the Niger Delta took credit for attacking an Italian oil giant Eni SpA pipeline, interrupting the flow of four thousand barrels of oil. It warned of more attacks in the Delta. The company confirmed the sabotage.

February 7, 2012—Nigeria—Boko Haram was suspected of setting off car bombs at the army's First Mechanized Division Headquarters and the training command of the air force near Kaduna, causing several injuries. The group released a video claiming to welcome peace talks with the government. A third bomb went off near a highway overpass. One of the car bombers at the headquarters was wearing a military uniform. Soldiers fired at him, killing him. Air force officials said the bomber was stopped before getting past the gate, so he threw an explosive 550 yards from the outer fence of the base.

February 8, 2012—Somalia—Al-Shabaab set off a car bomb in Mogadishu that killed eight people and wounded two members of parliament.

February 9, 2012—Somalia—As-Sahab Media released a fifteen-minute video in which Ayman al-Zawahiri and Harakat al-Shabaab al-Mujahideen leader Mukhtar Abdurahman Abu az–Zubeir, alias Godane, announced that al-Shabaab had pledged bayat (an oath of allegiance) to the al Qaeda leader. The duo had recorded their presentations separately; the comments were then spliced. Al-Zawahiri said, "Today I bring glad tidings to our Muslim Ummah, happy tidings that pleased the believers and displeases the crusaders, which is the joining of Shabaab al-Mujahideen in Somalia to Qaida't al-Jihad in support of the jihad unit in the face of the Zionist-Crusader campaign and their helpers of cooperative traitor rulers who brought in the crusader invasive forces to their countries." Az-Zubeir added, "The entire world attests that America's days are over and her rule has gone and her minions in the land of Muslims—their end has come."

February 10, 2012—Syria—Two suicide bombs went off in the commercial center of Aleppo, killing twenty-eight. No one claimed credit. Observers feared al Qaeda was trying to establish a foothold.

February 11, 2012—Syria—Three gunmen waiting outside Brig. Gen. Issa al-Kholi's his home in the Rukn Eddin neighborhood of Damascus shot him to death. Al-Kholi was director of a hospital.

February 12, 2012—Egypt—Nermeen Gomaa Khalil, 41, an Egyptian woman working as a consultant for a UN fund for women, was fatally shot in the head by gunmen in a passing car while driving through Mohandiseen, a Cairo neighborhood.

February 12, 2012—Internet—Ayman al-Zawahiri released a video onto the Internet entitled *Onwards, Lions of Syria* in which he called for Syrians to overthrown Bashar al-Assad without Arab or

Western government assistance. He called on Muslims in Turkey, Iraq, Lebanon, and Jordan to aid Syrian rebels.

Wounded Syria still bleeds day after day, while the butcher, son of the butcher Bashar bin Hafiz, is not deterred to stop. But the resistance of our people in Syria despite all the pain, sacrifice, and bloodshed escalates and grows. [Muslims should help] his brothers in Syria with all that he can, with his life, money, opinion, as well as information ... Our people in Syria, don't rely on the West, or the United States or Arab governments and Turkey. You know better what they are planning against you. Our people in Syria, don't depend on the Arab League and its corrupt governments supporting it. If we want freedom, we must be liberated from this regime. If we want justice, we must retaliate against this regime. Continue your revolt and anger. Don't accept anything else apart from independent, respectful governments.

February 13, 2012—United Kingdom—The United Kingdom released Abu Qatada, al Qaeda's seniormost operative in Europe.

February 13, 2012—India—A bomb exploded under an Israeli Embassy van in New Delhi, wounding four people, including the van's driver, its passenger—Tal Yehoshua-Koren, an embassy employee who is the wife of an Israeli defense envoy—and two people in a nearby car. The bomb was slapped onto the car by a passing motorcyclist as Yehoshua-Koren was on her way to pick up her children from the American Embassy School. The bomb went off a few hundred yards from the prime minister's residence. It was similar to the January 11 killing of an Iranian nuclear chemist in Tehran. On March 7, Indian police arrested a local journalist, Syed Mohammed Kazmi, 50, in connection with the attack. He claimed to work for an Iranian news organization, according to the Press Trust of India. Investigators said he had been in touch with the bomber. He was represented by attorney Vijay Aggarwal. On March 15, India issued arrest warrants for three Iranians—Housan Afshar, Syed Ali Mehdi Sadr, and Mohammed Reza Abolghasemi. On March 17, 2012, Indian police said the bombing attack was connected to the plot to attack Israelis in Thailand.

Indian police identified the bomber as Houshang Afshar Irani, whose passport showed he first visited New Delhi in April 2011 for ten days before returning to the city on January 29, 2012. He reached the city's airport seventy-five minutes after the bomb attack, and after waiting seven hours for a flight, left for Malaysia and on to Dubai, then Tehran. Investigators said the bomb

was a TNT variant. The shell was made outside India. The magnetic strips used in the limpet were the same as those used in the Bangkok and Tbilisi bombings.

On July 30, 2012, ABCNews.com reported that Interpol had issued arrest warrants for five members of Iran's Revolutionary Guard in the case. They were Houshang Afshar Irani, a builder who drove past the Israeli car on a motorcycle and attached the explosive device; Masoud Sedaghatzadeh, a salesman and alleged mastermind; Syed Ali Mahdiansadr, a mobile shopkeeper; and Mohammed Reza Abolghasemi, a clerk at a Tehran water authority. Two were also wanted by Thai police for the plot to attack Israeli targets in Bangkok the next day. Thai and Indian police were also searching for Ali Akbar Norouzishayan, a retired Tehran accountant, who was spotted on security camera footage leaving the Bangkok safe house after the explosion. 12021301

February 13, 2012—Georgia—A bomb found under an Israeli Embassy car in Tbilisi was defused without incident. 12021302

February 14, 2012—Thailand—The Israeli government blamed Iran for a bomb that exploded in Bangkok, blowing off a leg of Saeid Moradi, an Iranian man who was carrying it. Three Thai men and one Thai woman were treated at Kluaynamthai Hospital for their injuries from the blast. Two foreigners and the Iranian ran from the residence when some explosives went off. He tried to hail a cab, but the driver refused to take the blood-drenched Moradi. He then threw a bomb at the taxi and started running. Surrounded by police, he threw a grenade at them, but it bounced back, blowing off a leg. Police found Iranian currency, U.S. dollars, and Thai money in a satchel at the scene. Authorities found C4 explosives and two magnetic explosive devices in his house. His passport said he was Saeid Moradi from Iran. Mohammad Kharzei, 42, a second Iranian, was detained at Bangkok's international airport as he attempted to escape to Malaysia. A third man, Masoud Sedaghatzadeh, was arrested in Malaysia on February 15. A Bangkok court approved an arrest warrant for Leila Rohani, who rented the destroyed house before fleeing to Tehran. Thai police said on February 17 that they were searching for a fifth suspect who was seen on security cameras entering and exiting the house before the bomb went off. On February 27, Thai authorities arrested three more Iranians who were in contact with the key suspects.

Moradi arrived in Thailand from Seoul, South Korea, on February 8. He flew into Phuket, then stayed in a Chonburi hotel.

Israel said that the magnetic explosives were similar to those used in New Delhi and Tbilisi the previous day.

On March 15, Masoud Sedaghatzadeh, 31, an Iranian man held in Malaysia, told a Kuala Lumpur court that he was not involved and intended to fight extradition. Thai officials said he was seen leaving the building where the bomb went off. Malaysia ordered Sedaghatzadeh's extradition to Thailand on June 25, 2012. 12021401

February 17, 2012—Pakistan—A suicide bomber on a motorcycle killed twenty-three Shi'ite Muslims and wounded fifty people in a market in Parachinar near the Afghanistan border. Locals protested the attack and were fired on by security officials, who killed three people.

February 17, 2012—United States—Federal authorities arrested Amine el Khalifi, 29, a Moroccan illegally in the United States, as he walked to the U.S. Capitol wearing what he thought was a suicide vest. The Alexandria, Virginia, resident had been given an inerted vest and fake handgun by an FBI undercover agent. Retired patent attorney Frank Dynda, Khalifi's landlord, tipped off the FBI a year earlier about his suspicious behavior. For the rest of the year, the FBI learned he was considering attacking a synagogue, an Alexandria building with military offices, and a restaurant popular with military officers before settling on the Capitol target. He was arrested a few blocks from the Capitol at lunchtime, carrying the vest and an inoperable loaded automatic weapon which he believed had been provided by al Qaeda. He was charged in U.S. District Court in Alexandria, Virginia, with attempting to use a weapon of mass destruction against federal property. He faced life in prison.

He had arrived in the United States at age 16, then overstayed his visitor's visa while living in northern Virginia. He was evicted from an Arlington apartment in 2010 after missing rent payment. On December 1, 2011, Khalifi and Hussien, who Khalifi thought was an al Qaeda operative, met Yusuf, an undercover officer who Khalifi told he wanted to bomb an Alexandria building. On December 8, Khalifi told Hussien that he should attack a synagogue and an army general. On December 15, Khalifi told Hussien that he wanted to bomb a DC restaurant next to a government building; the duo visited the restaurant the next week. On January 7, 2012, Hussien told Khalifi that he worked for al Qaeda. They talked about conducting a second attack on a military site after Khalifi either shot up or bombed the restaurant. On January 8, Khalifi bought bomb-making materials. On January 15, Khalifi decided to conduct a suicide bombing against the Capitol. The duo set off a test bomb in a West Virginia quarry. Khalifi set the bombing date for February 17. The two visited the Capitol on January 28 and February 6. During the second surveillance and on February 12, Khalifi asked for a gun to shoot Capitol guards. On February 14, Yusuf gave Khalifi an inoperable weapon and what Khalifi thought was a suicide jacket. Khalifi tested its cell phone detonator. On February 17, Khalifi prayed at the northern Virginia Dar al-Hijrah mosque. The trio went to a parking garage near the Capitol, and Khalifi took what he thought would be his last walk. He was arrested several blocks away. Police raided a red brick rambler on Randolph Street in the Douglas Park neighborhood of Alexandria. A preliminary court hearing was set for February 22.

On June 22, 2012, Khalifi pleaded guilty in U.S. District Court in Alexandria to a charge of attempting to use a weapon of mass destruction against federal property. Under his plea bargain, he would serve twenty-five to thirty years. On September 14, 2012, Khalifi was sentenced to thirty years in prison. He was to be deported to Morocco after finishing his sentence.

February 22, 2012—Georgia—Five gunmen fired automatic rifles and grenade launchers and set off a roadside bomb under a motorcade at 8:30 a.m. in a failed attempt to kill Aleksandr Z. Ankvab, president of the Russian-backed rebel enclave Abkhazia. Ankvab was uninjured, but a bodyguard died and two others were seriously injured in the sixth assassination try against Ankvab in a decade. He had recently dismissed the entire staff of the immigration bureau on suspicion of corruption.

February 23, 2012—Pakistan—A Honda City car filled with 100 pounds of explosives and artillery shells was remotely detonated at a minibus depot in Peshawar, killing thirteen, including two children. No one claimed credit.

February 23, 2012—Afghanistan—As a wave of protests continued over inadvertent American burning of Qurans, a member of the Afghan Army shot to death two U.S. soldiers at a base in eastern Afghanistan.

February 24, 2012—Somalia—A missile strike in Kilometre 60, in the al-Shabaab-controlled Lower Shabelle region, killed an Egyptian and three Kenyan Islamists.

February 25, 2012—Yemen—A pickup truck bomb outside a presidential compound in Mukalla, Hadramout Province, killed twenty-five people hours after Yemen's new president, Abed Rabbo Mansour Hadi, was sworn in. Al Qaeda in the Arabian Peninsula was suspected.

February 25, 2012—Afghanistan—Abdul Saboor, an Afghan driver, turned his silenced pistol on his NATO counterparts, killing two U.S. officers inside the Interior Ministry building in Kabul. The duo were identified by the press as Air Force Lt. Col. John D. Loftis, 44, of Paducah, Kentucky and a Major Saboor, a Tajik from Parwan Province, did not appear to have Taliban links. He escaped from the Ministry.

February 26, 2012—Colombia—The Revolutionary Armed Forces of Colombia (FARC) announced that it would no longer kidnap civilians for ransom. It also said it would free its ten remaining "prisoners of war"—soldiers and policemen who had been held for more than a decade. It was believed to still hold one hundred civilian hostages. FARC did not mention their fate.

February 26, 2012—Afghanistan—Protestors demonstrating against the burning of Qurans threw a grenade, wounding at least six U.S. service members in the north.

February 26, 2012—Nigeria—A Boko Haram suicide bomber killed three people—a father, his child, and a woman—and hospitalized thirty-eight at the headquarters of the Church of Christ in Nigeria during an early morning service in Jos. The bomber hit a woman with his car while driving to the church compound. Boko Haram spokesman Abul Qaqa also claimed credit for burning down a primary school in Maiduguri and warned security agencies to not enter Islamic schools. "Our attacks have no distinction on any person, be him Muslim or Christian. For as long as they stand against us and our cause, their blood is legitimate to be shed."

February 28, 2012—Pakistan—Uniformed Sunni gunmen fired on a bus convoy ferrying Shi'ite passengers from Rawalpindi to Gilgit in Kohistan district in the north. They forced selected passengers to get off the bus, then shot to death all eighteen. The attack was conducted 102 miles north of Islamabad. The Pakistani Taliban claimed credit.

March 2012—Yemen—In two incidents, a Swiss woman and three Philippine nationals were kidnapped. As of March 28, they had not been released. 12039901-02

March 2012—Saudi Arabia—In mid–March, gunmen attacked a BBC news crew, killing a cameraman and critically wounding a senior correspondent as they tried to film a suspected terrorist's family home in the radical-infested Suweidi

neighborhood of Riyadh. The terrorist was identified as Ibrahim al-Rayyes, number 6 on the Saudis' Most Wanted Terrorists List. He was killed in early December 2011 in a shootout with police near a filling station in Suweidi. Eight security officers were wounded and a terrorist was killed in the gun battle. 12039903

March 2012—Saudi Arabia—In late March, two U.S. defense workers were gunned down outside their homes in Riyadh. 12039904-05

March 2012—Yemen—In two incidents, a Swiss woman and three Philippine nationals were kidnapped. As of March 28, they had not been released. On May 1, 2012, her kidnappers released a video of the Swiss hostage, who said that she was being held by al Qaeda and needed the Swiss government to help her. 12039906-07

March 1, 2012—Turkey—A remotely-detonated bomb injured fifteen police officers and a civilian in a police minibus near the Istanbul headquarters of the ruling Justice and Development Party (AK Party). No one claimed credit.

March 1, 2012—Afghanistan—An Afghan soldier and an Afghan civilian teaching a literacy course on a NATO-Afghan base in the Zhari district of southern Kandahar Province shot to death two U.S. troops and injured a third. NATO troops shot to death the gunmen. 12030101

March 1, 2012—Yemen—A gunman fired several shots at an armored vehicle carrying a U.S. security team training Yemeni soldiers. No one was injured. 12030102

March 2, 2012—Pakistan—A Pakistani Taliban suicide bomber killed twenty-three people when he attacked the headquarters of the rival Lashkar-e-Islam insurgent group in the northwest Tirah Valley.

March 3, 2012—Algeria—A four-wheel-drive Toyota crashed into the entrance of the headquarters of the national police in Tamanrasset, 1,200 miles south of Algiers, at 7:45 a.m., wounding fifteen officers, five firemen, and three bystanders. A local journalist said five police officers had died. Al Qaeda in the Islamic Maghreb was suspected.

March 4, 2012—Yemen—Ansar al-Sharia, a group linked to al Qaeda in the Arabian Peninsula (AQAP), conducted two suicide bomb attacks in Zinjibar, killing nearly two hundred soldiers. They also captured seventy soldiers. AQAP later claimed credit.

March 8, 2012—Thailand—Four soldiers escorting Buddhist villagers were killed by a bomb set by Islamist terrorists.

March 10, 2012—Kenya—The government blamed al-Shabaab for a series of grenade attacks in Nairobi that killed at least six and injured nearly seventy. People in a car threw three grenades at an outdoor bus terminal, killing four and wounding forty. The Red Cross said a dozen people were in critical condition. Among the injured was Frederick Shikutu, 36. 12031001

March 11, 2012—Pakistan—A suicide bomber killed at least fifteen mourners and wounded another thirty-seven at a funeral attended by anti–Taliban politician Khush Dil Khan, who was unhurt in the attack in Badhber in the Peshawar suburbs. Among the hospitalized was Zahir Khan, 32, whose brother was killed.

March 11, 2012—Afghanistan—U.S. Staff Sgt. Robert Bales, 38, wearing local garb and carrying a 9-mm pistol and an M-4 rifle with a grenade launcher, walked out of his base at 3:00 a.m. and went to Najeeban and Alokozo (also identified as Balandi and Alkozai), two villages in the Panjwai district of Kandahar Province, where he shot to death seventeen sleeping people, including three women and nine children, before coming back to his base and surrendering. At least eight other children were wounded. Bales was on his fourth war zone tour of duty; three others were in Iraq. He was flown to Kuwait, then later to Fort Leavenworth, Kansas, to await criminal charges for leaving his post, killing the people, and trying to burn their bodies. There was some evidence that he had returned to base before the second attack. He was from Joint Base Fort Lewis-McChord, in Washington State. The highly decorated soldier had been hurt twice in Iraq, suffering a concussion and losing part of his foot. The married father of two had received a diagnosis of traumatic brain injury. He was a member of the 3rd Stryker Brigade Combat Team, 2nd Infantry Division. The Taliban vowed to avenge the deaths, observing, "If the perpetrators of this massacre were in fact mentally ill, then this testifies to yet another moral transgression by the American military because they are arming lunatics in Afghanistan who turn their weapons against defenseless Afghans." Prosecutors at Fort Leavenworth, Kansas, charged Bales on March 23 with seventeen counts of murder, six counts of attempted murder and aggravated assault, and dereliction of duty. He was represented by attorney John Henry Browne of Seattle.

March 11, 2012—Nigeria—A suicide car bomber killed ten people during the day's final Mass at St. Finbar's Catholic Church in Jos. He had been stopped at the gate of the compound. Boko Haram was suspected.

March 11, 2012—France—Mohammed Merah, 23, a gunman on a motorcycle, shot and killed a French soldier of north African origin who was on his motorcycle. He used a .45 caliber pistol. The soldier was not in uniform and the motorcycle did not have military identification on it. Merah posted a video of the shooting, telling the soldier, "You kill my brothers, I kill you." Paratrooper Imad Ibn Ziaten answered an online ad to purchase a scooter in Toulouse. Ziaten had said he was in the military. Merah used his brother's IP address to set up the fatal meeting with Ziaten. 12031101

March 13, 2012—Ethiopia—Gunmen in the southwest killed nineteen people in an attack on a public bus in Gambella region.

March 14, 2012—Azerbaijan—The Ministry of National Security arrested twenty-two people accused of plotting terrorist attacks against Western, U.S. and Israeli embassies and other targets at the behest of the Iranian Revolutionary Guard Corps. The Azeri cell members were trained in "camps around Tehran" and elsewhere in Iran. Their Iranian handlers met them in Syria and Russia, according to the Ministry. The Ministry said the group can be traced back to 1999, and had been given money, weapons, and military training. The group had obtained weapons and explosives.

March 14, 2012—Afghanistan—An Afghan crashed a stolen pickup truck into a ditch near the plane of arriving U.S. Defense Secretary Leon E. Panetta. The man burst into flames but his truck did not. The Afghan was an interpreter working for the coalition forces at the Camp Bastion military airfield, a British complex adjoining Camp Leatherneck. The attacker had tried to run over a group of U.S. Marines and other dignitaries waiting on a runway ramp for the plane. The attacker died a day later of extensive burns. No explosives were found in the car or on the attacker, who was not wearing a suicide vest. He apparently tried to ignite gasoline containers in the cab of the truck. Secretary Panetta denied that he was the target. The man had hijacked the truck thirty minutes earlier, injuring a British soldier. A military dog who apparently pulled the attacker from the wreck sustained slight burn wounds. 12031401

March 15, 2012—United States—Bakhtiyor Jumaev, a Philadelphia resident believed to be from Uzbekistan, was arrested and charged in Philadelphia in an alleged plot to provide support to an Uzbek terrorist organization. He was represented by attorney Barnaby Wittels. Authorities said Jumaev sent $300 to Uzbek refugee Jamshid Muhtorov, who lived in Aurora, Colorado. Muhtorov was arrested on January 12, 2012, while traveling in Chicago. Investigators believed the duo was planning a "wedding"—a terrorist attack by the Islamic Jihad Union.

March 16, 2012—France—Black-clad gunman Mohammed Merah, riding a motorcycle, shot and killed two French paratroopers of North African and French Caribbean descent and injured a black soldier from the French Antilles while they were using an ATM in a shopping center in Montauban. Merah posted a video of the shooting, during which he yelled, "Allahu Akbar." He used a .45 caliber pistol to kill Abel Chennouf, 25, and Mohamed Legouade, 23. The wounded soldier went into a coma. 12031601

March 16, 2012—Pakistan/United States—The *Washington Post* reported that documents captured at Osama bin Laden's compound on May 2, 2011, showed that he planned to kill President Obama so that he could deal with an "unprepared" Vice President Biden and also planned to kill then–Commander of U.S. forces in Afghanistan Gen. David Petraeus. Bin Laden proposed an attack on Air Force One.

March 17, 2012—Syria—Two suicide car bombers killed 27 people and injured 140 others in front of the intelligence and security buildings in Damascus. Authorities said a third bomb went off at a Palestinian refugee camp in Damascus, but the two bombers were the only casualties.

March 18, 2012—Yemen—In Taiz, an al Qaeda in the Arabian Peninsula gunman riding on the back of a motorcycle shot to death Joel Shrum, 29, an American teacher serving as an advisor at a Swedish-affiliated institute. Shrum was on his way to work. The al Qaeda-linked Ansar al-Sharia texted to the news media, "This operation comes as a response to the campaign of Christian proselytizing that the West has launched against Muslims." Shrum, of Mount Joy, Pennsylvania, had gone to Yemen in 2009 to learn Arabic. He had been living in the country with his wife and two children. 12031801

March 18, 2012—Indonesia—Counterterrorism police killed five members of a Jemaah Islamiyah splinter group in Bali who were considering conducting a series of robberies of jewelry stores, including two that night. The police raided two hotels in the Denpasar area of Bali. Authorities seized two guns and ammunition. Police believed they were responsible for a bank robbery in Medan, North Sumatra, in 2010. The press later reported that they planned to bomb the Hard Rock Café and other Western targets.

March 18, 2012—Syria—A bomb went off at a government security building in Aleppo, killing a police officer and a civilian and injuring thirty people.

March 19, 2012—France—At 8:00 a.m., Mohammed Merah, 23, a French citizen of Algerian descent, riding a Yamaha T-Max 530 motor scooter, shot to death French Israeli Rabbi Jonathan Sandler, 30, and his two sons, Gabriel, 6, and Arieh, 3, and Miriam Monsonego, 8-year-old daughter of the school's director, at the Jewish elementary Ozar Hatorah school in Toulouse before escaping. He drove up and shot two pistols at a group of children waiting in front of the school, then followed others into a courtyard as they ran toward the building. Monsonego died in front of her father, Yaacov. All of the dead were dual Israeli French nationals and all were shot in the head. Another six students were wounded, including a 17-year-old boy who was in serious condition at a local hospital. Merah had used the same .45 caliber Colt semiautomatic pistol in his attacks on French paratroopers of North African descent on March 11 and 15.

Merah wounded three police officers in a shootout in a Toulouse house. On March 21 at 3:00 p.m., he was surrounded by three hundred police officers and said he would surrender at night "to be more discreet." He threw a pistol out the window in exchange for a "communication device," but police believed he retained other weapons, including an AK-47. Although he appeared to have acted alone, he told police negotiators that he had met al Qaeda leaders while in Pakistan in 2011. He said he was acting for "revenge for Palestinian children" and was attacking the French Army because of its involvement in Afghanistan and for French banning of Islamic veils. He claimed to be a member of al Qaeda who had been to Afghanistan twice and had trained in Waziristan. Authorities said he planned to kill another soldier and two police officers. His brother was implicated in a network sending foreign fighters to Iraq. After a thirty-two-hour siege, he was shot to death.

Also on March 21, police arrested another man at a separate location in connection with the school shooting.

Merah was well-known to authorities. The Toulouse-born delinquent who had worked in a body shop had been sentenced fifteen times in Toulouse juvenile court when he was a minor for such offenses as purse-snatching and possession of stolen goods. Acquaintances said he was not particularly devout as a juvenile and had taken to wearing punk garb. He had been represented on a charge of driving without a valid license by attorney Christian Etelin, who said his client was psychologically impaired. He twice tried to join the French armed forces. He was turned down in Lille because of prior convictions. In July 2010, he tried to join the Foreign Legion in Toulouse but left after the first round of tests.

France 24 said French intelligence had tracked Merah for several years. Merah was arrested in Afghanistan on December 19, 2007. He was sentenced to three years for planting bombs in Kandahar. He escaped from Kandahar prison in 2008. Afghan police picked him up at a traffic stop and sent him back to France, which placed him under surveillance. Merah became involved with a group of fifteen extremists upon returning to France. He was on a U.S. no-fly list.

Merah called Ebba Kalondo, the senior news editor of the television network France 24, two hours before police surrounded him in his hideout, to talk about the attacks.

The press said authorities found him after being tipped off by a Toulouse motorcycle shop owner, who reported that a man had asked how to turn off the GPS in his TMX scooter. When the police RAID team arrived at 3:00 a.m. at Merah's house 2 miles from the school, he shot through the door, injuring one officer in the knee, one in the shoulder, and wounding a third. Police detained his mother, elder brother, and two sisters, seeking to get their help in dealing with him. Merah said he was a member of Forsane Alizza (Knights of Glory), which the French government had banned in January for recruiting people to fight in Afghanistan. Before its banning, it posted on Facebook a call to attack Americans, Jews, and French soldiers.

On March 22 at 11:30 a.m., the siege ended when Merah, wearing a bulletproof vest, emerged from a bathroom and fired thirty shots at police, who returned fire, using at least three hundred rounds of ammunition. Merah jumped out a window onto a balcony, apparently was hit in the head, and toppled to the ground, dead. Two police officers were injured. Merah had two bullets left in his gun. Police found rifles and material for making bombs.

The little known Kazakhstan-based Jund al-Khilafah said "Yusuf of France" was responsible for the school attack. French officials said it was probably an opportunistic claim and that Merah had not heard of them.

The attacks came just before French national elections on April 23 and May 6.

Al-Jazeera said it had decided against broadcasting Merah's murder videos.

On March 25, investigating judges filed preliminary murder and terrorism charges against an Islamist radical with ties to a jihadi network—Abdelkader Merah, 29, the gunman's older brother. He denied the charges.

On June 11, 2012, Mohamed Benalel Merah, Mohammed Merah's father, filed a lawsuit in Paris alleging murder in the killing by police of his son. His legal team included terrorist Carlos's wife Isabelle Courtant-Peyre and Algerian lawyer Zahia Mokhtari. 12031901

March 19–20, 2012—Somalia—Al-Shabaab conducted nighttime mortar attacks on the Presidential Palace, killing five and injuring several others. The five mortar attack landed on a refugee camp next to the presidential compound, killing five. Abu Zubeyr, alias Ahmed Godane, an al-Shabaab commander, aired a twenty-five-minute message on the group's radio station calling for other Somalis to join the Jihad.

March 20, 2012—United Kingdom—Former Russian banker German Gorbuntsov was shot in East London; police viewed it as an attempted murder. Ten days later, prosecutors were attempting to deport a suspected Chechen government assassin.

March 21, 2012—United States—Shaima Alawadi, 32, an Iraqi woman whose family had been in the United States since the mid–1990s, was found severely beaten on the head with a tire iron, next to a threatening note saying, "Go back to your country, you terrorist." Fatima Al-Himidi, 17, her daughter, found her lying in a pool of blood that morning in the dining room of the house in El Cajon, California. The mother of five died on March 24. The family received a similar note earlier in the month but had not reported it to authorities. The family had moved from Michigan a few weeks earlier. Alawadi's husband had previously worked in San Diego as a private contractor for the U.S. Army, serving as a cultural adviser to train soldiers deploying to the Middle East. Police were investigating whether the murder was a hate crime. She was buried in Iraq on March 31.

March 22, 2012—Internet—Al Qaeda message forums al-Shamukh al-Islam, al-Fidaa, and Ansar al-Mujahideen Arabic Forum started going offline, possibly from a cyber attack. Al-Mujahidin and al-Shamukh returned briefly. The administrator of another al Qaeda site posted, "The media arena is witnessing a vicious attack by the cross and its helpers on the jihadi media castles." Al-Shamukh returned on April 4, noting, "The enemies of Allah who boast of their freedoms have not spared any effort to eradicate our blessed media." Five other sites remained offline.

March 25, 2012—United Kingdom—The *Sunday Times* received a four-minute video from Wal-iur Rehman, deputy commander of the Pakistani Tehrik-e-Taliban, in which he claimed that Muslim prisoners, including Bilal Abdullah, the Glasgow airport bomber, and Dhiren Barot, a "dirty bomb" plotter, were being mistreated in U.K. jails. The video was filmed the previous week near Miranshah, capital of North Waziristan. He threatened "severe revenge" if Muslim prisoners were not released. "If the British government does not comply with this, then our revenge against the British government will be very severe. These are not just words. We will show them in practice. We will show them how we take revenge for the mistreatment of our brothers." He claimed Abdullah and Barot were "stripped naked and their dignity violated." "They poured hot kerosene oil on [Barot's] face."

March 26, 2012—Afghanistan—An Afghan Army soldier shot to death two U.K. troops at the entrance of the provincial reconstruction team headquarters in Lashkar Gah, capital of Helmand Province. Foreign forces returned fire, killing him. A member of a U.S.-trained Afghan Local Police Force fatally shot a NATO soldier as troops approached a militia checkpoint. Since May 2007, Afghan security forces had killed at least eighty NATO troops.

March 27, 2012—Spain—Police in Valencia arrested Muhrad Hussein Almalki, "al Qaeda's librarian," on charges of broadcasting videos on the Internet to incite terrorist attacks. He had been under investigation since February 2011. He was suspected of working with al Qaeda in the Arabian Peninsula and al Qaeda in the Islamic Mahgreb. He supervised one of the al Qaeda sites that went dark in late March 2012 and posted often under aliases on two others.

March 27, 2012—Afghanistan—The Defense Ministry went into lockdown after the discovery of ten suicide vests, mostly in guard sheds around a parking lot, and the arrests of sixteen soldiers and civilians suspected of planning to attack the ministry and the intelligence agency and bomb commuter buses carrying government employees home. Two suspected bombers reportedly were at large.

March 28, 2012—Yemen—Unknown gunmen kidnapped Saudi deputy consul Abdullah al-Khalidi from his vehicle near his residence in Rimi, in the Mansoora district. On April 17, 2012, Saudi Interior Ministry spokesman Maj. Gen. Mansour al-Turki said that al Qaeda had claimed credit and was demanding the release of prisoners and a ransom payment. He said Saudi terror suspect Mashaal Rasheed al-Shawdakhi had phoned the Saudi Embassy in Yemen, threatening to kill al-Khalidi if the government did not release senior al Qaeda prisoners, both Saudi and Yemeni, and six female prisoners in Saudi jails. Shawdakhi claimed that Nasser al-Washidi, leader of al Qaeda in the Arabian Peninsula (AQAP) had appointed him to release the demands. AQAP released al-Khalidi on August 11, 2012, after tribal mediation efforts. The terms of his release were not disclosed. 12032801

March 28, 2012—Pakistan—Gunmen conducted two attacks in Baluchistan's Mastung district. In one attack, gunmen fired on a car carrying local staff of the UN Food and Agriculture Organization, killing a driver and a member of the group's project staff. Another member of the staff was wounded. In Quetta, gunmen on motorcycles fired on a passenger van, killing four Shi'ites. 1203 2802

March 30, 2012—Afghanistan—A member of the Afghan Local Police in Paktika Province shot to death nine drugged colleagues in their sleep, then escaped in a government vehicle full of guns and ammunition.

March 30, 2012—Afghanistan—Acid was thrown into the faces and the mouths of two children. The Afghan National Army brought their bodies to the local hospital after villagers found them in Nani village in eastern Ghazni Province's Andar district. The identity of their parents was unknown.

March 30, 2012—Afghanistan—Asadullah, alias Mujahid Sanaullah, 22, a member of the Afghan Local Police in Paktika Province, shot to death nine colleagues—including eight police officers—whom he had drugged, in their sleep, then escaped with two terrorists in a Toyota Ranger police pickup truck filled with ten rifles and twenty-five magazines of ammunition. He had been a Taliban fighter for several years. His neighbors said he had given the Taliban permission to kill his father, Ehsanulah, a government official and religious leader in the Yayakhil district of Paktika Province. Authorities detained two of Asadullah's brothers following the shootings. Among the dead was Mohammed Ramazan, a police commander who had supported Asadullah's participation in a reintegration program for former Taliban insurgents, and two of Ramazan's sons.

March 30, 2012—France—Police arrested nineteen or twenty Islamic militants in early morning raids in Toulouse, Paris, and southern and western cities including Nantes, seizing Kalashnikov assault rifles. Among those detained was Mohammed Achamlane, leader of the small militant group Forsan al-Izza. He denied that the group seeks jihadi recruits. President Nicolas Sarkozy said at least some of the detainees would be expelled. Seven were held for questioning; two were released.

On April 4, 2012, thirteen of those arrested were placed under formal investigation for "criminal conspiracy in connection with a terrorist enterprise," and possession and transportation of weapons. Nine of the thirteen were jailed, including Achamlane. The other four were released on April 3 but remained "under judicial control." Achamlane was represented by attorney Philippe Missamou. French prosecutor Francois Molins said the detainees were "calling for the establishment of an Islamic caliphate in France and calling for the implementation of Sharia law and inciting Muslims in France to unite for the preparation of a civil war." Prosecutors said Achamlane's followers held "discussions during a meeting held in Lyon in September 2011 about a plan to kidnap a judge based in Lyon."

March 31, 2012—Thailand—Bombs killed 14 and wounded more than 500 in Yala and Songkhla provinces. Buildings, cars, and motorcycles were damaged in the attacks on shoppers and a high-rise hotel. Bombs hidden in two stolen trucks went off in Yala, setting fire to nearby vehicles and buildings and killing 11 and injuring 110. The second bomb went off twenty minutes after the first, injuring numerous people who had gathered after the initial attack. An hour later, a car bomb went off in the underground parking of the 405-room Lee Gardens Plaza Hotel in Songkhla Province, killing at least 3, including a Malaysian tourist, and injuring 400, mostly from smoke inhalation. The bomb set off a fire at a high rise hotel in Hat Yai city and badly damaged a McDonald's. A fourth bomb on a motorcycle went off 50 meters from a local police station in the Mae Lan district of Pattani Province, wounding a police officer. Islamist insurgents were suspected. 12033101

March 31, 2012—Kenya—Two nighttime grenade attacks killed one person and injured thirty-three others. One grenade went off in the southeastern town of Mtwapa, killing one and injuring thirty-one. Another was thrown into a stadium in the coastal city of Mombasa, injuring two others. No one claimed credit, but al-Shabaab posted an Internet message that observed,

The deteriorating insecurity in Kenyan cities is an embodiment of Kenya's misguided policies that place foreign interests above its national interests and the security of Western nations above the security of its citizens, thereby wasting the lives of its men and its resources for no real gain.... The Kenyan public must be aware that the more Kenyan troops continue to persecute innocent Muslims of Somalia, the less secure Kenyan cities will be; and the more oppression the Muslims of Somalia feel, the more constricted Kenyan life will be.... Such is the law of Retribution. Your security depends on our security. It is a long, protracted war and Kenyans must neither harbor a reason for optimism nor hope for triumph.

March 31, 2012—Nigeria—Security forces raided a suspected Boko Haram bomb factory in Okene in Kogi State. During the raid, the group killed a soldier and a member of the State Security Service. Elsewhere, Boko Haram shot to death local politician Wanangu Kachuwa after returning to his home in Maiduguri following a church service. Also that night, the group burned down two police stations in separate cities in Yobe State, injuring two police officers.

March 31, 2012—Saudi Arabia—Al Qaeda in the Arabian Peninsula (AQAP) abducted Paul Johnson, 49, of Stafford Township, New Jersey, a Lockheed Martin employee. The kidnappers released a video on April 3 showing a blindfolded Johnson and threatened to kill him within seventy-two hours if the government did not release al Qaeda prisoners. The video showed a man reading a statement and holding an AK-47. A subtitle said that he was Abdulaziz al-Moqrin, head of the Saudi branch of AQAP.

April 2012—Mali—Gunmen claiming to be acting under the orders of al Qaeda in the Islamic Maghreb kidnapped a Swiss missionary in Timbuktu. She was later freed after negotiations. 1204 9901

April 2012—Georgia—Authorities arrested smugglers from Abkhazia who were bringing three glass containers with 2.2 pounds of yellowcake uranium.

April 2012—Georgia—Authorities arrested three men in a hotel suite in Batumi offering radioactive cesium. One of the Turkish men said he could provide uranium. The buyers, undercover agents, said they would photograph the four cylinders and see if their leader was interested. Police then arrested the trio. The arrests were linked to Soslan Oniani. One lead cylinder held cesium–137, two held strontium–90, and the fourth held a spent nuclear material which could be used to make a radioactive dispersal device (dirty bomb). The two Turks and Oniani were convicted in a Georgian court in September 2012 and sentenced to six years in prison.

April 2012—Turkey—Ankara authorities arrested three Turkish men with a kilogram of cesium–135. Georgian officials said they were residents of Germany and were driving a German-plated car. The material originated in Abkhazia. Turkish authorities said the trio entered the country from Georgia.

April 2, 2012—Colombia—A loaned Brazilian Air Force helicopter took off from an airstrip in central Colombia to pick up six police officers and four soldiers who were being released by the Revolutionary Armed Forces of Colombia (FARC), who had kidnapped them a dozen years earlier. They were FARC's last group of government hostages, although hundreds of civilians remained captive.

April 2, 2012—United Kingdom—Government lawyers accused E1, 45, a Chechen-born former elite soldier described as "a henchman" of President Ramzan A. Kadyrov of Chechnya, of seeking to assassinate Akhmed K. Zakayev, a prominent Chechen politician who was granted asylum in 2003 in London. Government attorneys said E1 was involved in a 2009 Kadyrov-sponsored assassination in Vienna, Austria.

April 2, 2012—Internet—Jihadi forums posted a photo of the New York City skyline at sunset, overlaid with the text "Al Qaeda: Coming Soon Again in New York."

April 2, 2012—Pakistan—Judge Shahrukh Arjumand sentenced thee wives and two adult daughters of Osama bin Laden to serve six weeks and pay a fine of $110 for violating immigration laws. They were formally arrested on March 3. They were to be deported to their respective countries on April 15. Kharia Hussain Sabir and Siham Sharif were Saudis, as were the two adult daughters. Amal Ahmad Abdul Fateh, 30, is a Yemeni who was wounded when bin Laden was shot in a SEAL raid on May 2, 2011, in Abbotabad. Fateh had born him five children. They had faced five years, but Pakistan wanted them and their children out of the country.

April 4, 2012—Somalia—A young Al-Shabaab female suicide bomber killed six people, including two senior sports officials—Said Mohamed Nur Mugambe, head of the Somali football federation, and Somali Olympic Committee president Adan Hagi Yabarow Wiish—and injured a dozen, including Prime Minister Abdiweli Mohamed Ali,

ten journalists, and a lawmaker, during a celebration of the first anniversary of Somali national television in Somalia's newly reopened National Theater in Mogadishu. The skinny woman, in her early 20s, was carrying a police ID. Al-Shabaab said that it had planted explosives at the theater ahead of time.

April 4, 2012—France—DCRI authorities arrested another ten Islamists in Roubaix, Lyon, Bordeaux, Valence, Pau, Marseille, Carpentras, and in the Lot et Garonne region. They were suspected of links to Islamist Web sites and threatening violence in online postings. An official said some of them might have been trying to obtain terrorist training on the Afghanistan-Pakistan border.

April 4, 2012—Lebanon—A sniper fired bullets past the head and torso of Samir Geagea, leader of the Lebanese Forces, one of the country's main Christian parties, as he bent down to pick up a flower. The sniper was on a hilltop, one kilometer away. Hizballah was suspected.

April 5, 2012—China—The Ministry of Public Security added six Turkic Uighur men to its list of terrorists, accusing them of involvement in East Turkestan Islamic Movement terrorist attacks in Zinjiang. They remained at large. The Ministry said they had recruited and trained members for the organization, provided funding, and incited violence, including suicide bombings.

April 5, 2012—Mali—Unidentified gunmen kidnapped Algeria's consul in Gao and five consular officials. The town was under control of Tuareg separatists. The Movement for Oneness and Jihad in West Africa (MUJAO), an ally of al Qaeda in the Islamic Maghreb, was suspected. Authorities later changed the number of hostages to seven. As of April 30, the hostages remained detained. On September 2, 2012, MUJAO spokesman Oumar Ould Hamaha said the group had killed the Algerian diplomat. "We did this so that Algeria learns a lesson and understands that when we give an ultimatum, they need to take us seriously. And so that other countries know that when we give an ultimatum in regards to their hostages, they need to act." 12040501

April 6, 2012—Libya—Explosives were thrown over the wall of the U.S. Consulate in Benghazi. No one was injured. Two former Libyan guards hired by a security contractor were taken into custody. They drove a car owned by compound guard Ahmed Marimi. They were released by the Libyan government for lack of "hard evidence." Ibrahim Faqzi Etwear was a former employee of Blue

Mountain Group of Carmarthen, Wales, who had been fired four days earlier for vandalism. The other suspect was Mohe el-Dean Bacher, a recently demoted guard. 12040601

April 6, 2012—Yemen—An al Qaeda in the Arabian Peninsula bomber died when his explosives detonated prematurely as he attempted to attack an intelligence office in Mansoura in southern Aden Province. A motorcyclist he had tricked into giving him a ride also died.

April 8, 2012—Nigeria—A suicide car bomber killed forty-one people in front of the All Nations Christian Assembly Church in Kaduna on Easter morning. The car exploded at a roadside junction where men sold black market gasoline, which caught fire. Boko Haram was blamed. As of April 10, it had not spoken of the attack.

Later that day, a bomb went off in Jos, killing sixteen.

April 9, 2012—Somalia—Al-Shabaab bombed a vegetable market in Baidoa, killing a dozen people and wounding thirty. Police arrested one suspect. The group posted on its Web site, "The explosion has targeted Ethiopians and their apostate companions. Then they opened fire at the civilians in the market, killing five people on the spot."

April 9, 2012—Nigeria—Suspected Boko Haram gunmen fired on a policeman and his family in Potiskum, a city in the northeast, killing the policeman's 6-year-old daughter. Meanwhile, gunmen killed three people in attacks on a police station, church, and bank in the northeastern border town of Dikwa. A local politician, a police officer, a civilian, and three gunmen died in the attacks, which were blamed on Boko Haram.

April 9, 2012—Egypt—An explosion went off at the Egyptian pipeline carrying gas to Israel and Jordan in the northern Sinai at the entrance of the town of al-Arish. No group claimed credit. It was the fourteenth attack on the pipeline since the uprising against former President Hosni Mubarak. The pipeline is run by Gasco, a subsidiary of the national gas company EGAS. 12040901

April 9, 2012—Peru—Masked Shining Path gunmen took nearly forty oil and gas workers hostage near natural gas fields near Kepashiato in a bid to foil an army capture operation. The employees work for the Swedish firm Skanska, which services Peru's main natural gas pipeline. Some fifteen hundred troops and police joined the search for the hostages. The Shining Path fired on a military helicopter that was part of the dragnet, killing a police captain and injuring two people. The group demanded a $10 million ransom, along with explosives and weapons. The government said it would not negotiate. The Maoist faction, led by Martin Quispe, alias Comrade Gabriel, freed the hostages after being surrounded by government troops on April 14. At least six security agents were killed during the rescue. Quispe appeared on television to say that his group was now named the Militarized Communist Party of Peru. 1204 0902

April 12, 2012—Nigeria—Boko Haram leader Imam Abubakar Shekau posted a fourteen-minute Internet video addressing Nigerian President Goodluck Jonathan. "You the helpless, we heard that you intend and want to destroy us, but this talk is useless when it is said by an infidel because only God can destroy us. Until now, nobody was able to do that, and you, too, will not be able to do anything, with God's help.... One day you kill one thousand and then we turn back, then after two days we kill your own one hundred. We're turning it around like the way it is in the Quran." Shekau was in a white robe; he was joined by gunmen holding Kalashnikov rifles. He spoke in Arabic and Hausa. The video included a Hausa song about the sect, saying it was ready to kill nonbelievers. The video included the group's logo of two crossed Kalashnikovs around a Quran and a black Islamist flag, similar to that used by al Qaeda in the Islamic Mahgreb.

April 14, 2012—Colombia—Four bombs exploded in the country apparently in protest of the visit of President Barack Obama for the Summit of the Americas. Leftist rebels were suspected. Two bombs went off in a ditch in a residential area near the attorney general's office and the U.S. Embassy, breaking windows but causing no casualties. Two other bombs went off in Cartagena.

April 15, 2012—Afghanistan—The Taliban conducted coordinated attacks at 1:45 p.m. against several Western embassies in Kabul's diplomatic quarter. Taliban spokesman Zabihullah Mujahid credited a "spring offensive" that it had planned for months. "This is a message to those foreign commanders who claim that the Taliban lost momentum. We just showed that we are here and we will launch and stage attacks whenever we want." Local police captured two terrorists with suicide-bomb vests and destroyed a car bomb near the parliament building. U.S. Embassy staff were reported safe but under lockdown. The Taliban said it had targeted the U.K. and German embassies, the headquarters of NATO's International Security Assistance Force (ISAF), and President Hamid Karzai's presidential palace compound. Two rockets hit a British Embassy guard tower and a rocket-propelled grenade landed outside the front gate of a house used by British diplomats. Rockets were also fired at the Russian, U.K., German, and Canadian embassies and the parliament building. Fighting was reported at seven locations, including near the U.S., Russian, and German embassies. Three rockets hit a supermarket that is popular with foreigners near the German Embassy. The Taliban attacked the Star Hotel complex near the presidential palace and the Iranian Embassy. Gun battles went on for at least fourteen hours. The Pakistan-based Haqqani branch of the Taliban was blamed. The Interior Ministry said seventeen terrorists were killed and seventeen police officers and fourteen civilians were injured in the attacks in Kabul and several outlying areas. 12041501-05

April 15, 2012—Mali—Islamists believed linked to al Qaeda in the Islamic Mahgreb (AQIM) kidnapped Swiss missionary Beatrice Stockly. She was released on October 24, 2012. 12041501

April 16, 2012—Nigeria—Boko Haram shot dead two people in Maiduguri.

April 17, 2012—Afghanistan—The Taliban was suspected of poisoning the well of a school for girls in Rostaq in Takhar Province, hospitalizing 171 women and girls ranging in age from 14 to 30. Police took 2 school caretakers into custody.

April 17, 2012—Nigeria—Authorities raided Boko Haram sites in Maiduguri, killed one member and arrested thirteen others.

April 18, 2012—Nigeria—The US Embassy warned Americans that "Boko Haram may be planning attacks in Abuja, Nigeria, including against hotels frequently visited by Westerners." In November 2011, the embassy had warned of possible attacks against the Hilton, Sheraton, and Nicon Luxury hotels in Abuja.

April 18, 2012—Azerbaijan—The Ministry of National Security announced that it had disbanded a terrorist cell of twenty al Qaeda-linked operatives who were planning to attack "shrines, mosques, and prayer houses," as well as "law enforcement agencies" to "create [an] atmosphere of ... confusion and horror among the population." The Ministry noted that some members of the cell had logged two months receiving "weapons and physical training in the Islamic Republic of Iran." The *Weekly Standard* reported that the cell was aided by Ibrahimkhalil "Saleh" Davudov before he was killed by Russian security forces in 2012. Davudov had been head of Dagestani terrorists and reported to Chechen terrorist leader Doku Umarov. The government said some of the terror-

ists were trained in northern Pakistan by the Islamic Jihad Union, which is affiliated with al Qaeda.

April 19, 2012—Nigeria—Suspected Boko Haram gunmen attacked a bakery and shot others in a Maiduguri street, killing seven people, including an officer of the Nigeria Customs Service, a man selling drinking water in the street, and five people working overnight in the bakery near a branch of Nigeria's Central Bank.

April 19, 2012—Tajikistan—A court in Khujand convicted thirty-four people of participation in a terrorist group and sentenced them to terms ranging from eight to twenty-eight years. Some were charged with murder and attempting the violent overthrow of the country. They were believed to be members of the Islamic Movement of Uzbekistan.

April 19, 2012—Kazakhstan—A court sentenced forty-seven people to up to fifteen years on terrorism charges after a month-long secret trial in the western region of the country. Some forty-two defendants were jailed on charges of forming a terrorist group, financing extremist activity, and organizing a series of attacks. The other five were linked to Jund al-Khilafah attacks in Atyrau, a western oil city, in October 2011; only a bomber was killed. The defendants were between 22 and 32 years old. Two were from Uzbekistan.

April 20, 2012—United Kingdom—West Midlands Counter Terrorism Unit police at Heathrow Airport arrested three Birmingham men on suspicion of "possessing articles and documents with intent to use them for terrorist purposes overseas." The trio, aged 33 to 39, had arrived that night from Oman.

April 20, 2012—United Kingdom—Al-Shabaab posted a warning on jihadi Web sites that the United Kingdom faced terrorist attacks if it deported radical Muslim cleric Abu Qatada.

April 21, 2012—Afghanistan—The National Directorate of Security (NDS) intelligence agency said that it had arrested Haqqani terrorists planning to kill Second Vice President Karim Khalili and a second group of three Pakistanis and two Afghans who were smuggling 11 tons of explosives into Kabul hidden in a truck of potatoes. A government spokesman said that the trio, all Afghans, hailed from Paktia, Ghazni, and Wardak provinces, and "all the detained individuals confessed their involvement during the preliminary investigations and admitted that they had been dispatched to military, terrorist, and suicide training camps in Miran Shah, Pakistan." NDS said the smuggling was organized by the Pakistani Taliban and the Qari Baryal group.

April 23, 2012—Kenya—The U.S. Embassy warned U.S. citizens "residing in or visiting Kenya that the U.S. Embassy in Nairobi has received credible information regarding a possible attack on Nairobi hotels and prominent Kenyan government buildings." The attacks could include "suicide operations, bombings, kidnappings, attacks on civil aviation, and attacks on maritime vessels in or near Kenyan ports."

April 24, 2012—Nigeria—A bomb exploded at a bar in a Christian neighborhood in Jos where people were watching Chelsea play Barcelona in the Champions League. One person was killed and nine others injured. Boko Haram was suspected.

April 24, 2012—Pakistan—A time bomb containing between 13 and 18 pounds of explosives went off in Lahore's busiest rail station, killing two and injuring twenty-seven who were in the waiting area of Business Express, a luxury train service linking Lahore and Karachi. Lashkar-e-Baluchistan (Army of Baluchistan) claimed credit.

April 24, 2012—United Kingdom—In morning raids in Luton, members of the counterterrorism unit of London's Metropolitan Police Service arrested five men, aged 21 to 35, on "the suspicion of the commission, preparation, or instigation of acts of terrorism."

April 25, 2012—Syria—An explosion killed sixteen people when it flattened a block of houses in Hama. The government claimed rebel bomb makers accidentally set off the bomb, but anti-government activists blamed government shelling and said the death toll was seventy.

April 26, 2012—Nigeria—A suicide car bomber in Abuja and a man driving a car and armed with explosives in Kaduna attacked two Nigerian newspapers—*ThisDay* in Abuja and an office building it shares with *The Moment* and *The Daily Sun* newspapers in Kaduna—killing seven and wounding twenty-six. Boko Haram claimed credit. The Abuja attack killed three and injured others. In Kaduna, locals allowed a car bomber to open the trunk of his car; he pulled out a bomb and threw it, killing four people. He was arrested. Boko Haram said it would continue attacking the media because of inaccurate coverage. On May 1, Boko Haram posted an eighteen-minute video to YouTube that showed the smiling suicide bomber driving into the newspaper offices. The group included threats to continue attacks against journalists, major Nigerian newspapers, Voice of America, Radio France Internationale, and the Nigerian government, saying, "If they destroy one brick from our building, we will destroy five hundred from theirs."

April 26, 2012—Afghanistan—An Afghan special forces soldier opened fire with a machine gun from the top of a building, shooting to death Andrew Britton, 25, a Green Beret soldier in the Shah Wali Kot district of Kandahar and wounding three other coalition troops and a local interpreter before he was killed. Taliban spokesman Qari Yousuf Ahmadi posted on an insurgent Web site that it had planted the terrorist in the elite unit. The Taliban identified the killer as Zakirullah, a resident of Nangarhar Province.

April 27, 2012—Afghanistan—During an argument between Afghan and Western troops, an Afghan police officer opened fire, injuring two U.S. troops. NATO troops fired back, killing two local police officers.

April 27, 2012—Syria—State television reported that a suicide bomber killed ten and wounded nearly thirty across the street from a Damascus mosque.

April 27, 2012—Denmark—Authorities arrested three people—a 22-year-old Jordanian citizen, a 23-year-old Turkish citizen who lives in Denmark, and a 21-year-old Danish citizen who lives in Egypt—on suspicion of planning a terror attack. They were charged with illegal possession of automatic weapons and ammunition, which police had confiscated. They were arrested at two locations. Police seized three cars in Herlev, a suburb of Copenhagen; witnesses also saw police activity in the Valby neighborhood.

April 27, 2012—Ukraine—Four bombs went off within seventy-two minutes of each other, injuring twenty-nine people, including nine children, in Dnipropetrovsk. Authorities blamed terrorists. The first bomb, which went off at 11:50 a.m., was hidden in a trash can at a tram stop, and injured thirteen. Forty minutes later, a bomb went off near a movie theater, injuring eleven, including nine children. A third bomb went off near a park entrance, injuring three people. The fourth bomb went off in the city center, causing no injuries. At least twenty-four people were hospitalized. The city is the home of jailed former Prime Minister Yulia V. Tymoshenko.

April 28, 2012—Afghanistan—At 11:15 a.m., two Taliban gunmen who hid their Spanish-made Astra Cub pistols and explosives in their boots failed to assassinate Kandahar Governor Tooryalai Wesa when they were stopped in his reception area by police who fired on them. Wesa is U.S.-educated. The terrorists and two Afghan police officers died in the twenty-minute exchange. Wesa's office said it was the ninth assassination attempt on him. The Astra holds eleven .22 caliber bullets and has a 2-inch barrel. The attackers left behind two vehicles that were packed with explosives, which authorities defused.

April 28, 2012—Colombia—The Revolutionary Armed Forces of Colombia (FARC) kidnapped French television journalist Romeo Langlois, 35. On May 6, 2012, a FARC squadron commander identifying himself as Ancizar, alias Monaso, dressed in olive fatigues and carrying an assault rifle, released a video in which he said that Langlois was a "prisoner of war" who was receiving medical treatment for an injured arm. Langlois was captured in Caqueta while with Colombian military and police forces on an antidrug mission when they engaged in a gun battle with FARC during which four Colombian soldiers and a policeman were killed. The spokesman said he was reading from a script dated April 30. Langlois was working freelance for France 24, a news channel. On May 30, FARC released Langlois in the village of San Isidro, Caqueta Department, to an international delegation including a representative of the French government, the International Red Cross, and former Colombian Senator Piedad Cordoba. Langlois said that FARC treated him with respect, "They never tied me up.... They always treated me like a guest." He told a meeting in the town square that "the government has sold the idea that this conflict was almost over, that there were just a few hot zones left. That has always been false. The fact that they had to hold an independent journalist for thirty-three days to remind people of the situation, shows how tremendously degraded the conflict has become." He said the guerrillas held up his release to coincide with the group's forty-eighth anniversary. 12042801

April 29, 2012—Kenya—A grenade was thrown into God's House of Miracles International Church in Nairobi's Ngara enclave during Sunday services, killing one person and injuring more than a dozen. Al-Shabaab was suspected. On May 15, 2012, police charged Kenyan citizen Ibrahim Kibe Kagwa with six counts of causing grievous bodily harm.

April 29, 2012—Algeria—Security forces killed twenty members of the Movement for Oneness and Jihad in West Africa, an al Qaeda splinter group, as they were about to attack two fuel tankers near the Mali border. The group had earlier kidnapped seven Algerian diplomats from their consulate in Gao, in northern Mali.

April 30, 2012—Nigeria—A suicide bomber drove his motorcycle into a convoy carrying Police Commissioner Mamman Sule to his offices near the governor's office in Jalingo, capital of Taraba State. Sule was uninjured, but the explosives caused massive damage at a roadside market, killing eleven people—including the suicide bomber—injuring twenty-six, and blowing out the windows of the state Ministry of Finance building. Boko Haram was suspected.

April 30, 2012—Syria—Government media said nine people died and one hundred were wounded in two suicide bombings against local branches of army and air force intelligence in Idlib. The U.K.-based Syrian Observatory for Human Rights said twenty were killed, most with the security services.

April 30, 2012—United States—The FBI's Joint Terrorism Task Force arrested five men planning to blow up Cleveland's Brecksville–Northfield High Level Bridge at Route 82 that crosses from Brecksville to Sagamore Hills over the Cuyahoga Valley National Park. An undercover FBI agent gave them inoperable explosive devices. The FBI arrested them after the individuals planted the device. Douglas L. Wright, 26, Brandon L. Baxter, 20, and Anthony Hayne, 35, were held on charges of conspiracy and attempted use of explosive materials to damage physical property affecting interstate commerce. Charges were pending against Connor C. Stevens, 20, and Joshua S. Stafford, 23. Three of the men claimed to be anarchists. The Bureau said the group wanted to "topple financial institution signs atop high rise buildings in downtown Cleveland" while co-conspirators used smoke grenades to distract law enforcement. The group ratcheted up the plan into using explosives to destroy bridges or other targets. Some of the bombers were to set off the bombs from a safe distance that they thought could provide an alibi. The FBI had tracked the individuals since a confidential source met Wright at a Cleveland-area protest event in November 2011. Wright told the source that his group of anarchists "had been discussing plans involving violence and destruction to physical property ... to send a message to corporations and the United States government." The charges carried possible sentences of twenty-plus years in prison. The five had been associated with the Occupy Cleveland movement, which denied involvement and canceled its planned May Day protest following the arrests.

May 2012—Libya—Rocket-propelled grenades were fired at the Benghazi offices of the International Committee of the Red Cross. The Brigades of Imprisoned Sheikh Omar Abdel-Rahman, a Libyan jihadi group named after the "blind sheikh," claimed credit. The group said the Red Cross was targeted as "one of the strongholds of Christian missionary activity." The group released a three-minute video of the nighttime attack. 12059901

May 2012—Congo—Villagers unhappy with the UN for not protecting them fired at a UN base, injuring eleven Pakistani peacekeepers who were part of the UN mission. 12059902

May 2012—Egypt—Bedouin tribesman kidnapped ten Fijian soldiers attached to the UN Multinational Force and Observers, holding them for two days. 12059903

May 2012—Syria—As of January 9, 2013, nine Lebanese Shi'ites, part of a group kidnapped in Aleppo, remained hostages. Lebanese, Turkish, and Qatari officials had tried to broker a deal. 12059904

May 1, 2012—Germany—Berlin police found three pipe bombs, about 16 inches long and filled with an explosive made of chlorate and sugar, on sidewalks in Berlin's western Kreuzberg neighborhood near a May 1 protest march that attracted ten thousand leftist demonstrators.

May 1, 2012—Yemen—Five suspected al Qaeda gunmen attacked Yemeni and French employees of the French oil company Total as they were driving from an oil field in Hadramout Province to the airport in Seiyun. Two kilometers away from the airport, the gunmen fired rifles at the car, killing a Yemeni escort soldier who was sitting in the front passenger seat and wounding a Frenchman in the leg and another Yemeni employee, who was hit three times in the chest. 12050101

May 1, 2012—United Kingdom—Authorities arrested six men and one woman suspected of financing terrorism in Somalia by smuggling khat leaf into the United States and Canada. The raids took place at four residences in London, Coventry, and Cardiff, Wales. Police searched seven other residences and a business in Coventry.

May 1, 2012—United Kingdom—Police charged Kamran Ahmed, 21, from Birmingham, with six counts of terrorism offenses, saying that he possessed documents and records that could be used to commit terrorism. He was out on bail until a hearing scheduled for May 4 in Westminster Magistrates Court.

May 2, 2012—Internet—The first two new editions of al Qaeda in the Arabian Peninsula's e-magazine *Inspire* since the death of editor Samir Khan and operations chief Anwar al-Aulaqi offered instructions on building remotely-detonated bombs and how to set off forest fires in the United States with timed explosives. The ninth edition eulogized the duo, saying:

> To the disappointment of our enemies, issue 9 of *Inspire* magazine is out against all odds.... The Zionists and the Crusaders thought that the magazine was gone with the martyrdom of Shaykh Anwar and brother Samir. Yet again, they have failed to come to terms with the fact that the Muslim ummah is the most fertile and most generous mother that gives birth to thousands and thousands of the likes of Shaykh Anwar and brother Samir ... *Inspire* is and will be an effective tool regardless of who is in charge of it.

Articles in the ninth edition included, "It Is of Your Freedom to Ignite a Firebomb," and suggested Montana as a good place for an "ember bomb." "In America, there are more houses built in the [countryside] than in the cities. It is difficult to choose a better place [than] in the valleys of Montana." Articles in the eighth edition included, "Training with the Handgun" and "Remote Control Detonation," and apparently al-Aulaqi's final article, in which he said, "Explosives ... firearms ... poisons, or chemical and biological weapons against population centers is allowed and is strongly recommended due to its great effect on the enemy." The magazine said it is "still publishing America's worst nightmare." The magazine's new editors did not have the English-language fluency of their predecessors, publishing such passages as "What does it take to be an effective urbanite assassin? This is an inquiry that recurs in the psyche of the personage who apprehends the potency of this policy upon his preys."

May 2, 2012—Afghanistan—At 6:15 a.m., at least four Taliban insurgents, armed with mortars, machine guns, hand grenades, and suicide vests attacked the main gate of the Green Village, a fortified compound run by Stratex Hospitality that houses two thousand Westerners in Kabul, killing at least six people, including one foreign guard and one Afghan student. The attack came hours after President Barack Obama left the country after a surprise visit. The Taliban announced, "This delivers a message to President Obama that he is not welcome in Afghanistan. When he is in Afghanistan, we want him to hear the sound of explosions. Afghanistan does not want his imposed strategy." The terrorists had worn burqas to hide their weapons. They set off at least three explosions, possibly car bombs, at the gate. Two insurgents entered the compound and seized the laundry and maintenance building. Afghan special police forces and Norwegian military personnel conducted a three-hour gun battle, killing at least one terrorist. 12050201

May 3, 2012—Russia—Two suicide car bombers set off their 175 pounds of explosives fifteen minutes apart during the night near a traffic police post in Makhachkala, Dagestan, killing thirteen and wounding more than one hundred. Islamist insurgents were suspected. The first bomb went off at 10:10 p.m.; the second killed police officers and rescue workers arriving at the scene. Shrapnel went through a natural gas pipeline, starting a fire that kept rescue workers away from the victims.

May 3, 2012—Germany—Four men were charged in Berlin with membership in a terrorist organization and planning to carry out an attack for al Qaeda in Germany against an undetermined target. Abdeladim el-Kebir, the group's 30-year-old Moroccan leader, was also charged with training at a terrorist camp near the Afghanistan-Pakistan border. He also recruited and indoctrinated the group's other members. Jamil S., 32, a German Moroccan, was charged with helping to make explosives. Amid C., 20, a German Iranian, and Halil S., 27, a German, were believed to have been involved in logistics. Halil S. was accused of involvement in the plot after the other three Duesseldorf Cell members were arrested in Duesseldorf and Bochum on April 29, 2011. Halil S. was arrested in Bochum on December 8, 2011.

May 3, 2012—Afghanistan—The national intelligence agency said it had arrested a Pakistani suicide truck bomber on the main road in eastern Kabul. The target was unspecified.

May 4, 2012—United States—The news media reported that the Department of Homeland Security's Industrial Control Systems Cyber Emergency Response Team (ICS-CERT) issued a monthly note in which it indicated that cyber attacks had been targeting gas pipeline companies since December 2011. DHS spokesman Peter Boogaard confirmed that the team "has been working since March 2012 with critical infrastructure owners and operators in the oil and natural gas sector to address a series of cyber intrusions targeting natural gas pipeline companies. The cyber intrusion involves sophisticated spear-phishing activities targeting personnel within the private companies." The memo added, "Analysis shows that the spear-phishing attempts have targeted a variety of personnel within these organizations; however, the number of persons targeted appears to be tightly focused. In addition, the emails have been convincingly crafted to appear as though they were sent from a trusted member

internal to the organization." The hacking was first spotted in March. National Security Agency Director Gen. Keith Alexander told a Senate Committee that a similar attack that occurred in March 2011 was believed to have originated on Chinese servers.

May 4, 2012—Pakistan—An 8:00 a.m. suicide bombing in the Bajur tribal area near the Afghanistan border killed twenty-six people—five of them local members of the security forces, including one who had received an award for bravery in fighting jihadis—and injuring at least seventy-five people. The terrorist set off the bomb as he approached a security checkpoint, killing a woman and several schoolchildren. The Pakistani Taliban claimed credit, saying two senior security officials had been targeted to avenge the death at the hands of security forces in Bajur in 2011 of Sheik Marwan, an al Qaeda commander. Ihsanullah Ihsan said, "We will continue to attack government-sponsored militias and security forces." Taliban commander Dadullah was believed behind the attack.

May 5, 2012—Mali—Al Qaeda-linked Ansar Dine Islamists torched the tomb of Sidi Mahmoud Ben Amar, a Sufi saint in Timbuktu, which was designated by UN Educational, Scientific, and Cultural Organization (UNESCO) as a World Heritage Site.

May 7, 2012—Yemen/United States—The news media reported that the CIA in April had foiled a plot by al-Qaida's affiliate in Yemen to bomb a U.S.-bound airliner around the first anniversary of the death of Osama bin Laden. The bomb contained lead azide and had a new dual-detonator design that improved upon the earlier "underwear bomber" method that failed on Christmas 2009. The bomb did not have any metal parts, which would make it more difficult to detect by current screening mechanisms, although U.S. authorities said that it would probably be spotted by U.S. scanners. U.S. officials said it was still designed to be hidden in the terrorist's underwear. The FBI's Quantico facility was testing the device, which had been seized within the previous ten days. The Bureau credited the "close cooperation with our security and intelligence partners overseas." Officials said the bomb was seized in transit in the Middle East outside Yemen, but not at an airport. The United States had been aware of the plot for about one month. The bomber had been told to pick a target of opportunity.

The next day, the press reported that the would-be bomber was a Saudi intelligence service source who passed the bomb to the Agency via the Saudis rather than detonate it on a plane. In a joint operation with the Saudi intelligence service, the CIA tracked the device for several weeks. The plotters, including Fahd al-Quso, later died in an air strike because of information provided by the source, according to the *Washington Post*. NBC News reported on May 10 that source was a Western-documented British national of Middle Eastern origin. Other news reports said that the British MI5 and MI6 intelligence services were also involved in the individual's recruitment. Members of the U.S. Congress called for an investigation of the plethora of leaks regarding the case.

Authorities believed the bomb was designed by al Qaeda in the Arabian Peninsula bomb maker Ibrahim Hassan Tali al-Asiri or an apprentice. Asiri had designed the first underwear bomb and the printer ink cartridge bombs that were discovered in 2010 before they could explode inside cargo planes. Asiri had also inserted a bomb inside his brother in the latter's 2009 attempt to assassinate Prince Mohammed bin Nayef, the Saudi deputy interior minister. The press later reported that the would-be terrorist was a Yemeni born in Jeddah, Saudi Arabia, who studied and worked in the United Kingdom, where he obtained a U.K. passport.

May 7, 2012—Yemen—Al Qaeda in the Arabian Peninsula (AQAP) attacked a Yemeni army base in Abyan Province, killing twenty-two soldiers, injuring twelve, and capturing twenty-five a few hours after a drone strike had killed AQAP operations chief Fahd al-Quso. The terrorists arrived by sea and land, and stole weapons and other military hardware.

May 8, 2012—United States—Southwest Airlines flight 811 and flight 1184 flying from Orange County, California, to Phoenix, Arizona, were the subjects of nonspecific bomb threats. Passengers and bags were screened. No bombs were found.

May 8, 2012—Algeria—The U.S. Department of State announced in a travel advisory that "the U.S. government considers the potential threat to U.S. Embassy personnel assigned to Algiers sufficiently serious to require them to live and work under significant security restrictions."

May 9, 2012—Syria—A bomb hit a Syrian military convoy escorting the head of the UN observer mission, injuring eight Syrian soldiers. The opposition Free Syrian Army denied involvement. None of the UN monitors, led by Norwegian Maj. Gen. Robert Mood, were injured. The convoy went on to Daraa. 12050901

May 9, 2012—Internet—Al Qaeda leader Ayman al-Zawahiri called on Muslims to avenge the February Quran burnings at a U.S. air base in Afghanistan by fighting "those aggressors who occupied your countries, stole your wealth, and violated your sanctities." He deemed the American apology for the mistake a "silly farce."

May 9, 2012—Nigeria—Boko Haram (BH) was believed responsible for shooting to death two traders in a market in Maiduguri. Soldiers killed one suspected BH member and arrested two others who carried out an attack on a military post.

May 10, 2012—Russia—Russian media announced that earlier in the week Russia's security service in a joint operation with Abkhazian security services arrested three men in Georgia's breakaway republic of Abkhazia on charges of plotting to attack the 2014 Winter Olympics in the Black Sea city of Sochi. The trio was believed to be leaders of a regional cell of the North Caucasus–based Chechen terrorist group Caucasus Emirate. Police seized weapons, including three portable surface-to-air missiles, two antitank guided missiles, a mortar, and a flamethrower.

Meanwhile, the U.S. Department of State added the Caucasus Emirate to its list of foreign terrorist groups and authorized a reward of up to $5 million for information leading to the location of its leader, Doku Umarov.

May 10, 2012—Syria—Syria's Interior Ministry claimed that terrorists had set off two "booby-trapped cars" filled with more than a ton of explosives, killing dozens and wounding more than 400 near an intersection on a busy highway during the morning rush hour in Damascus. No one claimed credit. The opposition Syrian Observatory for Human Rights said 59 died and the nation's intelligence agency building was destroyed in the 8:00 a.m. blasts. The Interior Ministry said the dead included 55 civilians and security force members and 372 injured at an intersection in the densely populated neighborhood of Qazzaz. The Health Ministry's tally was 55 dead and circa 400 wounded. At least one foreign expert suggested that the al Qaeda–linked Al-Nusrah Front for the People of the Levant or the jihadi Al-Baraa Ibn Malik Martyrdom Brigade was responsible. The target was the headquarters of the Syrian security services' Palestine Branch; the building housing the Patrols Branch was also damaged. The explosions destroyed twenty-one vehicles and damaged more than one hundred others. The Al-Nusrah Front released a video on May 11 claiming credit, saying, "We fulfilled our promise to respond with strikes and explosions" to avenge the Assad regime's attacks on residential areas. "We promised the regime in our last declaration to respond to its killing of families, women, children, and old men in a number of Syrian provinces, and here we kept our promise.... We tell this regime: stop your massacres against the Sunni people. If not, you will bear the sin of the Alawites. What is coming will be more calamitous, God willing."

May 11, 2012—Afghanistan—A man wearing an Afghan Army uniform shot to death a U.S. soldier in Konar Province. It was the fifteenth attack in which Afghan soldiers or insurgents wearing military uniforms had shot foreign troops. The Taliban claimed credit. The terrorist, Mahmood, died in a precision air strike in Kunar Province on September 15. 12051101

May 11, 2012—Syria—Authorities said they had foiled a suicide minivan bombing that would have set off 1,200 kilograms of explosives in Aleppo. The non–Syrian bomber was shot to death in his van in the al Shaar district. 12051201

May 11, 2012—Internet—Ayman al-Zawahiri released a video calling for al-Shabaab to continue attacks and ignore drone strikes.

May 12, 2012—Afghanistan—At 3:00 p.m., gunmen wearing Afghan police uniforms shot to death two British NATO soldiers in a joint NATO-Afghan coalition compound in Helmand Province. A third policeman shot to death one of the attackers and wounded the second, who escaped. The duo had been members of the Afghan National Police for one year. 12051202

May 12, 2012—Nigeria—Nigerian police captured Suleiman Mohammed, a leading Boko Haram figure in Kano, along with his wife and children in his hideout. The Yoruba terrorist was flown to Abuja. Police recovered explosives, ammunition, and guns.

May 13, 2012—Afghanistan—Gunmen shot to death Maulvi Arsala Rahmani, who was stuck in traffic in Kabul. Occupants of a car beside his opened fire. Rahmani was a Taliban defector who had served on the seventy-member High Peace Council set up two years earlier to liaise with the insurgents. Taliban spokesman Zabihullah Majihid denied involvement, saying, "Others are involved in this."

May 14, 2012—United States—Federal authorities arrested and charged three self-proclaimed anarchist members of the Black Bloc who had traveled from Florida to Chicago planning to commit violence as a protest against the NATO summit. They had plotted to attack President Obama's Chicago campaign headquarters, the Chicago

mayor's home, and four Chicago police district stations. The Black Bloc name was used by anarchists who conducted violence during the Occupy protests, including in Rome in 2011 when ski-masked terrorists torched cars and clashed with police and other Occupiers. An Illinois judge set bail at $1.5 million. The trio were identified as Brian Church, 22, of Fort Lauderdale, Florida; Jared Chase, 27, of Keene, New Hampshire; and Brent Vincent Betterly, 24, of Massachusetts and Oakland Park, Florida. Charges included providing material support for terrorism, conspiracy to commit terrorism, and possession of explosives or incendiary devices. Authorities said Church planned to recruit four teams of four each and that reconnaissance had already been done on the Chicago Police Department headquarters. Police seized improvised explosive or incendiary devices, a mortar gun, swords, a hunting bow, throwing stars, and knives with brass-knuckle handles. Prosecutors said they had also stockpiled Molotov cocktails. They were represented by the National Lawyers Guild and attorney Sarah Gelsomino of the People's Law Office.

May 14, 2012—Afghanistan—Some 389 boys at a school in the Ismail Khan Mandokhil district of southeastern Khost Province fell ill after drinking water from a well that may have been poisoned. Eighty of them remained in a hospital as of May 20.

May 15, 2012—Colombia—A bomb targeting former Interior Minister Fernando Londono exploded in Bogota's commercial district, killing two people and injuring nineteen, including Londono.

May 15, 2012—Kenya—Gunmen fired shots and threw four grenades outside Mombasa's Velle Vista nightclub after they were denied entry, killing a security guard and wounding five people, including a terrorist. Authorities blamed al-Shabaab. The terrorist was hospitalized with shrapnel from a grenade. He was identified as Thabit Jamal Din Yahya, a Nairobi resident who had traveled to Mombasa days before the attack. He was to depart for Nairobi at 10:00 p.m. via bus. Authorities searched the bus terminal and found that his luggage contained a pistol magazine and eight rounds of ammunition.

May 15, 2012—Kenya—A bomb exploded at the world's largest refugee camp, near the Kenya-Somalia border, killing one policeman and seriously wounding four others when the bomb went off under their car. Al-Shabaab was suspected.

May 15, 2012—Internet—Al Qaeda leader Ayman al-Zawahiri issued an audio message on jihadi Web sites entitled *Yemen: Between a Fugitive Pup-*

pet and a Collaborating Stooge. It was recorded before the latest underwear bomber attempt.

May 18, 2012—Internet—Al Qaeda leader Ayman al-Zawahiri issued a video lasting six minutes and nineteen seconds on jihadi Web sites in which he called for Muslims to rise up against the Saudi monarchy using the model of Arab Spring revolutions in Egypt, Libya, and Tunisia.

> Why don't you rise up, for you are the sons of the strong and proud tribes that look down upon death in order to lift up humiliation and oppression? Are you afraid of the forces of the Saudi regime and its security and army? The Family of Saud might be able to kill tens, hundreds, or thousands from amongst you, but if hundreds of thousands come out, then they will be shocked and will end up, Allah permitting, in the state that their brethren ended up in amongst the ousted tyrants.

He also observed, regarding a Yemeni government change, "So, Ali Abdallah Saleh is gone, and his successor Abed Rabbo Mansour Hadi has taken over."

May 19, 2012—Italy—A bomb went off at 7:45 a.m. at a high school in Brindisi, killing a 16-year-old girl and injuring ten. Police did not think it was the work of the Sacred United Crown, a Mafia group, suggesting anarchists were behind it. The school was named after anti–Mafia prosecutor Giovanni Falcone and his wife, Francesca Morvillo, a judge who was also killed in the 1992 bombing on a highway in Sicily by La Cosa Nostra. The bomb consisted of three cooking-gas canisters and a remotely-controlled detonator. It had been placed on a low wall ringing the school. Police later ruled out the Mafia and said it appeared to be the work of a lone man. Two men were taken into custody for questioning. On June 7, 2012, Giovanni Vantaggiato, 68, confessed to acting alone in building and placing the Brindisi school bomb. He had been arrested a day earlier. Surveillance video showed him driving his own car and his wife's car in front of the school in the days before the attack. He used a remote detonator. He owns a gas station, giving him access to gas and gas tanks used in the bombing. His motive remained unclear.

May 19, 2012—Syria—A suicide car bomber in Deir al-Zor killed nine and wounded one hundred. The regime blamed al Qaeda.

May 20, 2012—Yemen—Three American contractors working with the Yemen Coast Guard were wounded in a shooting in the port city of Hodeida. One person was arrested in the attack. 12052001

May 20, 2012—United States—Sebastian Senakiewicz, 24, of Chicago, was charged with falsely making a terrorist threat. Mark Neiweem, 28, believed to be from Chicago, was charged with attempted possession of explosives or incendiary devices. Bond was set at $750,000 for Senakiewicz and $500,000 for Neiweem. Authorities said they were not part of the previous week's plot to set off bombs throughout Chicago as part of the anti–NATO demonstrations by the Black Bloc. Senakiewicz, a native of Poland, told friends he had made two homemade explosive devices that could "blow up half of an overpass for a train" and was planning to use them during the summit. He said that they were stored in a Chicago home in a hollowed-out Harry Potter book. He also said he had a vehicle "filled with explosives and weapons." A search turned up no explosives. Neiweem told an associate that he wanted to obtain materials to make a pipe bomb. Senakiewicz claimed to be a member of the Black Bloc and "an anarchist who is upset with the lack of chaos in Chicago."

May 21, 2012—Yemen—At 10:00 a.m., a suicide bomber dressed in a military uniform killed 105 soldiers and injured 300, some critically, at a military parade rehearsal in Sabeen Square, 220 meters from the presidential palace in Sana'a. The parade was to commemorate National Day, when in 1990 the two countries of North Yemen and South Yemen united. Ansar al-Shariah posted on Facebook that it was aiming at Mohammed Nasser Ahmed, Yemen's defense minister, and was retaliating for attacks on Al Qaeda in the Arabian Peninsula (AQAP) southern safe houses in May. AQAP said it was avenging the U.S. and local military's war on its followers in southern Yemen. The attack missed killing the defense minister, the target of the bomber. The group issued a message to military commanders that said, "We will take revenge, God willing, and the flames of war will reach you everywhere, and what happened is but the start of a jihad project in defense of honor and sanctities." The group had heretofore attacked targets in the south, ignoring the capital. Observers suggested that the bomber was an AQAP penetration of the armed forces. Yemeni President Abdu Rabbu Mansour Hadi announced the sacking of four senior commanders. Among the injured was Mahdi al-Jarbani, the drill major for the brigade; he sustained shrapnel wounds. On January 14, 2013, nine Yemenis accused of complicity in the suicide bombing appeared in court.

May 21, 2012—Colombia—Between sixty and eighty Revolutionary Armed Forces of Colombia (FARC) members staged an attack from Venezuelan soil into Colombia on an army patrol guarding a telecommunications tower, killing twelve soldiers, including a second lieutenant, and wounding four others during an hour-long firefight. Venezuelan President Hugo Chavez announced that he had sent additional troops to guard against rebels passing into his country. The Nuevo Arco Iris foundation Bogota reported that FARC had conducted 550 attacks in the first four months of 2012, an increase of 3 percent from 2011 and 15 percent from four years earlier.

May 22, 2012—France—U.S. Airways flight 787, a B-767 flying from Paris to Charlotte with 188 people on board, was diverted safely to Bangor, Maine, after a female French citizen born in Cameroon handed a note to a flight attendant saying that she had a surgically implanted bomb. The plane was trailed by two F-15s. She was removed from the aircraft, questioned by U.S. Customs and Border Protection, and placed in FBI custody. Earlier in the month there were reports that al Qaeda in the Arabian Peninsula was looking into such an attack. U.S. Attorney Thomas Delahanty, II, said that there was not sufficient evidence to support charges against Lucie Zeeko Marigot, 41, and she would soon be headed back home.

May 22, 2012—Syria—Syrian rebels kidnapped eleven Lebanese Shi'ites and their Syrian driver in Aleppo Province while they were coming home via two buses from a pilgrimage in Iran. The rebels released the women they had detained, saying they should go to a security headquarters in Aleppo and arrange for the release of rebels being held by the Syrian government. The Free Syrian Army denied involvement. The Lebanese victims' neighborhoods saw rioting, with streets blocked by burning tires. Hizballah leader Hassan Nasrallah urged calm, saying, "We don't want to create a conflict. That is illegitimate. Those Syrian immigrants are our brothers, and we don't want any violent actions, which do not help the cause."

As of December 15, the kidnappers had released two hostages as a goodwill gesture but insisted that the other nine were Hizballah members. The group was led by Amar al-Dadikhi of the North Storm Brigade, who demanded the release by Syria of two prominent opposition figures—Tal al-Mallohi and Lt. Col. Hussein Harmoush—and the release by Lebanon of all Syrian activists in detention. Mallohi was a teen female blogger who was jailed in 2009 on accusations of espionage. Harmoush was the first prominent Syrian Army defector in June 2011 and disappeared in Turkey in August 2011, soon appearing on Syrian television to recant his claims that the government had or-

dered troops to fire on civilians. Dadikhi permitted two *New York Times* journalists on December 13 to meet with hostages Ali Abbas, 30, and Ali Tormos, 54. 12052201

May 22, 2012—Argentina—Police defused a bomb at the Gran Rex Theater in Buenos Aires, a day before former Colombian President Alvaro Uribe was scheduled to speak. The bomb was set to go off at 4:30 p.m. during Uribe's presentation at an international conference of entrepreneurs. 12052202

May 22, 2012—United States—The Senate Committee on Homeland Security and Government Affairs released an al Qaeda video calling for "covert mujahideen" to conduct "electronic jihad" against the U.S. government and critical infrastructure, including the electronic grid. The video exhorted Muslims "with expertise in this domain to target the Web sites and information systems of big companies and government agencies." The Department of Homeland Security reported receiving more than fifty thousand reports of cyber intrusions or attempted intrusions in the United States since October 2011. The call for cyber jihad was part of a two-hour al Qaeda online video.

May 22, 2012—Afghanistan—At 4:00 p.m., gunmen kidnapped four workers—Helen Johnston, 28, of the United Kingdom; Moragwa Oirere, 26, of Kenya; and their two Afghan colleagues—who were on assignment for Medair, an international humanitarian organization based in Lausanne, Switzerland. Medair specializes in emergency relief work, food aid, and nutrition projects. The hostages were grabbed as they were traveling on horseback on a rural road near a project site between Yaftal and Raghistan districts in Badakhshan Province. Afghan elders worked to free the hostages during negotiations over the terrorists' demand for a $10 million ransom. The hostages were freed from a mountain cave on June 2 in a 1:00 a.m. raid by helicopter-borne U.K. and NATO forces. Seven terrorists were killed. The terrorists had links to the Taliban and were armed with heavy machine guns, rocket-propelled grenades, and AK-47s. They had held the hostages in Gulati, a village in Shahri Buzurg district, a mountainous and forested area near the border with Tajikistan. 12052202

May 23, 2012—Afghanistan—Terrorists poisoned 122 girls and 3 teachers at the Bibi Hajera girls' school in the provincial capital of Talokhan. The Taliban was suspected.

May 23, 2012—Internet—U.S. Secretary of State Hillary Clinton said that cyber experts in the U.S.

Department of State's Center for Strategic Counterterrorism Communications had hacked into al Qaeda in the Arabian Peninsula Web sites that posted information on al Qaeda attacks against Yemeni citizens.

May 24, 2012—Pakistan—Two missiles fired from a drone hit a house in the Mirali area of North Waziristan, killing ten militants, including five Central Asians linked to al Qaeda, and injuring several individuals.

May 25, 2012—Yemen—Two al Qaeda-linked suicide bombers killed twelve Shi'ites at a school and a protest march in the north. Ansar al-Sharia (Partisans of Islamic Law), an al Qaeda-linked Sunni group, claimed credit, saying it was avenging the deaths of Sunnis in the north. A suicide bomber set off his explosive belt at a Shi'ite protest march in Saada Province but caused no casualties. Later that day, in al-Jawf Province, a suicide bomber attacked a school in which Shi'ite rebels, known as Houthis, were praying, killing twelve of them. Ansar said more than twenty "apostates" had died. The group said, "O apostates, don't think that we have forgotten you or that our battle against the crusaders and their allies in Abyan will stop us from fighting you. For, by God, we will not cease until we purify the Arabian Peninsula of you."

May 25, 2012—Turkey—Two suspected suicide bombers set off their car bomb outside a police station in Pinarbasi, Kayseri Province, killing a police officer and wounding eighteen people. The Kurdistan Workers Party claimed credit. The media said the bombers had entered the country from Syria. Authorities detained four people. Police had followed the car from Goksun district in Kahramanmaras to Pinarbasi after it blew through a checkpoint. Police fired on the car as it passed the Pinarbasi police station.

May 25–26, 2012—Mexico—Five warehouses and parking lots of Sabritas, a PepsiCo subsidiary, were firebombed in Michoacan and Guanajuato states by masked men who attacked dozens of the firm's distribution trucks and some warehouses. No injuries were reported. On May 28, authorities detained a Knights Templar drug cartel lieutenant and three other drug cartel suspects for the first multiple attacks on a foreign firm in the country's five and a half years of drug wars. The cartel left Michoacan's La Familia group in 2011 and traffics mostly in methamphetamines and marijuana. The Knights Templar claimed credit for the attacks. 12052501, 12052601

May 26, 2012—Kenya—Terrorists threw grenades at a hotel and a refugee camp in the north-

east, wounding five people. Al-Shabaab was suspected.

May 27, 2012—Benin—A U.S. Department of State official told the press that an American had been kidnapped in Benin. The United States was providing "consular assistance." 12052701

May 27, 2012—Iraq—A roadside bomb injured twenty-four Pakistan pilgrims whose bus overturned en route to a Shi'ite shrine near Saqlawiyah, 45 miles west of Baghdad. The pilgrims were on their way from Syria to a northern Baghdad shrine in the Kazimiyah neighborhood. At least nineteen people were hurt by the explosion; another five were hurt when the bus overturned. 12052702

May 27, 2012—Dubai—British sailor Timothy Andrew MacColl, 27, vanished after leaving the Rock Bottom Bar at the Regent Hotel in the area of Deira and getting into a taxi at 2:00 a.m. The bar was fifteen minutes from Port Rashid, where his ship, the HMS *Westminster*, had docked the previous day. He is married with two children, aged 4 and 6. Rachel MacColl was expecting their third child in October.

May 28, 2012—Kenya—The government blamed terrorists for a 1:15 p.m. explosion in a shopping center on Moi Avenue in downtown Nairobi that injured thirty-three people, five of them critically. Police and hospital officials said it was an accidental electrical fire. An official later suggested that it was a fertilizer bomb. Witnesses smelled ammonia at the scene and noted that a bearded man had left behind a bag shortly before the explosion.

May 28, 2012—Denmark—Authorities arrested two Somali-origin Danish brothers, aged 18 and 23, "in the process of preparing an act of terror." One was detained in Aarhus and one as he got off the plane at Copenhagen International Airport. The Danish Security and Intelligence Service (PET) said they were overheard talking about weapons, targets, and methods. One had been to an al-Shabaab training camp. They had lived in Denmark for sixteen years.

May 29, 2012—Afghanistan—The Taliban was suspected when 160 schoolgirls, aged 10 to 20, were poisoned in Takhar Province. A police official suggested that the classrooms had been sprayed with a toxin before the girls entered the Aahan Dara Girls School in Taluqan.

May 29, 2012—Somalia—Al-Shabaab gunmen attacked the Somali president's convoy as it was traveling from Afgoye to Mogadishu. African Union forces intervened; the president was unhurt.

May 30, 2012—Nigeria—Gunmen kidnapped an Italian engineer working for a construction company in the south. 12053001

May 30, 2012—Azerbaijan—The government announced the arrest of forty individuals planning to attack the Eurovision Song Contest venue at Baku Crystal Hall, religious pilgrimage sites, police stations, and Marriott and Hilton hotels in Baku, as well as conduct an April assassination against President Ilham Aliyev. Authorities seized 13 assault rifles, a machine gun, 12 handguns, 3 rifles, 3,400 rounds of ammunition, 62 hand grenades, and several kilograms of explosives.

May 30, 2012—Kenya—Al-Shabaab posted on a Web site a threat that "something big is coming" and that Kenyans would "watch your towers coming down. Two weeks from now you will weep."

May 31, 2012—Egypt—Two 31-year-old American tourists were kidnapped from their car in Dahab on their way to Nuweiba, another resort town on the Red Sea's Gulf of Aqaba in the Egyptian Sinai region. They were released the same day. One of the hostages was Brandon Kutz. The Bedouin gunmen had demanded the release of Eid Suleiman Etaiwy, a man arrested on May 30 for drug possession.

June 2012—Georgia—Acting on a tip from the Germans, local authorities arrested five suspects with nine vials of cesium–135.

June 2012—Argentina—Police arrested seven Peruvians with ties to the Shining Path on suspicion of trafficking cocaine in Buenos Aires. Authorities seized twenty thousand doses of paco, a smokable cocaine residue.

June 1, 2012—Mexico—Gunmen torched a delivery truck belonging to Sabritas, a local division of PepsiCo. The criminal organization Knights Templar, an offshoot of La Familia, claimed credit for similar attacks earlier in the week.

June 3, 2012—Nigeria—Boko Haram claimed credit for bombing two churches in Bauchi, killing fifteen people and injuring thirty-eight, including six children, during Sunday morning services. The group also threatened journalists over what it claimed was biased reporting. The bombs struck the Church of Christ and the Living Faith church in the Yelwatudu area of Bauchi State. The group on occasion calls itself the Nigerian Taliban.

June 3, 2012—Internet—Al Qaeda leader Ayman al-Zawahiri posted an Internet video entitled *Days with the Imam, Part Two,* in which he said that Osama bin Laden had lived cheaply, spending his money on attacks against the West and providing hospitality with good food.

When you entered his house you would be surprised. It was a very simple house, with some wooden beds and plastic coverings and very little furniture. If the Sheikh invited us to his house, he would give us what he had in the way of bread, vegetables, rice—whatever was available he would give us.... He was known for his generosity with guests by slaughtering sheep for them and because of continuous visitors, he once bought a herd of sheep so that he would be always ready for them. He would slaughter livestock for them and give them tasty food.... He spent all his money on jihad.... Luxury is the enemy of jihad and if the mujahideen were brought up to live in asceticism, they would tolerate the burden of jihad.

He thus claimed that bin Laden swore off electricity to live a simpler life. Al-Zawahiri claimed that bin Laden spent $50,000 to finance the U.S. African embassy bombings in 1998, depleting his $55,000 savings.

June 4, 2012—Italy—The Olga Nucleus of the Informal Anarchist Federation-International Revolutionary (FAI), an Italian anarchist group, shot Roberto Adinolfi, the CEO of Ansaldo Nucleare in Genoa. The company is part of the Italian industrial conglomerate Finmeccanica and builds, operates, and decommissions nuclear power plants. Two gunmen ambushed him near his Genoa home and shot him in the legs. They fled on motorbikes.

June 4, 2012—Iraq—A suicide car bomber killed 18 and wounded 125 at the offices of Shi'ite religious affairs in the Bab al-Mouadham district in north-central Baghdad.

June 4, 2012—Pakistan—A pre-dawn drone strike on a compound and nearby pickup truck in Hassu Khel (variant Hesokhel), a small North Waziristan village south of Mir Ali, Pakistan, killed al Qaeda's deputy commander Abu Yahya al-Libi, true name Mohamed Hassan Qaid, 49, and fourteen other terrorists, including several of Arab or Central Asian descent. Al-Qaida's top-ranked, password-protected Shamukh Web forum confirmed the death. The *New York Times* reported that al-Libi was at the compound recuperating from injuries suffered in a May 28 drone strike. The key propagandist escaped a U.S. military prison at Bagram Air Base in Afghanistan on the night of July 10, 2005. He later appeared in more than thirty videos produced by As-Sahab. In December 2009, Pakistani officials erroneously reported he had been killed in a Predator strike. The Rewards for Justice Program had offered $1 million for information leading to his detention. He had been attempting to lure Libyans into al

Qaeda, posting a video in December 2011 that said, "At this crossroads you have found yourselves: You either choose a secular regime that pleases the greedy crocodiles of the West and for them to use it as a means to fulfill their goals, or you take a strong position and establish the religion of Allah."

On June 12, 2012, As-Sahab released a video of al-Libi that was produced some time after November 2011 and dated Islamic year 1433. He called Syrian President Bashar al-Assad a "tyrant" and his government a "criminal regime." He said that the "West and their agent assistants" were complicit in Assad's crimes. He called "on our brothers in Iraq, Jordan, and Turkey to go help their brothers and to sacrifice themselves for them" in Syria. "If your revolution was to be peaceful, God would have chosen it that way, but now the illusion of peaceful means after these great sacrifices ... would show weakness." He did not refer to the May 25 massacre in Houla, Syria, in which the UN said more than one hundred people, nearly half of them children, were executed. The video used honorifics for al-Libi that generally are given only to the living.

June 6, 2012—Afghanistan—Two suicide bombers attacked a bazaar in southern Kandahar Province, killing twenty-two and injuring more than fifty. The market is on the main highway to Pakistan. A Taliban spokesman credited Islamic insurgents but claimed that the dead were all foreign soldiers.

June 6, 2012—Libya—A bomb thrown from a passing vehicle exploded next to a wall of the U.S. Consulate in Benghazi causing no casualties. The Brigades of Imprisoned Sheikh Omar Abdel-Rahman, a Libyan jihadi group named after the "blind sheikh," claimed credit. The group said it was responding to the drone strike that killed Abu Yahya al-Libi on June 4. 12060601

June 6, 2012—Colombia—The Colombian military bombed a Revolutionary Armed Forces of Colombia (FARC) camp in Antioquia state, killing eight rebels, including Luis Enrique Benitez, the leader of the 37th Front of the FARC.

June 7, 2012—United States/Somalia—The State Department's Rewards for Justice program offered $7 million for information on the whereabouts of al-Shabaab founder and commander Ahmed Abdi aw-Mohammed. It offered $5 million for Ibrahim Haji Jama, an al-Shabaab co-founder; Fuad Mohamed Khalaf, al-Shabaab financer; al-Shabaab military commander Bashir Mohamed Mahamoud; and al-Shabaab spokesman Mukhtar Robow. The program offered $3 million for al-

Shabaab intelligence chief Zakariya Ismail Ahmed Hersi and senior al-Shabaab figure Abdullahi Yare. On June 11, 2012, al-Shabaab fund-raiser Fuad Mohamed Khalaf posted an audio statement on jihadi Web sites offering a bounty of ten camels for U.S. President Barack Obama and twenty chickens (ten hens, ten cocks) for information on Secretary of State Hillary Clinton. "Whoever brings the mujahideen information about the whereabouts of infidel Obama and the lady of Bill Clinton, the woman named Hillary Clinton, I will give a reward." The Western press reported that the going rate for a camel in Somalia is $700. Khalaf observed, "There is nothing new in the fact that infidels pay to have Muslim leaders killed. They already did that by offering camels for the head of Prophet Mohammed, and $5 million is equivalent to two hundred camels today."

June 8, 2012—Nigeria—A suicide bomber set off his car outside Maiduguri police headquarters, killing eight and wounding nineteen people.

A few hours later, another bomber died when his explosives went off prematurely elsewhere in the city.

June 8, 2012—Pakistan—An 18-pound time bomb went off in a bus filled with government employees and other civilians in Peshawar, killing nineteen, including seven women and a child, and wounding forty-two. Passengers included twenty-two employees of the Peshawar Civil Secretariat and another thirty civilians en route to Charsadda.

June 8, 2012—Ivory Coast—Gunmen snuck across the border with Liberia and killed eight civilians, one or two Ivorian soldiers, and seven Nigerien UN peacekeeping troops on patrol south of Tai in the southwest. 12060801

June 8, 2012—Internet—Omaima Hassan, wife of al Qaeda leader Ayman al-Zawahiri, posted a seven-page letter praising Muslim women for their role in the Arab Spring.

I congratulate all females of the world for these blessed revolutions and I salute every mother who sacrificed her loved ones in the revolutions. It is really an Arab Spring and will soon become an Islamic Spring.... These revolutions toppled the tyrant criminals, and thanks to your efforts, patience, and raising your sons in dignity.... Much of what happened was something we had wished, pleaded, and called for, for decades, but unfortunately, only few had responded. But today, the balance has tipped—with the grace of God—and things have changed.... We did not leave our homes, nor were we persecuted in our nations except to implement the will of God and uphold His word. But if we were made to choose between going back to our lands and compromising our principles, then we would choose expatriation, even if we continued to be immigrants for the rest of our lives ... Every righteous Muslim mother shall raise her son as the new Saladin and say to him: you will be the one to bring back the glory of the Islamic Umma, and you will be the one to liberate Jerusalem, God willing ... The veil is the Muslim woman's identity and the West wants to remove this identity so she will be without an identity. My advice to you sisters is to raise your children on the love of martyrdom ... and to prepare them for restoring the glories of Islam and the liberation of Jerusalem ... We will have a new Islamic state based on sharia arbitration, and we will free Palestine and build a state of succession to the prophecy.

She had posted a similar message in 2009.

June 10, 2012—Nigeria—A suicide car bomber crashed into the Christ Chosen Church of God in Jos, killing six and injuring forty-eight people. Meanwhile, 230 miles away, gunmen fired into the Church of the Brethren (EYN) chapel in Biu, killing an usher and another worshiper and wounding several people. Boko Haram claimed credit for both attacks.

June 11, 2012—Internet—CNN reported that al Qaeda in the Arabian Peninsula (AQAP) posted on the Shumukh and al-Fidaa jihadi forums that it was seeking Western recruits. The posting, by the military committee of AQAP, noted, "Corresponding with those who yearn for martyrdom operations and the brothers who are searching to execute an operation that would cause great damage to the enemies, the goal now is to activate those brothers who reside in the land of the enemy ... whether Jewish, Christian, or apostates as clearly individual jihad or the so-called lone wolf has become popular." AQAP included three e-mails to use to contact them, using downloadable encryption software. They had earlier published the e-mails in *Inspire.*

June 11, 2012—Libya—Gunmen fired on a convoy transporting British Ambassador Dominic Asquith near a university in Benghazi, injuring two security guards. 12061101

June 12, 2012—Libya—A bomb went off at the Misrata offices of the International Committee of the Red Cross, wounding the landowner's son and seriously damaging the building. 12061201

June 13, 2012—Iraq—A series of twenty-two roadside and suicide car bombings throughout the country killed more than 90 and injured at least 270. Many of them were Shi'ite pilgrims walking and driving to the Imam Kadhim shrine in the Kadhimiya neighborhood of Baghdad. Imam Moussa al-Kadhim is one of twelve revered imams and a saint in Shi'ite Islam. One of the bombs, in Hilla, killed twenty people and injured forty. One Hilla bomb hit a restaurant near a local police academy, killing several recruits eating breakfast. Shi'ite mosques in Hilla were also damaged, although no casualties were reported. Other bombs went off in Kadhimiya and other Baghdad neighborhoods, including Balad and Kirkuk, north of Baghdad, Hindiya and Madaan, south of Baghdad, and Samarra, Mosul, Falluja, and Ramadi. A truck bomb went off at 5:00 a.m. in Kadhimiya. Five parked cars exploded in Baghdad, killing 29 and injuring 80. A group of day laborers were hit by an explosion in a village east of Karbala. In Kirkuk, four car bombs exploded, two near Kurdish political offices, including that of Kurdish leader Massoud Barzani's party. Two car bombs exploded in Balad, killing five and wounding thirty. Gunfire and bombs killed five in Diyala Province. A morning bomb in Mosul was aimed at an office of Iraqi President Jalal Talabani's party, killing two people. A second afternoon blast killed a soldier. Two other Mosul explosions wounded five other people. No one claimed credit, although al Qaeda in Iraq was suspected.

June 14, 2012—Germany—Some 850 police officers raided homes, meeting halls, and mosques in seven of the country's sixteen states, focusing on the radical Islamist organizations Dawa FFM and The True Religion (DWR). The government banned the Salafist organization Millatu Ibrahim after it called on Muslims to fight against the country's "constitutional order." Police seized videos, laptops, cell phones, and other items to determine whether those groups should also be banned.

June 16, 2012—Iraq—Car bombs at religious processions killed at least twenty-six people. The first bomb went off after noon near Shi'ite pilgrims in the Shula neighborhood in Baghdad, killing fourteen people headed toward the shrine of Imam Moussa al-Kadhim. At 1:00 p.m., a car bomb went off in the Kadhimiyah neighborhood, killing another dozen.

June 16, 2012—Pakistan—Two bombs killed thirty-two people in the Khyber tribal region. The first bomb was hidden in a pickup truck that exploded in the Zakhakhel bus stop in Landi Kotal, 30 miles west of Peshawar, killing twenty-five people and injuring dozens. The Zakhakhel tribe had formed a pro-government militia that had battled

Lashkar-i-Islam in the Tirah Valley. Later that day, a bomb exploded in a handcart in Kohat district, killing seven people, including police officers. Lashkar was suspected.

June 16, 2012—Pakistan—The terrorist group led by Hafiz Gul Bahadur threatened to attack anyone conducting polio vaccinations in North Waziristan as long as the United States conducted drone missile strikes in Pakistan. "No one will have the right to complain about damage in case of any violation ... Polio campaigns are also used to spy for America against the mujahideen, one example of which is Dr. Shakil Afridi."

June 17, 2012—Iraq—A roadside bomb went off during the morning under a two-vehicle convoy in Kirkuk, killing an Iraqi security contractor and injuring three other Iraqis. The four were working for a Turkish firm providing security for a Turkish construction project. 12061701

June 17, 2012—Nigeria—Boko Haram bombed three churches in Damaturu during Sunday services, killing 25 people, including 20 civilians, and sparking a wave of violence leading to the deaths of at least 138 people and injuries to 130 others over the next few days. In the first attack, a suicide bomber crashed through a barricade at the EWCA Goodnews Wusasa Zaria church around 9:00 a.m., killing 24 and injuring 125, according to a Kaduna state government official (the Nigerian Red Cross Society said there were 2 dead and 22 injured). Minutes later, a bomb went off at the Christ the King Catholic Church in Zaria, killing 10 and injuring more than 50, according to the same official. (The Red Cross said 16 died and 31 were injured.) Another 10 died in a 9:25 a.m. bombing of a Kaduna church. The Red Cross said 32 were killed and 78 were injured in the bombing and a series of reprisals by Christian youths in Zaria and Kaduna. An Associated Press reporter said he saw a fourth bombed church, a police station punctured by bullets, and a crumbling police outpost. Five primary schools were also bombed. Nigerian authorities arrested a bomber who survived. Boko Haram said in a Hausa-language e-mail, "Allah has given us victory in the attacks we launched against churches in Kaduna and Zaria towns which resulted in the deaths of many Christians and security personnel."

June 18, 2012—Pakistan—Ghazala Javed, a popular female Pakistani singer who defied the Taliban's decree against singing and dancing, was shot to death during the night. Her ex-husband was a suspect, against whom she had filed for divorce after finding he had a second wife. Authorities said it did not appear that the Taliban was involved.

She was driving home with her father after leaving a hair salon when gunmen on a motorcycle fired on her car. She was hit with six bullets and pronounced dead at a Peshawar hospital.

June 18, 2012—Israel—The Mujahideen Shura Council of Jerusalem, a group claiming al Qaeda ties, infiltrated Israel from the Egyptian Sinai desert and killed a civilian Israeli construction worker on a team building a border fence 20 miles south of the Gaza Strip near the border community of Nitzana. At 6:00 a.m., three terrorists ambushed two cars carrying civilians to the site, fired a rocket-propelled grenade and an AK-47 assault rifle, and set off bombs which hit one of the vehicles. The vehicle went into a ditch, killing Sayed Fashafsheh, 36, an Arab citizen of Israel from Haifa. Israeli forces killed two gunmen that the group said were an Egyptian and a Saudi. Israeli gunfire set off explosives that the terrorists were carrying on their bodies. A third terrorist was believed to have escaped back to Egypt. An Israeli military spokesman said the explosives and gear—flak jackets, camouflage uniforms, and helmets—were similar to those used in an August 2011 attack by the Popular Resistance Committees, a Palestinian group, in which eight Israelis were killed near Eilat resort. 12061801

June 18, 2012—Iraq—A suicide bomber set off his explosive belt in a funeral tent in Baqouba, killing at least fifteen mourners of a Zubaidi Shi'ite tribal leader. Another forty people were wounded. Among the mourners was Lt. Gen. Ali Ghaidan, commander of the army's ground forces. He was not wounded but one of his bodyguards died and two others were wounded. The government blamed al Qaeda-linked Sunni terrorists.

June 18, 2012—Pakistan—A remotely-detonated car bomb exploded next to a bus going to the Baluchistan University of Information Technology in Quetta, killing five students and injuring more than fifty people.

June 18, 2012—Yemen—An al Qaeda in the Arabian Peninsula (AQAP) suicide bomber of Somali nationality jumped at a vehicle carrying Maj. Gen. Salem Ali Qatan to work in Aden. Qatan, who had led the anti–AQAP military campaign, died, as did his driver and a security guard escorting him in a three-car convoy. Five passersby, including two women, were seriously wounded. The group posted an Internet message to the "leaders of the joint American-Yemeni campaign ... The message ... consists of the blood and body parts of the martyrdom-seekers who swore to pluck your rotten heads, which agreed to be a vehicle for America in its war against the Muslims in Yemen."

Later that day, Yemeni security forces detained Sami Dayyan, a suspected AQAP leader, and two other suspected terrorists driving from Aden to Lahej Province. Explosives and suicide belts were found in the vehicle. Residents in Aden's al-Mansoura district said Dayyan was looking to rent a house in the neighborhood a few days earlier but was chased away.

June 19, 2012—Nigeria—A bomb went off prematurely, blowing off the arms and legs of the terrorist in Bauchi city. His intended target was not clear.

June 19, 2012—Yemen—The government announced that police in Sana'a stopped a vehicle carrying a trio who had weapons, explosives, and maps of foreign embassies and the homes of military and civilian notables marked out.

June 19, 2012—Kenya—Police arrested two Iranians in Nairobi, seizing bomb-making chemicals. The same day, police in Mombasa impounded an Iraq-origin container suspected of containing explosives. One of the Iranians was flown to Mombasa. He led police to 15 kilograms of RDX powder, which the forensic lab was examining. The duo was charged on June 25 with intent to conduct bombings. The Associated Press reported on July 2 that the Iranians planned to attack Israeli, U.S., U.K., or Saudi targets inside Kenya. They were believed to be members of the Islamic Revolutionary Guards Corps Quds Force, an elite Iranian unit. The charge sheet said that Ahmad Abolfathi Mohammad and Sayed Mansour Mousavi had explosives "in circumstances that indicated they were armed with the intent to commit a felony, namely, acts intended to cause grievous harm." The duo was represented by attorney David Kirimi.

June 20, 2012—France—A man claiming membership in al Qaeda took four hostages during a botched robbery of the CIC bank branch in Toulouse at 10:30 a.m. during which he fired a shot. The hostages, including the bank manager, were freed after several hours. He was slightly injured during his arrest at 4:00 p.m. Several gunshots were heard at the scene.

June 21, 2012—Sweden—Authorities found explosives on a truck at the southwestern Ringhals atomic power station. Technicians said the material lacked a detonator. Security was increased at the country's three nuclear power plants.

June 21, 2012—Afghanistan—At 11:30 p.m., seven Taliban gunmen attacked Kabul's Spozhmai Hotel, taking dozens of hostages and conducting an eleven-hour siege that left twenty-six people dead in a gun battle with Afghan and NATO troops. They jumped out of a minivan wearing burqas, which they pulled off to reveal their automatic weapons. They ran into the hotel yelling, "Where are the prostitutes," before shooting the manager and three unarmed hotel guards. Some terrorists attacked the Spugmay restaurant. Others went to the rooftop terrace and to the garden, attacking diners. They fired on any male they found but appeared to be sparing women and children. The terrorists killed fifteen civilians, a police officer, and three security guards before they were killed. Police said ten people were wounded. One of the dead was a young Afghan man who had emigrated and returned from London for a visit. Two terrorists died by setting off their suicide vests. Police rescued the remaining fifty hostages. Four civilians had escaped by jumping into nearby Qargha Lake; one drowned. Police found burqas in the terrorists' minivan, which was used to bring in explosives. Police disarmed the explosives by firing a rocket-propelled grenade into the van.

Taliban spokesman Zabiullah Mujahid said the gunmen targeted Westerners and were armed with suicide vests, rocket-propelled grenades, and heavy machine guns. In an e-mail during the siege, he wrote, "Every night people come here for different types of debauchery, but on Thursday night, the number increases, including foreigners who come here and they hold anti–Islamic ceremonies. Tonight, according to our information, a number of ISAF [International Security Assistance Force] and embassy diplomats from foreign countries have been invited by some senior Kabul administration officials and are now under attack." Claiming that there was drinking and dancing going on, he observed, "These acts are illegal and strictly prohibited in Islam. Women dancers were sexually misused there." Apparently there were no foreigners at the site at the time of the attack. 12062101

June 22, 2012—Iraq—Two bombs went off within minutes of each other in an open-air market in the Shi'te neighborhood of Husseiniyah in northeastern Baghdad, killing fourteen and wounding more than one hundred people. A car bomb went off in Samarra near the Shi'ite al-Askari shrine, killing one pilgrim and injuring thirteen. Gunmen fired on a police checkpoint in Baghdad, killing three officers.

June 24, 2012—Pakistan—Pakistani Taliban gunmen crossed the border from Afghanistan to attack a Pakistani patrol in Upper Dir, killing eighteen troops and beheading seventeen of them. Another four troops were missing. Pakistani troops killed fourteen terrorists. Reuters reported that the gunmen were led by Fazlullah, alias FM Mullah, who had terrorized the Swat Valley before being pushed out by Pakistani forces three years ago. He was the cousin of Sirajuddin Ahmad, who served as his spokesman.

June 24, 2012—Uganda—Authorities arrested five Pakistanis and a Congolese guide in the western oil region of Ntoroki after they crossed the border with Congo. Police said while in the Congo, they had met with Allied Democratic Forces, a group of Ugandan rebels formed in the mid–1990s who hoped to create an Islamic state. Police spokeswoman Judith Nabakoba said, "They are suspected to be involved in terrorism." Ugandan police issued a terrorist alert, suggesting that attacks could be conducted against fans watching the European soccer championship.

June 25, 2012—Pakistan—Taliban gunmen fired on the Karachi offices of Aaj TV, injuring a guard and employee. Spokesman Ahsanullah Ahsan said Aaj had not broadcast the group's claim for the previous day's attack in Upper Dir and threatened further attacks on stations that did not broadcast Taliban statements.

June 25, 2012—Norway—The Associated Press cited three European security agencies as indicating that a Norwegian man had been trained by al Qaeda in the Arabian Peninsula and was awaiting orders to carry out an attack against the West. The *New York Daily News* said it was to be against a U.S. jet; the *Times of London* said it would be an Olympics attack. He was believed to be in his 30s with no immigrant background. He converted to Islam in 2008, became radicalized, then traveled to Yemen for terrorist training. He was believed to have been in Yemen for several months and was still there. He had no criminal record and used the *kunya* Muslim Abu Abdurrahman.

June 25, 2012—United States—NPR reported that the FBI was investigating more than one hundred suspected Islamic extremists within the U.S. armed forces. At least a dozen cases were considered serious.

June 25, 2012—United Kingdom—Reuters and *The Guardian* quoted Security Service (MI5) Director Gen. Jonathan Evans as saying in a rare speech "today parts of the Arab world have once more become a permissive environment for al Qaeda ... A small number of British would-be jihadis are also making their way to Arab countries to seek training and opportunities for militant activity, as they do in Somalia and Yemen. Some will return to the United Kingdom and post a threat here." He also said the Olympic Games were an attractive terrorist target.

June 25, 2012—Yemen—The Yemeni Defense Ministry said that al Qaeda landmines had killed seventy-three people, including twenty-three soldiers, in Abyan Province since al Qaeda fighters were defeated two weeks earlier. The Defense Ministry said tens of thousands of mines were planted.

June 26, 2012—Nigeria—Terrorists bombed a police outpost in Damaturu and police station in Kano at 6:00 p.m. The terrorists then conducted a gun battle with the Damaturu police in which four policemen, four civilians, and nineteen terrorists died. They later set fire to two blocks of empty classrooms at the Federal Polytechnic Damaturu during the night. Boko Haram was suspected.

June 26, 2012—Yemen—At least twenty-three inmates, including five al Qaeda in the Arabian Peninsula (AQAP) members, escaped a Yemeni prison by tunneling out from a cell to a nearby graveyard. Several AQAP terrorists were believed to have gone across the border to Oman.

June 26, 2012—Kenya—The U.S. Embassy issued a travel warning against Americans visiting the country.

June 27, 2012—Northern Ireland—Queen Elizabeth II shook hands with former Irish Republican Army (IRA) commander Martin McGuinness in a show of support for the peace process. The IRA had killed her cousin, Lord Louis Mountbatten, in a 1979 bombing. The Queen and McGuinness, now the deputy first minister of Northern Ireland, met at an arts event in Belfast.

June 27, 2012—Pakistan—A bomb exploded in a Sibi railway station tea shop, killing seven and injuring twenty. Baloch separatists were suspected of targeting Punjabis traveling through the area.

June 27, 2012—Mali—Mokhtar Belmokhtar, an Algerian founder of al Qaeda in the Islamic Maghreb (AQIM), was reported killed in a battle between Islamists and secular Tuareg separatist rebels belonging to the National Movement for the Liberation of Azawad (MNLA) in northern Mali. The gun battle left twenty dead in Gao, Mali. Belmokhtar led one of AQIM's two battalions in Algeria's southern desert. An Algerian court had sentenced him to life in absentia for the killing of ten Algerian customs agents in 2007.

June 27, 2012—West Bank—A Palestinian crashed his vehicle into an Israeli police car, attacked a security guard, and tried to grab his gun. The Palestinian was shot and taken to a Jerusalem hospital. Police investigators believed it was an attempted terrorist attack.

June 27, 2012—Syria—Kamal Ghanaja, a senior Hamas operative, was assassinated in his Damascus home in the Quidsia neighborhood by gunmen who seized rifles and set the house on fire. His charred body showed signs of torture. Observers attributed the killing to a rift with the Syrian government; other blamed Israel. A Syrian opposition group blamed the Shabiha, a Syrian progovernment militia. Ghanaja, a former deputy of Mahmoud al-Mabhouh, who was assassinated in a Dubai hotel room in 2010, was believed to have run guns into the Gaza Strip. A public statement by Hamas did not specifically blame Israel.

June 28, 2012—United Kingdom—East London police arrested two British Muslim converts planning to conduct terrorist attacks. Friends identified the detainees as Jamal ud–Din, 18, and Zakariya, 32. Ud-Din had posted a YouTube video in 2011 in which he denigrated democracy and non–Muslims, praised jailed Egyptian radical preacher Abu Hamza, and expressed anger at the Danish cartoons of Muhammad. It was not determined whether they planned to attack the upcoming Olympics.

June 28, 2012—Pakistan—Sunni terrorists set off a bomb against a bus carrying forty Shi'ite pilgrims from Iran to Quetta, killing ten people and wounding twenty-five, including four police officers escorting the bus. 12062801

June 28, 2012—Iraq—A bomb in a parked taxi exploded at the entrance of a Baghdad market in the Shi'ite district of Washash, killing eight people. In Baqubah, 35 miles away, six people died when a bomb in a parked car went off near shops and cafés in a Shi'ite area. Bombs also went off in the Sunni town of Taji, in the Shi'ite area of Abu Dsheer in southern Baghdad, and in Fallujah, a Sunni area. At least twenty-one people were killed and more than one hundred were wounded during the day's attacks.

June 29, 2012—China—Ten minutes after a Tianjin Airlines flight took off from Hotan in southern Xinjiang, toward Urumqi, six people tried to hijack it and set off explosives but were subdued by the passengers, crew, and a group of police officers who happened to be on the flight. The hijackers disassembled a crutch into metal rods which they tried to use to break into the cockpit. The hijackers, all ethnic Uighurs, sustained minor injuries, as did two air marshals and two flight attendants. The hijackers were arrested once the plane landed. On December 11, a Chinese court in Xinjiang sentenced three hijackers to death and gave a fourth a life sentence in what the media deemed religious-inspired terrorism.

The two other hijackers were injured during the scuffle and died in custody. Those sentenced to death were Musa Yusuf, Arsdikali Yimin, and Omar Yimin. Alimu Musa, sentenced to life, showed "a good attitude in admitting his crimes," according to Xinhua news agency. 12062901

June 29, 2012—United States—The U.S. Department of the Treasury imposed sanctions on two hawalas—informal money exchange networks in Afghanistan and Pakistan—in an effort to slow Taliban cash used to pay salaries and purchase weapons. Treasury said Afghan Taliban commanders kept accounts with the Haji Khairullah Haji Sattar Money Exchange and the Roshan Money Exchange. Much of the cash came from narcotics sales. The UN added those exchanges to its list of backers of Taliban terrorists.

June 29, 2012—Kenya—In late June, four foreign aid workers from Norway, Pakistan, the Philippines, and Canada, and two Kenyans, all affiliated with the Norwegian Refugee Council, were kidnapped from their convoy in the Dadaab refugee complex near the Somalia border. Their driver was killed and the Pakistani hostage was shot in the leg. Two other injured staff members were treated at a Nairobi hospital. The kidnappers made off with a Norwegian Refugee Council vehicle. On July 1, they were freed following a rescue by Kenya Defense Forces and Somali soldiers, who killed a kidnapper. Two terrorists escaped while trying to flee with the hostages, none of whom were hurt in the rescue. The Pakistani underwent surgery at the base. 12062902

June 29, 2012—Nigeria—Authorities destroyed a Boko Haram hideout in Damaturu, killing at least three sect members.

June 29, 2012—France—Authorities in Toulon arrested a 35-year-old Tunisian man believed to have administered a radical Web site that served as the conduit of messages between al Qaeda-linked jihadis, including al Qaeda in the Arabian Peninsula, al Qaeda in the Islamic Mahgreb, Fatah al-Islam in Lebanon, and groups in Yemen, Africa, Pakistan, Afghanistan, and elsewhere. He was accused of raising funds, recruiting and transporting jihadis for indoctrination and military training, and providing information about bomb making and potential targets. In 2003, he arrived in France, living there on a valid residence permit. Extremist leaders in 2008 tasked him with running the Web site. He was spotted in 2007 when investigators in Paris arrested a recruitment network of volunteers for Afghanistan. A French official said, "We've already got two emails from Fatah al-Islam in Lebanon thanking [him] for the money and saying the funds bought Kalashnikovs and rocket launchers."

June 30, 2012—Nigeria—Soldiers continued the offensive against Boko Haram in the Nyanya and Obansanjo Estates neighborhoods of Damaturu, firing mortar rounds while the terrorists used gunfire and improvised explosive devices.

July 2012—Kenya—Local authorities arrested two Iranian men who brought more than 220 pounds of RDX explosives into the country as part of a plot to bomb several Western and Israeli businesses.

July 2012—Melilla—Authorities arrested two Spanish citizens in the Spanish enclave in North Africa on suspicion of terrorism.

July 2012—Libya—On October 6, 2012, seven members of the Iranian Red Crescent were released to the Iranian Embassy after sixty-five days in captivity.

July 2012—Congo—March 23 Movement rebels killed a UN peacekeeper and fired on a UN peacekeeping base at Kiwanja. 12079901

July 1, 2012—Kenya—At 10:15 a.m., masked "goons" wearing balaclavas attacked churchgoers at the Catholic church and the African Inland Church with guns and grenades, killing at least seventeen, including two police officers, and wounding fifty. The attacks occurred in Garissa, a town used as a base for anti-al-Shabaab operations. Four gunmen attacked the African Inland Church, throwing two grenades and shooting to death two police officers guarding the door. They scooped up the police officers' rifles and turned them on the worshipers. Two other terrorists threw grenades into the Roman Catholic church, wounding three people.

July 1, 2012—Nigeria—Boko Haram was suspected of slashing throats in a nighttime attack in Maiduguri. One victim was found the next day barely breathing, bleeding at the neck. A neighbor saw fourteen bodies, some of them from the Christian south.

July 1, 2012—Afghanistan—The latest "green on blue" attack involved an Afghan wearing the uniform of the Afghan National Civil Order Police who turned his gun on British soldiers during an argument, killing three of them as they left a meeting with local elders in Helmand Province. A spokesman for the provincial government said that the attacker was a member of the Civil Order Police and had been fatally wounded in the 5:00 p.m. firefight with the British troops at a checkpoint in the Nahr-e Saraj district.

July 1, 2012—Yemen—Yemeni authorities announced that they had foiled at least thirteen al Qaeda in the Arabian Peninsula (AQAP) plots to attack foreign diplomats, embassies, and senior military and government officials in Sana'a and other cities. The attacks would include assassinations, bombings, and kidnappings of foreign diplomats. AQAP prisoners provided the tipoff information.

July 1, 2012—West Bank—Palestinian parliamentarian Shami al-Shami was shot twice in the leg by gunmen as he got out of his car at 1:30 a.m. as he returned to his Jenin home. Six bullets missed him; one hit the side mirror. He is a member of Fatah.

July 3, 2012—Cyprus—Authorities detained a 24-year-old Lebanese Palestinian carrying a Swedish passport on suspicion of involvement in a Hizballah plot to attack Israeli interests in Limassol. He admitted to Hizballah affiliation. He said he was planning to attack planes and buses used by Israeli tourists. Police searching his hotel room found plans to blow up a plane or tour bus. He was collecting flight schedules of charter planes from Israel and tour bus routes. Police said he acted alone. He was ordered to stand trial on September 12 on seventeen terrorism-related charges, including espionage and conspiracy to commit a terrorist attack. He faced life in prison. He was represented by attorney Antonis Georgiades.

July 3–5, 2012—United Kingdom—Police in West Midlands arrested seven men on suspicion of the commission, preparation, or instigation of acts of terrorism. The arrests followed a weekend discovery of two guns and a small amount of ammunition in a car stopped by police who believed it was uninsured. The detainees included six men from the West Midlands, all in their 20s, and a 43-year-old man from West Yorkshire.

On July 9, 2012, three men were ordered held, pending a July 31 hearing at London's Central Criminal Court. Jewel Uddin, 26, Omar Mohammed Khan, 27, and Mohammed Hasseen, 23, all from Birmingham, were charged with "engaging in conduct in preparation for an act or acts of terrorism, with the intention of committing such acts." Prosecutors said that they manufactured an improvised explosive device, acquired firearms and other weapons, and purchased cars connected with their plans, between May 1 and July 4.

On July 11, 2012, another three men, Anzal Hussain, 24, Mohammed Saud, 22, and Zohaib Ahmed, 22, appeared at Westminster Magistrates' Court to face charges of preparing an act of terrorism in a plot to set off a bomb at a rally of U.K.'s far-right English Defense League, which carries a potential life sentence. Deputy Chief Magistrate Daphne Wickham ordered the Birmingham-based trio held in prison custody until a July 31 hearing with the other three at London's Central Criminal Court.

July 5, 2012—United Kingdom—London police used smoke grenades and a stun gun to arrest five men and a woman, aged 18 to 30, on suspicion of the commission, preparation, or instigation of acts of terrorism. The raids occurred against homes in east, west, and north London and businesses in east London. Police said the operation was not linked to the Olympic and Paralympic Games. Three brothers were arrested in Stratford, a neighborhood that contains Olympic Park. They did not have any links to the individuals arrested in West Midlands. On July 11, 2012, London police released without charge two of the men detained on July 5–7—an 18-year-old man and a 24-year-old man detained at an address close to the Olympic stadium. The 24-year-old was hit by a taser during his arrest. A 30-year-old woman was released earlier.

On July 18, 2012, Scotland Yard charged three British Muslims with traveling to Pakistan for terrorist training. Richard Dart, 29, Imran Mahmood, 21, and Jahangir Alom, 26, went to Pakistan between 2010 and 2012 "with the intention of committing acts of terrorism or assisting another to commit such acts." The indictment said they provided others with advice on how to get to Pakistan, get trained, and stay safe in Pakistan. Ruksana Begum, 22, and Khalid Javed Baqa, 47, were charged with having material likely to be useful for terrorism. The five had been arrested earlier in July. Dart, a Muslim convert, was featured in *My Brother the Islamist*, a BBC documentary. Former police support officer Alom appeared in a YouTube video to talk about his hardline stance. Begum was detained while carrying a memory chip with issues of al Qaeda in the Arabian Peninsula's *Inspire*. Baqa also had copies of *Inspire* and a CD containing "39 Ways to Support and Participate in Jihad." Alom lives a mile from London's Olympic Stadium. Mahmood lives down the street from the site of Royal Air Force Northolt in northwest London.

July 6, 2012—Nigeria—Authorities discovered and safely detonated a bomb in Jos. Boko Haram was suspected.

July 7, 2012—Nigeria—Terrorist attacks and reprisal raids in thirteen Christian villages near Jos left thirty-seven people—including fourteen civilians, twenty-one terrorists, and two police of-ficers—dead and more than three hundred people displaced. Police conducted a four-hour gun battle with the attackers. The Nigerian Red Cross tallied fifty-eight killed after a federal lawmaker and a state lawmaker were ambushed on July 8 on their way to a mass burial for the victims. They were identified as Senator Gyang Dantong and majority leader of the Plateau State House of Assembly Gyang Fulani. Another seven people, including one lawmaker, were injured in the ambush. A government spokesman said the terrorists "came in hundreds. Some had (police) uniforms and some even had bulletproof vests." Muslim Fulani herdsmen were initially suspected until Boko Haram claimed credit.

July 9, 2012—Pakistan—Pakistani Taliban gunmen attacked a Pakistani Army camp on the outskirts of Gujrat at 5:20 a.m., killing eight people. Thousands of Islamist Difah-e-Pakistan (Defense of Pakistan) protestors had spent the night nearby before going to Islamabad to protest the decision to reopen the NATO supply line to Afghanistan.

July 13, 2012—Egypt—Bedouin gunmen jumped from two cars and kidnapped two American tourists and their local tour guide from their tour bus in the Sinai en route to Taba. One of the Americans was Michel Louis, 61, a pastor of Boston's Free Pentecostal Church of God, from Dorchester, Massachusetts, who was traveling with a group of clergy and church members; the other American was Lisa Alphonse, 39, a woman from another church who worked closely with Louis's congregation. The kidnappers wanted the release of their relative who was detained in Alexandria, Egypt, on drug charges. Bedouin sheikhs acting as mediators between the kidnappers and the government said that the hostages were unharmed and well fed. Authorities said the principal hostage taker was Germy Abu Masouh, a member of a prominent Bedouin tribe in the Sinai. He wanted Egyptian police to free his uncle, who was caught in Alexandria with a half-ton of drugs. He threatened to kidnap more tourists if the demands were not met. The three hostages were freed unharmed on July 16. The government said it did not give in to the kidnappers' demands. 12071301

July 13, 2012—Nigeria—A suicide bomber set off his explosives outside the Central Mosque in Maiduguri, killing five people. Alhaji Zanna Umar Mustapha, deputy governor of Borno State, said that the young boy was targeting him and the Shehu of Borno; neither was hurt. Boko Haram was suspected.

July 13, 2012—Syria—Islamic gunmen kidnapped two Western photojournalists—Jeroen Oerlemans, a Dutch freelance photographer with the British agency Panos Picture, and John Cantlie, a British freelancer who had worked for the *Sunday Times* of London—after they entered Bab al-Hawa, a border crossing with Turkey. The two were freed on July 27 by another group of rebels. Oerlemans sustained two gunshot wounds while trying to escape; Cantlie was also shot during the failed escape. Oerlemans was hit in the groin; Cantlie in the arm. Oerlemans said in an interview in Turkey with Business News Radio of the Netherlands that he was sure that the gunmen were not Syrians. "They all claimed they came from countries like Pakistan and Bangladesh and Chechnya," and the United Kingdom. The terrorists accused the journalists of working for the CIA and took their equipment and documents. Between thirty and one hundred jihadi gunmen kept the two hooded and blindfolded and often threatened to kill them. Oerlemans said,

> They were definitely quite extreme in their religious beliefs. All day we were spoken to about the Quran and how they would bring shariah law to Syria. I don't think they were al Qaeda; they seemed too amateurish for that. They said, "We're not al Qaeda, but al Qaeda is down the road." Guantanamo was constantly on their minds, and they were saying, "This is what you do to our guys." They would cock their weapons and say, "Prepare for the afterlife," or, "You better repent and accept Islam." It was pretty terrifying, I can assure you.

He assumed their rescuers were from the Free Syrian Army, who fired into the air to intimidate the jihadis. By October 9, British police were investigating whether a British man and woman, both 26, who were arrested at Heathrow Airport after arriving on a flight from Egypt, were involved in the kidnapping. The two were arrested on suspicion of "commission, preparation, or instigation of acts of terrorism" in Syria. The former hostages had said that some of the kidnappers had British accents. The British press said Cantlie said one of the kidnappers claimed to be a U.K. medic who was on sabbatical to treat Syrian fighters. On October 17, 2012, Shajul Islam, 26, was indicted in Westminster Magistrates Court in the United Kingdom for the kidnapping. He had been arrested at Heathrow Airport on October 9. A 26-year-old woman arrested with Islam was released without charge. The British duo had flown to Heathrow from Egypt. Islam was a trainee doctor who studied at St. Bart's and University of London Hospital. He joined a jihadi group in Syria, serving as a medic. He said there could be fifteen Britons in a jihadi camp in Syria. A follow-up hearing was scheduled for November 2 at the Old Bailey. 12071302

July 14, 2012—Afghanistan—A suicide bomber set off his suicide vest at a wedding in Aybak, capital of Samangan Province, killing twenty-two guests, including a senior politician, and injuring forty-three. The politician was identified as Ahmad Khan Samangani, a member of the Afghan parliament, who was hosting his daughter's wedding. He had been an anti–Taliban militia leader. Also dead was the provincial head of the Afghan intelligence service.

July 15, 2012—Yemen—An al Qaeda in the Arabian Peninsula terrorist killed himself and injured another person when the bomb he was making exploded in a metal workshop in the southern Hizzayz district of Sana'a.

July 15, 2012—Netherlands—Needles were inserted into six turkey sandwiches prepared in an Amsterdam catering company for four Delta Airlines flights to Minneapolis, Atlanta, and Seattle. One passenger on a flight to Minneapolis was injured, although the individual refused medical treatment. Some of the sandwiches were served to business class passengers.

July 15, 2012—Libya—Ahmad Nabil al-Alam, president of the Libyan Olympic Committee, was kidnapped in central Tripoli at 4:00 p.m. Unidentified gunmen in two vehicles seized him. He was freed on July 22. He was scheduled to head the Libyan delegation in London for the Olympic Games.

July 17, 2012—United States—Brian Hedglin, 40, a SkyWest Airlines pilot who killed Christina Cornejo, 39, a Colorado woman found dead of stab wounds in Colorado Springs on July 13, attempted to steal a SkyWest CRJ200 commercial jetliner that was not in service at St. George Municipal Airport. He killed himself before the plane became airborne. Hedglin and Cornejo both served in the Colorado Army National Guard. Hedglin was on administrative leave from SkyWest. 12071701

July 17, 2012—Nigeria—Terrorists fired a rocket-propelled grenade at a Muslim school in Jos, killing a 10-year-old boy when it missed the school and hit a nearby house.

July 17, 2012—Pakistan—Gunmen fired on a UN vehicle in Karachi's northwestern Gadap neighborhood, seriously wounding in the abdomen a Ghanaian doctor working on vaccinating people against polio. The doctor's driver was less seriously wounded. The Taliban had made threats against the World Health Organization's program. 12071702

July 18, 2012—Syria—A bomb killed Assef Shaw-kat, President Bashar al-Assad's brother-in-law (Shawkat was married to al-Assad's elder sister Bushra) and deputy chief of staff of the Syrian armed forces; Minister of Defense Dawoud Rajha, who was the most prominent Christian in the government; and former Minister of Defense Hassan Turkmani, who headed the country's crisis management cell and was the senior military aide to Vice President Farouk al-Sharaa. The trio was attending a meeting of the central command unit for crisis management at the National Security Building in Damascus's Rawda neighborhood. Interior Minister Lt. Gen. Mohammad Ibrahim al-Shaar and Lt. Gen. Hisham Baktiar, the national security chief, were hospitalized. Baktiar later died of his wounds. Al-Dunia TV said it was a suicide bombing; the Free Syrian Army, which claimed credit, said the bomb was remotely detonated in the conference room. The Brigade of Islam and the Islamic Battalions also claimed credit.

July 18, 2012—Bulgaria—Israel blamed Iran-backed Islamic Jihad, Hamas, or Hizballah terrorists when a suicide bomber set off explosives in his backpack on a tour bus carrying forty-seven Israelis that killed six—including five Israeli tourists and the Bulgarian bus driver—and injured thirty-two (three were in intensive care), including two Russians, an Italian, and a Slovak, in a parking lot outside Burgas Airport on the Black Sea. The Israelis had just arrived from Tel Aviv and were going to a beach resort 30 miles away. The dead included childhood friends Itzik Kolengi, 28, and Amir Menashe, 27. Their plane had landed at 5:00 p.m. The bus was one of seven that were to transport the tourists.

Bulgaria's Interior Ministry said the male suicide bomber was carrying a fake Michigan driver's license with a Louisiana address. The Bulgarian press said the bomber was Stockholm-born Mehdi Ghezali, 33, a Swede captured in Afghanistan in 2001, sent to Guantanamo on January 7, 2002, and detained for two years at Guantanamo Bay. Sweden denied that the man repatriated from Gitmo on July 8, 2004, was the bomber. The Bulgarian Interior Minister said Ghezali had been in the country for twenty days before the attack. Video of the bomber showed an individual with long hair wearing a hat, glasses, shorts, and T-shirt, and carrying a large backpack. The *New York Times* said U.S. officials believed the bomber was a Hizballah member. On July 20, Israeli Prime Minister Benjamin Netanyahu narrowed the suspect list to Hizballah. Over the week, a Lebanese newspaper received a claim of credit by al Qaeda.

Police said the foreign bomber used 7 pounds of TNT to build the bomb. They were searching for local accomplices. He had been driven by taxi from the seaside town of Ravda. A man with a faked Michigan driver's license had tried to rent a car earlier that week at the Tourist Office Afrodita agency in Pomorie but left when they tried to photocopy his license. Bulgarian Prime Minister Boiko Borisov told the press on July 24 that the conspirators rented several cars, met in several cities, and were never photographed together. On August 16, Bulgaria announced that a suspected accomplice used a faked Michigan driver's license for Ralph William Rico. A computer-generated image showed a heavyset man wearing glasses with short hair and stubble. 12071801

July 18, 2012—Afghanistan—Taliban gunmen destroyed twenty-two trucks, including eighteen fuel tankers, carrying supplies for NATO forces in Samangan Province in northern Afghanistan. One person was wounded in the bombing.

July 19, 2012—Russia—Assassins in Kazan, capital of Tatarstan, killed Valiulla Yakupov, a deputy mufti, and hospitalized Ildus Faizov, Tatarstan's chief mufti. Radical Islamists were suspected of attacking the traditionalist Islamic leaders, who had criticized Salafis. Yakupov died in the lobby of his house as he was leaving for work. A bomb exploded in Faizov's Toyota Land Cruiser an hour later. He was thrown from the car and broke both his legs. Russian investigators arrested five suspects, one of whom headed a firm that arranges hajj travel. On August 4, 2012, Jihad Muhammad, emir of the previously unknown Mujahideen of Tatarstan, released a video on a Muslim Caucasus radical Web site in which he said, "On July 19, 2012, on my orders an operation was conducted against the enemies of Allah.... All praise Allah. We believe the operation was a success.... If any of the imams do not want or cannot carry out the points established by Shariah, they should leave their posts. That way, you will be protected from the mujahideen." By then, investigators had detained six suspects and released photographs of Robert R. Valeev, 35, and Rais R. Mingaleev, 36, the two men at large suspected of organizing the killing and deemed "extremely dangerous." By the end of August, dozens of Muslim men were arrested; most were released. October 24, 2012, police and security services killed three Islamic terrorists suspected of conducting the attacks on Faizov and Yakupov. While the police attempted to arrest the terrorists, a bomb went off, killing a security officer. The officers broke into the first-floor apartment in Kazan, where they found guns and materials to be used for bomb making.

July 20, 2012—United States—James Egan Holmes, 24, walked into the Century Aurora 16 multiplex's theater 9 in Aurora, Colorado, thirty minutes after the beginning of the midnight showing of the new Batman movie, *The Dark Knight Rises*. He threw two tear gas canisters, then opened fire, killing a dozen people and injuring fifty-nine, including a 3-month-old. He fired an AR-15 rifle, a 12-gauge shotgun, and two .40 caliber handguns while wearing body armor, a helmet, and a gas mask. He surrendered peacefully in the parking lot to police, telling them that he was the Joker. He sported dyed red hair.

Holmes had sat in the front row by himself. He feigned taking a phone call, then walked out the emergency exit, propping open the door. He put on his gear, then returned through the door.

He told police there were explosives in his white Hyundai and in his apartment, which he had booby-trapped with incendiaries and chemical devices attached to tripwires. Police found a Soldiers of Misfortune poster in the 800-square-foot third-floor apartment, as well as sixty incendiary and chemical devices linked to wire-filament tripwires. A posting in Adult Friend Finder by "classicjimbo" appeared to have been of Holmes, who asked, "Will you visit me in prison?" He had legally purchased the guns from Gander Mountain and Bass Pro Shop. He also amassed six thousand rounds of ammunition online. He had had numerous boxes delivered to his apartment in the previous few months.

Holmes appeared in an Arapahoe County, Colorado, courtroom on July 23, sporting an amateurish orange hair dye job and looking distant. He was represented by public defenders Tamara Brady and Daniel King. On July 30, he was charged with 24 counts of first-degree murder (12 counts of murder with deliberation and 12 of murder with extreme indifference to the value of human life), 116 counts of attempted murder, a charge of possession of explosive or incendiary devices, and one charge of a crime of violence—a weapons charge of using deadly weapons during the commission of murder and attempted murder.

Holmes was about to drop out of the doctoral program in neurosciences at the University of Colorado. He had recently given a presentation on the biological basis of psychiatric and neurological disorders.

Those killed were:

- Alex Sullivan, 27, who was celebrating his birthday and had worked at the theater
- John Larimer, 27, who served in the U.S. Navy as a petty officer third class with the cyber command of the U.S. Tenth Fleet at Buckley Air Force Base in Aurora. He was a native of Crystal Lake, Illinois.
- Jessica Ghawi, 24, an aspiring sports journalist who had survived the June 2 Toronto mall shooting that left two dead and several wounded. She had graduated from the University of Texas at San Antonio.
- Micayla Medek, 23, a community college student working at a restaurant
- Jon Blunk, 26, who died shielding girlfriend Jansen Young. The navy veteran was the father of two.
- Alex Teves, 24, who recently earned a master's degree in counseling psychology from the University of Denver
- Alexander "AJ" Boik, 18, who recently graduated from high school, planned to attend Rocky Mountain College of Art and Design. He had not yet told his parents that he was engaged to Lasamoa Croft.
- Gordon Cowden, 51, father of two, from Centennial, Colorado
- Rebecca Wingo, 32, a waitress and mother of two
- Matt R. McQuinn, 27, who died shielding his girlfriend, Samantha Yowler, 27, along with her brother, Nick Yowler, 32, who had stood up to shield Samantha. McQuinn was hit in the chest, leg, and back. He had recently come to Denver from Ohio. He worked at a local Target with Samantha.
- Veronica Moser-Sullivan, 6; her mother, Ashley Moser, 25, was in critical condition. Ashley Moser miscarried on July 29 and was paralyzed from the waist down. Ashley was studying to be a nurse.
- Jesse Childress, 29, an Air Force Reserves staff sergeant on active duty at Buckley Air Force Base, serving as a cyber systems operator with the 310 Force Support Squadron.

Those injured included:

- Brent Lowak, a Texan who was at the film with Jessica Ghawi
- Patricia Legarreta, a Texan, who brought her 4-year-old daughter and boyfriend Jamie Rohrs's 4-month old son, Ethan. Legarreta was hospitalized with a bullet wound. At the hospital, Rohrs proposed.
- Samantha Yowler, 27, underwent surgery for a bullet to her knee.
- Brandon Axelrod, 30, was sitting in the tenth row with Denise Traynom, 24, his wife of two weeks and a friend, Josh Nowlan. The couple suffered minor injuries from shrapnel.

- Josh Nowlan, 32, was shot twice; one bullet broke his right arm and the other damaged his leg.
- Pierce O'Farrill, 22, wounded in the left arm by a shotgun blast, was on a cross-country bike trip after graduating from Syracuse University, where he gave the student commencement speech. He was scheduled to teach English in Russia on a Fulbright grant.
- Rita Paulina, hit in the left leg
- Caleb Medely, 23, an aspiring comic who remained in a coma as of August 12, 2012
- Allie Young, 19, saved by Stephanie Davies, 21, who applied pressure to Young's gushing neck wound and led her to safety
- Stephen Barton, of Southbury, Connecticut
- Zack Golditch, 17, a Gateway High School student who was shot in the back of the neck
- Petra Anderson, 22, a violinist who was hit by four shotgun pellets, one of which lodged in her brain. She had been accepted into the graduate program at the University of Maryland School of Music.
- Jennifer Seeger, another Gateway student and aspiring firefighter, who was burned on her legs by the hot shell casings
- Farrah Soudani, 22, who lost a kidney and her spleen and needed reconstructive surgery on her left calf. Her left lung and pancreas were damaged and three ribs were broken. She was working her way through masseuse school at a local Red Robin restaurant. She did not have health insurance

CNN reported on August 2 that Lynne Fenton, medical director of student mental health services at the university and Holmes's psychiatrist, had warned police about her patient. Holmes had mailed to Fenton a journal that foreshadowed a massacre, but the package was not opened before the killings.

The United States experienced 645 incidents of the killing of at least four victims between 1976 and 2010.

July 20, 2012—Iraq—An 11:00 p.m. explosion damaged a pipeline carrying oil from Kirkuk, Iraq, to Ceyhan, Turkey, causing no injuries. Authorities also shut down a parallel pipeline as a precaution. Officials blamed the Kurdistan Workers Party (PKK). Firat News, a PKK-linked Web site, said the group was responsible. 12072001

July 20, 2012—Iraq—Abu Bakr al-Baghdadi, emir of al Qaeda in Iraq, released an audiotape for the opening of Ramadan in which it threatened to strike at the "heart" of the United States. "You will soon witness how attacks will resound in the heart of your land, because our war with you has now started." He also praised the Syrian uprising and announced a new campaign of violence against the Iraqi government. "We are starting a new phase in our struggle with a plan we named 'Breaking the Walls,' and we remind you of your priority to free the Muslim prisoners. At the top of your priorities regarding targets is to chase and liquidate the judges, the investigators, and the guards."

July 21, 2012—Somalia—Puntland authorities seized a boat carrying explosives, switches, rockets, guns, ammunition, and rocket-propelled grenades believed going from al Qaeda in the Arabian Peninsula in Yemen to al-Shabaab in Somalia.

July 21, 2012—Pakistan—A suicide vehicle bomber killed twelve people, including four children—three girls and a boy—and wounded thirteen in Orakzai tribal agency, near the home of Maulvi Nabi, a pro-government militant commander who was not wounded. Local authorities said his group has battled an organization led by Mullah Toofan with links to Tehrik-i-Taliban Pakistan. A Taliban spokesman claimed credit.

July 22, 2012—Egypt—Terrorists blew up a gas pipeline in the Sinai Peninsula that transports fuel to Israel. It was the fifteenth such attack since the ouster of Hosni Mubarak in 2011. The blast caused moderate damage but set fire to some gas left in the pipeline. 12072201

July 22, 2012—Afghanistan—A man wearing an Afghan National Security Forces uniform shot to death three NATO contractors. 12072202

July 23, 2012—Yemen—Security forces defused a remote-controlled bomb planted at the entrance of an intelligence services building in Aden.

July 23, 2012—Turkey—Some 2,000 Turkish troops in an air-power-assisted offensive killed 115 suspected Kurdish rebels in Semdinli between July 23 and August 5.

July 24, 2012—Afghanistan—The National Directorate of Security claimed to have broken up a terrorist plan to attack a five-star international hotel in Kabul.

July 24, 2012—Afghanistan—Gunmen ambushed three people in a van in the northern province of Parwan, killing all three, including a U.S. electrical engineer who had lived in Afghanistan for decades, an Afghan colleague, and their Afghan driver. The Taliban took credit. 12072401

July 24, 2012—Pakistan—Gunmen fired on a NATO troop convoy, killing a driver and wounding a second driver and his assistant, in Jamrud in the Khyber tribal area. The Pakistani Taliban was suspected.

July 25, 2012—Nigeria—Boko Haram killed two Indian businessmen and injured a third in a morning attack on their shop in Maiduguri. 12072501

July 25, 2012—Philippines—In a day-long gun battle between Philippine troops and Abu Sayyaf, twelve army soldiers and four terrorists died at a terrorist encampment on Basilan Island in the Sumisip township. At least thirty-three soldiers and two terrorists were wounded.

July 26, 2012—Nigeria—Gunmen shot to death three police officers at a highway checkpoint in Bauchi State. A fourth policeman was injured in the morning attack. The terrorists stole the police officers' rifles.

July 27, 2012—Russia—During the night, security forces killed eight terrorists in Alburikent, Dagestan, in the suburbs of Makhachkala, after storming a house where they had holed up with women and children. Negotiations failed and the terrorists fired on the troops. One woman pretended to turn herself in, but when she approached the special forces, she set off an explosive belt, killing herself but not harming any troops. At least eight bodies were found in the house.

July 27, 2012—Nigeria—Gunmen on a motorcycle shot to death two air force officers in Kano.

July 28, 2012—Nigeria—Three gunmen shot to death a shoe shiner in a morning attack outside an uninhabited house in Zaria belonging to Vice President Namadi Sambo. The house was under renovation.

July 29, 2012—Yemen—A guard at the Italian Embassy who was a member of the Carabinieri was kidnapped in broad daylight and driven off in a car. No one took credit. 12072901

July 30, 2012—Nigeria—Suicide bombers killed themselves and three other people in Sokoto. One bomber hit a compound containing a police station and regional police officers. Another hit a police station two miles away. Among the dead were a civilian and a police officer. One injured man at the Specialist Hospital Sokoto said he saw a car drive through the main gate of the compound. The blast threw him from his bicycle. Motorcycle-riding gunmen shot at a third police station in Sokoto.

July 31, 2012—Spain—Authorities arrested three suspected al Qaeda terrorists planning to conduct an attack in a Gibraltar-area shopping mall, coinciding with the London Olympics. Authorities

found equipment for three motorized paragliding machines and explosives in the rented La Linea de la Concepcion home of Cengiz Yalcin. Police believed one of their targets was the Puerta de Europa commercial complex in Algeciras, across the Strait of Gibraltar. Cengiz Yalcin, the cell's Turkish facilitator, was asked to take photos of a Gibraltar shopping mall. The cell tested a remote-controlled plane as a potential bomb delivery system. Investigators found a video of Yalcin flying a 3-meter-long remote-controlled airplane in a descent; two packets dropped from either wing of the plane. Authorities arrested Chechen Russian Eldar Magomedov, alias Ahmad Avar, and Chechen Russian Muhammad Ankari Adamov on a bus near Valdepenas and Ciudad Real, 125 miles south of Madrid, en route to France. Magomedov violently resisted arrest. The duo gave fake names but were identified by Russian authorities.

Magomedov, the group's suspected leader, was a former member of the Russian Spetsnaz special forces. He had trained as a sniper and was an expert in poisons. He had joined training camps in Afghanistan and Pakistan, including those run by Lashkar-e-Tayyiba, after leaving the Spetsnaz. Between 2008 and 2011, he operated in Dagestan and North and South Waziristan. Adamov received explosives training in Afghanistan. He was suspected of participating in a recent bombing in Moscow. They were charged with membership in a terrorist group and possession or storage of explosives. They were believed to have been tasked with conducting the attack; they had been trained in motor-paragliding near La Linea. Authorities found a Russian-language paragliding handbook in their possession. Yalcin was accused of possession of explosive substances. He had worked at a construction company. The Chechens also lived near La Linea. The French had been monitoring the duo's phone calls and tipped off the Spanish in May, according to CNN. The London *Mirror* said the two were going to conduct a Mumbai-style attack against British tourists and military personnel watching the Olympics on an outdoor screen and in bars. They would crash the explosives-laden plane, then machine-gun other tourists and soldiers. The *Mirror* said other gunmen were at large and that 300 pounds of explosives were seized. The paper also said the cell considered using an explosives-laden boat against a ship moored off Gibraltar.

July 31, 2012—Libya—Seven Iranian relief workers who were official guests of the Libyan Red Crescent Association were kidnapped in Benghazi. As of August 21, their whereabouts were unknown. Qadhafi loyalists were suspected. 1207 3101

August 2012—Djibouti—Local authorities arrested Swedish citizens Ali Yasin Ahmed, 27, and Mohamed Yusuf, 29, and former U.K. resident Mahdi Hashi, 23, as they were on their way to Yemen. The trio was of Somali extraction. Hashi's U.K. citizenship had been revoked.

The United States accused them of participating in weapons and explosives training with al-Shabaab. A U.S. federal grand jury secretly indicted the trio on October 18. The FBI took custody of them on November 14. They appeared in a Brooklyn, New York, federal court on December 21, 2012, to face charges that they had supported al-Shabaab, illegally used high-powered firearms, and participated in "an elite al-Shabaab suicide-bomber program." They were accompanied in court by a Swedish interpreter. The case had been under seal for several months. Attorney Ephraim Savitt, a former federal prosecutor, represented one of the Swedes. British attorney Saghir Hussain represented Hashi's family and claimed that the case had the "hallmarks of rendition." U.S. attorney Harry Batchelder represented Hashi. Susan Kellman was the U.S. defense attorney for Ahmed.

August 2012—Syria—Syrian rebels posted to YouTube a video in which they threatened to kill 48 Iranian Shi'ite pilgrims from Iran if Tehran and Damascus did not comply with their demands. "Unless they start releasing our people from their prisons and cease the shelling of the innocent civilians in our cities and the ongoing random slaughter, within forty-eight hours, starting from the moment this statement is read, we inform you that for every martyr who gets killed by the Syrian regime, we will kill one of the Iranian hostages."

The government announced on January 9, 2013, that it would free 2,130 prisoners, including dozens of women and children and some Turkish nationals, in exchange for the 48 Iranian hostages. The governments of Turkey and Qatar, along with the Turkish humanitarian aid agency IHH, brokered the deal with the al-Baraa rebel brigade. Iran had eventually admitted that the 48 were part of a delegation from the Revolutionary Guard Corps and its paramilitary Basij militia, backing off from its story that they were civilian pilgrims. The hostages were turned over to an Iranian Embassy delegation at a Damascus hotel.

August 2012—Colombia—Guerrillas toppled three electricity towers in the Pacific coast port town of Tumaco, cutting electrical service for more than one week. Landmines killed at least five people, including two repairmen.

August 1, 2012—Egypt—Jihadis posted a statement on Internet forums to announce the creation of the Soldiers of Islamic Law, which listed five demands of the Egyptian and U.S. governments, including establishment of shariah law throughout Egypt starting in the Sinai, release of prisoners, and withdrawal of U.S. peacekeeping troops stationed along the border.

August 1, 2012—India—Between 7:37 p.m. and 8:15 p.m., four bombs went off in Pune. One person was seriously injured at a theater. Another bomb was defused at the theater. Other bombs went off near a McDonald's restaurant, a bank, and a bridge. At least one bomb was on a bicycle. 12080101

August 1, 2012—Somalia—A failed suicide attack involving two bomb explosions in Mogadishu did not stop the National Constituent Assembly from adopting a new constitution that established shariah as the basis for all laws. The two bombers made it to the gate of the meeting but killed only themselves while wounding a Somali soldier.

August 4, 2012—Nigeria—Gunmen attacked two ships belonging to Sea Trucks Group, an oil and gas contractor with offices in the Netherlands, 35 nautical miles off the Niger Delta. They kidnapped an Indonesian, an Iranian, a Malaysian, and a Thai before fleeing. No immediate ransom demand or credit claim was made. 12080401

August 4, 2012—Yemen—A suspected al Qaeda suicide bomber set off his explosives during an evening funeral in Jaar, killing forty-five people and injuring forty, most of them civilian militia fighters who aided the government in its retaking of Jaar from al Qaeda in the Arabian Peninsula.

August 4, 2012—Syria—Shortly before noon, gunmen kidnapped forty-eight Iranians. Tehran claimed those kidnapped were pilgrims from a tour bus group in Damascus, en route to the Shi'ite shrine of Sayeda Zeinab and the Hotel al-Faradis in Damascus. The bus was the last in a convoy of six and was stopped at an opposition checkpoint when the kidnapping took place. The Iranian government had canceled official tours. One bus sustained a bullet hole in its windshield. No group claimed credit. The trip was organized by Samen al Aemmeh Industries' travel agency owned by Iran's Revolutionary Guard Corps (IRGC), according to the rebels. The firm was under UN Security Council and U.S. Treasury sanctions for its role in the Iranian missile and nuclear programs. The *Wall Street Journal* quoted local sources as saying that the IRGC members were on a mission to provide counterinsurgency training to Syrian forces to use in Aleppo. The Free Syrian Army (FSA) posted a video of the hostages, showing IRGC ID cards. The rebels said three Iranians and several FSA soldiers died in Damascus during a government bombardment and threatened to kill the rest of the hostages if the bombing continued. Iran asked Qatar and Turkey for assistance in obtaining the hostages' release. 12080402

August 5, 2012—United States—At 10:25 a.m., Wade Michael Page, 40, opened fire on the Sikh Temple of Wisconsin in Oak Creek, south of Milwaukee, killing six before he killed himself after being hit by police gunfire. Earlier reports said a police officer shot him to death with a rifle. The gunman shot police Lt. Brian Murphy, 51, several times. Page started firing in the parking lot, killing one person, walked into the temple and fired, then fired at responding police vehicles. The temple's president, Satwant Singh Kaleka, 65, was among the dead. Police identified four other dead men as Sita Singh, 41, Ranjit Singh, 49, Suveg Singh, 84, and Prakash Singh, 39, a priest who had recently immigrated to the United States. One woman, Paramjit Kaur, 41, was also killed. Two other Sikhs were hospitalized in critical condition, as was Lt. Murphy, a 21-year police veteran. A third was treated and released. Members of the Sikh community praised two children who saw the shooting in the parking lot and ran into the temple to warn others, saving a dozen people who hid in a pantry.

The army veteran played guitar in Thirteen Knots—the number of knots in a noose—and End Apathy, Max Resist, Blue Eyed Devil, and Intimidation One, all far-right punk bands. He had been involved in the "hate music" subculture for a decade. Local authorities deemed it a domestic terrorist attack. Page had legally purchased his 9-mm semiautomatic handgun with multiple ammunition magazines. Police said he was a white supremacist. He had a 9/11 tattoo on his arm. Page, born on Veterans' Day 1971, served in the army from 1992 to 1998, stationed at Fort Bliss and Fort Bragg as a missile system repairman and a psychological operations specialist. He obtained an honorable discharge, despite a service record with "patterns of misconduct." His criminal record included DUI (driving under the influence) convictions in Colorado in 1999, writing a bad check in October 1997, and criminal mischief in Texas in 1994. He bummed around the United States with a backpack and motorcycle. He bought a house in Fayetteville, North Carolina,

in 2007 for $165,000, but it was foreclosed in January 2012. He was issued five gun permits on May 5, 2008. He moved to Wisconsin in 2012, living in a two-story apartment in South Milwaukee with his girlfriend and her son. On August 7, South Milwaukee police arrested Page's former girlfriend, Misty Cook, for felony firearm possession.

August 5, 2012—Egypt—At sunset, thirty-five masked Islamist gunmen armed with automatic rifles and weapons mounted on three Land Cruisers killed sixteen border guards and wounded seven others sitting down to their post-sunset Ramadan dinner at a checkpoint along the border with Gaza and Israel. The attackers were supported by mortar fire by Gaza. The terrorists commandeered an armored vehicle and a truck, which they used in an attack across the Israel border. The truck contained a half ton of explosives. The driver set off the explosives at 8:00 p.m. at the Israel border fence, killing himself. The armored car then entered Israel but was stopped by three Israeli air strikes that killed six or seven men, most of them carrying explosives. Egyptian officials said militants in the Sinai were aided by Palestinians in Gaza. On August 10, troops and security forces arrested nine sleeping suspects at a house close to the Rafah border crossing into the Gaza Strip. The suspects believed behind the attack included Selmi Zeyoud, a "dangerous element" and brother of a slain jihadi. Egypt indefinitely closed the border crossing at Rafah. Israel returned to Egypt the armored car and the bodies of those killed at the Kerem Shalom crossing. Egyptian President Mohamed Morsi fired intelligence chief Gen. Mohamed Murad Mowafi and other senior defense officials. On August 8, the Egyptian Army conducted helicopter missile attacks in the Sinai, killing twenty terrorists. 12080501

August 5, 2012—Libya—Gunmen attacked the International Committee of the Red Cross compound in Misrata with grenades and rockets. The Red Cross suspended its work in the port city and Benghazi. Seven aid workers were inside the residence but none were hurt. Building damage was extensive.

August 5, 2012—Nigeria—Boko Haram set off a suicide car bomb in Damaturu, killing six soldiers and two civilians.

August 6, 2012—Russia—A Chechen suicide bomber killed three Russian soldiers and wounded another three outside a Chechen department store in Grozny. A separate branch of the Interior Ministry said two suicide bombers had killed four soldiers.

August 6, 2012—United States—At 3:30 a.m., the mosque of the Islamic Society in Joplin, Missouri, burned to the ground. No injuries were reported. Arson was the cause of a July 4 fire at the mosque that caused minor damage; no arrests were made in that case. The mosque's sign was torched in 2008.

August 6, 2012—Nigeria—Three gunmen entered the Deeper Life evangelical church in Otite, a suburb of Okene, in Kogi State, 155 miles southwest of Abuja, and fired assault rifles on an evening Bible study group, killing nineteen people. At least twenty worshipers, including Lawan, Saliu, were injured. Two gunmen fired on the parishioners while the third switched off the generator, putting the church into darkness, and preventing the victims from seeing to flee. Boko Haram was suspected.

August 7, 2012—Nigeria—Three motorcycle-riding gunmen shot at a military patrol in Okene, killing two soldiers.

August 7, 2012—Afghanistan—A remotely-detonated bomb hidden under a bridge hit a mini-van in Paghman Valley in the western suburbs of Kabul, killing eight civilians and wounding several other local residents. Irate residents badly pummeled a man captured with the remote device. Observers suggested the intended target was a group of Afghan troops passing the bridge at the time; none of them were hurt. The Taliban was suspected.

August 7, 2012—Afghanistan—Two foreign soldiers died when a suicide bomber set off explosives at a joint NATO-Afghan base. Several foreign troops and Afghan civilians were wounded.

August 8, 2012—Afghanistan—A suicide bomber killed a USAID worker along with an Afghan civilian and three coalition troops. Ragaei Abdelfattah, 43, was on his second voluntary tour with USAID. He was a former master planner for Prince George's County, Maryland, who had emigrated from Egypt. He had established schools and health clinics. He was a doctoral candidate at Virginia Tech. He became a naturalized U.S. citizen several years earlier.

August 9, 2012—Turkey—Two roadside bombs hit a bus carrying Turkish troops en route to a naval base outside the Aegean resort town of Foca, killing a soldier. Eleven people were wounded, including six soldiers and five civilians who worked for the military. The Kurdistan Workers Party (PKK) was blamed for the 8:00 a.m. attack.

August 10, 2012—Afghanistan—A gunman wearing an Afghan police uniform shot to death three U.S. Special Forces troops during a nighttime meeting with tribal leaders at an Afghan checkpoint in the Sangin district of Helmand Province. The gunman, identified as police officer Asadullah, escaped. Asadullah's father, Shamsullah Sahraye Alokozai, denied the allegations. Taliban spokesman Qari Yousef Ahmadi said the gunman was safe with the Taliban.

August 10, 2012—Afghanistan—At 8:30 p.m., three U.S. Marines were shot to death by Aynoddin, 15, an Afghan police affiliate, while they were exercising at the U.S.-Afghan base Delhi in Garmsir district in Helmand Province. They were pronounced dead just before midnight. They were assigned to Kilo Company, 3rd Battalion, 8th Marine Regiment. The detained Taliban killer was a personal assistant to the district police chief, Sarwar Jan, and had not been vetted. The teen grabbed a Kalashnikov rifle that was in an unlocked barracks. He walked to the gym where four unarmed Marines were exercising and emptied the clip. The fourth Marine was badly injured. The teen walked out of the gym, still armed, and yelled, "I just did jihad. Don't you want to do jihad, too? If not, I will kill you."

August 11, 2012—Afghanistan—The National Directorate of Security said it had arrested four Afghans and a Pakistani in Kabul who were planning to attack the parliament and the home of Karim Khalili, the country's second vice president and leader of the Hezb-i-Wahdat party. Authorities seized weapons, ammunition, suicide vests, Afghan army uniforms, and Pakistani ID cards, money, and phone numbers.

August 12, 2012—Sudan—An armed gang in Nyala, capital of South Darfur State, shot to death a UN peacekeeper from Bangladesh's Formed Police Unit and injured another in the mission's policing center inside the Otash camp for internally displaced persons. 12081201

August 12, 2012—Turkey—Members of the Kurdistan Workers Party (PKK) kidnapped Huseyin Aygun, a parliamentarian from the opposition Republican People's Party, during the evening at a roadblock between Ovacik and Tunceli. The gunmen freed a journalist and Deniz Tunc, an advisor traveling with him. Aygun represents Tunceli, where he was an attorney for fourteen years.

August 12, 2012—Ivory Coast—Gunmen crossed the Liberia border to attack army checkpoints in Pekambly and Pahoubly in the west, wounding one soldier in the fifth attack against the armed forces during August. Officials blamed loyalists of ousted President Laurent Gbagbo, who refused to concede defeat in the November 2010 election; the resulting violence left three thousand dead. Eleven soldiers had died in earlier pre-dawn raids against the military in Abidjan. The gunmen had also attacked Abengorour, near the Ghana border, and Agboville. Gbagbo's Ivorian Popular Front party condemned the attacks. Human Rights Watch claimed gunmen had forced child soldiers to conduct attacks. On August 14, the Liberian government announced the arrest of six individuals who attacked two Ivorian military checkpoints while they were trying to cross into Liberia while armed.

August 12, 2012—Egypt—Security forces killed seven suspected terrorists in raids on hideouts in al-Ghora and al-Mahdiyah villages in near el-Arish in northern Sinai. Police seized landmines, an antiaircraft missile, heavy machine guns, and grenades. The terrorists died following a firefight in which the authorities shelled their safe house.

August 12, 2012—Lebanon—The Military Tribunal charged former Lebanese Information Minister Michel Samaha—believed to be an ally of Syria, Iran, and Hizballah—and two Syrians—Chief of the Syrian National Security Bureau Gen. Ali Mamlouk and Syrian Army Brig. Gen. Adnan—with conspiring to conduct terrorist attacks in Lebanon and plotting to assassinate politicians and religious officials. The charge sheet said Samaha transported and stored explosives provided by Mamlouk and Adnan. The trio set up an armed group to incite sectarian unrest and undermine "the authority of the state and its civil and military institutions." They were accused of working with the "intelligence ministry of a foreign country to undertake attacks in Lebanon." Lebanese authorities arrested Samaha on August 7 at his home in the Metn Mountains and seized equipment, computers, and documents from his offices in Beirut and Metn.

August 13, 2012—Syria—Gunmen kidnapped Ahmad Sattouf, a correspondent for Iran's state-run Arabic-language TV Al-Alam from his office in Homs. 12081301

August 13, 2012—Syria—U.S. freelance journalist Austin Tice, 31, disappeared in Darayya, a Damascus suburb. On September 26, 2012, khalidfree75 posted a forty-seven-second video clip entitled *Austin Tice Still Alive* on YouTube. The video was reposted on a Facebook page called "The Media Channel of Al-Assad's Syria." He was surrounded by masked gunmen holding assault rifles. Tice wrote stories for such outlets as the *Washington Post* and McClatchy Newspapers. The men were shown driving through the mountains,

then leading Tice up a mountain path while they called out, "Allahu al-Akbar." Tice was on his knees, initially praying in Arabic, then said, "Oh Jesus, oh Jesus," before returning to Arabic. Observers noted that the gunmen were wearing freshly pressed and clean Afghan-style tunic and pants, which Syrian rebels do not wear. Another video posting blamed the al-Nusrah Front as being responsible. Some observers believed that the video was faked by the Syrian government, which was holding Tice.

Tice was a Georgetown University law school student and a former Marine infantry officer. He had crossed into Syria from Turkey in May. His parents made a plea for his release during a November 12, 2012, news conference in Beirut, Lebanon, and another on December 20, 2012. 1208 1302

August 14, 2012—Syria—The Saudi-owned al-Arabiya television channel broadcast a Syrian rebel video showing a kidnapped Lebanese Shi'ite believed linked to Hizballah. Hassane Salim al-Mikdad (variant Hassan al-Meqdad) said his group was told by Hizballah leader Sheik Hassan Narullah to help "the Shi'ite army against Sunni gangs." He was surrounded by three masked gunmen. He noted, "Most of those who entered were snipers." He said his group was sent to Syria on August 3. Hizballah denied that he was a group member. 12081401

August 15, 2012—Lebanon—Members of a clan hoping to obtain the release of a relative kidnapped by the Free Syrian Army (FSA) kidnapped a Turk and forty Syrians with ties to the FSA. They showed a video of three gunmen standing behind two Syrians in front of a banner for the al-Meqdad Clan. The first hostage said he was Mohammed Musa Issa, a member of the FSA from Daraa, who recruited and obtained weapons for the FSA in Lebanon. The second hostage, Maher al-Housarnabi, said he assisted Issa. Ramzi Meqdad, a clan spokesman, asked for International Committee of the Red Cross mediation for a hostage swap. By August 24, clan spokesman Maher Mokdad (he spells it differently) said twenty-two Syrian hostages had been released, but they were still holding more than twenty Syrians and the Turk. 12081501

August 15, 2012—Lebanon—Members of the Meqdad clan, in interviews with local news channels, threatened to kidnap Qatari and Saudi nationals in Lebanon.

August 16, 2012—Israel—Jewish extremist settlers were believed responsible for throwing firebombs at a Palestinian taxi, hospitalizing the driver and four members of a Palestinian family with several burns. The attack occurred south of Jerusalem at 5:30 p.m. Driver Bassam Ghayada, from Nahalin, a Palestinian village, was driving construction worker Ayman Ghayada, his wife, brother, and three children to the Rami Levy supermarket on the West Bank. A young masked man wearing sidelocks threw a Molotov cocktail from 30 feet away. Another group of settlers threw a second firebomb that missed the taxi. Investigators believed the attacks came from the Bat Ayin settlement, which had been the base of a Jewish network that planned to bomb a Palestinian girls' school in 2002. Five of the victims remained hospitalized with burns after a week; the father was in intensive care. On August 26, Israeli police arrested three suspects, aged 12 or 13, living in Bat Ayin.

August 16, 2012—Indonesia—Two gunmen shot at a police post in Solo, injuring two officers.

August 17, 2012—Indonesia—A terrorist threw a grenade at a police post, wounding two police officers.

August 17, 2012—Afghanistan—An Afghan Local Police officer shot to death two American soldiers during a training exercise in Farah Province.

August 17, 2012—Kazakhstan—In a dawn raid in a village 16 miles outside Almaty, police killed nine terrorists suspected of bombing a house and killing eight people a month earlier. One police officer was wounded. The terrorists were also linked to a July 11 house fire that killed eight people. Police later found guns and ammunition in an adjacent garage.

August 18, 2012—Yemen—Al Qaeda in the Arabian Peninsula was suspected in the morning attack on the intelligence services headquarters in Aden that killed fourteen Yemeni soldiers and security guards and wounded seven others. The terrorists set off a car bomb next to the headquarters, then fired rocket-propelled grenades and guns, breaking windows and setting the building on fire.

August 18, 2012—Russia—A suicide bomber in Ingushetia killed seven people and wounded eleven at a house in rural Sagopshi of Ilez Korigov Malgobek. The home was the site of a funeral for a police officer who was killed in a shootout with terrorists that day. The government blamed Islamists.

August 18, 2012—Russia—Two masked gunmen fired inside a Shi'ite mosque in Khasavyurtin in the North Caucasus, injuring six people. The government blamed Islamists looking to form a caliphate.

August 18, 2012—Libya—A bomb exploded near a military vehicle outside the Four Seasons Hotel in Tripoli. No one was injured.

August 19, 2012—Afghanistan—An Afghan police officer shot to death a NATO service member and wounded another in Spin Boldak district of Kandahar Province. He had been arguing with his Western colleague before turning his gun on him. 12081901

August 19, 2012—Libya—Three car bombs exploded near Interior Ministry and security buildings on Omar al-Mukhtar road in Tripoli, killing two people. One bomb went off near the Interior Ministry's administrative offices, causing no casualties. Police found another car bomb that did not explode. Thirty minutes later, two car bombs detonated near the former headquarters of a women's police academy, which the defense ministry had used for interrogations and detentions. Two men were killed and another two wounded.

August 20, 2012—United States—Treasury officials in New York seized $150 million from the account of Beirut's Societe Generale de Banque au Liban/Lebanese Canadian Bank in connection with the laundering of hundreds of millions of dollars of illegal money belonging to Hizballah.

August 20, 2012—Turkey—A remotely-controlled car bomb exploded at a bus stop near a police station in Gaziantep, killing nine people, including a 12-year-old girl and three other children, and wounding sixty-one. The government blamed the Kurdistan Workers' Party (PKK) and arrested more than a dozen people. The PKK denied involvement. A Gaziantep lawmaker said the raid was planned with Syrian intelligence to retaliate for the government's policy toward Syria.

August 20, 2012—Pakistan—The Taliban tried to kidnap the brother and other relatives of Dr. Shakil Afridi, accused of helping the CIA find Osama bin Laden.

August 20, 2012—Sudan—Gunmen kidnapped two Jordanian police officers on patrol as African Union-United Nations Mission in Darfur (UNAMID) peacekeepers in Kabkabiya, 87 miles west of El-Fasher. Hasan Al-Mazawdeh and Qasim Al-Sarhan were freed on January 3, 2013, in Darfur. They had been held for 136 days but were unharmed and in good health. The UNAMID worked with the government of Sudan and Jordan and the governor of North Darfur to secure their release. 12082001

August 21, 2012—Libya—Authorities defused a car bomb in a Tripoli suburb.

August 21, 2012—Libya—The car of an Egyptian diplomat was blown up in Benghazi, causing no injuries. Security forces arrested thirty-two Qadhafi loyalists who were accused of involvement in the string of bombings the past week. 12082101

August 25, 2012—Yemen—Shots were fired in Aden at the car of Transport Minister Waed Abdullah Bathib; no one was hurt.

August 26, 2012—Saudi Arabia—Authorities arrested six Yemeni members of an al Qaeda cell preparing to set off explosives in Riyadh. Their arrest followed the detention of their Saudi leader, who was picked up in Jeddah for preparing chemicals to be used in explosives.

August 26, 2012—Russia—A car carrying three men who had an automatic rifle and Islamic pamphlets exploded in Zelenodolsk in what appeared to be an accidental detonation of a homemade bomb. Authorities blamed Tatarstan Islamists.

August 27, 2012—United States—Prosecutors near Fort Stewart in Georgia said that four army soldiers who belonged to an anarchist militia group plotted several anti-government domestic terrorist attacks and killed a former colleague and his girlfriend. The four included active and former U.S. military members who spent $87,000 to purchase eighteen rifles and handguns and bomb components in Washington and Georgia. Authorities seized uncompleted pipe bombs.

Prosecutors said the group on December 4, 2011, shot to death former soldier Michael Roark, 19, and his girlfriend, Tiffany York, 17; their bodies were found the next day by fishermen in the woods near the base. The group also planned to take over Fort Stewart and seize its ammunition control point; bomb vehicles of local and state judicial and political figureheads and federal representatives to include the local Department of Homeland Security; bomb the Forsyth Park fountain in Savannah, Georgia; bomb a dam; poison Washington State's apple crop; overthrow the government; and assassinate President Barack Obama. Army Pfc. Michael Burnett told a southeast Long County, Georgia, court that the group killed the duo because Roark took money from the group, which he planned to leave. Also accused was Pvt. Isaac Aguigui, 21, the leader of the group, who recruited disaffected soldiers at Fort Stewart. Also accused were Sgt. Anthony Peden and Pvt. Christopher Salmon, who created the group FEAR (Forever Enduring Always Ready). Burnett said Peden shot York; Salmon shot Roark. Burnett had a plea deal in which he pleaded guilty to several charges, including manslaughter, rather than capital murder. The army dismissed military murder charges initially brought in March, ceding jurisdiction to the civilian court system. Civilian prosecutors sought the death penalty for the remaining three defendants, who were each charged with thirteen counts of malice murder, felony murder, and illegal gang activity. Salmon's wife, Heather, was charged with murder and other counts, but the prosecution did not seek the death penalty for her.

Investigators later said that Aguigui was a suspect in the murder of his wife, Army Sgt. Deirdre Wetzker Aguigui, 24, in July 2011. She was five months pregnant. She had served in Iraq as an Arab-language linguist. He was believed to have founded FEAR with circa $500,000 in life insurance benefits he collected after his wife's death. The couple met at the U.S. Military Preparatory Academy in Fort Monmouth, New Jersey. Aguigui was initially represented by attorney Keith Higgins.

August 27, 2012—Kenya—Radical cleric Sheik Aboud Rogo Mohammed, accused by the UN and United States of being a fund-raiser and recruiter for al-Shabaab, was shot to death in Mombasa by gunmen who sprayed his minivan with bullets. He faced Kenyan charges of orchestrating terrorist attacks. The U.S. Treasury Department had imposed sanctions on him in July 2012 for facilitating travel of recruits and raising money for al-Shabaab. The UN Security Council imposed sanctions on him in July for his "campaign to promote violence throughout East Africa." Local police said he was assassinated by al Qaeda rivals; his followers and family said he was killed by police. The crime scene was destroyed in rioting that followed his death.

August 28, 2012—Kenya—Grenades were thrown at a police truck during a riot in Mombasa, killing fourteen people, including a local police officer. The protestors were reacting to the murder of radical cleric Sheik Aboud Rogo Mohammed the previous day. Muslims accused police of the murder.

August 28, 2012—Russia—Female suicide bomber Aminat Kurbanova, 30, set off an explosive belt, killing herself and six other people, including Sheik Said Afandi Atsayev, 74, a Sufi scholar and spiritual leader of Muslims in Dagestan. She entered his home in Chirkey disguised as a pilgrim. The explosive belt, which was packed with nails and ball bearings, also killed an 11-year-old boy who was visiting with his parents. The terrorist lived in Makhachkala, Dagestan's capital.

A border guard shot to death seven of his fellow soldiers belonging to a special rapid response unit before he was killed in Belidzhi village in the Republic of Dagestan in the North Caucasus. The press suggested that he had been recruited by Wahhabi extremists.

August 29, 2012—Afghanistan—A gunman wearing an Afghan National Army uniform opened fire during the night at Australian soldiers who were relaxing at a base in Uruzgan Province, killing three and wounding two. Australian soldiers returned fire, but the gunman hopped a fence and escaped. One of the wounded soldiers was medevaced to another base. 12082901

August 29, 2012—Georgia—Authorities conducted a gun battle against twenty heavily armed terrorists who had crossed the Russia border from Dagestan and took hostage five Georgian villagers in Lapankuri, 13 miles from the border. At least three Georgian officers and eleven terrorists died in the exchange. Among the dead was a Defense Ministry doctor, Vladimir Khvedelidze, and two members of the Interior Ministry's special forces—Solomon Tsiklauri and Archil Chokheli. Georgian President Mikheil Saakashvili said Russia was "exporting its disorder."

Georgian authorities had attempted to negotiate with the gunmen, who refused to surrender. They accepted a swap of border guards in place of the civilian hostages; the border guards were later exchanged for other officers. A gunfight broke out when the government forces were conducting a rescue operation. By mid-day, five hostages were freed and the terrorists were surrounded. One young former hostage, Levan Khutsurauili, was seen on a government video saying, "We went for a picnic to the forest, I and my friends. When we were returning along the river we met several men; they were armed and had beards. They told us we are hostages now and must follow them. They threatened they would kill us if we tried to run away." The government said the terrorists wore camouflage uniforms and carried Russian passports and Qurans. The government seized automatic weapons, ammunition, grenade launchers, sniper rifles, radios, maps, binoculars, and other equipment. The government said at least six terrorists had escaped and were hiding in the woods. Swiss diplomats had conveyed information from Georgia to the Russian government regarding the attack. 12082902

August 30, 2012—Indonesia—Two gunmen on a motorbike killed a police officer in Solo following the arrest of a member of a terrorist cell in Bandung, West Java Province. He was identified as computer expert Maman Kurniawan and believed to be a Muslim terrorist and a key member of a new terrorist cell in North Sumatra's Medan city. He had helped the group hack several Web sites and raise $700,000. Police seized computers and bank transfer documents.

August 31, 2012—Indonesia—An Indonesian antiterrorist squad shot to death two terrorists and arrested a third, who was wounded, at a food stall in central Java's Solo town, hometown of Abu Bakar Baasyir, Jemaah Islamiya's spiritual leader. Police had been tipped that the group was planning more attacks on Java. The terrorists fired at police, who returned fire. Police were investigating their ties to Jemaah Anshorut Tauhid.

August 31, 2012—Pakistan—A car bomb exploded in a market in Mattani near Peshawar, killing eleven, injuring twenty, and damaging thirty shops.

August 31, 2012—Afghanistan—Villagers found the decapitated body of a 12-year-old boy in the rural Panjwai district of Kandahar Province. Local observers said the Taliban killed him because his brother and uncle were members of the local police. The Taliban denied the charge.

August 31, 2012—Afghanistan—The decapitated body of a 7-year-old girl was found in a garden in the Tagab district of eastern Kapisa Province.

September 2012—Indonesia—Jakarta police found bomb-making materials at a house believed occupied by suspected bomb maker Muhammad Toriq, who fled during a police raid.

September 2012—Kenya—Following the assassination of a radical Islamic cleric, two Christian churches were burned and looted and two civilians killed.

September 2012—France—A grenade exploded at a kosher grocery store. A jihadi cell of young French converts was suspected. On October 6, 2012, police killed a man whose DNA was found at the scene. He had fired on police in Strasbourg. Police arrested eleven other suspects across the country.

September 2, 2012—Libya—A bomb that was planted in a car went off in a shopping district on Gamal Abdel-Nasser Street in Benghazi, killing the driver, who was a Libyan intelligence officer, and wounding a second.

September 4, 2012—Pakistan—A suicide bomber crashed his car bomb into a U.S. Consulate SUV near the U.S. Consulate in Peshawar during the morning, killing two Pakistanis and wounding twenty-five other people, including two U.S. consular staffers and two Pakistani employees of the consulate. A U.S. backup vehicle immediately rescued the four who were injured and took them to the consulate. The two Pakistanis were killed outside the vehicle. The Taliban was suspected. The U.S. vehicle was passing a UN High Commissioner for Refugees guesthouse on Abdara Road when the vehicle hit it and set off 200 pounds of explosives. 12090401

September 4, 2012—Afghanistan—At 3:30 p.m., a suicide bomber killed between twenty-five and thirty-five mourners and injured another forty-five at a funeral for Hajji Rasi, a prominent businessman, in the Durbaba district of Nangarhar Province. A Shinwari tribal leader said the target was probably district Governor Hamisha Gul, who was wounded. Among the dead was Gul's son, Nek Wali, 26. The Taliban disputed government charges of involvement.

September 4, 2012—United States—Jonathan Jimenez, 28, an Orange County man, pleaded guilty to two federal charges in connection with a plot to kill members of the U.S. military serving overseas. He admitted in an Orlando Federal courtroom to tax fraud and lying to the FBI regarding the plot to wage violent jihad. An FBI phone tap established that he had received terrorist training, including martial arts, firearms, and knife training, from convicted felon Marcus Robertson, the former imam of an east Orange County mosque.

September 4, 2012—Canada—Richard H. Bain, 61, fired an assault rifle and shot to death Denis Blanchette, 48, a stagehand, and wounded another person at a nighttime victory rally in Montreal's concert hall by Pauline Marois, 63, Quebec's newly elected premier. The gunman was dressed in a blue bathrobe, balaclava, black underwear, and a face mask. He carried two guns and had five more in his car. Police discovered that he owned at least twenty firearms; all but one were registered. He set fire at the hall's back door before being arrested. As he was being placed into a police cruiser, he yelled, "The English are waking up!" in French. He was initially taken to a hospital, but later jailed. Police said it might have been an assassination attempt against Marois, leader of the separatist Parti Quebecois. Bain owned an outdoor outfitting business near the Mont Tremblant resort and lived in La Conception. He was charged in a Montreal courtroom with sixteen counts, including first-degree murder, attempted murder, and arson. Many in rural Quebec viewed him as a kilt-wearing eccentric.

September 5–6, 2012—Nigeria—Boko Haram was suspected of damaging thirty-one cell phone towers in six states, including Adamawa, Yobe,

Gombe, Bauchi, Kano, and Borno. One of the burned towers was in Maiduguri's main office for the South Africa–based MTN group, Ltd., Nigeria's largest cell network provider. Other firms hit included Bharti Airtel, Ltd., of India, Abu Dhabi-based Etisalat, the local Globacom, Ltd., and five other local firms. The group had threatened cell phone companies six months earlier for cooperating with the government against its members. 12090501-03

September 6, 2012—Gaza Strip—Israeli soldiers shot to death three Palestinian men who were "part of a terrorist squad that was planting an explosive device" near the security fence in Beit Hanoun on the border with Israel. Two of the men were brothers.

September 7, 2012—United States—The U.S. Department of State announced that as of September 17, the Haqqani network would be the fifty-second entry on the Department's Foreign Terrorist Organizations list, thereby prohibiting network members from traveling to the United States, freezing its assets in the United States, and barring Americans from providing financial/material support.

September 7, 2012—Philippines—Seven Abu Sayyaf gunmen attacked 120 rubber plantation workers in four trucks heading home for lunch in Sumisip township on Basilan Island, killing one and wounding 35.

September 8, 2012—Afghanistan—A 14-year-old Taliban suicide bomber killed six people, most of them children, in a high-security zone in Kabul 150 feet from the headquarters of the International Security Assistance Force.

September 8, 2012—Indonesia—A bomb exploded during the night in a terrorist bomb-making safe house in Depok, a suburb near Jakarta, injuring five people, including three passersby and two fleeing terrorists on a motorbike. The terrorists were seriously wounded on their hands. Police found one man at the site whose left hand had been severed and had burns over 70 percent of his face and body. A woman sustained slight wounds to her head. The house was listed as an orphanage foundation and herbal clinic but was never opened to the public. Police confiscated six pipe bombs, three grenades, two machine guns, a Beretta pistol, bomb guide books, and several jihadi books. The bombs were packed with nails. Police ran a DNA test to determine whether the injured man was bomb maker Muhammad Toriq. He was believed linked to a terrorist group planning to shoot police and bomb the parliament building as part of a jihad to establish a caliphate. The Associated Press reported on September 10 that Toriq had surrendered on September 9 while carrying a gun and ammunition and wearing an empty suicide bomber belt. He told police he had planned to conduct a suicide bombing on September 10 against police, an antiterrorism squad, or Buddhists to protest mistreatment of minority Rohingya Muslims in Myanmar. Although he had written a suicide note, he reconsidered after thinking about the pain it would cause his mother, wife, and son.

September 9, 2012—Israel—A rocket fired from the Gaza Strip hit the roof of the southern Israel home of Pini Azoulay. Palestinian terrorists were suspected. 12090901

September 9, 2012—Iraq—A car bomb went off outside a French consular building in Nassiriya, 185 miles south of Baghdad, wounding two people. No one claimed credit. 12090902

September 11, 2012—Internet—Ayman al-Zawahiri posted a video on Islamist sites entitled *Truth Has Come and Falsehood Has Perished,* in which he said, "I proudly announce to the Muslim umma and to the Mujahideen ... the news of the martyrdom of the lion of Libya Sheikh Hassan Mohammed Qaed," one of the names of Abu Yahya al-Libi, a senior al Qaeda member who died in a U.S. drone strike in June in Pakistan. He called for revenge. "His blood urges you and incites you to fight and kill the crusaders." Al-Zawahiri said Libi was a "lion of jihad and knowledge." Referring to President Obama, he said, "This liar is trying to fool Americans into believing that he will defeat al Qaeda by killing this person or that person. But he escapes from the fact that he was defeated in Iraq and Afghanistan." Adam Gadahn, American-born al Qaeda propagandist, added, "America is crystal clear about its opposition to Islam as a political system, Islam as a ruling system ... and the essence of Islam. So, how can America say that it is not at war with Islam?"

September 11, 2012—Turkey—A Revolutionary People's Liberation Party-Front (DHKP-C) suicide bomber threw a hand grenade and detonated his explosives at the entrance to a police station in Istanbul, killing a police officer and injuring seven others. The attacker had participated in prison hunger strikes.

September 11, 2012—Nigeria—Authorities arrested eleven Boko Haram members and seized a submachinegun, 7 AK-47s, 1,568 rounds of ammunition, 12 empty shells, and 19 bombs in the Waka-Biu region of Borno State.

September 11, 2012—Yemen—A car bomb went off alongside a convoy in Sana'a that included Yemeni Defense Minister Maj. Gen. Mohammed Nasser Ahmed, killing seven bodyguards and five civilians and wounding fifteen other people. Ahmed was unhurt. Ali al-Ansi, head of the National Security Agency, was fired. No group claimed credit, although al Qaeda in the Arabian Peninsula was suspected.

September 11, 2012—Afghanistan—Taliban attackers killed three Afghan intelligence employees and destroyed a NATO helicopter.

September 11, 2012—Libya—At 10:00 p.m., RPGs and mortars slammed into a building in the U.S. Consulate compound, killing the U.S. ambassador and three other U.S. diplomats and wounding another two. Two diplomats died in the building; another two were killed in a midnight firefight while another facility was still under siege. The Islamic terrorist group Ansar al-Shariah was suspected; the group denied responsibility. The group was believed led by Sufyan bin Qumu, a Libyan released from Gitmo in 2007 and transferred to Libya on condition he be kept in jail; Qadhafi released him in 2008. He was believed to have had ties to the 9/11 financiers and to the Libyan Islamic Fighting Group. Other observers pointed to al Qaeda in the Islamic Maghreb (AQIM) or to individuals with AQIM ties.

The dead U.S. diplomats included:

- Ambassador J. Christopher Stevens, a career State Department officer who spoke Arabic and French and had twice served in Libya. He had run the liaison office with the rebels in Benghazi during the overthrow of Muammar Qadhafi. He was the sixth U.S. ambassador to be killed by terrorists.

- Sean Smith, 34, who had worked as an information management specialist for the State Department for a decade in Brussels, Baghdad, Pretoria, and Libya. The online gamer enlisted in the U.S. Air Force in 1995 at age 17. He served for six years as a ground radio maintenance specialist and deployed to Oman. He left the service in 2002 as a staff sergeant, having earned the Air Force Commendation Medal. He had served for the State Department in Brussels, Baghdad, Pretoria, Montreal, and The Hague. Smith was survived by his wife and two children.

- Glen Anthony Doherty, 42, a former U.S. Navy SEAL who worked for a private security firm protecting the Benghazi consulate. He was a pilot and paramedic, and had coauthored a book about being a military sniper. He had told ABC News that he was tracking down MANPADS shoulder-fired surface-to-air missiles left over from Qadhafi's arsenal. He attended Embry-Riddle Aeronautical University in Arizona. He had joined the U.S. Navy in 1996 and left active duty in 2005 as a petty officer first class. He had served two tours in Iraq, earning the Navy and Marine Corps Commendation Medal with Combat Distinguished Device. He was lauded in the book *The Red Circle* by colleague Brandon Webb.

- Tyrone S. Woods, 52, a former U.S. Navy SEAL who had served several tours in Iraq and Afghanistan. He was a registered nurse and paramedic. He enlisted in the U.S. Navy out of high school in 1990. Decorations included the Bronze Star with Combat V. He retired as a senior chief petty officer in 2007. He had protected U.S. diplomats in Central America and the Middle East since 2010. He was survived by his wife and three sons.

The news media initially reported that the attackers and demonstrators in numerous other countries were protesting an inflammatory anti–Islam video. Authorities scrambled to determine the authorship of the thirteen-minute *Innocence of Islam* trailer, which portrays Muhammad and his followers as child abusers and perverts. It was eventually attributed to a handful of California-based Coptic Christian extremists. The amateurish film had been available on the Internet since July but only recently was made available in Arabic. The apparent producer of the film, Nakoula Basseley Nakoula, 55, was arrested on September 27 for violating terms of his probation.

News reports later pieced together the chronology of the attack. At around 9:00 p.m., gunmen attacked the compound from three directions. Smith and Stevens were mortally injured. Stevens was taken to a local hospital where he was pronounced dead. A group of Americans escaped to a second compound a mile away but were attacked in a firefight. The two former SEALs were killed.

On September 16, Mohamed al-Magariaf, leader of the General National Congress, said fifty people had been arrested in connection with the attack. He said they included individuals from Mali and Algeria and several with ties to al Qaeda. Al-Magariaf said that the attack was planned and organized by foreigners. Some observers said the attack was led by the Ansar al-Sharia. The *Wall Street Journal* reported on October 2 that the gunmen were linked to Muhammad Jamal Abu Ahmad, who had asked Ayman al-Zawahiri for permission to open an al Qaeda franchise in Libya.

On September 19, during testimony to Congress, Matthew Olsen, director of the National Counterterrorism Center, said that it was an "opportunistic attack" by heavily armed militants. He told the Senate Homeland Security Committee that the Americans "were killed in the course of a terrorist attack on our embassy."

Within a week the United States had shuttered its consulates in Alexandria, Peshawar, Lahore, and Karachi.

On September 21, U.S. officials said that the fifty attackers, many of them masked, used military-style tactics to steer the Americans toward an ambush. The terrorists used gun trucks and set up a perimeter. The first attack moved the Americans to their fallback building, which was then hit by mortars.

FBI investigators were accompanied by several dozen Special Operations forces in examining the ruins of the Benghazi consulate on October 3. Two days earlier, the State Department had withdrawn all official U.S. government personnel from Benghazi; nonessential personnel were withdrawn from the U.S. Embassy in Tripoli, as well.

Turkish authorities announced on October 4 that they had arrested two Tunisian men carrying fake Austrian passports who had attempted to arrive at Istanbul's Ataturk Airport. They were believed involved in the Libya attack. The Omar Abdul Rahman Brigades, which had claimed credit for setting off a small bomb outside the Benghazi consulate in June, was also suspected.

Ahmed Abu Khattalah was seen at the diplomatic mission where two of the Americans died. The founder of Ansar al-Sharia reportedly propagates an al Qaeda-style ideology. The militia leader lives in the Leithi neighborhood of Benghazi. He was believed to be in his mid–40s as of October 2012. He trained to become an auto mechanic while a teen. He spent most of his adult life in Qadhafi's Abu Salem prison. He was released in February 2011.

On October 24, 2012, the Tunisian government arrested Ali al-Harzi, 28, a Tunisian, in connection with the September 11, 2012, attack in Benghazi, Libya, in which the U.S. ambassador and three other Americans were killed. He was represented by attorney Oulad Ali Anwar, who claimed his client was working in Benghazi painting a house at the time of the attack. He had been arrested in Turkey on October 3 along with another Tunisian; the duo were carrying fake passports and were on their way to Syria from Libya.

On October 25, 2012, Egyptian police arrested five Libyan and two Egyptian members of al Qaeda, killed Karim Ahmed Essam al-Azizi, alias Hazem, a Libyan suspected of involvement in the

September 11, 2012 assault on the U.S. Consulate in Benghazi, and seized two trucks carrying 25 rockets, 102 rocket-propelled grenades, and 102 mortar rounds. Al-Azizi died in a raid on his rented apartment in the Cairo suburb of Medinat Nasser. He threw a bomb at the police, but it bounced back and exploded in his apartment. Police seized 17 bombs, 4 rocket-propelled grenades, 3 automatic weapons, and large quantities of ammunition. Police said the group had been using several apartments in the neighborhood to store arms. The trucks were halted on the highway near Marsa Matrouh, 270 miles northwest of Cairo.

In early December, Egyptian authorities announced the arrest of Muhammad Jamal Abu Ahmad, 45, whose supporters were believed involved in the attack. He had been released from an Egyptian prison in March 2011. The former Egyptian Islamic Jihad member had been arrested in mid–November in Sharkia Province on charges of leading a militant cell of Libyans and Egyptians. Police found 2 machine guns, ammunition, and a laptop. Egyptian authorities said his cell, with al Qaeda in the Arabian Peninsula assistance, was planning attacks in Egypt and abroad. He had set up training camps in Libya and Egypt. The group became known as the Jamal Network. He held a master's degree in sharia law. He had asked Ayman al-Zawahiri to establish an affiliate called al Qaeda in Egypt. Authorities also believed he was a founder and leader of the Nasr City Cell in Cairo. In October 2012, Egyptian authorities raided an apartment in Nasr City, arresting five terrorists after a gun battle during which a terrorist set off a bomb. Ahmad speaks English, is 5 foot, 7 inches, and has a thick beard.

In December 2012, Ali Harzi, alias Abdelbasset Ben Mbarek, a Tunisian suspected of involvement, refused to be interrogated by FBI agents, according to his lawyer, Anwar Oued-Ali. He was freed by Tunisian authorities on January 8, 2013, for lack of evidence. He had been detained in October 2012 at a Turkish airport.

Ahmed Abu Khattala, another suspect, on January 6, 2013, survived a car bombing in Benghazi that killed his would-be assassin. It was unclear what happened to the other man who was planting the bomb under Abu Khattala's car. 12091101

September 11, 2012—Egypt—Protestors climbed the compound wall to attack the U.S. Embassy, burning a U.S. flag. At least two thousand demonstrators were involved but only a dozen climbed the wall.

September 12, 2012—Somalia—Three suicide bombers attacked the temporary residence of new Somali President Hassan Sheik Mohamud, 56, who was elected by the new parliament on September 10, during a news conference. The terrorists killed an African Union soldier but did not assassinate any political leaders. One terrorist struck near the gate, and one struck at the back of the Jazeera Hotel near the airport. The third attacker was shot trying to go over the wall of the compound. One terrorist was wearing a military uniform. An African Union spokesman said four people died, plus the three terrorists. Three other African Union troops were injured. Al-Shabaab claimed credit. Mohamud did not stop his speech during the gunfire, telling visiting Kenyan Foreign Minister Sam Ongeri, "Things like what's happening now outside will continue for some time ... Somalia has the momentum to move ahead." 12091201

September 13, 2012—Iraq—Qais al-Khazali, leader of the Asaib al-Haq militia, threatened to attack Americans as part of the Islamic demonstrations against the anti–Muhammad film. "The offence caused to the Messenger will put all American interests in danger and we will not forgive them for that." Hundreds of protestors were on the streets of Baghdad and Basra.

September 13, 2012—Internet—Ayman al-Zawahiri released another audio, calling on Muslims to back Syrian rebels and demanding Egypt revoke its 1979 peace treaty with Israel, saying Cairo represented a "government for sale and an army for rent." "Supporting jihad in Syria to establish a Muslim state is a basic step towards Jerusalem, and thus America is giving the secular Baathist regime one chance after another for fear that a government is established in Syria that would threaten Israel." "I appeal to the honorable members of the Egyptian Army, and there are many of them, not to be guards for the borders of Israel, and not to defend its borders or participate in besieging our people in Gaza."

September 13, 2012—Yemen—Protests over the anti–Muhammad film led to the death of four demonstrators during a battle between security forces and thousands of demonstrators outside the U.S. Embassy. Some twenty-four security force members and eleven protestors were injured. The protestors had hopped a compound wall and stormed the embassy, but no diplomats were harmed. One of the compound's buildings was set on fire. 12091301

September 13, 2012—Egypt—Police fired warning shots and tear gas at protestors outside the U.S. Embassy in Cairo. Minor injuries were reported.

Protests also took place in Tunisia, Morocco, Iran, and other locations throughout the Middle East.

September 14, 2012—Middle East/Asia—Anti-U.S. protests were reported in Tunisia, Turkey, Lebanon, Libya, Egypt, Sudan, Qatar, Yemen, Iraq, Iran, Syria, Afghanistan, Pakistan, India, Bangladesh, Malaysia, and Indonesia. Protestors torched Kentucky Fried Chicken and Hardee's restaurants in Tripoli, Lebanon; police fired on the arsonists, killing one. Protestors broke into the U.S. embassies in Sudan and Tunisia. Sudan refused to let the United States send more Marines to defend the facility. 12091401-04

September 14, 2012—Sudan—Protestors set alight the German Embassy, then tried to attack the U.S. Embassy. Police opened fire. Casualties were not reported. 12091405

September 14, 2012—Lebanon—Demonstrators torched a Kentucky Fried Chicken restaurant in Tripoli. One man was killed and more than a dozen injured in clashes with police. 12091406

September 14, 2012—Kenya—Local police arrested two people with two explosive devices, four suicide vests containing hundreds of ball bears, four AK-47 assault rifles, twelve grenades, and ammunition and were searching for eight more would-be bombers and masterminds of a plot to conduct a terrorist attack in Nairobi. The group was believed linked to al-Shabaab.

September 14, 2012—United States—Authorities arrested Adel Daoud, 18, a U.S. citizen residing in Chicago's Hillside suburb, following an undercover operation in which FBI agents provided him with a fake Jeep bomb he planned to use against a downtown bar. He was charged the next day with attempting to use a weapon of mass destruction and attempting to damage and destroy a building with an explosive. He had posted material on the Internet about "violent jihad" and the killing of Americans. Daoud had listed twenty-nine potential targets, including military recruiting centers, bars, malls, and other tourist attractions in Chicago. The U.S. Attorney's office noted that at 7:15 p.m., he met the undercover agent in Villa Park and drove with him to downtown Chicago.

During the drive, Daoud led the undercover agent in a prayer that Daoud and the agent succeed in their attack, kill many people, and cause destruction. They entered a parking lot where a Jeep containing the purported explosive device was parked. Daoud then drove the Jeep out of the parking lot and parked the vehicle in front of a bar in downtown Chicago, which was the target that he had previously selected. According to the affidavit, Daoud exited the vehicle and walked to an alley approximately a block away, and in the presence of the undercover agent, attempted to detonate the device by pressing the triggering mechanism. He was then arrested.

He was charged the next day with one count of attempting to use a weapon of mass destruction, namely explosives, and one count of attempting to damage and destroy a building by means of an explosive. He faced life plus twenty years in prison if convicted.

September 15, 2012—Tunisia—During anti–U.S. riots, a school building on the grounds of the American school in Tunis was destroyed. Four people died and fifty injured during a firebomb attack on the U.S. Embassy. The United States announced that it was withdrawing embassy staff in Tunisia and Sudan. Local authorities blamed Salafist thugs and announced the arrests of 96 suspects. Police were searching for Salafist leader Saif Allah bin Hussein, alias Abu Ayyad, leader of the Tunisian wing of Ansar al-Sharia. He had been jailed under the former Tunisian government and released in 2011 at the start of the Arab Spring. He had delivered a sermon the previous day that authorities believed incited the attack on the school and embassy. The government detained 144 people, mostly Salafists, including 2 leaders of Ansar al-Sharia, after the attack on the embassy. Some conducted a prison hunger strike.

On October 14, U.S. Ambassador Jacob Walles sent a letter to the Tunisian government in which he called "upon the Tunisian government to conduct its investigation and bring the perpetrators and instigators of this attack to justice." On October 24, a Tunisian court sentenced Abu Ayyad (variant Abu Ayub, variant Abu Ayoub), leader of Ansar al-Sharia in Tunisia, to a year in prison on charges of disturbing public security and incitement to violence, including the attack on the U.S. Embassy. His attorney, Rafik Ghak, said he would appeal. Bachir al-Gholi and Mohammed Bakhti, prominent Tunisian members of the Salafist movement, died on November 15 and 17, 2012, from their hunger strikes. They were held in the attack on the U.S. Embassy. 12091501-02

September 15, 2012—Afghanistan—An Afghan Local Police officer fired on British NATO coalition soldiers, killing two and wounding four, before he was shot to death by another soldier in Gereshk town. 12091501

September 15, 2012—Yemen—Al Qaeda in the Arabian Peninsula called for killing more U.S. diplomats. Yemen's parliament demanded that all foreign troops leave, including the fifty U.S. Marines protecting the U.S. Embassy.

September 16, 2012—Pakistan/Afghanistan/Australia—Anti-U.S. protests continued. In Karachi, one protester died and eighteen were injured when hundreds of people broke through a barricade and tried to enter the U.S. Consulate.

September 16, 2012—Pakistan—A remotely-detonated bomb hit a passenger van in the Lower Dir district near Bunr village in Khyber Pakhtunkhwa Province, killing fourteen and injuring six.

September 16, 2012—Turkey—Police officers hit a landmine while they were driving from Karliova to their base in Bingol Province in the predominantly Kurdish southeast. Eight officers died and nine were wounded. Kurdish separatists were suspected.

September 16, 2012—Afghanistan—A member of the Afghan security forces fired on U.S. troops at a remote checkpoint near a NATO installation in Zabul Province, killing four. 12091601

September 16, 2012—Afghanistan—An Afghan National Army soldier fired on six Lebanese civilian contractors working for NATO forces, causing minor injuries to some of them. The six were riding in a vehicle near Camp Garmsir in southern Helmand Province. 12091602

September 16, 2012—Egypt—Salafist preacher Ahmad Ashoush issued a fatwa saying, "The killing of the director, producer, actors, and everyone else involved in the film is mandatory."

September 16, 2012—Somalia—Gunmen shot in the head and chest freelance cameraman Zakariye Mohamed Mohamud Moallim, killing him.

September 16, 2012—Nigeria—Boko Haram shot to death a security agent and three of his family members in Kano.

Gunmen attacked a Bauchi suburb, killing eight people playing poker.

Gunmen shot to death a moderate Muslim cleric in Maiduguri.

September 17, 2012—Lebanon—Hizballah led tens of thousands of protestors in Beirut. The group was addressed by Hizballah leader Hasan Nasrallah, who noted, "The world should know our anger will not be a passing outburst but that this is the start of a serious movement that will continue all over the Muslim world to defend the prophet of God." He said that the release of a full-length version of the thirteen-minute video would entail "dangerous consequences."

September 17, 2012—Nigeria—Soldiers at a checkpoint in Mariri shot to death two Boko Haram (BH) leaders. One was the BH spokesman, Abul Qaqa; another was the commander of the Kogi state BH group. The commander's wife and children, who were also in the BH vehicle, were taken into military custody.

Meanwhile, a Nigerian Army soldier and thirteen suspected BH members were killed in Maiduguri when terrorists threw an explosive at a military vehicle. The bomb killed the soldier and injured three others. During a subsequent firefight, the thirteen BH members were killed.

September 18, 2012—Afghanistan—At 6:45 a.m., a 22-year-old female suicide bomber driving a Toyota Corolla attacked a van carrying foreigners near Kabul Airport, killing fourteen people, among them ten foreigners, including eight foreign civilians working for Air Charter Service Balmoral, an international aviation company. Two Afghan bystanders were killed and ten wounded. South Africa said most of the dead were South Africans. Kabul police said only six South Africans were killed, including one woman, and that a Filipino died, along with the Afghan driver. Afghan President Hamid Karzai said one of the dead was from Kyrgyzstan. Russian casualties were also reported. Haroon Zarghoon, a spokesman for Hizb-i-Islam terrorists, claimed credit, saying the bomber, Fatima, was protesting the anti–Muhammad film. Observers noted that Afghan women rarely drive, and this was the first female suicide bombing in the country. A second Hizb-i-Islam spokesman, Zubair Sediqqi, said, "A woman wearing a suicide vest blew herself up in response to the anti–Islam video." 12091801

September 18, 2012—Turkey—Kurdish rebels were blamed for an attack on a military convoy in Bingol Province that killed ten soldiers and wounded more than seventy.

September 18, 2012—Pakistan—Two bombs exploded within minutes of each other at a market in the Nazim Abad neighborhood of Karachi, killing six and wounding fifteen. No one claimed credit.

September 18, 2012—Mali—Al Qaeda in the Islamic Maghreb threatened new anti–U.S. attacks in Algeria, Tunisia, Morocco, and Mauritania, encouraging "all Muslims to continue to demonstrate and escalate their protests ... kill their ambassadors and representatives or to expel them to cleanse our land from their wickedness.... We congratulate our Muslim rebel brothers who defended our Prophet's honor ... and we tell them: the killing of the U.S. ambassador is the best gift you give to his arrogant unjust government."

September 19, 2012—Pakistan—A remotely-detonated car bomb went off near a passing Pakistani Air Force vehicle close to Badaber Air Base, killing ten and wounding twenty-seven at a busy intersection in Peshawar. The Pakistani Taliban was suspected.

September 19, 2012—Nigeria—The Nigerian Army announced it had killed two more Boko Haram leaders at a highway checkpoint near Maiduguri. The men had weapons in their car.

September 19, 2012—France—A grenade attack against a Jewish grocery store in Sarcelles, a Paris suburb, injured one person. On October 6, 2012, French authorities conducted raids in Strasbourg, Paris, Nice, and Cannes, detaining twelve French-born suspects and killing one suspected of involvement in the grenade attack. Police found weapons, $35,200 in cash (27,000 Euros), a printed al Qaeda publication, martyr wills, and a list of Jewish groups in the Paris area. Authorities said a jihadi network was targeting the Jewish community.

The dead suspect was Jeremie Louis-Sidney, 33, whose DNA was found on the remains of the grenade. Sidney emptied six shots from his .357 caliber pistol at police as they forced open the door of his wife's home. They fired back, killing him. One police officer was wounded in the gun battle. Louis-Sydney had earlier served two years in prison from 2008 to 2010 for drug trafficking. He was born of Caribbean descent and raised as a Christian. He was radicalized in prison. Hours after Sidney was killed, blank shots were fired at a synagogue in Argenteuil, a working-class suburb of Paris.

Another one of the detainees was captured near Paris carrying a loaded pistol. French President Francois Hollande said a proposed law would make it illegal to travel to militant training camps. Some of the suspects were admirers of Mohammed Merah, who conducted anti–Semitic attacks in March 2012 in Toulouse before being killed in a shootout with police. Prosecutors said that the dozen suspects were planning attacks on French soil and wanted to recruit people to fight against the Syrian regime and in other countries.

On October 11, 2012, five of the detainees were freed. The other seven were recent Islamic converts. The suspects ranged in age from 18 to 25. Also on October 11, French police announced that the Sarcelles bombing was planned by Jeremy Bailly. Investigators found during a raid of his home a key to a storage unit in Torcy outside Paris

that contained bomb-making material, including bags of chemicals, batteries, alarm clocks, car headlights, and a pressure cooker. A prosecutor said the bomb he was building was "exactly" the type used by an Algerian terrorist group in the mid–1990s.

September 20, 2012—Somalia—Two suicide bombers attacked a Mogadishu restaurant, killing fifteen people, including three local journalists and two police officers. The dead journalists included Abdisatar Dahir Sabriye, news producer for the state-run Somali National TV; Liban Ali Nor, a TV news editor; and Abdirahman Yasin Ali, a radio director. Five other journalists were wounded. Al-Shabaab was suspected of the attack on the Village Restaurant, which is owned by Ahmed Jama, 46, a British Somali. The restaurant is next door to Radio Kulmiye, a station where Somali comedian Abdi Jeylani Malaq, who had twitted al-Shabaab, was shot to death in August. 12092001

September 20, 2012—Internet—Al Qaeda American-born spokesman Adam Gadahn released an eighty-four-minute As-Sahab video entitled *Advice and Support to Our Rebel Brothers Against Injustice*. It was believed to have been produced on April 30. Gadahn spoke in Arabic.

September 21, 2012—Somalia—Gunmen shot to death a radio reporter.

September 21, 2012—Worldwide—France closed diplomatic facilities in twenty countries after *Charles Hebdo*, a French satire magazine, printed anti–Mohammed cartoons. Germany closed its embassy in the Sudan in preparation for likely protests. A few dozen people stood in front of the French Embassy in Cairo in protest.

September 21, 2012—Pakistan—During protests against the anti–Mohammed film, 19 people died and 160-plus were injured in demonstrations throughout the country. Mobs in Peshawar torched two movie theaters; TV reporter Muhammad Amir and another person were killed. Demonstrators in Rawalpindi set alight a tollbooth and vehicles. Police prevented the protestors from getting to U.S. diplomatic facilities in Rawalpindi, Lahore, Peshawar, and Islamabad. Arsonists in Karachi hit movie theaters, banks, American food franchises, and police vehicles and threw stones at the Sheraton hotel. A mob burned an Anglican church in Mardan.

September 21, 2012—Worldwide—Protests against the anti–Islam film were also reported in Lebanon, Bangladesh, and Malaysia.

September 21, 2012—United States—The *Washington Post* reported that the State Department had decided to remove the Iranian Mujahideen-e Khalq from the list of terrorist groups.

September 21, 2012—Israel—Three gunmen wearing camouflage uniforms crossed the Sinai border in a mountainous area but were shot to death in a firefight with Israeli troops, who lost soldier Netanel Yahalomi, 20; a second soldier was wounded. Yahalomi was posthumously promoted to corporal. The terrorists had fired on Israeli soldiers who were securing a construction zone for a security fence at Mount Harif between the Gaza Strip and Eilat. An explosives belt worn by one of the terrorists detonated. The gunmen had three rocket-propelled grenade launchers and a machine gun hidden in a nearby pit. The Supporters of the Holy Places (Ansar Bait al-Maqdis, variant Partisans of Jerusalem) claimed credit, saying it was retaliating for the anti–Muhammad video. The group also claimed credit for the August 18, 2011, attack near Eilat that killed eight and wounded more than thirty people. The group said one of its leaders, Ibrahim Aweida, helped lead the Eilat attack, and that he died in an Israeli attack in the Sinai village of Khreiza in August 2012. The most recent attack was also to avenge his death. 1209 2101

September 21, 2012—Afghanistan—A joint Afghan-NATO special operations team foiled two men preparing to attack a coalition base in Logar Province. The two "known insider attack facilitators" planned to set off homemade bombs, recruit terrorists, and infiltrate the Afghan security forces. Interrogators were trying to determine their affiliation.

September 21–22, 2012—Russia—Four police officers and four Chechen terrorists were killed in gun battles in the southern Vedeno region. Eleven police officers were wounded.

September 22, 2012—Somalia—Unidentified gunmen shot to death Mustaf Haji Mohamed, a Somali lawmaker, after evening prayers in Mogadishu's Waberi district.

September 22, 2012—Yemen—Abdul-Latif al-Sayed, a former Islamist who helped drive al Qaeda in the Arabian Peninsula out of Jaar, escaped an assassination attempt when a suicide bomber set off his explosives. Al-Sayed had entered a parked car with three others after dining in an Aden restaurant. The terrorist died; four victims had serious injuries. An August attack against Sayed killed forty-five.

September 22, 2012—Pakistan—Federal Railways Minister Ghulam Ahmad Bilour told a news conference that he would personally finance a $100,000 reward for the death of the person behind the anti–Muhammad video. Although incitement to murder is illegal, Bilour was "ready to be hanged in the name of the Prophet Muhammad" and called on the Taliban and al Qaeda to join him as "partners in this noble deed." The prime minister's press secretary said, "We completely dissociate ourselves from the statement of Mr. Bilour." Nakoula Basseley Nakoula, 55, who lives in California, was believed to be the target of the hit. The Pakistani Taliban took Bilour off its hit list. The Dadullah Group of the Taliban in Afghanistan offered a bounty of 8 kilograms of gold (roughly $487,000) for the killing of those behind the film.

September 22, 2012—Bangladesh—Clashes between police and Islamists protesting the anti–Muhammad video left more than one hundred people injured in Dhaka.

September 22, 2012—Indonesia—An antiterrorist squad arrested ten Islamist militants and seized a dozen homemade bombs, three rifles, four swords, and several jihadi books from the homes of three suspects. The team defused five bombs in Solo. The group was planning suicide attacks against security forces and the government; attacks would include a bombing of parliament, shooting of police, and attacking members of the antiterrorist team. Two terrorists were picked up in Central Java's Solo town after being fingered by detainees; they were identified as Mohammad Toriq, a bomb maker who surrendered a fortnight earlier in Jakarta while carrying a gun and ammunition and wearing an empty suicide belt, and Yusuf Rizaldi, who surrendered to police in North Sumatra three days later. They in turn fingered six other terrorists arrested later in Solo. A ninth suspect was grabbed in West Kalimantan, Borneo. The tenth suspect, Joko Partit, brother of Eko Joko Supriyanto, a terrorist shot dead by police in 2009, was arrested in Solo on September 23. Badri Hartono and Rudi Kurnia Putra, both 45, reportedly recruited young men and taught them to make bombs.

September 23, 2012—Nigeria—At 9:00 a.m., a suicide car bomber attacked a Catholic Mass ceremony in St. John's Catholic Church in Bauchi, killing two and wounding forty-five. Boko Haram was suspected.

September 24, 2012—Nigeria—The military announced it had arrested more than 150 people and killed 36 others in a crackdown against Boko Haram in towns in Adamawa and Yobe states. Two soldiers were wounded in the operations that had taken place during the previous few days.

September 24, 2012—Yemen—Gunmen shot to death Col. Abdullah al-Ashwal, the most senior intelligence officer killed in Sana'a. Al Qaeda in the Arabian Peninsula was suspected of the drive-by shooting.

September 25, 2012—India—During a gun battle in a forest village in Kashmir, a terrorist and a soldier were killed. Two soldiers were wounded.

September 25, 2012—Turkey—A bomb exploded under a vehicle carrying Turkish security forces in Tunceli, killing six soldiers and a civilian walking in the road. Kurdish rebels were suspected.

September 26, 2012—Syria—Suicide bombers attacked the Syrian Army's General Staff Command headquarters in Damascus in a morning attack, setting off a white van on the main highway outside the perimeter fence. A second explosion went off on the grounds. Four guards were killed and fourteen people were wounded. The Free Syrian Army's Damascus Military Council and the jihadi Tajamo Ansar al-Islam claimed credit on Facebook.

September 27, 2012—Internet—Ayman al-Zawahiri released a video on a jihadi Web site, *Days with the Imam, Part III*, about his memories of Osama bin Laden. He noted that bin Laden was blind in the right eye after an accident in his youth when he was a member of the Saudi branch of the Muslim Brotherhood in Jeddah. The group tossed him out for insisting on conducting jihad against the Soviet presence in Afghanistan in the late 1980s.

September 28, 2012—Iraq—During a prison break in Tikrit, forty-seven al Qaeda terrorists escaped. Al Qaeda in Iraq claimed credit on October 12, saying it had smuggled weapons to the prisoners. The dozens of prisoners, many on death row, killed sixteen members of the security forces. The group said it set off a car bomb outside the prison gate.

September 29, 2012—Thailand—Islamist insurgents were blamed for firing two grenades at a security checkpoint near a trade fair in Bajoh District, Narathiwat Province, injuring thirty people, four seriously.

September 29, 2012—Afghanistan Guards at an Afghan Army checkpoint fired on a platoon of twenty U.S. soldiers during an afternoon patrol in Wardak Province. The senior American was killed when an Afghan opened fire without warning. A second Afghan killed a U.S. civilian contractor and wounded two U.S. soldiers. Afghan soldiers and insurgents fired from different directions at

4:00 p.m. north of Sisay in the Tangi Valley. Three Afghan soldiers were killed and several wounded in the gun battle.

September 30, 2012—Nigeria—Gunmen set off a bomb near an Islamic boarding school in the Gaskiya neighborhood of Zaria, in northern Kaduna State, injuring several. They then conducted a gun battle with authorities that resulted in two deaths. The terrorists ordered the students out of the school before setting off the bomb, which destroyed several nearby homes. Boko Haram was suspected. The school is run by Awwal Adam Albani, a critic of Boko Haram and himself a Salafi.

September 30, 2012—Kenya—At 10:30 a.m., a grenade was thrown into a church in the Eastleigh neighborhood of Nairobi, killing a 9-year-old boy and injuring several children. Al-Shabaab sympathizers were suspected.

September 30, 2012—Iraq—Bombs in Kirkuk, Taji, and Kut killed twenty-six and wounded ninety-four people. Al Qaeda in Iraq was suspected. At 7:15 a.m., three car bombs went off in a Shi'ite neighborhood in Taji, killing eight and wounding twenty-eight. At the same time, a suicide bomber set off his car bomb in Shula, Baghdad, killing one person and injuring seven. A suicide bomber drove his minibus into a security checkpoint in Kut, killing three police officers and wounding five.

October 2012—Syria—Rebel gunmen kidnapped Ukrainian journalist Anhar Kochneva, 40. On November 7, the group released a video of her admitting to working for Russian military intelligence agent Pyotr Petrov, translating for Russian and Syrian military officers. Her captors said on Ukrainian television, "Let not a single Russian, Ukrainian or Iranian come out of Syria alive." She had grown up in Odessa, where she learned Arabic. She ran a Moscow travel agency that specialized in the Middle East. Following her divorce, she moved to Damascus. She worked on getting out of the Syrian government's message, often appearing on Syrian television. She phoned family and friends to say she had been kidnapped. She said the Free Syrian Army had saved her from a group of violent thugs but then held on to her as a hostage. 12109901

October 2012—Pakistan—The Pakistani Taliban conducted an acid attack on a Kohat University van filled with graduate students in Doranai near Parachinar in northern Pakistan, leaving two girls, Zahida and Nabila, with severe burns to their faces and one boy, Mohammad Ali, with gunshot wounds. Another boy was also burned by acid. The terrorists left pamphlets warning local girls against going to school. Local Pakistani Taliban leader Qari Muhavia told CNN, "We will never allow the girls of this area to go and get a Western education.... If and when we find any girl from Parachinar going to university for an education, we will target her [in] the same way, so that she might not be able to unveil her face before others."

October 2012—Gaza Strip—Palestinians for the first time fired a Strela shoulder-launched missile at an Israeli helicopter early in the month. Israeli officials believed the missile originated from Libyan stockpiles that were smuggled through tunnels along the Egypt-Gaza border.

October 2012—Lebanon—In late October, Beirut authorities arrested two Malaysians on suspicion of having al Qaeda links. They were represented by local attorney Marwan Sinno, who said they were accused of planning a terrorist attack in Syria.

October 1, 2012—Afghanistan—At 9:00 a.m. in Khost, a Taliban suicide bomber set off his explosives-packed motorcycle near a joint International Security Assistance Force and Afghan police patrol in the east, killing nineteen people, including three NATO service members, their local interpreter, and fifteen Afghan police and civilians. Fifty-nine others were wounded.

October 2, 2012—Nigeria—Gunmen and knife-wielding terrorists killed twenty-five to twenty-seven people at the Federal Polytechnic college in Mubi in Adamawa State. Gang members of warring religious fraternities were suspected. Police said most who were killed were executive leaders elected in a campus election that week. Among the dead were nineteen Polytechnic students, three students from another college, a former soldier, a guard, and an elderly man. Police had raided the campus the previous week in a search for Boko Haram members, seizing weapons and bombs.

October 2, 2012—Sudan—Four Nigerian soldiers belonging to the UN–African Union peacekeeping mission in western Darfur were ambushed and shot to death during the evening. Eight soldiers were injured by unknown gunmen. 12100201

October 3, 2012—Syria—Car bombs exploded in Aleppo at a social club and a hotel in the central Saadallah al-Jabri Square, killing 40 and wounding between 90 and 130. Al Qaeda-inspired terrorists belonging to al-Nusrah were suspected.

October 3, 2012—Lebanon—Three Hizballah members were killed when explosives went off in a weapons warehouse in Nabi Sheet, south of Baalbek.

October 4, 2012—Nigeria—A bomb at an outdoor bar in Jalingo in Taraba State killed two people and wounded fourteen others at 8:00 p.m. Boko Haram was suspected.

October 5, 2012—Israel—New York native William Hershkovitz, 23, a U.S. tourist at the Red Sea resort of Eilat, attacked a security guard at the seaside Leonardo Club hotel, grabbed his gun, and shot to death a hotel chef. Hershkovitz then barricaded himself in the hotel's kitchen before being shot dead by a military counterterrorism team. 12100501

October 5, 2012—Nigeria—A bomb went off during the night in Jalingo in Taraba State, wounding eight people. Boko Haram was suspected.

October 6, 2012—Israel—Israeli authorities shot down a Hizballah drone that entered Israeli airspace. Hizballah leader Seyed Hassan Nasrallah said it was an Iranian-built reconnaissance drone. Israeli officials said the drone was spotted over the Mediterranean, near the Gaza Strip. Israeli officials suggested it was photographing the Dimona nuclear research center. Israeli officials said it was Hizballah's third drone flight.

October 6, 2012—Peru—The Shining Path destroyed three helicopters belonging to Transportadora de Gas Del Peru (TGP), leaving the natural gas pipeline from the Camisea gas fields without maintenance services. The firm is owned by Argentina's Pluspetrol, U.S.-based Hunt Oil, South Korea's SK Energy, Suez-Tractebel, and others. 12100601

October 7, 2012—Philippines—The press reported that the government and the Moro Islamic Liberation Front had come to an agreement that set the stage for a final agreement that would end the insurgency. Muslims in the southern Philippines would be granted broad autonomy in a new administrative region, Bangsamoro. The October 15 signing was witnessed by Malaysian Prime Minister Najib Razak, whose emissaries served as mediators, Philippine President Benigno Aquino, III, and rebel chairman Al-Haj Murad Ebrahim.

October 7, 2012—Iraq—Six people died in bombings in Mosul, Tal Afar, Sulaiman Bek, and Baghdad. In Mosul, gunmen killed Judge Abbas al-Abadi in a drive-by shooting.

October 7, 2012—Nigeria—Boko Haram was suspected in the shooting death of a Chinese citizen outside of Maiduguri. 12100701

October 8, 2012—Yemen—Local authorities detained an American suspected of having links to al Qaeda. He was arrested in a hotel in Ataq, capital of Shabwa Province, carrying two U.S. passports and a German one. He had been visiting mosques in Marib. He had earlier been in Saudi Arabia before entering Yemen a few months ago. He was on a list of wanted al Qaeda suspects. He spoke English, claiming to be a Muslim.

October 8, 2012—Nigeria—Boko Haram was suspected of setting off a bomb that killed an army lieutenant and wounded two others in Maiduguri.

October 8, 2012—Nigeria—Boko Haram killed fourteen people, including a mother and her three children, belonging to a Christian ethnic group in the Riyom local government area of Plateau State. Gunmen fired on a car in Barkin Ladi near the local airport, killing two Christians; local villagers killed a Muslim man in retaliation.

October 8, 2012—Afghanistan—Caitlan Coleman, 27, a pregnant American woman, was reported missing with her Canadian husband. She was due to deliver in January and was suffering from a liver ailment. The family said on December 30, 2012, that they last heard from son-in-law Josh on October 8 from an Internet café. No ransom demand had been made. No terrorist group claimed credit. Observers suggested that they had been kidnapped. 12100801

October 9, 2012—Pakistan—A masked Pakistani Taliban gunman shot in the head and critically wounded Malala Yousafzai, 14 (although her school records listed her birth date as July 12, 1997), a ninth-grade girl who had spoken out against Taliban attempts to intimidate girls from going to school. The gunman jumped into her school bus, asked for her by name, and shot her. A second gunman was in the rear of the bus. She was flown to a military hospital in Peshawar, then sent to a U.K. surgical hospital. Thousands of Pakistanis demonstrated against the Taliban's attack. In early 2009, she wrote in a diary about Taliban attacks for the BBC's Urdu service. She lived in Mingora, in the Swat Valley. In 2011, the Pakistani government awarded her a 1 million rupee ($10,500) peace prize. She was a finalist that year for the International Children's Peace Prize, awarded by a Dutch organization. Two other girls were shot, including a seventh grader who was hit in the leg. The Pakistani Taliban vowed to kill her if she survived surgery. Spokesman Ihsanullah Ihsan said she was responsible for "negative propaganda" about Muslims. "She considers President Obama as her ideal leader. Malala is the symbol of the infidels and obscenity."

Authorities said they had identified an attacker who traveled from eastern Afghanistan and offered a $100,000 reward for his capture. On October 19, the Taliban threatened to attack media outlets that covered the Malala story. Pakistani police detained the relatives of Attaullah, believed to be the gunman. The detainees included his brother, Ehsanullah, 18, who was picked up a month earlier. Also detained were Attaullah's brother-in-law and an uncle. He had earlier been arrested on suspicion of militant activity in 2009 during a military operation in Swat, Pakistan, but was freed for lack of evidence. His family home is in Sangota, 4 miles from Mingora. Two other men accused of sheltering the gunman for a night were arrested. One was a driving instructor from Mingora named Abdul Haleem. Authorities believed Attaullah had fled to Afghanistan. The press reported that the head of the Swat Taliban, Maulana Fazlullah, alias Mullah Radio (he once ran a private FM station), had ordered the murder from his hideout in Konar Province, Afghanistan.

October 9, 2012—Yemen—Authorities found three decapitated bodies in a market in Marib. CDs next to the bodies showed them confessing to being government informants against al Qaeda and placing tracking devices on cars that were targets of U.S. drones. One man said he worked in a tire repair shop and planted chips in terrorist vehicles.

October 9, 2012—Nigeria—Gunmen shot to death two police officers in Kano who were guarding workers trying to give polio shots to local children. Police arrested several suspects.

October 9, 2012—Syria—The Sunni jihadi Al-Nusrah Front for the People of Levant claimed credit for a nighttime three-stage suicide attack on a compound of the air force intelligence service in Harasta. The group named the suicide bomber and said the car contained 9 tons of explosives. After twenty-five minutes, another man drove an ambulance carrying explosives to the scene to kill first responders. The group then shelled the area.

October 10, 2012—Nigeria—Gunmen outside of Kano shot to death two officers of the Federal Road Safety Corps who were on a routine assignment checking vehicles. Another officer was wounded. Boko Haram was suspected.

October 10, 2012—Libya—Gunmen in a passing car shot to death Army Gen. Mohammed al-Fitori as he was leaving Friday prayers in Benghazi. He had defected from the Qadhafi regime and rose to become head of ammunition and armament for the army.

October 10, 2012—Afghanistan—Six members of the Afghan Local Police died when a police vehicle ran over a roadside bomb in the Nad Ali district of Helmand Province.

October 11, 2012—Pakistan—Gunmen kidnapped a retired Army Brig. Gen. who was working on a counterterrorism contract with the Inter-Services Intelligence agency. He was grabbed on the outskirts of Islamabad shortly after leaving his home for work. His driver resisted and was shot to death.

October 11, 2012—Yemen—Al Qaeda in the Arabian Peninsula was blamed in the drive-by shooting by a masked terrorist of Qassem M. Aqlani, a security official for the U.S. Embassy in Sana'a. The terrorist escaped on a motorcycle driven by a colleague after intercepting Aqlani near his house. He had worked for the embassy for eleven years. 12101101

October 12, 2012—Internet—Al Qaeda leader Ayman al-Zawahiri released an audio on Mujahedin al-Ansar, an Islamist Web site, in which he called for "free and distinguished zealots for Islam" to "continue their opposition to American crusader Zionist aggression against Islam and Muslims." He called for more protests outside U.S. embassies. He praised the assassination of the U.S. ambassador to Libya the previous month. He claimed U.S. authorities permitted the anti–Muhammed film "in the name of personal freedom and freedom of expression" that is not given to Muslim prisoners in Iraq, Afghanistan, and Guantanamo Bay.

October 13, 2012—Libya—A bomb exploded beneath the car of a police colonel in Benghazi's al-Hadayeq neighborhood. Col. Mohammed Ben Haleem was uninjured when he went to warm up his engine then stepped back into his house. No injuries were reported.

October 13, 2012—Pakistan—A car bomb exploded in a Darra Adam Khel bazaar outside an office of anti–Taliban tribal elders, killing seventeen people, injuring forty, and destroying thirty-five shops and eight vehicles. The Pakistani Taliban was suspected of the attack in Khyber Pakhtunkhwa Province.

October 13, 2012—Mali—Al Qaeda-linked members of the Movement for Unity and Jihad in West Africa (MUJAO) threatened to "open the doors of hell" for French citizens if Paris continued to press for armed intervention by Economic Community of West African States.

October 13, 2012—Afghanistan—An insider attack, this time by a member of the Afghan intelligence service, killed two Americans and four Afghan National Directorate of Security colleagues when a suicide bomber set off his vest at the intelligence office in the Maruf district in Kandahar Province. The dead included former U.S. military officer Dario Lorenzetti, 42 (according to the *Fort Worth Star-Telegram*); Ghulam Rasool, deputy intelligence director for Kandahar Province; two of his bodyguards; and another intelligence employee. The terrorist was identified as Abdul Wali from Zirak village in Maruf district. Wali's 9-year-old brother was killed in a revenge attack later that day. The *New York Times*, Reuters, CNN, *Daily Mail*, Google, and Associated Press reported on October 17 that one of the Americans killed worked for the CIA. The *Wall Street Journal* on October 17 said that the Department of Defense identified the U.S. military casualty as Spc. Brittany B. Gordon, 24, of St. Petersburg, Florida, assigned to the 572nd Military Intelligence Company, 2nd Stryker Brigade Combat Team, 2nd Infantry Division. 12101301

October 14, 2012—Nigeria—Fifty gunmen firing assault rifles killed twenty-four people, including those leaving a mosque after dawn prayers, in Dogon Dawa, a village in Kaduna State. Observers suggested the attack was part of a clash between Muslim farmers and Muslim nomadic cattlemen.

October 14, 2012—Nigeria—Boko Haram shot to death Mala Kaka, a traditional ruler in Maiduguri who had called for an end to attacks.

October 14–15, 2012—Ivory Coast—Gunmen attacked a power station and security facilities in Abidjan during the night and early morning. Supporters of deposed President Laurent Gbagbo were suspected. Among the sites was the Azito thermal power station in Abidjan's Yopougon neighborhood, where ten attackers were arrested. Gunmen also attacked a police station in Bonoua in an attempt to steal weapons.

October 15, 2012—Nigeria—At least fifteen bombs went off during a hail of gunfire in Maiduguri. Boko Haram was suspected. A gunman shot to death a police traffic warden. Fighting between the police and the terrorists killed at least twenty-four people; one soldier was injured. Boko Haram used small arms and rocket-propelled grenades. One school was burned down.

October 16, 2012—Yemen—A gunman on a motorcycle shot to death Gen. Khaled al-Hashim, a senior Yemeni intelligence officer. Al Qaeda in the Arabian Peninsula was suspected. Al-Hashim was one of several Iraqi military experts hired by the

Yemeni government after the end of the Saddam Hussein regime in 2003. 12101601

October 16, 2012—Tunisia—Five masked men set alight the 500-year-old shrine of Sayyeda Aicha Manoubia, a thirteenth-century Muslim female saint, in Tunis. The men then stole valuables from four women staying overnight at the shrine. Salafis oppose the veneration of saints.

October 17, 2012—Norway—The government of Colombia began closed-door peace talks with representatives of the Revolutionary Armed Forces of Colombia.

October 17, 2012—United States—The FBI arrested Quazi Mohammad Rezwanul Ahsan Nafis, 21, a Bangladeshi living in Queens who tried to bomb the Federal Reserve Bank of New York on 33 Liberty Street with what he believed was a 1,000-pound bomb in a van. He came to the United States on a student visa in January 2012, looking to perform jihad in the United States. His parents (his father is a banker) in Dhaka said he was a terrible student, on probation in Bangladesh's North South University, and he had come to study in the United States to improve his job prospects. He enrolled in cybersecurity at Southeast Missouri State University, becoming vice president of the school's Muslim student association. He withdrew after a semester and requested that his records be transferred to a Brooklyn-area school. He contacted an individual who was an FBI informant. He claimed to have had overseas connections with al Qaeda (AQ), although the FBI said there was no evidence that AQ was involved. He suggested several targets, including a senior New York Stock Exchange official and President Obama. The undercover agent provided twenty 50-pound bags of inerted explosives, which Nafis stored in a warehouse, then moved to a van. He parked the van, recorded a confessor video in a nearby hotel, phoned a number he believed would set off a detonator, and was arrested. His Plan B was to conduct a suicide attack, although he preferred to stay alive to carry out more attacks. In the video, he warned, "We will not stop until we attain victory or martyrdom." Nafis hoped the bomb would disrupt the presidential election and the U.S. economy. He also wrote an article claiming credit; he asked the agent to give the article to an al Qaeda magazine.

Nafis was charged with attempting to use a weapon of mass destruction and attempting to provide material support to al Qaeda. He was assigned a public defender. He made an initial court appearance at a federal courthouse in Brooklyn. Magistrate Judge Roanne L. Mann ordered him held without bail. He had claimed that he was going to attend school in Missouri. He was working as a busboy at a Manhattan restaurant when arrested.

Nafis communicated via Facebook with the undercover FBI agent and someone named "Yaqeen." They discussed whether it was permissible under Islamic rulings to wage jihad while on a student visa. On October 18, 2012, the FBI arrested the man they believed to be "Yaqeen" and Nafis's accomplice. Howard Willie Carter, II, was arrested after the Bureau found one thousand images and three video files of child pornography on a laptop and hard drive in the trash near his apartment in San Diego. He was held on child pornography charges. Carter was named as a co-conspirator in the Nafis indictment. Nafis said that Yaqeen had told him about a Baltimore military base that had only one guard. 12101701

October 17, 2012—Nigeria—Gunmen kidnapped six Russian sailors and an Estonian in an attack on the Bourbon *Liberty 249*, an anchor handling ship operated by the Paris-based Bourbon SA oil and gas services firm off the coast of the Niger Delta. The attack occurred near the Pennington River off Bayelsa State, near the Pennington Export Terminal run by the U.S.-based Chevron Corporation. The company works with the Chinese-owned Addax Petroleum Company, among others. Another nine sailors on the ship sailed to the firm's port on Onne in Rivers State. 12101702

October 18, 2012—Turkey—Security forces killed a dozen Kurdish rebels in the southeast, bringing the death toll in two days of fighting to eighteen.

October 18, 2012—Turkey—A midnight explosion outside Eleskirt wounded twenty-eight soldiers and damaged a military vehicle and a state-owned Boru Hatlari ile Petrol Tasima AS (BOTAS) pipeline, disrupting the flow of natural gas from Iran. BOTAS transports oil and gas from Iran, Iraq, Russia, and Azerbaijan. No group claimed credit, although the Kurdistan Workers' Party was suspected. 12101801

October 18, 2012—United States—The U.S. State Department's Rewards for Justice Program offered multi-million dollar rewards for the arrest of two al Qaeda (AQ) members moving money and terrorists through Iran. The administration offered $7 million for Iran-based financier Muhsin al-Fadhli, who had received advanced notification of the 9/11 plot. Another $5 million was offered for Fadhli's deputy, Adel Radi Saqr al-Wahabi al-Harbi, which moved AQ money and terrorists through South Asia and the Middle East. The U.S. Treasury imposed financial sanctions against al-Harbi, prohibiting U.S. citizens from dealing with him and freezing his U.S.-based assets. Al-Fadhli was blacklisted by the Treasury in 2005.

October 18, 2012—Afghanistan—At 6:00 a.m., a roadside mine exploded near a minibus carrying people to a wedding reception at the groom's house in the Dawlat Abad district of northern Balkh Province, killing nineteen, including six children and seven women, and wounding sixteen.

October 18, 2012—Algeria—Gunmen stopped a bus at their checkpoint in the Boumerdes region, checked passengers' IDs, and pulled aside two members of the military, dragging them out and shooting them dead.

October 19, 2012—Lebanon—During the afternoon rush hour, a remotely-detonated car bomb exploded in East Beirut's Ashrafiyeh district near Sassine Square in the mostly Christian Ashrafiyeh area, killing Brig. Gen. Wissam al-Hassan, chief of the Internal Security Forces Information Branch, and seven other people, including his bodyguard and a civilian, and injuring 110. The bomb was hidden in a stolen car parked on a narrow street near a safe house he had used to meet sources. He and his bodyguard were driving an unarmored, rented Honda Accord. He was outspoken in his opposition to the Syrian regime and was leading an investigation into jailed Lebanese politician Michel Samaha, who was believed to be plotting with two Syrian officials to conduct political and religious assassination in Lebanon. Many Lebanese observers blamed Hizballah and suggested it was an inside job. Hizballah deemed the attack a "sinful attempt to target the stability and national unity." Al-Hassan had returned from Paris to Lebanon the night before, traveling under a false name. Some officials suggested that airport workers in thrall to Hizballah leaked his whereabouts to the terrorists. 12101901

October 20, 2012—Iraq—Two bombs went off near a Baghdad checkpoint in front of a Shi'ite shrine in the Khadimiya neighborhood, killing eleven and wounding forty-eight.

October 19, 2012—Yemen—In an al Qaeda in the Arabian Peninsula attack on an army base in Abyan, thirteen soldiers and thirteen terrorists were killed. Two terrorists wearing army uniforms drove their truck bomb into the base, killing themselves and ten soldiers and injuring more than twenty soldiers. Another group of terrorists attacked the base from the sea, spurring a gun battle in which eleven more terrorists and three soldiers died.

October 21, 2012—Russia—The Russian National Anti-Terrorism Committee announced that it had killed forty-nine rebels and captured dozens more in the North Caucasus in a two-month period of raids against ninety militant bases and twenty-six weapons caches. The government said the terrorists were responsible for bombings, murders of police officers, and attacks on schools in the Dagestan and Kabardino-Balkaria Republics.

October 21, 2012—Jordan—The government announced the arrest of eleven Jordanians who had been planning since June to attack shopping centers, cafés, government buildings, and diplomatic targets, including the U.S. Embassy, using car bombs, mortars, machine guns, grenades, and other heavy weapons that would have killed hundreds of people. The group named itself 11-9 the Second, referring to the November 9, 2005, series of Amman hotel bombings that killed 60 people and wounded 115. Minister for Media and Communication Samih Maayta said that the group had traveled to Syria to obtain weapons, including TNT, and had taken "counsel from al Qaeda in Iraq via the terrorist sites on the Internet." Several targets were in the affluent Abdoun neighborhood in southern Amman. Authorities seized weapons, computers, cameras, and forged documents. A week earlier, Jordanian officials had arrested three Jordanians trying to sneak into Syria to join radical jihadis fighting Assad loyalists.

The *Washington Post* reported on December 3, 2012, that the attacks would have been conducted in three phases. First, they planned suicide bombings of two shopping centers. Second, they planned gun and bomb attacks against luxury hotels frequented by foreigners, cafes, and government buildings, to draw police away from the final target. Third, the U.S. Embassy and the affluent Abdoun district would be subjected to heavy mortar and machinegun fire.

The detainees were identified as Mohammed Raed Moustafa Khater, Abdullah Khalil Mohammad Hamdam, Abdul Rahman Sabri Abdul Rahman al-Heyari, Ahmed Abd al Hadi Abu Taha, Mahmoud Younis Manaa, Ala al-Deen Derbas, Fawzi abd al-Jabbar Hussein, Abdal-Fattah Saud Dardas, Tareq Ali al-Shari, Jafar Saud el-Fatah Dardas, and Ayman Ahmed Salam Abu Selek. They had met while fighting the Assad government in Syria and were in their 20s and 30s. They had smuggled across the border cases of TNT, mortar shells, grenade launchers, and belt-fed machine guns. Authorities had kept them under surveillance after penetrating the cell. They arrested the group, seizing their weapons, computers, and forged documents.

October 21, 2012—Jordan—In a separate attack, government forces battled sixteen armed terrorists trying to sneak into Syria. A Jordanian soldier and four terrorists died in the twenty-minute gun battle.

October 22, 2012—Nigeria—The government set a 4:00 p.m. to 7:00 a.m. curfew in Potiskum, Yobe State, after twenty-three people were killed by Boko Haram attacks. The dead included a state government official and his two children. Gunmen burned down three schools and threw a bomb at a military convoy, injuring two soldiers.

October 24, 2012—Yemen—Two masked motorcyclists shot to death Ali al-Yamani, a counterterrorism official, in Damar Province. The fleeing gunmen were suspected of al Qaeda in the Arabian Peninsula membership.

October 24, 2012—Afghanistan—An Afghan soldier not wearing his uniform shot to death two British soldiers and an Afghan police officer in Helmand Province. 12102401

October 25, 2012—Yemen—A gunman firing from a motorcycle failed to assassinate Abdulkader Ali Hilal, mayor of Sana'a. The gunman and the driver of the motorbike were arrested.

October 25, 2012—Afghanistan—Taliban spokesman said a uniformed member of the Afghan security forces shot two U.S. service members in Uruzgan Province. 12102501

October 25–26, 2012—Indonesia—Antiterrorist authorities conducted raids in four provinces and arrested eleven members of Harakah Sunni for Indonesian Society (HASMI) of planning terrorist attacks on local and foreign targets, including the U.S. Embassy, the local office of U.S. mining firm Freeport-McMoRan, the U.S. Consulate in Surabaya, a plaza near the Australian Embassy, and the headquarters of a special police force in Central Java. Police confiscated bombs, explosives, bomb-making material, ammunition, and a 6.6-pound gas cylinder filled with explosives that had been assembled at a house in Madiun, East Java. They also found videos and images of attacks on Muslims elsewhere in the world.

October 26, 2012—Afghanistan—At least forty-one people died and seventy were injured when a suicide bomber attacked a mosque in Meymaneh, capital of Faryab Province, on the first day of the Eid al-Adha holiday. Casualties included police officers and soldiers plus fourteen civilians.

October 27, 2012—Internet—Ayman al-Zawahiri released a two-hour and twelve-minute video calling for kidnapping of Westerners, imposition of sharia in Egypt, and assisting the rebellion in Syria. "We are seeking, by the help of Allah, to capture others and to incite Muslims to capture the citizens of the countries that are fighting Muslims in order to release our captives." He complained that the international community had given Bashar al-Assad "a license to kill ... I incite Muslims everywhere, especially in the countries that are contiguous to Syria, to rise to support their brothers in Syria with all that they can and not to spare anything that they can offer." Turning, to Egypt, he observed, "The battle in Egypt is very clear. It is a battle between the secular minority that is allied with the church and that is leaning on the support of the army, who are made by [former president Hosni] Mubarak and the Americans ... and the Muslim ummah in Egypt that is seeking to implement the sharia." He demanded the release of "blind sheik" Omar Abdel Rahman from the United States.

October 28, 2012—Nigeria—At 9:00 a.m., a suicide bomber crashed his explosives-carrying Jeep SUV at St. Rita's Catholic Church in Kaduna's Malali neighborhood, killing seven and wounding more than one hundred. Boko Haram was suspected.

October 28, 2012—France—Police arrested two Basque Homeland and Liberty (ETA) members—Izaskun Lesaka, 37, responsible for its weapons and explosives caches, and Joseba Iturbide Ochoteco, 35—in a hotel in Macon in eastern France. Both were armed. Lesaka was considered one of ETA's top three leaders. Police seized "abundant computer equipment and a stolen car with false number plates."

October 29, 2012—Afghanistan—A man in an Afghan police uniform shot to death two NATO soldiers during a joint patrol in Girishk, Helmand Province. The attacker escaped. 12102901

October 31, 2012—Egypt—Authorities arrested a dozen jihadis, including a Tunisian and a Libyan suspected of al Qaeda links, planning to conduct terrorist operations inside Egypt and abroad. The terrorists had rented apartments and used false names. They belonged to Cairo cells in Nasser City, Sayyida Zeinab and Heliopolis, and an area on the Cairo-Alexandria desert road. Police seized arms, explosives, and rocket-propelled grenade launchers. Three of the terrorists were trying to sneak into Libya.

November 2012—Nigeria—The Ansaru faction of Boko Haram kidnapped a French engineer in the north near the Nigeria border, citing the French ban on Islamic veils and preparations for a military operation in Mali. 12119901

November 1, 2012—Northern Ireland—Irish Republican Army (IRA) terrorists were suspected in the death of a prison guard during a gun ambush as David Black, 52, drove to work on the M1 freeway southwest of Belfast. His car crashed down a grassy embankment into a ditch. The burned-out getaway car was found in Lurgan, a power base of two factions of the IRA—the Real IRA and Continuity IRA. The car had Dublin, Ireland, license plates. It was the first murder of a guard in two decades. No one claimed credit 12110101

November 2, 2012—Afghanistan—Rival police officers shot to death four Afghan colleagues in Helmand's Grish District during a shift change by arriving officers.

November 2, 2012—Nigeria—Boko Haram was suspected of shooting to death a retired general at his Maiduguri home while he was sitting with guests during an afternoon visit.

November 3, 2012—Pakistan—A suicide bomber set off his explosives near a vehicle carrying Fateh Khan, head of a local anti–Taliban militia, killing him, three guards, and two passersby. Several others were wounded at a gas station in Buner District in Khyber Pakhtunkhwa Province. Khan was a leader of the Awami National Party.

November 3, 2012—Somalia—Two suicide bombers set off explosives at a Mogadishu restaurant when a security guard stopped them from entering the building. The attack killed one person and damaged cars.

November 4, 2012—Libya—A homemade bomb exploded under a police car in front of the central Hadayeq police station in Benghazi, injuring three police officers.

November 4, 2012—Kenya—Al-Shabaab was suspected in a grenade attack on a church service in a police camp in the north that wounded ten people.

November 5, 2012—Bahrain—A series of five bomb explosions killed two Asian men working as street cleaners, including a trash collector, and seriously injured a third Asian in Manama's Qudaibiya and Adliya districts, an area popular with tourists and Westerners. 12110501-05

November 5, 2012—Saudi Arabia—Al Qaeda killed two Saudi border guards.

November 6, 2012—Iraq—A suicide car bomber killed thirty-three people and wounded fifty-six at an Iraqi military base during shift change in Taji. Among the dead were twenty-two soldiers, as were many of the wounded.

November 6, 2012—Internet—Al Qaeda leader Ayman al-Zawahiri said in a video posted on a jihadi Web site that Muslims should join al-Shabaab in fighting "crusader invaders" after Kenyan soldiers forced them out of their redoubts. He suggested guerrilla tactics and suicide bombings. "Show them the fire of jihad and its heat. Chase them with guerrilla warfare, ambushes, martyrdom.... With God's grace, these people are to be defeated. They have been defeated in Iraq, they are withdrawing from Afghanistan, their ambassador was killed in Benghazi and their flags lowered in Cairo and Sana'a." He observed that al-Shabaab was pushed out of Kismayo thanks to "clear, direct, and flagrant support from the Americans." He believed that American "awe is lost and their might is gone and they don't dare to carry out a new campaign like their past ones in Iraq and Afghanistan."

November 7, 2012—Pakistan—A suicide bomber targeted the vehicle of a senior police officer outside a Peshawar police station in a crowded market, killing the officer, two other policemen, and two bystanders. Twenty people were injured. No one claimed credit.

November 7, 2012—Yemen—A drive-by gunman on a motorbike shot in the head and killed Mohammed El-Fil, a Yemeni intelligence officer. Al Qaeda in the Arabian Peninsula was suspected.

November 8, 2012—Pakistan—In a morning attack, a Taliban suicide truck bomber crashed into housing for the Rangers paramilitary force in Karachi, killing three security officers and injuring twenty.

November 8, 2012—Gaza Strip—Explosives hidden in a tunnel blew up near soldiers on the Gaza-Israel fence, injuring one soldier. The Hamas tunnel was the largest seen in years. An army spokeswoman said, "A kidnapping attempt is a possibility. Killing soldiers is a possibility."

November 9, 2012—Poland—Internal Security Agency investigators arrested a 45-year-old Polish researcher employed at the University of Agriculture in Krakow for illegal possession of explosive materials, munitions, and guns. He was planning to set off a four-ton bomb in front of Warsaw's parliament building when President Bronislaw Komorowski, Prime Minister Donald Tusk, government ministers, and 460 lower chamber legislators were inside. Police discovered the plot while looking into Polish links to Anders Breivik, the Norwegian right-wing terrorist. Police believed he had purchased bomb-making materials in Poland. The researcher had nationalistic, xenophobic, and anti–Semitic ideas, although he did not belong to a political group. He refused psychiatric testing. He was building bombs and had detonators. He was a chemist who conducted research at the university. He faced five years in prison. Two accomplices were arrested for illegal possession of weapons.

November 11, 2012—Afghanistan—A gunman wearing an Afghan Army uniform shot to death a British member of the coalition forces. Coalition forces returned fire, killing a member of the Afghan Army. 12111101

November 14, 2012—Gaza Strip—An Israeli air strike killed Ahmed al-Ja'abari, chief of the Ezzedin Qassam Brigades, Hamas's military wing. Israel and Palestinians exchanged rocket fire for several days. Israel called up sixteen thousand reservists while hundreds of rockets were aimed at Israeli territory, including Tel Aviv. Three Israelis—Yitzhak Amsalem, Mira Scharf, and Rabbi Aharon Smadja—were killed on November 15 when a rocket fired from the Gaza strip hit an apartment house in Kiryat Malachi.

November 14, 2012—Internet—Ayman al-Zawahiri issued a statement entitled *Supporting Islam* on the Internet, in which he called for the resumption of the caliphate and rejected the idea of nation states or the UN in dealing with conflict. Sharia should be supreme for Muslims who "refuse judgment by any other principles, beliefs, and laws." The caliphate "does not recognize nation state, national links, or the borders imposed by the occupiers, but establishes a rightly guided caliphate following in the footsteps of the Prophet Mohammed.... These are the objectives of the Document of Supporting Islam, and we call on all those who believe in them to call for them, support them, and try to spread them in every way possible among the people of the nation." Muslims should liberate occupied lands, including the British Mandate Palestine, Chechnya, Kashmir, Ceuta and Melilla, and East Turkestan.

November 16, 2012—Afghanistan—A roadside bomb went off under a minivan carrying thirty-one Afghans to a wedding party in Farah Province, killing seventeen people, including nine women and one child.

November 18, 2012—Pakistan—A roadside bomb went off against a fifteen-vehicle military convoy in the Mir Ali area 21 miles east of Miran Shah, killing two Pakistani soldiers and wounding seven.

November 18, 2012—Pakistan—A bomb exploded on a motorcycle outside a Shi'ite mosque in Karachi, killing two and injuring ten people celebrating the holy month of Muharram.

November 18, 2012—Kenya—A bomb exploded in a minibus in Nairobi's predominantly Somali Eastleigh neighborhood, killing nine and damaging two cars. Al-Shabaab was suspected. Three people were detained. Rioters attacked Somalis in Nairobi and looted their homes.

November 19, 2012—Kenya—Al-Shabaab was suspected when gunmen shot to death three Kenyan Army soldiers in the north. They were part of an African Union force fighting al-Shabaab in Somalia. They were in the border town of Garissa on their way back to Somalia. Five soldiers had gone to a garage to change a flat tire when they were fired on by seven gunmen; two soldiers survived. Rioters attacked ethnic Somalis a day later; thirteen people were shot and hundreds of shops in Garissa were torched. 12111901

November 19, 2012—Pakistan—A female suicide bomber detonated her explosives near the convoy of Husain Ahmad, former leader of Jamaat-e-Islami Pakistan, the country's largest Islamist party. He was unharmed in the attack in Mohmand tribal region, but three of his aides were injured. No one claimed credit, but the Pakistani Taliban was suspected.

November 19, 2012—United States—Bashir Ahmad, 57, an Afghan immigrant who operates a Manhattan food cart and issues the morning call to prayer at a Kew Gardens mosque in Queens, was stabbed by a stranger. The attacker approached him from behind yelling anti–Muslim comments, bit his nose, threatened to kill him, and slashed him a dozen times with a knife. Police said the attacker was 35 to 45 years old, 6 feet tall, weighed 180 pounds, and had blue eyes. He was wearing a blue baseball cap, black jacket, and blue jeans. 12111902

November 19, 2012—Colombia—Ivan Marquez, spokesman for the Revolutionary Armed Forces of Colombia, unilaterally declared a two-month cease-fire as his team started peace talks with the government, hosted in Havana. The government refused to reciprocate.

November 20, 2012—United States—Four men—Sohiel Omar Kabir, 34, a naturalized U.S. citizen from Afghanistan; Ralph Deleon, 23, a permanent U.S. resident from the Philippines; Miguel Alejandro Santana Vidriales, 21, a permanent U.S. resident from Mexico; and Arifeen David Gojali, 21, an American of Vietnamese descent living in Riverside, California—were charged with conspiracy to provide material support to al Qaeda and the Taliban in Afghanistan and wage war against Americans overseas by attacking U.S. bases.

Kabir converted and recruited Santana and Deleon to Islam in 2010, introducing them to the teachings of Anwar al-Aulaqi. The two converts then recruited Gojali in September 2012. They played paintball as part of their training. Kabir went to Afghanistan in July 2012 to set up training for the other three. Vidriales and Deleon told an FBI informant of their plans to fly from Mexico City to Istanbul en route to Afghanistan. Authorities arrested Santana, Gojali, and Deleon in Chino on November 15, a day after they booked their tickets. Kabir was captured by U.S. Special Forces in Kabul on November 17, 2012.

Kabir had lived in Pomona and served in the U.S. Air Force from 2000 to 2001. The plotters lived in Ontario, Upland, and Riverside, California. Deleon went to Ontario High School in 2006, playing on the football team and making the Homecoming Court.

Kabir returned to the United States for his first court appearance on December 4, 2012, and was represented by Deputy Federal Public Defender Jeffrey Aaron. He was charged with conspiracy to provide material support to terrorists. He was held without bond and scheduled for a December 11 court date. Deleon, Gojali, and Vidriales pleaded not guilty on December 5 to the same charge. They all faced fifteen years in prison.

November 20, 2012—Mali—Seven masked and turbaned gunmen kidnapped French citizen Gilberto Rodriguez Leal, 61, a retiree who was touring western Mali in a camper. He was chatting with youths in Diema when the gunmen grabbed him. Several days later, the terrorists released a video of him pleading for his release. 12112001

November 21, 2012—Israel—A man threw a bag of explosives into a bus as it passed army headquarters, injuring twenty-two people, three seriously. Hamas praised the attack.

November 21, 2012—Libya—Three gunmen assassinated Col. Farag al-Dersi, head of Benghazi police, in front of his home as he was returning from work. The trio fled.

November 21, 2012—Pakistan—A bomb went off near an army vehicle, killing three soldiers and two civilians in Quetta. Hours later, two bombs exploded outside a Shi'ite mosque in Karachi, killing one person.

November 21, 2012—Afghanistan—Two Taliban men set off their suicide vests near a U.S. base in Kabul's Wazir Akbar Khan neighborhood after 8:00 a.m., killing two Afghan guards and injuring five civilians In what might have been intended as an attack against Camp Eggers.

November 22, 2012—Syria—Unknown gunmen kidnapped freelance U.S. war correspondent James Foley, 39, of Rochester, New Hampshire, in Taftanaz, Idlib Province, in northwestern Syria. He contributed several videos to Agence France Presse regarding the Syrian conflict. His family made public his plight on January 2, 2013. The name of another journalist taken with Foley was not released. No group claimed credit. 12112201

November 23, 2012—Afghanistan—A Taliban suicide bomber set off his explosives hidden in a water tanker truck, killing three Afghan civilians, including one woman, and wounding more than ninety people, including twenty prisoners, fifteen police officers, and several Afghan and NATO troops in a morning explosion in Maidan Shahr, capital of Wardak Province. The wounded including seventy-five men, eleven women, and four children; six NATO troops were injured. The bomb damaged several government offices and a jail. Taliban spokesman Zabiullah Mujahid said the group was retaliating for the execution of four Taliban prisoners at the Kabul detention center. 12112301

November 23, 2012—Nigeria—A military task force offered $1.8 million for information leading to the arrest of Boko Haram leaders.

November 24, 2012—Pakistan—The Pakistani Taliban set off a 10-kilogram bomb in a garbage container in Dera Ismail Khan during a Shi'ite religious procession during the two-day Ashura holiday, killing seven people, including four children. Thirty people were injured, including five children and two police officers. The Houthi tribe in northern Yemen said four Yemenis were killed in the attack. 12112401

November 25, 2012—Pakistan—Yet another bomb went off near a Shi'ite Muslim procession in Dera Ismail, killing six and injuring more than ninety. The bomb went off inside a bicycle repair shop. The Pakistani Taliban claimed credit.

November 25, 2012—Nigeria—Two suicide car bombs went off at the St. Andrew Military Protestant Church in Jaji inside the barracks of the Armed Forces Command and Staff College, killing thirty and wounding another thirty. The second bomb went off ten minutes after noon, ten minutes after the first, targeting first responders. Boko Haram was suspected. A bus bomb rammed the church's walls before exploding. A sedan parked nearby then went off.

November 26, 2012—Nigeria—Gunmen conducted a nighttime drive-by shooting on a road leading to the airport in Plateau State, killing ten people in a Christian town. The gunmen wore military uniforms.

November 26, 2012—Pakistan—A bomb was found under the car of Hamid Mir, a journalist who hosts a popular political talk show. The Pakistani Taliban was suspected. Mir had criticized the Taliban's attempted assassination of 14-year-old Malala Yousafzai. The Taliban affiliate Tariq Geedar had earlier in the month threatened to kill Mir. A black box attached with magnets to the bottom of his car contained a half kilogram of plastic explosive and a landmine detonator.

November 27, 2012—Pakistan—Acting on a tip, police detained three boys, aged 12 to 14, who were to be trained as suicide bombers, along with their handler. The group was going from Karachi to Miranshah and was halted while boarding a bus in Norang town. They were from South Waziristan, but living in Karachi. The boys and handler, Yahya Mehsud, part of a gang that recruits young boys for suicide attacks, appeared before an antiterror court the next day.

November 27, 2012—Iraq—Car bombs in Shi'ite mosques in Baghdad killed thirty and wounded dozens. Car bombs went off at three mosques, killing twenty-one. The first bomb went off in the Hurriyah neighborhood, killing nine and wounding twenty. Another bomb went off near Gaereat mosque, killing five. A third bomb killed seven and wounded twenty-one in the Shula neighborhood in the north. Meanwhile, three car bombs went off in Kirkuk. One went off near the main Kurdish party headquarters, killing five, including a Kurdish security guard, and injuring fifty-eight. Minutes later, two bombs went off in a market in Hawija west of Kirkuk, killing two civilians and wounding five others. Bombs injured five Iraqi Army soldiers at their houses in nearby Tuz Khortmato.

November 28, 2012—Yemen—Saudi military attaché Sgt. Khalid al-Onizi and his Yemeni bodyguard were shot to death on a busy street in Sana'a. His 4-wheel-drive vehicle was blocked at noon by another vehicle. Gunmen jumped out and fired on his vehicle, hitting both men in the head. Al Qaeda in the Arabian Peninsula was suspected. 12112801

November 29, 2012—Iraq—Two car bombs killed 32 Shi'ite pilgrims and wounded 138 in Hilla. The second car bomb was aimed at first responders. Another car bomb exploded at the shrine of Imam Hussein in Karbala, killing six Shi'ites. Bombs in Falluja, Mosul, Baghdad, and Karbala killed another ten and wounded seventy.

November 29, 2012—United States—Authorities in Fort Lauderdale, Florida, arrested Sheheryar Alam Qazi, 30, and his brother, Raees Alam Qazi, 20, two naturalized U.S. citizens from Pakistan, for plotting to provide material support to terrorists and to use a weapon of mass destruction by providing money, property, housing, and communications equipment to conspirators. A bail hearing was set for December 7.

December 2012—Algeria—The Salafist Group for Preaching and Combat posted an Internet video of its bomb attack on a bus transporting Algerian oil workers.

December 2, 2012—Nigeria—Ten people died when gunmen attacked a church in Chibok, Borno State. Boko Haram was suspected. Gunmen also torched government buildings in Gamboru village.

December 3, 2012—Pakistan—Two police officers died when a bomb exploded outside a police van on patrol in Peshawar.

December 4, 2012—Somalia—Al-Shabaab attacked an army outpost in the Galgala Mountains in Puntland, killing a dozen soldiers.

December 5, 2012—Pakistan—Two suicide bombers set off their truck bomb at the gate of an army camp in Wana, South Waziristan, killing three soldiers and wounding twenty. Soldiers had unsuccessfully fired an RPG at the truck. The Ahmadzai Wazir tribe was suspected.

December 5, 2012—Kenya—A remotely-detonated bomb exploded during the evening rush hour in Eastleigh, a rundown Somali neighborhood in Nairobi, wounding nine people, three critically. Al-Shabaab was suspected. 12120501

December 5, 2012—Afghanistan—The Taliban kidnapped American doctor Dilip Joseph of Colorado Springs, Colorado, and two of his Afghan colleagues while driving to a rural medical clinic in the Sarobi district of Kabul Province. Dr. Joseph worked for the U.S. nonprofit Morning Star Development. Following two days of negotiations, the kidnappers released the Afghan hostages. Dr. Joseph was held 50 miles from the border with Pakistan. The Taliban was believed to have demanded a $100,000 ransom. U.S. forces rescued him in a helicopter raid in Sarobi on December 9 after intelligence showed he was in "imminent danger of injury or death," according to U.S. Gen. John R. Allen. On December 9, President Obama announced that Nicolas D. Checque, 28, of Pennsylvania, a member of the U.S. Special Forces SEAL 6 team, was killed in the hostage rescue. Seven Taliban armed with machine guns and AK-47s were killed. Two Taliban leaders were arrested. 12120502

December 6, 2012—Syria—A car bomb exploded in Damascus's southern Zahraa district, killing one person and damaging the headquarters of the Syrian Arab Red Crescent relief organization. Observers believed the target was Prime Minister Wael al-Halki; the bomb killed his driver outside the latter's home.

December 6, 2012—Lebanon—Snipers killed two men in Tripoli in a battle between pro– and anti–Syrian gunmen. During the past three days, eight people died and fifty-eight were wounded in the gunfights.

December 6, 2012—Afghanistan—A suicide bomber posing as a Taliban peace negotiator seriously injured Asadullah Khan Khalid, 43, head of the National Directorate of Security intelligence organization, inside one of the organizations guesthouses in Kabul's Taimani neighborhood. Khalid underwent emergency surgery on the lower part of his body. One of his bodyguards died in the 3:00 p.m. bombing. The bomber had hidden explosives in his underwear. Khalid had served as governor of Kandahar and Ghazni provinces and minister of Tribal and Border Affairs. Afghan President Hamid Karzai claimed that the bomber came from Pakistan, where the plot had been "designed" as a "very sophisticated and complicated act by a professional intelligence service." He said the Taliban could not have organized such a sophisticated attack alone.

December 7, 2012—Pakistan—CNN reported that a Predator drone strike killed Sheikh Khalid Bin Abdul Rehman Al-Hussainan, aka Abu-Zaid al-Kuwaiti, 46, who was eating breakfast. He was seen as a possible successor to al Qaeda leader Ayman al-Zawahiri. He had written several books on religious topics and had trained al Qaeda operatives in religion.

December 7, 2012—Kenya—A bomb went off in Eastleigh, a Somali district in Nairobi, killing three and wounding eight, including parliamentarian Yusuf Hassan. Al-Shabaab was blamed.

December 7, 2012—Corsica—At least seventeen houses were bombed and a man was shot to death. Authorities suggested separatist terrorists or criminal gangs were responsible.

December 10, 2012—Pakistan—Taliban attackers using a rocket, hand grenades, and automatic weapons killed six people—three police officers and three civilians—at a police station in Bannu during an hour-long gun battle. The civilians were coming out of a neighboring mosque. Another eight people—three police officers and five civilians—were injured. Three terrorists were killed; another escaped.

December 11, 2012—Yemen—Suspected masked al Qaeda in the Arabian Peninsula gunmen riding a motorcycle shot to death Col. Ahmed Barmadah, deputy head of the Political Security Office, as he left his house in Mukalla in Hadramut Province.

December 11, 2012—United States—The FBI arrested one U.S. citizen at a bus station in Augusta, Georgia, and one U.S. citizen at Atlanta's airport on charges that they were leaving the United States for North Africa "intending to prepare to wage violent jihad." Mohammad Abdul Rahman Abukhadair and Randy Wilson, alias Rasheed Wilson, both 25, were charged with conspiracy to "kill persons or damage property outside the United States." They had run a men's fragrance store in Mobile, Alabama. The criminal complaint said the duo exchanged e-mails two years earlier, then told an FBI source that they planned to use fake passports to join terrorists in Mauritania or Morocco. Abukhdair suggested buying firearms and taking hostages in the United States. He allegedly told Wilson and the source that "jihad means people are going to die. This is what jihad is. This is what war is." Wilson added, "One way or the other, everyone's gonna have to fight ... Jihad is the pinnacle of Islam. There's no dead better than jihad."

Born in Mobile, Wilson and his wife have two small children. He was a former roommate of Omar Hammami, who had joined al-Shabaab. Abukhdair, from Syracuse, New York, was single. He had been jailed in Egypt for terrorist ties. He was deported to the United States. He moved to Mobile in October 2011. The duo watched videos of guerrilla tactics, bombings, beheadings, and mutilations of women and children. They spoke in codes, such Nevada for Nigeria, San Francisco for Sudan, and San Diego for Somalia.

December 10, 2012—United States—The State Department blacklisted the jihadist Jabhat al-Nusrah in Syria as a foreign terrorist organization linked to al Qaeda in Iraq. The U.S. Department of the Treasury imposed sanctions on its leaders. The *Federal Register* indicated that the name was an alias of al Qaeda in Iraq.

December 12, 2012—Syria—An NBC News team led by Richard Engel, 39, chief foreign correspondent, was ambushed, forced out of their car and into a container truck, blindfolded, and held for five days by fifteen masked members of an unknown group. Also on the team was NBC producer Ghazi Balkiz, cameraman John Kooistra, and Aziz Akyavas, a Turkish reporter working with NBC. One of their rebel escorts was immediately killed during the ambush. The hostages were moved to several safe houses. They were freed on December 17 at 11:00 p.m. during a firefight at an Ahrar al-Sham Islamist rebel checkpoint. Two kidnappers were killed; the rest escaped. NBC said no ransom was demanded, and no contact had been made with the kidnappers. News services had kept the kidnapping under wraps to avoid endangering the hostages.

Engel said he believed the kidnappers were pro–Assad Shabiha militia members trained by the Iranian Revolutionary Guard and allied with Hizballah. "They were talking openly about their loyalty to the government, openly expressing their Shi'ite faith." The team returned unharmed to Turkey. Engel noted, "There was a lot of psychological torture, threats of being killed. They made us choose which one of us would be shot first and when we refused, there were mock shootings. They pretended to shoot Ghazi several times. When you're blindfolded and then they fire the gun up in the air, it can be a very traumatic experience." He said the kidnappers wanted the release of four Iranians and two Lebanese from a Shi'ite political party who were held by rebels. On December 19, Ian Rivers, part of the kidnapped team who became separated from the other hostages during the escape, reached safety in Turkey. 12121201

December 13, 2012—Afghanistan—At 5:00 p.m., a suicide car bomber attacked an armored military vehicle outside Kandahar Airfield, killing an American and two Afghan civilians and wounding several other people. U.S. Secretary of Defense Leon Panetta had been at the base a few hours earlier.

December 14, 2012—Philippines—Mohd Noor Fikrie Bin Abd Kahar, a suspected 26-year-old Malaysian terrorist planning a bomb attack, was shot to death by Philippine police outside a Davao hotel. He and his Filipino wife, Annabel Nieva Lee, a Muslim convert, were checking out. He tried to grab her backpack, which contained a bomb. He threatened to set off the bomb, saying, "You want the bomb? You want the bomb? Shoot me! Shoot me! I will explode the bomb!" The couple ran outside, and he grabbed the backpack and ran toward a park where there were people

partying. Police arrested her. Guards locked the park gate. Kahar ran into a packed restaurant but was shot twice in the chest. Other officers shot and killed him. Police defused the bomb, which was fashioned from a mortar shell. Kahar's passport indicated he had left Malaysia via Sabah on April 27, arriving in the Philippines on April 28. He had stayed in southern Zamboanga City, moved to Cotabato City, then went to Davao on December 14. 12121401

December 15, 2012—Pakistan—At 8:30 p.m., Pakistani Taliban gunmen fired five rocket-propelled grenades at Peshawar's Bacha Khan International Airport, killing nine people. Two of the rockets landed in a nearby neighborhood. The terrorists failed to drive a car bomb into the airport. The vehicle hit the airport's outer wall and exploded, killing five terrorists and four civilians and wounding more than forty people. Police removed and defused suicide jackets found on the terrorist corpses. The next day, police raided a residence that the terrorists had taken over, taking the homeowner hostage. The terrorists set off their explosives, killing two terrorists, while three other terrorists died in the gun battle with the police. One police officer died in the skirmish. Pakistani Taliban spokesman Ehsanullah Ehsan said the terrorists were targeting the nearby air base. "We have planned more attacks on Pakistani forces and its installations as it works to please the USA." Several of the attackers were Uzbeks, suggesting an al Qaeda link. 12121501

December 16, 2012—Libya—Gunmen fired rocket-propelled grenades on a security compound in Benghazi, killing four policemen. Police said the gunmen had planned to break into a detention center holding a man involved in the November 21 assassination of Col. Farag el-Dersi, National Security chief.

December 17, 2012—Syria—Gunmen kidnapped two Russian steel plant workers and an Italian colleague and demanded more than $700,000. 12121701

December 17, 2012—Afghanistan—A landmine exploded as several girls, aged 9 to 13, were gathering wood outside Dawlatzai village in Nangarhar Province's Chaperhar District. Ten girls died; another two were in critical condition at a local hospital. A boy was also injured. A police spokesman said the device went off when the children hit it with an axe and that it probably dated from the civil war or from the Soviet occupation.

December 17, 2012—Afghanistan—A Taliban suicide bomber set off a car bomb at the compound of McLean, Virginia-based Contrack International, a private military contractor in the Kabul suburbs, killing one person and injuring fifteen, including foreigners, among them five American and South African citizens. The construction maintenance company provides logistics services for the Afghan Army, police, and NATO coalition bases. Among the injured was Roheen Fedai, 19, a member of the company's call center, who was hit in the hand and eye. The bomb destroyed a two-story office. A director of the firm was wounded. 12121702

December 17, 2012—Pakistan—Gunmen shot to death Khadim Hussain Noori, provincial spokesman and Shi'ite Muslim, in Quetta. The motorcycle-riding gunmen then shot to death two policemen and wounded a third.

December 17, 2012—Pakistan—A car bomb loaded with 90 pounds of explosives was remotely detonated near government offices in Jamrud, the Khyber tribal agency, killing seventeen people, including four Afghan women and three children, and hospitalizing forty-four, who had been near the women's waiting area of a bus stop. No one claimed credit. It was unclear whether the attackers were targeting the government or the anti–Taliban Zakakhel subtribe. 12121703

December 17, 2012—Nigeria—Gunmen kidnapped four South Korean workers and their Nigerian colleague in the Niger Delta. They were freed on December 22 after Hyundai Heavy Industries Company paid $187,000 to the kidnappers. 12121704

December 18, 2012—Pakistan—Gunmen on motorcycles shot to death five female health workers providing polio immunizations to children in Karachi. Three victims were teens. Two male health workers were wounded. Gunmen fired on two sisters providing vaccinations in Peshawar; one died. The next day, a male health worker was shot in Peshawar, and a female health supervisor and her driver in Charsadda were shot dead in a car. The government suspended vaccinations in two cities. A local doctor, Shakil Afridi, who was involved with a vaccination program, had visited Osama bin Laden's compound before the U.S. raid in May 2011, leading local terrorists to suspect all vaccination programs. After three days of attacks, eight workers had died and the World Health Organization and UNICEF had suspended anti-polio work in Pakistan. The Pakistani Taliban in Mohmand was suspected, although spokesman Ahsanullah Ahsan denied involvement. Police shot two suspects and arrested a dozen people in connection with the attacks.

December 19, 2012—Nigeria—Up to thirty gunmen were believed involved in the nighttime kidnapping in Rimi of a French engineer working for Bergnet, a French renewable-energy contractor. The gunmen killed a guard and another man at the victim's home. Members of al Qaeda in the Arabaian Peninsula or another Islamist group in northern Mali were blamed. 12121901

December 20, 2012—Libya—Terrorists fired rocket-propelled grenades and threw hand grenades at the security directorate headquarters in Benghazi during the night, killing four people, including a national guard soldier, a police officer, and two militia members. Police said it was another attempt to free suspects in the November 21 assassination of Col. Farag el-Dersi, National Security chief. The detainees included Salah al-Hami, a member of an Islamist clan and a suspect in the killings of former Qadhafi regime officials. He is the brother of Mohamed al-Hami, former leader of the Libyan Islamic Fighting Group, who, along with two other brothers and an uncle, was killed by Qadhafi's security services.

December 20, 2012—Iraq—Iraqi Finance Minister Rafia al-Issawi said a "militia" force had kidnapped members of his staff. He called for a no-confidence vote against Prime Minister Nouri al-Maliki, who he held responsible for the hostages' safety.

December 21, 2012—Kenya—Pokomo farmers wielding AK-47s raided a village of Orma herders in the Tana River Delta. At least thirty-nine people died in the attack, including thirteen children, six women, eleven men, and nine terrorists. The Pokomo tribesmen torched forty-five houses.

December 21, 2012—South Sudan—A UN helicopter was shot down while conducting reconnaissance in Jonglei State. All four Russian crew members were killed. The UN blamed the government, which in turn blamed rebel fighters.

December 21, 2012—Yemen—Tribesmen in Sana'a kidnapped a Finnish couple and an Austrian man who were studying Arabic. The Finnish woman was grabbed from a busy street. The hostages were sold to al Qaeda in the Arabian Peninsula (AQAP), who demanded a ransom and was holding them in al-Bayda Province as of January 15, 2013. Hundreds of AQAP terrorists flowed into the south to bolster the kidnappers after negotiations broke down. Some four thousand Yemeni troops conducted a ground assault. 12122101

December 22, 2012—Pakistan—A suicide bomber set off his explosives at a political rally for the Awami National Party, which opposes the Taliban, killing nine people, including Bashir Bilour, second-ranking member of the provincial cabinet.

December 22, 2012—Nigeria—Boko Haram was suspected when two suicide bombers attacked two mobile phone switching stations of the South Africa–based MTN Group, Ltd., and Bharti Airtel, Ltd., of India at 8:00 a.m. in Kano. The Airtel bomber crashed his car bomb into the gate, injuring a staffer. A security guard shot the MTN bomber before he could pass the gate and get onto the premises. The stations control Kano's mobile phone network. 12122201-02

December 24, 2012—Afghanistan—An Afghan policewoman shot to death Joseph Griffin, 49, of Mansfield, Georgia, an American civilian member of the International Security Assistance Forces who served as a logistics adviser to the Kabul police. She shot him in the heart in the office of a local police chief as he looked at a case full of decorative medals. The shooter, Sgt. Nargis, 33, one of 1,850 female police officers trained in Afghanistan since 2002, was arrested and faced prosecution in an Afghan court. Griffin worked for DynCorp International of Falls Church, Virginia, since November 2000. It appeared to have been the first insider attack by a woman. A senior Afghan official later said Nargis was an Iranian who had infiltrated the Afghan National Police. She married an Afghan refugee in Tehran a decade before moving to Afghanistan with him. They had three children. He helped her obtain Afghan documents. Afghan officials showed a press conference her Iranian passport. She had returned from a monthly police training program in Egypt less than a month earlier. She had gone AWOL for two days in Egypt. She told police that she wanted to kill someone "important." She initially tried to get access to the offices of the Kabul governor's office and the Kabul police chief's office but after being turned away, settled for Griffin, who had just bought an Afghan flag at a police canteen. 12122401

December 25, 2012—Nigeria—Boko Haram was suspected when gunmen fired on a church in a village west of Potiskum, Yobe State, killing five people and wounding four others.

December 26, 2012—United Arab Emirates—The government announced the arrest of U.A.E. and Saudi citizens planning attacks in the two countries and other states. Authorities confiscated equipment to be used in al-Islah terrorist operations.

December 26, 2012—Russia—Gunmen shot to death Islamic cleric Ibragim Dudarov, 34, North

Ossetia's deputy mufti, as he was driving near Vladikavkaz.

December 27, 2012—Pakistan—At least twenty-three police officers were kidnapped when the Pakistan Taliban attacked two police posts in Frontier Region Peshawar with rocket-propelled grenades and automatic weapons, killing two police officers. Some twenty-one officers were found shot to death in the Jabai area of Frontier Region Peshawar on December 30, after one officer escaped. Another officer was found seriously wounded. The police were lined up on a cricket pitch on December 29 and gunned down.

December 28, 2012—Yemen—Al Qaeda-linked tribesmen were believed responsible for an attack on an oil pipeline in Marib Province, hours after it had been repaired.

December 29, 2012—Nigeria—Boko Haram was suspected of attacking Musari village near Maiduguri during the morning, lining up men, women, and children, then slitting their throats. At least fifteen people were killed.

December 29, 2012—Pakistan—An explosion went off on a passenger bus at a Karachi bus terminal, killed six and wounding fifty-two. Police suspected a bomb or gas canister.

December 30, 2012—Pakistan—The Taliban was suspected when a car bomb went off near a convoy of buses taking Shi'ite pilgrims to Iran, killing nineteen and wounding thirty in the Mastung district in the southwest of the country. The explosion destroyed the bus and damaged another that was carrying Shi'ites. It was unclear whether it was a suicide bomb or a remotely-detonated device.

December 30, 2012—Northern Ireland—An Irish Republican Army splinter group placed a booby-trapped bomb under the car of a Northern Irish policeman. The officer found the bomb near the Northern Irish parliament in east Belfast, just before he was going out to lunch with his family.

December 30, 2012—Libya—A bomb went off at an Egyptian Coptic church in Misrata, killing two Egyptian citizens working at the church in preparation for New Year's Eve Mass and wounding two other people. 12123001

December 31, 2012—Yemen—Al Qaeda in the Arabian Peninsula (AQAP) offered 3 kilograms (more than 105 ounces, worth $160,000) of gold for the killing of U.S. Ambassador to Yemen Gerald Feierstein and 5 million Yemeni rials ($23,350) to anyone who kills any American soldier in Yemen. The offer was good for six months to "encourage our Muslim Ummah [nation], and to expand the circle of the jihad by the masses." The audio recording, posted on the Internet, was made by AQAP's Malahem Foundation media group.

December 31, 2012—Colombia—The police said the Revolutionary Armed Forces of Colombia was behind a grenade attack that injured four civilians and two police officers at a police station in Guapi village.

Updates of
1950–2007 Incidents

February 21, 1965—United States—The only man who admitted involvement in the assassination of Malcolm X at the Audubon Ballroom in Harlem, Thomas Hagan, 69, was paroled from a Manhattan prison on April 27, 2010.

November 24, 1968—United States—On October 11, 2009, Luis Armando Pena Soltren, 66, surrendered to federal authorities at John F. Kennedy Airport, from which he had hijacked Pan Am flight 281 in 1968. He had flown from Havana under the custody of State Department diplomatic security personnel. A December 1968 indictment said that Soltren, Jose Rafael Rios Cruz, Miguel Castro, and Alejandro Figueroa conspired to hijack the flight. They brought concealed guns and knives aboard, forced their way into the plane's cabin, and demanded to go to Havana. Figueroa was acquitted in 1969. Rios and Castro were sentenced in the 1970s after pleading guilty in U.S. District Court in New York. They received fifteen-year and twelve-year sentences, respectively.

May 8, 1972—Belgium—Reginald Levy, 88, the pilot of Sabena flight 571, died on August 1, 2010, in Dover, United Kingdom, of a suspected heart attack or blood clot. He had been flying during his fiftieth birthday when the plane was hijacked by Black September. One of the passengers was his wife, Dora, with whom he was planning to celebrate with a dinner in Tel Aviv. He kept calmly talking to the hijackers and passed information on to authorities. The plane was stormed by a rescue team that included eventual Israeli Defense Minister Ehud Barak and eventual Prime Minister Binyamin Netanyahu. Levy, born in Blackpool, United Kingdom, earned the Distinguished Flying Cross for piloting Royal Air Force bombers during World War II. He flew in the Berlin Air

Lift before joining Sabena, from which he retired in 1982.

July 31, 1972—United States—Five Black Panther Party sympathizers were accompanied by their three children when they hijacked Delta Airlines flight 841, a DC8 flying from Detroit to Miami on July 31, 1972. George E. Wright, alias Burgess, was one of them. They demanded $1 million and to be flown to Algeria. The ransom was paid in Miami where the hostages were freed, and the plane went on to Algiers the next day. They were taken into custody but freed on August 4. The money was returned to Delta on August 23, 1972. On September 26, 2011, Wright, 68, was taken into Portuguese police custody at the request of the United States. He had lived in a local hamlet with his Portuguese wife and two children. He had escaped from a New Jersey jail after his conviction of killing a gas station attendant. The United States requested his extradition.

April 1977—West Germany—On September 4, 2009, UPI reported that former Red Army Faction (RAF) member Verena Becker had been arrested in her Berlin apartment in connection with the April 1977 murder of Siegfried Buback. She reportedly had been paid $70,000 by the German intelligence service for tips that led to the arrests of several terrorists. Although RAF terrorists Christian Klar, Knut Folkerts, Guenter Sonnenberg, and Brigitte Mohnhaupt were convicted of planning and carrying out the killing, several observers had questioned the verdict. Becker had been sentenced to life in prison in 1977 for seriously injuring a police officer, but was pardoned in 1989. When she and Sonnenberg were arrested, they had the Buback murder weapon, but she was never tried in the case. She then alerted police to the hiding places of Klar and Mohnhaupt.

November 4, 1979—Iran—Former hostage at the U.S. Embassy in Iran Gary E. Lee, 67, a State Department officer, died on October 10, 2010, in Fulton, Texas, of cancer. Lee survived mock executions, beatings, and near starvation. On October 11, 2010, fellow hostage and Consul General Richard Morefield, 81, died at a hospital in Raleigh, North Carolina, of pneumonia. He was kept in isolation during his confinement. Three times his captors placed a gun against his head and clicked the trigger.

February 21, 1981—West Germany—Richard Cummings, writing in the Spring 2008 edition of *Intelligencer*, established that the Carlos group was responsible for the bombing of the Radio Free Europe/Radio Liberty facility in Munich. This was the only terrorist attack attributable to Carlos for which he did not claim credit. Among those involved in the attack were Johannes Weinrich, alias Steve, from the German Revolutionary Cells; Bruno Breguet, alias Luca, from the Swiss Primea Linea; Jose Maria Larretxea, alias Schep, from Basque Nation and Liberty (ETA); and another woman from the ETA.

May 13, 1981—Italy—On January 18, 2010, Turkey released would-be papal assassin Mehmet Ali Agca, 52, from Sincan's prison. He was taken to the psychiatry department of the military hospital, GATA, to be assessed for compulsory military service, but a 2006 military hospital report said his "severe anti-social personality disorder" made him unfit for duty. He released a statement saying, "I proclaim the end of the world. All the world will be destroyed in this century. Every human being will die in this century ... I am the Christ eternal." He was represented by attorneys Melahat Uzunoglu and Gokay Gultekin.

1982—Lebanon—David Stuart Dodge, 86, the former acting president of the American University of Beirut, who was abducted in Lebanon in 1982 and released in 1983, died of cancer in Princeton, New Jersey, on January 20, 2009.

May 12, 1982—Portugal—On October 15, 2008, the Vatican announced that in 1982, Pope John Paul II was wounded by ultraconservative Spanish priest Juan Fernandez Krohn in a knife attack in Fatima. The injury had been kept secret for a quarter century, according to the documentary *Testimony*, made by Cardinal Stanislaw Dziwisz and narrated by Michael York. Krohn was arrested, served several years in a Portuguese prison, and was expelled from the country.

1983—United States—On May 10, 2011, the FBI arrested Norberto Gonzalez Claudio in Puerto Rico. He was the last of sixteen alleged accomplices in the 1983 theft of $7 million from a West Hartford armored car depot by a militant Puerto Rican independence group. The only remaining at-large suspect was Victor Gerena, who had been on the FBI's Ten Most Wanted List longer than any other fugitive. He was believed to be living in Cuba.

April 18, 1983—Lebanon—On May 22, 2012, CIA's Office of Public Affairs announced that fifteen names had been inscribed on the Memorial Wall. Among the names were those killed in the attack on the Beirut Embassy: Phyliss Nancy Faraci, Deborah M. Hixon (a friend of the author), Frank J. Johnson, James F. Lewis, and his wife, Monique N. Lewis, who was on her first day on the job.

1985—Greece—On July 7, 2008, Ibrahim Fatayer Abdelatif, 43, was ordered freed from a temporary holding center for illegal immigrants in Rome, having served his twenty-five-year sentence (reduced for good behavior) for the 1985 *Achille Lauro* shipjacking. Italy attempted to expel him, but his attorneys argued that since he was stateless, he should be permitted to stay for humanitarian reasons.

On April 30, 2009, Youssef Magied al-Molqi, the leader of the hijackers, was released early from a prison in Palermo, Italy. He had served nearly twenty-four years of his thirty-year sentence and was freed for "good behavior." He was transferred to a holding center for immigrants in Trapani while officials worked on expulsion orders. Stella Cavallo, his attorney, said she would fight any expulsion order. She noted that he had married an Italian woman but was stateless. In 1996, he had disappeared during a furlough but was captured in Spain three weeks later.

March 25, 1985—Lebanon—The remains of Alec Collett, who was 63 when he was abducted, were found on November 23, 2009, in eastern Lebanon. In April 1986, the Revolutionary Organization of Muslim Socialists sent to a Beirut television station a video showing the British UN worker being hanged. His Austrian driver was also kidnapped but later released. Collett was married to U.S. citizen Elaine Collett; their son Karim was 11 at the time of the kidnapping.

1986—Lebanon—On February 26, 2009, a U.S. federal court dismissed a lawsuit against Libya brought by the estate of U.S. librarian Peter Kilburn, who was kidnapped and eventually killed following the U.S. raid on Libya in 1986. His relatives and the U.S. government had requested the dismissal so that the family could seek compensation from the $1.8 billion fund created to compensate victims of Libyan-sponsored terrorism.

September 5, 1986—Pakistan—On January 9, 2010, a U.S. missile strike in North Waziristan, Pakistan, killed Jamal Saeed Abdul Rahim, a Palestinian with possible Lebanese citizenship who was a member of Abu Nidal and possibly of al Qaeda. He was wanted by the United States for his role in the September 5, 1986, hijacking of Pan Am 73 during a stop in Karachi in which twenty people, including two Americans, were killed when the terrorists threw grenades and fired automatic weapons at the passengers. He was tried and convicted in Pakistan, but he and three accomplices were released in January 2008. The four were placed on the FBI's Most Wanted Terrorist List in 2009.

1987—France—On October 14, 2008, Marseille airport authorities arrested Algerian diplomat Mohamed Ziane Hasseni for complicity in the 1987 murder of exiled Algerian dissident Ali Mecili, an attorney killed by three gunshots in his Paris apartment on the Left Bank. Preliminary charges were filed against Hasseni, chief of protocol of the Algerian Foreign Ministry. He was released but barred from leaving the country. Mecili had been jailed in Algeria in the 1960s. Upon release, he moved to France, studied law, and became a French citizen. Another suspect in the killing had been arrested soon after but was sent to Algeria because he was a senior Algerian military security agent.

July 11, 1988—Greece—On March 1, 2012, a special French antiterrorism court convicted three radical Palestinian members of the Fatah Revolutionary Council in absentia and sentenced them to thirty years in prison for the attack on the *City of Poros* cruise ship that left nine dead, including three French citizens. Adnan Sojod was convicted of murder and attempted murder. Samir Khaidir and Abdul Hamid Amoud were convicted of conspiracy to commit murder and conspiracy to attempt murder. New arrest warrants were issued.

December 21, 1988—United Kingdom—On August 4, 2008, President Bush signed legislation directing the Department of State to settle all remaining lawsuits against Libya regarding the downing of Pan Am 103. The legislation gave Libya immunity from further lawsuits once compensation is paid.

On November 15, 2008, an Edinburgh court refused to release on bail Libyan terrorist Abdel Basset Ali al-Megrahi, who was serving a life sentence for the bombing, despite his cancer.

On May 22, 2012, CIA's Office of Public Affairs announced that fifteen names had been inscribed on the Memorial Wall. Among the names was Matthew K. Gannon, who was killed in the Lockerbie bombing.

May 21, 1991—India—On October 17, 2012, Sri Lanka released Selvarasa Pathmanathan, the leader of the former Liberation Tigers of Tamil, wanted by India for the 1991 assassination of former Indian Prime Minister Rajiv Gandhi. He remained on Interpol's wanted list. Sri Lanka said he could continue working for a nongovernmental development organization in the north.

June 1993—United States—On February 15, 2011, Dr. Charles Epstein, the Unabomber's target, died in Tiburon, California, at age 77 of pancreatic cancer.

July 18, 1994—Argentina—On May 20, 2009, Argentina issued an international arrest warrant for Samuel Salman El-Reda, a Colombian of Lebanese descent, in connection with the bombing of a Jewish charities building in Buenos Aires that killed eighty-five and injured three hundred. On January 29, 2013, Israel protested to the Argentine ambassador regarding a January 26, 2013, agreement between Iran and Argentina to jointly investigate the attack.

July 26, 1994—Cambodia—The Khmer Rouge kidnapped three Westerners from a train in the southeast near Phnom Voar at the direction of Sam Bith. Bith ordered the trio killed on September 28, 1994, after negotiations broke down. He defected to the government in 1997 and received the rank of general in the Cambodian Army. However, he was arrested in May 2002 after another Khmer Rouge leader implicated him in the killings. Bith was sentenced to life in December 2002 after being found guilty of conspiracy to kidnap Australian David Wilson, Briton Mark Slater, and French citizen Jean-Michel Braquet. Nuon Paet and Chhouk Rin were also sentenced to life for their involvement in the kidnapping and murders. Bith, 74, died in prison on February 15, 2008.

March 1995—Pakistan—May 22, 2012, CIA's Office of Public Affairs announced that fifteen names had been inscribed on the Memorial Wall. Among the names was Jacqueline K. Van Landingham, who was in the van that was attacked.

March 20, 1995—Japan—On June 4, 2012, police in Sagamihara, Japan, arrested Naoko Kikuchi, 40, a follower of the Aum Supreme Truth cult. Kikuchi had admitted to making the sarin but did not know about the details of the planned attack. She was held on suspicion of murder and attempted murder. After seventeen years on the run, she was living in a small, run-down house made out of rusted metal panels. A 41-year-old man was detained for hiding the suspect. Police acted on a tipoff, possibly sparked by their doubling the reward for her arrest to ten million yen ($125,000).

On June 15, 2012, Japanese police arrested the final at-large suspect, Katsuya Takahashi, 54, former bodyguard for Aum leader Shoko Asahara, in front of a comic book café on suspicion of murder and attempted murder for the attack. He had altered his appearance and was using an alias when captured.

December 27, 1995—Philippines—On December 17, 2010, a federal judge in Washington, DC, sentenced Madhatta Asagal Haipe, 48, a charter member and deputy chief of the Abu Sayyaf (al–Harakat al-Islamiyyah) terrorist group to twenty-five years in prison for his role in the 1995 ransom kidnapping of sixteen tourists, including four Americans. He left the group in 1997 for Malaysia and was arrested there in June 2006. He was transferred to the Philippines, then extradited to the United States in summer 2010. He pleaded guilty in July 2010.

November 1996—Comoros—May 22, 2012, CIA's Office of Public Affairs announced that fifteen names had been inscribed on the Memorial Wall. Among the names was Leslianne Shedd, who was on the hijacked plane. Witnesses said she "spent her final moments comforting those around her."

1997—Cuba—On December 2, 2010, an official government Web site reported that Cuba's Supreme Court had begun the review of the death sentence of Raul Ernesto Cruz Leon, a Salvadoran who had been convicted of terrorism after confessing to five hotel bombings in 1997.

December 1997—Colombia—The Revolutionary Armed Forces of Colombia (FARC) kidnapped Army Cpl. Pablo Emilio Moncayo, 19, after overrunning his base in Putumayo State near the southern border with Ecuador. Proof of life came only in 2007, when FARC released a video of him asking President Uribe to open peace negotiations with the rebels. Moncayo was released on March 30, 2010, two days after the release of Pvt. Josue Daniel Calvo in Meta State after Calvo was held for eleven months. Moncayo, now 31, was handed over in Caqueta State to officials of the International Committee of the Red Cross and leftist Colombian Senator Piedad Cordoba, who had served as a liaison between the government and FARC. A Brazilian helicopter crew flew Moncayo to Floencia, the state capital.

August 7, 1998—Kenya/Tanzania—On August 3, 2008, Fazul Abdullah Mohammed escaped a police raid in Kenya. He was seeking treatment for a kidney problem. He planned the attacks on the U.S. embassies in Kenya and Tanzania that killed 225 and wounded 5,000.

On November 17, 2010, Ahmed Ghailani, 36, was found guilty of one count of conspiracy to damage or destroy U.S. property. He was acquitted of 284 counts of murder and attempted murder. He faced twenty years to life. Sentencing was set for January 25, 2011.

On June 7, 2011, Somali officials killed Fazul Abdullah Mohammed, alias Harun Fazul, and a second al Qaeda operative in a shootout after they had stopped their luxury car at a government checkpoint in Mogadishu. The terrorists opened fire when security found a pistol on one of the men. Mohammed was wanted for planning the embassy bombings. A security official said Mohammed was carrying a false South African passport for "Daniel Robinson," maps, weapons, $40,000 in cash, and documents about a plot he was considering to attack Eton College and luxury hotels in London, including the Ritz Carlton, and mainland Europe. Al Qaeda operatives would check into hotels, then set their rooms alight.

On May 22, 2012, CIA's Office of Public Affairs announced that fifteen names had been inscribed on the Memorial Wall. Among the names was Molly N. Hardy, killed in the Nairobi Embassy bombing.

August 15, 1998—Northern Ireland—On June 9, 2009, the Belfast High Court ruled that the families of the victims of the Omagh bombing of 1998 could collect $2.4 million in damages from the Real Irish Republican Army terrorists responsible for the attack—Real IRA leader Michael McKevitt, Liam Campbell, Colm Murphy, and Seamus Daly.

February 25, 1999—Colombia—The 45th Front of the Revolutionary Armed Forces of Colombia (FARC) kidnapped three Americans who had been helping an Indian group in a land dispute with a U.S. oil company. Terence Freitas, 24, an environmentalist from Los Angeles; Ingrid Inawatuk (or Washinawatok), 41, a member of the Menominee Nation of Wisconsin; and Gay Laheenae (variant Lahe'ena'e Gay), 39, who was Sioux and headed the Hawaii-based Pacific Cultural Conservancy International, were grabbed during the morning near Royota village in Arauca Province. The trio was studying the U'wa culture, which was in conflict with the Colombian government.

The bodies of the three Americans were found on March 5, 1999, amid signs that they had been tortured. The blindfolded and bound bodies were on the Venezuelan side of the Arauca River in the Venezuelan hamlet of Los Pajaros. The two women were shot four times each in the face and chest with 9-mm weapons; Freitas was shot six times. Colombian and U.S. officials said that the killings were on the orders of senior insurgent commanders, citing eyewitness accounts and electronic intercepts of two rebel conversations, including a recording of the order to execute them. One of the intercepted cellular phone conversations was between the 45th Front and German Briceno, Front commander and brother of Jorge Briceno, FARC's leading military strategist. The 45th Front was one of the groups most closely tied to drug trafficking. German Briceno protected large cocaine laboratories in the jungle.

Raul Reyes, a member of FARC's seven-man ruling junta, said on March 8, 1999, that FARC would investigate, but he had seen no sign of any rebel role.

FARC admitted to the murders on March 10, 1999, but refused to extradite the killers to the United States, saying that they would be "sanctioned" by their code of revolutionary justice. The killers believed the activists worked for CIA. The killers were identified as German Briceno Suarez, alias Grannobles, and the brother of Mono Jojoy, alias Rafael, alias Marrano, alias Alveiro, alias Reynaldo. Washinatwatok was bitten by a snake and taken to a clinic in Arauca Department for first aid. The doctors told FARC that she would have to stay there, but the kidnappers took her away. When she became seriously ill with life-threatening complications, El Marrano called German Briceno, or "Grannobles," who gave the order to kill the Americans. The group received a second radio communication rescinding the kill order, but it arrived too late. Senior FARC leaders apparently did not support the killings.

On March 25, 1999, authorities ordered the arrest of German Briceno, who on July 16, 1999, was charged with ordering the killings. Gustavo Bogota, a member of the U'wa tribe, was charged as an accomplice. The duo remained at large. FARC claimed that Briceno was not responsible and that a lower-ranking squad leader and two fighters under his command were involved.

On March 22, 2012, Venezuela detained William Alberto Asprilla, alias Marquetaliano, 62, a mid-level FARC leader, on the road between Caracas and La Guaira port. Colombian authorities said he was in Venezuela for the previous six months doing support work for the rebels. He was wanted for his role in the kidnapping and murder, along with rebellion and conspiracy. Colombia had issued an international arrest order via Interpol. He was very close to Jorge Briceno. He had planned the kidnappings with the Briceno brothers. 99022501

December 15, 1999—United States—On March 13, 2012, in a 7–4 ruling, the full U.S. Ninth Circuit Court of Appeals ruled that Ahmed Ressam's twenty-two-year sentence was unreasonably lenient and sent the case back to U.S. District Judge John Coughenour in Seattle for resentencing. Current federal sentencing guidelines called for sixty-five years to life. On October 24, 2012, Judge Coughenour, having had his twenty-two-year sentence of Ahmed Ressam twice overturned by federal appeals court panels, sentenced Ressam to thirty-seven years, refusing to impose a life sentence. Ressam was represented by public defender Thomas W. Hillier.

December 31, 1999—United States—On October 20, 2008, a court in Kalamazoo, Michigan, sentenced to nine years in prison Frank Ambrose, 33, a former environmental activist, for his New Year's Eve arson attack at Michigan State University's Agriculture Hall in the name of the Earth Liberation Front. He was also ordered to pay $3.7 million to MSU and to other sabotaged sites; the MSU damage was estimated at $1 million. He was sentenced to a lifetime of supervisory release after prison. He later became a government informant. He had pleaded guilty to conspiracy to set a fire and explosion. He had been protesting genetically modified crops.

October 12, 2000—Yemen—In mid–April 2010, sixty-one relatives of the seventeen sailors who were killed sued Sudan in U.S. District Court in Norfolk, Virginia, for $282.5 million in emotional damages that were rejected in a previous lawsuit. Three years earlier, thirty-three family members received $8 million in damages.

On December 16, 2010, the news media reported that a photo had surfaced of Fahd al-Quso, an al Qaeda terrorist wanted for the USS *Cole* bombing, who had been believed to have died in an air strike in Pakistan in October 2010. He was photographed during an early December interview with Arafat Mudabish, a Yemeni journalist. Al-Quso was indicted in 2003 by a federal grand jury for the USS *Cole* attack and was believed to have attended a meeting in Malaysia regarding 9/11 planning.

On January 31, 2012, an air strike killed a dozen al Qaeda in the Arabian Peninsula (AQAP) terrorists, including Abdul Monem al-Fahtani, a mid-level AQAP leader believed to have participated in the 2000 USS *Cole* attack. Yemeni forces had attacked him in late 2010; his death was never confirmed.

On May 6, 2012, an air strike killed two Yemeni al Qaeda terrorists, including Fahd al-Quso, 37, who was wanted in the USS *Cole* bombing, in their car in southern Yemen's Wadi Rafad valley in Shabwa Province. The second terrorist was identified as Fahed Salem al-Akdam. The al Qaida-linked Ansar al-Sharia group said, "Al-Qaida affirms the martyrdom of the Fahd al-Quso in an American attack this afternoon in Rafad." Al-Quso was also linked to the 2009 Christmas airliner attack, apparently having met with the suspected underwear bomber, Umar Farouk Abdulmutallab. Yemeni government officials reported in 2009 that al-Quso was killed in an air strike in Rafd, but he later resurfaced.

September 11, 2001—United States—On January 17, 2002, attorneys for Zacarias Moussaoui filed a 202-page appeal of his life sentence. He had pleaded guilty in April 2005 of complicity in the 9/11 attacks and was sentenced to life without the possibility of parole in May 2006. He asked to rescind his guilty plea. On February 15, 2008, the court papers were unsealed and revealed that his attorneys, Justin S. Antonipillai and Barbara L. Hartung, asked the U.S. Court of Appeals for the Fourth Circuit to overturn the guilty plea and life prison sentence because he could not choose his own counsel or learn much of the evidence against him.

September 11, 2001—United States—On February 11, 2008, the Pentagon announced that it would seek the death penalty in the war crimes charges of six individuals detained at Guantanamo who were believed to have planned the 9/11 attacks: Khalid Sheikh Muhammad (KSM), Ramzi bin al-Shibh, Ali Abd al-Aziz Ali alias Ammar al-Baluchi, Mohammed al-Qahtani, Mustafa Ahmed al-Hawsawi, and Walid bin Attash alias Khallad. The six were charged with conspiracy, murder in violation of the laws of war, attacking civilians, attacking civilian objects, intentionally causing bodily injury, destruction of property, terrorism, and material support for terrorism. KSM, bin Attash, Binalshibh, and Ali were also charged with hijacking or hazarding an aircraft.

On March 1, 2008, Dorothy England, wife of Deputy Defense Secretary Gordon England, christened the USS *New York* in Avondale, Louisiana. The bow stem contains 7.5 tons of scrap steel from Ground Zero.

On July 13, 2010, workers at Ground Zero found an eighteenth century 32-foot-long ship hull under the site. A 100-pound anchor was found a few yards from the ship; it was unclear whether it was part of the vessel.

On April 4, 2011, Attorney General Eric Holder announced that five 9/11 suspects (Khalid Sheik Muhammad; Ramzi Binalshibh; Walid Muhammad bin Attash, alias Tawfiq bin Attash; Amar al-Baluchi, alias Ali Abd al-Aziz Ali; and Mustafa Ahmed al-Hawsawi) would be tried before a military commission at Guantanamo Bay. The Department of Justice unsealed a December 2009 indictment, which was dismissed by a federal judge at the request of the civilian prosecutors. The announcement reversed an earlier decision to try the group in a federal courthouse in Manhattan.

The U.S. Navy SEAL Team 6 killed bin Laden in a raid at his Abbotabad, Pakistan compound on May 1, 2011 (*see also* Incident entry May 1, 2011—Pakistan).

On June 17, 2011, New York City's medical examiner ruled that Jerry Borg, 63, who died in 2010, had succumbed to complications caused by pulmonary sarcoidosis, which he got from inhaling dust at Ground Zero. He was the 2753th World Trade Center victim, only the third person to be added to the medical examiner's list.

The five terrorists accused of organizing 9/11 were arraigned on May 5, 2012, in a military commission in Gitmo. Following the lead of Khalid Sheikh Mohammed, they refused to speak. They were charged with conspiracy, attacking civilians, intentionally causing serious bodily injury, murder in violation of the law of war, hijacking, terrorism, and other crimes. They deferred entering a plea. Mohammed's civilian attorney was David Nevin. Ali Abdul Aziz Ali, Mohammed's nephew, was represented by civilian attorney James Connell. Brig. Gen. Mark Martins was the chief military prosecutor. Walid bin Attash was represented by civilian attorney Cheryl Borman, who wore a black hijab. Mustafa al-Hawsawi was represented by Navy Cdr. Walter Ruiz. Also on trial was Ramzi bin al-Shibh.

On July 28, 2012, the U.S. Navy christened the USS *Somerset*, the last of three navy ships named for 9/11 attack sites.

On October 15, 2012, the week-long pretrial hearing began before a military commission at Guantanamo Bay. Khalid Sheikh Mohammed, Mustafa Ahmed al-Hawsawi, Ramzi bin al-Shibh, Ali Abd al Aziz Ali (alias Ammar al Baluchi), and Walid bin Attash sat calmly and spoke directly to Judge Col. James L. Pohl.

October 2001—United States—On June 27, 2008, the U.S. Department of Justice agreed to a $5.85 million settlement with Dr. Steven J. Hatfill, who agreed to drop his 2003 lawsuit against the government after he had been declared a "person of interest" by former Attorney General John D. Ashcroft in the investigation of the October 2001 anthrax attacks. The government did not admit wrongdoing. On July 14, 2008, the U.S. Court of Appeals for the Fourth Circuit in Richmond, Virginia, unanimously dismissed Hatfill's libel lawsuit against the *New York Times*, saying that he had become a public figure and that the *Times* had not acted with malice.

On July 29, 2008, Bruce E. Ivins, a 62-year-old biodefense scientist who worked at the U.S. Army lab at Fort Detrick, Maryland, committed suicide via an overdose of Tylenol when he learned that federal prosecutors were going to indict him for the October 2001 anthrax attacks in the United States. Prosecutors were going to offer a plea bargain of life in prison, but he died two hours before the meeting was scheduled. He was represented by Bethesda, Maryland, attorney Paul F. Kemp. Some observers suggested that he conducted the attacks for financial gain; he had two patents that were used by the California company Vax Gen to create anthrax vaccines after the attacks. Others pointed out that he had developed mental problems. In March 2008, he was found unconscious in his home. The same thing happened in late July. A Frederick social worker, Jean Duley, had told the FBI on July 21 that he had made mass homicidal threats and asked for judicial protection from Ivins. She cited his psychiatrist, who called him a threat.

On November 28, 2011, the U.S. government agreed to pay $2.5 million to the family of Robert Stevens, an employee of American Media, who died after his exposure to the anthrax spores. The government filed documents in U.S. District Court in West Palm Beach, Florida, in which it agreed to the settlement but did not admit liability or negligence. The family had sued the government for $50 million.

2002—Gulf of Aden—On August 19, 2010, al Qaeda member Hazem al-Mujali turned himself in to Yemeni authorities. He had been accused of taking part in the bombing of a French oil tanker in 2002.

February 2002—Colombia—On January 10, 2008, the Revolutionary Armed Forces of Colombia (FARC) released Consuelo Gonzalez, a politician who had been kidnapped in 2001, and Clara Rojas, who was grabbed in February 2002 with Presidential candidate Ingrid Betancourt. Rojas's son, who was born in captivity, had been quietly passed to foster care three years earlier. The release was mediated by Venezuelan President Hugo Chavez, who called FARC and National Liberation Army rebels "true armies" rather than terrorists. On February 27, 2008, French President Nicolas Sarkozy pleaded for FARC to free Betancourt, who was ill, according to two of the four hostages who were freed that day. The hostages were former Colombian legislators Gloria Polanco, Orlando Beltran, Jorge Eduardo Gechem, and Luis Eladio Perez. The International Committee of the Red Cross met the hostages in a Colombian jungle and flew them to Caracas, where they met Chavez, who brokered their freedom.

On April 8, 2008, Spain, Switzerland, and France closed their humanitarian mission to free the hostages. FARC had claimed that the group had not coordinated its plane landing in Colombia with them ahead of time. The plane had arrived on April 3 with diplomats and doctors to help Betancourt, who reportedly was dying from hepatitis B.

On July 2, 2008, in a daring rescue called Operation Check, the Colombian Army tricked the Revolutionary Armed Forces of Colombia (FARC) commander Gerardo Antonio Aguilar Ramirez, alias Cesar, and his fellow hostage-takers into believing that an Army Mi-17 helicopter that landed in a remote jungle clearing 45 miles southeast of San Jose del Guaviare belonged to a humanitarian group and was going to move several hostages to another FARC-controlled locale to meet new FARC commander Alfonso Cano. After the FARC moved several of its highest-value hostages to the site—it had rarely kept all of its major hostages in the same place—the army sprung the trap, flying off, capturing two FARC rebels, including Cesar and his deputy, Alexander Farfan, alias Gafas, on board without firing a shot, and freeing former Colombian presidential candidate Ingrid Betancourt (held since February 23, 2002), 46; American Northrop Grumman military contractors Marc Gonsalves, Keith Stansell, and Thomas Howes (held since February 13, 2003); and eleven Colombian soldiers, including Army Capt. Juan Carlos Bermeo, Lt. Raimundo Malagon, and army nurse William Perez. The rebels still held seven hundred hostages.

On July 9, 2010, Betancourt sued the Colombian government for $6.5 million in compensation for her captivity.

February 27, 2002—India—On February 22, 2011, a court in Gujarat found thirty-one Muslims guilty of murder and criminal conspiracy by setting alight the Sabarmati Express train coach in Godhra and killing fifty-nine Hindu passengers. Another sixty-three were acquitted, among them Maulana Hussain Umarji, 70, who was believed to be a key conspirator. The defense said it would appeal. On March 1, 2011, the court sentenced eleven Muslims to death for being part of the criminal conspiracy; twenty were sentenced to life in prison.

April 2002—Colombia—In May 2012, Sigifredo Lopez, 48, one of the hostages freed after being held for more than seven years, was arrested in Colombia on May 16, 2012, on suspicion of helping to carry out the kidnapping of a dozen provincial parliamentarians in Cali by the Revolutionary Armed Forces of Colombia (FARC).

As of May 21, 2012, he had not been charged. FARC kidnappers had scuffled with another FARC team and thinking that they were under military attack, killed the other eleven hostages, sparking Lopez, to prevent a rescue. Lopez was freed in February 2009.

April 11, 2002—Tunisia—On February 5, 2009, a French court sentenced German citizen Christian Ganczarski to eighteen years in jail for his part in the suicide bombing of a synagogue in Tunisia that killed twenty-one people in 2002. French authorities had arrested him in 2003. The court also sentenced Walid Naouar, the suicide bomber's brother, to twelve years.

May 8, 2002—United States—U.S. District Judge Marcia G. Cooke announced on January 16, 2008, that Jose Padilla, 37, the alleged "dirty bomber," his alleged recruiter Adham Amin Hassoun, and Kifah Wael Jayyousi, a former San Diego school administrator accused of aiding overseas Islamist fighters, should spend at least thirty years to life in prison. On January 22, 2008, Judge Cooke sentenced Padilla to seventeen years and four months on conspiracy charges; Hassoun to fifteen years and eight months; and Jayyousi to twelve years and eight months. Attorneys for the trio promised appeals. On February 17, 2011, U.S. District Judge Richard Gergel threw out Padilla's claim that he was tortured while in a navy brig in Charleston, South Carolina, saying that the enemy combatant had no right to sue for constitutional violations and that the defendants had qualified immunity. On September 19, 2011, a three-judge panel of the U.S. Court of Appeals for the Eleventh Circuit said that Padilla's January 2008 seventeen-year sentence was too lenient and ordered the case sent back to federal court for resentencing.

August 2002—Indonesia/Papua New Guinea—Gunmen attacked a convoy of international teachers for forty-five minutes, killing three people, including Rick Spiers, who had been teaching children of U.S. mining workers, the school's American superintendent, and an Indonesian colleague, and wounding eight others, including Patsy Spier, Rick's wife. In late 2008, at age 51, she became a coordinator in the U.S. Department of Justice's (DOJ) Office of Justice for Victims of Overseas Terrorism, where she tracked down victims and determined their need for money, counseling, and other assistance. She also trained FBI agents and DOJ prosecutors in working with families.

October 2002—United States—On September 24, 2008, U.S. District Judge Liam O'Grady in Alexandria, Virginia, rejected sniper John Allen Muhammad's appeal of the death sentence he received for the murder of Dean H. Meyers near Manassas, Virginia. O'Grady lifted the stay of execution. On September 16, 2009, Prince William County Circuit Court Judge Mary Grace O'Brien set November 10 as the execution date. On November 10, 2009, John Allen Muhammad was executed by lethal injection. At 9:06 p.m., thiopental sodium knocked him out, pancuronium bromide stopped his breathing, and potassium chloride stopped his heart. He was pronounced dead five minutes later at the Greensville Correctional Center in Jarratt, Virginia.

In a taping for an A&E cable television interview scheduled to air on July 29, 2010, sniper Lee Boyd Malvo told William Shatner that the duo had killed forty-two people in 2002. He claimed that the duo had three conspirators, two of whom they killed.

October 6, 2002—Yemen—On August 31, 2012, Khaled Batis, variant Khalid Batees, a senior al Qaeda terrorist wanted for masterminding the October 6, 2002, attack on the French oil tanker *Limburg*, was killed along with four other terrorists riding in a vehicle that was struck by a drone missile on August 31, 2012, in Hadramawt, Yemen.

October 12, 2002—Indonesia/Bali—On November 8, 2008, the Indonesian government executed Islamic militants Imam Samudra, Amrozi Nurhasyim, and Ali Ghufron (the last two are brothers) at 11:20 p.m. for helping plan and conduct the Bali bombing by Jemaah Islamiyah (al Qaeda sympathizers) that killed 202 people, many of them Australian tourists.

On March 9, 2010, police raided an Internet café in Pamulang, Banten Province, and killed Dulmatin, 40, alias Joko Pitoyo, a senior member of Jemaah Islamiyah who was believed behind the Bali bombings. Two other terrorists died in the raid. Police arrested twenty-one suspects in Aceh and Java and seized books on jihad, rifles, and military uniforms. The electronics specialist had trained in al Qaeda camps in Afghanistan and had a $10 million bounty on his head. His group called itself the Aceh branch of al Qaeda for Southeast Asia (Tandzim al-Qoidah Indonesia Wilayah Serambi Makkah).

On January 25, 2011, Pakistani security officials arrested al Qaeda operative Umar Patek, 40, a Javanese Arabic man suspected of membership in Jemaah Islamiyah, in connection with the Bali bombings. He was believed to be the deputy field commander for those bombings, as well as suicide bombings in Jakarta in 2003 and 2009. The United States had offered a $1 million reward for his arrest.

On June 9, 2011, Indonesian authorities in central Java arrested Heru Kuncoro, who was suspected in the bombing, along with two other men with ties to terrorist leaders, after security officials foiled a plot by sixteen detainees to kill police with cyanide. Police said he was a facilitator who bought electronic equipment used in the bombings.

The trial of Hisyam Bin Alizein, alias Umar Patek, 41, for the Bali bombings began on February 13, 2012, in the West Jakarta District Court. He was charged with premeditated murder, hiding information about terrorism, illegal possession of explosives, and conspiracy to commit terrorism. Prosecutors said he had confessed to being a key participant in the Bali bombings, assembling the 2,250-pound bomb that was hidden inside a van. He also said he made the bombs used in the December 24, 2000, attacks on churches that killed nineteen. He faced death by firing squad. He was represented by ten lawyers, including attorney Ashluddin Hatjani.

He told interrogators he had hidden in a rented house while he built a 700-kilogram bomb using a rice ladle, grocer's scale, and plastic bags. His band hid the bomb in four filing cabinets, then loaded them in a Mitsubishi L300 van along with a TNT vest bomb. He said a small explosion occurred while they were loading the bomb onto the van.

He claimed to have learned bomb making while at a militant academy in Pakistan's Sadda Province from 1991 to 1994 and later at Turkhom, Afghanistan.

While he was living in Solo, Indonesia, he was pitched by Imam Samudra to make the Bali bomb. He flew to Denpasar, Bali, and went to the rented house with co-conspirator Sawad. Dulmatin worked on the electronic circuits used for the detonators. Patek and Dulmatin joined Abu Sayyaf in the Philippines after the bombings. Nadeem Akhtar, 37, a Pakistani in Indonesia, helped Patek get a Pakistani visa from his embassy in Jakarta.

On June 21, 2012, an Indonesian court sentenced Umar Patek, 45, to twenty years, after finding him guilty of helping assemble the Bali bomb, premeditated murder, and conspiracy to smuggle explosives and firearms for use in terror attacks. He was also charged with smuggling firearms from the Philippines to Indonesia and planning a militant camp in Aceh in 2010. He told the court that upon arrival in Bali, 950 kilograms of the explosives had already been mixed, and he agreed to mix the rest. "When I saw Sawada, aka Sarjiyo, looking exhausted and nervous, finally I agreed to help him and both of us mixed the explosive ingredients that were less than 50 kg. I did it lazily because it didn't come from my soul and it was contrary to my conscience."

November 28, 2002—Kenya—On September 14, 2002, U.S. commandos killed Saleh Ali Saleh Nabhan, ringleader of the attackers of the Mombasa hotel, in Baraawe, Somalia. He might also have played a role in the August 1998 bombings of the U.S. embassies in Kenya and Tanzania.

2003—India—Bombs went off at Mumbai's Gateway of India and Zaveri gold market, killing fifty-four people. The Lashkar-e-Tayyiba was blamed. On July 27, 2009, an India court convicted a married couple and another man for the attacks. On August 4, 2009, the prosecution demanded the death sentence for the married couple—Mohammad Hanif and his wife Fahmida (who goes by one name)—and their accomplice Ashrat Ansari.

2003—Morocco—Al-Jazeera reported on April 10, 2008, that nine Casablanca-based Moroccan men jailed for the bombings that killed forty-five people in 2003 had tunneled out of Kenitra prison, north of Rabat. One of the escapees had been on death row; six others were serving life sentences; the other two had been sentenced to twenty years.

2003—Venezuela—On April 30, 2008, a Venezuelan court sentenced dissident former Gen. Felipe Rodriguez to ten years in prison for conspiracy and aggravated burning of property in the 2003 bombings of the Spanish and Colombian embassies that injured four people. He had been involved in the 2002 failed coup attempt against President Hugo Chavez.

2003—Gulf of Aden—On April 22, 2012, Mohammed Said al-Umdah, alias Ghareeb al-Taizi, who provided logistical and financial support for al Qaeda in the Arabian Peninsula, and two others were killed when an air strike hit his SUV in northeast Yemen. He had received military training in Afghanistan under Osama bin Laden's supervision. He had been convicted for his role in the 2003 bombing of the French oil tanker *Limburg* in the Gulf of Aden. He was one of the twenty-three convicts who escaped from a Yemeni prison in February 2006. The Yemeni Embassy in Washington, DC, said he was number 4 on its most wanted list.

2003—Georgia—Armenian citizen Garik Dadaian was arrested after setting off a radiation detector at a checkpoint on the border with Armenia. He was returned to Armenia a few days later. In 2010, his name was found on a bank transfer slip carried by one of two smugglers arrested with highly enriched uranium, which the duo had obtained from Dadaian. Forensic analysis said it was from the same batch as the 2003 material. Russian authorities suggested he got the material from a manufacturing plant in Novosibirsk, Russia. The duo was identified as bankrupt dairy farmer Sumbat Tonoyan and Hrant Ohanian, a former physicist at a nuclear research facility in Yerevan, Armenia. They were sentenced to thirteen to fourteen years.

January 5, 2003—United Kingdom—In a bloody gun battle, British authorities arrested seven al Qaeda members planning to use ricin in the London underground. The terrorists were commanded by al-Zarqawi.

February 13, 2003—Colombia—On February 2, 2008, the Colombian Army detained near the Venezuela border Luz Dari Condo Rubio, a Colombian female rebel wanted in the kidnapping of three U.S. contractors in February 2003.

On February 27, 2008, Luis Eladio Perez, one of the four Colombian legislators who were freed by the Revolutionary Armed Forces of Colombia (FARC), said that the three Americans had given him letters to give to President Bush and other U.S. politicians but that the rebels confiscated them.

On July 2, 2008, the Colombian Army fooled FARC into believing that its helicopter was a FARC chopper that was to move several hostages out of the area. When the FARC placed its hostages onto the helicopter, government troops announced the ruse, freed the hostages, including Betancourt and the three Americans, and detained the FARC members (*see also* Updates February 2002—Colombia).

On August 1, 2008, the United States indicted Hely Mejia Mendoza, alias Martin Sombra, in U.S. District Court for conspiring with other guerrillas to abduct the trio.

On August 22, 2009, Colombian police captured Jose Armando Cadena Cabrera, alias Bronco, a FARC guerrilla who was believed to have killed U.S. citizen Thomas John Janis and soldier Luis Alcides Cruz and kidnapped the other three Americans whose helicopter had crashed. The three Northrop Grumman contractors wrote in their 2009 memoir that a FARC member named Sonia told them that she had killed the duo.

On September 19, 2009, Colombia extradited to Florida Nancy Conde Rubio, 37, who led a finance and supply operation for the Revolutionary Armed Forces of Colombia. She faced charges of terrorism in a U.S. federal court. She was the former girlfriend of a FARC member who helped guard fifteen hostages, including Ingrid Betancourt and three U.S. military contractors, who were rescued by the Colombian military in July 2008. Conde's intercepted phone calls helped locate the rebel hideout.

On December 14, 2010, a U.S. federal grand jury of the U.S. District Court for the District of Columbia indicted eighteen FARC members on terrorism and weapons charges in connection with the taking of the three U.S. hostages. Sixteen of them were charged for the first time. This was the first time senior FARC general staff members were accused of telling their American hostages that the kidnapping would increase international pressure on Bogota to accede to their demands. Among those indicted were

- Tanja Anamary Nijmeijer, 32, a former Dutch schoolteacher who rose to senior FARC levels. She recently was shown in a fifty-three-second video broadcast by Dutch news services in which she wore military fatigues and held an assault rifle. She had written a diary recovered from a FARC camp in 2007. She was an aide to Victor Suarez, alias Jorse Briceno, alias El Mono Jojoy, the senior FARC military strategist who was killed in a Colombian raid in August 2010.
- Carlos Alberto Garcia, alias El Paisa
- Jose Ignacio Gonzalez Perdomo, alias Alfred Arenas

FARC member Alexander Beltran Herrera was extradited to the United States in mid–March 2012. On March 12, 2012, the 35-year-old pleaded not guilty in a U.S. court to taking three U.S. citizens hostage after their plane crashed in Colombia in February 2003. He was represented by court-appointed attorney John Machado. Herrera was one of eighteen FARC members indicted in February 2012. The others remained at large.

August 19, 2003—Iraq—On June 26, 2009, Iraqi officials arrested Ali Hussein Azzawi, 54, a former Iraqi Airways commercial airline pilot and senior member of al Qaeda in Iraq, at his home in eastern Baghdad. On January 16, 2010, authorities released a videotaped confession in which he said he was a senior member of the Sunni group. Iraqi officials said he orchestrated the 2003 bombing of the UN headquarters in Baghdad that killed twenty-two people.

September 10, 2003—Sweden—On August 29, 2011, assassin Mijailo Mijailovic said he faked mental illness at his trial so he would get a less severe sentence. He blamed politicians for his failings in life; the hatred led to his attack.

2004—Israel—On April 26, 2010, Israeli forces killed Ali Sweiti, 42, who was a senior member of the Izzidin al-Qassam Brigade, the Hamas armed movement, who was believed to have killed an Israeli soldier. He refused to leave a house where he was hiding during a late night raid. After a gun battle, Israeli soldiers bulldozed the house with him in it; his body was found in the rubble. He had two wives and fourteen children.

2004—Saudi Arabia—On April 8, 2012, Saudi Arabia began the trial of fifty men suspected of al Qaeda links. They were charged with killing an American who was kidnapped in 2004, bombing the al-Muhaya foreign housing compound in Riyadh and other compounds in the Eastern Province in 2003, and planning to attack the U.S. and U.K. embassies.

February 26, 2004—United States—Members of the White Aryan Resistance set off a bomb that injured Don Logan, the black director of diversity at Scottsdale, Arizona. Logan underwent four surgeries on his hand and arm. The bomb also injured a secretary. The group had called on "lone wolves" to attack non-whites and the government. In January 2012, a six-week trial began for identical twins Dennis and Daniel Mahon, 61, of Illinois. On February 24, 2012, the jury convicted Dennis Mahon on three charges but said Daniel was not guilty of conspiracy to damage buildings and property by means of explosives. On May 21, 2012, U.S. District Judge David Campbell sentenced Dennis Mahon to forty years in prison.

March 11, 2004—Spain—On July 17, 2008, Spain's Supreme Court upheld the acquittal of Rabei Osman Sayed Ahmed, an Egyptian, on charges of leading the group that bombed several Madrid trains on March 11, 2004, killing 191 people. It also cleared four men convicted by a lower court in the case. In October 2007, the National Court

had convicted three men of murder. European investigators determined that the attacks cost only $80,000 to conduct.

On December 18, 2008, a Moroccan criminal court convicted Abdelilah Ahriz, 31, of belonging to the group that conducted the train attacks. He was sentenced to twenty years. Prosecutors had requested a life sentence, noting that witness testimony and DNA sampling proved his involvement.

In November 2009, National Court Judge Eloy Velasco indicted seven Islamic militants for helping the bombers of Madrid trains on March 11, 2004. The suspects were said to have provided money, housing, food, and forged documents to the six key suspects, whom they also hid and then helped escape from Spain. Six suspects were charged with membership in a terrorist group; the seventh with collaborating with terrorists. Three of the fugitives were believed to have later conducted suicide bombings in Iraq against Western soldiers. A fourth was caught and convicted in Morocco for his role in the training bombings. A fifth faced trial in Morocco. The sixth, initially believed to have gone to ground in Belgium, remained at large. The seven defendants included four Moroccans, an Algerian, and a Tunisian. Zohair Khadiri, a Moroccan, was the only one in jail. The judge linked him to three others convicted last May in Spain for helping train bomb suspects to flee. The six faced twelve-year prison sentences; the collaborator faced ten years in prison. A procedural hearing was scheduled for November 20, 2009.

On January 12, 2010, Spanish terrorism expert Fernando Reinares claimed that the train bombings were orchestrated by terrorists in North Waziristan. A ringleader was a Moroccan, Amer Azizi, who had been in northwest Pakistan in 2004 and worked with al Qaeda's head of external operations, Egyptian citizen Hamza Rabia. Azizi had recruited the leaders of the bombers' cell. The two were killed in a U.S. missile attack in 2005 on Haisori village near Miranshah in North Waziristan.

April 9, 2004—Iraq—The U.S. military announced on March 30, 2008, the discovery of the remains of Army Sgt. Keith Matthew Maupin, 20, who had been kidnapped in 2004 when his fuel convoy was ambushed west of Baghdad.

October 18, 2004—Spain—Spanish police arrested thirty suspected Islamic militants planning to set off a 500-kilogram bomb at Madrid's antiterrorism National Court. They hoped to destroy files against other Islamist terrorist suspects, including those held in the 3/11 Madrid train bombings in 2004. Among them were nineteen Algerians, five Moroccans, and defendants from Mauritania, Afghanistan, Palestine, Lebanon, and Spain. They were identified by a Moroccan who was a police informant, by wiretaps, and intercepted correspondence. Their trial began in October 2007 and ended on January 14, 2008. On February 4, 2008, a Spanish court provisionally released ten of them. Five were kept in jail on other charges. Those who were freed must report to the police station every Monday, surrender their passports, and not leave Spain.

On February 27, 2008, a Spanish court acquitted twenty of the suspects of charges of conspiracy to blow up the court but convicted them of lesser offenses. The twenty were convicted of creating jihadi cells in jail by recruiting other prisoners. The three-judge court convicted eighteen of belonging to a terrorist organization. The other two were convicted of collaborating with the group. Sentences ranged from five to fourteen years. The final ten were acquitted of all charges.

October 19, 2004—Iraq—On June 2, 2009, a Baghdad court convicted Iraqi citizen Ali Lutfi al-Rawi and sentenced him to life in prison for the 2004 kidnapping and murder of U.K. aid worker Margaret Hassan. On August 22, 2010, Iraq's deputy justice minister confirmed that al-Rawi had escaped from prison in September 2009.

2005—Australia—On February 15, 2010, five Australian Muslims who were found guilty in October 2009 of conspiring to commit an attack between July 2004 and November 2005 were sentenced by the New South Wales State Supreme Court Judge Anthony Whealy to terms ranging from twenty-three to twenty-eight years. Authorities had confiscated twenty-eight thousand rounds of ammunition, weapons, and chemicals to make bombs that were to be used in retaliation for Australian involvement in the wars in Iraq and Afghanistan. The men, aged 25 to 44, were arrested in Sydney in 2005.

February 12, 2005—Brazil—Vitalmiro Bastos de Moura was one of two ranchers who were alleged to have ordered the February 12, 2005, murder of Sister Dorothy Stang, 73, a U.S. nun and rain forest activist. He was convicted and sentenced to thirty years, but on retrial (Brazil requires retrials for first offenders sentenced to twenty-plus years) in Para State's seniormost court, he was acquitted on a technicality on May 6, 2008. On April 7, 2009, a Brazilian court ordered his arrest and retrial. Prosecutors refiled charges on April 12, 2010.

On December 31, 2008, Brazilian police arrested Regivaldo Pereira Galvao, who had been seen at the site of Stang's murder. Pereira was held on charges of land fraud and slavery. He had earlier been charged with conspiracy to murder Stang. He had been held in prison for a year after Stang's murder until his release by the Brazilian Supreme Court in 2006; as of December 31, 2008, he had yet to be tried.

A documentary movie released in 2008, *They Killed Sister Dorothy*, was narrated by Martin Sheen. Brazilian investigators said some of the interviews in the film would be used against those accused in the case.

February 14, 2005—Lebanon—On April 19, 2009, Dubai authorities arrested Syrian intelligence officer Muhammed Zuhair Siddiq on suspicion of involvement in the February 2005 assassination of Rafiq Hariri. France had put him under house arrest in October 2005 on the recommendation of a UN commission investigating the killing, but he disappeared in March 2008.

On April 29, 2009, Lebanon released Jamil Sayyed, Ali Hajj, Raymond Azar, and Mustafa Hamdan, the four generals it had held for nearly four years in the case, after an internal tribunal in The Hague ordered them freed. Prosecutors said they did not have enough evidence to continue the detention.

On May 24, 2009, Hizballah denied *Der Spiegel*'s claim that the group was involved in the attack.

On March 31, 2010, UN special investigator, Canadian prosecutor David Bellemare, summoned twelve Hizballah members for questioning.

In November 2010, the Canadian Broadcasting Company (CBC) reported that the UN International Independent Investigation Commission had determined that phone records implicated Hizballah in the Hariri assassination. Pundits speculated that the UN would indict a Hizballah member by the end of the year. CBC also reported that an internal UN document had suggested that Col. Wissam al-Hassan, a Lebanese intelligence official who was a liaison with UN investigators, was implicated in the case because although he was in charge of Hariri's security, he had taken that day off to take a university exam.

On January 12, 2011, on the eve of potential indictments against Hizballah members in the Hariri assassination, eleven cabinet ministers from Hizballah and its allies withdrew from the Lebanese government coalition of Prime Minister Saad Hariri, ensuring that the government would fall and sparking a crisis in regime stability. The UN prosecutor issued a sealed indictment against suspects on January 17, 2011.

On July 29, 2011, the UN-based international court announced the names of four Hizballah members wanted on suspicion of the murder—Mustafa Amine Badreddine, Hizballah's deputy military commander; Salim Jamil Ayyash; Hussein Hassan Oneissi; and Assad Hassan Sabra. On August 17, 2011, the UN tribunal released its forty-seven-page indictment against Hizballah members, following its June 30 arrest warrants for four Hizballah members who remained at large.

July 7, 2005—United Kingdom—Investigators determined that the London subway and train bombings cost only $15,000 to conduct.

On January 21, 2009, authorities in Peshawar, Pakistan, arrested Taifi, a Saudi from Taif, and six other insurgents in a pre-dawn raid on the house of an Afghan refugee. Taifi was believed involved in the London bombings.

On April 28, 2009, Kingston Crown Court west of London acquitted in a retrial Mohammed Shakil, 32, Sadeer Saleem, 28, and Waheed Ali, 25, of aiding the bombers by scouting locations for the attacks. A jury in the first trial in 2008 failed to reach a verdict. The trio were found not guilty of conspiracy to cause explosions. Ali and Shakil were convicted of conspiring to attend a terrorist training camp in Pakistan in 2001 and 2003, where they were instructed in the use of automatic weapons and grenade launchers. The next day, they were sentenced to seven years in prison. Saleem was represented by attorney Imran Khan. Prosecutors had claimed that the trio had joined three of the bombers for a test run in December 2004, when they visited subway stations and tourist locales.

Martine Wright, 37, who lost both legs in the Aldgate blast, five years later to the day was a member of the British women's sitting volleyball team that was training to compete in the 2012 London Paralympics.

July 21, 2005—United Kingdom—A London court on February 5, 2008, convicted Siraj Ali, 33, Muhedin Ali, 29, Ismail Abduraham, 25, Wahbi Mohammed, 25, and Abdul Sherif, 30, of twenty-two charges of failing to disclose information about terrorism and assisting an offender in connection with the failed copycat bombing of the London transit system in July 2005. Mohammed was sentenced to seventeen years, Siraj Ali to twelve years, Sherif and Abdurahman to ten years, and Muhedin Ali to seven years. The five provided safe houses, passports, clothing, and food for the would-be bombers after the failed attacks. Siraj Ali and Mohammed were also charged and convicted of having prior knowledge of the attacks. Sherif is the brother of Hussain Osman, a convicted bomber. Mohammed is the brother of Ramzi Mohammed, another bomber.

On February 26, 2008, the self-appointed Osama bin London, Mohammed Hamid, 50, was convicted of running terrorist training camps in the U.K. countryside, including one attended by the five men convicted of the failed bombing plot. He was also convicted of encouraging Muslims to attend the camps and holding recruiting sessions in his London home aiming at murdering "non-believers." Prosecutors told the Woolwich Crown Court that he had deemed the fifty-two deaths in the 7/7 London train and bus bombings in 2005 as "not even breakfast for me." He was an associate of Abu Hamza al-Masri, the radical Islamic cleric. Hamid, who often gave fiery speeches at Speakers' Corner in Hyde Park, ran a bookstall in central London.

On February 13, 2009, British prosecutors announced that they would not seek charges against the police officers who shot to death Jean Charles de Menezes, 27, on July 22, 2005, in the mistaken belief that he was another would-be suicide bomber.

September 2005—Belarus—Two explosions wounded forty-eight people in Vitebsk.

December 27, 2005—Philippines—On August 28, 2009, Manila extradited to the United States Filipino citizen Commander Madhatta Haipe in connection with a hostage-taking by Abu Sayyaf. He had been held in the Philippines for at least three months. He was indicted in November 2000 on charges of leading a group that kidnapped sixteen people, including four Californians, from the mountainous Tran-Kine Spring Resort at Lake Sebu, 640 miles southeast of Manila, on December 27, 2005. Most of the hostages were held for five days. The rest were released on December 31 after payment of a $57,000 ransom. A week later, troops in helicopter gunships raided the kidnappers' safe haven, killing seven, and capturing three, including Haipe, who was wounded. Haipe was a former professor of Islamic studies at Mindanao State University in the Philippines. On August 29, 2009, U.S. Magistrate Judge Alan Kay in Washington, DC, ordered him held without bond pending trial.

2006—Israel—On October 20, 2010, Chief Judge Royce C. Lamberth of the U.S. District Court for the District of Columbia ruled that the Bank of China could be sued for supporting terrorism in a case brought by the family of Daniel Wultz, 16, an American residing in south Florida who was killed in a 2006 suicide bombing at a Tel Aviv restaurant. Islamic Jihad (IJ) claimed credit. His parents, Yekutiel and Sheryl Wultz, sought $300 million in damages in 2008 from Iran, Syria, and the Bank of China. Israel had claimed that IJ was financing its bombings via a bank account in the United States maintained by Said al-Shurafa, a senior IJ officer.

January 7, 2006—Iraq—Jill Carroll, who had been kidnapped and held hostage for three months, on August 18, 2008, left her job as a journalist with the *Christian Science Monitor* to begin five months of training to become a firefighter and EMT for Fairfax County Fire and Rescue in northern Virginia.

In late August 2008, coalition forces announced that on August 11 and 17, 2008, they had detained two suspected masterminds of several kidnappings, including Carroll's, identified as Salim Abdallah Ashur al-Shujayri, alias Abu Uthman, and Ali Rash Nasir Jiyad al-Shammari, alias Abu Tiba. They were also believed behind car and suicide bombings against Iraqis. Abu Tiba was believed to have led fifteen al Qaeda in Iraq attack cells by giving them money, weapons, and explosives.

March 2006—United States—On August 26, 2008, Mohammed Taheri-Azar, 25, was sentenced to up to thirty-three years in prison after pleading guilty to nine counts of attempted murder when he drove his SUV into a crowd at the University of North Carolina bar The Pit. He was a naturalized U.S. citizen from Iran. He grew up near Charlotte, North Carolina, and graduated from the university.

March 2006—United States—On June 11, 2009, a federal judge in Atlanta, Georgia, convicted Syed Haris Ahmed, 24, of conspiracy to support terrorists. He had gone to Washington, DC, in April 2005, where he made short digital videos of the U.S. Capitol, Pentagon, George Washington National Masonic Memorial, the World Bank, and fuel tanks near I-95 in northern Virginia. He shared the videos with Younis Tsouli, believed to be a recruiter for al Qaeda in Iraq, and Aabid Hussein Khan, who has ties to Pakistani Islamists, including Lashkar-i-Taiba. The duo had been convicted of terrorist crimes in the United Kingdom. Ahmed was arrested in March 2006.

March 2, 2006—Pakistan—On February 24, 2010, a missile strike in Dargah Mandi in North Waziristan, Pakistan, killed thirteen terrorists, including Qari Mohammad Zafar, who was wanted for questioning in the March 2, 2006, bombing near the U.S. Consulate in Karachi that killed three Pakistanis and U.S. diplomat David Foy. The

United States had put a $5 million reward out for the pro–Taliban Zafar, who was a member of Lashkar-e Jangvi.

May 29, 2006—Iraq—The 500-pound car bomb killed cameraman Paul Douglas and soundman James Brolan, Army Capt. James Funkhouser, and Iraqi translator Sam. Four other soldiers and CBS News correspondent Kimberly Dozier were injured. She ultimately returned to Iraq with Adm. Mike Millen, chairman of the Joint Chiefs of Staff, in December 2009 during a United Service Organizations (USO) trip.

June 2, 2006—Canada—Toronto police arrested eighteen terrorists—fourteen adults and four youths—planning to conduct three days of bombing attacks in "the Battle of Toronto," starting on the fifth anniversary of 9/11. The group hoped to shut down the downtown core, harm the economy, and kill civilians by parking three explosives-packed U-Haul vans at the Toronto Stock Exchange, the Front Street offices of Canada's intelligence agency, and a military base off Highway 401 between Toronto and Ottawa. They intended to use three tons of ammonium nitrate fertilizer and nitric acid. Three months later, they planned to attack the Sears Building in Chicago or the UN headquarters in New York City. The group also had plans to bomb nuclear power stations, storm the parliament buildings in Ottawa, and kidnap and behead Prime Minister Stephen Harper. The group hoped to pressure the government to withdraw Canadian troops from Afghanistan. Police relied on the work of undercover police agent Shaher Elsohemy, who talked to the deputy chief of the group about its plans.

On September 25, 2008, an Ontario court declared guilty one of the "Toronto 18" who was 17 at the time of his arrest.

The sentencing hearing in a Brampton court began on June 22, 2009, against Saad Khalid, 22, from Mississauga. Khalid was charged with knowingly participating in a terrorist group, receiving training for the purpose of enhancing the ability of a terrorist group, and doing anything with "intent to cause an explosion of an explosive substance that was likely to cause serious bodily harm or death." He pleaded guilty to the last count—he rented warehouse space in Newmarket to store the fertilizer and received the delivery truck—the only one who admitted to the existence of a bomb plot. Police arrested Khalid and others while they were unloading the truck. Prosecutors said Khalid attended a jihadist training camp in Washago, Ontario, in December 2005. He was represented by attorney Russell Silverstein.

Since the arrests and Khalid's hearing, charges against seven defendants were stayed by the court.

By March 2006, the group's two ringleaders—one from Scarborough and one from Mississauga—had clashed. The Mississauga leader is alleged to have developed the bomb plot.

One plotter was sentenced to fourteen years on June 23, 2009. Ringleader Zacariah Amara faced life in prison, which in Canada translates to twenty-five years. Sentencing was scheduled for January 2010.

June 22, 2006—United States—Federal authorities in Miami's impoverished Liberty City district arrested six individuals aged 22 to 32 who were plotting to attack the Sears Tower in Chicago, the James Lawrence King Federal Justice Building, federal courthouse buildings, the Federal Detention Center, the Miami Police Department, and the FBI office in Miami. Those arrested included Lyglenson Lemorin, Stanley Grant Phanor, Narseale Batiste, Patrick Abraham, Naudimar Herrera, Burson Augustin, and Rotschild Augustine.

On December 13, 2007, Judge Lenard declared a mistrial for six of the defendants. Lyglenson Lemorin was acquitted of all charges but remained in detention as there was an "immigration hold" on him.

The retrial began on January 22, 2008. On February 6, 2008, federal immigration prosecutors charged Lemorin with nearly identical offenses. On May 12, 2009, a Miami federal jury convicted five of the remaining Liberty City Six in their third trial of charges of planning to blow up the Sears Tower in Chicago. Sentencing was scheduled for July 27, 2009. Herrera was acquitted.

July 8, 2006—Germany—On February 7, 2008, Lebanese citizen Youssef Mohammed el-Hajdib told a German court that he took part in the attempt to bomb two German commuter trains in July 2006 and that the ringleader was Jihad Hamad, who was sentenced in Lebanon in December 2007 to twelve years in prison. The bombing was to be revenge for German newspapers reprinting caricatures of Muhammad. On December 9, 2008, a German court in Duesseldorf found the 24-year-old college student guilty of attempted murder and other crimes. He had claimed that the devices would not have exploded. He was sentenced to life in prison. Defense attorney Bernd Rosenkranz said he would appeal.

August 10, 2006—United Kingdom—On April 2, 2008, jury selection began in the trial of eight British Muslims who had been arrested in a terrorist plot to use liquid explosives to destroy ten commercial jetliners flying to the United States.

Most of them were in their 20s and of Pakistani extraction. The plot led to major changes in how airport security is handled. The group pleaded not guilty. Police had searched sixty-nine sites, arrested twenty-one people, and confiscated four hundred computers, two hundred cell phones, eight thousand computer-related items, including DVDs, CDs, and memory sticks, and several martyrdom videos. Among the seized bomb-making equipment were empty sports drink bottles to hold the explosive liquids, batteries, syringes, food coloring, an amp-volt reader, a pH reader, electronic scales, a digital thermometer, bulbs, wiring, hydrogen peroxide, and citric acid. The group planned to down United flight 925 to Washington, United flight 931 to San Francisco, United flight 959 to Chicago, American Airlines flight 139 to New York, American Airlines flight 91 to Chicago, Air Canada flight 849 to Toronto, and Air Canada flight 865 to Montreal. The prosecution ran six "martyrdom tapes" recorded by the defendants. One of the plotters planned attacks on nuclear power plants, gas pipelines, oil refineries, tunnels, electric grids, Internet service providers, the London financial district, and Heathrow Airport's control tower.

On June 2, 2008, defendant Ali Ahmed Khan told the jury that he was not involved in an airliner plot, but had looked into setting off a non-lethal bomb at the British Parliament to protest U.K. participation in the wars in Iraq and Afghanistan. He said he and fellow defendant Assad Sarwar went to Pakistan to work with Afghan refugees and that they had considered bombing the Bank of England and the Canary Wharf financial district.

Khan's family had moved to the United Kingdom from Pakistan in the 1960s.

On July 14, 2008, the trio pleaded guilty to conspiracy to set off bombs but not guilty to conspiracy to murder, saying that they did not target planes and did not intend to cause injuries. Defendants Abdulla Ahmed Ali and Assad Sarwar testified that they intended to bomb Parliament and other high profile sites as a publicity stunt. Ali, Sarwar, Tanvir Hussain, Ibrahim Savant, 27, and Umar Islam, 30, pleaded guilty to conspiracy to cause public nuisance by distributing their confessor videos.

The jury of the Woolwich Crown Court issued a split decision on September 8, 2008, convicting Abdullah Ahmed Ali, 27, Assad Sarwar, 28, and Tanvir Hussain, 27, of "conspiracy to murder persons unknown" but not deciding whether any of the eight defendants intended to destroy the planes with liquid bombs. Mohammed Guilzar,

27, was acquitted of all charges and set free. The jury did not decide on the murder conspiracy charges against Ibrahim Savant, 27, Arafat Waheed Khan, 27, Waheed Zaman, 24, and Umar Islam, 30. Those four had earlier pleaded guilty on public nuisance charges and were kept in detention. The seven faced life in prison. The prosecution said it would seek a retrial, as the jury had not come to a verdict on some of the charges.

On September 7, 2009, at the end of Britain's longest counterterrorist investigation, the Woolwich Crown Court found Tanvir Hussain, Assad Sarwar, and Abdulla Ahmed Ali guilty of plotting to kill more than 1,500 people. Not guilty were Ibrahim Savant, Arafat Waheed Khan, Waheed Zaman, and Donald Stewart-Whyte, who had converted to Islam four months before his arrest. Umar Islam was found guilty of a separate charge of conspiracy to commit murder, for which Ali, Hussain, and Sarwar had been convicted at the group's first trial that ended in September 2008. The jury hung on whether to convict Ibrahim Savant, Arafat Waheed Khan, and Waheed Zaman on conspiracy to murder persons unknown; the prosecutor said he would retry the trio. On September 14, 2009, Justice Richard Henriques sentenced Ali to life in prison with a minimum of forty years before becoming eligible for parole; Sarwar to life with a minimum of thirty-six years; Hussain to life with a minimum of thirty-two years; and Umar Islam to twenty-two years.

On December 9, 2009, the jury at Woolwich Crown Court found Adam Khatib, 22, guilty of conspiring to commit murder with Abdulla Ahmed Ali. Khatib, then a 19-year-old factory worker, was willing to become a suicide bomber on one of the planes. Nabeel Hussain, 25, was guilty of acts preparatory to terrorism. Police found a martyr's will, dated September 2005, in which he said, "Why should I worry when I die a Muslim in the manner in which I am to die? I go to my death for the sake of my maker, who if he wishes can bless limbs torn away." Mohammed Shamin Uddin, 39, was convicted of possessing a document likely to be useful to terrorists. He had researched how to buy hydrogen peroxide, a precursor for liquid explosives. Authorities found a CD containing information on making poisons and explosives.

On July 8, 2010, following their third trial, this one lasting three months, Ibrahim Savant, Arafat Waheed Khan, and Waheed Zaman were found guilty in a U.K. court of conspiracy to murder. Zaman had recorded a martyrdom video in which he said, "I warn you today so that you will have no cause for complaint. Remember, as you kill us, you will be killed; as you bomb us, you will be bombed." On July 12, 2010, they were sentenced to life in prison.

Scotland Yard said the police operation in the case cost circa $40 million and involved twenty-nine surveillance teams.

October 2006—United Kingdom—Sohail Anjum Qureshi, 30, originally of Pakistan, was arrested at Heathrow Airport as he was about to board a plane for Islamabad. He was carrying what he said were "gifts" for the mujahideen he was going to meet in Pakistan. The gifts were a night-vision optical device, backpacks, police-style ASP batons, sleeping bags, and camping gear. He was also carrying a computer hard drive with several "combat manuals" in its files, 9,000 pounds (worth $16,800) and an eight-page al-wida (farewell message) in which he said, "If I am to become a Shaheed [martyr] then cry not and celebrate that day as if you celebrate a happy occasion." He had told an Internet contact that he had trained at an al Qaeda camp in Pakistan in 1996 and led another in 1998. He had contacted Samina Malik, the lyrical terrorist, who worked in a Heathrow Airport store and told him about airport security measures. She was sentenced to nine months in prison in November 2007 for possession of articles useful for terrorist purposes. He claimed he was a terrorism financier and fund-raiser, observing that "bullets cost money." He said that he wanted to "kill many" in an overseas operation. On January 8, 2008, a British court sentenced him to four and a half years in prison.

November 16, 2006—Iraq—Forty gunmen took hostage six Western contractors in two incidents six weeks apart. On March 13, 2008, the media announced that severed fingers of the hostages were sent to the U.S. military in Baghdad in February 2008. DNA tests confirmed that the fingers belonged to the hostages.

Five men—Paul Reuben, 41, of Buffalo, Minnesota; Jonathon Cote, 25, of Getzville, New York; former Marine Joshua Munns, 25, of Redding, California; and Bert Nussbaumer, 26, of Vienna, Austria—were kidnapped near the Kuwait border on November 16. They worked for the Kuwait-based Crescent Security Group. John Young, 45, of Lee's Summit, Missouri, was also taken, although his fingers did not show up in the March 2008 case. He was the security team's leader. Reuben appeared in a video that was released on January 3, 2007. The video was time-stamped December 21–22.

On January 5, 2007, Ronald J. Withrow, 40, of Lubbock, Texas, a contractor working for JPI Worldwide, was abducted near Basra.

On March 23, 2008, the FBI reported the recovery of the bodies of Young and Withrow and three unidentified bodies. They were attempting to recover another corpse near Basra, near where the convoy attack occurred.

On April 23, 2008, U.S. authorities identified Cote's body in Basra. His was the last to be recovered.

December 2006—Ceuta—Eleven Islamist militants were arrested on charges of plotting terrorist attacks in Ceuta and Mellia, two Spanish enclaves on Morocco's north coast. Police seized forged documents, computers, an air pistol, a bulletproof vest, and a large machete. The group went on trial at Spain's National Court in Madrid on March 20, 2012. Prosecutor Carlos Bautista sought sentences of eight years in prison for seven of the defendants and sentences of up to eleven years for the two other defendants, who were also charged with robbery and forgery. Charges had been dropped against two others. The group pleaded innocent. Among the defendants was Mohamed Fuad Abdeselam, 40, a social worker and father of five, who was believed to be the group's ringleader. He denied giving radical jihadi videos to the others. Prosecutors said the group planned to steal explosives from a local military base and had photographs of the busy passenger ferry that links Ceuta to the Spanish mainland.

2007—United States—John Tomkins, a machinist from Dubuque, Iowa, was arrested for mailing two inoperable pipe bombs and letters threatening violence against investment firms whose stock picks had not performed as well as he had expected. On May 3, 2012, he told a federal jury that he was guilty and expressed remorse. He wanted to force the firms' executive to boost the stock valuation of two companies.

2007—United States—On December 15, 2010, the U.S. Eastern District Court of New York sentenced Abdul Kadir to life in prison after he was convicted in a 2007 plot to explode fuel tanks and the fuel pipeline under John F. Kennedy International Airport in New York.

January 31, 2007—United Kingdom—Birmingham police, Midlands Counterterrorism Unit officers, West Midlands Police, and London's Metropolitan Police raided eight homes and four businesses in two predominantly Muslim neighborhoods beginning at 4:30 a.m. and detained eight Muslim radicals planning to kidnap, torture, and kill a Muslim soldier serving in the U.K. Army, then post the execution video on the Internet.

On February 9, 2007, U.K. police charged six men in the case. They were Parviz Khan, 36, Mohammed Irfan, 30, Zahoor Iqbal, 29, Hamid Elasmar, 43, and Amjad Mahmood, 31. Khan, as the group's leader, was charged with providing equipment and funding for the plan. The five were ordered held until February 23, when a hearing was scheduled. The sixth defendant, Basiru Gassama, 29, was charged under the Terrorism Act with failing to inform authorities about the plot.

In mid–January 2008, Khan pleaded guilty to sending night-vision equipment, sleeping bags, walkie-talkies, computer equipment, and other gear to Pakistan to be used by extremists. The shipments were made in 2005 and 2006. His plea was made public on January 29 at the opening of the trial of two co-defendants. He planned to kidnap the serviceman in the Broad Street entertainment area of Birmingham. Khan had been stopped by U.K. authorities on his return from Pakistan in July 2006 when they found him carrying a notebook with "a shopping list from terrorist contacts of materials they wanted sent back in the next delivery." He was under surveillance until his arrest.

Gassama, Irfan, and Elsamar pleaded guilty to helping Khan or failing to report the plot. Iqbal and Mahmood pleaded not guilty to assisting Khan and knowing of his plot and not reporting it to police. Police found in Iqbal's computer the *Encyclopedia Jihad*, plus videos and books that included a "mujahideen poison book."

March 2007—Iran—On December 9, 2011, a year-old, fifty-seven-second video was released by the family of Robert Levinson, now 63, a former FBI agent who vanished from the Iranian resort island of Kish in March 2007. It was unclear who his abductors were; Iran denied involvement. Levinson said, "Please help me get home. Thirty-three years of service to the United States deserves something.... I need the help of the United States government to answer the requests of the group that has held me." He vanished while serving as a private investigator into a cigarette smuggling case. The video had been mailed to his family a year earlier but was kept under wraps while U.S. officials examined it and the still images also sent to the family. Some observers suggested he was held by Hizballah. Levinson had briefly met with Dawud Salahuddin, a U.S. fugitive in Iran who had assassinated a former aide to the deposed Shah in 1980.

April 2007—Iraq—The Shi'ite-dominated parliament was bombed, killing a parliamentarian. On February 22, 2009, Iraqi security forces said hard-line Sunni Mohammed al-Daini, a member of parliament, had been named by two body-guards as involved in the attack. Security forces said he was also involved in burying victims alive and robbing gold stores. He remained free because of parliamentary immunity and said the allegations were baseless.

May 2007—Colombia—The Revolutionary Armed Forces of Colombia (FARC) took hostage Erik Roland Larsson, 67, and his Colombian wife from the Cielito Lindo ranch where the couple had retired. She escaped less than a month later during a gun battle between FARC and police. The terrorists demanded a $5 million ransom for the Swede's release. He had worked on a hydro-electric project in northern Colombia before retiring. He was released on March 17, 2009, the final remaining foreign hostage held by FARC. His right arm, right leg, and parts of his face were paralyzed, apparently as a result of a stroke he suffered in captivity. It was not disclosed whether a ransom had been paid. 07059901

May 7, 2007—United States—On January 3, 2008, U.S. District Judge Robert Kugler ruled in Camden, New Jersey, against bail for the five foreign-born Muslims who were charged in May with conspiring to kill soldiers at Fort Dix. They faced life in prison. Mohamad Shnewer was represented by attorney Rocco Cipparone.

On December 21, 2008, a judge found the five guilty of conspiracy to kill U.S. soldiers and other charges but not guilty of attempted murder. Sentencing was set for April 2009.

May 29, 2007—Iraq—The hostage takers of five U.K. citizens released a video, dated November 18, 2007, but released in December, that showed hostage "Jason," who was to be killed if the United Kingdom did not withdraw its troops from Iraq in ten days. On July 20, 2008, the kidnappers said that Jason had killed himself on May 25.

On February 26, 2008, Peter Moore, one of five U.K. citizens, along with two Iraqis, who were kidnapped in 2007 from a Finance Ministry building in Baghdad, was on an Al-Arabiya video broadcast, pleading with British Prime Minister Gordon Brown to release nine Iraqi prisoners in return for the hostages' freedom. "It's a simple exchange—release those that they want so we can go home. It's as simple as that. It is a simple exchange of people. This is all they want, just have their people released." Moore worked as a computer consultant for BearingPoint, a Virginia-based management and technology consulting firm. The video was signed by the previously-unknown Shi'ite Islamic Resistance in Iraq. Iraqi government officials blamed Muqtada al-Sadr's Mehdi Army militia.

British cleric Canon Andrew White had unsuccessfully attempted to negotiate in July 2007.

In March 2009, a videotape showing Moore in good health was delivered to the British Embassy in Baghdad.

The Islamic Shi'ite Resistance of Iraq kidnappers released a video on March 22, 2009, of one of the five British hostages who were kidnapped in May 2007. The British Embassy did not release the hostage's name. The video also included footage of fellow British hostage Peter Moore.

On June 7, 2009, Laith al-Khazali was released by the Iraqi government following reports that several Iran-linked militiamen would be released in exchange for the freedom of five British hostages. Government spokesmen denied such a deal took place. He and his brother Qasi had been held since March 2007 for the January 2007 attack in Karbala that killed five U.S. soldiers, who were identified as Capt. Brian S. Freeman, 31, of Temecula, California; 1st Lt. Jacob N. Fritz, 25, of Verdon, Nebraska; Spc. Johnathan B. Chism, 22, of Gonzales, Louisiana; Pfc. Shawn P. Falter, 25, of Cortland, New York; and Pfc. Johnathon M. Millican, 20, of Trafford, Alabama. They were believed to be among the nine to twelve gunmen in five SUVs who drove through checkpoints before firing on the soldiers in the government compound. One of the soldiers died at the scene; four others were kidnapped—three of them were later found fatally shot—the last was alive with a gunshot wound, but died en route to the hospital. Al-Khazali's Shi'ite group was identified as the League of the Righteous, alias Asaib Ahl al-Haq (AAH), which had claimed more than six thousand attacks against foreign military forces. Four of the British hostages worked for GardaWorld, a Canada-based security firm, and were protecting the fifth Briton, a computer analyst with U.S.-based BearingPoint. Qasi remained in custody.

On June 21, 2009, U.K. officials identified two bodies recovered in Iraq, saying they were likely to be two of the hostages, Jason Creswell, originally from Glasgow, Scotland, and Jason Swindlehurst, originally from Skelmersdale.

On July 29, 2009, U.K. Prime Minister Gordon Brown told the families that British hostages Alan McMenemy and Alec MacLachlan were probably dead. He also said he believed Peter Moore was alive. The bodies of two other hostages—Jason Creswell and Jason Swindlehurst—were recovered and returned to the United Kingdom in June 2009.

In August 2009, Moore's kidnappers, Asaib Ahl al-Haq (League of the Righteous), said it would disarm and join the political process.

On September 2, 2009, the remains of Alec MacLachlan were handed over to the U.K. Embassy in Baghdad following negotiations between the Iraqi government and the kidnappers.

On the morning of December 30, 2009, Moore, 36, was handed over to Iraqi authorities, apparently the only survivor of the hostage taking. The United Kingdom said it made no concessions to the terrorists but would not comment as to whether the Iraqi government did so. Reuters reported that Moore had been in Iran during some of his captivity. British officials called on the terrorists to release the body of Alan McMenemy, 34, one of the four bodyguards kidnapped with Moore and believed to have been killed.

June 2, 2007—United States—On February 17, 2011, U.S. District Judge Dora Irizarry sentenced Russell Defreitas to life in prison.

June 30, 2007—United Kingdom—On December 17, 2008, Bilal Abdulla, 29, was sentenced to two consecutive life terms for the failed car bomb attacks in Glasgow and London. Under British law, he would serve at least thirty-two years in prison. Mohammed Asha, 28, was acquitted.

August 4, 2007—United States—Ahmed Abdellatif Sherif Mohamed (also identified as Mohamed Ahmed), 24, and Youssef Samir Megahed, 21, two Egyptian students from the University of South Florida in Tampa, were stopped for speeding in their 2000 Toyota Camry near a navy base in Goose Creek, South Carolina. They were jailed after authorities discovered explosives in the car's trunk. The material included a mixture of fertilizer, kitty litter, and sugar; 20 feet of fuse cord; and a box of .22 caliber bullets. On August 31, they were indicted by a federal grand jury on charges of carrying explosive materials across state lines. One of them faced terrorist-related charges of demonstrating how to use pipe bomb explosives, including the use of remotely-controlled toys, to the other. The duo claimed they were going to the beach with fireworks purchased from Wal-Mart. With federal charges in place, state charges were expected to be dismissed as of September 4.

Authorities later determined that Ahmed had posted on YouTube a twelve-minute video on how to use a remotely-controlled toy car to set off a bomb. His computer had bomb-making files in a folder called "Bomb Shock."

On December 1, 2007, Mohamed said in a defense filing that the explosives were cheap "sugar rocket" fireworks he had made that would travel only a few feet. On January 31, 2008, the FBI announced that the items were low-grade fireworks.

But prosecutors countered on February 5, 2008, that the FBI report had been mischaracterized and that the items met the U.S. legal definition of explosives.

September 2007—Germany—On April 22, 2009, a Berlin court began a trial of three Germans and a Turk who had by September 2007 accumulated enough chemicals to make a half ton of explosives, which were to be used in bombing U.S. military bases, dance clubs, bars, and other American hangouts in Germany. Two Germans and a Turk were arrested in September 2007; the other German was arrested later. Those accused were Fritz Gelowicz, 29; Adem Yilmaz, 30, a Turk who grew up in Germany; Daniel Schneider, 22, a Muslim convert; and Attila Selek, a German citizen of Turkish descent. While overseas, Gelowicz, Yilmaz, and Schneider met a recruiter for the Pakistan-based Islamic Jihad Union, which had been accused of bombing the U.S. and Israeli embassies in Tashkent, Uzbekistan, in 2004. The threesome trained in an al Qaeda affiliate's Pakistan-based camp.

On March 4, 2010, a German court convicted four men in connection with a foiled terrorist plot against Ramstein Air Base and other U.S. and Uzbek military and diplomatic installations in Germany. They were mixing explosives that would have been more destructive than the 3/11 Madrid train bombings. Three were convicted of membership in a terrorist organization. German citizens Gelowicz and Schneider were sentenced to twelve years in prison for membership in a terrorist organization. Turkish citizen Yilmaz received eleven years for membership in a terrorist organization. German citizen Selek was sentenced to five years for supporting the organization.

September 2007—Denmark—On October 21, 2008, the City Court in Glostrup convicted Hammad Khuershid, a Danish citizen of Pakistani origin, and Abdoulghani Tokhi, an Afghan citizen, of preparing a terrorist attack. The duo was clandestinely filmed mixing triacetone triperoxide, the same kind of explosive used in the July 7, 2005, suicide bombings of the London transit system. Prosecutors linked Khuershid to an al Qaeda member. Police had found handwritten bomb-making manuals in the suspects' homes; Khuershid allegedly had copied them at the pro–Taliban Red Mosque in Islamabad. The duo had spent time in Waziristan; Khuershid denied receiving military training while he was there. The duo faced life in prison, although such sentences are often reduced to sixteen years. They had been arrested in Copenhagen in September 2007.

September 2007—Maldives—A bomb exploded in Sultan Park outside the office of Minister of Islamic Affairs Abdul Majeed Abdul Bari, wounding twelve tourists. Within a week, authorities rounded up fifty extremists in a raid on a makeshift mosque on Himandhoo Island. The mosque was patrolled by masked men carrying swords and iron rods. Six terrorism suspects were transferred to a prison and counseled by ministry officials for more than a year. They eventually were declared rehabilitated.

In early August 2008, Maldives President Maumoon Abdul Gayoom pardoned immigration officer Warahumath Ahmed, 21, of M. Radium Kokaa, who was sentenced on February 21, 2008, to a year in prison. He had assisted the escape of detained bombing suspects Abdul Latheef Ibrahim of Green Villa, Laamu atoll Kalhaidhoo, and Ali Shameem of Dhoores, Shaviyani atoll Komandoo. They remained at large.

September 29, 2007—Sudan—One thousand rebels attacked an African Union camp in Haskanita, killing a dozen African Union peacekeepers in Darfur.

On November 20, 2008, an International Criminal Court prosecutor requested arrest warrants on charges of war crimes for three of the rebel commanders believed responsible. Their names were not released.

October 2007—Chad—U.S. missionary Steven Godbold, 48, was taken hostage by the Movement for Democracy and Justice in Chad (MDJT). MDJT spokesman Choua Dazi accused him of being a spy for the local government. He was released on July 24, 2008.

October 18, 2007—Pakistan—On February 25, 2008, Pakistani authorities arrested suspected al Qaeda member Qari Saifullah Akhtar in Lahore for involvement in the October suicide bombing in Karachi of the homecoming parade of former Prime Minister Benazir Bhutto. The attack killed 140.

December 2007—France—Authorities arrested eight French Algerians and Algerians in the Paris suburbs, seizing computers, electronic material, night-vision goggles, global positioning equipment, cell phones, weapons-making machinery, and 20,000 Euros ($30,000). Authorities said they were sending logistical equipment for an attack in Algeria. By mid–June 2008, six of the men had been released.

December 24, 2007—Mauritania—A family of four French tourists was murdered by al Qaeda in the Islamic Maghreb terrorists who fired AK-47s at them. Three gunmen in a black Mercedes attacked five French tourists from Lyon as they were having a midafternoon picnic near Aleg, 1,700 miles southwest of Algiers. Francois Tollet, 74, a retired chemist, survived when the body of one of his two dying sons fell on him. His brother and a friend also died. The gunmen escaped into Senegal and Gambia, but were eventually captured by French intelligence in Guinea-Bissau. 07122401

December 26, 2007—Somalia—A female Spanish doctor and a female Argentine nurse working for Medicins sans Frontieres were kidnapped in Puntland. They were released on January 2, 2008. No ransom was paid, according to Nicolas Martin Cinto, the Spanish ambassador to Kenya, who participated in the negotiations for their release. 07122601

December 27, 2007—Pakistan—Authorities in the Northwest Frontier Province on January 17, 2008, arrested Aitazaz Shah, 15, who said he had been trained as a suicide bomber to kill Benazir Bhutto if the first group did not kill her, and Sher Zaman, 32, his handler in Dera Ismail Khan. The former prime minister was murdered in a gun and bomb attack in Rawalpindi on December 27, 2007. The duo was arrested while driving on a rural road near the border. Police found explosives in the car. Three other males were later detained. On February 7, 2008, Scotland Yard investigators concluded that she was killed when the blast forced her head against the SUV's open roof and that she was not killed by bullets.

On February 7, 2008, Pakistani authorities arrested Husnain Gul and Rafaqat in connection with the attack. One of them was the brother of the suicide bomber. Police later arrested Gul's cousin, taxi driver Abdul Rashid.

On March 1, 2008, Zaman and Shah appeared in court to be formally charged with aiding the assassination plot. Rashid, Gul, and Rafaqat were accused of providing transportation and other assistance. Police also charged Baitullah Mehsud, leader of Tehrik-e-Taliban, the umbrella movement of Pakistani Taliban, who remained at large but had denied the charges. Investigators said Mehsud gave the equivalent of $6,500 to Qari Ismail, who belongs to a Taliban-linked seminar, to organize the assassination. On June 14, 2009, Pakistan announced that it would conduct a military strike against Mehsud.

On November 5, 2011, seven men, including two senior police officers, were indicted for conspiracy to kill former Pakistani Prime Minister Benazir Bhutto. Police officers Saud Aziz, former Rawalpindi police chief, and Khurram Shahzad were accused of security breaches and covering up evidence by hosing down the crime scene. The duo pleaded not guilty and were released on bail. The other five defendants, members of the Pakistani Taliban, were indicted in an antiterror court in Rawalpindi for terrorism, murder, attempted murder, and criminal conspiracy. They were suspected of having links with Beitullah Mehsud, the former leader of the Pakistani Taliban. They were identified as Sher Zaman, Hasnain Gul, Rafaqat Hussain, Abdul Rasheed, and Aitzaz Shah. All hailed from northwest Pakistan.

BIBLIOGRAPHY

General

Abadie, Alberto. "Poverty, Political Freedom, and the Roots of Terrorism." *American Economic Review* 96.2 (2006): 50–6.

Abadie, Alberto, and Javier Gardeazabal. "Terrorism and the World Economy." *European Economic Review* 52.1 (2008): 1–27.

Aboul-Enein, Commander Youssef H. *Militant Islamist Ideology: Understanding the Global Threat.* Annapolis: Naval Institute Press, 2010.

Aid, Matthew M. *Intel Wars: The Secret History of the Fight Against Terror.* New York: Bloomsbury, 2012.

Alaolmolki, Nozar. *Militant Islamists: Terrorists Without Frontiers.* Santa Barbara: Praeger, 2009.

Alexander, Yonah, and Tyler B. Richardson. *Terror on the High Seas: From Piracy to Strategic Challenge.* Santa Barbara: Praeger, 2009.

Ballen, Ken. *Terrorists in Love: The Real Lives of Islamic Radicals.* New York: Free Press, 2011.

Baracskay, Daniel. *The Palestine Liberation Organization: Terrorism and Prospects for Peace in the Holy Land.* Santa Barbara: ABC-CLIO, 2011.

Behling, John. *The DNA of Terrorism: Setting the Stage for World War IV.* In preparation.

Berko, Anat. *The Path to Paradise: The Inner World of Suicide Bombers and Their Dispatchers.* Washington, DC: Potomac Books, 2009.

Berman, Eli, and David Laitin, "Hard Targets: Theory and Evidence on Suicide Attacks." National Bureau of Economic Research, Working Paper No. W 11740 (November 2005).

Berman, Eli, and David Laitin. "Religion, Terrorism, and Public Goods: Testing the Club Model." *Journal of Public Economics* (March 2008): 1942–67.

Berntsen, Gary. *Human Intelligence, Counterterrorism, and National Leadership: A Practical Guide.* Washington, DC: Potomac Books, 2008.

Berrebi, Claude, and Darius Lakdawalla. "How Does Terrorism Risk Vary Across Space and Time? An Analysis Based on the Israeli Experience." *Defence and Peace Economics* 18.2 (2007): 113–31.

Bjorgo, Tore, and John Horgan, eds. *Leaving Terrorism Behind: Individual and Collective Disengagement.* New York: Routledge, 2009.

Blomberg, S. Brock, Rozlyn C. Engel, and Reid Sawyer. "On the Duration and Sustainability of Transnational Terrorist Organizations." *Journal of Conflict Resolution* 54 (2010): 303ff.

Blomberg, S. Brock, and Gregory D. Hess. "From (No) Butter to Guns? Understanding the Economic Role in Transnational Terrorism." In *Terrorism, Economic Development, and Political Openness,* edited by Philip Keefer and Norman Loayza, 83–115. Cambridge: Cambridge University Press, 2009.

Blomberg, S. Brock, and Gregory D. Hess. "The Lexus and the Olive Branch." In *Terrorism, Economic Development, and Political Openness,* edited by Philip Keefer and Norman Loayza, 116–47. Cambridge: Cambridge University Press, 2009.

Blomberg, S. Brock, and Peter Rosendorff. "A Gravity Model of Globalization, Democracy and Transnational Terrorism." In *Guns and Butter,* edited by Gregory Hess, 125–56. Cambridge: MIT Press, 2009.

Bloom, Mia. *Bombshell: Women and Terror.* Philadelphia: University of Pennsylvania Press, 2011.

Bloom, Mia. *Dying to Kill: The Allure of Suicide Terror.* New York: Columbia University Press, 2007.

Bobbitt, Philip. *Terror and Consent: The Wars for the Twenty-First Century.* New York: Knopf, 2008.

Bolt, Paul J., Su Changhe, and Sharyl Cross, eds. *The United States, Russia, and China: Confronting Global Terrorism and Security Challenges in the 21st Century.* Westport, CT: Praeger Security International, 2008.

Brandt, Patrick, and Todd Sandler. "What Do Transnational Terrorists Target? Has It Changed? Are We Safer?" *Journal of Conflict Resolution* 54.2 (2010): 214–36.

Burleigh, Michael. *Blood and Rage: A Cultural History of Terrorism.* New York: HarperCollins, 2009.

Butterworth, Alex. *The World That Never Was: A True Story of Dreamers, Schemers, Anarchists and Secret Agents.* New York: Pantheon, 2010.

Caravelli, Jack. *Nuclear Insecurity: Understanding the Threat from Rogue Nations and Terrorists.* Westport, CT: Praeger Security International, 2007.

Ciment, James, ed. *World Terrorism: An Encyclopedia of Political Violence from Ancient Times to the Post–911 Era.* 3 vols. 2nd ed. Armonk, NY: Sharpe Reference, 2011.

Clauset, Aaron, and Ryan Woodard. "Estimating the Historical and Future Probabilities of Large Terrorist Events." *arXiv* 1209.0089v1 (September 1, 2012).

Combs, Cindy C. *Terrorism in the 21st Century.* 6th ed. Upper Saddle River, NJ: Pearson, 2010.

Commission on the Prevention of Weapons of Mass Destruction, Proliferation, and Terrorism. *World at Risk: The Report of the Commission on the Prevention of Weapons of Mass Destruction, Proliferation, and Terrorism.* New York: Vintage, 2008.

Cragin, R. Kim, and Sara A. Daly. *Women as Terrorists: Mothers, Recruiters, and Martyrs.* Santa Barbara: Praeger, 2009.

Cronin, Audrey. "How al-Qaida Ends: The Decline and Demise of Terrorist Groups." *International Security* 31.2 (2006): 7–48.

_____. *How Terrorism Ends: Understanding the Decline and Demise of Terrorist Campaigns.* Princeton: Princeton University Press, 2009.

Curry, Andrew. "The Mathematics of Terror." *Discover* July/August 2010: 38–43.

Davis, Paul K., and Kim Cragin. *Social Science for Counterterrorism: Putting the Pieces Together.* Santa Monica: RAND, 2009.

Drakos, Konstantinos. "Terrorism-Induced Structural Shifts in Financial Risk: Airline Stocks in the Aftermath of the September 11th Terror Attacks." *European Journal of Political Economy* 20.2 (2004): 436–46.

Drakos, Konstantinos, and Ali M. Kutan. "Regional Effects of Terrorism on Tourism in Three Mediterranean Countries." *Journal of Conflict Resolution* 47.5 (2003): 621–41.

Dugan, Laura, Gary LaFree, and E. Miller. "Organizational Trajectories of Terrorism Activity." Presentation at the American Society of Criminology Annual Meeting, Atlanta, November 2007.

Dugan, Laura, Gary LaFree, and A. Piquero. "Testing a Rational Choice Model of Airline Hijackings." *Criminology* 43 (2005): 1031–66.

Dzikansky, Mordecai, Gil Kleiman, and Robert Slater. *Terrorist Suicide Bombings: Attack Interdiction, Mitigation, and Response.* Boca Raton: CRC Press, 2012.

East-West Institute. "Countering Violent Extremism: Video-Power and Cyber-Space." *Report of the 5th Annual Security Conference of the East-West Institute,* 2008.

Enders, Walter, Todd Sandler, and Khusrav Gaibulloev. "Domestic versus Transnational Terrorism: Data, Decomposition, and Dynamics." *Journal of Peace Research* 48.3 (2011): 319–38.

Faure, Guy Olivier, and I. William Zartman, eds. *Negotiating with Terrorists: Strategy, Tactics, and Politics.* New York: Routledge, 2010.

Forest, James J. F. "Global Trends in Kidnapping by Terrorist Groups." *Global Change, Peace and Security* 24.3 (2012): 311–30.

Forest, James J. F. *Teaching Terror: Strategic and Tactical Learning in the Terrorist World.* Lanham, MD: Rowman and Littlefield, 2006.

Forest, James J. F., ed. *Influence Warfare: How Terrorists and Governments Fight to Shape Perceptions in a War of Ideas.* Santa Barbara: Praeger, 2009.

Frey, Bruno, and Dominic Rohner. "Protecting Cultural Monuments from Terrorism." *Defence and Peace Economics* 18.3 (2007): 245–52.

Galeotti, Mark. "Spirited Away: The Rise of Global Kidnapping Trends." *Jane's Intelligence Review* (April 2010).

Ganor, Boaz. "Terrorism as a Strategy of Psychological Warfare." *Journal of Aggression, Maltreatment, and Trauma* 9.1/2 (2005): 33–43.

Goerzig, Carolin. *Talking to Terrorists: Concessions and the Renunciation of Violence.* New York: Routledge, 2010.

Goldsmith, Benjamin E., and Yusaku Horiuchi. "Living with Hegemony: High and Low Crisis Periods and Perceptions of the U.S. in Global Public Opinion." Australasian Political Studies Association Meeting, Newcastle, Australia, September 2006.

Goulden, Joseph C. "Espionage, Terrorism, Oil, Propaganda and the Horrors of War: Intelligence Literature Reviews." *Intelligencer: Journal of U.S. Intelligence Studies* 16.2 (2008): 111–17.

Hassan, Riaz. *Life as a Weapon: The Global Rise of Suicide Bombings.* New York: Routledge, 2010.

Hawkesworth, Mary, and Karen Alexander, eds. *War and Terror: Feminist Perspectives.* Chicago: University of Chicago Press Journals, 2008.

Herridge, Catherine. *The Next Wave: On the Hunt for al Qaeda's American Recruits.* New York: Crown Forum, 2011.

Hoffman, Bruce. "The Myth of Grass-Roots Terrorism." *Foreign Affairs* 87.3 (2008).

Horgan, John. *Walking Away from Terrorism: Accounts of Disengagement from Radical and Extremist Movements.* New York: Routledge, 2009.

Jones, Seth G. *Hunting in the Shadows: The Pursuit of al Qa'ida Since 9/11.* New York: Norton, 2012.

Jones, Seth G., and Martin Libicki. *How Terrorist Groups End: Lessons for Countering al Qa'ida.* Santa Monica: RAND, 2008.

Khalsa, Sundri. *Forecasting Terrorism: Indicators and*

Proven Analytic Techniques. Lanham, MD: Scarecrow Press, 2004.

LaFree, Gary, and Laura Dugan. "Introducing the Global Terrorism Database." *Terrorism and Political Violence* 19 (2007): 181–204.

LaFree, Gary, and Laura Dugan. "Tracking Global Terrorism." In *To Protect and to Serve: Police and Policing in an Age of Terrorism*, edited by D. Weisburd, T. Feucht, I. Hakimi, L. Mock, and S. Perry. New York: Springer, 2009.

LaFree, Gary, and Laura Dugan. "Research on Terrorism and Countering Terrorism." In *Crime and Justice*, Vol. 38, edited by M. Tonry. Chicago: University of Chicago Press, 2009.

LaFree, Gary, Laura Dugan, and K. Cragin. "The State of Global Terrorism." In *Peace and Conflict*, edited by J. J. Hewitt, Jonathan Wilkenfeld, and Ted Robert Gurr. Boulder: Paradigm, 2009.

LaFree, Gary, and D. Franke. "The Impact of Legitimacy on Attitudes toward Terrorism." Paper presented at the annual meeting of the International Studies Association, Chicago, February 2007.

LaFree, Gary, Nancy A. Morris, and Laura Dugan. "Cross-National Patterns of Terrorism: Comparing Trajectories for Total, Attributed and Fatal Attacks, 1970–2006." *British Journal of Criminology* 50 (2010): 622–49.

LaFree, Gary, Nancy A. Morris, Laura Dugan, and S. Fahey. "Identifying Global Terrorist Hot Spots." In *Tangled Roots: Social and Psychological Factors in the Genesis of Terrorism*, edited by J. Victoroff, 98–114. Amsterdam: IOS Press, 2006.

LaFree, Gary, S. M. Yang, and Martha Crenshaw. "Trajectory of Terrorism: Attack Patterns of Foreign Groups That Have Targeted the United States, 1970 to 2004." *Criminology and Public Policy* 8 (2009): 445–73.

Lewis, Jeffrey William. *The Business of Martyrdom: A History of Suicide Bombing.* Annapolis: Naval Institute Press, 2012.

Likar, Lawrence E. *Eco-Warriors, Nihilistic Terrorists, and the Environment.* Santa Barbara: ABC-CLIO, 2011.

LoCicero, Alice, and Samuel J. Sinclair. *Creating Young Martyrs: Conditions That Make Dying in a Terrorist Attack Seem Like a Good Idea.* Westport, CT: Praeger Security International, 2008.

Lowther, Adam B., and Beverly Lindsay. *Terrorism in the 21st Century: Unanswered Questions.* Westport, CT: Praeger Security International, 2008.

Masse, Todd M. *Nuclear Jihad: A Clear and Present Danger?* Washington, DC: Potomac Books, 2011.

Matusitz, Jonathan. *Terrorism and Communication.* New York: Sage, 2012.

McCauley, Clark, and Sophia Moskalenko. *Friction: How Radicalization Happens to Them and Us.* New York: Oxford University Press, 2011.

Merari, Ariel. *Driven to Death: Psychological and So-cial Aspects of Suicide Terrorists.* New York: Oxford University Press, 2010.

Moghaddam, Fathali M. *The New Global Insecurity: How Terrorism, Environmental Collapse, Economic Inequalities, and Resource Shortages Are Changing Our World.* Santa Barbara: Praeger, 2010.

Mueller, John. "Six Rather Unusual Propositions About Terrorism." *Terrorism and Political Violence* 17 (2005): 487–505.

Mueller, John, and Mark Stewart. "Hardly Existential: Thinking Rationally About Terrorism." *Foreign Affairs,* 2 April 2010.

Mullins, Chris, and Joseph K. Young. "Cultures of Violence and Acts of Terror: Applying a Legitimation-Habituation Model to Terrorism." *Crime and Delinquency* 58.1 (2012): 28–56.

Nacos, Brigitte. *Terrorism and Counterterrorism.* 3rd ed. New York: Penguin, 2010.

National Counterterrorism Center. *Counterterrorism Calendar 2009.* Washington, DC: NCTC, 2009.

National Counterterrorism Center. *Counterterrorism Calendar 2010.* Washington, DC: NCTC, 2011.

National Counterterrorism Center. *2011 Report on Terrorism.* Washington, DC: NCTC, 2012.

Ness, Cindy D., ed. *Female Terrorism and Militancy: Agency, Utility, and Organization.* New York: Routledge, 2008.

Piazza, James. "Incubators of Terror: Do Failed and Failing States Promote Transnational Terrorism?" *International Studies Quarterly* 52 (2008): 469–88.

Pluchinsky, Dennis. "Ethnic Terrorism and Insurgencies." In *Understanding and Managing Insurgent Movements.* Singapore: Marshall Cavendish Academic, 2006.

_____, "Ethnic Terrorism: Themes and Variations." In *The Politics of Terror,* edited by Andrew Tan. London: Routledge, 2006.

_____. "The Evolution of the U.S. Government's Annual Report on Terrorism: A Personal Commentary." *Studies in Conflict and Terrorism* 29 (2006): 91–8.

_____. "The Migration of Terrorist Tactics, Techniques, and Creativity (TTC)." *Revue de L'Électricité et de L'Électonique* 10 (2007): 37–43.

_____. "Typology and Anatomy of Terrorist Operations." In *The McGraw-Hill Homeland Security Handbook,* edited by David Kamien, New York: McGraw-Hill, 2006.

Poindexter, John M. *The Closing of the Muslim Mind: How Intellectual Suicide Created the Modern Islamist Crisis.* Wilmington, DE: ISI Books, 2010.

Post, Jerrold. *The Mind of the Terrorist: The Psychology of Terrorism from the IRA to al-Qaeda.* New York: Palgrave Macmillan, 2007.

Poteat, Gene. "Maritime Security: Piracy and Terrorism." *Intelligencer: Journal of U.S. Intelligence Studies* 16.2 (2008): 118.

Price, Daniel E. *Sacred Terror: How Faith Becomes Lethal.* Santa Barbara: ABC-CLIO, 2012.

Sageman, Daniel E. *Leaderless Jihad: Terror Networks in the 21st Century.* Philadelphia: University of Pennsylvania Press, 2007.

Sandler, Todd, Daniel G. Arce, and Walter Enders. "Transnational Terrorism." In *Global Crises, Global Solutions.* 2nd ed., edited by Bjørn Lomborg, 516–62. Cambridge: Cambridge University Press, 2009.

Schmid, Alex P., ed. *The Routledge Handbook of Terrorism Research.* New York: Routledge, 2011.

Schultz, Richard H., Jr., and Andrea J. Dew. *Insurgents, Terrorists and Militias: The Warriors of Contemporary Combat.* New York: Columbia University Press, 2006.

Sinai, Joshua. "Radicalization into Extremism and Terrorism: A Conceptual Model." *Intelligencer: Journal of U.S. Intelligence Studies* 19 (2012): 21–5.

Sinai, Joshua. "Top 50 Books on Terrorism and Counterterrorism." *Intelligencer: Journal of U.S. Intelligence Studies.* 19.1 (2012): 105–8.

Skaine, Rosemary. *Suicide Warfare: Culture, the Military, and the Individual as a Weapon.* Santa Barbara: ABC-CLIO, 2013.

Smith, B. L., and K. R. Damphousse. "Terrorism in Time and Space." Paper presented at the American Association for the Advancement of Science Meeting, Boston, 2008.

Streatfield, Dominic. *A History of the World Since 9/11: Disaster, Deception, and Destruction in the War on Terror.* London: Bloomsbury, 2011.

Stern, Jessica. *Denial: A Memoir of Terror.* New York: Ecco, 2010.

Stevenson, Jonathan. *Thinking Beyond the Unthinkable: Harnessing Doom from the Cold War to the Age of Terror.* New York: Viking, 2008.

Stohl, Cynthia, and Michael Stohl. "Networks of Terror: Theoretical Assumptions and Pragmatic Consequences." *Communication Theory* 17.2 (2007): 93–124.

Stohl, Michael. "Don't Confuse Me with the Facts: Knowledge Claims and Terrorism." *Critical Studies on Terrorism* 5.1 (2012): 31–49.

Stohl, Michael. "State Terror: The Theoretical and Practical Utilities and Implications of a Contested Concept." In *Contemporary Debates on Terrorism,* edited by Richard Jackson and S. Justin Sinclair. Oxon: Routledge, 2011.

Stohl, Michael, and Peter Grabosky. *Crime and Terrorism.* London: Sage, 2010.

United States. Dept. of State. *Country Reports on Terrorism 2007.* Washington: GPO, 2008.

United States. Dept. of State. *Country Reports on Terrorism 2010.* Washington: GPO, 2011.

Verton, Dan. *Black Ice: The Invisible Threat of Cyber-Terrorism.* New York: McGraw-Hill Osborne Media, 2003.

Vittori, Jodi. *Terrorist Financing and Resourcing.* New York: Palgrave Macmillan, 2011.

Walker, Clive. *Terrorism and the Law.* New York: Oxford University Press, 2011.

Walton, Timothy. *Challenges in Intelligence Analysis: Lessons from 1300 BCE to the Present.* New York: Cambridge University Press, 2010.

Weinberg, Leonard. *The End of Terrorism?* New York: Routledge, 2011.

Young, Joseph K. "State Capacity, Democracy, and the Violation of Personal Integrity Rights." *Journal of Human Rights* 8.4 (2009): 283–300.

Young, Joseph K., and Laura Dugan. "Veto Players and Terror." *Journal of Peace Research* 48.1 (2010): 19–33.

Young, Joseph K., and Mike Findley. "Terrorism, Democracy, and Credible Commitments." *International Studies Quarterly* 55 (2011): 1–22.

Young, Joseph K., and David Siegel. "Simulating Terror: Credible Commitment, Costly Signaling, and Strategic Behavior." *PS: Politics & Political Science* 42.4 (2009): 765–71.

Africa

Eichstaedt, Peter. *First Kill Your Family: Child Soldiers of Uganda and the Lord's Resistance Army.* Chicago: Chicago Review Press, 2009.

Fowler, Robert. *A Season in Hell: My 130 Days in the Sahara with Al Qaeda.* New York: HarperCollins, 2011.

Gaibulloev, Khusrav, and Todd Sandler. "The Adverse Effect of Transnational and Domestic Terrorism on Growth in Africa." *Journal of Peace Research* 48.3 (2011): 355–71.

Prunier, Gerard. *Africa's World War: Congo, the Rwandan Genocide, and the Making of a Continental Catastrophe.* New York: Oxford University Press, 2011.

Raffaele, Paul. *Among the Cannibals: Adventures on the Trail of Man's Darkest Ritual.* Washington, DC: Smithsonian Institution, 2008.

Asia

Gaibulloev, Khusrav, and Todd Sandler. "The Impact of Terrorism and Conflicts on Growth in Asia." *Economics and Politics* 21.3 (2009): 359–83.

Hastings, Justin V. *No Man's Land: Globalization, Territory, and Clandestine Groups in Southeast Asia.* Ithaca: Cornell University Press, 2010.

Hiro, Dilip. *Apocalyptic Realm: Jihadists in South Asia.* New Haven: Yale University Press, 2012.

Jayasekara, S. "How the LTTE Was Destroyed." *Asian Conflict Reports* 6 (2009): 3–4.

Lieven, Anatol. *Pakistan: A Hard Country.* New York: Public Affairs, 2012.

Mahadevan, Prem. *The Politics of Counterterrorism in India: Strategic Intelligence and National Security in South Asia.* New York: Tauris, 2012.

Ramakrishna, Kumar. *Radical Pathways: Understanding Muslim Radicalization in Indonesia.* Santa Barbara: Praeger, 2009.

Reed, J. Todd, and Diana Raschke. *The ETIM: China's*

Islamic Militants and the Global Terrorist Threat. Santa Barbara: Praeger, 2010.

Ressa, Maria. *Seeds of Terror: An Eyewitness Account of al-Qaeda's Newest Center of Operations in Southeast Asia.* New York: Free Press, 2003.

Rohner, Dominic, and Bruno Frey. "Blood and Ink! The Common-Interest-Game Between Terrorists and the Media." *Public Choice* 133.1/2 (2007): 129–45.

Roy, Arundhati. *Walking with the Comrades.* New York: Penguin.

Samad, Yunas. *The Pakistan-US Conundrum: Jihadists, the Military and the People—The Struggle for Control.* New York: Columbia University Press, 2011.

Santos, Anne Noronha Dos. *Military Intervention and Secession in South Asia: The Cases of Bangladesh, Sri Lanka, Kashmir, and Punjab.* Westport, CT: Praeger Security International, 2007.

Singh, Bilveer. *The Talibanization of Southeast Asia: Losing the War on Terror to Islamist Extremists.* Westport, CT: Praeger Security International, 2007.

Subrahmanian, V. S., Aaron Mannes, Amy Sliva, Jana Shakarian, and John P. Dickerson. *Computational Analysis of Terrorist Groups: Lashkar-e-Taiba.* New York: Springer, 2012.

Tankel, Stephen. *Storming the World Stage: The Story of Lashkar-i-Taiba.* New York: Columbia University Press, 2011.

Europe

Aust, Stefan. *Baader-Meinhof: The Inside Story of the R.A.F,* translated by Anthea Bell. New York: Oxford University Press, 2009.

Barros, Carlos P., Jose Passos, and Luis A. Gil-Alana. "The Timing of ETA Terrorist Attacks." *Journal of Policy Modeling* 28 (2006): 335–46.

Bodansky, Yossef. *Chechen Jihad: Al-Qaeda's Training Ground and the Next Wave of Terror.* New York: Harper, 2007.

Bowen, Wayne H., and Jose E. Alvarez, eds. *A Military History of Modern Spain: From the Napoleonic Era to the International War on Terror.* Westport, CT: Praeger Security International, 2007.

Chenoweth, Erika. "Italy and the Red Brigades: The Success of Repentance Policy in Counterterrorism." In *Countering Terrorism and Insurgency in the 21st Century: International Perspectives,* edited by James J. F. Forest, 352–65. Westport, CT: Praeger, 2007.

Coolaet, Rik, ed. *Jihadi Terrorism and the Radicalisation Challenge: European and American Experiences.* 2nd ed. Burlington, VT: Ashgate, 2011.

Cummings, Richard. "Carlos the Jackal and the Bombing of Radio Free Europe/Radio Liberty in Munich." *Intelligencer: Journal of U.S. Intelligence Studies* 16.1 (2008): 41–54.

Demirel, Emin. *Al Qaeda Elements in Turkey.* n.p., 2008.

Dingley, James. *The IRA.* Santa Barbara: ABC-CLIO, 2012.

Dolnik, Adam. "The Siege of Beslan's School No. 1." In *Countering Terrorism and Insurgency in the 21st Century: International Perspectives,* edited by James J. F. Forest. Westport, CT: Praeger, 2007.

Dunlop, John B. *The 2002 Dubrovka and 2004 Beslan Hostage Crises.* Amsterdam: Ibidem-Verlag, 2006.

Foy, Michael T. *Michael Collins's Intelligence War: The Struggle Between the British and the IRA 1919–1921.* Stroud: History Press, 2008.

Gaibulloev, Khusrav, and Todd Sandler. "Growth Consequences of Terrorism in Western Europe." *Kyklos* 61.3 (2008): 411–24.

Greenbaum, R., Laura Dugan, and Gary LaFree. "The Impact of Terrorism on Italian Employment and Business Activity." *Urban Studies* 44 (2007): 1093–108.

Hahn, Gordon M. *Russia's Islamic Threat: Nationalism, Islam and Islamism.* New Haven: Yale University Press, 2007.

Hughes, James. *Chechnya: From Nationalism to Jihad.* Philadelphia: University of Pennsylvania Press, 2007.

Kopp, Magdalena. *Die Terrorjahre: Mein Leben an der Seite von Carlos.* Munich: DVA Sachbuch, 2007.

LaFree, Gary, Laura Dugan, and R. Korte. "The Impact of British Counter Terrorist Strategies on Political Violence in Northern Ireland: Comparing Deterrence and Backlash Models." *Criminology* 47 (2009): 17–45.

Large, David Clay. *Munich 1972: Tragedy, Terror, and Triumph at the Olympic Games.* New York: Rowman & Littlefield, 2012.

Leiken, Robert S. *Europe's Angry Muslims: The Revolt of the Second Generation.* London: Oxford University Press, 2012.

Mahon, Tom, and James J. Gillogly. *Decoding the IRA.* Cork: Mercier Press, 2008.

Merriman, John. *The Dynamite Club: How a Bombing in Fin-de-Siecle Paris Ignited the Age of Modern Terror.* New York: Houghton Mifflin Harcourt, 2009.

Murphy, Paul J. *Allah's Angels: Chechen Women in War.* Annapolis: Naval Institute Press, 2010.

Phillips, Timothy. *Beslan: The Tragedy of School No. 1.* London: Granta, 2008.

Robbins, James S. "Insurgent Seizure of an Urban Area: Grozny, 1996." In *Countering Terrorism and Insurgency in the 21st Century: International Perspectives,* edited by James J. F. Forest, 88–102. Westport, CT: Praeger, 2007.

Shlapentokh, Dmitry V. "Terrorism in Chechnya: An Assessment of Recent Works." *Intelligencer: Journal of U.S. Intelligence Studies* 16. 2 (2008): 97–100.

Silber, Mitchell D. *The Al Qaeda Factor: Plots Against the West.* Philadelphia: University of Pennsylvania Press, 2012.

Simcox, Robin. *Islamist Terrorism: The British Connections Radicalization, Linkage and Diversity: Cur-

rent Trends in Terrorism in Europe. Santa Monica: RAND, 2011.

Souleimanov, Emil. *An Endless War: The Russian-Chechen Conflict in Perspective.* Frankfurt: Oxford House, 2007.

Waugh, Billy. *Hunting the Jackal.* New York: Harper-Collins, 2004.

Widlanski, Michael. *Battle for Our Minds: Western Elites and the Terror Threat.* New York: Simon & Schuster, 2012.

Wright, Joanne. "Countering West Germany's Red Army Faction: What Can We Learn?" In *Countering Terrorism and Insurgency in the 21st Century: International Perspective,* edited by James J. F. Forest, 275–91. Westport, CT: Praeger, 2007.

Latin America

Araujo, Fernando. *El Trarecista.* Bogota: Planeta, 2008.

Artunduaga, Lucy. *The Love That Kidnapping Kills.* n.p., 2008.

Duncan, Gustavo. *Los Senores de La Guerra: De Paramilitares, Mafioses y Autodensas en Colombia (The Gentlemen of War).* Bogota: Planeta, 2006.

Gadea, Hilda. *My Life with Che: The Making of a Revolutionary.* New York: Palgrave Macmillan, 2008.

Gonsalves, Marc, Keith Stansell, and Tom Howes, with Gary Brozek. *Out of Captivity: Surviving 1,967 Days in the Colombian Jungle.* New York: Morrow, 2009.

Latell, Brian. *After Fidel: The Inside Story of Castro's Regime and Cuba's Next Leader.* New York: Palgrave Macmillan, 2005.

Moreno, Gustavo Bolivar, and Jorge Eduardo Gechem Turbay. *El Capo.* n.p., n.d.

Perez, Luis Eladio. *Held Hostage Seven Years by the FARC.* Bogota: Aguilar, 2008.

Pinchao, John Frank. *My Escape.* Bogota: Planeta, 2008.

Schoen, Douglas, and Michael Rowan. *The Threat Closer to Home: Huge Chavez and the War Against America.* New York: Free Press, 2009.

Middle East

Ackerman, Gary, and Jeremy Tamsett. *Jihadists and Weapons of Mass Destruction.* London: CRC, 2008.

Alexander, Matthew. *Kill or Capture: How a Special Operations Task Force Took Down a Notorious al Qaeda Terrorist.* New York: St. Martin's, 2011.

Al-Jamhi, Saeed Ali Obaid. *Al-Qaeda: Establishment, Ideological Background, and Continuity.* Cairo: Madbooli Press, 2007.

Amis, Martin. *The Second Plane: September 11: Terror and Boredom.* New York: Knopf, 2008.

Bawer, Brue. *Surrender: Appeasing Islam, Sacrificing Freedom.* New York: Doubleday, 2009.

Bergen, Peter L. *The Longest War: The Enduring Conflict Between America and al-Qaeda.* New York: Free Press, 2011.

Bergen, Peter L. *Manhunt: The Ten-Year Search for Bin Laden from 9/11 to Abbottabad.* New York: Crown, 2012.

Bergen, Peter L., and Katherine Tiedemann. "The Almanac of Al Qaeda: FP's Definitive Guide to What's Left of the Terrorist Group." *Foreign Policy* 179 (2010): n.p.

Bergen, Peter L., and Katherine Tiedemann. *Talibanistan: Negotiating the Borders Between Terror, Politics and Religion.* New York: Oxford University Press, 2013.

bin Laden, Najwa, Omar bin Laden, and Jean Sasson. *Growing Up Bin Laden: Osama's Wife and Son Take Us Inside Their Secret World.* New York: St. Martin's, 2009.

Blais, Allison, and Lynn Rasic. *A Place of Remembrance: The Official Book of the National September 11 Memorial* Washington, DC: National Geographic, 2011.

Blanford, Nicholas. *Warriors of God: Inside Hezbollah's Thirty-Year Struggle Against Israel.* New York: Random House, 2011.

Bradley, John R. *After the Arab Spring: How Islamists Hijacked the Middle East Revolts.* New York: Palgrave Macmillan, 2012.

Butt, Hassan, and Shiv Malik. *Leaving al Qaeda: Inside the Mind of a British Jihadist.* London: Constable and Robinson, 2008.

Cambanis, Thanassis. *A Privilege to Die: Inside Hezbollah's Legions and Their Endless War Against Israel.* New York: Free Press, 2010.

Cigar, Norman. *Al-Qa'ida's Doctrine for Insurgency: 'Abd al'-Aziz Al-Muqrin's "A Practical Course for Guerrilla War."* Washington, DC: Potomac Books, 2009.

Cockbur, Patrick. *Muqtada: Muqtada al-Sadr, the Shia Revival, and the Struggle for Iraq.* New York: Scribner, 2008.

Coll, Steve. *The Bin Ladens: An Arabian Family in the American Century.* New York: Penguin, 2008.

Eccarius-Kelly, Vera. *The Militant Kurds: A Dual Strategy for Freedom.* Santa Barbara: Praeger, 2010.

Evans, Harold. *My Paper Chase.* London: Little, Brown, 2009.

Evans, Martin, and John Phillips. *Algeria: Anger of the Dispossessed.* New Haven: Yale University Press, 2008.

Falk, Avner. *Islamic Terror: Conscious and Unconscious Motives.* Westport, CT: Praeger Security International, 2008.

Farral, L. "How al Qaeda Works: What the Organization's Subsidiaries Say about Its Strength." *Foreign Affairs* 90.2 (2011): 128–38.

Gartenstein-Ross, Daveed. *Bin Laden's Legacy: Why We're Still Losing the War on Terror.* New York: Wiley, 2011.

Gerges, Fawaz A. *The Rise and Fall of al Qaeda.* London: Oxford University Press, 2011.

Giustoizzi, Antonio, ed. *Decoding the New Taliban: Insights from the Afghan Field.* New York: Columbia University Press, 2010.

Gunaratna, Rohan. "Ideology in Terrorism and Counter Terrorism: Lessons from al-Qa'ida." In *The Ideological War on Terror: Worldwide Strategies for Counter-Terrorism,* edited by Anne Aldis and Graeme P. Herd, 21–34. London: Routledge, 2007.

Hafez, Mohammed M. *Suicide Bombers in Iraq: The Strategy and Ideology of Martyrdom.* Washington, DC: U.S. Institute of Peace Press, 2007.

Hafez, Mohammed M. "Suicide Terrorism in Iraq: A Preliminary Assessment of the Quantitative Data and Documentary Evidence." *Studies in Conflict and Terrorism* 29.6 (2006): 616–19.

Hastings, Michael. *The Operators: The Wild and Terrifying Inside Story of America's War in Afghanistan.* New York: Blue Rider Press, 2012.

Hertog, Steffen, and Diego Gambetta. *Engineers of Jihad.* Princeton: Princeton University Press, in preparation.

Hicks, David. *Guantanamo: My Journey.* North Sydney: William Heinemann, 2010.

Intel Center. *Afghanistan 2000–2007.* Terrorism Incident Reference Series. New York: Tempest, 2009.

Intel Center. *Algeria 2000–2007.* Terrorism Incident Reference Series. New York: Tempest, 2009.

Intel Center. *Al-Qaeda Messaging/Attacks Timeline 1992–2007.* New York: Tempest, 2009.

Intel Center. *Arabian Peninsula 2000–2007.* Terrorism Incident Reference Series. New York: Tempest, 2009.

Intel Center. *Iraq 2000–2005.* Terrorism Incident Reference Series. New York: Tempest, 2009.

Intel Center. *Iraq 2006.* Terrorism Incident Reference Series. New York: Tempest, 2009.

Intel Center. *Iraq 2007.* Terrorism Incident Reference Series. New York: Tempest, 2009.

Intel Center. *Pakistan 2000–2007.* Terrorism Incident Reference Series. New York: Tempest, 2009.

Intel Center. *Philippines 2000–2007.* Terrorism Incident Reference Series. New York: Tempest, 2009.

Intel Center. *Terrorist and Rebel Logo Identification Guide.* New York: Tempest, 2009.

Intel Center. *Words of Ayman al-Zawahiri.* Vol. 1. New York: Tempest, 2009.

Intel Center. *Words of Osama bin Laden.* Vol. 1. New York: Tempest, 2009.

Janjora, John W. *States Without Citizens: Understanding the Islamic Crisis.* Westport, CT: Praeger Security International, 2008.

Johnson, Gregory D. *The Last Refuge: Yemen, al-Qaeda, and America's War in Arabia.* New York: W.W. Norton, 2012.

Johnsen, Gregory D., and Brian O'Neill. "Islam and Insurgency in Yemen." *Waq el-Waq.* blogspot.com, n.d.

Jones, Seth G. "Think Again: al Qaeda." *Foreign Policy* (May/June 2012): 47–51.

Katz, Mark N. *Leaving Without Losing: The War on Terror After Iraq and Afghanistan.* Baltimore: Johns Hopkins University Press, 2012.

Keuh, Felix, and Faisal Devji. *Poetry of the Taliban.* London: C. Hurst, 2012.

Khan, Nyla Ali. *Islam, Women, and the Violence in Kashmir: Between India and Pakistan.* Westport, CT: Praeger Security International, 2008.

Khan, Samir. *Expectations Full.* Jihadi Manual. Internet. 2011.

Khurasani, Mukhtar. *Training Lessons or Better Preparation of the Mujahideen.* Terrorism Guide. Afghanistan: al Qaeda, 2008.

Kimmage, Daniel. "The Al Qaeda Media Nexus: The Virtual Network Behind the Global Message." Radio Free Europe/Radio Liberty Special Report, May 2008.

Koehler-Derrick, Gabriel. "The Abbottabad Documents: Bin Laden's Cautious Strategy in Yemen." *CTC Sentinel* 5.5 (2012): 15–18.

Kurzman, Charles. *The Missing Martyrs: Why There Are So Few Muslim Terrorists.* New York: Oxford University Press, 2011.

Lacey, Jim, ed. *The Canons of Jihad: Terrorists' Strategy for Defeating America.* Annapolis: Naval Institute Press, 2008.

Lacey, Jim, ed. *A Terrorist's Call to Global Jihad: Deciphering Abu Musab al-Suri's Islamic Jihad Manifesto.* Annapolis: Naval Institute Press, 2008.

Lacey, Robert. *Inside the Kingdom: Kings, Clerics, Modernists, Terrorists, and the Struggle for Saudi Arabia.* New York: Viking, 2009.

Lahoud, Nelly, Stuart Caudill, Liam Collins, Gabriel Koehler-Derrick, Don Rassler, and Muhammad al-'Ubaydi. *Letters from Abbottabad: Bin Ladin Sidelined?* West Point, NY: Combating Terrorism Center, 2012.

Lansford, Tom. *9/11 and the Wars in Afghanistan and Iraq: A Chronology and Reference Guide.* E-book. Santa Barbara: ABC-CLIO, 2011.

Lappin, Yaakov. *Virtual Caliphate: Exposing the Islamist State on the Internet.* Washington, DC: Potomac Books, 2010.

Curtis, Brian, ed. *The Legacy Letters: Messages of Life and Hope from 9/11 Family Members.* New York: Perigee, 2011.

Lentini, Pete, and Muhammad Bakashmar. "Jihadist Beheading: A Convergence of Technology, Theology and Teleology?" *Studies in Conflict and Terrorism* 30.4 (2007): 303–25.

Lia, Brynjar. *Architect of Global Jihad: The Life of Al Qaeda Strategist Abu Mus'ab al-Suri.* New York: Columbia University Press, 2008.

Lippold, Kurt. *Front Burner: Al Qaeda's Attack on the USS Cole.* New York: Public Affairs, 2012.

Maalouf, Amin. *Disordered World: Setting a New Course for the 21st Century.* London: Bloomsbury, 2011.

MacFarquhar, Neil. *The Media Relations Department*

of Hizbollah Wishes You a Happy Birthday: Unexpected Encounters in the Changing Middle East. New York: Public Affairs, 2009.

Mannes, Aaron. *Profiles in Terror: The Guide to Middle East Terrorist Organizations.* Lanham, MD: Rowman & Littlefield, 2004.

Marcus, Aliza. *Blood and Belief: The PKK and the Kurdish Fight for Independence.* New York: New York University Press, 2009.

McDermott, Terry, and Josh Meyer. *The Hunt for KSM: Inside the Pursuit and Takedown of the Real 9/11 Mastermind, Khalid Sheikh Mohammed.* New York: Little, Brown, 2012.

McGeough, Paul. *Kill Khalid: The Failed Mossad Assassination of Khalid Mishal and the Rise of Hamas.* New York: New Press, 2009.

McGregor, Andrew. "Will al-Qaeda Survive the Loss of Its Leadership?" *Terrorism Monitor* 8.24 (2010): n.p.

Miller, Flagg. "Object Lesson: Voices from Jihad." *Yale Alumni Magazine* 72.3 (2009): 48.

Mockaitis, Thomas R. *Iraq and the Challenge of Counterinsurgency.* Westport, CT: Praeger Security International, 2008.

Moghadam, Assaf, and Brian Fishman, eds. *Fault Lines in Global Jihad: Organizational, Strategic, and Ideological Fissures.* New York: Routledge, 2011.

Morgan, Matthew J. *A Democracy Is Born: An Insider's Account of the Battle Against Terrorism in Afghanistan.* Westport, CT: Praeger Security International, 2007.

Morris, Benny. *1948: A History of the First Arab–Israeli War.* New Haven: Yale University Press, 2008.

Mowatt-Larssen, Rolf. "Al-Qaeda's Pursuit of Weapons of Mass Destruction." *Foreign Policy* (2010, January 25): n.p. Web.

Nawaz, Shuja. *Crossed Swords: Pakistan, Its Army, and the Wars Within.* New York: Oxford University Press, 2008.

O'Hern, Steven. *Iran's Revolutionary Guard: The Threat That Grows While America Sleeps.* Washington, DC: Potomac Books, 2012.

Olsson, Peter Alan. *The Cult of Osama: Psychoanalyzing Bin Laden and His Magnetism for Muslim Youths.* Westport, CT: Praeger Security International, 2007.

Owen, Mark, and Kevin Maurer. *No Easy Day: The Firsthand Account of the Mission That Killed Osama bin Laden: The Autobiography of a Navy SEAL.* New York: Dutton, 2012.

Pedahzur, Ami. *The Israeli Secret Services and the Struggle Against Terrorism.* New York: Columbia University Press, 2009.

Peters, Gretchen. *Haqqani Network Financing: The Evolution of an Industry.* West Point, NY: Combating Terrorism Center, 2012.

Peters, Gretchen. *Seeds of Terror: How Drugs, Thugs, and Crime Are Reshaping the Afghan War.* New York: Thomas Dunne Books, 2009.

Phares, Walid. *The Confrontation: Winning the War Against Future Jihad.* New York: Palgrave Macmillan, 2008.

Pluchinsky, Dennis. "Global Jihadist Recidivism: A Red Flag." *Studies in Conflict and Terrorism* 31 (2008): 182–200.

Rashid, Ahmed. *Descent into Chaos: The United States and the Failure of Nation Building in Pakistan, Afghanistan, and Central Asia.* New York: Viking, 2008.

Raviv, Dan, and Yossi Melman. *Spies Against Armageddon: Inside Israel's Secret Wars.* Sea Cliff, NY: Levant Books, 2012.

Riedel, Bruce. *Deadly Embrace: Pakistan, America, and the Future of Global Jihad.* Washington, DC: Brookings Institution Press, 2011.

Riedel, Bruce. *The Search for al Qaeda: Its Leadership, Ideology and Future.* Washington, DC: Brookings Institution Press, 2008.

Ross, Michael, with Jonathan Kay. *The Volunteer: The Incredible True Story of an Israeli Spy on the Trail of International Terrorists.* New York: Skyhorse, 2007.

Scheuer, Michael. *Marching Toward Hell: America and Islam After Iraq.* New York: Free Press, 2008.

Scheuer, Michael. *Osama bin Laden.* New York: Oxford University Press, 2011.

Schmitt, Eric, and Thom Shanker. *Counterstrike: The Untold Story of America's Secret Campaign Against Al Qaeda.* New York: Times Books, 2011.

Scroggin, Deborah. *Wanted Women: Faith, Lies, and the War on Terror: The Lives of Ayaan Hiri Ali and Aafia Siddiqui.* New York: Harper.

Shanty, Frank. *The Nexus: International Terrorism and Drug Trafficking from Afghanistan.* Santa Barbara: ABC-CLIO, 2011.

Shay, Shaul. *Islamic Terror Abductions in the Middle East.* Brighton, UK: Sussex Academic Press, 2007.

Sheikh, Naveed S. *Saudi State, Wahhabi World: The Globalization of Muslim Radicalism.* Westport, CT: Praeger Security International, 2010.

Skalka, Jennifer. "Silent Stars: The Secretive Life of Jennifer Matthews and an Inside Look at a Bloody, Unfinished War." *Intelligencer: Journal of U.S. Intelligence Studies* 19.1 (2012): 25–34.

Smith, Clive Stafford. *Eight O'Clock Ferry to the Windward Side: Seeking Justice in Guantanamo Bay.* New York: Nation Books, 2008.

Springer, Devin R., James L. Regens, and David N. Edger. *Islamic Radicalism and Global Jihad.* Washington, DC: Georgetown University Press, 2009.

Stout, Mark E., Jessica M. Huckabey, and John R. Schindler, with Jim Lacey. *The Terrorist Perspectives Project: Strategic and Operational Views of al Qaida and Associated Movements.* Annapolis: Naval Institute Press.

Strozier, Charles N. *Until the Fires Stopped Burning.* New York: Columbia University Press, 2011.

Summers, Anthony, and Robbyn Swa. *The Eleventh Day: The Full Story of 9/11 and Osama Bin Laden.* New York: Ballantine, 2011.

Tomsen, Peter. *The Wars of Afghanistan: Messianic Terrorism, Tribal Conflicts, and the Failures of Great Powers.* New York: Public Affairs, 2011.

Tribute WTC Visitor Center. *9/11: The World Speaks.* Guilford, CT: Lyons Press, 2011.

Tschirgi, Dan. *Turning Point: The Arab World's Marginalization and International Security After 9/11.* Westport, CT: Praeger Security International, 2007.

Tyler, Patrick. *A World of Trouble: The White House and the Middle East—From the Cold War to the War on Terror.* New York: Farrar, Straus and Giroux, 2009.

Van Dyk, Jere. *Captive: My Time as a Prisoner of the Taliban.* New York: St. Martin's Griffin, 2011.

Warrick, Joby. *The Triple Agent: The al Qaeda Mole Who Infiltrated the CIA.* New York: Doubleday, 2011.

Weiss, Deborah. *Saudi Arabia and the Global Islamist Terrorist Network.* New York: Palgrave Macmillan, 2011.

Williams, Phil. *Criminals, Militias and Insurgents: Organized Crime in Iraq.* Carlisle, PA: U.S. Army War College, Strategic Studies Institute, 2009.

Wissing, Douglas A. *Funding the Enemy: How U.S. Taxpayers Bankroll the Taliban.* Amherst, NY: Prometheus Books, 2012.

Wolfe, Wojtek Mackiewicz. *Winning the War of Words: Selling the War on Terror from Afghanistan to Iraq.* Westport, CT: Praeger Security International, 2008.

Wright, Robin. *Rock the Casbah: Rage and Rebellion Across the Islamic World.* New York: Simon & Schuster, 2011.

Yousef, Mosab Hassan, and Ron Brackin. *Son of Hamas: A Gripping Account of Terror, Betrayal, Political Intrigue, and Unthinkable Choices.* Carol Stream, IL: SaltRiver/Tyndale, 2010.

Zaeef, Abdul Salam. *My Life with the Taliban*, edited by Alex Strick van Linschoten and Felix Kuehn. New York: Columbia University Press, 2010.

United States/North America

Albarus, Carmeta. *The Making of Lee Boyd Malvo: The D.C. Sniper.* New York: Columbia University Press, 2012.

Alexander, Yonah. *Terrorists in Our Midst: Combating Foreign-Affinity Terrorism in America.* Santa Barbara: Praeger, 2010.

Asal, Victor, R. K. Rethemeyer, Ian Anderson, Jeff Rizzo, Matthew M Rozea, and Allyson Stein. "The Softest of Targets: A Study of Terrorist Target Selection." *Journal of Applied Security Research* 4.3 (2009): 258–278.

Atkins, Stephen E. *The 9/11 Encyclopedia.* Westport, CT: Praeger Security International, 2008.

Bartoletti, Susan Campbell. *They Called Themselves the K.K.K.: The Birth of an American Terrorist Group.* New York: Houghton Mifflin, 2010.

Benfante, Michael, and Dave Hollande. *Reluctant Hero: A 9/11 Survivor Speaks Out About That Unthinkable Day, What He's Learned, How He's Struggled, and What No One Should Ever Forget.* New York: Skyhorse, 2011.

Bergen, Peter, and Bruce Hoffman. *Assessing the Terrorist Threat.* Report of the Bipartisan Policy Center's National Security Preparedness Group. Collingdale, PA: Diane, 2010.

Berger, J. M. *Jihad Joe: Americans Who Go to War in the Name of Islam.* Washington, DC: Potomac Books, 2011.

Boykin, William J., Harry Edward Soyster, Henry Cooper, Stephen C. Coughlin, Michael Del Rosso, John Guandolo, Clare M. Lopez, Andrew C. McCarthy, Patrick Poole, Joseph E. Schmitz, Tom Trento, J. Michael Waller, Diana West, R. James Woolsey, Brian Kennedy, and Frank J. Gaffney, Jr. *Shariah: The Threat to America: An Exercise in Competitive Analysis, Report of Team B II.* Washington, DC: Center for Security Policy, 2010.

Bullaty, Sonja, Angelo Lomeo, and Paul Goldberger. *The World Trade Center Remembered.* New York: Abbeville, 2011.

Castagnera, James Ottavio. *Al-Qaeda Goes to College: Impact of the War on Terror on American Higher Education.* Santa Barbara: Praeger, 2009.

CBS News. *What We Saw: The Events of September 11, 2001, in Words, Pictures, and Video.* New York: Simon & Schuster, 2011.

Chomsky, Noam. *9/11: Was There an Alternative?* New York: Seven Stories, 2011.

Clark, Mary Marshall, Peter Bearman, Catherine Ellis, and Stephen Drury Smith, eds. *After the Fall: New Yorkers Remember September 2001 and the Years That Followed.* New York: New Press, 2011.

Cooper, Martha. *Remembering 9/11.* New York: Mark Batty, 2011.

Curtis, Brian. *The Legacy Letters: Messages of Life and Hope from 9/11 Family Members.* New York: Perigee, 2011.

Darton, Eric. *Divided We Stand: A Biography of the World Trade Center.* New York: Basic, 2011.

Davis, Danny W. *The Phinehas Priesthood: Violent Vanguard of the Christian Identity Movement.* Santa Barbara: Praeger, 2010.

Dunbar, David, and Brad Reagan, eds. *Debunking 9/11 Myths: Why Conspiracy Theories Can't Stand Up to the Facts.* New York: Hearst, 2011.

Dunleavy, Patrick J. *The Fertile Soil of Jihad: Terrorism's Prison Connection.* Washington, DC: Potomac Books, 2011.

Dwyer, Jim, and Kevin Flynn. *102 Minutes: The Unforgettable Story of the Fight to Survive Inside the Twin Towers.* New York: Times, 2011.

Eisner, Harvey, ed. *WTC: In Their Own Words—A Highly Detailed, In-Depth Look at the Response to the Worst Terrorist Attack on American Soil on September 11, 2001.* New York: Cygnus Business Media, 2011.

Evans, Jocelyn J. *One Nation Under Siege: Congress, Terrorism, and the Fate of American Democracy.* Lexington: University Press of Kentucky, 2012.

FDNY Foundation. *FDNY 2001–2011: A Decade of Remembrance and Resilience.* New York: M. T., 2011.

Gage, Beverly. *The Day Wall Street Exploded: A Story of America in Its First Age of Terror.* New York: Oxford University Press, 2009.

Gray, Geoffrey. *Skyjack: The Hunt for D.B. Cooper.* New York: Crown, 2011.

Guillemin, Jeanne. *American Anthrax: Fear, Crime, and the Investigation of the Nation's Deadliest Bioterror Attack.* New York: Henry Holt, 2011.

Gumbel, Andrew, and Roger G. Charles. *Oklahoma City.* New York: Morrow, 2012.

Harris, Shane. "Interview with John Brennan, Former Director, National Counterterrorism Center—Advisor to Barack Obama." *Intelligencer: Journal of U.S. Intelligence Studies* 16.1 (2008): 7–10.

Hawley, Kip, and Nathan Means. *Permanent Emergency: Inside the TSA and the Fight for the Future of American Security.* New York: Palgrave Macmillan, 2012.

Herridge, Catherine. *The Next Wave: On the Hunt for al Qaeda's American Recruits.* New York: Crown Forum, 2011.

Hewitt, Christopher. *Catching Terrorists in America.* Santa Barbara: Praeger, 2010.

Hingson, Michael, with Susy Flory. *Thunder Dog: The True Story of a Blind Man, His Guide Dog and the Triumph of Trust at Ground Zero.* New York: Thomas Nelson, 2011.

Hunter, Stephen, and John Bainbridge, Jr. *American Gunfight: The Plot to Kill Harry Truman and the Shoot-Out That Stopped It.* New York: Simon & Schuster, 2005.

Ito, Harumi, and Darin Lee. "Assessing the Impact of the September 11th Terrorist Attacks on U.S. Airline Demand." *Journal of Economics and Business* 57.1 (2005): 75–95.

Jefferis, Jennifer. *Armed for Life: The Army of God and Anti-Abortion Terror in the United States.* Santa Barbara: ABC-CLIO, 2011.

Jenkins, Brian Michael, and John Paul Godges, eds. *The Long Shadow of 9/11: America's Response to Terrorism.* Santa Monica: RAND, 2011.

Johnson, Dennis Loy, and Valerie Merians. *Poetry After 9/11: An Anthology of New York Poets.* New York: Melville House, 2011.

Kaczynski, David. "My Brother Ted: Long Before Ted Kaczynski Became the Unabomber." *Playboy* 56.3 (2009): 36–38, 98–101.

Kessler, Ron. *The Secrets of the FBI.* New York: Crown, 2011.

Lance, Peter. "The Spy Who Came in for the Heat." *Playboy* 57.8 (2010): 46–8, 118–22.

Levi, Michael, and Graham Allison. "How Likely Is a Nuclear Terrorist Attack on the United States? A Discussion." *Intelligencer: Journal of U.S. Intelligence Studies* 16.2 (2008): 23–6.

Life Magazine. *One Nation: America Remembers September 11, 2001, Ten Years Later.* New York: Little, Brown, 2011.

Likar, Lawrence E. *Eco-Warriors, Nihilistic Terrorists and the Environment.* Westport, CT: Praeger, 2011.

Lioy, Paul J. *Dust: The Inside Story of Its Role in the September 11th Aftermath.* Lanham, MD: Rowman & Littlefield, 2011.

Luft, Benjamin J. *We're Not Leaving: 9/11 Responders Tell Their Stories of Courage, Sacrifice and Renewal.* New York: Greenpoint, 2011.

Manning, Lauren. *Unmeasured Strength.* New York: Henry Holt, 2011.

McEneaney, Bonnie. *Messages: Signs, Visits, and Premonitions from Loved Ones Lost on 9/11.* New York: Harper, 2011.

Millard, Candice. *Destiny of the Republic: A Tale of Madness, Medicine and the Murder of a President.* New York: Doubleday, 2012.

Miller, Scott. *The President and the Assassin: McKinley, Terror, and the Empire at the Dawn of the American Century.* New York: Random House, 2011.

Neumayer, Eric, and Thomas Plumper. "Foreign Terror on Americans." *Journal of Peace Research* 48.1 (2011): 3–17.

New York Police Department Intelligence Division. *Radicalization in the West: The Homegrown Threat.* New York: NYPD, 2007.

9/11 Ten Years Later. Spec. issue of *Granta* 116 (2011): n.p.

Rascoff, Samuel. "The Law of Homegrown (Counter) Terrorism." *Texas Law Review* 88.7 (2010): 1715.

Rollins, John. *American Jihadist Terrorism: Combating a Complex Threat.* Washington, DC: Congressional Research Service, 2010.

Rudd, Mark. *Underground: My Life with SDS and the Weathermen.* New York: Morrow, 2009.

Secunda, Eugene, and Terence P. Moran. *Selling War to America: From the Spanish American War to the Global War on Terror.* Westport, CT: Praeger Security International, 2007.

Shenon, Philip. *The Commission: The Uncensored History of the 9/11 Commission.* New York: Twelve, 2008.

Silber, Mitchell, and Arvin Bhatt. "Radicalization and the West: The Homegrown Threat." Paper presented at the 26th Annual Government and Industry Conference on International Terrorism of the American Society for Industrial Security (ASIS-International), Miami, Florida, March 17, 2008.

Sides, Hampton. *Hellhound on His Trail: The Stalking of Martin Luther King, Jr., and the International Hunt for His Assassin.* New York: Doubleday, 2010.

Smith, Dennis, with Deirdre Smith. *A Decade of Hope: Stories of Grief and Endurance from 9/11 Families and Friends.* New York: Viking, 2011.

Soufan, Ali H., with Daniel Freedman. *The Black Ban-*

ners: *The Inside Story of 9/11 and the War Against al-Qaeda*. New York: Norton, 2011.

Stern, Robin, and Courtney E. Martin. *Project Rebirth: Survival and the Strength of the Human Spirit from 9/11 Survivors*. New York: Dutton, 2011.

Strozier, Charles B. *Until the Fires Stopped Burning: 9/11 and New York City in the Words and Experiences of Survivors and Witnesses*. New York: Columbia University Press, 2011.

Takacs, Stacy. *Terrorism TV: Popular Entertainment in Post–9/11 America*. Lawrence: University of Kansas, 2012.

Temple-Raston, Dina, and Marguerite Gavin. *The Jihad Next Door: The Lackawanna Six and Rough Justice in the Age of Terror*. New York: Public Affairs, 2007.

Torres, Frances. *Memory Remains: 9/11 Artifacts at Hangar 17*. New York: National Geographic, 2011.

Triller, Marie. *Ten Years: Remembering 9/11*. New York: John Isaacs, 2011.

Trulson, Jennifer Gardner. *Where You Left Me: A Memoir*. New York: Gallery, 2011.

United States. Senate Committee on Homeland Security and Governmental Affairs. *A Ticking Time Bomb: Counterterrorism Lessons from the U.S. Government's Failure to Prevent the Fort Hood Attack*. Washington, DC: GPO, 2011.

United States. Senate Committee on Homeland Security and Governmental Affairs. *Violent Islamist Extremism, the Internet, and the Homegrown Terrorist Threat*. Washington, DC: GPO, 2008.

Welsh-Huggins, Andrew. *Hatred at Home: Al Qaida on Trial in the American Midwest*. Athens: Ohio University Press, 2011.

Willman, Andrew. *The Mirage Man: Bruce Ivins, the Anthrax Attacks, and America's Rush to War*. New York: Bantam, 2011.

Zagat, Tim, comp. *9/11: Stories of Courage, Heroism and Generosity*. New York: Zagat Survey, 2011.

Zegart, Amy. *Spying Blind: The CIA, the FBI, and the Origins of 9/11*. Princeton: Princeton University Press, 2009.

Responses

Abrams, Norman. *Anti-Terrorism and Criminal Enforcement*. 4th ed. St. Paul: West, 2012.

Alden, Edward. *The Closing of the American Border: Terrorism, Immigration and Security Since 9/11*. New York: Harper Perennial, 2009.

Alexander, Matthew, and John R. Bruning. *How to Break a Terrorist: The U.S. Interrogators Who Used Brains, Not Brutality, to Take Down the Deadliest Man in Iraq*. New York: St. Martin's Griffin, 2011.

Alexander, Yonah. "United States." In *Counterterrorism Strategies: Successes and Failures of Six Nations*, edited by Yonah Alexander, 9–43. Washington, DC: Potomac Books, 2006.

Alexander, Yonah, and Michael B. Kraft, eds. *Evolu-*

tion of U.S. Counterterrorism Policy. 3 vols. Westport, CT: Praeger Security International, 2007.

Anderson, Sean, and Peter Spagnolo. "The *Achille Lauro* Hijacking." In *Countering Terrorism and Insurgency in the 21st Century: International Perspectives*, edited by James J. F. Forest. Westport, CT: Praeger, 2007.

Art, Robert J., and Louise Richardson. *Democracy and Counterterrorism: Lessons from the Past*. Washington, DC: U.S. Institute of Peace Press, 2007.

Baker, John, Meghan Wool, Adrian Smith, Jerome Kahan, Clarke Ansel, Philip Hammar, David McGarvey, Matthew Phillips. *Risk Analysis and Intelligence Communities Collaborative Framework*. Arlington, VA: Homeland Security Institute, 2009.

Baker, Stewart. *Skating on Stilts: Why We Aren't Stopping Tomorrow's Terrorism*. Stanford: Hoover Institution, 2010.

Bamford, James. *The Shadow Factory: The Ultra-Secret NSA from 9/11 to the Eavesdropping on America*. New York: Doubleday, 2008.

Ben-Veniste, Richard. *The Emperor's New Clothes: Exposing the Truth from Watergate to 9/11*. New York: Thomas Dunne, 2009.

Bennett, Gina M. *National Security Mom: Why "Going Soft" Will Make America Strong*. Deadwood, OR: Wyatt-McKenzie, 2008.

Bjoro, Tore, and John Horgan, eds. *Leaving Terrorism Behind: Individual and Collective Disengagement*. New York: Routledge, 2009.

Bobbitt, Philip. *Terror and Consent: The Wars for the Twenty-First Century*. New York: Knopf, 2008.

Bock, Andreas M. "Containment Revived: An Alternative Way to Cope with Terrorism." *Journal of Strategic Security* 2.1 (2009): 25–38.

Bonner, David. *Executive Measures, Terrorism, and National Security—Have the Rules of the Game Changed?* Aldershot, UK: Ashgate, 2007.

Bowden, Mark. *The Finish: The Killing of Osama bin Laden*. New York: Grove/Atlantic, 2012.

Bracken, Paul, Ian Bremmer, and David Gordon, eds. *Managing Strategic Surprise: Lessons from Risk Management and Risk Assessment*. New York: Cambridge University Press, 2008.

Brandt, Patrick, and Todd Sandler. "Hostage Taking: Understanding Terrorism Event Dynamics." *Journal of Policy Modeling* 31.5 (2009): 758–78.

Brzezinski, Zbigniew. "The Simple Power of Weakness, the Complex Vulnerability of Power." In *After Terror: Promoting Dialogue Among Civilizations*, edited by Akbar Ahmed and Brian Forst, 15–20. Cambridge, MA: Polity Press, 2005.

Bush, George W. *Decision Points*. New York: Crown/Random House, 2010.

Byman, Daniel. "Biggest Think: All of Our Ideas About Terrorism Are Wrong, a Scholar Argues." *Washington Post Book World* 20 April 2008: 2.

Byman, Daniel. *The Five Front War: The Better Way to Fight Global Jihad*. New York: Wiley, 2007.

Byman, Daniel. "U.S. Counter-Terrorism Options: A Taxonomy." *Survival* 49.3 (2007): 121–50.

Chermak, Steven M., Joshua D. Freilich, and David Caspi. "Policymakers and Law Enforcement Must Consider the Unintended Consequences of Their Proposed Interventions/Responses to Extremist and Terrorist Groups." In *Contemporary Issues in Criminal Justice Policy: Policy Proposals from the American Society of Criminology Conference,* edited by N. D. Frost, J. D. Freilich, and T. R. Clear, 139–150. New York: Wadsworth, 2010.

Chertoff, Michael. *Homeland Security: Assessing the First Five Years.* Philadelphia: University of Pennsylvania Press, 2009.

Cole, J. Michael. *Smokescreen: Canadian Security Intelligence After September 11, 2001.* iUniverse, 2008.

Collins, Pamela A., and Ryan K. Baggett. *Homeland Security and Critical Infrastructure Protection.* Santa Barbara: Praeger, 2009.

Coombs, W. Timothy. *PSI Handbook of Business Security.* 2 vols. Westport, CT: Praeger Security International, 2008.

Corn, David. *Showdown: The Inside Story of How Obama Fought Back Against Boehner, Cantor, and the Tea Party.* New York: Morrow, 2012.

Creed, Patrick, and Rick Newman. *Firefight: Inside the Battle to Save the Pentagon on 9/11.* New York: Ballantine, 2008.

Crumpton, Henry A. *The Art of Intelligence: Lessons from a Life in the CIA's Clandestine Service.* New York: Penguin, 2012.

Cummings, Melanie C., David C. McGarvey, and Peter M. Vinch. *Homeland Security Risk Assessment, Volume II: Methods, Techniques, and Tools.* Arlington, VA: Homeland Security Institute, 2006.

Darby, Joseph. "The Death of Osama bin Laden and Its Discontents." *Intelligencer: Journal of U.S. Intelligence Studies* 18.3 (2011) 7–10.

Dershowitz, Alan. *Finding Jefferson: A Lost Letter, a Remarkable Discovery, and the First Amendment in an Age of Terrorism.* New York: Wiley, 2007.

Dickey, Christopher. *Securing the City: Inside America's Best Counterterror Force—The NYPD.* New York: Simon & Schuster, 2009.

Doln, Adam, and Keith M. Fitzgerald. *Negotiating Hostage Crises with the New Terrorists.* Westport, CT: Praeger Security International, 2007.

Dorin, Adam Frederic. *Jihad and American Medicine: Thinking Like a Terrorist to Anticipate Attacks via Our Health System.* Westport, CT: Praeger Security International, 2007.

Eichenwald, Kurt. *500 Days: Secrets and Lies in the Terror Wars.* New York: Touchstone, 2012.

Ellis, James O. "Countering Terrorism with Knowledge." In *Terrorism Informatics: Knowledge Management and Data Mining for Homeland Security,* edited by Hsinchun Chen, Edna Reid, Joshua Sinai, Andrew Silke, and Boaz Ganor, 141–155. New York: Springer, 2008.

Ellis, James O. "Foreword." In *Terrorism and Global Security (Global Issues),* edited by Anne E. Robertson. New York: Facts on File, 2007.

Ellis, James O. "MIPT: Sharing Terrorism Information Resources." In *Intelligence and Security Informatics, Second Symposium on Intelligence and Security Informatics,* ISI Proceedings, 520–25. Berlin: Springer, 2004.

Ellis, James O. "Yesterday's News? The WMD Threat Today." In *Terrorism: Research, Readings, and Realities,* edited by Lynne L. Snowden and Bradley C. Whitsel. Upper Saddle River, NJ: Pearson Prentice Hall, 2005.

Ellis, James O., ed. *Terrorism: What's Coming: The Mutating Threat,* Introduction by Brian Jenkins. Contributions from Martha Crenshaw, Alex Schmid, L. Weinberg, B. Ganor, G. Gorriti, and Rohan Gunaratna. Oklahoma City: Memorial Institute for the Prevention of Terrorism (MIPT), 2007.

Feingold, Russ. *While America Sleeps: A Wake-Up Call for the Post–9/11 Era.* New York: Crown, 2010.

Feste, Karen. *Terminate Terrorism: Framing, Gaming, and Negotiating Conflicts.* Boulder: Paradigm, 2010.

Forst, Brian. *Terrorism, Crime, and Public Policy.* New York: Cambridge University Press, 2009.

Frey, Bruno S. *Dealing with Terrorism—Stick or Carrot?* London: Edward Elgar, 2004.

Gaffney, Frank J. "The Leaker Shield Act—Its Impact on Crime and Counterterrorism Investigations." *Intelligencer: Journal of U.S. Intelligence Studies* 16.1 (2008): 15–20.

Gaibulloev, Khusrav, and Todd Sandler. "Hostage Taking: Determinants of Terrorist Logistical and Negotiation Success." *Journal of Peace Research* 46.6 (2009): 739–56.

Ganor, Boaz. *The Counter-Terrorism Puzzle: A Guide for Decision Makers.* New Brunswick: Transaction, 2005.

Goldsmith, Jack. *Power and Constraint: The Accountable Presidency After 9/11.* New York: Norton, 2012.

Govier, Trudy. *A Delicate Balance: What Philosophy Can Tell Us About Terrorism.* Oxford: Basic Books, 2002.

de Graaf, Beatrice. *Evaluating Counterterrorism Performance: A Comparative Study.* New York; Routledge, 2011.

Graff, Garrett M. *The Threat Matrix: The FBI at War in the Age of Terror.* Boston: Little, Brown, 2011.

Graham, Thomas, Jr. *Unending Crisis: National Security Policy After 9/11.* Seattle: University of Washington Press, 2012.

Halliday, Fred. *Shocked and Awed: A Dictionary of the War on Terror.* Berkeley: University of California Press, 2011.

Hammer, Mitchell R. *Saving Lives: The S.A.F.E. Model for Resolving Hostage and Crisis Incidents.* Westport, CT: Praeger Security International, 2007.

Harmon, Christopher, Andrew Pratt, and Sebastian

Gorka. *Toward a Grand Strategy Against Terrorism.* New York: McGraw-Hill, 2010.

Harris, Shane. "Killer App: Have a Bunch of Silicon Valley Geeks Figured Out How to Stop Terrorists?" *Washingtonian* February 2012: 71–108.

Herman, Susan N., and Paul Finkelman, eds. *Terrorism, Government, and Law: National Authority and Local Autonomy in the War on Terror.* Westport, CT: Praeger Security International, 2008.

Howard, Russell D., Reid L. Sawyer, and Natasha E. Bajema. *Terrorism and Counterterrorism: Understanding the New Security Environment.* 3rd ed. New York: McGraw-Hill, 2009.

Jackson, Lee. "Increased Emphasis on Security U.S. Ports from Terrorist Attacks." *Defense Transportation Journal* 62.6 (2007): n.p.

Jenkins, Brian Michael. *Unconquerable Nation: Knowing Our Enemy, Strengthening Ourselves.* Santa Monica: RAND, 2006.

Johnson, Thomas A. *The War on Terrorism: A Collision of Value, Strategies, and Societies.* London: CRC, 2008.

Johnson, Thomas A., ed. *National Security Issues in Science, Law, and Technology: Confronting Weapons of Terrorism.* London: CRC, 2007.

Johnston, Douglas M., Jr. *Religion, Terror, and Error: U.S. Foreign Policy and the Challenge of Spiritual Engagement.* Santa Barbara: ABC-CLIO, 2011.

Johnston, R. William. *Bioterror: Anthrax, Influenza, and the Future of Public Health Security.* Westport, CT: Praeger Security International, 2008.

Jones, Seth, and Martin Libicki. *How Terrorist Groups End: Lessons for Countering al-Qaeda.* Santa Monica: RAND, 2008.

Kahn, Laura H. *Who's in Charge? Leadership During Epidemics, Bioterror Attacks, and Other Public Health Crises.* Santa Barbara: Praeger, 2009.

Kessler, Ronald. *The Terrorist Watch: Inside the Desperate Race to Stop the Next Attack.* New York: Crown Forum, 2007.

Kiriakou, John, with Michael Ruby. *The Reluctant Spy: My Secret Life in the CIA's War on Terror.* New York: Bantam, 2010.

Klaidman, Daniel. *Kill or Capture: The War on Terror and the Soul of the Obama Presidency.* New York: Houghton Mifflin Harcourt, 2012.

Knowles, Scott Gabriel. *The Disaster Experts: Mastering Risk in Modern America.* Philadelphia: University of Pennsylvania Press, 2011.

Kraft, Michael B., and Edward Marks. *U.S. Government Counterterrorism: A Guide to Who Does What.* Boca Raton: CRC Press, 2012.

Lichtblau, Eric. *Bush's Law: The Remaking of American Justice.* New York: Pantheon Books, 2008.

Linnan, David K., ed. *Enemy Combatants, Terrorism, and Armed Conflict Law: A Guide to the Issues.* Westport, CT: Praeger Security International, 2008.

Mahler, Jonathan. *The Challenge: Hamdan v. Rumsfeld and the Fight Over Presidential Power.* New York: Farrar, Straus and Giroux, 2008.

Makowski, Alexander. *Ferreting Out Bin Laden.* Poland: n.p., 2012.

Mandel, Robert. *Global Threat: Target-Centered Assessment and Management.* Westport, CT: Praeger Security International, 2008.

Mayer, Jane. *The Dark Side: The Inside Story of How the War on Terror Turned into a War on American Ideals.* New York: Doubleday, 2008.

Mendelso, Sarah. *Closing Guantanamo: From Bumper Sticker to Blue Print.* Washington, DC: Center for Strategic and International Studies, 2008.

Miles, Stephen. *Oath Betrayed: Torture, Medical Complicity, and the War on Terror.* New York: Random House, 2006.

Moghaddam, Fathali M. *How Globalization Spurs Terrorism: The Lopsided Benefits of "One World" and Why That Fuels Violence.* Westport, CT: Praeger Security International, 2008.

Mueller, Robert S., III. "Combating Threats in the Cyber World—Outsmarting Terrorists, Hackers, and Spies." *Intelligencer: Journal of U.S. Intelligence Studies* 19.1 (2012): 15–19.

Mueller, Robert S., III. "Protecting the United States from Terrorism and Crime: It Begins with Intelligence." *Intelligencer: Journal of U.S. Intelligence Studies* 16.2 (2008): 27–30.

Mukasey, Michael Bernard. *How Obama Has Mishandled the War on Terror.* New York: Encounter Books, 2010.

Nacos, Brigitte L. *Terrorism and Counterterrorism.* 4th ed. Boston: Longman, 2012.

Nance, Malcolm W. *Terrorist Recognition Handbook: A Practitioner's Manual for Predicting and Identifying Terrorist Activities.* 2nd ed. London: CRC, 2008.

Noesner, Gary. *Stalling for Time: My Life as an FBI Hostage Negotiator.* New York: Random House, 2010.

Omand, David. *Securing the State.* New York: Columbia University Press, 2010.

Parnell, G., R. Liebe, R. Dillon-Merrill, D. Buede, J. Scouras, B. Colletti, M. Cummings, D. McGarvey, R. Newport, P. Vinch, B. Ayyub, M. Kaminskiy, and J. Scouras. *Homeland Security Risk Assessment, Volume I: An Illustrative Framework.* Arlington, VA: Homeland Security Institute, 2006.

Patman, Robert. *Strategic Shortfall: The Somali Syndrome and the March to 9/11.* Westport, CT: Praeger Security International, 2008.

Peritz, Aki, and Eric Rosenbach. *Find, Fix, Finish: Inside the Counterterrorism Campaigns that Killed Bin Laden and Devastated al-Qaeda.* New York: Public Affairs, 2012.

Pettyjohn, Stacie Leigh. *Talking with Terrorists: American Policy Toward the PLO, Sinn Fein, and Hamas.* Diss. University of Virginia, 2010.

Pfarrer, Chuck. *SEAL Target Geronimo: The Inside Story of the Mission to Kill Osama bin Laden.* New York: St. Martin's, 2011.

Phares, Walid. *The Confrontation: Winning the War Against Future Jihad*. New York: Palgrave Macmillan, 2008.

Pillar, Paul. *Intelligence and U.S. Foreign Policy: Iraq, 9/11, and Misguided Reform*. New York: Columbia University Press, 2011.

Posner, Richard A. *Countering Terrorism: Blurred Focus, Halting Steps*. Lanham, MD: Rowman & Littlefield, 2007.

Ranstorp, Magnus, and Graeme P. Herd "*Approaches to Countering Terrorism and CIST.*" In *The Ideological War on Terror: Strategies for Counter-Terrorism*, edited by Anne Aldis and Graeme P. Herd, 3–20. London: Routledge, 2007.

Rees, Wyn. *Transatlantic Counter-Terrorism Cooperation: A New Imperative*. London: Routledge, 2006.

Reinke de Buitrago, Sybille. "Communication Patterns in the 'War on Terrorism' and Their Potential for Escalation or Deescalation of the Conflict." *S+F: Sicherheit und Frieden/Security and Peace* 2 August 2008: 105–109.

Reinke de Buitrago, Sybille. "The Impact of Psychological-Cultural Factors on Concepts of Fighting Terrorism." *Journal of Strategic Security* 2.1 (2009): 59–79.

Reuter, Dean, and John Yoo, eds. *Confronting Terror: 9/11 and the Future of American National Security*. New York: Encounter, 2011.

Richardson, Louise. *What Terrorists Want: Understanding the Enemy, Containing the Threat*. New York: Random House, 2006.

Richelson, Jeffrey T. *Defusing Armageddon: Inside NEST, America's Secret Nuclear Bomb Squad*. New York: W. W. Norton, 2009.

Ridge, Tom, with Lary Bloom. *The Test of Our Times: America Under Siege ... and How We Can Be Safe Again*. New York: Thomas Dunne, 2009.

Roach, Kent. *The 9/11 Effect: Comparative Counter-Terrorism*. London: Cambridge University Press, 2011.

Rodriguez, Jose A., Jr., with Bill Harlow. *Hard Measures: How Aggressive CIA Actions After 9/11 Saved American Lives*. New York: Threshold Editions, 2012.

Ronczkowski, Michael R. *Terrorism and Organized Hate Crime: Intelligence Gathering, Analysis and Investigations*. 2nd ed. London: CRC, 2007.

Ropeik, David. *How Risky Is It, Really? Why Our Fears Don't Always Match the Facts*. New York: McGraw Hill, 2010.

Rosell, Bruce. "Under-reactions: Lessons from Fort Hood." *T+D: Training Plus Development* 64.4 (2010): 6, 50–52.

Sandler, Todd, Daniel G. Arce, and Walter Enders. "An Evaluation of INTERPOL's Cooperative-Based Counterterrorism Linkages." *Journal of Law and Economics* 54.1 (2011).

Schmitt, Gary J., ed. *Safety, Liberty and Islamist Terrorism: American and European Approaches to Domestic Counterterrorism*. Washington, DC: AEI Press, 2010.

Schuber, Hiltmar. *Detection of Liquid Explosives and Flammable Agents in Connection with Terrorism*. New York: Springer, 2008.

Seidenstat, Paul, and Francis X. Splane, eds. *Protecting Airline Passengers in the Age of Terrorism*. Santa Barbara: Praeger, 2009.

Shanty, Frank. *Counter-terrorism from the Cold War to the War on Terror*. 2 vols. Santa Barbara: ABC-CLIO, 2012.

Shawcross, William. *Justice and the Enemy: Nuremberg, 9/11, and the Trial of Khalid Sheikh Mohammed*. New York: Public Affairs, 2012.

Sheehan, Michael. *Crush the Cell: How to Defeat Terrorism Without Terrorizing Ourselves*. New York: Crown, 2008.

Sinai, Joseph. "Terrorism on the Internet and Effective Countermeasures. *Intelligencer: Journal of U.S. Intelligence* 18.3 (2011): 21–4.

Strauss, Michael J. *The Leasing of Guantanamo Bay*. Santa Barbara: Praeger, 2009.

Tama, Jordan. *Terrorism and National Security Reform: How Commissions Can Drive Change During Crises*. London: Cambridge University Press, 2011.

Terry, James P. *The War on Terror: The Legal Dimension*. Annapolis: Naval Institute Press, 2011.

Thiessen, Marc A. *Courting Disaster: How the CIA Kept America Safe and How Barack Obama Is Inviting the Next Attack*. Washington, DC: Regnery, 2010.

Thomas, Andrew R., ed. *Aviation Security Management*. 3 vols. Westport, CT: Praeger Security International, 2008.

Travers, Russell E. "Evaluating Progress in the 'War on Terror.'" *Intelligencer: Journal of U.S. Intelligence Studies* 17.1 (2009): 11–4.

Treverton, Gregory F. *Assessing Counterterrorism-Focused Domestic Intelligence*. Santa Monica: RAND, 2008.

Tsang, Steve, ed. *Combating Transnational Terrorism: Searching for a New Paradigm*. Santa Barbara: Praeger, 2009.

Turchie, Terry D., and Kathleen M. Puckett. *Hunting the American Terrorist: The FBI's War on Homegrown Terror*. Palisades, NY: History, 2007.

Ulph, Stephen, John H. Moore, John Lenczowski, and Robert R. Reilly. *Fighting the Ideological War: Winning Strategies from Communism to Islamism*. McLean, VA: Westminster Institute; Isaac, 2012.

Ungar, David C. *The Emergency State: America's Pursuit of Absolute Security at All Costs*. New York: Penguin, 2012.

United States. Department of Homeland Security. Office for Civil Rights and Civil Liberties. "Terminology to Define the Terrorists: Recommendations from American Muslims." Washington, DC, January 2008: 1–9. Web.

United States. Federal Bureau of Investigation (FBI).

"Help Bring Bob Levinson Home—$1 Million Reward Offering for Missing Retired FBI Agent." *Intelligencer: Journal of U.S. Intelligence Studies* 19.1 (2012): 41–44.

United States. Government Accountability Office (GAO). *The United States Lacks Comprehensive Plan to Destroy the Terrorist Threat and Close the Safe Haven in Pakistan's Federally Administered Tribal Areas.* Washington: GPO, 2008.

Unites States. State Department. National Counter Terrorism Center (NCTC). "Words That Work and Words That Don't: A Guide for Counter-Terrorism Communication." *Counterterrorism Communications Center (CTCC)* 2.10 (2008): 1–3.

Viotti, Paul, Michael Opheim, and Nicholas Bowen, eds. *Terrorism and Homeland Security: Thinking Strategically About Policy.* London: CRC, 2008.

Wallace, Robert W., H. Keith Melton, and Henry R. Schlesinger. *Spycraft: The Secret History of the CIA's Spytechs from Communism to Al Qaeda.* New York: Dutton, 2008.

Wax, Steven T. *Kafka Comes to America: Fighting for Justice in the War on Terror: A Public Defender's Inside Account.* New York: Other Press, 2008.

Weinberger, Seth. Restoring *the Balance: War Powers in an Age of Terror.* Santa Barbara: Praeger, 2009.

Willis, Henry H., Andrew R. Morral, and Jamison Jo Medby. *Estimating Terrorism Risk.* Santa Monica: RAND, 2005.

Wittes, Benjamin. *Law and the Long War: The Future of Justice in the Age of Terror.* New York: Penguin, 2008.

Woodward, Bob. *The War Within: A Secret White House History 2006–2008.* New York: Simon & Schuster, 2008.

Wrona, Richard M., Jr. "Beginning of a War: The United States and the Hijacking of TWA Flight 847." In *Countering Terrorism and Insurgency in the 21st Century: International Perspectives,* Vol. 3, edited by James J. F. Forest. Westport, CT: Praeger, 2007.

Wuthnow, Robert. *Be Very Afraid: The Cultural Response to Terror, Pandemics, Environmental Devastation, Nuclear Annihilation, and Other Threats.* Cambridge: Oxford University Press, 2010.

Zabel, Richard B., and James J. Benjamin. *In Pursuit of Justice: Prosecuting Terrorism Cases in the Federal Courts.* Human Rights First White Paper, May 2008.

Fiction

Baldacci, David. *First Family.* New York: Grand Central, 2009.

Berenson, Alex. *The Faithful Spy.* New York: Jove, 2008.

Berenson, Alex. *The Silent Man.* New York: Putnam Adult, 2009.

Carey, Peter. *His Illegal Self.* New York: Knopf, 2008.

Child, Lee. *Gone Tomorrow.* New York: Delacorte, 2009.

Choi, Susan. *A Person of Interest.* New York: Viking Adult.

Deaver, Jeffery, Lisa Scottoline, Lee Child, Joseph Finder, David Hewson, Peter Spiegelman, S. J. Rozan, Erica Spindler, John Ramsey Miller, James Grady, P. J. Parrish, Jim Fusilli, David Corbett, John Gilstrap, and Ralph Pezzullo. *Watchlist: Part I: The Chopin Manuscript: A Serial Thriller.* Audio narrated by Alfred Molina. 1st broadcast September 25–November 13, 2007. MP-3, Brilliance Audio, 2008. E-book, Vook, 2011.

Deaver, Jeffery, Gayle Lynds, David Hewson, Jim Fusilli, John Gilstrap, Joseph Finder, Lisa Scottoline, David Corbett, Linda Barnes, Jenny Siler, David Liss, P. J. Parrish, Brett Battles, Lee Child, Jon Land, and James Phelan. *Watchlist: Part II: The Copper Bracelet.* Audio narrated by Alfred Molina. MP-3, Brilliance Audio, 2010. E-book, Vook, 2011.

Doyle, Roddy. *The Dead Republic.* New York: Viking, 2010.

Dubus, Andre, III. *The Garden of Last Day.* New York: Norton, 2008.

Evans, Duane. *North From Calcutta.* Secaucus, NJ: Pecos Moon, 2009.

Fesperman, Dan. *The Amateur Spy.* New York: Knopf, 2008.

Gilleo, Mark. *Love Thy Neighbor.* Stamford, CT: Story Plant, 2012.

Graham, Bob. *Keys to the Kingdom.* New York: Vanguard, 2011.

Gruber, Michael. *The Good Son.* New York: Henry Holt, 2010.

Hamilton, Marsha. *31 Hours.* Cave Creek, AZ: Unbridled, 2009.

Higgins, Jack. *The Killing Ground.* New York: Putnam, 2008.

Hillhouse, R. J. *Outsourced: A Novel.* New York: Forge Books, 2007.

Hunter, Stephen. *I, Sniper.* New York: Simon & Schuster, 2009.

Hynes, James. *Next.* Boston: Reagan Arthur/Little, Brown, 2010.

Johnson, Diane. *Lulu in Marrakech.* New York: Dutton, 2008.

Lavalle, Victor. *Big Machine.* New York: Spiegel and Grau, 2009.

Le Carre, John. *A Most Wanted Man.* New York: Scribner, 2008.

LeGallo, Andre. *The Caliphate.* New York: Dorchester, 2010.

Neville, Stuart. *The Ghosts of Belfast.* New York: Soho, 2009.

Palahniu, Chuck. *Pygmy.* New York: Doubleday, 2009.

Patterson, James. *Kill Alex Cross.* Boston: Little, Brown, 2011.

Patterson, Richard North. *The Devil's Light.* New York: Scribner, 2011.

Reich, Christopher. *Rules of Deception*. New York: Doubleday, 2008.

Rubenfeld, Jed. *The Death Instinct*. New York: Riverhead/Penguin, 2011.

Ruff, Matt. *The Mirage*. New York: Harper, 2012.

Silva, Daniel. *Moscow Rules*. New York: Putnam, 2008.

Smolens, John. *The Anarchist*. New York: Three Rivers Press, 2009.

Spurlock, Morgan. *Where in the World Is Osama Bin Laden?* New York: Random House, 2008.

Thor, Brad. *The Apostle*. New York: Atria, 2009.

Thor, Brad. *The First Commandment*. New York: Pocket, 2007.

Van Lustbade, Eric. *Robert Ludlum's The Bourne Sanction*. New York: Grand Central, 2009.

Waldman, Amy. *The Submission*. New York: Farrar, Straus and Giroux, 2011.

Weisman, John. *KBL: Kill bin Laden: A Novel Based on True Events*. New York: William Morrow, 2011.

Westlake, Donald E. *The Comedy Is Finished*. New York: Hard Case Crime, 2012.

Internet

http://internet-haganah.com/haganah/. Site hosted by A. Aaron Weisburd, senior fellow at Homeland Security Policy Institute, that tracks jihadi fora.

www.alemarah1.com. Site often used by the Taliban to announce daily attacks on coalition forces.

www.toorabora.com. Taliban Tora Bora Front site that claims attacks on coalition forces. Includes some interviews with Taliban commanders in English, Dari, and Pashto.

INDEX TO COUNTRIES AND PLACES

References are to entry dates.